10th Workshop on the Representation and Processing of Sign Languages: Multilingual Sign Language Resources (sign-lang@LREC 2022)

Held at LREC 2022

Marseille, France
20 – 25 June 2022

Editors:

Eleni Efthimiou
Stavroula-Evita Fotinea
Thomas Hanke
Julie A. Hochgesang
Jette Kristoffersen
Johanna Mesch
Marc Schulder

ISBN: 978-1-7138-6137-9

Printed from e-media with permission by:

Curran Associates, Inc.
57 Morehouse Lane
Red Hook, NY 12571

Some format issues inherent in the e-media version may also appear in this print version.

Printed with permission by Curran Associates, Inc. (2023)

For permission requests, please contact the Association for Computational Linguistics at the address below.

Association for Computational Linguistics
209 N. Eighth Street
Stroudsburg, Pennsylvania 18360

Phone: 1-570-476-8006
Fax: 1-570-476-0860

acl@aclweb.org

Additional copies of this publication are available from:

Curran Associates, Inc.
57 Morehouse Lane
Red Hook, NY 12571 USA
Phone: 845-758-0400
Fax: 845-758-2633
Email: curran@proceedings.com
Web: www.proceedings.com

LREC 2022 Workshop
Language Resources and Evaluation Conference
20-25 June 2022

10th Workshop on the Representation and Processing of Sign Languages: Multilingual Sign Language Resources (sign-lang@LREC 2022)

PROCEEDINGS

Eleni Efthimiou, Stavroula-Evita Fotinea, Thomas Hanke, Julie A. Hochgesang, Jette Kristoffersen, Johanna Mesch, Marc Schulder (eds.)

Proceedings of the LREC 2022 10th Workshop on the Representation and Processing of Sign Languages: Multilingual Sign Language Resources (sign-lang@LREC 2022)

Edited by: Eleni Efthimiou, Stavroula-Evita Fotinea, Thomas Hanke, Julie A. Hochgesang, Jette Kristoffersen, Johanna Mesch, and Marc Schulder

For more information:
European Language Resources Association (ELRA)
9 rue des Cordelières
75013, Paris
France
http://www.elra.info
Email: lrec@elda.org

Preface

This collection of papers stems from the 10th Workshop on the Representation and Processing of Sign Languages which takes place as a satellite workshop to the Language Resources and Evaluation Conference in Marseille (France).

While there has been occasional attention to sign languages at the main LREC conference, the focus there is on spoken languages in their written and spoken forms. This series of workshops, however, offers a forum for researchers focussing on sign languages, especially on corpus data and corpus technology for sign languages.

This year's hot topic "Multilingual Sign Language Resources" aligns with one of the main conference's hot topics. It stresses the importance of looking across sign languages whenever testing claims about signed modality, but it also addresses the problem that for many sign languages only very few languages resources are available. Combining resources across languages is a promising perspective to draw on richer sets of data.

Please note that this year LREC has two workshops on sign languages: SLTAT7 covers the topics automatic translation and avatar technology. In the corresponding proceedings, you find 19 more sign language-related papers.

The contributions composing this volume are presented in alphabetical order by the first author. For the reader's convenience, an author index is provided as well.

Once again, we would like to thank all members of the program committee who helped us tremendously by reviewing the submissions to the workshop within a very short timeframe!

Finally, we would like to point the reader to the proceedings of the previous workshops that form important resources in a growing field of research. They are all available online from the sign-lang@LREC Anthology at

`https://www.sign-lang.uni-hamburg.de/lrec/`

The site offers an author index across all workshops as well as stable URLs for all workshop papers and posters. If you need bibliographical (BibTeX) data for all workshops, the site now has them per paper, per workshop, per author or all in one. Happy browsing!

The Editors

Organizers

Eleni Efthimiou, Institute for Language and Speech Processing, Athens, Greece
Stavroula-Evita Fotinea, Institute for Language and Speech Processing, Athens, Greece
Thomas Hanke, Institute of German Sign Language, University of Hamburg, Germany
Julie A. Hochgesang, Gallaudet University, Washington, USA
Jette Kristoffersen, Centre for Sign Language, Copenhagen, Denmark
Johanna Mesch, Stockholm University, Sweden
Marc Schulder, Institute of German Sign Language, University of Hamburg, Germany

Program Committee:

Penny Boyes-Braem, University of Zurich, Zurich, Switzerland
Annelies Braffort, LIMSI/CNRS, Orsay, France
Carl Börstell, University of Bergen, Bergen, Norway
Kearsy Cormier, University College London, London, United Kingdom
Onno Crasborn, Radboud University, Nijmegen, The Netherlands
Eleni Efthimiou, Institute for Language and Speech Processing, Athens, Greece
Michael Filhol, LIMSI/CNRS, Orsay, France
Stavroula-Evita Fotinea, Institute for Language and Speech Processing, Athens, Greece
Thomas Hanke, University of Hamburg, Hamburg, Germany
Julie A. Hochgesang, Gallaudet University, Washington, USA
Amy Isard, University of Hamburg, Hamburg, Germany
Trevor Johnston, Macquarie University, Sydney, Australia
Vadim Kimmelman, University of Bergen, Bergen, Norway
Reiner Konrad, University of Hamburg, Hamburg, Germany
Jette Kristoffersen, Centre for Sign Language, Copenhagen, Denmark
Anna Kuder, University of Warsaw, Warsaw, Poland
Lorraine Leeson, Trinity College Dublin, Dublin, Ireland
John McDonald, DePaul University, Chicago, USA
Johanna Mesch, Stockholm University, Stockholm, Sweden
Hope E. Morgan, Radboud University, Nijmegen, The Netherlands
Carol Neidle, Boston University, Boston, USA
Justin Power, University of Texas, Austin, USA
Paweł Rutkowski, University of Warsaw, Warsaw, Poland
Marc Schulder, University of Hamburg, Hamburg, Germany
Rose Stamp, Bar-Ilan University, Ramat Gan, Israel
Anna Vacalopoulou, Institute for Language and Speech Processing, Athens, Greece
Rosalee Wolfe, Institute for Language and Speech Processing, Athens, Greece

Table of Contents

PeruSIL: A Framework to Build a Continuous Peruvian Sign Language Interpretation Dataset
Gissella Bejarano, Joe Huamani-Malca, Francisco Cerna-Herrera, Fernando Alva-Manchego and Pablo Rivas 1

Introducing Sign Languages to a Multilingual Wordnet: Bootstrapping Corpora and Lexical Resources of Greek Sign Language and German Sign Language
Sam Bigeard, Marc Schulder, Maria Kopf, Thomas Hanke, Kyriaki Vasilaki, Anna Vacalopoulou, Theodore Goulas, Athanasia-Lida Dimou, Stavroula-Evita Fotinea and Eleni Efthimiou 9

Introducing the signglossR Package
Carl Börstell 16

Moving towards a Functional Approach in the Flemish Sign Language Dictionary Making Process
Caro Brosens, Margot Janssens, Sam Verstraete, Thijs Vandamme and Hannes De Durpel 24

Phonetics of Negative Headshake in Russian Sign Language: A Small-Scale Corpus Study
Anastasia Chizhikova and Vadim Kimmelman 29

Documenting the Use of Iranian Sign Language (ZEI) in Kermanshah
Yassaman Choubsaz, Onno Crasborn, Sara Siyavoshi and Farzaneh Soleimanbeigi 37

Applying the Transcription System Typannot to Mouth Gestures
Claire Danet, Chloé Thomas, Adrien Contesse, Morgane Rébulard, Claudia S. Bianchini, Léa Chevrefils and Patrick Doan 42

Libras Portal: A Way of Documentation, a Way of Sharing
Ronice de Quadros, Renata Krusser and Daniela Saito 48

Representation and Synthesis of Geometric Relocations
Michael Filhol and John McDonald 53

Sign Language Phonetic Annotator-Analyzer: Open-Source Software for Form-Based Analysis of Sign Languages
Kathleen Currie Hall, Yurika Aonuki, Kaili Vesik, April Poy and Nico Tolmie 59

ASL-Homework-RGBD Dataset: An Annotated Dataset of 45 Fluent and Non-fluent Signers Performing American Sign Language Homeworks
Saad Hassan, Matthew Seita, Larwan Berke, Yingli Tian, Elaine Gale, Sooyeon Lee and Matt Huenerfauth 67

MY DGS – ANNIS: ANNIS and the Public DGS Corpus
Amy Isard and Reiner Konrad 73

Outreach and Science Communication in the DGS-Korpus Project: Accessibility of Data and the Benefit of Interactive Exchange between Communities
Elena Jahn, Calvin Khan and Annika Herrmann 80

MC-TRISLAN: A Large 3D Motion Capture Sign Language Data-set
Pavel Jedlička, Zdeněk Krňoul, Milos Zelezny and Ludek Muller 88

A Machine Learning-based Segmentation Approach for Measuring Similarity between Sign Languages
Tonni Das Jui, Gissella Bejarano and Pablo Rivas 94

The Sign Language Dataset Compendium: Creating an Overview of Digital Linguistic Resources
Maria Kopf, Marc Schulder and Thomas Hanke 102

Making Sign Language Corpora Comparable: A Study of Palm-Up and Throw-Away in Polish Sign Language, German Sign Language, and Russian Sign Language
Anna Kuder 110

Open Repository of the Polish Sign Language Corpus: Publication Project of the Polish Sign Language Corpus
Anna Kuder, Joanna Wójcicka, Piotr Mostowski and Paweł Rutkowski 118

Functional Data Analysis of Non-manual Marking of Questions in Kazakh-Russian Sign Language
Anna Kuznetsova, Alfarabi Imashev, Medet Mukushev, Anara Sandygulova and Vadim Kimmelman 124

Two New AZee Production Rules Refining Multiplicity in French Sign Language
Emmanuella Martinod, Claire Danet and Michael Filhol 132

Language Planning in Action: Depiction as a Driver of New Terminology in Irish Sign Language
Rachel Moiselle and Lorraine Leeson 139

Facilitating the Spread of New Sign Language Technologies across Europe
Hope Morgan, Onno Crasborn, Maria Kopf, Marc Schulder and Thomas Hanke 144

ISL-LEX v.1: An Online Lexical Resource of Israeli Sign Language
Hope Morgan, Wendy Sandler, Rose Stamp and Rama Novogrodsky 148

Towards Large Vocabulary Kazakh-Russian Sign Language Dataset: KRSL-OnlineSchool
Medet Mukushev, Aigerim Kydyrbekova, Vadim Kimmelman and Anara Sandygulova 154

Towards Semi-automatic Sign Language Annotation Tool: SLAN-tool
Medet Mukushev, Arman Sabyrov, Madina Sultanova, Vadim Kimmelman and Anara Sandygulova 159

Resources for Computer-Based Sign Recognition from Video, and the Criticality of Consistency of Gloss Labeling across Multiple Large ASL Video Corpora
Carol Neidle, Augustine Opoku, Carey Ballard, Konstantinos M. Dafnis, Evgenia Chroni and Dimitri Metaxas 165

Signed Language Transcription and the Creation of a Cross-linguistic Comparative Database
Justin Power, David Quinto-Pozos and Danny Law 173

Integrating Auslan Resources into the Language Data Commons of Australia
River Tae Smith, Louisa Willoughby and Trevor Johnston 181

Capturing Distalization
Rose Stamp, Lilyana Khatib and Hagit Hel-Or 187

The Corpus of Israeli Sign Language
Rose Stamp, Ora Ohanin and Sara Lanesman 192

Segmentation of Signs for Research Purposes: Comparing Humans and Machines
Bencie Woll, Neil Fox and Kearsy Cormier 198

Sign Language Video Anonymization
Zhaoyang Xia, Yuxiao Chen, Qilong Zhangli, Matt Huenerfauth, Carol Neidle and Dimitri Metaxas 202

Proceedings of the 10th Workshop on the Representation and Processing of Sign Languages (sign-lang@LREC 2022), pages 1–8
Language Resources and Evaluation Conference (LREC 2022), Marseille, 20-25 June 2022

PeruSIL: A Framework to Build a Continuous Peruvian Sign Language Interpretation Dataset

Gissella Bejarano[1,4], Joe Huamani-Malca[2], Francisco Cerna-Herrera[2], Fernando Alva-Manchego[3], Pablo Rivas[1]
[1]Baylor University, [2]Pontificia Universidad Católica del Perú,
[3]Cardiff University,[4]Universidad Peruana Cayetano Heredia
{gissella_bejaranonic, Pablo_Rivas}@baylor.edu,
{huamani.jn, francisco.cerna}@pucp.edu.pe,
alvamanchegof@cardiff.ac.uk

Abstract

Video-based datasets for Continuous Sign Language are scarce due to the challenging task of recording videos from native signers and the reduced number of people who can annotate sign language. COVID-19 has evidenced the key role of sign language interpreters in delivering nationwide health messages to deaf communities. In this paper, we present a framework for creating a multi-modal sign language interpretation dataset based on videos and we use it to create the first dataset for Peruvian Sign Language (LSP) interpretation annotated by hearing volunteers who have intermediate knowledge of PSL guided by the video audio. We rely on hearing people to produce a first version of the annotations, which should be reviewed by native signers in the future. Our contributions: i) we design a framework to annotate a sign Language dataset; ii) we release the first annotated LSP multi-modal interpretation dataset (AEC); iii) we evaluate the annotation done by hearing people by training a sign language recognition model. Our model reaches up to 80.3% of accuracy among a minimum of five classes (signs) AEC dataset, and 52.4% in a second dataset. Nevertheless, analysis by subject in the second dataset show variations worth to discuss.

Keywords: Continuous Sign Language, Peruvian Sign Language, multi-modal dataset

1. Introduction

An increasing number of calls highlight the need to research sign language, and develop technologies with a multidisciplinary approach. For instance, Bragg et al. (2019) introduced the term Sign Language Processing (SLP) to refer to the task of building models that are able to perform a complete translation process. Similarly, Yin et al. (2021) urges the inclusion of SLP in the more-developed research area of Natural Language Processing (NLP). This can bring enormous benefits in inheriting and adapting the advancements reached in machine translation to sign language translation. For example, several annotation systems have been developed for sign language research with focus in linguistics. However, these annotation systems might not be suitable when working with machine learning models.

Recent advancements in SLP based on computer-vision rely on datasets of *continuous* sign language interpretation. For example, several work is addressing sign language temporal segmentation (Renz et al., 2021a; Renz et al., 2021b) and even aligning subtitles to perform this task (Bull et al., 2020; Bull et al., 2021). On the other hand, (Camgoz et al., 2020b; Camgoz et al., 2018; Camgoz et al., 2020a) focus on sign language recognition and translation. All of these works use at least one dataset of sign language interpreters, such as RWTH-PHOENIX-Weather (Forster et al., 2012) or BSL-1k (Albanie et al., 2020). In that sense, Continuous Sign Language performed by interpreters, and properly reviewed by deaf people, can contribute to the development of more resources for the task. However, to really develop sign language technology and to include deaf people in its design and construction, we need more standardized annotation conventions, less background-controlled videos, and more variations in the topics covered in the datasets.

2. Peruvian Sign Language (LSP)

Peruvian Sign Language (LSP by its acronym in Spanish) is the aboriginal sign language from Peru. There are around half a million deaf people in the country (INEI and CONADIS, 2012), and at least 10,000 people have LSP as their mother tongue (INEI, 2018). LSP is an understudied language that has only recently been officially recognized by the government (MIMP, 2017). Although both public and private institutions are required to provide sign language interpretation in Peru, not many do so since the law is not properly enforced. There are almost no resources in LSP, and the few existing research has primarily studied its grammatical properties (Madrid Vega, 2018) and aspects of their users (Elizabeth and Parks, 2010), or has built a dictionary from a partially annotated dataset (PUCP-DGI) (Rodríguez Mondoñedo and Arnaiz, 2015). On the other hand, computational approaches have only focused on isolated sign language alphabet recognition (Lazo et al., 2019; Mejía Gamarra et al., 2020; Berrú-Novoa et al., 2018; Nureña-Jara et al., 2020).

Although more technological tools are accessible to people with hearing disabilities, they are still based on the written version of a spoken language and not on the main language in which deaf people communicate, for instance. To contribute to bridging that gap, we introduce PeruSIL – a framework for building multi-modal datasets for Continuous Peruvian Sign Language interpretation. Our framework proposes an annotation convention based on the glossing system but simplified, and a pipeline to combine manual and automatic multimodal annotations (Section 2). In addition, we use our framework to create the first multi-modal dataset for Peruvian Sign Language interpretation (Section 3), which includes videos, unaligned audio, transcripts, text, and keypoint landmarks (pose, hands, and facial). For this dataset, original videos were acquired from a Peruvian government's TV program developed for remote school education during the COVID-19 pandemic. We also evaluate the usefulness of our annotated dataset as training data for a sign recognition model, tested in both in-domain and out-of-domain settings (Section 4). Our framework and dataset are part of a larger project aiming to create a larger and online Peruvian Sign language/Spanish dictionary, and an automatic Peruvian Sign Language Translation framework.

3. PeruSIL Framework

In this section, we detail our proposed annotation convention and the pipeline used to build a multi-modal sign language interpretation dataset. We highlight the challenge of collecting sign language datasets due to the lack of videos from native signers, and the limited availability of experts for their annotation, as mentioned by Dreuw and Ney (2008).

3.1. Convention for Annotation

We used two levels of annotation: one for a Spanish word representing the sign, and another for the sentences in Spanish. Sentence annotation can contribute to future sentence segmentation and translation models. As mentioned in Cormier et al. (2012), the annotation of a sign language corpus should be machine-readable through a systematic annotation. Even when to a large extent, a sign could be easily related to a unique English word, this is not always straightforward. It is the case that sometimes there are several options of glosses for just one sign. This is particularly sensitive when a sign can be interpreted both as a verb or a noun. In that sense, it is usually necessary to rely on grammatical knowledge of the sign language being annotated and also to establish a particular criteria for the annotation based on the needs of the investigation. Due to the few LSP users that know an annotation convention such as the glossing system, we simplify it to a convention that is more suitable to use in a machine learning approach. We expect that machine learning models extract and learn the more specific nuances from the visual information rather than from costly annotation of variants and classifiers in the glosses. Some of the criteria that we simplified are as follows. We relate one sign with only one token or Spanish word in lowercase. We use infinite forms for verbs and singular masculine forms for nouns. We expect to use uppercase only for entities for future identification. For the sentence level annotation, we keep the modifiers of the words (i.e. time, number) and expect the machine learning models to learn from them to match it to a final translation statement. Sign is related to more than one word. In those cases, we assign the closest word related to the sign as if it was seen isolated. For example, this is the case for "helado" ("ice cream") in LSP and "comer helado" ("to eat ice cream"), whose sign are the same. Table 1 shows and explain all the conventions that we considered when instructing the volunteers to annotate the signs and sign sentences.

3.2. Multi-modal Pipeline

In this section we describe the pipeline or information process that we followed to combine the manual annotations and the addition of unaligned audio and keypoint landmarks annotation in an automatic manner. Figure 1 shows more details about the process and structure of the final files of a multi-modal dataset generated by our framework. We provide code of our scripts in our GitHub repository.[1]

3.2.1. Manual Annotation

To obtained the two levels of annotations defined in the annotation convention in two stages. First, we asked a group of volunteers to transcript the video in text files with proper punctuation. Then, we merged them with the YouTube automatically-generated transcripts and time boundaries of subtitles. Given that we are creating an interpretation dataset, the hearing volunteers performed oral-based punctuation by listening to the audio. Note that sign language sentence segmentation might need more understanding such as the one shown in Fenlon et al. (2007) that analyses visual markers as boundaries in intonational phrase of British Sign Language. After the merge of the files, we obtained corrected and punctuated SRT files that can be used as a raw approach to automatic segmentation based on audio that is unaligned to the signing. Second, considering the audio from the video, other group of three volunteers identified repetitive spoken words and aligned them with repetitive signs in the videos. In other words, they used the unaligned audio and punctuated transcript as a reference to identify temporal boundaries of the two levels of annotations, described in 3.1, by signs and by sign sentences. For this second part, these three volunteers used ELAN (Wittenburg et al., 2006), an annotation tool for audio and video, as shown in Figure 2. These volunteers had intermediate knowledge of LSP and rely also in the audio to identify vocabulary in for this task.

3.2.2. Automatic Multi-modal Annotation

After the video segmentation is done manually using ELAN for each tier, we cut each original video using

[1]https://github.com/gissemari/PeruvianSignLanguage

Criteria	Explanation	Example
Lower case	The gloss at the 1st tier, except proper nouns should be written with lower case. In that way, it could be easier to identify them in future works.	1st tier:"Peru","yo","vivir"(Peru, I, live) 2nd tier: "Yo vivo en Peru" (I live in Peru)
Uppercase	Entities and following convention of writing sentences in Spanish in 2nd tier	
Fingerspelling	They should be annotated separated by a hyphen	1st tier: "yo", "P-A-T-R-I-C-I-A" (I, Patricia) 2nd tier: "Yo soy Patricia" (I am Patricia)
One sign - several words	Assign the closest single word to the sign in the 1st tier level, as if it was isolated. Use both words in the 2nd tier	1st tier:"helado" (ice cream) 2nd tier: "Comer helado" (to eat ice cream)
Gender & Number	If a sign could have both genres, prefer the male genre in the 1st tier, and the correct reference in the 2nd tier	1st tier: "niño","niño" (boy, boy) or "dos","niño" (two, boy) 2nd tier: "Dos niños" (Two boys or boys)
Verbs	Annotate the verb in present and the sign of the time	1st tier: "antes","yo","ir","Cusco" (past, I, go, Cusco) 2nd tier: "Yo fui a Cusco" (I went to Cusco)
Unknown sign	When a sign is not identifiable, "NNN" should be used in both tiers	1st tier:"antes","comí","NNN" (past, eat, NNN) 2nd tier: "Ayer comí NNN" (yesterday I ate NNN)

Table 1: Annotation Convention

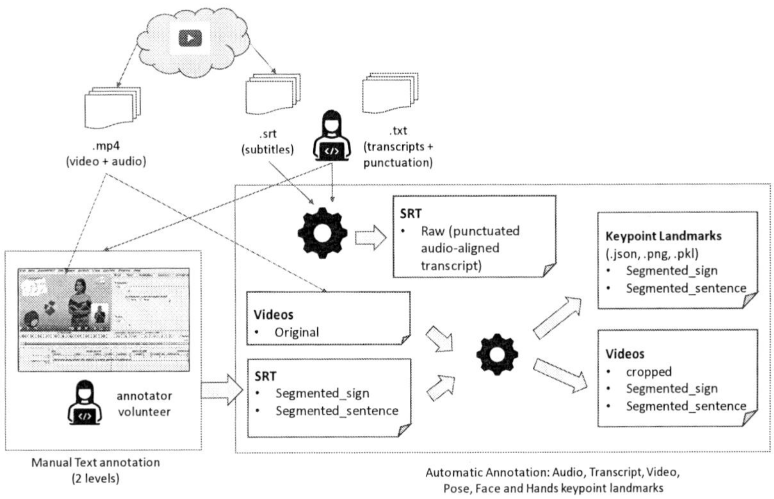

Figure 1: Pipeline for the manual and automatic annotation of PeruSIL

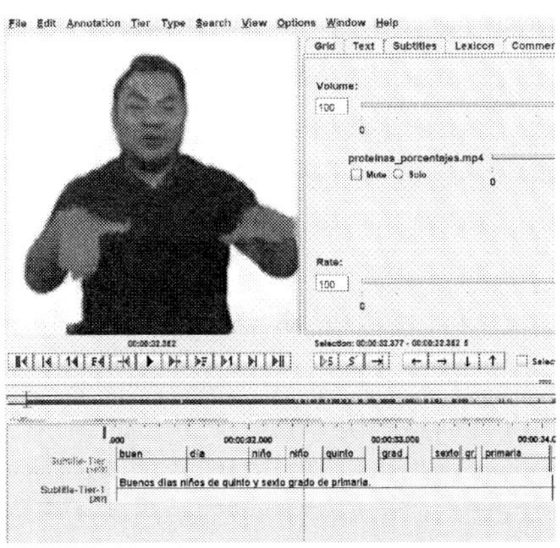

Figure 2: Tiers for the two-level annotation: individual sign y sign sentence (AEC dataset)

the exported two SRT files and save new videos of isolated signs and of sentences in different folders. We use the opencv and pysrt libraries to work with the videos and the SRTs files. Then, we use the MediaPipe open-source platform from Google to annotate the keynote landmarks for each frame at every new video (Lugaresi et al., 2019). The MediaPipe platform provides different sets of landmarks around a body: face, pose, hands, and a set called holistic to retrieve all the previous sets. Our framework generates this annotation in three different types of files for every frame of the segmented videos: visualization in images (.png), data interchange format (.json), and object structure serialization or intermediate storage (.pkl). These two steps are executed as part of the process implemented in our repository to generate the three types of files. In our repository we also provide the link to our dataset. In Figure 3 we show the keypoint landmarks annotation for the sequence of frames of two video instances for the same sign *IDEA*.

Figure 3: Sequence of frames for the sign IDEA performed by two subjects of AEC

4. Peruvian Sign Language Interpretation: AEC Dataset

During the 2020 and 2021 lockdowns, the Peruvian Government offered remote public school education through a show called "Aprendo en Casa" (AEC, or *I learn at home* in English). Episodes of this show were released on TV channels, social media, and the YouTube channel PeruEduca. In this section, we detail how we leveraged the publicly-available videos from AEC to build a multi-modal dataset for Peruvian SLP using the proposed framework in the previous section.

We selected two subject-videos (of 20 to 30 minutes each). We processed two videos where interpreters translate audio-visual content in the right-most bottom white square, using black clothing and a white background. The rate of a sample of the original downloaded video and the segmented videos is 29.97 fps (frames per second), and the interpretation part had a size of 220 x 220 pixels.

We created a dataset consisting of >500 unique signs, >2000 instances, and >150 sentences. In Figure 4, we show the histogram of instances per unique sign. More than 400 signs have less than 10 instances, and only a few signs, like TO-EAT and PERCENTAGE, have more than 50 instances. This is due to the topics related to the two selected videos, one about knowing our emotions in the subject of socio-cultural development,[2] and the other about healthy food, proportions, and percentages in the Math course.[3] On the other hand, the average number of words in a sentence is 8.80, with a minimum of 1 and a maximum of 34 words. Figure 5 shows the frequency of sentences with a different number of signs/words, and most of them have less than 15 words. We provide direct access to the dataset generated by our pipeline in our github repository.

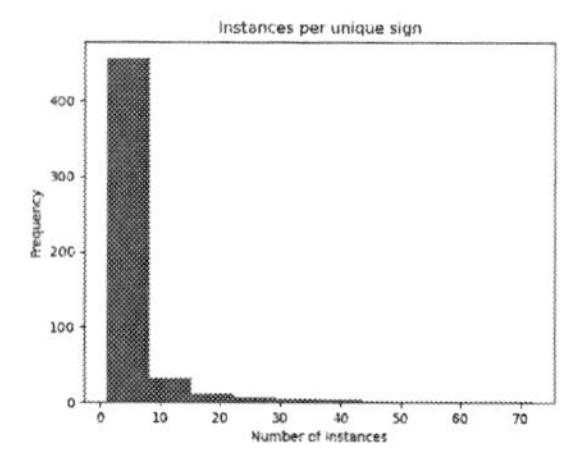

Figure 4: Distribution of instances of signs

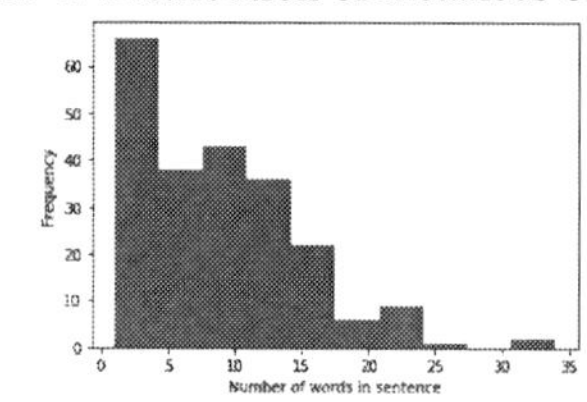

Figure 5: Distribution of sentences lengths

5. Evaluation through a Sign Language Recognition Model

To assess the usefulness of the annotations produced with the PeruSIL framework, we trained and tested a machine learning model in our interpreter-based dataset, AEC, annotated by hearing people for sign language recognition. We also evaluated its performance on common signs found in an additional LSP dataset, PUCP-DGI (Rodriguez Mondoñedo and Arnaiz Fernandez-Concha, 2022), which provides annotations by sign with a gloss convention that lacks standardization for computational processing. In other words, they assign variations of gloss depending on conjugation, number and gender of the translation in context. We identified some of those variations and modified their gloss manually in order to obtain a few more instances.

5.1. ChaLearn Model

The selected machine learning architecture corresponds to one of the 26 participants in 2021 Looking at People Large Scale Signer Independent Isolated SLR CVPR Challenge (De Coster et al., 2021).[4] The challenge consists of performing sign language recognition in a dataset of 226 classes and 36,302 videos.[5] In this subsection we explain the preprocessing needed to perform the feature extraction process to feed the model.

[2] https://youtu.be/7fGAIL2dtk8

[3] https://youtu.be/P4IckOY9P3w

[4] https://github.com/m-decoster/ChaLearn-2021-LAP

[5] https://chalearnlap.cvc.uab.es/dataset/40/description/

5.1.1. Preprocessing

The preprocessing step of this existing model consists of two main phases. The first phase occurs before training, when the keypoints from each video are used to obtain the pose flow data. Then, the original authors estimated keypoints of every frame using the OpenPose library, and substract the keypoints landmarks of the previous frame to calculate the direction of the signer's pose's movement. Due to technical restrictions in our server, we used MediaPipe instead of OpenPose to provide similar landmark estimations. In case the frame count number is lower than the defined sequence length, the missing data is filled by repeating the last video frame, as in a padding form. The second phase occurs during training. The process begins by cropping both hands in a timestep (frame). This cropped area is calculated based on the direction from the elbow to the wrist, where the size of the crop is defined by half the sum of the distance between the shoulders and the distance between the center of the hand and their respective shoulder. The final result is two cropped frames from each signer's hand, which is called RGB data.

5.1.2. Feature Extraction and Training

The model starts by creating batches of preprocessed data: pose flow data and RGB data. The starting RGB data dimension is $B * T * X * C * H * W$ where B is the batch size, T is the number of timesteps, X the number of hands (always 2), C is the channel size, H the height, and W the width of each the frames. This RGB data is modified to $B * (T.X) * C * H * W$ to have both hands sequentially in order from their respective timestep. Then, the dimensions are modified again to $(B.T.X) * C * H * W$ to convert each cropped hand at each time step in an instance to be processed by a pretrained ResNet (He et al., 2016). In that way, the ResNet processes all sequential data in parallel, reducing time for feature extraction. The ResNet output is transformed using a 2D convolutional network to an embedding of certain size (default 512), and then matched to the batch size $(B.T.X) * (FeatureSize)$. Each feature embedding is concatenated with a pose flow data according to timestep-and-batch order, and then normalized. The result of this union is passed to a linear neural network with a Relu function activation, and used as input to a positional encoding that feeds a self-attention model that works similarly to a recurrent neural network whose inner parts consist of a series of a Multi head attention model and position wise Feedforward, using a hidden layer size of 2*embedding size and 2 heads. The model is trained with an Adam optimizer. Lastly, the result is used to learn a cross-entropy layer to do sign recognition of the classes defined. Figure 6 shows the Feature extraction process together with how the model calculates the output through the neural network.

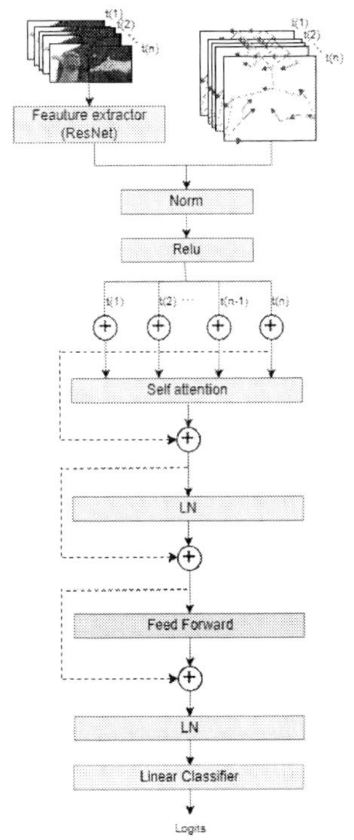

Figure 6: Feature extraction and model

5.2. Experiments

We tested the ChaLearn model in a subset of 5 signs with at least 10 instances per sign: think, see, feel, say, do/make. Figure 7 shows the distribution of the number of frames or length of the video signs for both datasets. The PUCP-DGI dataset shows a broader range of lengths compared to AEC. We hypothesize that this reflects that the pace in native LSP is lower than the interpretation of the LSP. To perform hyperparametrization tuning, we run 3 experiments for each combination in GPUs.

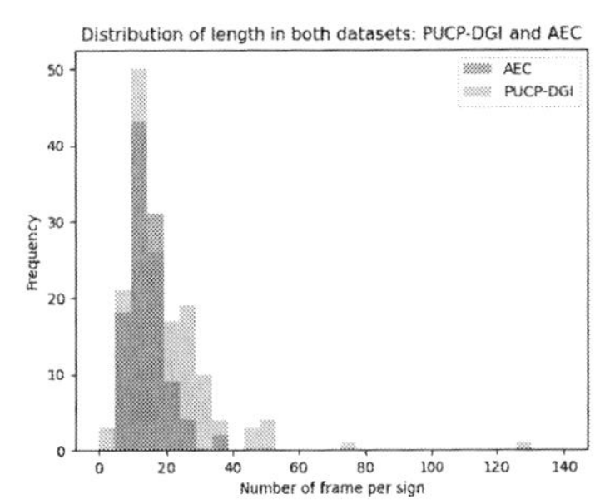

Figure 7. Distribution of length in both datasets: AEC and PUCP-DGI

5.2.1. In-domain Dataset

We did not experiment with hyper-parameter values such as number of *hidden units* or *number of attention heads* due to the good results the ChaLearn model already provided. However, we tested the ResNet architecture used for feature extraction (*rn18* or *rn34*) and *length* of the videos or number of frames as: 10, 15, 20. Also, the *stride* hyperparameter influences how this frames are selected within the set of original frames in a sign video: 1 or 2. Another hyperparameter that we tested was *learning rate* with values 1e-4, 1e-5 and 1e-6.

In Table 2, we show the results of our experiments for the set of 5 classes. In this section we analyze our F1 micro for AEC, which can be interpreted as a direct value to the accuracy through sign classes. In general, the hyperparameter that seems to impact the most in the results is the learning rate. In addition, more consistent results in AEC are reached by 1e-4. For example, for both feature extraction architectures (rn18 and rn34), we found higher F1 results with 1e-4, such as 80.3%. Additionally, higher values remain accross different values of sequence length and stride.

5.2.2. Out-of-Domain Dataset

The PUCP-DGI dataset was created by the Linguistics Department at the Pontificia Universidad Católica del Perú. This dataset includes video recordings of 27 deaf individuals in different classrooms, and each lasts between 1 to 9 minutes approximately. This dataset contains three tiers or levels of annotation: *gloss*, *description* and *classification*, as can be seen in Figure 8. The importance of this dataset is that it was annotated by one deaf person who is an expert in LSP and Spanish. However, we consider this dataset to be partially annotated because the gloss used in the first tier is not completely standardized.

For instance, for this dataset, we identify that variations of a gloss can correspond to the same sign, such as plural and feminine of a certain word. Considering that, we identify 1,382 different tokens, which can include modified tokens of the same sign. However, in order to balance the common classes, we modify these gloss variations and standardize the annotation of some of the instances of this dataset. Additionally, to deal with the problem of some camera movement in videos, frame-by-frame processing has been done to keep the signer in focus.

As shown in Table 2, the best-averaged F1 for PUCP-DGI dataset for rn18 is 51.8%, reached by a sequence length of 10, stride 1 and learning rate of 1e-6 for the group of 5 classes, and best averaged F1 for rn34 is with length 15 and learning rate of 1e-6 as well. We focus on the F1 micro metric due to class imbalance in PUCP-DGI dataset. We also experiment with sets of 10 and 15 classes and they had worse results than random guessing in the test set. It is interesting to notice that while 1e-4 result in higher F1 values for AEC, 1e-6 was a better hyperparameter value for PUCP-DGI results across feature extractor architectures, 51.8% and 52.4% respectively. We hypothesize the reasons can be the class imbalance in this second dataset, the quality of pose estimation, the difference in the pace of recording, and clothing or background of the signers. These results equate to a baseline of 53.2% calculated using the DummyClassifier in scikit-learn with a stratified strategy . We disaggregate PUCP-DGI F1 values by each signer. Table 3 shows the setting with the higher value of accuracy for the PUCP-DGI dataset, and analyzes the accuracy by subject in the two settings where the best results were achieved (rn18 and rn34). Using rn18, we found that subjects that represent 59% of the instances reach individual accuracy of more than 50%.

Feature extractor	Sequence Length	Learning Rate	Stride	F1 micro AEC (%)	F1 micro PUCP-DGI (%)
rn18	10	1.0E-04	1	**80.3 ± 2.6**	20.2 ± 6
rn18	10	1.0E-05	1	59.1 ± 4.5	46.4 ± 4.9
rn18	10	1.0E-06	1	30.3 ± 5.2	49.6 ± 2.7
rn18	10	1.0E-04	2	78.8 ± 2.6	20.8 ± 7.9
rn18	10	1.0E-05	2	53 ± 6.9	48.8 ± 7.3
rn18	10	1.0E-06	2	30.3 ± 6.9	**51.8 ± 3.6**
rn18	15	1.0E-04	1	78.8 ± 2.6	22.2 ± 4.5
rn18	15	1.0E-05	1	57.6 ± 6.9	50.6 ± 9.8
rn18	15	1.0E-06	1	31.8 ± 4.5	49.8 ± 4.1
rn18	15	1.0E-04	2	74.2 ± 5.2	30 ± 11.5
rn18	15	1.0E-05	2	50 ± 4.5	50.4 ± 9.5
rn18	15	1.0E-06	2	31.8 ± 0	51 ± 1.5
rn34	10	1.0E-04	1	80.3 ± 2.6	27.6 ± 10.5
rn34	10	1.0E-05	1	56.1 ± 2.6	39.9 ± 5.2
rn34	10	1.0E-06	1	38.3 ± 11.4	34.7 ± 6.9
rn34	10	1.0E-04	2	74.2 ± 2.6	27.2 ± 7.5
rn34	10	1.0E-05	2	57.6 ± 2.6	40.7 ± 2.3
rn34	10	1.0E-06	2	38.3 ± 11.4	36.5 ± 6.2
rn34	15	1.0E-04	1	78.8 ± 2.6	27.2 ± 3.1
rn34	15	1.0E-05	1	53 ± 9.5	51.4 ± 4.2
rn34	15	1.0E-06	1	30.3 ± 2.6	**52.4 ± 1.2**
rn34	15	1.0E-04	2	75.8 ± 6.9	23.6 ± 4.3
rn34	15	1.0E-05	2	42.4 ± 6.9	50.6 ± 3.1
rn34	15	1.0E-06	2	33.3 ± 2.6	49.6 ± 2.5

Table 2: Comparison of F1 micro and macro for both datasets

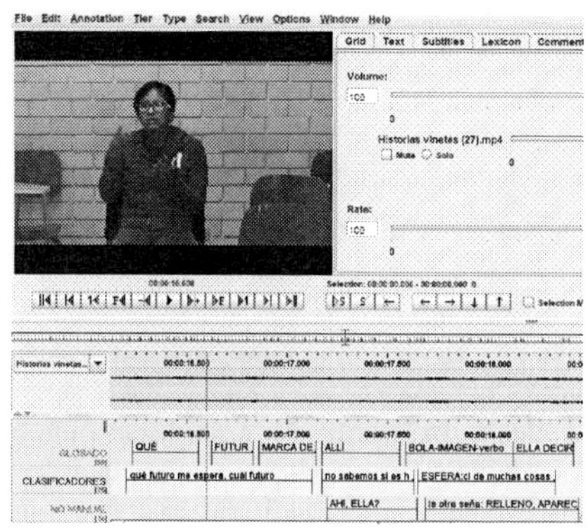

Figure 8: PUCP-DGI tiers for three-level annotation: gloss, description and classification

6. Conclusions

In this paper, we have presented PERUSIL, a framework to annotate sign language. We use this framework to annotate a continuous Peruvian Sign Language inter-

Subject	Number of instances	F1 in rn18	F1 in rn34
Subject15	1	0 %	0 %
Subject4	5	0 %	20 %
Subject8	1	0 %	0 %
Subject9	9	22 %	22 %
Subject13	4	25 %	100 %
Subject14	6	33 %	33 %
Subject2	3	33 %	0 %
Subject17	5	40 %	20 %
Subject19	5	40 %	60 %
Subject23	5	40 %	40 %
Subject27	8	50 %	38 %
Subject30	2	50 %	50 %
Subject6	14	50 %	50 %
Subject3	37	62 %	68 %
Subject12	3	67 %	33 %
Subject24	5	80 %	100 %
Subject18	15	87 %	87 %
Subject22	16	88 %	44 %
Subject20	7	100 %	57 %
Subject21	5	100 %	80 %
Subject25	3	100 %	100 %
Subject29	2	100 %	0 %
Subject37	5	100 %	20 %
Subject42	1	100 %	100 %
Subject5	1	100 %	0 %

Table 3: Frequency of instances within the set of 5 selected classes for training in PUCP-DGI dataset and accuracy by subject

pretation dataset of >500 unique signs and >150 sign sentences. We share publicly a multi-modal Sign Language interpretation resources. For the Peruvian LSP research community, this dataset becomes the first one to provide not only annotated isolated signs but annotation of continuous sign sentences. Our work can trigger the development of other sign language processing stages such as sign segmentation, sign classification (recognition), machine translation, language generation, human computing interaction, etc. Moreover, our proposed framework can help reduce the need of several experts by allowing hearing volunteers to annotate sign language interpretation videos based on audio. Further analysis in the inter-rater reliability of volunteer annotations needs to be tested. Nevertheless, it is highly recommended that the deaf community gets involved in the annotation task. This approach can help automate and scale annotation, as well as to build resources for low-resource sign language.

We demonstrated that a sign language recognition model trained on our dataset achieves moderate results when evaluated in a second dataset of native signers which was partially annotated by one deaf person. We expect that the dataset helps build better sign language processing models that a manage other challenges, such as non-controlled video environments and different rates and settings of recordings. We reached an accuracy of 80.3% in the same dataset, and an accuracy of 52.4% by testing the model in a second dataset. Although these results correspond to a reduced number of classes. Our future work will explore the development of sign language recognition models based on transfer learning, and data augmentation, which can allow working with a higher number of classes.

7. Acknowledgments

We thank all the volunteers who gathered to follow our proposed annotation framework, specially to Jessica Bornas, Edwin Diaz and Sandra Arana; our partners for volunteers training, José Ortiz (Capacitadero) and Alexandra Arnaiz; and Miguel Rodriguez-Mondoñedo for the review. The GPUs we used were provided by Chameleon Resource provided by NSF Keahey et al. (2020) and the Artificial Intelligence Research Group at PUCP (IAPUCP).

8. Bibliographical References

Albanie, S., Varol, G., Momeni, L., Afouras, T., Chung, J. S., Fox, N., and Zisserman, A. (2020). Bsl-1k: Scaling up co-articulated sign language recognition using mouthing cues. In Andrea Vedaldi, et al., editors, *Computer Vision – ECCV 2020*, pages 35–53, Cham. Springer International Publishing.

Berrú-Novoa, B., González-Valenzuela, R., and Shiguihara-Juárez, P. (2018). Peruvian sign language recognition using low resolution cameras. In *2018 IEEE XXV International Conference on Electronics, Electrical Engineering and Computing (INTERCON)*, pages 1–4.

Bragg, D., Koller, O., Bellard, M., Berke, L., Boudreault, P., Braffort, A., Caselli, N., Huenerfauth, M., Kacorri, H., Verhoef, T., Vogler, C., and Ringel Morris, M. (2019). Sign language recognition, generation, and translation: An interdisciplinary perspective. In *The 21st International ACM SIGACCESS Conference on Computers and Accessibility*, ASSETS '19, page 16–31, New York, NY, USA. Association for Computing Machinery.

Bull, H., Gouiffès, M., and Braffort, A. (2020). Automatic segmentation of sign language into subtitle-units. In *European Conference on Computer Vision*, pages 186–198. Springer.

Bull, H., Afouras, T., Varol, G., Albanie, S., Momeni, L., and Zisserman, A. (2021). Aligning subtitles in sign language videos. *CoRR*, abs/2105.02877.

Camgoz, N. C., Hadfield, S., Koller, O., Ney, H., and Bowden, R. (2018). Neural sign language translation. In *2018 IEEE/CVF Conference on Computer Vision and Pattern Recognition*, pages 7784–7793.

Camgoz, N. C., Koller, O., Hadfield, S., and Bowden, R. (2020a). Multi-channel transformers for multi-articulatory sign language translation. In *European Conference on Computer Vision*, pages 301–319. Springer.

Camgoz, N. C., Koller, O., Hadfield, S., and Bowden, R. (2020b). Sign language transformers: Joint end-to-end sign language recognition and translation. In *Proceedings of the IEEE/CVF conference on computer vision and pattern recognition*, pages 10023–10033.

Cormier, K., Fenlon, J., Johnston, T., Rentelis, R., Schembri, A., Rowley, K., Adam, R., and Woll,

B. (2012). From corpus to lexical database to online dictionary: Issues in annotation of the BSL corpus and the development of BSL SignBank. In Onno Crasborn, et al., editors, *Proceedings of the LREC2012 5th Workshop on the Representation and Processing of Sign Languages: Interactions between Corpus and Lexicon*, pages 7–12, Istanbul, Turkey, May. European Language Resources Association (ELRA).

De Coster, M., Van Herreweghe, M., and Dambre, J. (2021). Isolated sign recognition from rgb video using pose flow and self-attention. In *Proceedings of the IEEE/CVF Conference on Computer Vision and Pattern Recognition*, pages 3441–3450.

Dreuw, P. and Ney, H. (2008). Towards automatic sign language annotation for the elan tool. In *Workshop Programme*, volume 50.

Elizabeth and Parks, J. (2010). A sociolinguistic profile of the peruvian deaf community. *Sign Language Studies*, 10(4):409–441.

Fenlon, J., Denmark, T., Campbell, R., and Woll, B. (2007). Seeing sentence boundaries. *Sign Language & Linguistics*, 10(2):177–200.

Forster, J., Schmidt, C., Hoyoux, T., Koller, O., Zelle, U., Piater, J., and Ney, H. (2012). RWTH-PHOENIX-Weather: A large vocabulary sign language recognition and translation corpus. In Nicoletta Calzolari, et al., editors, *8th International Conference on Language Resources and Evaluation (LREC 2012)*, pages 3785–3789, Istanbul, Turkey, May. European Language Resources Association (ELRA).

He, K., Zhang, X., Ren, S., and Sun, J. (2016). Deep residual learning for image recognition. In *Proceedings of the IEEE conference on computer vision and pattern recognition*, pages 770–778.

INEI and CONADIS. (2012). Primera encuesta nacional especializada sobre discapacidad 2012.

INEI. (2018). Resultados definitivos de los censos nacionales 2017.

Keahey, K., Anderson, J., Zhen, Z., Riteau, P., Ruth, P., Stanzione, D., Cevik, M., Colleran, J., Gunawi, H. S., Hammock, C., Mambretti, J., Barnes, A., Halbach, F., Rocha, A., and Stubbs, J. (2020). Lessons learned from the chameleon testbed. In *Proceedings of the 2020 USENIX Annual Technical Conference (USENIX ATC '20)*. USENIX Association, July.

Lazo, C., Sanchez, Z., and del Carpio, C. (2019). A static hand gesture recognition for peruvian sign language using digital image processing and deep learning. In Yuzo Iano, et al., editors, *Proceedings of the 4th Brazilian Technology Symposium (BTSym'18)*, pages 281–290, Cham. Springer International Publishing.

Lugaresi, C., Tang, J., Nash, H., McClanahan, C., Uboweja, E., Hays, M., Zhang, F., Chang, C.-L., Yong, M. G., Lee, J., Chang, W.-T., Hua, W., Georg, M., and Grundmann, M. (2019). Mediapipe: A framework for building perception pipelines.

Madrid Vega, R. M. (2018). Clasificadores en la lengua de señas peruana (LSP). BSc dissertation, Pontificia Universidad Católica del Perú, Lima, Perú.

Mejía Gamarra, J. E., Alonso Salazar Cubas, M., Sosa Silupú, J. D., and Enrique Córdova Chirinos, C. (2020). Prototype for peruvian sign language translation based on an artificial neural network approach. In *2020 IEEE XXVII International Conference on Electronics, Electrical Engineering and Computing (INTERCON)*, pages 1–4.

MIMP. (2017). Decreto supremo que aprueba el reglamento de la ley n° 29535, ley que otorga reconocimiento oficial a la lengua de señas peruana.

Nureña-Jara, R., Ramos-Carrión, C., and Shiguihara-Juárez, P. (2020). Data collection of 3d spatial features of gestures from static peruvian sign language alphabet for sign language recognition. In *2020 IEEE Engineering International Research Conference (EIRCON)*, pages 1–4.

Renz, K., Stache, N. C., Albanie, S., and Varol, G. (2021a). Sign language segmentation with temporal convolutional networks. In *ICASSP 2021-2021 IEEE International Conference on Acoustics, Speech and Signal Processing (ICASSP)*, pages 2135–2139. IEEE.

Renz, K., Stache, N. C., Fox, N., Varol, G., and Albanie, S. (2021b). Sign segmentation with changepoint-modulated pseudo-labelling. *CoRR*, abs/2104.13817.

Wittenburg, P., Brugman, H., Russel, A., Klassmann, A., and Sloetjes, H. (2006). ELAN: a professional framework for multimodality research. In Nicoletta Calzolari, et al., editors, *5th International Conference on Language Resources and Evaluation (LREC 2006)*, pages 1556–1559, Genoa, Italy, May. European Language Resources Association (ELRA).

Yin, K., Moryossef, A., Hochgesang, J., Goldberg, Y., and Alikhani, M. (2021). Including signed languages in natural language processing. *arXiv preprint arXiv:2105.05222*.

9. Language Resource References

Rodriguez Mondoñedo, Miguel and Arnaiz Fernandez-Concha, Alexandra. (2022). *Archivos de videos en mp4*. Pontificia Universidad Católica del Perú.

Rodríguez Mondoñedo, Miguel and Arnaiz, Alexandra. (2015). *Repositorio Lengua de Señas Peruana*.

Proceedings of the 10th Workshop on the Representation and Processing of Sign Languages (sign-lang@LREC 2022), pages 9–15
Language Resources and Evaluation Conference (LREC 2022), Marseille, 20-25 June 2022

Introducing Sign Languages to a Multilingual Wordnet: Bootstrapping Corpora and Lexical Resources of Greek Sign Language and German Sign Language

Sam Bigeard*, Marc Schulder*, Maria Kopf*, Thomas Hanke*, Kyriaki Vasilaki‡, Anna Vacalopoulou‡, Theodoros Goulas‡, Athanasia–Lida Dimou‡, Stavroula–Evita Fotinea‡, Eleni Efthimiou‡

*Institute of German Sign Language and Communication of the Deaf (IDGS), University of Hamburg, Germany
{sam.bigeard, marc.schulder, maria.kopf, thomas.hanke}@uni-hamburg.de
‡Institute for Language and Speech Processing (ILSP), Athena Research Center, Greece
{kvasilaki, avacalop, tgoulas, ndimou, evita, eleni_e}@athenarc.gr

Abstract

Wordnets have been a popular lexical resource type for many years. Their sense-based representation of lexical items and numerous relation structures have been used for a variety of computational and linguistic applications. The inclusion of different wordnets into multilingual wordnet networks has further extended their use into the realm of cross-lingual research. Wordnets have been released for many spoken languages. Research has also been carried out into the creation of wordnets for several sign languages, but none have yet resulted in publicly available datasets. This article presents our own efforts towards an inclusion of sign languages in a multilingual wordnet, starting with Greek Sign Language (GSL) and German Sign Language (DGS). Based on differences in available language resources between GSL and DGS, we trial two workflows with different coverage priorities. We also explore how synergies between both workflows can be leveraged and how future work on additional sign languages could profit from building on existing sign language wordnet data. The results of our work are made publicly available.

Keywords: Multilingual Wordnet, Sign Language Wordnet, Semi-automatic resource creation

1. Introduction

Multilingual resources like wordnets are still scarce in the field of sign language research. A multilingual sign language wordnet could open doors for computational linguistics as well as lexicographers working on sign language dictionaries. Sign language resources such as corpora and lexicons are often searchable only through spoken language translation, due to the lack of a common and easy to use sign writing system. Multilingual indexation is hindered by research-specific lemmatisation approaches which are difficult to combine. These conditions are a challenge for both human users and computational applications, the latter lacking machine-readable resources of all kinds for sign languages. To make sign language resources more searchable, more machine-readable, and their sense descriptions more precise and accessible, we aim at creating a multilingual sign language wordnet.

In this paper, we present our approach towards such a sign wordnet. We use a combination of automatic and manual methods to bootstrap the integration of sign languages into a multilingual wordnet. For this we are working on two languages in parallel: Greek Sign Language (GSL) and German Sign Language (DGS). The two languages are very different with regard to available resources, which gives us the opportunity to test different approaches and see which works best for what kind of resource. By describing our method and the issues we have encountered we hope to provide a helpful guide to other researchers working on multilingual sign language resources.

The results of our work are made publicly available and will be updated as our efforts progress.[1]

[1] https://doi.org/10.25592/uhhfdm.10169

2. Background

In this section we outline the relevant background on wordnets, describing the history of spoken language wordnets (Section 2.1) and existing work on sign language wordnets (Section 2.2).

2.1. Wordnets for Spoken Languages

The concept of a wordnet was first introduced by Miller et al. (1990) as the idea of a dictionary based on psycholinguistic principles. The new approach was that words are not organised alphabetically but in so-called synonym sets (synsets), each representing an underlying concept. The synsets are interconnected via directional relations such as hyponymy, antonymy and meronymy. For example, the concept of a dog, the animal, is expressed by a synset consisting of the words 'dog', 'domestic dog' and 'Canis familiaris'. This synset is a hyponym (i. e. a more specific form of) the 'domestic animal' synset. Other word senses of 'dog' are covered by other synsets with their own relations, such as the concept of a reprehensible person expressed by the terms 'dog', 'cad', 'blackguard' and others.

While the original Princeton Wordnet (PWN) was designed for English, wordnets for many other languages have since been created. Several efforts to interconnect these into a multilingual wordnet have been undertaken. The most prominent effort that is still actively supported is the Open Multilingual WordNet (OMW) (Bond and Paik, 2012).

Most wordnet projects use Princeton Wordnet as a basis to expand upon, rather than developing their own wordnet from scratch (Bond et al., 2016). This approach is known as the *expand model*. While this creates a bias toward English, it significantly reduces the amount of work needed to create a new wordnet and connect existing ones.

While the construction of a wordnet for well resourced spoken languages is relatively straightforward, the process has to be revisited for less resourced languages. Commonly used resources like dictionaries, wikis, and others may not be available. Bosch and Griesel (2017) use the *expand model* to create a wordnet of five South African languages. One of their findings is that 'similarities shared on levels such as morphology or grammar and semantics allow the language teams to learn from one another, to share and thus to fast-track the development of the individual wordnets in this way' (Bosch and Griesel, 2017, p. 11). On this basis, we expect that once a wordnet for one sign language is established, subsequent sign language wordnets will be able to build on it, significantly reducing the amount of work needed.

2.2. Wordnets for Sign Languages

Work on creating wordnets for individual signed languages has been reported for Swiss-German Sign Language (DSGS) (Ebling et al., 2012), Italian Sign Language (LIS) (Shoaib et al., 2014) and American Sign Language (ASL) (Lualdi et al., 2021), although no publicly available resource have yet been released. All of these works have in common that they seek to link wordnet structures to existing lexical resources of the respective signed language. This approach allows them to leverage existing video recordings and lexicographic information for individual signs, drastically reducing the cost of creating the wordnet. In the case of ASL, several lexical resources are used to increase the available vocabulary (Lualdi et al., 2021).

Other works do not seek to publish full signed language wordnets, but rather use existing wordnets for a spoken language as an aid to internal work. Troelsgård and Kristoffersen (2018) link entries in their lexical database of Danish Sign Language (DTS) to roughly matching synsets in DanNet. These links are used as an aid to lexicographers and to automatically determine potential synonyms. The authors stress that the wordnet senses do not necessarily correspond exactly to the sign senses. Langer and Schulder (2020) match lexical entries of the DGS Corpus (see Section 3.2) with wordnet lemmas to extract supersense categories for use in coarse semantic clustering for lexicographic work. The matching is done automatically, based on existing German translational equivalents for the signs and does not take into account word sense disambiguation.

3. Resources

Following the approach of other signed language wordnet creation efforts, we build directly on existing resources for Greek Sign Language (GSL), German Sign Language (DGS), Greek, and German. While the resources for GSL and DGS each include a corpus and a lexical resource, their history of creation and resulting available information structures are very different. However, among their main similarities lies the fact that they are both built with their respective sign languages (SLs) as a starting point; in other words, they are SL-based and produced and verified by both deaf and hearing experts of GSL and DGS.

3.1. GSL Lexical Resources

The repository of GSL lexical resources has been collected, built, and annotated for years by the Institute for Language and Speech Processing (ILSP). It mainly consists of the Noema+ bilingual dictionary (GSL and Modern Greek) and the underlying Polytropon parallel corpus, which provides example utterances involving specific signs. These were based on utterances from expert discussions which were then re-recorded in a studio environment and annotated to serve as a 'golden' corpus open to SL technologies research (Efthimiou et al., 2016; Efthimiou et al., 2018). These two resources comprise the most extensive reference pool for GSL to date and include more than 3,600 clauses in GSL.

The lexical database currently consists of approximately 12,000 entries and it has been annotated in its entirety on the basis of the Polytropon corpus. The construction and maintenance of the database is facilitated with the use of a dedicated web-based open environment that supports the creation and interlinking of GSL resources, namely, the SiS-Builder (Goulas et al., 2010).

As the Polytropon corpus consists of isolated utterances chosen to illustrate specific signs, the contribution relating to GSL is more lexicon- than corpus-based. While this has the drawback of not providing the full context and authenticity of natural discourse, the advantage of this more controlled environment is the more explicit correspondence between GSL sign and sense-appropriate Greek translation.

3.2. DGS Corpus Resources

The DGS Corpus is an annotated corpus of 560 hours of natural discourse in DGS (Prillwitz et al., 2008). A subset of the corpus has been released publicly as the Public DGS Corpus (Jahn et al., 2018).

The DGS Corpus implements a type hierarchy, called 'double glossing' (Konrad et al., 2012, p. 88). Each type represents a distinct sign and is further subdivided into subtypes, each of which represents a lexicalised meaning of that sign. Glosses for types and subtypes in the DGS Corpus are available in English and German.

In addition to the gloss name, each subtype can have one or more concept entries associated with it in the lexical database of the DGS Corpus. Concept entries are written with German or English orthography (as opposed to the all-caps glosses) and specify possible meanings. In the DTS corpus, which uses the same lexical database structure as DGS Corpus, these concept entries are in fact used to represent the DanNet synsets (Troelsgård and Kristoffersen, 2018). In the DGS Corpus, however, concepts are only disambiguated in relation to the German and English terms. If sign and word have the same sense ambiguity, only one concept is created. This makes DGS Corpus concepts coarser than wordnet synsets but more fine grained than glosses.

On the basis of the DGS Corpus a digital dictionary for DGS is currently being created, called DW-DGS (Müller et al., 2020). The dictionary provides more nuanced information on signs and their senses. The first pre-release entries are already published[2] and can be used to further feed the sign wordnet for DGS.

[2] http://dw-dgs.de

3.3. Greek WordNet

OMW covers a wide range of spoken languages, created in individual projects. The Greek WordNet included in OMW consists of 18,049 synsets. The Greek synsets were originally developed in the context of BalkaNet, a multilingual wordnet of Balkan languages (Grigoriadou et al., 2004). They were based on a series of Greek lexicons and corpora. In the course of our work we found that the entries of the Greek WordNet that we inspected mainly included glossed explanations of each lexical item with minimal, if any, usage examples.

3.4. GermaNet

The largest wordnet for German is GermaNet (Hamp and Feldweg, 1997). As of version 17 it contains 159,514 synsets. Due to licence restrictions it is not directly integrated into OMW. However, for 28,564 of its synsets a mapping to PWN exists, from which OMW identifiers can be inferred. For our mutlilingual wordnet we decided to use GermaNet and expand the connections to OMW.

4. Wordnet Creation

To create the multilingual sign wordnet both teams — the GSL and DGS team — first work independently on their respective language with frequent exchanges regarding method and implementation.
The GSL team follows a high precision approach of identifying strong synset matches for entries in the GSL lexical database. They prioritise providing at least one sign for many different synsets over specifying every possible synonym. This approach is outlined in Section 4.1.
The DGS team follows a high recall approach of automatically matching its corpus type inventory to wordnet lemmas and then verifying these matches. They prioritise validating many potential synonyms of fewer synsets over partially covering many synsets. This is described in Section 4.2.
The intermediate progress of both teams is compared in Section 4.3.
As work progresses, lists of linked synsets are exchanged between the teams to allow them to prioritise those synsets also covered by the other group. Additional cross-lingual factors are also considered, as described in Section 4.4. This pushes forward the progress towards a large interlingual index.

4.1. Linking the GSL Lexical Resources

The GSL team uses data that is collected by a semi-automatic process of mapping synsets from the Greek part of OMW to the GSL lexical database. As the only common element of both databases are Greek lemmas, this is done by matching the 'Greek equivalent' entries of GSL signs with the Greek lemmas in OMW synsets; at the end of this process, each GSL entry whose Greek equivalent also appears in OMW is mapped to the respective OMW entry.
In the next stage of the process, these automatically generated associations are checked by deaf and hearing GSL experts for validity against the respective videos offered for each sign, resulting in a new 'clean' database of wordnet synsets and their GSL equivalents. Of course, this is hardly a one-to-one connection, as a lot of false equivalents are revealed in the process. For instance, the GSL entry 'ανέκδοτο' has been automatically linked via the Greek equivalent to synset 07220586-n, which matches the English word 'anecdote'. However, this sense of the Greek equivalent does not correspond to the respective entry in the GSL database, where the word is associated with its much more frequent sense of 'joke'. The more fitting synset 06778102-n was not found during automatic matching because it has no Greek entry. All such instances are manually corrected by GSL experts.
The accuracy of the equivalents is tested against GSL examples that are linked to each of the lexical resource's entries to make sure that each corresponds to the correct definition, or rather glossed explanation (Fellbaum, 1998), in Greek WordNet. A secondary way of double-checking whether the correct sense of each entry is selected is reviewing the other available language versions in OMW with which annotators are familiar, namely, English and French.
In addition to that, the Greek WordNet proves to be rather limited for the purposes of this experiment, as it comprises 18,049 synsets compared to the English data of PWN, which consists of 117,659 synsets in version 3.0. These numbers limit the linking process even more. To compensate for this, it was decided to extend the mapping of the GSL material to the richer English part of OMW at a second level. At the time of writing, 1819 GSL signs have been linked to 4214 wordnet synsets.

4.2. Linking DGS Corpus

The DGS team uses a three-step method: automatic generation of candidate matches between synsets and subtypes, automatic verification of certain simple cases, and manual verification of all remaining cases.
Automatic matching is done between the lemmas of OMW synsets and the concept entries of DGS Corpus subtypes. Both German and English are used for this, although German is preferred, as concept values are more precise in that languages. Where no concept entry is available for a subtype, its gloss name is used as a fallback.
As mentioned in Section 2.1, we use GermaNet as our German wordnet resource and connect its entries to OMW through its partial mapping to PWN. If a German word is not present in GermaNet or a GermaNet synset has no connection to OMW, the English concept entry or gloss is used instead. For the case that there is no English translation in the DGS Corpus or no corresponding synset in OMW, a fallback solution of automatic translation of the German gloss to English is used.
At the time of writing, automatic candidate matches between 11,856 DGS subtypes and 27,020 synsets were found. Subtypes were associated with a mean of 8.6 synsets and a median of 2. This is a 'long tail' situation, where most subtypes have very few senses, while heavily polysemous terms such as 'have' or 'good' (and their DGS counterparts) have 20 synsets or more associated with them. In many cases, the two synsets associated with the sign represent a basic and a figurative sense.
In a second automatic processing step, candidate matches with a high likelihood of being correct are identified and marked as provisionally validated. This automatic valida-

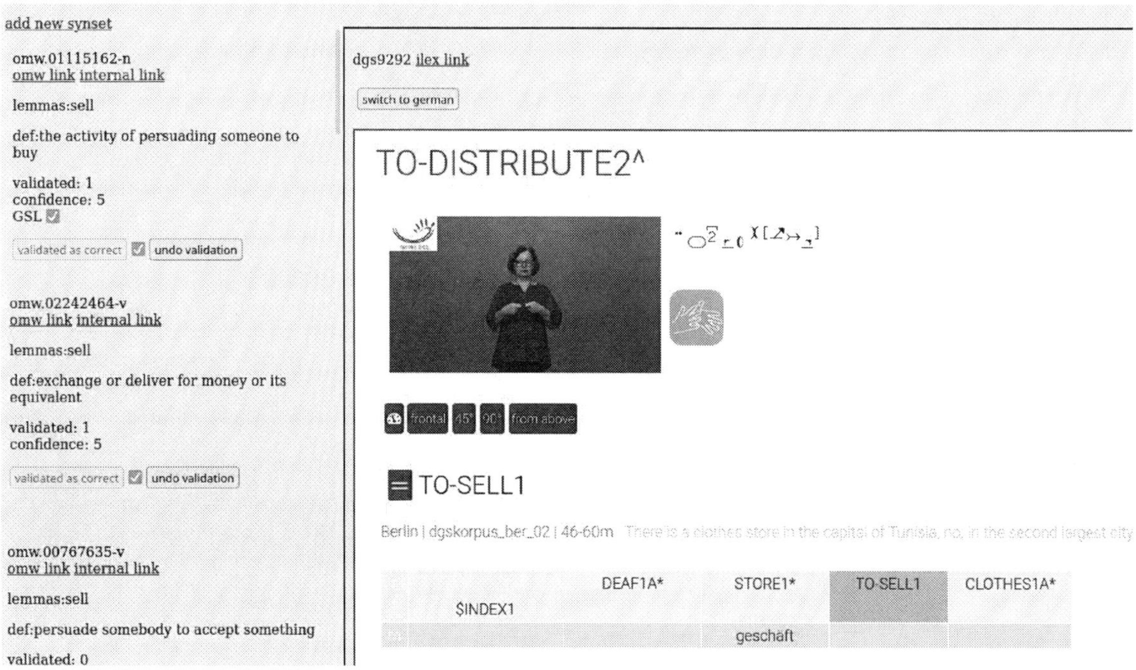

Figure 1: Manual validation interface listing all synsets associated with a specific DGS sign. The left side lists the associated synsets and their validation status for DGS and GSL, while the right side shows the DGS signs' type entry page from the Public DGS Corpus website.

tion step selects subtypes which were matched with only a single synset and using strong match conditions, i. e. not via automatic translation. Such single match-pairs mainly occur among the long tail of homonymous expressions. As they are based on high quality human translations (concept entries or glosses), the chance of such matches introducing incorrect senses for a sign is very low.

In the final step, the remaining automatic matches are validated manually by using corpus evidence and the expert's own acceptability judgements. Ideally such verifications would only be performed by L1 language users. Due to the large number of matches (over 100,000 subtype-synset pairs) this is currently not possible for us. Instead we follow a two-tiered approach in which L2 language users validate cases for which they have high confidence and mark the remaining cases for later review by an L1 user. This method allows us to have more annotators involved, resulting in a quicker workflow.

Figure 1 shows the validation interface for confirming or rejecting all synsets that were automatically matched to a specific sign. At the time of writing, 2230 DGS signs with one or more synsets have been validated.

4.3. Progress

Statistics on the current progress of linking both languages to OMW are outlined in Table 1. A notable difference between the languages can be seen regarding the number of signs and synsets covered relative to the overall number of sign-synset pairs. For GSL the number of validated pairs is close to the number of distinct synsets but greater than the number of signs, meaning that each sign is on average linked to 2.3 synsets, but only few synsets are linked to more than one sign. The number of validated DGS pairs, on the other hand, shows the inverse pattern, with most signs linking to only one synset, but covered synsets containing an average 2.4 signs each.

The difference between the languages is caused by both the difference in workflow between the teams already described in Section 4.1 and Section 4.2 and by the nature of the datasets on which they build. As described in Section 3.1, the GSL lexicon is primarily based on work for the Noema+ bilingual dictionary. Its focus was on providing GSL signs for many concepts. Following in this vein, the GSL team covered a wide variety of different concepts during their validation.

The DGS vocabulary, on the other hand, stems from the sign inventory encountered in the natural conversations of the DGS Corpus (see Section 3.2), reflecting the many variations in participants' vocabulary due to regional differences, age group, register, and other factors, leading to the presence of many synonyms. In addition, the DGS team started out by validating comparatively unambiguous concepts such as the names of months, which are straightforward to validate, but can be expressed by a large number of different signs in DGS. Because of this, comparatively few synsets are covered, but each with a higher number of signs associated with it.

It should be noted that the current ratios are due to the preliminary nature of the work. As the dataset size growths, both languages will start exhibiting the many-to-many ratio of more complete wordnets, with considerably more pairs than synsets or signs. This development is already hinted

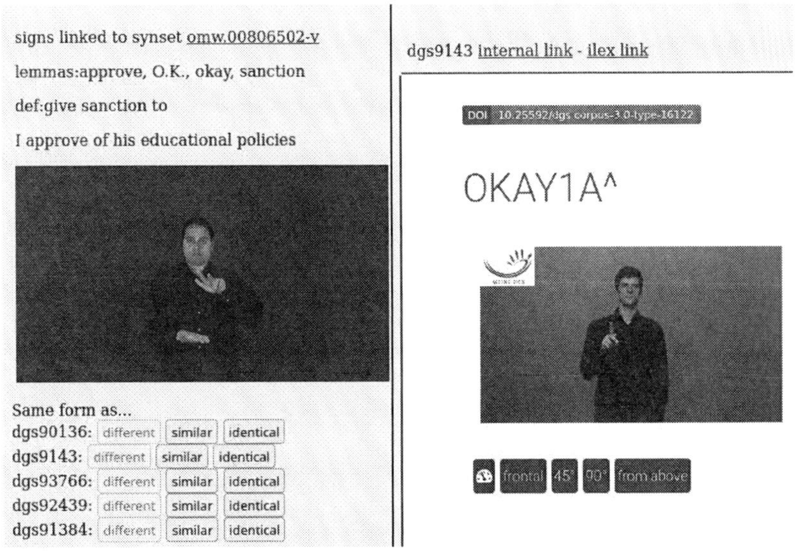

Figure 2: Manual validation interface for comparing GSL and DGS entries associated with the same synset. The interface integrates GSL video from Noema+ (left) and DGS type entry pages from the Public DGS Corpus website (right). The lower left corner lists DGS types that should be compared to the given GSL video to specify whether their sign form is identical, similar or different.

	GSL validated	DGS candidates	DGS validated	GSL/DGS overlap
distinct synsets	4214	27,020	969	278
distinct signs	1819	11,856	2230	*n/a*
sign-synset pairs	4347	138,518	2330	*n/a*

Table 1: Statistics on the current state of linking GSL and DGS vocabulary to OMW.

at by the ratio of automatic DGS candidates, which mirrors the word-synset ratios of the GermaNet entries that they are based on. Some difference, caused by the differences in source data, can however be expected to remain.

4.4. Cross-lingual Connections

Like other wordnet efforts for less-resourced languages, we apply the *expand model* of building on other languages already represented by a wordnet. While spoken language wordnet information is used for this out of necessity, it would be preferable to build on other sign languages where available to be hindered less by modality-specific assumptions.

As we are working on integrating two sign languages in parallel, synergies are used where they present themselves. As the GSL team had already produced a number of synset-sign matches when the DGS team started their manual validation phase, they prioritised synsets which were covered by both automatic DGS matching and GSL.

In addition to validating synset-sign matches, the DGS team also compared the form of the GSL and DGS signs (apart from mouthing) to identify identical and similar signs. The interface for this is shown in Figure 2. Such overlaps between languages can indicate shared iconicity (incidental or otherwise) or other kinds of linguistic relatedness. Annotating these overlaps adds a cross-lingual phonetic relation that is not usually covered by wordnets, but is of great use to research, for example for sign language technologies struggling with data sparsity.

Once signs from both languages are established for a synset, members of either team can inspect which other synsets the sign of the opposing language is connected to. They can then consider whether to expand their own sign to those synsets as well. Synsets with identical/similar forms across languages make particularly good candidates for this step.

5. Conclusion

In this paper we have presented our work on integrating Greek Sign Language and German Sign Language into the Open Multilingual Wordnet. To achieve this, we explore different workflows for working with lexicon-based and corpus-based data and for cross-lingual workflows.

This work has so far resulted in a publicly available dataset of 1819 GSL signs and 2230 DGS signs from existing language resources being linked to 4214 and 969 OMW synsets respectively, including 278 synsets that are covered by both languages. The state of this dataset is preliminary and it will be significantly expanded in size through future updates.[3]

In the long run we intend to add additional languages to this effort. Based on the experience of Bosch and Griesel (2017)

[3] For the latest version of the dataset, see https://doi.org/10.25592/uhhfdm.10168.

with using the *expand model* for less-resourced languages, we expect the required effort for adding new languages will become progressively more manageable as other sign languages can be built upon.

6. Acknowledgements

This work is supported in part by the EASIER (Intelligent Automatic Sign Language Translation) Project. EASIER has received funding from the European Union's Horizon 2020 research and innovation programme, grant agreement n° 101016982.
This publication has been produced in part in the context of the joint research funding of the German Federal Government and Federal States in the Academies' Programme, with funding from the Federal Ministry of Education and Research and the Free and Hanseatic City of Hamburg. The Academies' Programme is coordinated by the Union of the Academies of Sciences and Humanities.

7. Bibliographical References

Bond, F. and Paik, K. (2012). A survey of wordnets and their licenses. In *Proceedings of the 6th Global WordNet Conference*, page 8, Matsue, Japan.

Bond, F., Vossen, P., McCrae, J. P., and Fellbaum, C. (2016). CILI: the collaborative interlingual index. In *Proceedings of the Eighth Global WordNet Conference*, pages 50–57, Bucharest, Romania. University of Iasi.

Bosch, S. E. and Griesel, M. (2017). Strategies for building wordnets for under-resourced languages: The case of African languages. *Literator*, 38(1):1–12. DOI: 10.4102/lit.v38i1.1351.

Ebling, S., Tissi, K., and Volk, M. (2012). Semi-automatic annotation of semantic relations in a Swiss German Sign Language lexicon. In Crasborn, O., et al., editors, *Proceedings of the LREC2012 5th Workshop on the Representation and Processing of Sign Languages: Interactions between Corpus and Lexicon*, pages 31–36, Istanbul, Turkey. European Language Resources Association (ELRA).

Efthimiou, E., Fotinea, S.-E., Dimou, A.-L., Goulas, T., Karioris, P., Vasilaki, K., Vacalopoulou, A., and Pissaris, M. (2016). From a sign lexical database to an SL golden corpus – the POLYTROPON SL resource. In Efthimiou, E., et al., editors, *Proceedings of the LREC2016 7th Workshop on the Representation and Processing of Sign Languages: Corpus Mining*, pages 63–68, Portorož, Slovenia. European Language Resources Association (ELRA).

Efthimiou, E., Vasilaki, K., Fotinea, S.-E., Vacalopoulou, A., Goulas, T., and Dimou, A.-L. (2018). The POLYTROPON parallel corpus. In Bono, M., et al., editors, *Proceedings of the LREC2018 8th Workshop on the Representation and Processing of Sign Languages: Involving the Language Community*, pages 39–44, Miyazaki, Japan. European Language Resources Association (ELRA).

Fellbaum, C., editor. (1998). *WordNet: an electronic lexical database*. Language, Speech, and Communication. MIT Press.

Goulas, T., Fotinea, S.-E., Efthimiou, E., and Pissaris, M. (2010). SiS-Builder: A sign synthesis support tool. In Dreuw, P., et al., editors, *Proceedings of the LREC2010 4th Workshop on the Representation and Processing of Sign Languages: Corpora and Sign Language Technologies*, pages 102–105, Valletta, Malta. European Language Resources Association (ELRA).

Grigoriadou, M., Kornilakis, H., Galiotou, E., Stamou, S., and Papakitsos, E. C. (2004). The software infrastructure for the development and validation of the greek wordnet. *Romanian Journal of Information, Science and Technology*, pages 89–105.

Hamp, B. and Feldweg, H. (1997). GermaNet - a lexical-semantic net for German. In *Proceedings of the ACL Workshop on Automatic Information Extraction and Building of Lexical Semantic Resources for NLP Applications*, pages 9–15, Madrid, Spain. Association for Computational Linguistics.

Jahn, E., Konrad, R., Langer, G., Wagner, S., and Hanke, T. (2018). Publishing DGS Corpus data: Different formats for different needs. In Bono, M., et al., editors, *Proceedings of the LREC2018 8th Workshop on the Representation and Processing of Sign Languages: Involving the Language Community*, pages 83–90, Miyazaki, Japan. European Language Resources Association (ELRA).

Konrad, R., Hanke, T., König, S., Langer, G., Matthes, S., Nishio, R., and Regen, A. (2012). From form to function. a database approach to handle lexicon building and spotting token forms in sign languages. In Crasborn, O., et al., editors, *Proceedings of the LREC2012 5th Workshop on the Representation and Processing of Sign Languages: Interactions between Corpus and Lexicon*, pages 87–94, Istanbul, Turkey. European Language Resources Association (ELRA).

Langer, G. and Schulder, M. (2020). Collocations in sign language lexicography: Towards semantic abstractions for word sense discrimination. In Efthimiou, E., et al., editors, *Proceedings of the LREC2020 9th Workshop on the Representation and Processing of Sign Languages: Sign Language Resources in the Service of the Language Community, Technological Challenges and Application Perspectives*, pages 127–134, Marseille, France. European Language Resources Association (ELRA).

Lualdi, C. P., Wright, E., Hudson, J., Caselli, N. K., and Fellbaum, C. (2021). Implementing ASLNet v1.0: Progress and plans. In *Proceedings of the 11th Global Wordnet Conference*, pages 63–72, Potchefstroom, South Africa. South African Centre for Digital Language Resources (SADiLaR).

Miller, G. A., Beckwith, R., Fellbaum, C., Gross, D., and Miller, K. (1990). Introduction to wordnet: An on-line lexical database. *International Journal of Lexicography*, 3. DOI: 10.1093/ijl/3.4.235.

Müller, A., Hanke, T., Konrad, R., Langer, G., and Wähl, S. (2020). From dictionary to corpus and back again – linking heterogeneous language resources for DGS. In Efthimiou, E., et al., editors, *Proceedings of the LREC2020 9th Workshop on the Representation and Processing of Sign Languages: Sign Language Resources in the Service of the Language Community, Technological Challenges and Application Perspectives*, pages 157–164, Marseille, France. European Language Resources Association (ELRA).

Prillwitz, S., Hanke, T., König, S., Konrad, R., Langer, G., and Schwarz, A. (2008). DGS Corpus project – development of a corpus based electronic dictionary German Sign Language / German. In Crasborn, O., et al., editors, *Proceedings of the LREC2008 3rd Workshop on the Representation and Processing of Sign Languages: Construction and Exploitation of Sign Language Corpora*, pages 159–164, Marrakech, Morocco. European Language Resources Association (ELRA).

Shoaib, U., Ahmad, N., Prinetto, P., and Tiotto, G. (2014). Integrating MultiWordNet with Italian Sign Language lexical resources. *Expert Systems with Applications*, 41(5):2300–2308. DOI: 10.1016/j.eswa.2013.09.027.

Troelsgård, T. and Kristoffersen, J. (2018). Improving lemmatisation consistency without a phonological description. the Danish Sign Language corpus and dictionary project. In Bono, M., et al., editors, *Proceedings of the LREC2018 8th Workshop on the Representation and Processing of Sign Languages: Involving the Language Community*, pages 195–198, Miyazaki, Japan. European Language Resources Association (ELRA).

Proceedings of the 10th Workshop on the Representation and Processing of Sign Languages (sign-lang@LREC 2022), pages 16–23
Language Resources and Evaluation Conference (LREC 2022), Marseille, 20-25 June 2022

Introducing the `signglossR` Package

Carl Börstell
University of Bergen
Sydnesplassen 7, 5007, Bergen, Norway
carl.borstell@uib.no

Abstract

The `signglossR` package is a library written in the programming language R, intended as an easy-to-use resource for those who work with signed language data and are familiar with R. The package contains a variety of functions designed specifically towards signed language research, facilitating a single-pipeline workflow with R when accessing public language resources remotely (online) or a user's own files and data. The package specifically targets processing of image and video files, but also features some interaction with software commonly used by researchers working on signed language and gesture, such as *ELAN* and *OpenPose*. The `signglossR` package combines features and functionality from many other libraries and tools in order to simplify and collect existing resources in one place, as well as adding some new functionality, and adapt everything to the needs of researchers working with visual language data. In this paper, the main features of this package are introduced.

Keywords: sign language, signed language, multimedia, annotation, R, software

1. Introduction

Signed languages are (unless tactile) primarily visual languages. This differentiates them from spoken languages, which although also multimodal at their core (by virtue of being interactive, contextualized and simultaneously vocal and gestural) have established conventions for representing linguistic form in writing, either as (adapted) orthographic writing – e.g. conventionalized spelling or Jefferson transcription (Jefferson, 2004) – or phonetic transcription – e.g. the International Phonetic Alphabet. Although transcription even for spoken languages is only a partial representation of the multidimensional and highly variable properties of actual speech, the situation for signed languages is arguably much worse. Standard practice for representing signs in writing – since the earliest days of signed language research – has been based on so-called *sign glosses* (Miller, 2006; van der Hulst and Channon, 2010; Frishberg et al., 2012; Crasborn, 2015), representing signs with approximate written language translations rendered in small caps – e.g. TOMATO for the American Sign Language (ASL) sign meaning 'tomato', or even by combining the historical parts of the sign as a compound: RED+SLICE. While some notation systems have been developed to render a visually recognizable form of a sign, most notably *SignWriting* (Sutton, 1996) – shown to be useful for linguists and non-linguist signers alike in representing and recreating sign forms through transcription (Pizzuto et al., 2008) – others have sought to represent sign forms through combinations of symbols each representing a form segment of a sign, most notably the phonemic notation system introduced by Stokoe (1960) or later the phonetic machine-readable strings of *HamNoSys* (Prillwitz et al., 1989; Hanke, 2004). Nonetheless, the dominant convention has arguably been the use of sign glosses, which has continued to be used in corpus annotation work for signed languages (Johnston, 2010; Johnston, 2014; Schembri and Crasborn, 2010). However, sign glossing has been criticized for its complete disregard from representing signed languages in their true modality, with scholars arguing for a practice in which signed language examples are always represented in a visual form – preferably video, but possibly still images (Hochgesang, 2022) or a visually motivated transcription (Pizzuto et al., 2008).

Stepping away from the practice of only using written glosses for signed language examples has been lobbied for by Julie Hochgesang, sometimes under the Twitter hashtag #TyrannyOfGlossing. Later, an attempt to phrase this concretely, the Twitter hashtag #GlossGesang was defined as *"Always present sign language data in a visual format (videos/images) without relying solely on glossing"*. As such, even if sign glosses are used, for reasons of keeping unique, machine-readable labels in a database, they should always be accompanied by a visual representation – e.g. Figure 1.[1]

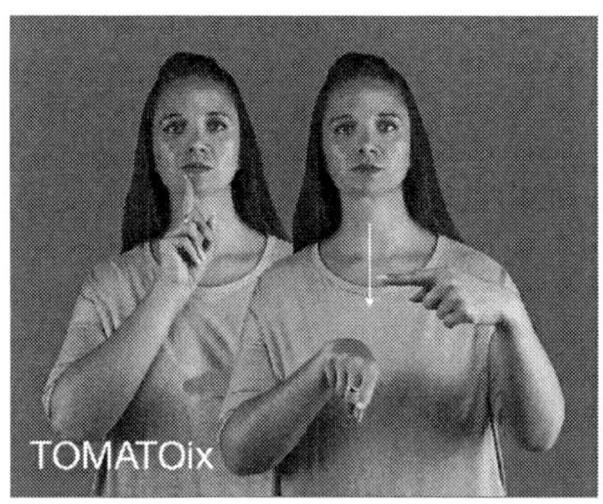

Figure 1: The ASL sign TOMATOix from ASL Signbank (Hochgesang et al., 2022, 1253).

[1] `https://aslsignbank.haskins.yale.edu/dictionary/gloss/1253.html`

The R package `signglossR` was directly inspired by the work of Julie Hochgesang and was originally intended to help researchers work towards visual representation of signed language data by facilitating the access to tools for collecting and modifying image and video data. In the following sections, I will present the main functionalities of the `signglossR` package and how it can be used to work with signed language data.

2. The signglossR package

The `signglossR` package is a library written in the programming language R, intended as an easy-to-use resource for those who work with signed language data and are familiar with R. The package contains a variety of functions designed specifically towards signed language research, facilitating a single-pipeline workflow with R when accessing public language resources remotely (online) or modifying and combining a user's own files and data, such as files locally on your own computer. The `signglossR` package combines features and functionality from several other libraries and tools, either implementations in the R language or external software and tools that need to be installed separately. The goal here has been to simplify and collect existing resources in one place, such that a variety of functions and tools useful for signed language research are all available in a single package for easier workflow without the need to switch between programming languages and without the need for command-line programming. The package specifically targets processing of image and video files (§2.2–2.4), but also features some interaction with software commonly used by researchers working on signed language and gesture, such as *ELAN* (§2.5.1) and *OpenPose* (§2.5.2).

2.1. Installation and Dependencies

2.1.1. Installing signglossR

Since the `signglossR` package is not hosted on CRAN[2], it needs to be installed directly from the GitHub repository.[3] In order to do this, users will need to have the `devtools` (Wickham et al., 2021) or `remotes` package (Csárdi et al., 2021) installed, then install the `signglossR` package from the remote GitHub repository:

```
install.packages("devtools")
library(devtools)
# or ...
install.packages("remotes")
library(remotes)

install_github(
  "borstell/signglossR")
```

When the package has been (successfully) installed, it can be accessed in the R environment by loading it in the R session: `library(signglossR)`

[2] https://cran.r-project.org

[3] https://github.com/borstell/signglossR

2.1.2. Installing Dependencies

The `signglossR` package is built on top of – and combining functions from – several other R packages, which are included as dependencies. However, some of the video and image processing functions depend on additional software external to R. In such cases, the `signglossR` functions will run commands on the local system externally in the background, which requires an external (prior) install of these tools: for video processing functions, this concerns `FFmpeg` (FFmpeg Team, 2022); for image processing, this concerns `ImageMagick` (ImageMagick Development Team, 2021), when possible in its R implementation using the `magick` package (Ooms, 2021). Running certain video or image processing functions in `signglossR` would therefore result in errors if these dependencies are not installed on the computer executing the code: follow instructions on their respective websites regarding installation!

These tools/packages are very powerful on their own and the main benefit of running them through `signglossR` is to facilitate the work for users familiar with R, but inexperienced or uncomfortable with working directly in the command line. Furthermore, the `signglossR` package was written to align with the tidy-style workflow using the `magrittr` (Bache and Wickham, 2022) piping function `%>%`, such that the output of one function can be used as input for another, creating a sequence of multiple operations.

2.2. Accessing Online Resources

As of the current version of `signglossR` (v2.2.2), the package has functions to access data from three signed language resources: the Swedish Sign Language dictionary *Svenskt teckenspråkslexikon* (Svenskt teckenspråkslexikon, 2022) (§2.2.1); the ASL dictionary *ASL Signbank* (Hochgesang et al., 2022) (§2.2.2); and the Swedish Sign Language (STS) Corpus *Svensk teckenspråkskorpus* (Öqvist et al., 2020) (§2.2.3). These are resources freely available online and whose maintainers have been informed about the access and processing functions of `signglossR`: users are advised to acknowledge these sources accordingly – try the `cite_source()` function! – and follow their respective terms of use. Using material from other sources should be done according to *their* terms and license.

2.2.1. The Swedish Sign Language Dictionary

Svenskt teckenspråkslexikon[4] (Svenskt teckenspråkslexikon, 2022) is an online dictionary of Swedish Sign Language (*svenskt teckenspråk*, STS). The dictionary contains some 17 000 sign entries, many with form variants, along with example videos of signs used in sentences, still images of the sign, phonemic transcription, a unique ID number and sign glosses used for the corpus and dictionary projects (Mesch et al., 2012).

[4] https://teckensprakslexikon.su.se

With `signglossR`, you can convert ID numbers to sign glosses – and vice versa – using the `id2gloss()` and `gloss2id` functions. For example:

```
> id2gloss(123)
[1] "VEM"
> gloss2id("VEM")
[1] "00123"
```

These functions work better from ID to gloss than the reverse: the IDs are always unique, whereas the glosses are simply searched for in the database and can result in multiple (or no) string matches.
The function `get_image()` downloads a video based on the unique ID, saves the file to your local computer (destination path can be specified) and outputs the filename to the console. It is also possible to combine with the previous function, to go from sign gloss to ID and fetch that sign image.

```
> get_image(1241)
>
> get_image(gloss2id("VEM"))
```

Figure 2: The sign SVERIGE ('Sweden') (Svenskt teckenspråkslexikon, 2022, 1241).

As can be seen from Figure 2, the sign SWEDEN contains multiple still images in the dictionary, and thus they are combined automatically through the `signglossR` function into a side-by-side image as a single file. However, it is also possible to generate an overlay image. Here, the function runs an external `ImageMagick` command that takes the first image at 25% opacity and overlays it onto the second image, creating a "ghost" outline of the earlier part of the sign and a clear image of the later part – see Figure 3.

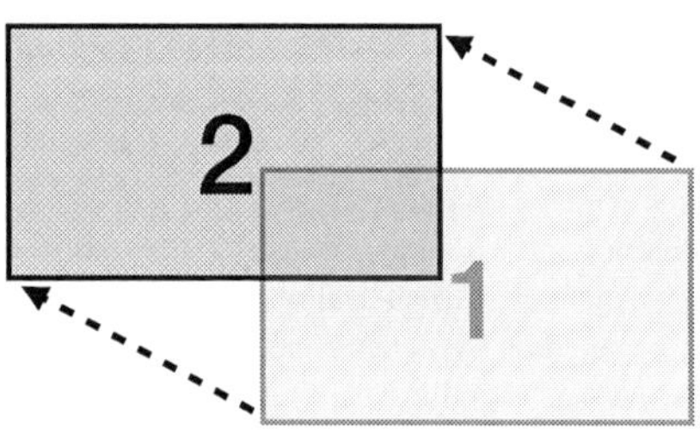

Figure 3: Producing an overlay image from two images with a 25% opacity "ghost" outline for the first image.

This can be achieved directly when downloading a file from the dictionary using the following function call:

```
> get_image(1241,
            overlay = TRUE)
```

This creates the following output, which can be useful as it takes up less horizontal space and illustrates the dynamic movement in a single frame – see Figure 4.

Figure 4: The sign SVERIGE ('Sweden') (Svenskt teckenspråkslexikon, 2022, 1241) with overlay.

Additionally, the functions `get_video()` and `get_gif()` can download a sign as video (`.mp4`) or GIF (`.gif`) directly:

```
> get_video(1241)
>
> get_gif(1241)
```

2.2.2. ASL Signbank

The second dictionary that can be accessed directly through `signglossR` is *ASL Signbank* (Hochgesang et al., 2022). The dictionary has videos and still images of signs, and both of these can be accessed directly. Converting between sign glosses and ID numbers is also possible. Note that the default language selection in `signglossR` is STS, so using general functions to access ASL resources requires specifying the language using `acronym = "ASL"`:

```
> id2gloss(1253,
           acronym = "ASL")
[1] "TOMATOix"
> gloss2id("TOMATOix",
           acronym = "ASL")
[1] "1253"
```

For the ASL Signbank images, we can directly specify that we want the sign gloss to be added to our downloaded image using `glosstext = TRUE`, and modify details about the fontsize and location of the label (`"southwest"` means bottom left) – the resulting image of the following code was seen in Figure 1:

```
> get_image(1253,
       acronym = "ASL",
```

```
            glosstext = TRUE,
            fontsize = 30,
            gravity = "southwest")
```

As with the STS dictionary, ASL Signbank sign videos can be downloaded directly using the `get_video()` function, again specifying `acronym = "ASL"`.

2.2.3. The Swedish Sign Language Corpus

The Swedish Sign Language (STS) Corpus (Mesch et al., 2012; Mesch et al., 2014) and specifically its online interface (Öqvist et al., 2020)[5] can be accessed using the function `search_corpus()`, for which a sign gloss is the input, and running the command opens a browser tab with the search hits for that sign gloss.

```
> search_corpus(id2gloss(1241))
```

2.3. Image Processing

Besides accessing image files directly from language resources online, `signglossR` also contains functions to process such files, either as part of the pipeline of accessing them from those resources, or applied to any image file locally.

2.3.1. Crop and Annotate

Trimming images can be done directly with the `get_image()` function, using the `trim` argument (`trim = .6` means 40% of the total width is cropped, equally on both sides with the image centered at the middle). This can be particularly useful when signs have many still images and you want side-by-side outputs but with efficient use of horizontal space – this is illustrated in Figure 5 in which the sign KÖPENHAMN ('Copenhagen') has four images representing the sign and each image is cropped to 60% of the original width:

```
> get_image(9979, trim = .6)
```

Figure 5: The sign KÖPENHAMN ('Copenhagen') (Svenskt teckenspråkslexikon, 2022, 9979).

Trimming and annotating can also be done on any image file using the `make_image_ex()` function and specifying a region to crop and a text annotation:

```
> make_image_ex("path/to/image",
            crop = TRUE,
            region = "400x300",
            text = "GLOSS")
```

[5] `https://teckensprakslexikon.su.se/`

2.3.2. Combine Images

Combining and overlaying images can also be done with local files. For example, if we try to directly create an overlay of the KÖPENHAMN sign from Figure 5, the result is what we find in Figure 6.

Figure 6: The sign KÖPENHAMN ('Copenhagen') (Svenskt teckenspråkslexikon, 2022, 9979) with overlay.

Because the ghost overlay is performed recursively, earlier frames are too weak to come through in the final output. Instead, we could process each individual image and combine them in stages, as in Figure 7:

```
> combine_images(
    c("image1", "image2"),
    overlay = TRUE,
    trim = .6)
> combine_images(
    c("image3", "image4"),
    overlay = TRUE,
    trim = .6)
> combine_images(
    c("image1-2", "image3-4"))
```

Figure 7: The sign KÖPENHAMN ('Copenhagen') (Svenskt teckenspråkslexikon, 2022, 9979) with segmented overlay.

Alternatively, images can also be combined vertically, allowing for a vertical stack to save horizontal space:

```
> combine_images(
    c("image1", "image2"),
```

```
    trim = .6)
> combine_images(
    c("image3", "image4"),
    trim = .6)
> combine_images(
    c("image1-2", "image3-4"),
    stack = TRUE)
```

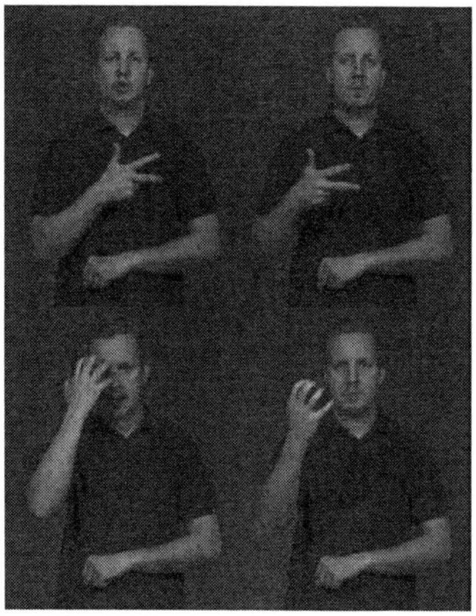

Figure 8: The sign KÖPENHAMN ('Copenhagen') (Svenskt teckenspråkslexikon, 2022, 9979) with segments stacked.

2.3.3. Censor Images

Sometimes we need to anonymize our data, for instance by blurring the face of the signer in an image. With signglossR, this can be achieved by using the censor_image() function, either by manually specifying the region to be censored (by an opaque square or by blurring), or by using an automated method from the opencv package (Ooms and Wijffels, 2021). As long as the face is not obstructed (e.g. by the signer's own hands), the automatic method works quite well, as illustrated in Figure 9. This function works with any local file, including one just piped as it was accessed from an online resource:

```
> get_image(1241,
        overlay = TRUE) %>%
    censor_image()
```

2.4. Video Processing

Besides the get_video() function described in §2.2, there are several functions to modify video files in different ways, described below.

2.4.1. Playback Speed and Repetition

The make_video_ex() function can be used to modify video files. For example, piping our SVERIGE sign

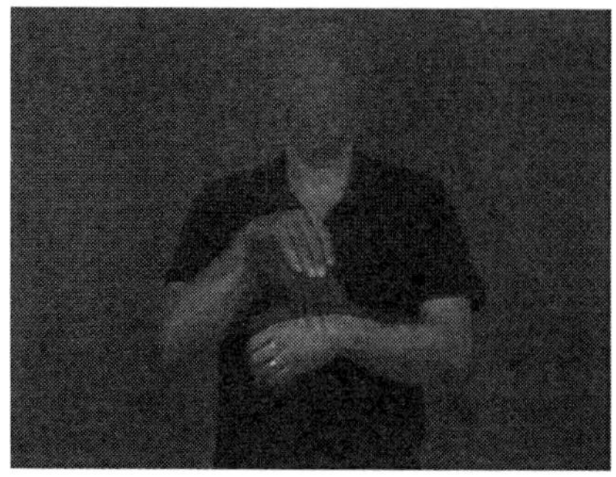

Figure 9: The sign SVERIGE ('Sweden') (Svenskt teckenspråkslexikon, 2022, 1241) with overlay and face censoring.

video, the first of the following commands would result in the video file being slowed down to 40% speed, and the second would result in a video file played once at original speed, then repeated at 30% speed:

```
> get_video(1241) %>%
    make_video_ex(speed = .4)
> get_video(1241) %>%
    make_video_ex(speed = .3,
                  rep = TRUE)
```

2.4.2. Making GIFs

The make_gif() function can be used to convert a video file to a GIF.

```
> get_video(1253,
        acronym = "ASL") %>%
    make_gif()
```

2.4.3. From ELAN to Multimedia Examples

Arguably the most advanced functions in the signglossR package are make_elan_image() and make_elan_video(), both of which input an ELAN file in order to generate image and video files, respectively, for use as linguistic examples (e.g. for a paper or presentation). How they work is that they input an ELAN file with specifications of a segmentation tier and a gloss tier, and then goes through these to create image or video outputs. Figure 10 shows a mock example, using data from the STS Corpus (Öqvist et al., 2020) with English glosses for illustration. Here, there are two tiers visible: *segment* and *gloss*.

What the ELAN segmentation function in signglossR does is that it groups annotation cells (annotations on the *gloss* tier) according to the segmentations made on the segmentation tier (annotations on the *segment* tier) – see Figure 11.

Using make_elan_video() with our mock example, the output would be a shorter video file spanning only the segment duration (if several segments are found, each can output a separate video) and annotating

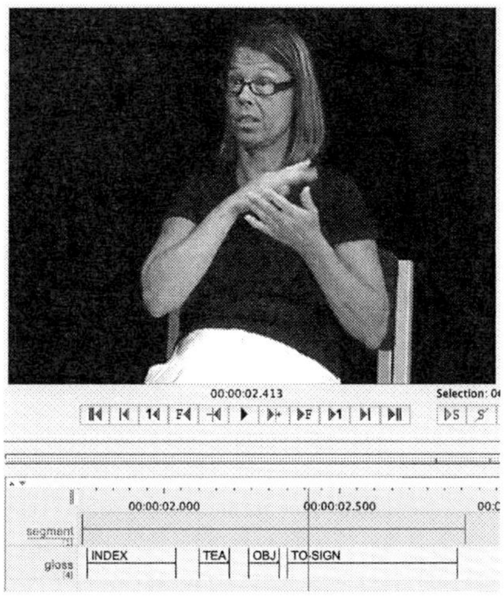

Figure 10: ELAN annotation view using a file from the STS Corpus (Öqvist et al., 2020) with glosses re-annotated in English. Original video sequence: SSLC01_021 00:04:08.

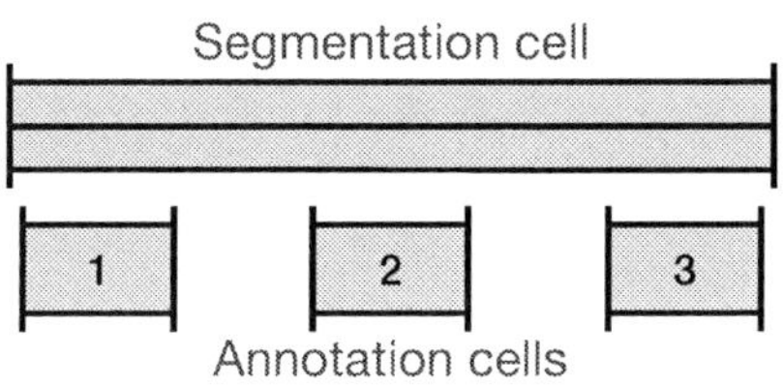

Figure 11: Schematic representation of annotation cells within the same segment.

the video with the sign glosses – thus, it can be used as a basic subtitling tool when illustrating examples.

```
> make_elan_video("file.eaf",
   segmentation_tier = "segment",
   gloss_tier1 = "gloss")
```

The function `make_elan_video()` retrieves the video path from within the ELAN file, but in case the video file is located elsewhere or there are multiple associated video files, users are advised to specify the video path explicitly as an argument to the function.

With `make_elan_image()`, the output will be an image sequence with each sign (what is segmented on the gloss tier) represented by an image. Here, there is an additional option of also creating overlaps for individual images. In this case, it selects the first and last frames of each gloss duration (the 1st and n^{th} frames of a sign of length n; see Figure 12) and creates an overlay for each, after which each sign image is combined into a horizontal sequence, as illustrated in Figure 13. If overlay is not selected (`combine = FALSE`), only the first frame of each sign is selected.

```
> make_elan_image("file.eaf",
   segmentation_tier = "segment",
   gloss_tier = "gloss")
```

The function `make_elan_image()` calls `make_image_ex()` internally and can therefore include a step of, for example, cropping each frame before combining. Furthermore, the output of these – and any image-generating – function can be piped to, e.g., `censor_image()` for an additional processing step censoring the face(s) in the image.

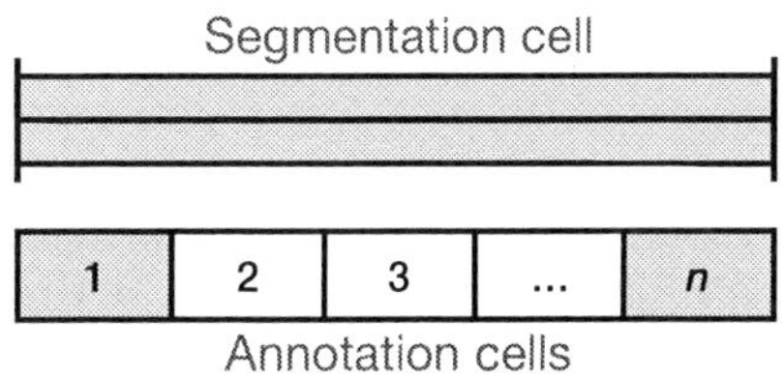

Figure 12: Schematic representation of video frames within the same annotation duration.

2.5. Processing Other File Types

In addition to image and video processing, there are a few functions in the `signglossR` package that aim to facilitate direct processing of file formats commonly found in signed language linguistics, namely ELAN files (§2.5.1) and OpenPose files (§2.5.2).

2.5.1. ELAN

ELAN (Brugman and Russel, 2004; Wittenburg et al., 2006; Crasborn and Sloetjes, 2008; ELAN (Version 6.3) [Computer software], 2022) is an annotation tool used by many researchers working on multimodal data, from signed languages to gesture and behavioral psychology. ELAN annotation files (`.eaf`) are underlyingly XML (`.xml`) files and can be processed as such. The `signglossR` function `read_elan()` inputs a path to a directory, parses all ELAN files in that directory and outputs a data frame (or, tibble) with the data in a typical long format of rows and columns, which lets the researcher get direct access to ELAN files from R without any intermediate export.

```
> path <- "path/to/directory"
> data <- read_elan(path)
```

2.5.2. OpenPose

OpenPose (Cao et al., 2017; Cao et al., 2019) is an open source tool used to input video (or image) files in order to estimate the body pose of any humans depicted, with keypoints for various anchor points on the body (e.g. nose, mouth, shoulders, wrists, etc.). This software has only just started gaining traction within signed language research, where it can be used to estimate signing activity and the location of hands/arms in signing space from videos. For each frame in a video, OpenPose outputs a JSON (`.json`) file linking each individual in the video to a key–value format

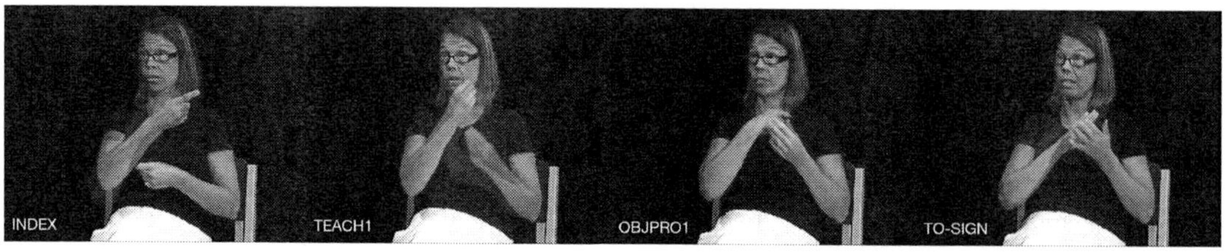

Figure 13: The output of make_elan_image() on a sequence from the Swedish Sign Language (STS) Corpus (Öqvist et al., 2020) with glosses re-annotated in English in ELAN, each sign represented by first-and-last frames overlaid and annotated with respective glosses and concatenated. Original video sequence: SSLC01_021 00:04:08

of keypoints and their respective estimated locations in the frame. The function read_openpose() inputs a path to a directory, parses all JSON files in that directory and outputs a data frame with the data either in a wide format (wide = TRUE is default), where each row represents a frame and each keypoint has its own column, or in a long format of rows and columns with each datapoint on a single row.

```
> path <- "path/to/directory"
> wide_data <-
    read_openpose(path)
> long_data <-
    read_openpose(path, wide=F)
```

3. Final remarks

In this paper, I have given a brief overview to the signglossR package and its functionality. Originally created with the intention to facilitate the use of visual representation of signed language data, it has grown to encompass other aspects of working with multimodal data and related software – e.g. ELAN – specifically in R, a language popular among linguists but with few packages dedicated to signed language data. It is then hopefully easier to proceed with work on such data with other R packages designated for, e.g., statistical analyses, although there is also more functionality and improvement in the planning stage by the author already. Since all the code is open source – just as most of the packages and software it is built on – other users are free to use, adapt or expand on the functionality and ideas of signglossR. Furthermore, if anyone using the package would encounter problems or wishes to relay feedback on their user experience, they are more than welcome to contact the author directly or file an issue in the GitHub repository.

4. Acknowledgments

Thanks to Julie Hochgesang whose presentation on glossing in Berlin on September 23rd 2019 (and advocacy using the Twitter hashtags #TyrannyOfGlossing and #GlossGesang) inspired a first (Python) prototype of an ELAN-to-image example generator. Thanks to three anonymous reviewers for comments on this paper. A special thanks to Jon Keane (https://github.com/jonkeane) for assistance and suggestions after the very first signglossR package launch in 2020.

5. Bibliographical References

Bache, S. M. and Wickham, H., (2022). *magrittr: A Forward-Pipe Operator for R.* R package v. 2.0.2.

Brugman, H. and Russel, A. (2004). Annotating multimedia/multi-modal resources with ELAN. In *Proceedings of the 4th International Conference on Language Resources and Evaluation (LREC 2004)*, pages 2065–2068.

Cao, Z., Simon, T., Wei, S.-E., and Sheikh, Y. (2017). Realtime multi-person 2d pose estimation using part affinity fields. In *CVPR*.

Cao, Z., Hidalgo Martinez, G., Simon, T., Wei, S., and Sheikh, Y. A. (2019). Openpose: Realtime multi-person 2d pose estimation using part affinity fields. *IEEE Transactions on Pattern Analysis and Machine Intelligence*.

Crasborn, O. and Sloetjes, H. (2008). Enhanced ELAN functionality for sign language corpora. In Onno Crasborn, et al., editors, *Proceedings of the LREC2008 3rd Workshop on the Representation and Processing of Sign Languages: Construction and Exploitation of Sign Language Corpora*, pages 39–43, Marrakech, June. European Language Resources Association (ELRA).

Crasborn, O. (2015). Transcription and Notation Methods. In Eleni Orfanidou, et al., editors, *Research Methods in Sign Language Studies*, pages 74–88. John Wiley & Sons, Ltd, Chichester.

Csárdi, G., Hester, J., Wickham, H., Chang, W., Morgan, M., and Tenenbaum, D., (2021). *remotes: R Package Installation from Remote Repositories, Including 'GitHub'.* R package v. 2.4.2.

ELAN (Version 6.3) [Computer software]. (2022). Max Planck Institute for Psycholinguistics, The Language Archive, Nijmegen.

FFmpeg Team. (2022). FFmpeg, v. 5.0.1.

Frishberg, N., Hoiting, N., and Slobin, D. I. (2012). Transcription. In Roland Pfau, et al., editors, *Sign language: An international handbook*, pages 1045–1075. De Gruyter Mouton, Berlin/Boston, MA.

Hanke, T. (2004). HamNoSys – Representing Sign Language Data in Language Resources and Language Processing Contexts. In Oliver Streiter et al., editors, *Proceedings of the LREC2004 Workshop on the Representation and Processing of Sign Languages: From SignWriting to Image Processing. Information techniques and their implications for teaching, documentation and communication*, pages 1–6, Lisbon, May. European Language Resources Association (ELRA).

Hochgesang, J. (2022). Managing Sign Language Acquisition Video Data: A Personal Journey in the Organization and Representation of Signed Data. In Andrea L. Berez-Kroeker, et al., editors, *The Open Handbook of Linguistic Data Management*, pages 367–383. The MIT Press.

ImageMagick Development Team. (2021). ImageMagick, v. 7.0.10.

Jefferson, G. (2004). Glossary of transcript symbols with an introduction. In Gene H. Lerner, editor, *Pragmatics & Beyond New Series*, volume 125, pages 13–31. John Benjamins Publishing Company, Amsterdam.

Johnston, T. (2010). From archive to corpus: Transcription and annotation in the creation of signed language corpora. *International Journal of Corpus Linguistics*, 15(1):106–131.

Johnston, T. (2014). The reluctant oracle: Adding value to, and extracting of value from, a signed language corpus through strategic annotations. *Corpora*, 9(2):155–189.

Mesch, J., Wallin, L., and Björkstrand, T. (2012). Sign language resources in Sweden: Dictionary and corpus. In Onno Crasborn, et al., editors, *Proceedings of the LREC2012 5th Workshop on the Representation and Processing of Sign Languages: Interactions between Corpus and Lexicon*, pages 127–130, Istanbul, May. European Language Resources Association (ELRA).

Miller, C. (2006). Sign language: Transcription, notation, and writing. In Keith Brown, editor, *Encyclopedia of Language & Linguistics*, number 1988, pages 353–354. Elsevier, Oxford.

Ooms, J. and Wijffels, J., (2021). *opencv: Bindings to 'OpenCV' Computer Vision Library*. R package v. 0.2.1.

Ooms, J., (2021). *magick: Advanced Graphics and Image-Processing in R*. R package v. 2.7.3.

Öqvist, Z., Riemer Kankkonen, N., and Mesch, J. (2020). STS-korpus: A sign language web corpus tool for teaching and public use. In Eleni Efthimiou, et al., editors, *Proceedings of the LREC2020 9th Workshop on the Representation and Processing of Sign Languages: Sign Language Resources in the Service of the Language Community, Technological Challenges and Application Perspectives*, pages 177–180, Marseille, May. European Language Resources Association (ELRA).

Pizzuto, E. A., Chiari, I., and Rossini, P. (2008). The representation issue and its multifaceted aspects in constructing sign language corpora: Questions, answers, further problems. In Onno Crasborn, et al., editors, *Proceedings of the LREC2008 3rd Workshop on the Representation and Processing of Sign Languages: Construction and Exploitation of Sign Language Corpora*, pages 150–158, Marrakech, June. European Language Resources Association (ELRA).

Prillwitz, S., Leven, R., Zienert, H., Hanke, T., and Henning, J. (1989). *HamNoSys Version 2.0: Hamburg Notation System for sign languages - An introductory guide*. Signum Verlag, Hamburg.

Schembri, A. and Crasborn, O. (2010). Issues in creating annotation standards for sign language description. In Philippe Dreuw, et al., editors, *Proceedings of the LREC2010 4th Workshop on the Representation and Processing of Sign Languages: Corpora and Sign Language Technologies*, pages 212–216, Valletta, May. European Language Resources Association (ELRA).

Stokoe, W. C. (1960). Sign language structure: An outline of the visual communication system of the American Deaf. In *Studies in linguistics: Occasional papers (No. 8)*, Buffalo, NY. Dept. of Anthropology and Linguistics, University of Buffalo.

Sutton, V. (1996). SignWriting. https://www.signwriting.org.

van der Hulst, H. and Channon, R. (2010). Notation systems. In Diane Brentari, editor, *Sign Languages*, pages 151–172. Cambridge University Press.

Wickham, H., Hester, J., Chang, W., and Bryan, J., (2021). *devtools: Tools to Make Developing R Packages Easier*. R package v. 2.4.3.

Wittenburg, P., Brugman, H., Russel, A., Klassmann, A., and Sloetjes, H. (2006). ELAN: A professional framework for multimodality research. In *Proceedings of the 5th International Conference on Language Resources and Evaluation (LREC 2006)*, pages 1556–1559.

6. Language Resource References

Hochgesang, J. A., Crasborn, O., and Lillo-Martin, D. (2022). ASL Signbank. Haskins Lab, Yale University, https://aslsignbank.haskins.yale.edu/.

Mesch, J., Wallin, L., Nilsson, A.-L., and Bergman, B. (2012). *Dataset. Swedish Sign Language Corpus project 2009–2011 (version 1)*. Department of Linguistics, Stockholm University.

Mesch, J., Rohdell, M., and Wallin, L. (2014). *Annotated files for the Swedish Sign Language Corpus. Version 2.* Department of Linguistics, Stockholm University.

Svenskt teckenspråkslexikon. (2022). Svenskt teckenspråkslexikon. Department of Linguistics, Stockholm University, https://teckenspraakslexikon.ling.su.se/.

Proceedings of the 10th Workshop on the Representation and Processing of Sign Languages (sign-lang@LREC 2022), pages 24–28
Language Resources and Evaluation Conference (LREC 2022), Marseille, 20-25 June 2022

Moving Towards a Functional Approach in the Flemish Sign Language Dictionary Making Process

Caro Brosens, Sam Verstraete, Thijs Vandamme, Hannes De Durpel, Margot Janssens
Vlaams GebarentaalCentrum (VGTC)
Sint-Jacobsmarkt 49, 2000 Antwerp, Belgium
caro.brosens@vgtc.be, sam.verstraete@vgtc.be, thijs.vandamme@vgtc.be,
hannes.de.durpel@vgtc.be, margot.janssens@vgtc.be

Abstract

This article outlines the dictionary making process of the new online Flemish Sign Language dictionary launched in 2019. First some necessary background information is provided, consisting of a brief history of Flemish Sign Language (VGT) lexicography. Then the three phases in the development of the renewed dictionary of VGT are explored: (i) user research, (ii) data-cleaning and modeling, and (iii) innovations. More than wanting to project a report of lexicographic research on a website, the goal was to make the new dictionary a practical, user-friendly reference tool that meets the needs, expectations, and skills of the dictionary users. Since 2017, VGTC has been using Signbank, an electronic database specifically developed to compile and manage lexicographic data for sign languages. Bringing together all this raw data inadvertently led to inconsistencies and small mistakes, therefore the data had to be manually revised and complemented. The VGT dictionary was mainly formally modernized, but there are also several substantive differences regarding the previous dictionary. Lastly, possible future innovations are briefly discussed. Future goals include adding definitions and sample sentences (preferably extracted from the corpus), as well as information on the etymology and common use of signs.

Keywords: Lexicography, Flemish Sign Language, Signbank, Sign Language Dictionary, Bilingual Dictionary, Bimodal Dictionary, Community Sourcing

1. Previous Lexicographic Work on VGT

When research into Flemish Sign Language (formerly called Flemish-Belgian Sign Language) started in the 1990s, the demand for a bilingual dictionary grew. From 1999 onwards, a number of small-scale lexicographic projects were set up all over Flanders, which resulted in the publication of the first online Dutch – Flemish Sign Language (VGT) dictionary gebaren.ugent.be in 2004.

In this bilingual dictionary, each sign was represented in three ways: a video clip, a Dutch translation, and Signwriting (a notation system that allows writing down signs in a visual way) (Van Herreweghe, 2001). This allowed for bidirectional search options, meaning that users could search for a sign by selecting its handshape, location or movement (based on the Signwriting), by scrolling through the Dutch words in alphabetical order, or by typing a Dutch word into a search bar (Vermeerbergen and Van Herreweghe, 2018). This was the first generation sign language dictionary in Flanders. For more information on the aims and the methodology of this dictionary, please see Vermeerbergen and Van Herreweghe (2018) and De Weerdt et al. (2003).

From 2012 until the launch of the new dictionary in 2019, gebaren.ugent.be was managed by the Flemish Sign Language Center (Vlaams GebarentaalCentrum / VGTC), the center of expertise for Flemish Sign Language. VGTC has pursued a further lexical extension of the dictionary since then, adopting the guidelines explained in the lexicographical research methodology of Oyserman et al. (2012).

VGTC has been lobbying for a thorough revision of the dictionary's interface. It seemed that, almost 15 years after the launch of the first dictionary, users' expectations were not fully met. After all, electronic technology had evolved very rapidly since 2004, greatly expanding the possibilities for an accessible online reference tool (McKee and McKee, 2013). Mixed methodology user research supported this hypothesis, as is explained in more depth later.

At the end of 2018, VGTC was awarded project funding, which enabled its employees, in collaboration with a software development company, to implement the large-scale renewal of the dictionary. In doing so, a practical lexicographical perspective was adopted: describing the language in a way that is faithful to the available lexicographic research, and always taking into account the expectations, needs and skills of those who will use the dictionary (Atkins and Rundell, 2008).

2. Developing the New Dictionary

2.1. User Research

When VGTC received the one-off project funding for the renewal of the online dictionary in 2018, the first meaningful steps were taken towards a new interface. In particular, extensive research regarding the users of the dictionary was conducted. More than wanting

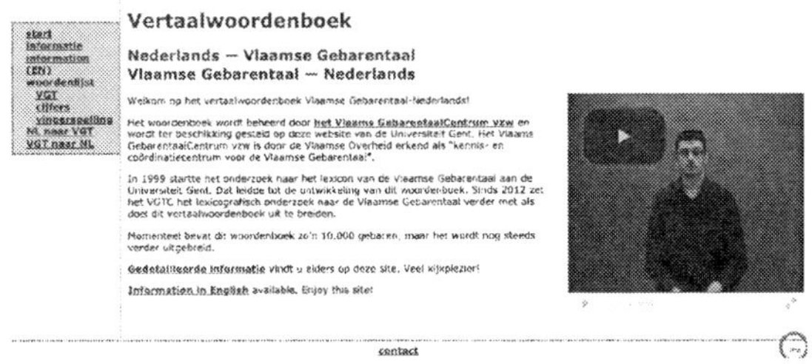

Figure 1: A screenshot of the home page of gebaren.ugent.be

to project a report of lexicographic research on a website, the goal was to make the new dictionary a practical, user-friendly reference tool that meets the needs, expectations and skills of the dictionary users. To gain a better understanding of who the users were, several sources were consulted: the user research by Oyserman (2013), the quantitative data from Google Analytics and VGTC's own user profiles.

An initial qualitative user study of gebaren.ugent.be was conducted by Joni Oyserman in 2013. In this preliminary study, a group of deaf and hearing teachers of VGT, interpreters, students of VGT, deaf and hearing parents of a deaf child and relatives of a deaf person were questioned about their usage pattern of the dictionary. One of the results of this survey is that users like to search from VGT to Dutch as well as vice versa. They would also like to search thematically to see all semantically related signs. Since the latter was not yet possible, this was taken into account and it was added during the development of the new VGT dictionary.

In addition, data from Google Analytics, a service from Google that gives website administrators access to usage statistics for that application, were also analysed. This tool keeps track of which signs are viewed the most, how long users visit a certain page and how they search. The data analysis showed that the search function VGT to Dutch was used only for a small percentage of the searches. This seems to be diametrically opposed to the result from the qualitative user study described above, in which informants indicated that this search direction is important. A possible explanation might be that the SignWriting symbols are not sufficiently accessible to the average user. Another assumption is that the search function yields too extensive a set of results to quickly arrive at the desired entry. In an attempt to make the VGT to Dutch search function more user friendly, it was decided SignWriting would no longer be used in the new dictionary.

Moreover, the percentage of new visitors was considerably larger than the number of returning visitors, which could indicate that the dictionary's content was, to some extent, inadequate. Also, whereas the website's interface was not responsive, meaning the web application is less accessible on smartphones and tablets, dictionary visitors did tend to use a mobile device in almost half of the sessions. Therefore, the need for a responsive website, which automatically adapts to other screen sizes and thus remains clear and user-friendly on different devices, became apparent. Because of this, it was necessary to develop a new web application.

In collaboration with AE, the software company that developed this new web application, fictitious user profiles were created to test the hypothesis from the above studies. During the development process, each version of the application was also tested by a small group of users. In April 2019 a testing session was held, in which eight volunteer informants (two deaf elderly, two young deaf people, two interpreters and two hearing interpreting students) carried out various assignments for one hour on the first version of the application. Their findings were included in the further development of the dictionary interface to make it as functional as possible. For instance, the testing session revealed the first iteration of the new VGT to Dutch search function needed to be adjusted.

2.2. Data Cleaning and Modelling

Since 2017, VGTC has been using Signbank, an electronic database specifically developed to compile and manage lexicographic data for sign languages. The precursor to Signbank originated in Australia by the work of Johnston (2001), and then further developed for AUSLAN and other sign languages like BSL (Cormier et al., 2012) and NGT (Crasborn et al., 2016). As sign languages are visual languages, it is important to use a database which allows for easy uploading and processing of video clips. In addition, this system offers the possibility to annotate signs morphologically, phonologically and semantically. These last two were used extensively, for the new VGT to Dutch search option and the thematic categories respectively.

Signs are added to Signbank by team members from various sources. For each sign that is added, the source is specified to enable further specific research. All data found in gebaren.ugent.be were added to Signbank, as were the results of the lexicographical research projects conducted by VGTC after 2004. Furthermore, the Signbank database enables VGTC to more easily collect signs on a larger scale through community sourcing. For example, employees can follow up on discussions about certain signs in Facebook groups and copy the data into Signbank. It should, however, be noted that this way of community sourcing is time consuming because of the manual effort it requires. In any case, Signbank has become the central hub where all lexicographic data for VGT are collected. These data are now used to directly feed the new dictionary. Currently Signbank holds about 20,000 entries, about half of which are published in the online dictionary.

Each entry contains a unique gloss, a gloss in this case being the closest representation of the meaning of the sign in written Dutch. One gloss represents one concept. The signs for both "poor" and "(an) arm" could be glossed as ARM in Dutch so in order to avoid confusion, "poor" was glossed as ARMOEDE, i.e. "poverty", a different possible translation of the same sign, instead. One gloss/concept can have several sign variants, in order to keep the glosses unique, a serial letter is added after each gloss, e.g. ARM-A, ARM-B, ... These glosses are only used in Signbank. The Dutch to VGT search bar on the dictionary uses the possible translations added to each entry.

Bringing together all these raw data from different sources inadvertently led to inconsistencies and small mistakes, for example: duplicate signs (i.e. signs which were accidentally added twice under a different gloss), inconsistent or confusing glosses (e.g. two concepts, like "poor" and "arm" under the same gloss), missing information, typos, etc. Because of this, the data had to be manually revised and complemented. Furthermore, in 2018 and 2019, part of the old video recordings of signs were renewed in Signbank to increase the video quality. This work will be continued until all recordings are dealt with.

Because SignWriting was not deemed very transparent, efficient and widely accessible, it would no longer be included in the new dictionary. In view of the new search function from VGT to Dutch, a phonological annotation was performed based on the hand shape and location of the signs. The sets of 34 handshapes and 20 locations were selected based on the research of Demey (2005). While the available SignWriting images were originally to be used for this annotation, it turned out this was not practically or technically feasible. In other words, all entries were annotated manually, mostly by the researching team (two deaf and one hearing) and to a lesser extent a volunteer (hard-of-hearing).

In order to enable thematic searches, signs were also assigned one or more semantic categories (e.g. nature, law, sports, medicine, family, ...) during this phase. The original lexicographic approach which was used to compile the previous dictionary, is at the basis of the semantic categories in the current dictionary. For more information, please see Vermeerbergen and Van Herreweghe (2018). The original list of semantic categories was reduced and reworked. There were three possibilities: (i) the category would be kept (and maybe renamed), (ii) the category would be merged with another category, or (iii) the category would cease to exist.

To decide which signs from Signbank are added to the dictionary, a committee of carefully selected deaf near-native signers (two from each of the five provinces in Flanders) meets 3 to 4 times a year. At least one of VGTC's employees is also present to guide and moderate the discussion. At these meetings, Signbank entries tagged as "expertgroep" ("group of experts") are discussed. The rather small size of the group allows for thorough and in-depth discussions. Leading up to the discussion, all participants received the necessary information to prepare in advance (i.e. think about the signs and concepts to be discussed and check with their own network of signers). Each participant would give a final "yes" or "no" at the end of the discussion as to whether to include the sign in the dictionary or not. If the sign was confirmed to be present in only some of the provinces, it would be included as a regional variant. However, the qualitative nature of this evaluative entity also means it is rather time consuming and inefficient, due to the practical difficulties of bringing everyone together physically and the manual processing of the data. It is therefore preferable to supplement it with quantitative data from the VGT corpus.

"In the last decade, much care, time, and resources have been invested in compiling the VGT corpus. This corpus consists of 5TB or 140 hours of video data produced by 120 deaf L1 signers" (Brosens et al., 2021). Approximately 40 hours of data was transcribed so far (Wille et al., 2022). Inspired by Crasborn et al. (2016), VGTC is still working on a link between Signbank and ELAN, the annotation program used by the annotators of the corpus. Through this form of corpus linguistics, the aim is to strengthen the lexicographic basis of Signbank in the future. Currently the corpus is used as much as possible for lemma selection (and thus to a lesser extent confirmation of existence). When – while annotating the corpus – signs are found that were not yet collected in Signbank, the annotator adds this sign manually. Future uses of the corpus hopefully include:

example material, sense discrimination, and description of regional variation. In the meantime, alternative ways of confirming the spread / existence of signs are being explored, for instance online questionnaires or polls using existing platforms or alternatively building a custom platform for this very purpose.

2.3. Innovations

As shown in figure two, the VGT dictionary was mainly formally modernised. However, there are also a number of substantive differences with regard to the previous dictionary. First of all, the search options were expanded. Because of this, users of the dictionary can now arrive at a certain sign in different ways. Just like in gebaren.ugent.be, people can search the Dutch equivalent of a sign in VGT via the hand shape or location of the sign. However, this no longer involves SignWriting, but images of the hand shapes and the locations on the body. Accessible information icons explain in a comprehensible way, both in VGT and in Dutch, what hand shapes and locations exactly are. Users can search Dutch to VGT via a search bar, in which a Dutch word can be typed. In addition, there is also the possibility to search by regional variant or by semantic category. Finally, a combination of search filters is possible with the aim of making the users of the dictionary find the searched entry faster.

Figure 2: A screenshot of the home page of the new dictionary

Once the searched entry is found, one click reveals the detail page where the phonology and semantic category of the sign are displayed. Thanks to cross-referencing, users are easily directed to signs that have the same meaning, but are used in a different region, or to signs that are phonologically related.

An interesting extension in the new application is the possibility to link different Dutch words to one lemma. In gebaren.ugent.be synonyms in Dutch (e.g. "climbing" and "scrambling") were placed under two different lemmata. The same applies to different parts of speech in Dutch (e.g. "relax" and "relaxation"). In the new dictionary, multiple possible Dutch translations can now be linked to a single sign.

As administrator of the new dictionary, VGTC is also more in touch with the user. Users can provide feedback, ranging from technical problems (e.g. a video that does not play properly) to more substantive comments (e.g. I suspect this sign is also used in my region), in an accessible way, through video and/or text. The sign is then appropriately tagged in Signbank and further research can be conducted. In addition, VGTC also receives a notification if users type a word in the dictionary and find no result. That way VGTC gets an overview of which lemmata users find lacking in the dictionary.

In addition to these substantive changes, the website has also been structurally changed. As mentioned earlier, the website is now responsive, so the interface adapts to the device on which people visit the website. In this way, the dictionary is as accessible on a smartphone or tablet as it is on a computer screen. The entire interface is also more visually organised. This is mainly the result of an initial user test. It was found desirable to avoid the Dutch text becoming a barrier for part of the target group.

3. Conclusions

Evidently, making a user-friendly bilingual and bidirectional online dictionary is a never ending process. VGTC aims to continuously improve both the user based interface and the content of the current dictionary. Future goals include, but are not limited to, adding definitions and sample sentences (preferably extracted from the corpus), as well as information on the etymology and common use of signs.

Even if the development of this new dictionary is a step forward, there are also limitations. It cannot be guaranteed, just like in gebaren.ugent.be, that every existing sign in VGT is included in the dictionary. Therefore, signs used by a sign language user that are not in the dictionary are no worse than or inferior to the ones found in the dictionary. Just as in the UGent project, VGTC naturally strives for a description of the language that is as complete as possible and is constantly working on expanding and deepening the dictionary.

As Atkins and Rundell (2008) state, "the content and design of every aspect of a dictionary must, centrally, take account of who the users will be and what they will use the dictionary for". VGTC, too, strongly believes that more in-depth users research, preceding, during and after the development of a sign language dictionary, is crucial in order to build a sustainable reference work, which dictionary users can continue to explore and enjoy using.

4. Bibliographical References

Atkins, B. and Rundell, M. (2008). *The Oxford Guide to a Practical Lexicography.* Oxford University Press Inc., New York.

Brosens, C., De Durpel, H., Beukeleers, I., and Wille, B. (2021). Towards a functional label set for the online dictionary of flemish sign language. In *FEAST*, pages 50–60, Hong Kong.

Cormier, K., Fenlon, J., Johnston, T., Rentelis, R., Schembri, A., Rowley, K., Adam, R., and Woll, B. (2012). From corpus to lexical database to online dictionary: Issues in annotation of the bsl corpus and the development of bsl signbank. In Crasborn, O., et al., editors, *Proceedings of the 5th Workshop on the Representation and Processing of Sign Languages: Interactions between Corpus and Lexicon (LREC'12)*, pages 7–12, Istanbul, Turkey. European Language Resource Association (ELRA).

Crasborn, O., Bank, R., Zwitserlood, I., Van der Kooij, E., Schüller, A., Ormel, E., Nauta, E., van Zuilen, M., van Winsum, F., and Ros, J. (2016). Linking lexical and corpus data for sign languages: Ngt signbank and the corpus ngt. In Efthimiou, E., et al., editors, *Proceedings of the 7th Workshop on the representation and processing of sign languages: Corpus Mining (LREC'16)*, pages 41–46, Portoroz, Slovenia. European Language Resource Association (ELRA).

De Weerdt, K., Vanhecke, E., Van Herreweghe, M., and Vermeerbergen, M. (2003). *De dovengemeenschap in Vlaanderen : Doorlichting, sensibilisering en standaardisering van de Vlaamse gebarentaal : Eindrapport, luik 2. Op onderzoek naar de Vlaamse gebaren-schat.* Fevlado-Diversus, Gent, BE.

Demey, E. (2005). *Fonologie van de Vlaamse Gebarentaal: distinctiviteit en iconiciteit.* Phd thesis, Universiteit Gent, Faculteit Letteren en Wijsbegeerte, Gent.

Johnston, T. (2001). The lexical database of auslan (australian sign language). *Sign Language and Linguistics*, 4(1-2):145–169.

McKee, R. and McKee, D. (2013). Making an online dictionary of new zealand sign language. *Lexikos*, 23(1):500–531.

Oyserman, J., Heyerick, I., and Huys, E. (2012). Onderzoeksmethodologie: Datacollectie voor lexicografisch onderzoek van de vlaamse gebarentaal. Vlaams GebarentaalCentrum.

Oyserman, J. (2013). Enquête resultaten gebruikersonderzoek online woordenboek vlaamse gebarentaal. Vlaams GebarentaalCentrum vzw.

Van Herreweghe, M. (2001). *SignWriting in de Vlaamse Gebarentaal.* Cultuur voor Doven, Gent, BE.

Vermeerbergen, M. and Van Herreweghe, M. (2018). Looking back while moving forward: The impact of societal and technological developments on flemish sign language lexicographic practices. *International Journal of Lexicography*, 31(2):167–195.

Wille, B., Beukeleers, I., Van Herreweghe, M., and Vermeerbergen, M. (2022). Big things often have small beginnings: on the development and use of small and big corpora for flemish sign language linguistic research. *Frontiers In Psychology*, 12. DOI: 10.3389/fpsyg.2021.779479.

Proceedings of the 10th Workshop on the Representation and Processing of Sign Languages (sign-lang@LREC 2022), pages 29–36
Language Resources and Evaluation Conference (LREC 2022), Marseille, 20-25 June 2022

Phonetics of Negative Headshake in Russian Sign Language: A Small-Scale Corpus Study

Anastasia Chizhikova, Vadim Kimmelman
HSE University, University of Bergen
Moscow (Russia), Bergen (Norway)
apchizhikova@edu.hse.ru, vadim.kimmelman@uib.no

Abstract

We analyzed negative headshake found in the online corpus of Russian Sign Language. We found that negative headshake can co-occur with negative manual signs, although most of these signs are not accompanied by it. We applied OpenFace, a Computer Vision toolkit, to extract head rotation measurements from video recordings, and analyzed the headshake in terms of the number of peaks (turns), the amplitude of the turns, and their frequency. We find that such basic phonetic measurements of headshake can be extracted using a combination of manual annotation and Computer Vision, and can be further used in comparative research across constructions and sign languages.

Keywords: negative headshake, nonmanual marking, Computer Vision

1. Introduction

While the importance of nonmanual markers in sign language grammar is well understood (Pfau and Quer, 2010; Wilbur, 2021; Lackner, 2021), only a small number of studies so far focused on phonetic properties of nonmanual movements (Baker-Shenk, 1983; De Vos et al., 2009; Weast, 2011; Dachkovsky et al., 2013; Puupponen et al., 2015; Tyrone and Mauk, 2016; Harmon, 2017). An important reason for the scarcity of phonetic investigation of nonmanuals has been methodological: manual annotation of nonmanuals is difficult, time-consuming and not very reliable while more reliable methods like using Motion Capture are expensive and also very time-consuming in terms of analysis of the data (Puupponen et al., 2015).

Recent advances is Deep Learning lead to significant breakthroughs in Computer Vision (CV): currently, multiple instruments exist that allow automatic detection and tracking of the human body in video recordings, OpenPose being probably the most famous to date (Wei et al., 2016; Cao et al., 2017; Cao et al., 2018). CV has been applied to sign language data especially in the context of automatic sign language recognition and translation (Ko et al., 2018; Koller et al., 2016; Saunders et al., 2020). However, only a few studies have used CV for linguistic analysis of sign language data, and especially for analyzing phonetic properties of nonmanuals (Kimmelman et al., 2020). At the moment, it is not well understood whether existing CV instruments are even suitable for linguistic analysis of sign languages, but it is already clear that extensive testing and adjusting of CV solutions is necessary before they can be applied to sign languages at scale (Kuznetsova et al., 2021).

In this paper, we report the results of an initial investigation of phonetics of nonmanual headshake in Russian Sign Language (RSL). We use naturalistic corpus data from the online corpus of Russian Sign Language (Burkova, 2015). We attempt to identify all negative utterances in the corpus, and then manually select the utterances containing negative headshakes. Consequently, we apply a CV instrument OpenFace (Baltrusaitis et al., 2018) to extract information about head rotation in these video files in order to further analyze phonetic properties of these movements quantitatively. The aim of the study is thus two-fold. First, we describe basic phonetic properties of negative headshake in RSL, which can be a first step towards more detailed research on phonetics of headshakes in this and other sign languages. Second, we test and discuss the applicability of CV-tools for phonetic analysis of headshake.

2. Negative Headshake in SLs

One of the most common linguistic nonmanuals cross-linguistically is the side-to-side negative headshake (Zeshan, 2006; Pfau, 2008; Oomen and Pfau, 2017).[1] In different sign languages, the headshake can accompany the negative sign alone or spread across parts or the whole sentence; in some sign languages (often called *non-manually dominant*), the headshake alone can express the negative polarity, without any manual negative sign. Recent studies based on corpus data have shown that, in naturalistic data, negative headshake can be frequent but by no means obligatory (Johnston, 2018; Kuder et al., 2018).

In a recent study (Rudnev and Kuznetsova, 2021), RSL has been classified as a manually-dominant sign language: negative sentences must contain a manual negative sign. The negative signs almost always occur in the clause-final position, as in (1). Negative headshake is also extensively used, and can also spread, as in (1).

(1) $\overline{\text{INDEX}_1\ \text{THINK NOT}}^{\text{neg}}$
'I did not think.'

[1] In some sign languages, backward head tilt is also used to mark negation, but the negative headshake is typically also attested (Zeshan, 2006).

Our knowledge of phonetic properties of negative headshake across sign languages is very limited.[2] In a recent small-scale study, Harmon (2017) described some aspects of phonetics of headshake in American Sign Language (ASL). She argued that ASL has two main types of headshake: canonical nonmanual negation, which begins with a wide arc and continues with smaller and smaller arcs, and intense negation, which has the same general shape, but with shorter (by 30-50%) arcs of movements. Both types of nonmanual negation can spread, and are generally temporally aligned with sign and sentence boundaries. Despite employing quantitative and CV-related techniques for data extraction, the paper does not report any quantitative results concerning phonetic properties of the headshake, and thus it is impossible to compare it to our findings below.

3. Methodology

In order to study phonetic properties of negative headshake in RSL, we applied the following steps, which we describe in more detail below: (1) Searching for negative signs and sentences in the online corpus of RSL (Burkova, 2015); (2) Manual identification of segments containing negative headshake; (3) Manual annotation of the boundaries of negative headshake and negative manual signs in ELAN (Crasborn and Sloetjes, 2008); (4) Extraction of head rotation measurements using OpenFace (Baltrusaitis et al., 2018); (5) Quantitative analysis of a subset of the measurements.

3.1. Corpus Data

The online corpus of RSL is a collection of over 230 video recordings produced by 43 RSL signers of different ages and from different regions, filmed mostly between 2010 and 2012 (Burkova, 2015). The total duration of the video recordings is approximately 4 hours 30 minutes, and it contains around 20 000 sign tokens. The corpus is fully available on-line, but registration is required to access the data. For more details and a case study, see Bauer and Kyuseva (2022).

Most recordings in the corpus are narrative monologues, although some dialogues are also included. Each recording is annotated on 3 tiers: right hand glosses, left hand glosses, and sentence translation, in Russian. The annotations were created in ELAN, but are also accessible and searchable via the on-line interface of the corpus.

In order to identify negative structures in the data, we searched in the ELAN annotation files for words that are used to express negation in Russian, including negative particles (most prominently *ne* 'not'), negative adverbs and negative pronouns. We then watched the found segments in order to identify (1) whether they were indeed negative structures and (2) whether they contained negative headshake.

3.2. Boundary Annotation

As mentioned above, the RSL corpus does not contain annotations of the nonmanual component. Because the horizontal position and the head movement along the horizontal plane are not exclusively associated with negation, we do not see an obvious way of automatically detecting negative headshake in the data. It might be possible to develop an ML solution, but we do not yet have sufficient data to train a model for automatic identification of headshake (see also a discussion in Section 5.3). Thus, we decided to manually annotate the boundaries of headshake in the segments that we selected before proceeding to further analysis of the data.

We used the following criteria. We consider the onset of the headshake to occur on the first frame of leftward or rightward turn of the head from the position that was maintained in the previous context. We consider the offset of the headshake to occur on the last frame of the leftward or rightward turn before the head is maintained in some position afterwards. Note that, in both cases, the maintained position is not always forward-facing, as head turns can be used for functions not related to negation (see further discussion in Section 5.2). This procedure is subjective and based on laborious visual inspection of the data. In fact, in order to test reliability, the two authors independently annotated 65 instances of headshake, and only found 68% of raw overlap between the annotations. However, if manual annotations are combined with visual inspection of the results of CV data extraction, it is possible to identify the boundaries more reliably (Section 5.2).

We also annotated the boundaries of the manual negative signs to explore alignment with the boundaries of the headshake. We used commonly accepted criteria (as used for example in the corpus of Sign Language of the Netherlands (Crasborn et al., 2008)): the sign starts in the frame where the (initial) handshape is fully formed and the initial location is reached, and ends in the frame where the hand starts moving away from the final location and/or the handshape starts to change from the (final) handshape.

3.3. Measurement Extraction and Analysis

We used a Python script to cut video fragments based on annotation boundaries extracted from ELAN annotation files. These fragments served as input to OpenFace, a toolkit for face landmark detection, head pose estimation, and facial action unit recognition. (Baltrusaitis et al., 2018). Importantly, this software reconstructs a 3D model of the face from 2D video recordings, and estimates not only facial landmark locations, but also head position along the 3 axes in radians. Most relevantly for us is the estimation of head position along the horizontal axis (also know as pitch), as negative headshake is rotation of the head on this axis.

[2] See also Coerts (1992) for some information on negative headshake in Sign Language of the Netherlands. Some research has also been done on formal aspects of negative headshake in co-speech gesture (Harrison, 2014).

We used the *find_peak* function from the Python *scipy* model (Virtanen et al., 2020) to automatically detect peaks in the estimated horizontal rotation of the head. Because the data is noisy, and even minimal head movements clearly not classifiable as head turns were detected, we applied an empirically calibrated filter set to ignore any peaks which differed from the neighbors by less than 0.01 radians (see Figure 1 for an illustration of the process).

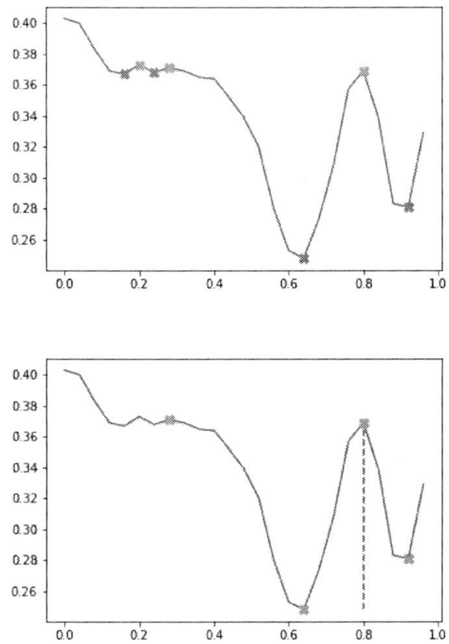

Figure 1: Top: peak identification before filtration. Bottom: peak identification after filtration and amplitude calculation.

For each headshake interval, we calculated the following measures:

- number of peaks;
- frequency: ((n_{peaks} - 1)/duration between the first and last peaks);
- the maximal amplitude.

The amplitude was calculated as the difference between the maximal and minimal peak for the interval. This is illustrated as the red dotted line in Figure 1.
The script used for cutting video fragments and extracting measurements from the data can be found here: `https://github.com/nastyachizhikova/Negative_Headshake_Phonetics_RSL`.
For the quantitative analysis, we only focused on the headshake that co-occurs with the three most frequent manual negative signs (see Section 4). We explore the distributions of the main phonetic measures above in these three types of constructions graphically and with basic descriptive statistics, using R and R Studio (R Core Team, 2019; RStudio Team, 2019).

4. Results

4.1. Basic Properties of RSL Negation

Using the methods discussed above, we found 663 potential instances of negative signs in the RSL corpus. However, unexpectedly, a vast majority of examples (476, 72%) did not contain visible headshake. This confirms earlier findings that RSL is a manually-dominant sign language, but it is still quite surprising that only a minority of negative sentences are also marked with headshake.[3]
Zooming in on the 187 examples that contain negative headshake, we can observe that a wide variety of manual negative markers are used in the data. The three most common types of manual negative signs are NEG, which is a side-to-side shaking of one or both palms used as the negative response sign 'no' or as a sentential negation (example 2, Figure 2, top line), NEG.EXIST which is the negative existential, but which can also be used as a sentential negation marker in combination with verbs (example 3, Figure 2, second line), and the class of irregular negative verbs (Zeshan, 2006), that is, verbs which have dedicated negative forms in RSL, such as NOT.KNOW and NOT.WANT (example 4, Figure 2, third line).

(2) ENTER $\overline{\text{NEG}}^{\text{neg}}$
'Do not enter!'

(3) CLOSE ALSO NOTHING $\overline{\text{NEG.EXIST}}^{\text{neg}}$
'In the one close by, there also was nothing.'

(4) INDEX_1 $\overline{\text{NOT.KNOW}}^{\text{neg}}$
'I don't know.'

Another frequent negative marker is the negative particle NE, which almost always expresses sentential negation, and directly follows the verb, often cliticizing to it, as in example (example 5, Figure 2, bottom line). It formally resembles the NEG sign, but contains only a single movement of the hand.

(5) $\overline{\text{NOBODY MEET NE}}^{\text{neg}}$
'Nobody is meeting me.'

As also discussed in earlier research, negative headshake can accompany the negative manual sign, but it also optionally spreads, as in (1). In our data, the

[3] This is not to say that all the cases without negative headshake were unmarked nonmanually. Other nonmanuals associated with negation, such as furrowed eyebrows and lowered mouth corners did occur, but we did not analyze them further.

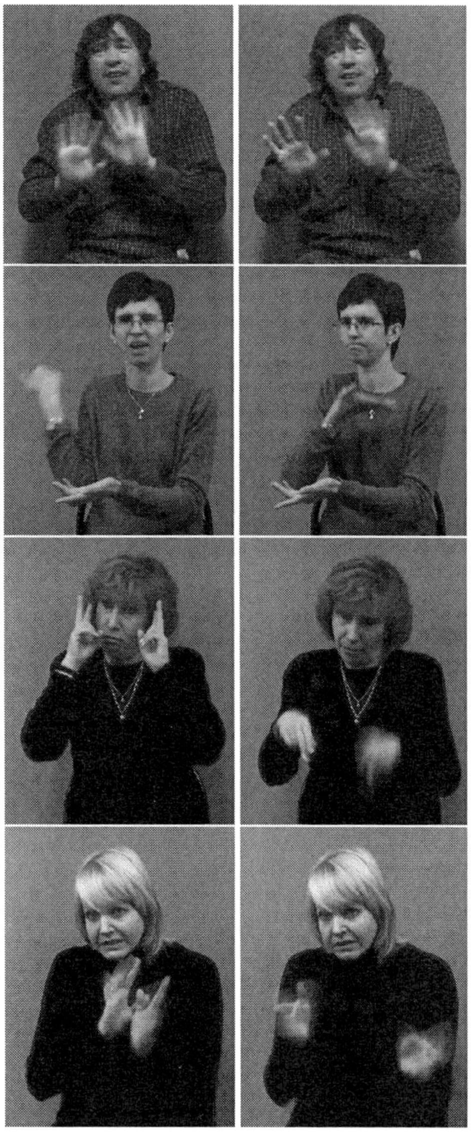

Figure 2: RSL signs NEG, NEG.EXIST, NOT.KNOW, NE from the examples.

spreading of the headshake was quite rare: it occurred in only 13% of the analyzed cases.

In the cases where there is no spreading, we observed remarkably precise alignment between the headshake and the manual negative sign. If we look in detail at the alignment between the headshake and the phases of the manual sign (Kita et al., 1998), the most common pattern is the following. The onset of the headshake coincides with the onset of the preparation phase of the negative sign, that is, when the hands start a transitional movement from a resting position or a preceding sign towards the negative manual sign, and the offset of the headshake coincides with the end of the stroke of the negative manual sign.

Consider Figure 3 which contains several screenshots from example (4). The first frame shows the last frame of the sign INDEX_1, and the head is in the neutral position. The second frame shows the retraction phase of this sign, initiating the transitional movement towards the manual negative sign, and the head starts a turning movement to the left. The third frame is in the middle of the transitional movement: the handshape of the negative sign NOT.KNOW is visible but not fully formed, and the initial location of the sign is not yet reached, while the head continues the turn. The fourth frame is the initial frame of the stroke of the negative sign, where the handshape and the initial location are fully formed, and the head starts a movement to the right. The fifth frame is the last frame of the stroke of the negative sign: the hands are still in the final location, and the head continues the turn from the headshake. Finally, in the sixth frame, the hands start moving towards the next sign, so this again is transitional movement, and the head starts another movement, a combination of turning and tilting, that is not a part of the negative headshake.

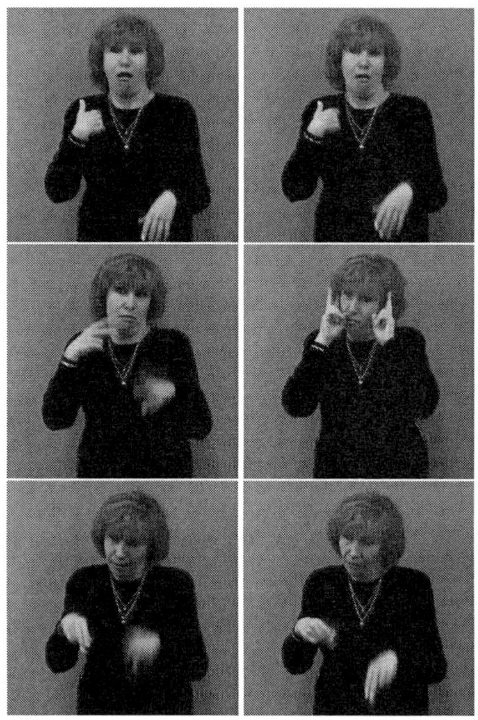

Figure 3: Selected frames from example (4), see the text for details.

In some cases the onset of the headshake is synchronized with the onset of the stroke of the manual sign, but this is less common.

4.2. Phonetic Properties of Negative Headshake

For the quantitative analysis of the phonetic properties of negative headshake, we focused on the three most common types of manual negative signs demonstrated in (2)-(4) above. In total, we analyzed 68 sentences negative headshakes.

The first measure that we considered is the number of peaks, that is, the number of turns of the head, where a turn towards one side is counted as a single turn. Most frequently, the negative signs were accompanied with 1 or 2 turns, although 3-5 turns were also quite common, and one instance contained 14 turns.

Looking at the three types of manual negative signs, some tendencies can be observed.[4] Specifically, while both NEG and NEG.EXIST most often co-occurred with a single turn of the head, irregular negation most often co-occurred with two turns, and never with one.

Concerning the amplitude of the turns, again, the three types were very similar. In general, the mean amplitude is 0.279 radians (16 degrees), and the median amplitude 0.23 radians (13.5 degrees), so the turns are relatively small. Irregular negation seems to be accompanied by headshake of a lower amplitude than the other groups, although the difference is not significant.

The final measurement we looked at was the frequency of turns, measured as the number of turns per second. The mean frequency was 7.9 turns per second. While no significant differences between the groups were found, the average frequency for the headshake co-occurring with the NEG.EXIST sign was slightly higher than for the other two types.

Finally, we visually explored the plots of the head position extracted from the video recordings. When looking at the cases with multiple peaks, we were interested whether we can observe the pattern previously reported for ASL, namely that the headshake starts with a wide arc, and that the following arcs decrease in amplitude. We indeed found many examples that conform to this pattern, as in Figure 4, upper panel. However, in some cases no decrease in amplitude was visible, and/or the first movement did not have the highest amplitude, as in Figure 4, lower panel.

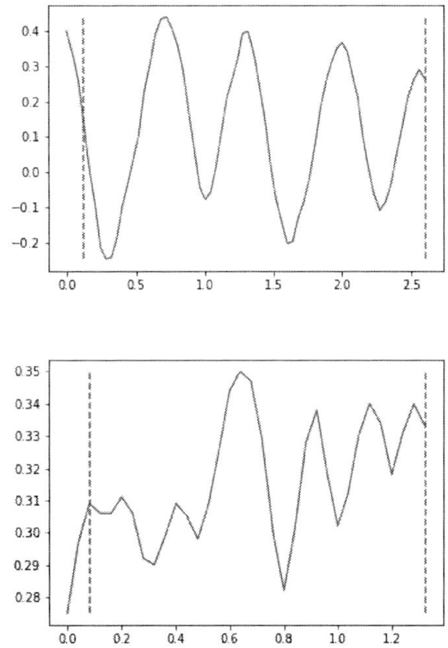

Figure 4: Example shapes of negative head movement in RSL. X-axis: time in seconds; y-axis: rotation in radians. Red lines: boundaries of the movement based on manual annotation.

5. Discussion and Outlook

5.1. Headshake in RSL

An important finding of this study is that headshake is a relatively infrequent marker of negation in RSL. Not only is headshake alone not enough to negate an utterance (a manual sign is required), but also under 30% of negative structures in the corpus contain headshake.

However, it is still important to be able to analyze phonetic properties of headshake, which we attempt to do in this study. We found that negative headshake in RSL most frequently contains only one or two turns of the head. This is also related to the fact that, in the majority of cases, the headshake does not spread from the negative manual sign.

On average, the head turns 16 degrees to the side when performing the headshake; the frequency of head turns in negative headshake is around 8/s. These measurements in isolation are not very useful. However, they open the perspective of comparative phonetic research. In a pilot follow-up, we looked at a small number of elicited RSL examples containing negation, and observed headshake with significantly larger amplitudes and number of peaks than in naturalistic corpus data. This is not completely unexpected, but should be investigated further.

Furthermore, while we did not find significant differences in phonetic properties of headshake accompanying the three types of negative signs, we observed some indications that there might be differences between them. For example, it seems that headshake with irregular negation typically has more peaks (at least two), and a smaller amplitude. It might be the case that different phonological types of negative headshake exist in RSL. Unfortunately we do not have a dataset that is sufficiently large to investigate this further.

Finally, similar measurements of phonetic properties of negative headshake can be conducted in future for

[4]None of the comparisons discussed in this section are statistically significant based on mixed effect regression models with signers as random effects. Given the very small size of the data set it is not surprising; but it does mean that all the discussed tendencies are only indications for future research.

other sign languages with sufficiently large published corpora. Thus it will be possible to test whether phonetics of headshake varies cross-linguistically.

5.2. Applicability of CV

An important goal of this study was to test the applicability of CV to phonetic analysis of nonmanuals in sign languages, specifically, to headshake.

The measurements of head rotation extracted with OpenFace agree with our perception of head rotation in the recordings. In other words, whenever a head rotation is visible in the recording, it will be visible in the curve representing horizontal rotation of the head extracted from OpenFace. Whenever there is a peak in the movement (the head reaches the maximal degree of turning and starts moving in the opposite direction), this peak is also visible in the graph. Thus, OpenFace measurements can be used to identify the number of peaks and calculate the frequency of rotations.

The creators of OpenFace (Baltrusaitis et al., 2018) report that the absolute mean error for head rotation in their model is 2.4 degrees. It is useful to relate this to the mean headshake amplitude detected in our data, which is 16 degrees, and the standard deviation, which is 11.2. The mean error for amplitude is thus around 0.2 SD of the headshake we found. This means that OpenFace measurements can be used to estimate amplitude of headshake to this degree of certainty. However, if very small differences in amplitude are to be investigated, the measurement error can become an obstacle. We do not know of any research indicating that very minimal differences in headshake amplitude in sign languages can be meaningful, but the lack of such findings can also be due to the lack of research at that level of precision.

Finally, while OpenFace seems to produce good measurements of head rotation for video recordings, these measurements cannot be easily applied to detect negative headshake in the data. As mentioned above, head position can be used for many different purposes in addition to expressing negation; thus, a non-neutral position or even a sequence of non-neutral positions do not necessarily mean a headshake. This is illustrated in Figure 5, which shows a large amount of horizontal head movements, but only a small part of the utterance actually contains headshake. The initial part of the head movement is in fact due to the signer imitating a person looking for something.

However, it appears that one can combine measurements extracted with OpenFace and manual inspection of video recordings. Manual inspection can help identify roughly where headshake occurs, and OpenFace measurements can be used to more precisely detect its boundaries and to measure the amplitude.

5.3. Comparison to Other Types of Headshake

An issue related to the applicability of CV is comparing negative headshake to other types of headshake in

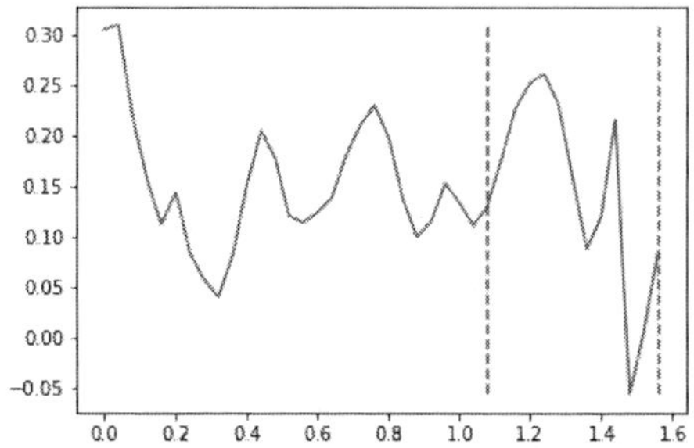

Figure 5: Example of head rotation in RSL. X-axis: time in seconds; y-axis: rotation in radians. Red lines: boundaries of the negative headshake.

RSL signers, and also comparing headshake produced by RSL signers to gestural headshake produced by e.g. speakers of Russian, in terms of phonetic characteristics. Such a comparison is necessary for quantitatively testing the claim in the literature that negative headshake in sign languages is different from gestural headshake, and that it is more grammaticalized (Pfau, 2008). Some recent corpus-based studies in fact directly question this conclusion, and argued that headshake produced by signers can be formally and functionally similar to headshake produced by non-signers (Johnston, 2018).

For the current study, we did not have the resources to compare negative headshake in RSL to headshake with other functions, or to headshake produced by non-signers. However, we think that the general methodology of using OpenFace to extract measurements of head rotation is fully applicable to conduct such a comparison in future. Furthermore, it seems conceptually possible and realistic to use output of OpenFace and Machine Learning to detect headshake in the data automatically, as the task of detecting headshake (vs. lack of headshake) is intuitively easier than distinguishing negative headshake (vs. other uses) based on measurements of head rotation alone. This automatic detection will likely need to be followed up by manual classification of the headshake detected, but this can still increase the speed of data collection and therefore sample sizes in future studies.

6. Bibliographical References

Baker-Shenk, C. L. (1983). *A microanalysis of the non-manual components of questions in American Sign Language*. Doctoral dissertation, University of California, Berkeley.

Baltrusaitis, T., Zadeh, A., Lim, Y. C., and Morency, L.-P. (2018). Openface 2.0: Facial behavior analysis toolkit. In *2018 13th IEEE International Conference on Automatic Face & Gesture Recognition (FG 2018)*, pages 59–66. IEEE.

Bauer, A. and Kyuseva, M. (2022). New Insights Into Mouthings: Evidence From a Corpus-Based Study of Russian Sign Language. *Frontiers in Psychology*, 12:779958. DOI: 10.3389/fpsyg.2021.779958.

Cao, Z., Simon, T., Wei, S.-E., and Sheikh, Y. (2017). Realtime multi-person 2D pose estimation using part affinity fields. In *Proceedings of the IEEE Conference on Computer Vision and Pattern Recognition (CVPR)*.

Cao, Z., Hidalgo, G., Simon, T., Wei, S.-E., and Sheikh, Y. (2018). OpenPose: realtime multi-person 2D pose estimation using Part Affinity Fields. In *arXiv preprint arXiv:1812.08008*.

Coerts, J. (1992). *Nonmanual Grammatical Markers. An Analysis of Interrogatives, Negation and Topicalisation in Sign Language of the Netherlands*. Doctoral dissertation, University of Amsterdam, Amsterdam.

Crasborn, O. and Sloetjes, H. (2008). Enhanced ELAN functionality for sign language corpora. In *Proceedings of the 3rd Workshop on the Representation and Processing of Sign Languages: Construction and Exploitation of Sign Language Corpora*, pages 39–43. ELRA, Paris.

Crasborn, O., Zwitserlood, I., and Ros, J. (2008). Corpus NGT. An open access digital corpus of movies with annotations of Sign Language of the Netherlands.

Dachkovsky, S., Healy, C., and Sandler, W. (2013). Visual intonation in two sign languages. *Phonology*, 30(02):211–252. DOI: 10.1017/S0952675713000122.

De Vos, C., Van der Kooij, E., and Crasborn, O. (2009). Mixed signals. Combining linguistic and affective functions of eye brows in questions in Sign Language of the Netherlands. *Language and Speech*, 52(2/3):315–339.

Harmon, J. (2017). Simultaneous articulation as a window into structure: nonmanuals in ASL. In Nee, J., et al., editors, *Proceedings of the Forthy-Third Annual Meeting of the Berkeley Linguistics Society*, volume I, pages 121–144. Berkeley Linguistics Society, Berkeley.

Harrison, S. (2014). 112. Head shakes: Variation in form, function, and cultural distribution of a head movement related to "no". In Müller, C., et al., editors, *Handbücher zur Sprach- und Kommunikationswissenschaft / Handbooks of Linguistics and Communication Science (HSK) 38/2*, pages 1496–1501. De Gruyter Mouton. DOI: 10.1515/9783110302028.1496.

Johnston, T. (2018). A corpus-based study of the role of headshaking in negation in Auslan (Australian Sign Language): Implications for signed language typology. *Linguistic Typology*, 22(2):185–231. DOI: 10.1515/lingty-2018-0008.

Kimmelman, V., Imashev, A., Mukushev, M., and Sandygulova, A. (2020). Eyebrow position in grammatical and emotional expressions in Kazakh-Russian Sign Language: A quantitative study. *PLOS ONE*, 15(6). DOI: 10.1371/journal.pone.0233731.

Kita, S., van Gijn, I., and van der Hulst, H. (1998). Movement phases in signs and co-speech gestures, and their transcription by human coders. In Wachsmuth, I. et al., editors, *Gesture and Sign Language in Human-Computer Interaction*, volume 1371, pages 23–35. Springer Berlin Heidelberg, Berlin, Heidelberg.

Ko, S.-K., Son, J. G., and Jung, H. (2018). Sign language recognition with recurrent neural network using human keypoint detection. In *Proceedings of the 2018 Conference on Research in Adaptive and Convergent Systems*, pages 326–328.

Koller, O., Ney, H., and Bowden, R. (2016). Deep hand: How to train a cnn on 1 million hand images when your data is continuous and weakly labelled. In *Proceedings of the IEEE conference on computer vision and pattern recognition*, pages 3793–3802.

Kuder, A., Filipczak, J., Mostowski, P., Rutkowski, P., and Johnston, T. (2018). What Corpus-Based Research on Negation in Auslan and PJM Tells Us About Building and Using Sign Language Corpora. In *Proceedings of the 8th Workshop on the Representation and Processing of Sign Languages: Involving the Language Community*, pages 101–106. ELRA, Paris.

Kuznetsova, A., Imashev, A., Mukushev, M., Sandygulova, A., and Kimmelman, V. (2021). Using Computer Vision to Analyze Non-manual Marking of Questions in KRSL. In *Proceedings of the 1st International Workshop on Automatic Translation for Signed and Spoken Languages (AT4SSL)*, pages 49–59, Virtual. Association for Machine Translation in the Americas.

Lackner, A. (2021). Nonmanuals in sign languages: a research desideratum. *Grazer Linguistische Studien*, pages 1–27. DOI: 10.25364/04.48:2021.93.1.

Oomen, M. and Pfau, R. (2017). Signing not (or not): A typological perspective on standard negation in Sign Language of the Netherlands. *Linguistic Typology*, 21(1):1–51. DOI: 10.1515/lingty-2017-0001.

Pfau, R. and Quer, J. (2010). Nonmanuals: their prosodic and grammatical roles. In Brentari, D., editor, *Sign Languages*, pages 381–402. Cambridge University Press, Cambridge.

Pfau, R. (2008). The grammar of headshake: a typological perspective on German Sign Language negation. *Linguistics in Amsterdam*, 1:37–74.

Puupponen, A., Wainio, T., Burger, B., and Jantunen, T. (2015). Head movements in Finnish Sign Language on the basis of Motion Capture data: A study of the form and function of nods, nodding, head thrusts, and head pulls. *Sign Language & Linguistics*, 18(1):41–89. DOI: 10.1075/sll.18.1.02puu.

R Core Team. (2019). *R: A Language and Environment for Statistical Computing*. R Foundation for Statistical Computing, Vienna, Austria.

RStudio Team. (2019). *RStudio: integrated development environment for R*. Boston, MA. tex.organization: RStudio, Inc.

Rudnev, P. and Kuznetsova, A. (2021). Linearization constraints on sentential negation in Russian Sign Language are prosodic. *Sign Language & Linguistics*, 24(2):259–273. DOI: 10.1075/sll.20007.rud.

Saunders, B., Camgoz, N. C., and Bowden, R. (2020). Everybody Sign Now: Translating Spoken Language to Photo Realistic Sign Language Video.

Tyrone, M. E. and Mauk, C. E. (2016). The Phonetics of Head and Body Movement in the Realization of American Sign Language Signs. *Phonetica*, 73(2):120–140. DOI: 10.1159/000443836.

Virtanen, P., Gommers, R., Oliphant, T. E., Haberland, M., Reddy, T., Cournapeau, D., Burovski, E., Peterson, P., Weckesser, W., Bright, J., van der Walt, S. J., Brett, M., Wilson, J., Millman, K. J., Mayorov, N., Nelson, A. R. J., Jones, E., Kern, R., Larson, E., Carey, C. J., Polat, L., Feng, Y., Moore, E. W., VanderPlas, J., Laxalde, D., Perktold, J., Cimrman, R., Henriksen, I., Quintero, E. A., Harris, C. R., Archibald, A. M., Ribeiro, A. H., Pedregosa, F., van Mulbregt, P., and SciPy 1.0 Contributors. (2020). SciPy 1.0: Fundamental algorithms for scientific computing in python. *Nature Methods*, 17:261–272. DOI: 10.1038/s41592-019-0686-2.

Weast, T. (2011). American Sign Language Tone and Intonation: A Phonetic Analysis of Eyebrow Properties. In Channon, R. et al., editors, *Formational Units in Sign Languages*, pages 203–226. De Gruyter, Berlin, Boston. DOI: 10.1515/9781614510680.203.

Wei, S.-E., Ramakrishna, V., Kanade, T., and Sheikh, Y. (2016). Convolutional pose machines. In *Proceedings of the IEEE Conference on Computer Vision and Pattern Recognition (CVPR)*, pages 4724–4732.

Wilbur, R. (2021). Non-manual markers: theoretical and experimental perspectives. In Quer, J., et al., editors, *The Routledge Handbook of Theoretical and Experimental Sign Language Research*, pages 530–565. Routledge, London; New York.

Zeshan, U., editor. (2006). *Interrogative and negative constructions in sign languages*. Number 1 in Sign Language Typology Series. Ishara Press, Nijmegen.

7. Language Resource References

Burkova, S. (2015). Russian Sign Language Corpus.

Proceedings of the 10th Workshop on the Representation and Processing of Sign Languages (sign-lang@LREC 2022), pages 37–41
Language Resources and Evaluation Conference (LREC 2022), Marseille, 20-25 June 2022

Documenting the Use of Iranian Sign Language (ZEI) in Kermanshah

Yassaman Choubsaz1, Onno Crasborn2, Sara Siyavoshi3, Farzaneh Soleimanbeigi4
1. Razi University, Kermanshah, Iran. 2. Centre for Language Studies, Radboud University.
3. Islamic Azad University, Fereshtegan International Branch. 4. Islamic Azad University, North Tehran Branch.
Address1: Postal code: 6714414971, Kermanshah, Iran. Address 2: PO Box 9103, 6500 HD Nijmegen, The Netherlands. Address3: Postal code: 13111-14656, Tehran, Iran.
Address4: Postal Code: 1651153311, Tehran, Iran
y.choobsaz@yahoo.com, onno.crasborn@ru.nl, ssiyavoshi@unm.edu, farzaneh.soleimanbeigi@gmail.com

Abstract

We describe a sign language documentation project funded by the Endangered Languages Documentation Project (ELDP) in the province of Kermanshah, a city in west of Iran. The deposit at ELDP archive (elararchive.org) includes recording of 38 native signers of Zaban Eshareh Irani living in Kermanshah. The recordings start with an elicitation of the signs of the Farsi alphabet along with fingerspelling of some words as well as vocabulary elicitation of some basic concepts. Subsequently, the participants are asked to watch short movies and then they are asked to retell the story. Later, the participants have natural conversations in pairs guided by a deaf moderator. Initial annotations of ID-glosses and translations to Persian and English were also archived. ID-glosses are stored as a dataset in Global Signbank, along with a citation form of signs and their phonological description. The resulting datasets and one-hour annotation of the conversations are available to other researchers in ELDP archive.

Keywords: ZEI, Iranian Sign Language, language documentation, data elicitation

1. The Situation of Sign Language and the Deaf Community in Iran

Zaban Eshareh Irani (henceforth referred to as ZEI), also referred to as Persian Sign Language (Lewis, Simons & Fennig 2017) or Iranian Sign Language (Behmanesh, 2006) is a sign language used by the Deaf community in Iran. It has been observed that there is regional variation among ZEI signers from different provinces of Iran (Siyavoshi, 2017). However, this variation does not impede their mutual intelligibility.

Although people in the Deaf community in Iran use ZEI to communicate with peers, it is not yet on a par with other spoken languages in Iran. In some reports, the population of the Deaf community in Iran has been estimated to be around one million and half (Noori, 2008). In a more recent report, it is claimed that about three million Deaf and hard of hearing people live in Iran (ZEI workshop, 2015). However, there is no estimate available for the number of ZEI users in this country (Jepsen et al., 2015).

2. Earlier Linguistic Studies and Documentation Projects

Before 2006, there had been no studies on the linguistic description of ZEI. However, since 1960s, there were a few academic publications which only focused on standardization of ZEI. This focus was under the influence of contact with American educators who were supporters of Signing Exact English or 'S.E.E.' Back then, publications had not gone beyond a four-volume dictionary in which the lexicon of the language is presented with Farsi, Arabic and English translations (Bahadori, 2005). Fortunately, within the past two decades, a few young Iranian linguists have put great effort to start and promote linguistic studies of ZEI. Sara Siyavoshi is one of those linguists who has started her research in 2006 as her MA thesis. In her thesis, she introduced the different aspects of morphology, syntax, and phonology of ZEI for the first time (2006). She continued her research on phonology and discourse analysis of ZEI (2009) and now she is working on semantics, narrative studies, and documentation of ZEI in the framework of cognitive linguistics (2015, 2017, 2019).

Ardavan Guity is another linguist who has put a lot of effort to support the use of natural sign language (ZEI in Iran's context) and training of ZEI interpreters. He and his co-authors have recently published two valuable books: *The Deaf book: an introduction to Iranian Sign Language and Deaf culture in Iran* (2020), and an *Introduction to* Iranian *Sign Language* (2021). These are both considered as the first attempts toward teaching and introducing the real and natural language of the Deaf community in Iran. At the moment, he is working on his PhD dissertation project at Gallaudet University which is a grammatical sketch of ZEI. In order to do this, he conducted a fieldwork project to gather and document ZEI in six different cities in Iran: Tehran, Mashhad, Shiraz, Isfahan, Zahedan, and Tabriz.

3. The Start of the project with ELDP's Support

The present study is the documentation of ZEI as used in Kermanshah, a city in West Iran. In Iran, the standard spoken language is Farsi, but in Kermanshah, Kurdish holds this status. As outlined above, it is not the first documentation project carried out on ZEI. Guity has been documenting ZEI in different cities of Iran. However, western area of Iran is not among the regions that he selected. The present study was funded and supported by ELDP (Endangered Languages Documentation Programme)[1], a program which provides funds for linguists all around the world to do fieldwork and archive the collected data in order to preserve endangered languages, making data publicly available. ELDP also provides training for grantees so that they can start their documentation project with some knowledge of documentary linguistics in theory and methods. Before starting the project, the first author took part in a one-week fall school on theory and methods in modern language documentation focusing on the MENA region (Middle East and North Africa) held by ELDP in October 2018. The workshop addressed the type of equipment to use for data collection, using software to annotate and transcribe data, doing fieldwork, how to write and apply for grants. Moreover, lectures introducing documentary linguistics and lexicography were presented in the workshop. At the end of the training, each of the participants were encouraged to apply for a 'small grant' at ELDP. The first author, having been in contact with the Deaf community of Kermanshah during research for her PhD dissertation, applied for this grant together with the second author, and was fortunately awarded with the grant.

The projected started in Kermanshah in September 2019 and ended almost a year later. However, ELDP has suggested that we continue the project and we like to do so. The main challenge here, though, is the pandemic. Before holding the recording sessions, the first author had some trainings and discussions at Radboud University, where researchers have had years of experience in studying sign languages and documenting NGT (Sign Language of the Netherlands). In the summer of 2019, the team of the project including the first author, Farzaneh Soleimanbeigi (a deaf linguist) and Sara Siyavoshi had a one-day training session with Ardavan Guity in which he shared his experience of working with ZEI data in ELAN and documenting ZEI. We discussed what to record, how to record and decided about the number of participants. He also talked about ethical and cultural issues we should have in mind throughout doing the project and answered our questions.

Back in Kermanshah, the first author and Soleimanbeigi held a workshop in sign language at the Deaf center for members of the Deaf community and introduced our project, the importance of documenting their language as well as their contribution to this project. We also clarified the steps which we were going through to carry out the project and answered their questions at the end of the workshop. It was surprising for the two organizers to realize that many signers were not much aware of their own natural sign language as independent from Farsi, the main spoken language of the country. Knowing this led us to go into details and examples in order to make them aware that ZEI is not signed Farsi and has its own grammar and lexicon.

4. What was Recorded and How?

The total number of participants in this project was 36, from which 18 were female and 18 were male. The decision to have 36 participants was based on the fact that we would need to have deaf participants of different age groups and genders in order to obtain a representative sample from the community. We decided to record deaf participants in 3 age groups: young (18 to 30 years old), middle aged (30 to 50 years old) and elderly participants (over 50). The group of young participants included 6 females and 6 males and the same held for the middle aged and elderly group. The first author had a local deaf assistant (henceforth referred to as the moderator) whose one of her responsibilities was to talk and communicate with the deaf candidates and invite them to participate in the study.

A SONY FDR AX33 video camera was used to record videos. This camera records two videos at the same time. One in the maximum quality XAVC format (3840x2160 = 4K) and another in MP4 format (1280x720), both at 25 frames per second. Having this feature helped us a lot since we had small files ready for instant sharing plus high-quality files for further editing. We only used one camera to record the videos in this project, since the budget would not allow us to have two cameras. The camera was located in a 2-meter distance from the participants. That was the furthest distance we could put the camera considering the limitation of space we had. We would zoom instead since we believed the further we put the camera, the more participants would look at the lens. The seat arrangement was in a way for the participants to carry on natural

[1] https://www.eldp.net/

conversations and for their maximum frame to be captured with regard to their faces and body.

Two participants who had almost the same age were recorded in each session. Prior to recording, the participants received an explanation of the project, a consent form (which would be translated into ZEI by the moderator) to sign, and some training about the tasks. The first task had two parts. The first part was elicitation of the signs of the Farsi alphabet. This task was designed to elicit how the participants sign the ZEI manual alphabet, Baghcheban (which is a manual alphabet system accepted and used by ZEI signers of Iran), and to see if there is any variant of the ZEI alphabet which we already knew of. In the second part of the task, the participants were asked to fingerspell 23 words written on a paper. This task was aimed to see how the participants spell Farsi words and to check whether or not the way ZEI alphabet is signed changes in the context of words.

The second task was the production of 100 signs elicited by picture clues on a laptop screen. These pictures included the most common animals, colors, food, as well as some basic concepts related to family, home, and city life in the context of Iran. These concepts were selected by the common sense of the authors and our judgment based on cultural intuition.

The third task was storytelling. We played two different (silent) stories for each signer in a session: "The Pear Story" and the "The Other Pair" (Rozik, 2014). Signer 1, for instance would watch the Pear Story on a laptop screen and tell the story of the movie to her/his partner. The benefit of asking the signer to retell the story to his/her partner rather than to the camera is that when signers are signing to each other, they feel the need to use more details and therefore they use more natural signs. Likewise, signer 2 would watch the other story (The Other Pair) and retell it to his/her partner.

As the last task, the moderator asked questions about different subjects. The moderator was trained by Farzaneh Soleimanbeigi on a number of video calls. We had prepared some questions about daily issues for the Deaf community in order to encourage them to sign in a natural context. The questions were asked only to inspire them to sign and there were not any true or false responses. Almost 16 hours of natural conversations were recorded in this task.
Finally, in addition to the four tasks, we also recorded a gathering of the deaf community in the Deaf club in order to document more natural conversations without any interventions or interruptions from our side. The deaf community in Kermanshah get together in the deaf club (Kanoon) once a week and they chat about their daily issues in life. This is where we recorded 1 hour of free interaction between about 14 Deaf people.

5. What was Annotated and How?

In this project, one hour of conversations between 18 signers in different sessions were annotated. In order to decide which sessions to choose to annotate from, we carefully went over all the recordings of conversations (Task 4). We decided not to start from the starting point of each conversation in task 4 to cover an hour of annotating. After reviewing the video files, we realized that interest in sharing ideas and the amount of linguistic information were not evenly distributed over the entire video session. Thus, we skipped some parts and started annotating some other parts that we realized the deaf person had entered into the discussion with more interest in a short period of time. In another word, the number of signs and variation of structures varied from one part of the videos to another. Our deaf colleague suggested that we consider the part of the video richer in signs.

To annotate the data, we used ELAN. At the time we started to annotate (May 2020), the pandemic had already struck and the research team could not meet in person regularly as it was planned. Therefore, we decided to meet online or talk on the phone when it was necessary to discuss things together. Difficulties arose when trying to send large video files. The low speed of internet connection in different areas of Iran was another technical difficulty.
In annotation phase, Soleimanbeigi (being a native signer) annotated most of the conversations and wrote ID-glosses and sentence translations in Farsi. Siyavoshi was responsible for double-checking the ID-glosses as well as sentence translations and she also translated ID-glosses into English. Finally, the first author translated the Farsi sentences into English and added some notes in the note tier of ELAN where ever an explanation was needed. It took almost 97 hours to annotate one hour of recordings.

ID-glosses were documented in a new dataset for ZEI in the lexical database Global Signbank[2], along with citation forms selected from the elicited data. Global Signbank was the only available option for hosting data in an existing multilingual database, and that it provides links to ELAN (by offering an ECV, external controlled vocabulary, for glossing in ELAN). The citation forms were re-created for the Signbank. We recorded the most frequent signs from a search result in ELAN. We aim to describe these signs in terms of their phonological and semantic properties in future.

[2] https://signbank.cls.ru.nl

Once we were done annotating the videos (Early October), the first author prepared the metadata in Lameta[3], checked the file naming according to ELDP conventions and sent the ELAN files along with all the source videos in MPEG-4 (h264) format to Radboud University, where all data were uploaded to the ELAR archive.

6. The Preliminary Results

A very brief look at the data collected in this study shows that three minor differences can be observed between the other variants of ZEI studied so far and the variant signers use in Kermanshah:

1. Some signs are different from the way they are signed in Tehrani (the capital city of Iran) ZEI which has been studied the most. These include the signs for "teacher", "man", "news", "village", "cheating", "exam", "train", and "math" (An example is provided in Figures 1 and 2).

2. A few alphabet letters are finger-spelled differently between participants from the way they are signed in Tehrani ZEI: te [t], če [tʃ], dâl [d], ze [z], že [ʒ], fe [f], and kâf [k] (here, shown with transcribed Persian alphabet followed by their corresponding IPA symbols). What is surprising is that more than one sign alphabet for some letters was observed in videos. A possible explanation for this might be that the deaf signers in Kermanshah have less often been to school than those in Tehran or maybe they have been to mainstream (hearing) schools instead. Consequently, since there was no one to teach them Baghcheban alphabet, they had learned these signs from each other, apparently with a wider range of variability [4] (An example is provided in figures 3 and 4).

3. The mouth patterns of some signs were different from those of Tehrani ZEI. We hypothesize that this is due to the use of Kurdish, which is the local spoken language in Kermanshah. It is notable that Fingerspelling is based on Farsi alphabet letters and the language that is used for teaching at schools. Kurdish is used as the spoken language in Kermanshah and does not have written form, therefore we cannot claim that the different fingerspelling of some manual alphabet is based on Kurdish.

Figure 1: The sign for "teacher" in Kermanshah.

Figure 2: The sign for "teacher" in Tehrani ZEI[5]

Figure 3: The sign for letter "te" [t] in Kermanshah

Figure 3: The sign for letter "te" [t] in Tehrani ZEI[6]

[3] www.lameta.org

[4]. It is notable that Fingerspelling is based on Farsi alphabet letters and the language that is used for teaching at schools. Kurdish is used as the spoken language in Kermanshah and does not have written form, therefore we cannot claim that the different fingerspelling of some manual alphabet is based on Kurdish.

[5]. The figure is taken from Soleimanbeigi, et al. 2021

[6]. The figure is taken from Soleimanbeigi et al. 2021

7. Future Plans

We are currently planning to continue recording more signers having natural conversations (doing task 4), with more participants from a wider range of age groups. To make this possible, at present this still involves making sure they are vaccinated completely against covid-19, and that it is safe for them and us to sit in a room with other people during the recordings. For that reason, it is hard to estimate when data collection will be completed.

Outside this project, one of the plans is to apply for another Small Grant at ELDP to document other variants of ZEI in other Western provinces of Iran which are less studied, like Ilam and Kurdestan.

8. Acknowledgments

The research reported on in this paper was funded by the Endangered Languages Documentation Programme (ELDP) (grant number: SG0561).

9. Bibliographical References

Bahadori, I. et al. (2005). Persian Sign Language (Vol. 2), fourth edition. Tehran: University of Social Welfare and Rehabilitation Sciences (First published in 1997).

Behmanesh, A. (2006). Iranian Deaf Culture. In *the Deaf Way II Reader: Perspectives from the Second International Conference on Deaf Culture*, vol. 2, H. Goodstein (Eds). Washington, DC: Gallaudet University Press, pp. 98-193.

Guity, Ardavan. In preparation. Esharani grammatical sketch; An initial description of the lexicon and grammar. Washington, DC: Gallaudet University dissertation.

Guity, A. & Siyavoshi, S. (2020). The Deaf Book: an introduction to Iranian Sign Language and Deaf culture in Iran". Tehran: Neveeseh Parsi Publication.

Jespen, J., De Clerck, G., Lutalo-Kiingi, S., & McGregor W. (2015). Sign Languages of the World: A Comparative Handbook. Berlin, München, Boston: De Gruyter Mouton.

Lewis, M. P., Simons, G. F., & Fennig, C. D. (Eds.) (2013). Ethnologue: Languages of the World (17th ed.). Dallas, TX: SIL International.

Noori, M. (2008). The Deaf Encyclopedia (Vol.1), in Noori M. (Eds.) Tehran: Farjam-e Jam-e Jam Publication.

Rozik, S. (2014). The Other Pair. Academy of Arts, High Institute of Cinema.

Siyavoshi, S. (2006). Structure of the Signs in Persian Sign Language. MA Thesis. Allameh Tabataba'i University, Tehran.

Siyavoshi, S. (2009). Manual Simultaneity in Persian Sign Language. MA Thesis. Radboud University, Nijmegen, the Netherlands.

Siyavoshi, S. (2015). Narrative Style and Grammar in ZEI. In *Proceedings of the 9th Iranian Conference on Linguistics*, vol 2, M. Dabir Moghaddam (Eds). Allameh Tabatana'i University, pp. 705-721.

Siyavoshi, S. (2017). The role of the non-dominant hand in ZEI discourse structure. Sign Language Studies, 18(1), pp. 58-72.

Siyavoshi, S. (2019). The expression of modality in ZEI. Doctoral Dissertation. University of New Mexico.

Soleimanbeigi, F., Guity, A., Siyavoshi, S., & Alemi, M. (2021). Introduction to Iranian Sign Language. Tehran: Sharif University of Technology, Institute of Scientific Publications.

ZEI workshop, April (2015). Linguistics Department and Deaf Iranian Visitors, Gallaudet University

Proceedings of the 10th Workshop on the Representation and Processing of Sign Languages (sign-lang@LREC 2022), pages 42–47
Language Resources and Evaluation Conference (LREC 2022), Marseille, 20-25 June 2022

Applying the Transcription System Typannot to Mouth Gestures

Claire Danet[1], Chloé Thomas[2], Adrien Contesse[1], Morgane Rébulard[1], Claudia S. Bianchini[3], Léa Chevrefils[2], Patrick Doan[1]
[1] Ecole d'Art et Design d'Amiens, 40 rue des Teinturiers, 80080 Amiens, France
{claire.danet, morgane.rebulard, adriencontesse, pdoan.atelier} @gmail.com
[2] Dynamique du langage in situ, Université Rouen-Normandie, 17 rue Lavoisier, 76130 Mont-Saint-Aignan, France
{thomaschloe2103, leachevrefils}@gmail.com
[3] Laboratoire Formes et Représentations en Linguistique, Littérature et dans les arts de l'Image et de la Scène, Université de Poitiers, 5 rue Lefebvre, 86073 Poitiers, France
claudia.savina.bianchini@univ-poitiers.fr

Abstract

Research on sign languages (SLs) requires dedicated, efficient and comprehensive transcription systems to analyze and compare the sign parameters; at present, many transcription systems focus on manual parameters, relegating the non-manual component to a lesser role. This article presents Typannot, a formal transcription system, and in particular its application to mouth gestures: 1) first, exposing its kinesiological approach, i.e. an intrinsic articulatory description anchored in the body; 2) then, showing its conception to integrate linguistic, graphic and technical aspects within a typeface; 3) finally, presenting its application to a corpus in French Sign Language (LSF) recorded with motion capture.

Keywords: Typannot, transcription system, mouth gestures

1. Introduction

Typannot is a transcription system designed to annotate every signed language (SLs), which takes into account all the SLs components, i.e. the manual parameters (Handshape, Initial location of the upper limb, and Movement) as well as the non-manual parameters (Mouth Action, Eye Action, Head, and Bust). It stands out from other current transcription systems, like HamNoSys (Hanke, 2004) or SignWriting (Bianchini, 2012), by adopting a descriptive model based on the articulatory possibilities of the body rather than the visuo-spatial characteristics of SLs gestures. This novel descriptive perspective is essential if we want to study the role of the body in the structuration of SLs next to the observations allowed by existing transcription systems.

2. State of the Art: Mouth Gesture

In SLs literature, the role of mouth has been the most studied among facial expressions: indeed, the lower part of the face plays one of the most important functions. Studies have reported a distinction between mouth movements, mouthings and mouth gestures. The mouthings would be the result of an oral education and/or a situation of contact with the hearing community and are labializations which resemble the surrounding vocal languages (Crasborn, 2006); moreover, mouthings generally tend to reproduce the most relevant phonetic part of a lemma of the spoken language. Conversely, mouth gestures are mouth movements specific to SLs (Crasborn *et al.*, 2008; Woll, 2001). It is generally recognized that the mouth assumes different roles, ranging from lexical to morphemic function (adjectival or adverbial). An example of the lexical role is given by the minimal pair [TOO BAD] (facial expression: frowned eyebrows, lips corners down) and [WIN] (facial expressions: wide eyes, eyebrows up, lips corners up) in French Sign Language (LSF), where both signs are textbook homonyms that are partially disambiguated by mouth gesture. In many signs, the mouth plays an important part and may be the only parameter in action, such as to express boredom in a story, i.e. the addition of puffy cheeks with outward airflow without any hand signs (Boyes Braem and Sutton-Spence, 2001).

These different studies show the importance of mouth movements on SLs research. To study these various movements within the corpus, it is necessary to have a complete and efficient transcription system. To date, there are already systems for annotating mouth movements, such as HamNoSys (Hanke, 2004), Vogt-Svendsen notation (2001) or Hohenberger and Happ notation (2001). The typographic system Typannot offers a complementary point of view based on the body articulatory possibilities to describe and note the movements made by the mouth, regardless of its function (mouth movements, mouthings or mouth gestures): in this paper we will focus on mouth gestures.

3. The Transcription System Typannot

The parameters for the description and study of SLs have gradually been established based on the work of Stokoe (1960). They include: the shape of the hand, its position and orientation, movement, and facial expression. Together they allow the description of language structure at a sub-lexical level. This categorization is found in the different types of representation systems, whether phonological (i.e., Stokoe) or phonetic (i.e., HamNoSys). In both cases, the transcription systems mainly rely on a **visuo-spatial** conception of these parameters. Indeed, those categorizations refer to an observation of gestural phenomena from a visual and spatial perspective: the hand has a **shape** and is in one **place**, is oriented in one **direction** and will follow a **trajectory**, the face has an **expression**. This mode of representation shows the gestures from an external point of view (visible) without seeking to precisely explain the bodily organization which partially underlies the forms / locations / orientations / trajectories / expressions (however, HamNoSys uses articulatory principles to represent manual shapes). Without contesting the strengths and merits of this approach, the fact is that currently it is not possible to systematically inform the way in which these forms are produced at a bodily level and consequently the role of the body in the language structure cannot be questioned. In view of the many works on embodied cognition (Varela *et al.*, 1991), the postulate is that the body is at least the vector of these forms, and at most the environment in which they **occur**, **articulate**, and **transform**. Being able to characterize SLs through a **specific body description model** would allow researchers to distinguish two levels of structuration that appear intrinsically linked: 1) a bodily level describing the way in which the articulatory possibilities of the body are dynamically organized; 2) a linguistic level describing how these bodily organizations can form meaningful structures within the language.

3.1 A Description Rooted in the Body: the Kinesiological Approach

The objective of Typannot is to propose a **phonetic** transcription system based on a **body articulatory** model. To do this, it follows a **kinesiological** perspective (Boutet, 2018; Chevrefils *et al.*, 2021), which makes it possible to understand the principles and mechanisms of movement at an anatomical and biomechanical level. The system adopts two registers of information referring to: 1) the articulatory structure; and 2) the mode of activation of the latter. The register of the articulatory structure is divided into three parameters: hand (Doan *et al.*, 2019), upper limbs (Bianchini *et al.*, 2018), and face; each of them has distinct parts (e.g., arms, forearms, hands) that can be arranged according to different degrees of freedom of their own (e.g., the upper limbs have seven degrees of freedom). The second register makes it possible to describe a specific body organization to which activation principles are associated (e.g., impulse, tension, amplitude). Together, these two registers allow investigating the dynamics of transformation of the gesture and questioning the processes of constitution and modulation of its meaning.

3.2 Appropriating a Bodily Perspective: a Grapholinguistic Reflection

At a grapholinguistic level, the design of Typannot, taken as a typographic transcription tool, poses several challenges related to the model and its use. Thanks to the involvement of typographic and UX/ UI[1] designers, it is possible to question how to typographically implement this model and help users to appropriate it. Once finalized, Typannot shall consist of a family of characters and an input interface covering the information registers. While existing transcription systems have traditionally to choose between a linear representation (linked to the decomposition and queryability of data) and a readable graphical synthesis of the sign (as in the case of SignWriting), Typannot is a system capable of combining the two (Fig. 1)

Figure 1: Typannot: description of a mouth gesture articulation in generic (middle) and in "composed glyph" (bottom).

Indeed, by exploiting the automatic ligature functionalities allowed by the OpenType[2] technology, the transcriptions in Typannot can be displayed either in a so-called "generic glyph", where the description has the form of a sequence of queryable characters, or in a so-called "composed glyph", which displays a thumbnail representing the articulatory subsystem (hands, upper limbs, face) in a simplified and visually explicit form. The purpose of this functionality is to be able to change the "focal point" of the observation, according to the needs and the context of use, without losing information. To succeed in producing the very large quantity of thumbnails corresponding to the possible combinations, a program to generate them automatically was created (Fig. 2).

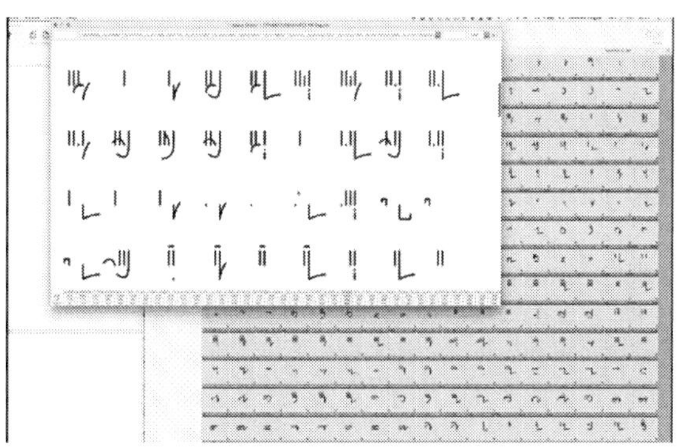

Figure 2: Automatic generation of "composed glyphs" for handshapes.

Alongside the actual typographical issues, a UX/UI approach favoring the assimilation of the model has also been developed for the input interface, named Typannot Keyboard. Indeed, by crossing the interactions allowed by the interface and visual feedbacks, the user can intuitively understand to what a variable corresponds (Fig. 3). This digital interface offering several input devices to adapt to a wide spectrum of transcription approaches and to allow

[1] UX/UI : User eXperience Design & User Interface.

[2] OpenType is a vectorial font format that allows encoding any character associated with Unicode, regardless of the platform (Mac, Windows, Android, etc.); OpenType fonts can have advanced typographic features that handle complex scripts and typographic effects like ligatures.

easy integration of the articulatory principles offered by the system; moreover, it allows easy access to composed glyphs without having to know the composition logic beforehand.
This interface is in progress and does not yet include mouth gestures. Despite this, the mouth gesture typeface with generic glyphs (see section 5) already exists and it is possible to use it on any software supporting OpenType (e.g. Word, Excel, ELAN, etc.).

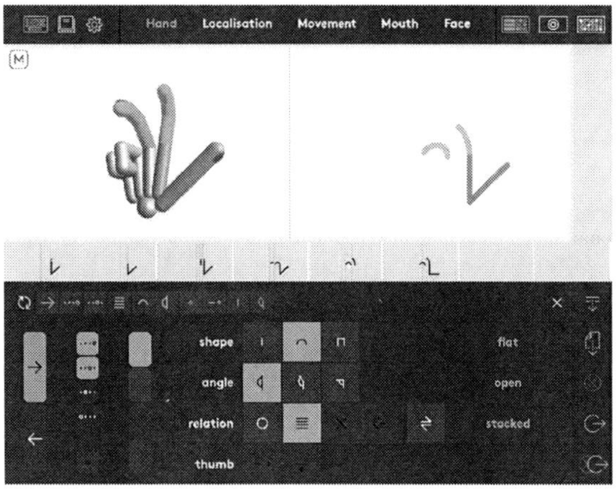

Figure 3: Typannot Keyboard for handshapes.

For a detailed description of the OpenType functionalities and of Typannot Keyboard, cfr. Danet *et al.* (2021) and Chevrefils *et al.* (2021).

4. The Case of the Mouth Gesture

In the Typannot system, mouth gestures are part of one of the two sub-parts of the face, i.e. Facial Action, which includes 1) Eye Action which concerns the upper part of the face and 2) Mouth Action (MA) which takes into account all the possibilities of the lower part and which corresponds to mouth gestures. In order to determine the description characteristics of MA, the work started with the observation of the existing formal descriptions in the literature (Boyes-Braem and Sutton-Spence, 2011), to understand the issues and the specific needs necessary for the realization of the mouth gestures in SLs (what is perceived by the interlocutor). Then, descriptions were reconsidered according to the principle of the articulatory approach and according to specific criteria of transcription (viewable, transferable, and searchable textual data) and design (genericity, readability, modularity, and hand-writability). This method allows a consistent coordination and unification of the typographic and graphic system for the different body parts (Danet *et al.*, 2021).

4.1 Articulatory Description of Features

To do so, gesture is deconstructed into discrete elements that can be divided into four levels of information:

- level 1. the articulatory parameter that the transcription refers to;
- level 2. the different parts that compose the parameter;
- level 3. the different variables associated with each parts;
- level 4. the values assigned to those variables.

Each of those levels have a limited set of characteristics that defines them like individual bricks of information.
After several iterations and thinking to optimize and organize these bricks, the XYZ axes were taken as the common referent: these allow to imagine the MA (parameter) composed of different face elements (parts) as fixed elements, having activable zones (variables) that carry transformations on these 3 axes (values).

PARTS

- ***Jaw, Lips[3] (i.e. corners, tubercles and vermilion borders), Tongue, Air***

VARIABLES and **values**

- ***CONVERGENCE*****:** indicates the approximation, one towards the other, of the two elements constituting the part in question (e.g., Lips Convergence = coming together of the lips)
- ***DIVERGENCE*****:** indicates the moving away, one opposite the other, of the two elements constituting the part in question (e.g., Jaw Divergence = opening of the mouth)
- ***CONTACT*****:** Alveolus, Dental arc, Vermilion, Corner, Cheek
- ***SELECTION*****:** Upper, Lower, Both Vermilion(s); Left, Right, Both Corner(s)
- ***POSITION*****:** Up, Down, Down+, Left, Right, Fore, Fore+, Back
- ***SHAPE*****:** Flat, Round, Tip, Blade
- ***CHANNEL*****:** Outward, Inward
- ***STREAM*****:** Obstructed, Restricted

Thereafter, it is necessary to order these elements in a robust syntax. The descriptive order was motivated by the logic of transformation and by the frequency of the activated elements. In this way, the Jaw comes first because it directly influences the openness of the lips. The lips may appear to diverge from each other when in reality they inherit the position of the jaw, they have not been activated and therefore remain in a "neutral" state. Thus, the graphematic formula of MA takes into account all the bricks, their levels of description and the logic of the transformation.

4.2 The Double Graphic Representation

Within the Typannot system, there are different graphic representations: generic glyphs and composed glyphs. The generic glyphs allow a detailed representation of each position of the articulators of the face, i.e. for the mouth

[3] The term Lips incorporates corners, tubercles and vermilion borders (the last two parts being refereed together as "vermilion").

gestures: Jaw, Lips, Tongue, Air; conversely, composed glyphs are an arrangement of the articulators position.

4.2.1 Generic Glyphs

Once defined, those characteristics form the generic components of the Typannot transcription system called generic glyphs. Graphic symbols can be assigned to them and later encoded into a font to perform like letters (Fig. 4).

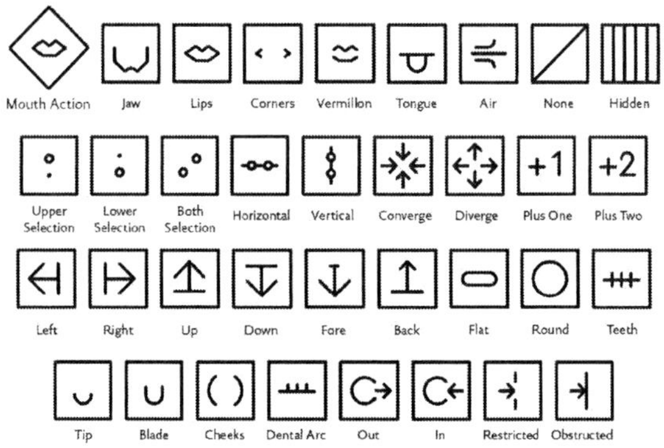

Figure 4: Table of generic glyphs for Mouth Action.

With these few generic components, it is thus possible to generate an infinite number of mouth gesture combinations (Fig. 5). The systematic organization of information into four levels supplemented by a syntax makes it possible to produce a manipulable and queryable transcription. Finally, thanks to the principle of genericity, Typannot allows annotators to query and compare data through different levels of analysis, from a single attribute to a combination of features.

Figure 5: Mouth Action examples, with pictures of the face and the corresponding generic glyphs, according to the established syntax.

4.2.2 Composed Glyphs

The decomposition into generic glyphs allows the generation of a multitude of mouth gestures combinations and the technical capabilities to analyze them. As they are arranged linearly (Fig. 5), the reader/transcriber must make an effort to visuo-spatially reconstruct the mouth gestures, to see them as units.

This is why it is important to propose the second graphic form of the Typannot system, which allows to "read" intuitively and quickly what is transcribed. This consists of producing a logographic representation (composed, unique and recognizable), which depicts the desired mouth gesture while retaining all the information bricks. Recent advances in font encoding technologies (e.g., OpenType properties) and typographical features (e.g., contextual ligatures) allow designing a system that gives users the ability to transparently display one shape or the other while maintaining data integrity.

However, due to a large number of strokes to be graphically represented in a small space, typographic choices were necessary. Typannot uses the modular design approach to be able to compose mouth gestures: each characteristic is symbolized by a graphic module, which can vary according to its transformation on the face and on the neighboring characteristics (Fig. 6). These modules are organized and transformed by respecting a grid and rules of composition. A specific graphical formula has been defined, which translates the generic element of information into a unified and visually explicit glyph (Fig. 7).

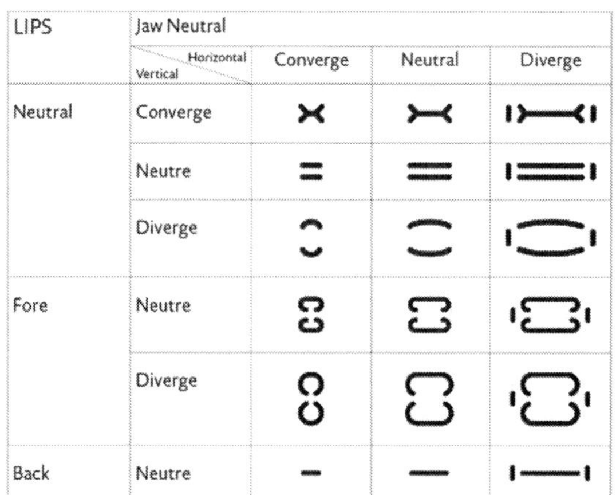

Figure 6: Modules and "composed glyphs" variations for Mouth Action.

Thanks to this modular framework and a scriptable font design environment (i.e., RoboFont[4]), it is possible to automate the modules composition in order to generate all the composed forms that users need.

[4] RoboFont is a software for typeface creation that can automatically generate contextual ligatures from graphic modules and layout instructions. For the development of Typannot, Frederik Berlaen, creator of RoboFont (https://robofont.com), has kindly provided GestualScript with a license to use his software.

Figure 7: Mouth Action examples, with pictures of the face and the corresponding composed glyphs.

5. Corpus Application

Thomas' thesis (in progress) identifies non-manual patterns within interrogative utterances in LSF. A corpus has been recorded, using different means such as Motion Capture (MoCap) through hardware solutions like *Perception Neuron®* and software solutions like *OpenFace®*, as well as three 4K and HD cameras. It originates from 6 deaf signers, 18 to 25 years-old, using LSF as their main language, and has a total duration of 1h43[5]. In order to conduct the transcription of this corpus, Thomas uses the Facial Action transcription system of Typannot in its entirety (MouthAction and EyeAction).

To transcribe this corpus, Thomas is using the multimodal software ELAN, developed by the Max Planck Institute for Psycholinguistics of Nijmegen, in the Netherland[6]. Two kinds of transcription have been used in this corpus: in French glosses for the translation and with the Typannot generic glyphs for the facial expressions. The use of generic glyphs implies having to annotate each articulator separately (lips, jaw, tongue, eyebrows, etc.). Indeed, when extracting data from a spreadsheet, each value of the articulators must be requested individually. If this had been transcribed in the same line, it would not be possible to know if, for example, the requested value "down" relates to the lips or the jaw; this problem arises from the system economicity, the same generic glyph being used for different articulators: composed glyphs solve this issue and simplify the annotation scheme.

During the transcription of this corpus, the transcription system had the advantage of being able to be implemented in the ELAN software as well as in a spreadsheet as a font, which allows to make numerous enquiries and analyses. The system – easy to learn and use[7] – is readable, thus allowing to quickly know what is annotated; moreover, it has the advantage of being useful to transcribe the different elements of the LSF.

A segment of annotated corpus follows (Fig. 8):

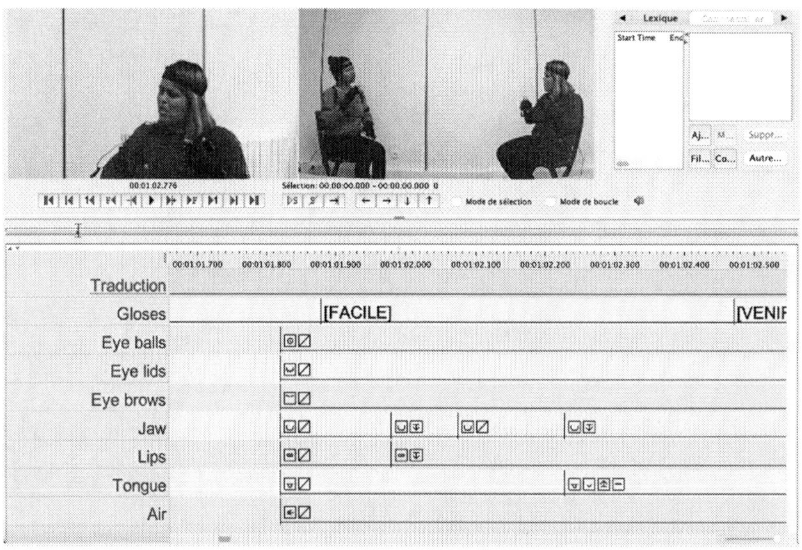

Figure 8: Frames from the visual corpus of gestures and a segment of its annotation with "generic glyphs" on ELAN.

6. Outlook

Typannot has a fine and precise grid for all the face articulators allowing to link the transcriptions to various data captured by MoCap systems such as the *OpenFace®* software. One of the objectives of Thomas' thesis (in progress) is to define thresholds between Typannot values and MoCap data. For example, for all the "lips diverge" within the corpus, limens will have to be issued on the 3 axes. Establishing these limens has the advantage of allowing (semi)-automatic transcriptions, resulting in reduced time in respect of manual transcriptions and/or the

[5] The corpus is composed of two types of elicited dialogues: 1) obtained by asking speakers to talk about the issue of accessibility (to culture, transport, health, etc.); 2) based on a questions&answers game (WH-questions and polar questions).

[6] https://www.mpi.nl/corpus/html/ELAN_ug/index.html

[7] Since 2019, students of the License "Sciences du Langage et Langue des Signes Française" at the University of Poitiers follow a 4-hour course explaining the basic principles of Typannot and the practical use of Typannot Handshape: they are then able to use the system in their linguistic analyses.

possibility of creating larger corpus to analyze. This limen principle has been experimented for the recognition of Typannot Handshape with *Leap Motion Controller®*[8] technology. However, for mouth gestures, the gestural phenomena to be recognized are limited to a smaller surface and therefore require a finer approach (Brumm and Grigat, 2020).

7. Acknowledgements

The project is funded by Ecole Supérieure d'Art et de Design (ESAD) de Amiens, the Hauts-de-France Region and the DGCA of the French Ministry of Culture.
For the corpus: Joëlle Mallet.

8. Bibliographical References

Bianchini, C.S. (2012). *Analyse métalinguistique de l'émergence d'un système d'écriture des Langues des Signes : SignWriting et son application à la Langue des Signes Italienne (LIS)*. Thèse de doctorat, Université de Paris 8 & Università degli Studi di Perugia. https://doi.org/10.13140/RG.2.1.3817.4563

Bianchini, C.S., Chevrefils, L., Danet, C., Doan, P., Rébulard, M, Contesse, A. and Dauphin, J.F. (2018). Coding movement in Sign Languages: the Typannot approach. In *Proceedings of the Fifth International Conference on Movement and Computing (MoCo'18), sect. 1(9), ACM*, pp. 1-8. https://doi.org/10.1145/3212721.3212808

Boutet, D. (2018). *Pour une approche kinésiologique de la gestualité*. Habilitation à diriger des recherches, Université de Rouen-Normandie.

Boyes-Braem, P. and Sutton-Spence, R. (Eds) (2001). *The hands are the head of the mouth: the mouth as articulator in sign language*. Hamburg: Signum Press.

Brumm, M., and Grigat, R.R. (2020). Optimised preprocessing for automatic mouth gesture classification. In Proceedings of the nineth Workshop on the Representation and Processing of Sign Languages *(LREC 2020)*, ELRA, pp. 27-32.

Chevrefils, L., Danet, C., Doan, P., Thomas, C., Rébulard, M., Contesse, A., Dauphin, J.-F., and Bianchini, C.S., (2021). The body between meaning and form: kinesiological analysis and typographical representation of movement in Sign Languages. Languages and Modalities, 1:49-63. https://doi.org/10.3897/lamo.1.68149

Crasborn, O.A. (2006). Nonmanual structures in sign language. In K. Brown (Ed.), *Encyclopedia of language & linguistics 8*. Oxford: Elsevier, pp. 668-672.

Crasborn, O.A., van der Kooij, E., Waters, D., Woll, B. and Mesch, J. (2008). Frequency distribution and spreading behavior of different types of mouth actions in three sign languages. *Sign Language & Linguistics*, 11(1):45-67. https://doi.org/10.1075/sll.11.1.04cra

Danet, C., Boutet, D., Doan, P., Bianchini, C.S., Contesse, A., Chevrefils, L., Rébulard, M., Thomas, C. and Dauphin, J.-F. (2021). Transcribing sign languages with Typannot: a typographic system which retains and displays layers of information. *Grapholinguistics and its Applications*, 5(2):1009-1037. https://doi.org/10.36824/020-graf-dane

Doan, P., Boutet, D., Bianchini, C.S., Danet, C., Rébulard, M., Dauphin, J.F., Chevrefils, L., Thomas, C. and Réguer, M. (2019). Handling sign language handshapes annotation with the Typannot typefont. *CogniTextes (AFLiCo)*, 19:1-24. https://doi.org/10.4000/cognitextes.1401

Hanke, T. (2004). HamNoSys: representing sign language data in language resources and language processing contexts. *Proceedings of the Fourth International Conference on Language Resources and Evaluation (LREC 2004)*, ELRA, pp. 1-6.

Hohenberger, A. and Happ, D. (2001). The linguistic primacy of signs and mouth gestures over mouthing: evidence from language production in German Sign Language (DGS). In P. Boyes-Braem, R. Sutton-Spence (Eds), *The hands are the head of the mouth: the mouth as articulator in sign language*. Hamburg: Signum Press, pp. 153-189.

Stokoe, W. (1960). Sign Language structure, an outline of the visual communications systems of American deaf. *Studies in Linguistics Occasional Paper*, 8. Reprinted as 2005. *Journal of Deaf Studies and Deaf Education*, 10(1):3-37. https://doi.org/10.1093/deafed/eni001

Thomas, C. (in progress). *Étude des paramètres non-manuels en LSF au sein d'énoncés interrogatifs : entre transcriptions manuelles et capture de mouvement*. Thèse de doctorat, Université de Rouen-Normandie.

Varela, F.J., Thompson, E. and Rosch, E. (1991). *The embodied mind: cognitive science and human experience*. Cambridge MA: MIT Press.

Vogt-Svendsen, M. (2001). A comparison of mouth gestures and mouthings in Norwegian Sign Language (NSL). In P. Boyes-Braem, R. Sutton-Spence (Eds), *The hands are the head of the mouth: the mouth as articulator in sign language*. Hamburg: Signum Press, pp. 9-40.

Woll, B. (2001). The sign that dares to speak its name: echo phonology in British Sign Language (BSL). In P. Boyes-Braem, R. Sutton-Spence (Eds), *The hands are the head of the mouth: the mouth as articulator in sign language*. Hamburg: Signum Press, pp. 87-98.

[8] Leap Motion Controller is an optical hand-tracking module that captures the hand movements of your hands with unparalleled accuracy.

Proceedings of the 10th Workshop on the Representation and Processing of Sign Languages (sign-lang@LREC 2022), pages 48–52
Language Resources and Evaluation Conference (LREC 2022), Marseille, 20-25 June 2022

Libras Portal: a Way of Documentation, a Way of Sharing

Ronice Müller de Quadros , Renata da Silva Krusser , Daniela Satomi Saito
Universidade Federal de Santa Catarina, Instituto Federal de Santa Catarina, Instituto Federal de Santa Catarina
ronice.quadros@ufsc.br, renata.krusser@ifsc.edu.br, daniela.saito@ifsc.edu.br

Abstract

The Libras Portal is a platform that makes available in one place a series of materials and tools related to the Brazilian Sign Language (Libras) that integrate the documentation of Libras. It can be used both for research and educational purposes. Among the artifacts developed are tools that support the constitution of an education network and/or community of practice, enabling the sharing of knowledge, data and interaction in Libras and Portuguese.

Keywords: Sign language documentation, Sign language visualization, Visual design

1. Introduction

Libras Portal (2022) involved the creation of a technology-mediated collaboration environment meets Davidson's (2008) definition of a generation of tools that is called Humanities 2.0: "openness about participation grounded in a different set of theoretical assumptions, which decenters knowledge and authority" (Davidson, 2008, p. 711-12). According to Wenger, McDermont, and Snyder (2002), communities of practice benefit from technologies, since they act as amplifiers of networks of relationships and encourage communication between people, stimulating learning and the social construction of knowledge through creative techniques and the use of new tools.

Considering the target audience of the platform and the constitution of the community of practice, which should be composed of deaf and hearing people, the Portal was designed considering aspects related to web accessibility and usability, especially with regard to communication in sign language. For this, the platform was implemented valuing the use of videos in Libras in the access to the menu and hyperlinks, as well as in other available artifacts related to the indexing of information and video upload.

Regarding the human-computer interface, the layout seeks to present a design that facilitates navigation by exploring visual and textual resources compatible with the visuality of deaf users.

The Libras Portal[1] offers resources for research and language teaching as the Grammar of Libras, Libras corpus, Bank of signs and literary anthology of Libras. In addition, we can highlight the repositories for sharing literary, academic and teaching materials, courses, glossaries, anthologies, sample lessons and grammar studies.

The development of this research and resources for accessibility will be described in this article.

2. Libras Portal Resources

2.1 Technical Architecture

The technical architecture of the Portal consists of two web applications: (1) the web app frontend (developed in the JavaScript language, in a reactive way using the Quasar Framework (https://quasar.dev) and the Node.js (https://nodejs.org); and, (2) the web app backend (which counts with all the application management rules), developed with the PHP language (https://www.php.net), with the Laravel Framework (https://laravel.com). To materialize the platform structure for the database Mysql (https://www.mysql.com) and Phpmyadmin (https://www.phpmyadmin.net) were used. For all applications the Linux OS Ubuntu (https://ubuntu.com) with Apache (https://www.apache.org) was used for service support.

2.2 Available Modules

As reported by Krusser, Saito & Quadros (2020), the Libras Portal contemplated the following resources:

a. materials module (literary, academic and didactic) with the tools of filters for searches, favorite materials, download materials and publication of new materials;
b. course module (courses offered in the country related to Libras, such as Libras courses, technical courses, undergraduate courses, graduate courses, other courses for the deaf and inclusion of new courses;
c. language module (different specific materials about Libras, including Libras Grammar, Libras Literary Anthologies, Reference for teaching Libras as L2, Libras corpus (Quadros et al., 2014) and Signbank of Libras[2] (Libras Signbank, 2021);
d. research module (registration of research in development and statistics of the Libras Portal);
e. evaluation module (the materials published in the Libras Portal can be evaluated by users);
f. user profile module (users can create a profile and save their preferences and materials in their profile)
g. interactive space which allows interaction in Libras and in Portuguese. This Portal includes tools that follow the philosophy of open source software design.

2.3 Educational Practices and Tools

With respect to educational practices, under the Libras Portal, a public environment was created that includes materials in different formats such as videos, images, animations, articles, theses, dissertations, teaching materials, on contemporary issues related to Libras, aiming to democratize access to information.

[1] https://portal-libras.org.br (not yet public; access through developer link: https://app-hmg-libras.levantelab.com.br/).

[2] https://signbank.libras.ufsc.br/

It should be considered that the technologies developed to enable this environment seek to make new forms of learning, called ubiquitous learning (Santaella, 2010), possible due to the advantages that networks present in terms of flexibility, speed, adaptability and open access to information.

The tools developed for the Libras Portal enable the management of resources in addition to favoring accessibility, evaluation of materials available, indexing information and uploading videos, constituting a possibility of research and development of products that can be reverted to the entire deaf and hearing community. It is noteworthy that these technologies and educational resources enable and enhance the guidance in Libras, with proven effectiveness in previous experiences.

Considering that the Libras Portal and the Community of Practice and / or Training Network aims to promote interaction in Libras and Portuguese, the following tools were developed, customized and / or integrated:

a. resources for visual search considering the specificities of Libras;
b. asynchronous interaction tools
c. collaboration tools
d. search system for signs in Libras.

To enable the implementation of all tools and educational practices, the Libras Portal comprised the following points:

a. generation of a multimedia database in Libras or about Libras and deaf education;
b. the possibility of users to manage their learning, from tools built for this purpose (e.g., reading progress, management of materials accessed, bookmarks, indication of related content, collaboration between users, etc.);
c. possibility of evaluating the learning materials according to detailed criteria that cover the pedagogical context, aspects of deaf culture, translation and interpretation, appropriateness and quality of digital media used and interface design;
d. support the implementation of research projects, public policies and dissemination of courses and materials in Libras that are in line with the philosophy of the digital humanities, especially Humanities 2.0;
e. organization and generation of a multimedia base for the Signbank on the Signbank global platform;
f. development of a search system in the portal by words in Portuguese or signs in Libras;
g. development of platform management tools with resources for material development, content and user management, information about the most accessed content, semantic and relational search tools;
h. integration of the information and statistics of use of the portal and the databases used and generated.

3. Human Computer Interaction (HCI)

The Libras Portal involved research in the design area for the development of a visual identity project that valued the deaf culture and the forms of visual orientation of the deaf. In addition to considering web accessibility guidelines, it observed recommendations from specific studies that analyzed the use of web environments by deaf people such as those of Flor (2016) and Fajardo, Parra, and Cañas (2010). Such studies highlight the importance of the use of sign language and the use of contextualized visual resources. According to the authors, the use of known and iconic images facilitates the understanding by the deaf, but abstract images or with unknown symbolism can hinder navigation.

The complexity of the information collected in the bilingual environment and the need to provide navigation that values visual and gestural orientation posed significant challenges for the designers. The information architecture design and interaction design took into account the user experience which was analyzed throughout the development of the project.

The portal was developed in a responsive format, aiming to make the Libras Portal a space that allows users to develop their communication skills at any time, through different devices.

The organization of the materials resulted in a layout that prioritized clarity, using a distribution of information with little depth, i.e., with few clicks required to access any content of the Libras Portal, following information architecture proposals designed by Rosenfeld, Morville and Arango (2015), cf. Figure 1.

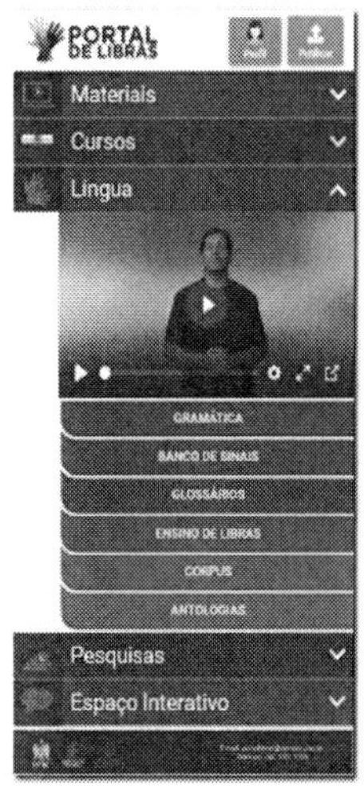

Figure 1: Interface of the Libras Portal, home page

The graphic interface, in turn, was designed to enable navigation through images, Libras, and written texts. In the presentation of the materials, we sought to explore visual resources along with filters to locate the information more efficiently. To this end, the option was included to view the materials with information such as the cover image and title of the material or photo and name of the authors (Figure 2 and Figure 3).

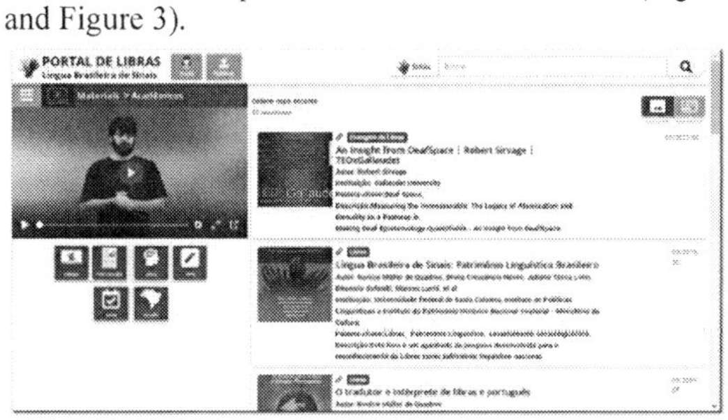

Figure 2: Presentation page of the Academic Materials list with the filters and view by cover.

Figure 3: Presentation page of the Academic Materials list with the filters and view by author.

4. Platform Features

Some of the main innovations of the portal, which required specific studies in doctoral research, are: the possibility of searching for content in the portal using a sign and the use of a tool for evaluating teaching materials developed considering the characteristics of deaf people and bilingual education.

4.1 Sign Searches

The project included in one of its stages the redesign of the Signbank interface to facilitate the search for signs in Libras. The redesign was one of the great challenges of the project, since the search in sign language dictionaries presents a much greater complexity due to the phonological parameters that sign languages present (Scolari, Braviano, and Crasborn, 2022).

The proposal was to develop a system of quick localization by image of the hand configuration using a slider resource. To this end, studies were conducted with usability tests considering the phonological parameter of hand configuration in order to identify the form of organization to be used. The choice for this organizational approach is based on Van der Helm's (2017) and Scolari's (2022) argument that the perceptual organization process is much faster than the thinking process.

Although there are systems that organize the signs for searches from some parameters such as hand configuration, number of hands used, location of articulation of the sign, type of movement, for example, most sign language dictionaries and glossaries do not use the search for signs, only the search for written words.

Studies around the world have sought to develop computer systems capable of recognizing a sign on video in sign language, but the contrasts between the color of the signer's skin and the clothes or the background of the video, and the different types of gestural expression in the execution of movements which vary according to each person and the communication context, make this recognition difficult, and there are still no efficient resources for this.

When the search for signs is offered, the process can be slow and discouraging, requiring choosing different parameters to then selecting the sign in a list of images extracted from the beginning of the video, and usually organized in alphabetical order, being necessary to click to view the sign.

In Libras, the initial selection is usually made by selecting one hand configuration from approximately 60 images that can be grouped by similarities for ease of localization. A word search follows an alphabetical order, which is widely known, but in Libras there is no standardized order or organization by categories of hand configurations that is adopted nationally.

According to Scolari and Braviano (2020) a systematic literature search showed that there are still no usability and design guidelines for the project of these interfaces, and the scientific production focused on the development and evaluation of bilingual interfaces with sign language search systems is still in its early stages.

From there, Scolari, Crasborn, and Braviano (2022) investigated how to classify and order images of hand configurations. To do this, a cluster analysis was performed using three variables, resulting in groups based on visual similarities between the hand configurations. The images were reordered based on similarity and shape gradation principles, aiming for an organization with good visualization, which can contribute to sign search by requiring less metalinguistic skills from users.

Based on these studies and the usability tests, we sought to classify and order the hand configurations within groups considering the visual similarities (Figure 4).

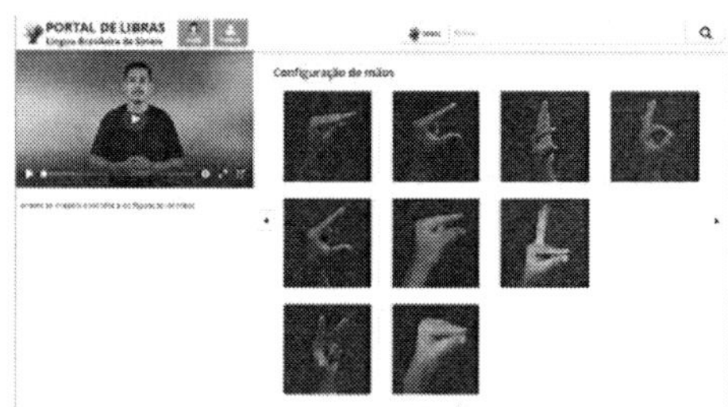

Figure 4: Sign search - Slider for locating a hand configuration.

Once a hand configuration is selected, a list of signals is presented in images with the frame in which the signal is made, making it easier to locate the signal. The organization of this list also allows the use of filters to choose to view only the signals made with one hand, two symmetrical hands, or two asymmetrical hands, and at a given location (Figure 5).

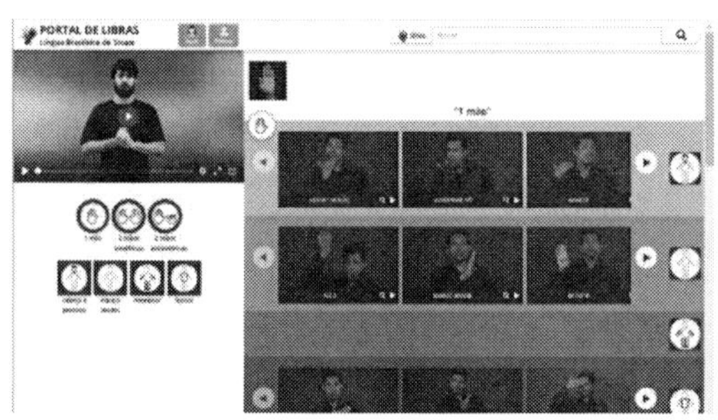

Figure 5: Signal search - finding a signal with a particular hand configuration.

Thus, with the integration of Signbank, it was possible to develop a search system in the portal that enables searches not only by the written word, but also by the sign in Libras. This was feasible because the cataloging of the signs was done in a database with phonological information about each sign: number of hands used to make the sign, hand configuration, location of the articulation of the sign, hand orientation, alternating movement, repeated movement, direction, form of movement, and type of contact between hands.

It is important to point out that the tools developed were designed to be easy to use on different equipment without the need for programming knowledge, and that the modules and materials produced will be available on the Portal for download in accordance with the open source philosophy. This definition aimed to disseminate the knowledge developed, as well as to stimulate the free contribution of the user community for the improvement of the tools and technologies developed.

4.2 Evaluation of the Design of Teaching Materials

Since the Libras Portal aims to enable the sharing of knowledge and resources for teachers, students, and translators-interpreters, we sought to develop a way to evaluate the different contributions received on the platform in order to facilitate the identification of the most appropriate materials for each audience.

According to Moraes et al. (2017), there has been a significant increase in the production of instructional materials for deaf students in the last ten years. However, research that addresses a way to evaluate and select materials for both teachers and students that are more congruent with the specificities of this audience is still scarce, considering that aspects such as the use of sign language and attention to different reading/writing skills should be considered in an evaluative process (Moraes, 2020, Debevc et al., 2014).

The evaluation categories were developed throughout the doctoral research of Moraes (2020), and they are: pedagogical context, deaf culture, translation and interpretation, digital media and interface design, which were implemented in the portal for the evaluation of teaching materials in the format of electronic form of quantitative/qualitative character.

5. Final Considerations

The development of the Libras Portal aimed to support the dissemination of content related to Libras and deaf education, promoting the formation of communities of practice (researchers, teachers, interpreters and translators of sign language and communities). The complexity of the relationship between information, the amount and variety of content available, the prospect of growth due to the demand for materials related to Libras, and the need to value the visual and Libras, required the development of different theoretical research on accessibility and perspectives of deaf people facing the choice of technologies to be used, as well as the development of innovative technological resources. The project involved studies for the development of an information architecture that would clarify the organization of the content, allowing its location by visual orientation and sign language. Studies were also developed for the construction of tools for searches in Libras, bilingual interaction, sharing, management and evaluation of multimedia materials, and the availability of statistical data about the types of users, authors, published materials and courses, aiming to serve as subsidies for research, teaching and public policies.

6. Acknowledgements

Current research was funded by the National Council for Scientific and Technological Development – CNPq (# 440337/2017-8).

7. Bibliographical References

Davidson, C. N. (2008). Humanities 2.0: Promise, Perils, Predictions. *Publications of the Modern Language Association of America.* 123(3):707–717. https://doi.org/10.1632/pmla.2008.123.3.707

Debevc, M., Stjepanovic, Z. and Holzinger, A. (2014). Development and evaluation of an e-learning course for deaf and hard of hearing based on the advanced Adapted Pedagogical Index method. *Interactive Learning Environments.* 22(1):35–50. https://doi.org/10.1080/10494820.2011.641673

Fajardo, I., Parra, E. and Cañas, J. J. 2010. Do sign language videos improve web navigation for deaf signer users? *Journal of Deaf Studies and Deaf Education,* 15(3):242–262. https://doi.org/10.1093/deafed/enq005

Flor, C. da S. (2016). *Recomendações para a criação de pistas proximais de navegação em websites voltadas para surdos pré-linguísticos.* Doctoral Thesis. Programa de Pós-graduação em Engenharia e Gestão do Conhecimento, Universidade Federal de Santa Catarina, Florianópolis. https://repositorio.ufsc.br/handle/123456789/174271

Krusser, R. da S., Saito, D. S., and Quadros, R. M. de (2020) Portal de Libras. *Forum Linguístico.* 17(4):5561–5574. https://doi.org/10.5007/1984-8412.2020.e77375

Moraes, L., Scandolara, D., Velloso, B.P., Bubniak, F. and Figueiredo, S. (2017). Interface Design and Accessibility. In: *International Technology, Education and Development Conference*, 2017. Valencia, pp. 7439–7444.

Moraes, L. (2020). *Um modelo para avaliação do design de Recursos Educacionais Digitais Bilíngues (Libras/Português).* Doctoral Thesis. Programa de Pós-graduação em Design, Centro de Comunicação e Expressão, Universidade Federal de Santa Catarina, Florianópolis. https://repositorio.ufsc.br/handle/123456789/219342

Rosenfeld, L., Morville, P., Arango, J. (2015). Information architecture: for the web and beyond. O'Reilly Media, 4th edition.

Santaella, L. (2010). A ecologia pluralista da comunicação: conectividade, mobilidade, ubiquidade. São Paulo: Paulus.

Scolari, S., Braviano, G. (2020). Usabilidade no design de sistemas de busca em língua de sinais: Revisão Sistemática da Literatura. In: Martins, N., Brandão, D. (Eds.) *DIGICOM, 4th International Conference on Design and Digital Communication.* IPCA - Instituto Politécnico do Cávado e do Ave. pp. 179–190. https://digicom.ipca.pt/docs/DIGICOM2020-Atas_PT-ES.pdf

Scolari, S., Braviano, G., Crasborn, O. (2022). Search Engines Interfaces for Sign Languages: Designing Multilanguage Questionnaire to Collect Signers Perception Similarities. In: Martins, N., Brandão, D. (Eds.) *Advances in Design and Digital Communication II.* pp. 31–43. https://doi.org/10.1007/978-3-030-89735-2_3

Scolari, S., Crasborn, O., Braviano, G. (2022) Searching for Signs: Developing a handshape taxonomy based on visual similarity. *International Journal of Lexicography*. ecac004:1–24. https://doi.org/10.1093/ijl/ecac004

Van der Helm, P. A. (2017). Human Visual Perceptual Organization Beats Thinking on Speed. *Attention, Perception, & Psychophysics*. 79:1227–1238. https://doi.org/10.3758/s13414-017-1281-1

Wenger, E., McDermont, R., Snyder, W. M. (2002) Cultivating communities of practice: a guide to managing knowledge. Boston, Massachusetts: Harvard Business School Press.

8. Language Resource References

Libras Portal (2021). Web Portal. https://portal-libras.org.br/

Libras Signbank (2021). Website. https://signbank.libras.ufsc.br/

Quadros, R. M. de, Schmitt, D., Lohn, J. T., Leite, T. de A., et al. (2014) *Corpus de Libras*. http://corpuslibras.ufsc.br/

Proceedings of the 10th Workshop on the Representation and Processing of Sign Languages (sign-lang@LREC 2022), pages 53–58
Language Resources and Evaluation Conference (LREC 2022), Marseille, 20-25 June 2022

Representation and Synthesis of Geometric Relocations

Michael Filhol[1], John McDonald[1,2]
[1] Laboratoire Interdisciplinaire des Sciences du Numérique (LISN), CNRS, Université Paris–Saclay, Orsay, France
[2] School of Computing, DePaul University, Chicago, IL, USA
michael.filhol@cnrs.fr, jmcdonald@cdm.depaul.edu

Abstract

One of the key features of signed discourse is the geometric placements of gestural units in signing space. Signers use the geometry of signing space to describe the placements and forms of objects and also use it to contrast participants or locales in a story. Depending on the specific functions of the placement in the discourse, features such as geometric precision, gaze redirection and timing will all differ. A signing avatar must capture these differences to sign such discourse naturally. This paper builds on prior work that animated geometric depictions to enable a signing avatar to more naturally use signing space for opposing participants and concepts in discourse. Building from a structured linguistic description of a signed newscast, they system automatically synthesizes animation that correctly utilizes signing space to lay out the opposing locales in the report. The efficacy of the approach is demonstrated through comparisons of the avatar's motion with the source signing.

Keywords: AZee, Sign Language, Avatar, Geometric Constructions, Relocation

1. Introduction

In the history of Sign Language study, there has been a long tradition of distinguishing the units composing signed sequences between conventional "lexical" units and the productive "depicting" ones (Cuxac, 2000; Johnston, 2010). The former are usually found in picture dictionaries, each given a fixed/canonical form (citation form), and labelled with a written language word equivalent (gloss) used in video stream annotations. These sometimes allow for variations such as hand location or movement direction change, which theories tend to analyse as spatial agreements ("relocated signs", "directional verbs") (Lillo-Martin and Meier, 2011; Quer, 2011; Wilbur, 2013), but much of the associated form remains invariant.

The latter usually escape the traditional grammatical qualifiers like verb or behaviour like agreement, and are described less systematically than, say, manual parameter values for signs. They make a productive use of space, and their iconicity is usually accepted, if not put forward, as their primary feature (Cogill-Koez, 2000; Liddell, 2003a; Liddell, 2003b). In contrast, the fact that the dictionary-type entries are often iconic too is mostly incidental to their common theoretical descriptions (Baus et al., 2013; Padden et al., 2013). Interestingly, we note that in closed vocabulary annotations, labels used for depicting units usually describe a wide generic category, e.g. "classifier placement" or "size and shape specification", covering highly variable forms and meaning. In contrast, glosses have a specific meaning, generally conveyed by the written word, and are coupled with forms that are largely invariant.

These categories can inform the way an avatar will need to move to correctly communicate the intended meaning. As signing is studied, however, the division between these two categories can become difficult to identify in practice due to the manner in which signers structure discourse. Further, computer animation sometimes has its own questions, techniques and considerations that make it difficult to align synthesis with traditional linguistic divisions.

This paper presents a linguistic framework and corresponding animation techniques that support the various relocating structures described above, and demonstrates their expressive efficacy by applying them to real-life discourse. The approach is validated by mapping the components of these descriptions to animated forms that are combined on the avatar to reproduce such discourse.

2. Related Prior Work

Over the recent past, we have been working to bridge the Sign description model AZee with the Paula Sign synthesis platform (Filhol et al., 2017). Both systems share two fundamental organising principles: multi-linear scheduling of motion processes as opposed to synchronous sequences, and a holistic view of the body as opposed to a-priori partitioning of the body articulators. The bridge leverages the principle of "the coarser the better", by which larger animation blocks yield more natural-looking animations, while also recognising the infinite variability of some SL productions, caused for example by the use of a continuous space in geometric constructions. Based on a top-down search for parameterised "shortcuts", it trades off composition of minimal units with reuse of coarser ones when available.

The stones were largely unturned in the area of depicting, i.e. non-glossable, productions, which led us to explore phenomena such as placements of objects (Huenerfauth, 2006; López-Colino and Colás, 2011; Filhol and McDonald, 2018) and deployments of shapes (Filhol and McDonald, 2020). The latest test has managed the synthesis of a description comprised mostly of depicting units, rendering an utterance of 20+ seconds (McDonald and Filhol, 2021). With this work, we could demonstrate that AZee provides efficient abstraction of articulated forms into semantic combinations, covering much of the language, even dealing with features left uncovered by other approaches. Plus, we have shown that this coverage was achieved with a limited number of combining production rules, making the case that AZee is a productive system. This point was recently generalised to the 120 videos of the *40 brèves* corpus[1],

[1]Parallel corpus of news items in French and French Sign Lan-

totalling 1 hour of LSF, and manually encoded in AZee (Challant and Filhol, 2022). The resulting AZee expressions were found to cover 94% of the signing time, with just 30+ combining production rules.

We also demonstrated that Paula was able to render natural and meaningful movement from the compiled AZee discourse expressions directly. This is thanks to AZee's specification not only of the forms to articulate but also the timing information to synchronise them, a feature that is essentially absent from gloss strings.

Finally, we observed that production rules that were initially found to order discourse constituents, were actually useful on all levels and in all types of productions, even the purely geometric ones. For example, rules `all-of` and `each-of` structured the table scene description on various levels of nested lists. For example, the utterance contained an `each-of` list of items on a table, which itself contained lists of plates, chairs, glasses, etc. Interestingly, `all-of` was also used to create a "knife & fork" compound to form a sign for "cutlery", which is close to the level usually considered lexical. We even found this rule inside units typically annotated as non-lexical and productive, as we studied shape deployments[2]. So we ended up with rules that are widely applicable regardless of divisions between lexical and non-lexical, between glossable and non-glossable, or between depicting and non-depicting.

This paper pushes our research on the use of space and geometric constructions further, this time taking advantage of the recently published corpus of 120 AZee expressions mentioned above.

3. Relocations in AZee

Looking at the AZee expressions recently added to the *40 brèves* repository[3], we can extract two types of AZee patterns that result in geometric relocations in the produced forms.

One is the use of the rule `about-point`, whose arguments are a locus point *pt* of the signing space and a score (signed utterance) *locsig*. Its form description involves a torso rotation and a brief glance towards the locus at the very beginning of the rotation, and *locsig* being signed normally, although seemingly displaced towards *pt*. The gestural units perceived as "at the locus" are performed with the torso rotation sustained until their completion. Its semantics is that *locsig* is information about what is anchored at *pt*. It is very similar to `info-about` (score arguments *topic* and *info*), except that the topic about which the information is given lies in the reference of the anchor, not in a signed argument.

A second AZee pattern found to relocate items is for a rule to use a geometric argument directly, e.g. a point of the signing space, on which its produced form depends. This generally affects the placement or movement of the more distal effectors controlled by the rule, like finger tips or hands, with less torso involvement and no gaze redirection. This pattern will typically be used for instances of units traditionally called "relocated", "directional" or "pointing" signs. Note that such arguments in AZee can be defined as optional (and given a default value, i.e. one to use if none is given when the rule is applied), or mandatory.

Let us take the "1R-JP" entry of the *40 brèves* corpus to exemplify these cases. The news report in question describes a French citizen who was held hostage in Iraq for 35 days, was released, and is about to return to France.

> *Le Français Bernard Planche, 52 ans, retenu en otage en Irak pendant 35 jours, a retrouvé samedi la liberté près de Bagdad, et devrait très prochainement regagner la France.*

The signed translation has the following structure (see fig. 1 for snapshots):

1. Iraq established on the right of the signing space (from the beginning to 2 s);
2. Bernard Planche, including nationality and age, established on the left (2–7.5 s);
3. reporting that he was held hostage 35 days, still signed on the left-hand side except for the last sign meaning "hostage", which ends on the right (7.5–11 s);
4. pausing with hands retracted together (11–11.3 s);
5. establishing a place near Baghdad that he is freed from, back on the right-hand side of the signing space (11.3–16 s);
6. reporting that he will be returning to France soon with a sign for "return" performed from right to left (from 16 s to the end).

The overall expression, given in file "1R-JP.az" of the corpus repository, connects the six segments mostly by means of the `context` rule, which we have covered in prior publications.

The first pattern with `about-point` is found in three instances, namely over segment 1 (locus on the right), over the pair of segments 2 and 3 (on the left), and over segment 5 (on the right again). The AZee expression for segment 1 for example is the following, where `category` with arguments *cat* and *elt* means "*elt* as an instance of *cat*", `pays` means "country" and `Irak` "Iraq". The `Rssp` reference stands for a point on the right of the signing space.

```
:about-point
  'pt
  ^Rssp
  'locsig
  :category    (*)
    'cat
    :pays
    'elt
    :Irak
```

guage, available at https://www.ortolang.fr/market/corpora/40-breves.

[2]See the description of the wall sections in (Filhol and McDonald, 2020)—direct link to video: https://zenodo.org/record/3904430/files/bedroom-walls.mp4?download=1.

[3]Permanent link to the corpus version used for this work: https://hdl.handle.net/11403/40-breves/v2.

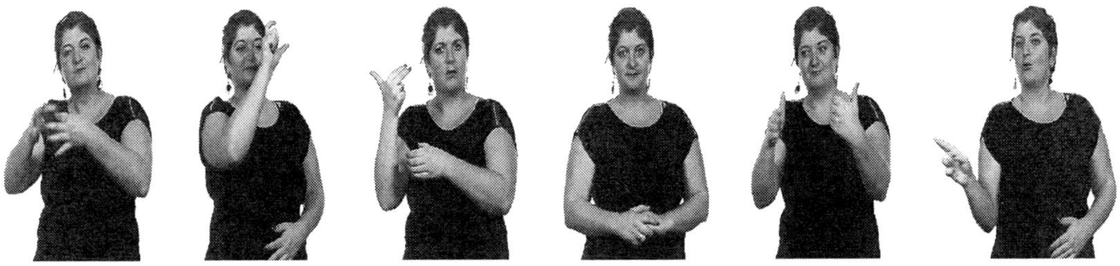

1. "country" 2. "person" 3. "hostage" 4. (pause) 5. "nearby" 6. "return"

Figure 1: Video snapshots of 1R-JP, one per segment described in section 3.

The second pattern is seen in various places. Below are three excerpts from the whole expression.

```
:otage       :retour       :pointage index
  'loc         'source       'target
  ^Rssp        ^Rssp         ^Lssp
               'dest
               ^Lssp
```

The first expression uses rule `otage`, which means "hostage" and produces the appropriate sign, allowing for a location point argument *loc* used to control the final position of the hands. The corresponding instance in the video is at 8 s (fig. 1.3). The `Rssp` argument point (signer's right-hand side of signing space in AZee) accounts for the fact that the sign ends on the right-hand side, which is interpreted as the location of the associated event. Note that neither the spine rotation nor the leading glance of the previous pattern are involved.

Similarly, the second expression uses rule `retour` for "return", which allows two point arguments *source* and *dest*, affecting the start/end points of the finger movement. The corresponding instance is visible at 17 s in the video (fig. 1.6).

Finally, the third expression captures the index pointing sign with rule `pointage index` and `Lssp` as its obligatory argument *target*, modifying the direction of the index. The corresponding instance is at 6 s in the video, and a similar one, pointing to the right (`Rssp`), can be found at 14 s.

Let us now look more closely at the AZee expressions shown above, and in particular how the part to which the geometric change is applied is inserted in the expression. The `about-point` expression, generating pattern 1, locates Iraq around `Rssp`. That geometric change is applied to what would otherwise be encoded as the sub-expression marked `(*)`. This sub-expression is inserted in the `about-point` operation with no change to it whatsoever. What the AZee formalism is telling us here is that this is an external change; nothing was changed inside of the relocated discourse itself. In contrast, the other three expressions relevant to the second form pattern, exhibit changes to, or the addition of, internal parameters of the original expressions. With no geometric change, `:otage` and `:retour` would be valid expressions, signed in the middle of the signing space (often referred to as neutral). In our current definition of `pointage index`, parameters could not be left out (one does not point at no target using that form), but any geometric change to it would still be encoded as a change to its *target* argument. This contrast in the formal representations indicates that geometric changes can be categorised in two groups: the external changes, i.e. operations applied to expressions as a whole, and internal ones, i.e. changes to the expression itself.

4. Animating Geometric Changes

In order to animate the full 1R-JP expression, the avatar must handle all of the contained geometric changes. We will see that the two types of modifications, *internal* and *external* defined above, need to be treated in distinct ways due to differences in how the human body moves to make these changes happen.

4.1. Animating External Changes

The `about-point` construction occurs several times in the discourse as elements relating to Iraq are placed to the right in segments 1, 3 and 5, and elements relating to France are placed to the left in segment 2. Analyzing the motion of the signer's body during these segments reveals the following common characteristics:

- the whole production of the sign is rotated to the relevant side of signing space with no other modification to the sign movement, supported by a shallow turn of the torso;
- the hands are not re-oriented to remain facing forward or to the side relative to the viewer, as can be clearly seen in the production of `une personne` in fig. 1.2 where the handshape is now facing to the right instead of forward as it would be in an unaltered production of `une personne`;
- there is an initial glance of short duration ($< .5$ s) at the beginning of the segment towards the target area.

To effectuate this change, all the avatar has to do is to rotate the torso and the shoulder joints without changing the rest of the motion in the production. Such a change is called a forward kinematic (FK) movement since the angles are being directly affected (Parent, 2012).

In many ways, this technique is similar to the forward kinematic rotations that were used in (Wolfe et al., 2012) to animate turn taking in reported dialog, except that the rotation of the torso is shallower because the signer is not actually shifting their torso to assume the position of a participant, nor is the signer's gaze locked on the target. In that prior

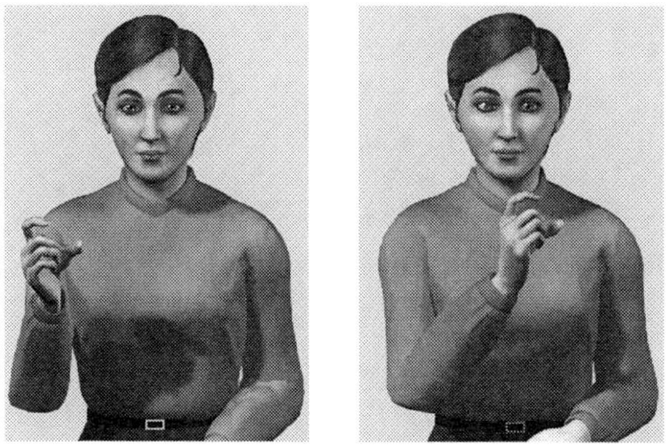

(a) Citation form (b) Relocated form

Figure 2: Relocation of `une personne` to the left.

work, the torso rotation carried all of the motion, whereas here, more of the rotation happens at the shoulder joints. In summary, the Paula avatar system can respond to AZee's `about-point` rule applied to a point p by taking the following actions:

1. compute the overall angle θ that needs to happen to shift the center to align with p;
2. apply $.45\theta$ to the spine's twist angle;
3. apply the remainder of θ to rotate the shoulder joints, and thus the arms, laterally;
4. raise or lower the elbow using the shoulder's swivel angle (Parent, 2012) by $.25\theta$ so that as the arm moves across the body the upper arm will not collide with the torso;
5. a small rotation of $.15\theta$ in the wrist is introduced to counter the arm's swivel rotation without bending the wrist too much;
6. apply a gaze of short duration with the rotation largely centered on the eyes rather than on the avatar's neck.

The results of these actions can be seen in fig. 2 wherein `une personne` is rotated to left signing space.
This technique stands in sharp contrast to the inverse kinematics (IK) computations used in prior work on geometric placements in both depictions (Filhol and McDonald, 2020) and agreement structures (Wolfe et al., 2012). The goal of IK is to compute the armature's angles based on the desired hand placement and orientation of the hand or finger.
There is another observation that supports the choice of FK here versus the IK techniques chosen for depictions. The placements of the hands show significant variance in position as the signer is describing Iraq and France on either side. Figure 3 compares the placement of `une personne` to `pointage index` in the left image, and to the form meaning "years old" generated by the rule `cpt-années` in the right image. These placements all arise in discourse segment 2. The overlays show significant differences in both vertical and lateral positions of the hands. This variance is generally higher than would be

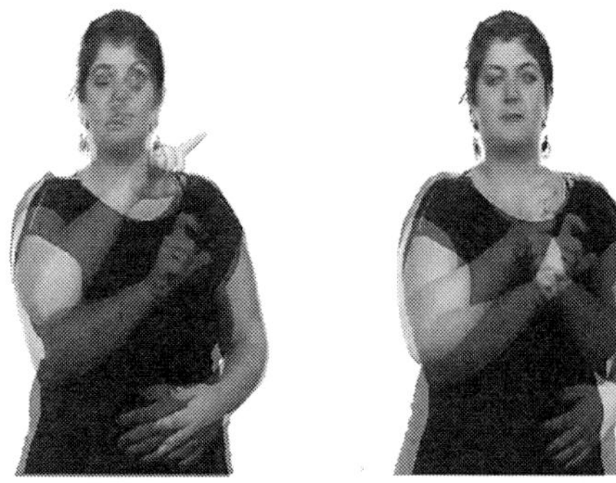

Figure 3: Variance in placement of signs.

found in depictions. In addition, the gaze is far less engaged than the sustained eye contact and neck rotations seen in that prior work.

4.2. Animating Internal Changes

The other three structures that cause geometric changes to signing in this discourse are `retour`, `otage` and `pointage index`. However, instead of the geometric information for the changes being provided at a higher level in the AZee expression (i.e. a containing structure like `about-point`), the geometric locations come internally in these expressions rather than externally. The only differences between them are that `retour` takes both a `source` and a `target` point, whereas the other two only take one[4]. To see how these changes occur on the body and may be implemented in the avatar, let us take `retour` as an example. Its motion is different from the prior `about-point` relocations since it affects the start and the end of the motion differently. It has very little accompanying torso rotation, and no redirection of the gaze. For these reasons, this motion falls under the traditional agreement pattern and Paula can shortcut to the system (Wolfe et al., 2012), wherein the artist not only animates a citation form of the sign, but provides a generic curve profile for the arms to follow, which is retargeted using IK. The rule `otage` can also be animated in this way.
The pointing signs actually have the same type of motion in the arms and torso as the `about-point` construction, and are even accompanied by the same type of glance. Since the handshape is pointing towards the target rather than being placed at the target, it can be animated with the same FK process by the avatar. The fact that the location is an internal parameter of the rule `pointage index`, instead of being a general process imposed externally, allows us to use a different animation scheme in this instance. It is worthy to note that the resulting avatar motion is different from the IK process that has been used previously for pointing signs in ASL (Wolfe et al., 2012). The pointing motions in

[4]Actually, the sign for `otage` is also contained in a surrounding `about-point` structure and therefore has its starting point altered externally. It also has one other interesting feature: the signer changes the form to mimic the action of the person being taken hostage at gunpoint causing changes to handshape, hand orientation and other parameters. These elements were included in the pre-animated sequence for `otage` for this demonstration.

that work were similar to the modifications to `otage` and `retour` above, and were accompanied by a stronger fixed gaze. Further study into pointing signs will be needed to determine whether the same type of motion and glance are used more widely across sign languages.

5. Discussion

The full synthesized discourse applies these processes to seamlessly synthesize the geometric changes discussed above. It can be viewed at `https://zenodo.org/record/6547654` and frames corresponding to the signer's positions in 1 are shown in fig. 4.

Throughout the animation, AZee rules such as `info-about`, `context` and `side-info` not only structure individual phrases but contribute associated nonmanual signals and rhythm that natively provide prosodic structure to the discourse. Also, we can notice an expressive mixing of the various patterns for locating signs or pieces of the discourse:

- segment 1 uses `about-point` with none of its content affected by internal changes;
- in segment 2, rule `pointage index` is applied inside an `about-point`, both with the same point argument `Lssp`;
- in segment 3, rule `otage` is applied to `Rssp` while nested in an `about-point` applied to `Lssp`;
- in segment 6, rule `return` uses two internal point arguments outside of any `about-point` operation;
- the very last unit, meaning "France", is performed with neither pattern applied.

All of these combinations are made possible by the existence of a single generic rule `about-point`, in addition to individual sign arguments.

Here again AZee proves to be a very productive system, i.e. very expressive, describing a wide range of types of communication while consisting of a limited set of combining rules. It is important to note that in the 120 examples contained in the *40 brèves v2* corpus of AZee expressions, about-point ranks third in application count (531 applications in total), after `info-about` and `side-info`. Thus, `about-point` is extensively used in common discourse, and the phenomenon of turning to a point reference after a quick eye glance is not rare. In contrast, the other pattern of direct point arguments, traditionally viewed as "agreement" structures, is surprisingly anecdotal, and do not generalize easily.

6. Conclusion and Future Work

The synthesis of the news report "1R-JP" provides a rich environment to test the ability of the AZee–Paula bridge to synthesize highly structured discourse featuring different types of geometric relocations. In particular, we can see that if the avatar is to convincingly reproduce such signing, it much be able to handle both precise IK styles of relocations used in depictions, as in prior efforts, and FK styles as in the `about-point` relocations explored here.

In addition, through this work, it can be seen that an avatar will struggle to animate even discourse such as the "1R-JP" example, that is of the kind that is often considered glossable, if the linguistic description is limited to a stream of glosses, albeit provided with a set of instructions for relocation of each gloss. Some relocations arise from external processes, i.e. larger in scope, and others from internal ones, i.e. only applying to the sign or a part of it. This distinction greatly impacts how the avatar must respond to produce natural movement.

This paper is a continuation of our effort to explore the description and synthesis of sign language, and there are still many unexplored avenues that will be pursued in future work. But, as in prior work in this area, we see that the interplay between linguistics and animation continues to be a rich field of study yielding insights on both sides.

Acknowledgement

This work is supported in part by the EASIER (Intelligent Automatic Sign Language Translation) Project. EASIER has received funding from the European Union's Horizon 2020 research and innovation programme, grant agreement n° 101016982. ■

7. Bibliographical References

Baus, C., Carreiras, M., and Emmorey, K. (2013). When does iconicity in sign language matter? *Language and cognitive processes*, 28(3):261–271.

Challant, C. and Filhol, M. (2022). A first corpus of azee discourse expressions. In *Language Resources and Evaluation Conference (LREC), Representation and Processing of Sign Languages, Marseilles, France*.

Cogill-Koez, D. (2000). A model of signed language classifier predicate as templated visual representation. *Sign Language & Linguistics*, 3:209–236.

Cuxac, C. (2000). *Langue des signes française, les voies de l'iconicité*, volume 15–16. Ophrys.

Filhol, M. and McDonald, J. (2018). Extending the azee-paula shortcuts to enable natural proform synthesis. In *Workshop on Representation and Processing of Sign Language, International Conference on Language Resources and Evaluation (LREC)*, pages 45–52.

Filhol, M. and McDonald, J. (2020). The synthesis of complex shape deployments in Sign Language. In *Proceedings of the 9th Workshop on the Representation and Processing of Sign Languages*, Marseille, France.

Filhol, M., McDonald, J., and Wolfe, R. (2017). Synthesizing Sign Language by connecting linguistically structured descriptions to a multi-track animation system. In *11th International Conference on Universal Access in Human-Computer Interaction (UAHCI 2017) Held as Part of HCI International 2017*, volume 10278 of *Universal Access in Human–Computer Interaction. Designing Novel Interactions*, Vancouver, Canada, July. Springer.

Huenerfauth, M. (2006). *Generating American Sign Language Classifier Predicates for English-to-ASL Machine Translation*. Ph.D. thesis, Pennsylvania, USA.

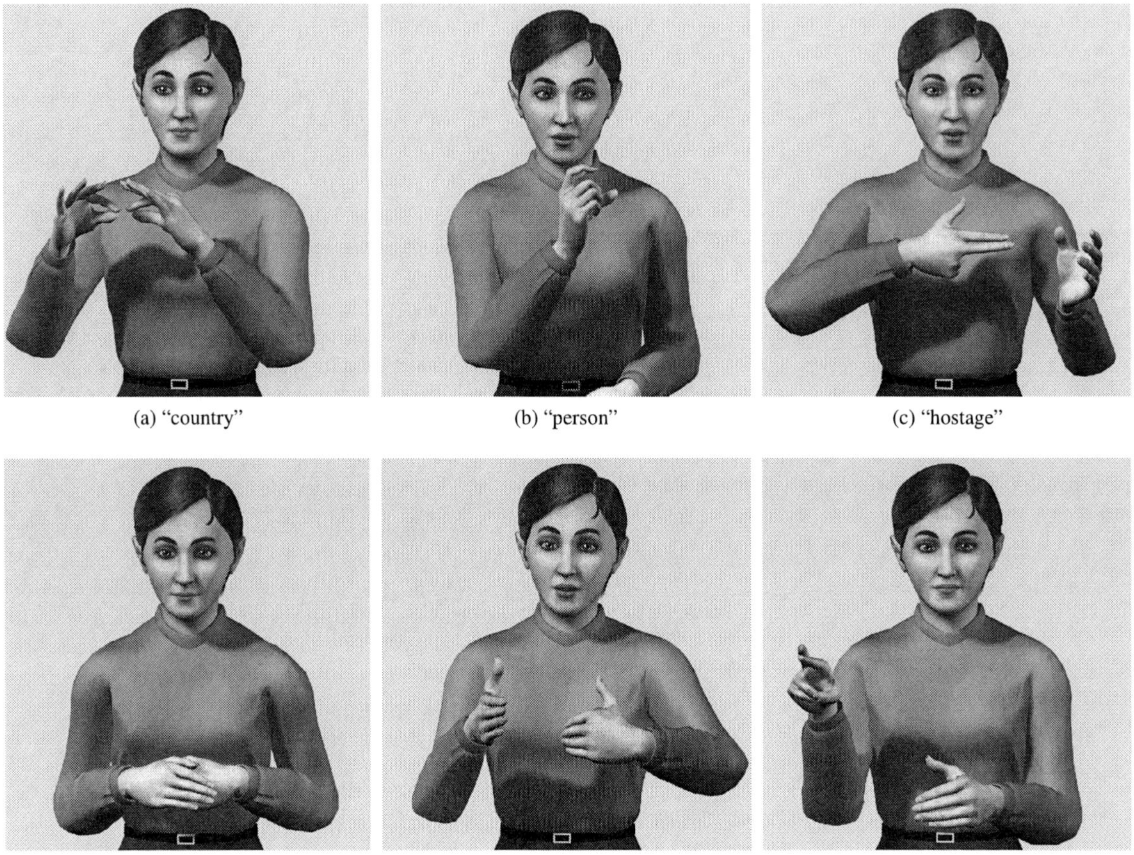

(a) "country" (b) "person" (c) "hostage"

(d) "pause" (e) "nearby" (f) "return"

Figure 4: Frames from the Paula Animation of 1R-JP.

Johnston, T. (2010). From archive to corpus: Transcription and annotation in the creation of signed language corpora. *International journal of corpus linguistics*, 15(1):106–131.

Liddell, S. K. (2003a). *Grammar, gesture, and meaning in American Sign Language*. Cambridge University Press.

Liddell, S. K., (2003b). *Perspectives on classifier constructions in sign languages*, chapter Sources of meaning in ASL classifier predicates, pages 199–220. Erlbaum, Mahwah, NJ.

Lillo-Martin, D. and Meier, R. P. (2011). On the linguistic status of 'agreement' in sign languages. *Theoretical Linguistics*, 37(3/4):95–141.

López-Colino, F. and Colás, J. (2011). The synthesis of lse classifiers: From representation to evaluation. *Journal of Universal Computer Science*, 17(3):399–425.

McDonald, J. and Filhol, M. (2021). Natural synthesis of productive forms from structured descriptions of sign language. *Machine Translation*, 35(3):363–386.

Padden, C. A., Meir, I., Hwang, S.-O., Lepic, R., Seegers, S., and Sampson, T. (2013). Patterned iconicity in sign language lexicons. *Gesture*, 13(3):287–308.

Parent, R. (2012). *Computer animation: algorithms and techniques*. Newnes.

Quer, J. (2011). When agreeing to disagree is not enough: further arguments for the linguistic status of sign language agreement. *Theoretical Linguistics*, 37(3/4):189–196.

Wilbur, R. B. (2013). The point of agreement: changing how we think about sign language, gesture, and agreement. *Sign Language & Linguistics*, 16(2):221–258.

Wolfe, R., McDonald, J. C., Toro, J., and Schnepp, J. (2012). A proposal for making corpora more accessible for synthesis: A case study involving pointing and agreement verbs. In *sign-lang@ LREC 2012*, pages 163–166. European Language Resources Association (ELRA).

Proceedings of the 10th Workshop on the Representation and Processing of Sign Languages (sign-lang@LREC 2022), pages 59–66
Language Resources and Evaluation Conference (LREC 2022), Marseille, 20-25 June 2022

Sign Language Phonetic Annotator-Analyzer: Open-Source Software for Form-Based Analysis of Sign Languages

Kathleen Currie Hall, Yurika Aonuki, Kaili Vesik, April Poy, and Nico Tolmie
University of British Columbia
2613 West Mall, Vancouver, BC V6T 1Z4 Canada
{kathleen.hall, yurika.aonuki, kaili.vesik}@ubc.ca
{aprilpoy, nhtolmie}@student.ubc.ca

Abstract

This paper provides an introduction to the Sign Language Phonetic Annotator-Analyzer (SLP-AA) software, a free and open-source tool currently under development, for facilitating detailed form-based transcription of signs. The software is designed to have a user-friendly interface that allows coders to transcribe a great deal of phonetic detail without being constrained to a particular phonetic annotation system or phonological framework. Here, we focus on the 'annotator' component of the software, outlining the functionality for transcribing movement, location, hand configuration, orientation, and contact, as well as the timing relations between them.

Keywords: sign language, phonetics, phonology, corpus, software

1. Background

Johnston (2010, 2014) made convincing arguments in favour of focusing resources on annotation rather than detailed phonetic transcription when it comes to building sign language corpora. Such advice makes sense when there is no widely agreed-upon system for transcription, video records are easily available, and priority needs to be placed on amassing larger datasets that are representative of individual sign languages (see also McEnery & Wilson, 2001; Gut & Voormann, 2014). At the same time, Johnston (2014: 157) also mentions that there can be a "value added" through transcription and that many teams have been interested in and invested in creating more detailed transcriptions. Indeed, our understanding of ways to represent the form of sign languages has been improved greatly by proposals for both phonological models (e.g., Padden & Perlmutter, 1987; Liddell & Johnson, 1989; Crasborn, 2001; Brentari, 1998; van der Kooij, 2002; Sandler & Lillo-Martin, 2006; Morgan, 2017) and phonetic transcription systems (e.g., Stokoe et al., 1965; Prillwitz et al., 1989; Hanke, 2004; Eccarius & Brentari, 2008; Johnson & Liddell, 2010, 2011a-b, 2012, 2021; Liddell & Johnson, 2019). Simultaneously, there has been increasing development of annotated corpora and databases of specific sign languages (e.g., the various SignBank corpora, including ASL-SignBank; ASL-LEX 2.0; the Corpus of Polish Sign Language (PJM); the German Sign Language corpus (DGS-Korpus); the database for Spanish Sign Language (LSE-Sign); the Swedish Sign Language Corpus; HandSpeak; Lifeprint.com).

As we have an increasing number of these 'broadbase' resources, it becomes more relevant to return to the idea of transcription in addition to annotation, to see whether there are new, more efficient ways to approach adding detailed phonetic transcriptions. Such transcriptions are necessary for doing more complete phonetic and phonological analyses of sign languages, as is illustrated by and discussed in Morgan (2017). Morgan's attention to detail in the documentation and description of the phonology of Kenyan Sign Language highlights both the previous lack of detail in many sign language descriptions and the new insights that can be gained by following more rigorous methods. As one example, Morgan (2017: §3.5-3.6) lays out a far more exacting method for deciding what 'counts' as a minimal pair in a signed language than many prior researchers have done and yet also points out that the oft-mentioned 'scarcity' of minimal pairs in sign languages is likely inaccurate. Instead, the way that minimal pairs are *distributed* in signed languages differs from that in spoken languages, such that a single parameter of contrast is simply likely to be the source of only a few pairs, rather than being re-used across many pairs as is common in spoken languages. As Morgan explains, however, "the process itself [of finding true minimal pairs] is painstaking and is probably impossible to do well without a digitized record of the formational content of signs that is easy to query on demand" (2017: 113).

It is in light of such observations that we are in the process of developing a new piece of software, Sign Language Phonetic Annotator-Analyzer (SLP-AA), a graphical user interface (GUI)-based software system for the form-based transcription and analysis of signs (see also Tkachman et al., 2016; Hall et al., 2017; and Lo & Hall, 2019 for descriptions of earlier versions). Three key components of this project that differentiate it from other similar endeavours are:

- the focus is on providing tools for facilitating form-based transcription and analysis, rather than being a more generalized linguistic annotation system or providing a database or corpus of already-coded forms;
- the system is intended to be relatively phonetic in nature and compatible with multiple phonological theories, enabling transcription of detailed variation across many sign languages, largely without relying on a specific notation system;
- the software and code are all completely free and open source (the Python code is available on GitHub), encouraging broad use and customization.

In this paper, we explain in more detail our vision and current implementation of the software in light of these features. Although our intention is for SLP-AA to be usable across all sign languages, most of our examples come from American Sign Language (ASL), as this is the sign language most in use in our local community and research setting.

2. Overview

There are two primary components to the SLP-AA software: the annotator portion, for which there is a version in development and which is the primary focus of this paper, and the analyzer portion, which is still pre-development. Both components make use of a relatively straightforward GUI that involves selecting from pre-set options written out in text in most cases, to maximize consistency and efficiency of coding.

2.1 Annotator

The annotator portion includes or will include modules for coding meta information and for transcribing sign type, movement, location, hand configuration, orientation, contact, and non-manual markers. Additionally, temporal relations among these modules can be encoded using a generic 'x-slot' framework (described in §3.8). There is also some ability for the software to auto-generate, auto-fill, and auto-link components. Details of all of these elements are described below in §3; see Figure 4 at the end of the paper for a visualization of how they all fit together.

2.2 Analyzer

The analyzer interface, intended to facilitate phonological searches and analyses, has not been developed yet, but is modelled on the *Phonological CorpusTools* software for spoken languages (Hall et al., 2019). It will allow users to search for any (combination of) specifications within the detailed coding, as well as to search for categories of signs that span specific combinations (e.g., searching for signs with three extended fingers, regardless of which fingers those are, or searching for multi-syllabic signs defined in a number of different ways). We also intend to have several pre-set search options (e.g., searching for dominance condition violations, cf. Battison (1978), or searching for typologically rare properties). In addition to the searches, other phonological analyses will be possible. For example, these might include finding minimal pairs, calculating the neighbourhood density of a given sign (Luce & Pisoni, 1998), calculating the functional load (Hockett, 1966) or informativity (Cohen Priva, 2015) of a particular phonological component, etc. Finally, we envision having a side-by-side comparison option, which will highlight form-based similarities or differences between signs selected by the user.

2.3 Integration

Currently, SLP-AA is stand-alone software that can be used to give detailed phonetic transcriptions of individual signs, one at a time. While these signs can come from any source, the software does not currently directly allow for the transcription of continuous signing. We are interested in seeing whether it can be integrated into other software that is equipped for this type of time-aligned transcription, e.g. iLex (Hanke & Storz, 2008), SignStream (Neidle et al., 2018), or ELAN (Crasborn & Sloetjes, 2008).

3. Annotator Functions

In this section, we briefly describe the specific functions available in the annotator component of the software. We preface this discussion, however, with the statement of an overarching general principle in our system design: our transcription system is intended to be phonetic in nature and as descriptive as possible. We try to cover all physically possible options and use physically based descriptions rather than relying on phonological categories that may be tied to specific languages or phonological theories. Our goal in doing so is to allow maximal flexibility and phonetic detail in the transcription of a variety of languages and dialects, registers, and phenomena (e.g., acquisition, poetic usage, slips of the hand). Of course, we recognize that *any* attempt to label components of signs is an act of categorization, and only the original production itself can be truly phonetic and maximally detailed. As others have pointed out, however, corpora are only useful for linguistic analysis insofar as they have been made machine-readable (e.g., Johnston, 2014; Crasborn, 2022), and our aim here is to help bridge the gap between broad annotations and original video recordings.

Another feature of our coding system is that it relies mostly on prose-based descriptions of phonetic characteristics (e.g., 'H1 [hand 1] and H2 [hand 2] maintain contact throughout the sign'). This bypasses the necessity for users to choose one of the multiple possible transcription systems listed in §1. As others have pointed out, no single system has yet achieved widespread acceptance (see discussion in, e.g., Hochgesang, 2014), and having to learn a notational system can itself be a barrier to both transcribing data in the first place and disseminating transcribed data (see discussion in Morgan, 2017: 60). In particular, using a text-based system means that the codings may be more accessible to a non-specialist audience—for example, a corpus or database that is coded using prose descriptions can be searched by teachers or learners of a sign language in order to find signs matching particular characteristics.

3.1 Metadata

Following guidelines set out for good data management practices (e.g., Crasborn, 2022; Kung, 2022; Mattern, 2022), SLP-AA includes built-in functions for managing metadata. For example, each signer, transcriber, source, and/or recording can be tagged with relevant demographic or reference information, and then each sign can be tagged with this source information. Each entry in the corpus is also automatically assigned a unique entry ID, according to information and formatting options selected by the user.

3.2 Sign-Level Information

Each entry has a variety of sign-level information that can be assigned to it. This includes the gloss and lemma / ID-gloss of the sign (see discussion in Johnston, 2008; Fenlon et al., 2015; Hochgesang et al., 2018), as well as the specific metadata for this token. Lemmas / ID-glosses have the potential to be imported from another source if desired, to maximize consistency. Labels can also be added here to flag additional information, e.g., compounds, finger-spelled items, or suboptimal video quality, with notes to explain the details. The list of these tags can also be modified by the user.

3.3 Sign Type

The sign type of a sign allows users to specify the overarching 'kind' of sign an entry is; at a basic level, this would cover types like one-handed (1H) and two-handed (2H). Within these larger types, additional phonetic detail can be added. For example, for 2H signs, users can specify the relation between the two hands in terms of shared or different handshapes, contact or lack thereof, and movement (see Figure 1). The sign type coding is a good example of how SLP-AA is more phonetically oriented than other systems. For instance, some existing corpora base their sign type distinctions on Battison's (1978) five sign types (e.g., ASL-Lex (Sehyr et al., 2021), LSE-Sign (Gutierrez-Sigut et al., 2016)). These sign types were developed with ASL in mind, and they combine logically separable features in ways that do not fully cover all possible combinations. For example, Battison's Type 1 signs are the only ones that involve both hands moving, and he further stipulates that in these signs, the movement must be identical or alternating. This precludes classifying signs like ASL RUN, which ASL-Lex 2.0 simply calls a "Symmetry Violation" sign. In SLP-AA, however, each component of the relation between the two hands is coded separately, so all signs can be described more exactly. Still, we recognize the utility of Battison's sign types, and plan to allow pre-defined searches in the Analyzer component that can find, e.g., all "Type 1" signs or all "Symmetry Violation" signs, regardless of the type of violation.

3.4 Movement Module

For each of the primary phonological parameters—movement, location, hand configuration, orientation, and, eventually, non-manual markers—SLP-AA works on a 'module' system. There is a pre-existing interface for each module, such as the movement module, and a user can invoke the module as many times as is relevant for achieving the desired level of phonetic detail, with each resulting specification tied to either H1 or H2. For example, in a sign like ASL DESTROY, there is both what is traditionally thought of as a 'path' movement, in which the two hands cross over each other and back along a horizontal axis, and what is traditionally thought of as a 'local' movement, in which the fingers of the two hands close and then open. In coding this sign in SLP-AA, then, a user would invoke two instances of the movement module per hand, one to represent each type of movement.[1]

This modularity allows a great deal of flexibility in terms of the variety of signs that can be coded as well as the internal conventions for coding. For example, a user could choose instead to invoke the movement module four times per hand in DESTROY, once for each direction of each movement (ipsi → contra, contra → ipsi for the 'path' movement and open → close, close → open for the 'local' movement), rather than twice with each movement being marked as bidirectional. While we recognize that this places a certain burden on the users of the system to be explicit and consistent about their own internal conventions, we also believe that this allows for the widest usability of the system across theoretical frameworks.

Similarly, we do not actually require users to classify movements into the traditional categories of 'path' / 'major' / 'primary' vs. 'local' / 'minor' / 'secondary' movements and instead have classifications for 1) "perceptual movements" (e.g., straight, circle, arc), "joint-specific movements" (e.g., twisting, closing), and "handshape changes" (e.g., fingerspelling). As Napoli et al. (2011: 19) point out, "the actual distinction between primary and secondary movement is not uncontroversial and is far from simple." For example, while wrist movements are typically considered local movements according to articulatory definitions of path and local movement categories (e.g., Brentari, 1998), some of them have been categorized as path movements (van der Kooij, 2002: 229; Sehyr et al., 2021: 269). Furthermore, forcing the choice between path and local movements at the level of phonetic transcription could mask empirical phenomena such as proximalization and distalization (Brentari, 1998), in which both path and local movements can be articulated by non-canonical joints. In response to these issues, our system allows any movement in which the hand or arm draws a perceptual shape in space to be classified as perceptual movement, with optional manual specifications of the exact (combination of) joints executing the movement under a separate "joint activity" section. Traditional local movements (relating to particular joints) defined in the literature are listed under the joint-specific movement section, with the associated joint activities optionally auto-filled (e.g., the joint-specific movement of "closing" can auto-fill to flexion of finger joints in the "joint activity" section).

In addition to the overall movement type and joint activity involved, each movement module allows for specification of the axis/axes, direction(s), and, if relevant, plane(s) of movement involved, along with characteristics like repetition and bidirectionality. Options in the movement module can be selected manually through a clickable menu system or typed in using keywords to allow for faster coding.

3.5 Location Module

As with movement, locations are specified in a modular system, such that users can invoke multiple instances of the location module to capture the position(s) of the hand(s) in space during the course of a sign in as much detail as the user wishes. At its most basic, this could be used to code positions of the hand at different timepoints in a sign (e.g., before and after a location-changing movement), though of course individual users could choose to code only one of these and leave the other unspecified / inferred from movement direction. Another use for multiple location modules, however, is to code the location of H1 both in space and with respect to H2. For example, in coding the ASL sign ROCKING CHAIR, a user could specify that H1 is in the location of the back of the index and middle fingers of H2, but also that both hands are simultaneously in neutral space.

While one could also use the modularity to encode what are traditionally called 'major' and 'minor' locations, we do allow for a single instance of the location module to be tagged with hierarchically nested locations. For example, in ASL EVERYDAY, a single location module could be used to transcribe that the sign is articulated on the head and at the cheek. Although users can specify their own custom set of locations, SLP-AA comes with a large set of pre-specified options, based on both body locations and signing space options.

[1] Note that the temporal relations between instances of a module will be covered in §3.8 and illustrated in Figure 3.

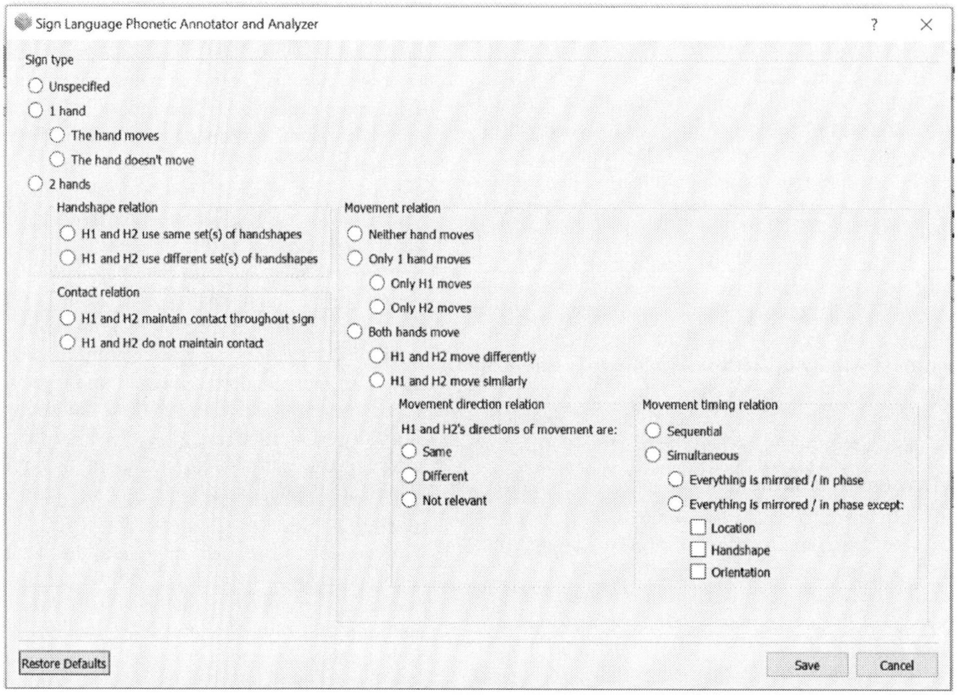

Figure 1: Screenshot of the "sign type" selector interface

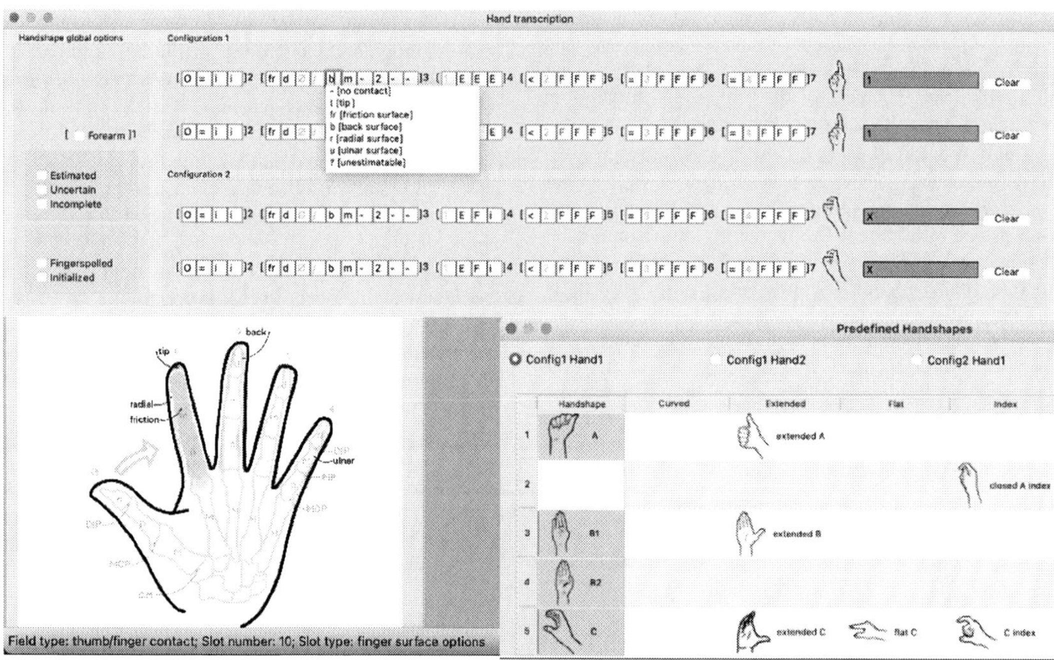

Figure 2: Elements from the hand configuration module for transcribing the handshapes in the ASL sign TEST. Top: Detailed phonetic coding following Johnson and Liddell (2011b, 2012), with the options for slot 10 ("thumb / finger contact") shown in a drop-down menu. Bottom left: Example drawing illustrating what type of information is expected in slot 10. Bottom right: Subset of the pre-defined handshapes selector, with phonologically unmarked base handshapes highlighted in green on the left and their variations in subsequent columns.

3.6 Hand Configuration Module

Each instance of the hand configuration module is used to transcribe a single configuration for one hand; a sign may consist of multiple sequential configurations. The transcription system for hand configuration is based closely on that proposed by Johnson and Liddell (2011b, 2012), and is also relatively thoroughly described elsewhere (Tkachman et al., 2016; Hall et al., 2017; Lo & Hall, 2019). There are 34 'slots' divided across seven 'fields' for transcribing a single hand configuration. Each slot is occupied by a letter, number, or symbol indicating characteristics like the degree of joint flexion, the degree of abduction / adduction from the adjacent finger, or points of contact within the hand configuration. Images and notes in the software remind the user what kind of information and choices are relevant for each slot (see Figure 2).

Recognizing that such a detailed coding can be tedious, we have also implemented a set of 'pre-defined' handshape options. For any given instance of the module, a pre-defined handshape can be selected (e.g., the ASL-based label 'extended-A,' associated with the following handshape:). Selecting the handshape then fills in the complete transcription, though any element may be modified to better represent a specific token if needed.

Finally, a user will be able to specify any given fingers within a hand configuration as 'selected.' This must be done manually, as it is a phonological rather than a phonetic characteristic; as van der Kooij and Crasborn (2016: 277) point out, the same phonetic handshape can have different 'selected fingers' based on the rest of the sign.

3.7 Additional Modules: Absolute Orientation, Handpart, and Contact

There are several additional characteristics that are coded with separate modules in SLP-AA. First, if absolute orientation is to be used (cf. Sandler, 1989), an orientation-specific module can be invoked. Each instance of the module involves specifying the absolute direction (e.g., up, distal, right) of both the palmar surface of the hand and the finger roots. Alternatively, if relative orientation is to be used (cf. Crasborn & van der Kooij, 1997), there is a handpart module that can be invoked to indicate which part of the hand is approaching a location or leading a movement, and the specified handpart can then be associated with a specific location or movement module.

Contact is also indicated with a separate module in SLP-AA. Each instance of the contact module is used to code the presence or absence of contact between an articulator and its target location, and, if relevant, the distance (e.g., close or far) and/or the relation (e.g., holding or continuous, cf. Friedman, 1976: 46-47) between them. Each instance of this module can be associated with a specific location module so that, e.g., in a phonetic description of a sign like ASL TIE, the brief initial contact between the two hands and the continuous contact between H1 and the torso can each be coded. The timing relations are coded through the linking of these contact modules to the x-slots, as will be described in §3.8.

3.8 Timing Relations

In order to fully represent a sign, it may also be necessary to specify the timing relations among the various instances of modules that have been coded. For example, in ASL DESTROY, the joint-specific finger closing-opening movements happen *simultaneously* with the *second* half of the perceptual straight movement of the hands (i.e., as each hand moves from contra to ipsi). In order to represent this timing, we make use of a generic 'x-slot' system. While the user can use these slots however they see fit, the system is built with the following choices in mind. In most cases, the basic timing structure of a sign is based on the single module that codes the most proximal movement. In ASL DESTROY, this 'foundational' movement would be the perceptual straight movement of the hands. Assuming this is treated as a bidirectional movement, the sign is associated with two 'x-slots.' Then, the bidirectional closing-opening movement is linked to the second x-slot.[2] This relation is shown in Figure 3.

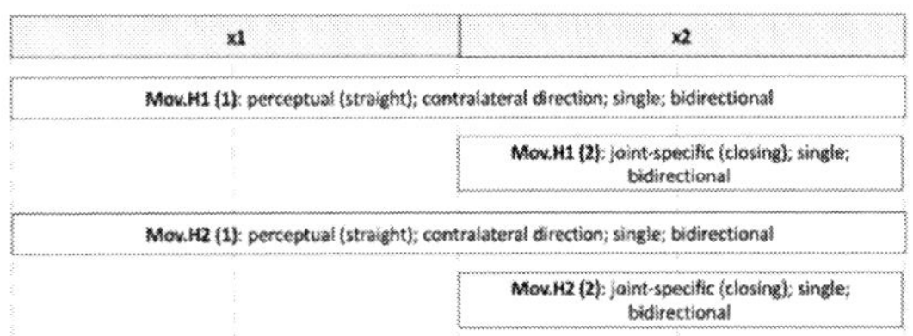

Figure 3: The movement components of the ASL sign DESTROY within an x-slot representation. Hand 1 ("H1") has two movements, with one being a bidirectional, unrepeated ("single"), straight perceptual movement that starts in a contralateral direction, and the second being a bidirectional joint-specific movement that starts with the fingers closing. The second movement starts halfway through the first movement, i.e., at the beginning of x2. Hand 2 ("H2") has two similar movements with the same timing.

In the full program, all of the modules are linked in this fashion, so that a fairly precise representation of the simultaneous and sequential components is attained, as is shown in Figure 4. This figure shows an example of the 'main' interface for SLP-AA, showing the summary of the transcription for a particular token of the ASL sign APPLE in the centre. Glosses of all signs in the corpus are shown on the left, and additional modules can be added and linked by clicking on the buttons on the right-hand side. Note that individual transcription modules can be linked as either intervals or timepoints to the x-slots (e.g., the movement, location, contact, and hand configuration modules are linked to intervals in Figure 4, while the orientations are linked to timepoints). The x-slots easily accommodate compounds or otherwise multisyllabic signs because any module, including the movement modules, can be sequentially ordered over any number of x-slots.

3.9 Auto-Generation/Filling/Linking

In many cases, the number of x-slots required for a given sign is predictable from the specified movements, as are the

[2] Recall that there are alternative ways of representing the bidirectionality in this sign (§3.4), which could lead to even more precise alignments of the closing-opening movement within the second x-slot.

number of instances of the location, hand configuration, and orientation modules, and how each instance would link to the x-slots. In these cases, SLP-AA will be able to generate x-slots and (un-filled) instances of the relevant modules and link the two to facilitate efficient and consistent transcription. For example, in ASL THROW-AWAY, the straight movement makes the hand travel in space, and the opening movement of the fingers changes the hand configuration. Once these movements are coded, auto-generation can begin. SLP-AA generates only one x-slot in this case, because the straight movement is unidirectional and unrepeated, and both the straight and opening movements are linked to the entirety of that single x-slot. Under the most detailed global transcription setting (see §3.10), two instances of the location module are auto-generated and auto-linked to the beginning and ending points of the x-slot, respectively, and the user is prompted to manually fill them in. Similarly, based on the existence of an opening movement, two instances of the hand configuration module are auto-generated and auto-linked to the beginning and ending points of the x-slot, respectively. Finally, given the lack of orientation-changing movement, the system auto-generates only one instance of the orientation module and links it to the entirety of the x-slot.

Moreover, for two-handed signs, some parameters of H2 may be predictable from those of H1 and the specification of the sign type. In those cases, some instances of modules for H2 can be auto-generated and auto-filled. For example, in two-handed signs with a shared handshape, like ASL MEET, once the user codes the hand configuration of H1 and links it to the x-slot, an identical instance of the hand configuration module is auto-generated for H2, which stretches for the same duration as its original H1 counterpart.

Any auto-generated information can be overwritten in the case of unusual sign types, but this feature helps streamline the process of doing such a detailed coding, while also facilitating inter-coder reliability.

3.10 Customization

To increase the flexibility of using the SLP-AA software with multiple different theoretical frameworks in mind, there are a number of customizations that can be done. Most menus will be modifiable so that individual menu items match those needed by a particular research team. Additionally, there are global settings that can be selected. These include whether to include timing relations (x-slots) at all; whether auto-generation/filling/linking should be done and if so how (e.g., should locations be coded as occurring before a location-changing movement, after, or both?); and how movement should be defined on the horizontal axis (i.e., in terms of ipsi / contra directions or in terms of right / left directions).

3.11 Additional features

There are a few other features of SLP-AA that are worth noting. First, individual transcriptions can be marked as being 'estimates,' 'uncertain,' or 'incomplete,' to capture and manage the realities of transcription. Additionally, each instance of each module can also be specified as being either a 'target' transcription or a 'token' transcription. In other words, coding may be done simultaneously for canonical productions and utterance forms. While a similar effect can also be achieved by linking individual signs to their lemma forms in a separately coded database, this feature allows for a fine-grained level of detail to be included. For instance, a particular utterance might be associated to a given lemma (e.g., it could be the ASL sign ADVERTISE), but then coded as having, say, a particular target handshape ("5") and phonetically realized as having the fingers more curved / relaxed than a canonical 5 handshape. Searches and analyses can be performed over targets, tokens, or both.

Finally, all transcriptions in the system will also be exportable to a plaintext format for use outside of the SLP-AA software itself, and the software is accompanied by detailed documentation.

While prompts within the software are currently all in English, the open-source nature of the project means that the prompts could be translated to another language (including e.g. having pop-up tool-tip videos in a sign language).

4. Conclusion

In sum, SLP-AA will be a tool for facilitating consistent and descriptively transparent transcriptions, and helps to set a precedent for the level of phonetic detail to be documented in signed languages. We believe that it is flexible enough to be used with a variety of languages, frameworks, and projects. As the software is still under development, we welcome feedback from other research teams as to what features and functionality would be most useful, and would like to work to integrate SLP-AA into other annotation and corpus-building workflows.

5. Acknowledgements

This research is supported in part by funding from the Social Sciences and Humanities Research Council. We are also grateful to numerous contributors and advisors on this project, including: Leanne Gallant and the Canadian Cultural Society of the Deaf, Ashley Chand, Paris Gappmayr, Julie Hochgesang, Cristina Lee, Roger Yu-Hsiang Lo, J. Scott Mackie, Hope Morgan, & Oksana Tkachman. All errors are our own. The handshape fonts are created by CSLDS, CUHK.

6. Bibliographical References

Battison, R. (1978). Lexical borrowing in American Sign Language. Silver Spring, MD: Linstok.

Brentari, D. (1998). A Prosodic Model of Sign Language Phonology. Cambridge, MA: MIT Press.

Cohen Priva, U. (2015). Informativity affects consonant duration and deletion rates. Laboratory Phonology, 6(2), pp. 243-278.

Crasborn, O. (2001). Phonetic implementation of phonological categories in Sign Language of the Netherlands. Doctoral dissertation. Universiteit Leiden.

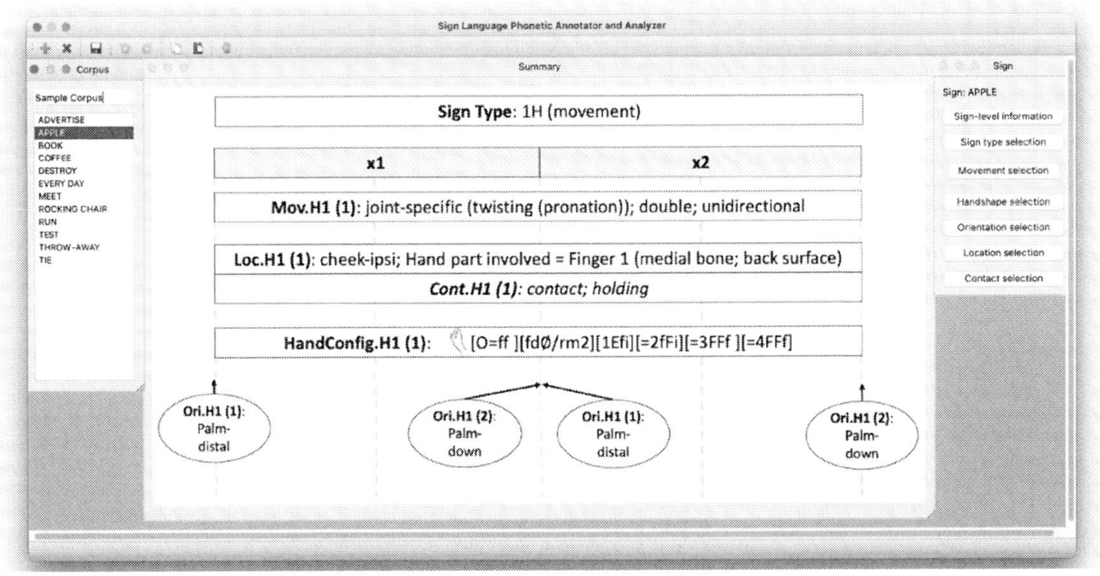

Figure 4: Mock-up of the SLP-AA interface, with a summary transcription for ASL APPLE. Note that this is a detailed phonetic transcription of this particular token of the sign; it is possible to link this to a lemma and/or do a less-detailed, more phonological transcription.

Crasborn, O. (2022). Managing data in sign language corpora. In A. L. Berez-Kroeker, B. McDonnell, E. Koller, L. B. Collister (Eds). The Open Handbook of Linguistic Data Management. Cambridge, MA pp. 463-470.

Crasborn, O., & van der Kooij, E. (1997). Relative orientation in sign language phonology. In J. Coerts, H. de Hoop (Eds.), Linguistics in the Netherlands. Amsterdam: John Benjamins, pp. 37-48.

Crasborn, O. & Sloetjes, H. (2008). Enhanced ELAN functionality for sign language corpora. In Proceedings of the 3rd LREC Workshop on the Representation and Processing of Sign Languages: Construction and exploitation of sign language corpora. Marrakesh: ELRA, pp. 39-43.

Eccarius, P. & Brentari, D. (2008). Handshape Coding Made Easier: A Theoreti-cally Based Notation for Phonological Transcription. Sign Language and Linguistics, 11(1), pp. 69-101.

Fenlon, J., Cormier, K. & Schembri, A. (2015). Building BSL SignBank: The lemma dilemma revisited. International Journal of Lexicography, 28, pp. 169-206.

Friedman, L. (1976). Phonology of a soundless language: Phonological structure of the American Sign Language. Doctoral dissertation. University of California, Berkeley.

Gut, U. & Voormann, H. (2014). Corpus Design. In J. Durand, U. Gut, G. Kristoffersen (Eds.), The Oxford Handbook of Corpus Phonology. Oxford: Oxford UP, pp. 13-26.

Gutiérrez-Sigut, E., Costello, B., Baus, C. & Carreiras, M. (2015). LSE-sign: A lexical database for Spanish Sign Language. Behavior Research Methods, 48, pp. 123-137.

Hall, K. C., Mackie, S., Fry, M. & Tkachman, O. (2017). SLPAnnotator: Tools for implementing Sign Language Phonetic Annotation. In Proceedings of the 18th Annual Conference of the International Speech Communication Association (INTERSPEECH 2017). Stockholm, Sweden: International Speech Communication Association, pp. 2083-2087.

Hall, K. C., Mackie, J. S. & Lo, R. Y-H. (2019). Phonological Corpus Tools: Software for doing phonological analysis on transcribed corpora. International Journal of Corpus Linguistics, 24(4), pp. 522-535.

Hanke, T. (2004). HamNoSys: Representing sign language data in language resources and language processing contexts. In Proceedings of the 4th LREC Workshop on the Representation and Processing of Sign Languages: From SignWriting to Image Processing. Paris: ELRA, pp. 1-6.

Hanke, T. & Storz, J. (2008). iLex: A database tool for integrating sign language corpus linguistics and sign language lexicography. In Proceedings of the 6th LREC Workshop on the Representation and Processing of Sign Languages: Construction and exploitation of sign language corpora. Paris: ELRA, pp. 64-67.

Hochgesang, J. A. (2014). Using Design Principles to Consider Representation of the Hand in Some Notation Systems. Sign Language Studies, 14(4), pp. 488-542.

Hochgesang, J., Crasborn, O. & Lillo-Martin, D. (2018). Building the ASL Signbank: Lemmatization Principles for ASL. In Proceedings of the 11th International Conference on Language Resources and Evaluation Workshop on the Representation and Processing of Sign Languages: Involving the Language Community. Paris: ELRA, pp. 69-74.

Hockett, C. F. (1966). The Quantification of functional load: A linguistic problem. U.S. Air Force Memorandum RM-5168-PR.

Johnson, R. E. & Liddell, S. K. (2010). Toward a phonetic representation of signs: sequentiality and contrast. Sign Language Studies, 11(2), pp. 271-74.

Johnson, R. E. & Liddell, S. K. (2011a). A segmental framework for representing signs phonetically. Sign Language Studies, 11(3), pp. 408-63.
Johnson, R. E. & Liddell, S. K. (2011b). Toward a phonetic representation: The fingers. Sign Language Studies, 12(1), pp. 4-45.
Johnson, R. E. & Liddell, S. K. (2012). Toward a phonetic representation of hand configuration: The thumb. Sign Language Studies, 12(2), pp. 316-33.
Johnson, R. E. & Liddell, S. K. (2012). Toward a phonetic description of hand placement on bearings. Sign Language Studies, 22(1), pp. 131-80.
Johnston, T. (2008). Corpus linguistics and signed languages: No lemmata, no corpus. In Proceedings of the 6th International Conference on Language Resources and Evaluation Workshop on the Representation and Processing of Sign Languages: Construction and Exploitation of Sign Language Corpora. Paris: ELRA. pp. 82-87.
Johnston, T. (2010). From archive to corpus: Transcription and annotation in the creation of signed language corpora. International Journal of Corpus Linguistics, 15(1), pp. 106–131.
Johnston, T. (2014). The reluctant oracle: Using strategic annotations to add value to, and extract value from, a signed language corpus. Corpora, 9(2), pp. 155-189.
Kooij, E. van der (2002). Phonological categories in Sign Language of the Netherlands: The role of phonetic implementation and iconicity. Doctoral dissertation. Netherlands Graduate School of Linguistics.
Kooij, E. van der and Crasborn, O. (2016). Phonology. In A. Baker, B. van den Bogaerde, R. Pfau, T. Schermer (Eds.), The linguistics of sign languages: An introduction. Amsterdam: John Benjamins, pp. 251-278.
Kung, S. S. (2022). Developing a data management plan. In A. L. Berez-Kroeker, B. McDonnell, E. Koller, L. B. Collister (Eds.), The Open Handbook of Linguistic Data Management. Cambridge, MA: MIT Press, pp.101-115.
Liddell, S. K. & Johnson, R. E. (1989). American Sign Language: The phonological base, Sign Language Studies, 64, pp. 195-277.
Liddell, S. K. & Johnson, R. E. (2019). Sign Language Articulators on Phonetic Bearings. Sign Language Studies, 20(1), pp. 132-172.
Lo, R. Y.-H. & Hall, K. C. (2019). SLP-AA: Tools for Sign Language Phonetic and Phonological Research. In Proceedings of the 20th Annual Conference of the International Speech Communication Association (INTERSPEECH 2019): Show & Tell Contribution, Graz, Austria: International Speech Communication Association, pp. 3679-3680.
Luce, P. A. & Pisoni, D. B. (1998). Recognizing spoken words: The neighborhood activation model. Ear and Hearing, 19, pp. 1-36.
Mattern, E. (2022). The Linguistic Data Life Cycle, Sustainability of Data, and Principles of Solid Data Management. In A. L. Berez-Kroeker, B. McDonnell, E. Koller, L. B. Collister (Eds.), The Open Handbook of Linguistic Data Management. Cambridge, MA: MIT Press, pp. 61-71.
Morgan, H. E. (2017). The phonology of Kenyan Sign Language (southwestern dialect). Doctoral dissertation. University of California, San Diego.
McEnery, A. M. & Wilson, A. (2001). Corpus Linguistics. Edinburgh: Edinburgh UP.
Napoli, D. J., Mai, M. & Gaw, N. (2011). Primary movement in sign languages: A study of six languages. Washington D.C.: Gallaudet UP.
Neidle, C., Opoku, A., Dimitriadis, G. & Metaxas, D. (2018). New shared & interconnected ASL resources: SignStream® 3 software; DAI 2 for web access to linguistically annotated video corpora; and a sign bank. In Proceedings of the 11th LREC Workshop on the Representation and Processing of Sign Languages: Involving the Language Community, Paris: ELRA.
Prillwitz, S., Leven, R., Zienert, H., Hanke, T. & Henning, J. (1989). HamNoSys. Version 2.0. International Studies on Sign Language and Communication of the Deaf, 7, pp. 225-231.
Padden, C. A. & Perlmutter, D. M. (1987). American Sign Language and the architecture of phonological theory. Natural Language & Linguistic Theory, 5(3), pp. 335-375.
Sandler, W. (1989). Phonological representation of the sign: Linearity and nonlinearity in American Sign Language (Vol. 32). Berlin: Walter de Gruyter.
Sandler, W. & Lillo-Martin, D. (2006). Sign language and linguistic universals. Cambridge: Cambridge UP.
Sehyr, Z. S., Caselli, N., Cohen-Goldberg, A. M. & Emmorey, K. (2021). The ASL-LEX 2.0 Project: A database of lexical and phonological properties for 2,723 signs in American Sign Language. The Journal of Deaf Studies and Deaf Education, 26(2), pp. 263-277.
Stokoe, W. C., Casterline, D. C. & Croneberg, C. G. (1965). A Dictionary of American Sign Language on Linguistic Principles. Silver Spring, MD: Linstok.
Tkachman, O., Hall, K. C., Xavier A. & Gick, B. (2016). Sign Language Phonetic Annotation meets Phonological CorpusTools: Towards a Sign Language Toolset for Phonetic Notation and Phonological Analysis. In Proceedings of the 2015 Annual Meeting on Phonology, Washington, DC: Linguistic Society of America, pp.1-9.

7. Language Resource References

ASL-LEX 2.0. (2020). Available at https://asl-lex.org/index.html
ASL-SignBank (2021). Available at https://aslsignbank.haskins.yale.edu/
Corpus of Polish Sign Language (PJM). (2013). Section for Sign Linguistics, University of Warsaw. Available at https://ses.library.usyd.edu.au/handle/2123/9841
DGS-Korpus. (2009). The Institute for German Sign Language and Communication of the Deaf at Hamburg University. Available at https://www.sign-lang.uni-hamburg.de/dgs-korpus/index.php/welcome.html
HandSpeak. (1995). American Sign Language dictionary. Available at www.handspeak.com
Lifeprint.com: ASL University. (n.d.). ASLU: English to ASL Dictionary. Available at https://www.lifeprint.com/
LSE-Sign. (2015). BCBL. Available on Portal LSE at http://lse-sign.bcbl.eu/web-busqueda/
SignBank. (n.d.). SignBank: Home for the various spinoffs of the Auslan Signbank. Available at https://github.com/Signbank
Swedish Sign Language Corpus (2020). Department of Sign Language, Department of Linguistics, Stockholm University. Available at teckensprakskorpus.su.se

Proceedings of the 10th Workshop on the Representation and Processing of Sign Languages (sign-lang@LREC 2022), pages 67–72
Language Resources and Evaluation Conference (LREC 2022), Marseille, 20-25 June 2022

ASL-Homework-RGBD Dataset: An annotated dataset of 45 fluent and non-fluent signers performing American Sign Language homeworks

Saad Hassan[1], Matthew Seita[1], Larwan Berke[1], Yingli Tian[2], Elaine Gale[3], Sooyeon Lee[1], Matt Huenerfauth[1]
[1] Rochester Institute of Technology, Rochester, NY 14623 USA
[2] The City College of New York, New York, NY 10031 US,
[3] Hunter College, City University of New York, 695 Park Ave, New York, NY 10065
sh2513@rit.edu , mss4296@rit.edu, lwb2627@rit.edu,
ytian@ccny.cuny.edu , egale@hunter.cuny.edu , slics@rit.edu , matt.huenerfauth@rit.edu

Abstract

We are releasing a dataset containing videos of both fluent and non-fluent signers using American Sign Language (ASL), which were collected using a Kinect v2 sensor. This dataset was collected as a part of a project to develop and evaluate computer vision algorithms to support new technologies for automatic detection of ASL fluency attributes. A total of 45 fluent and non-fluent participants were asked to perform signing homework assignments that are similar to the assignments used in introductory or intermediate level ASL courses. The data is annotated to identify several aspects of signing including grammatical features and non-manual markers. Sign language recognition is currently very data-driven and this dataset can support the design of recognition technologies, especially technologies that can benefit ASL learners. This dataset might also be interesting to ASL education researchers who want to contrast fluent and non-fluent signing.

Keywords: American Sign Language, Sign Languages, Dataset, Corpus, Annotation, ASL Annotation, ASL Learning, ASL Homeworks, Video data, ASL Grammar, Fingerspelling, ELAN, Continous Signing, ASL Fluency, Facial Expressions

1. Background and Related Work

Advancements in deep learning and sensor technologies as well as research on computer vision techniques have enabled the development of sign language recognition systems (Rastgoo et al., 2021). While the accuracy of sign language recognition technologies have improved, there are still some challenges that need to be resolved. Modern machine learning approaches to sign-recognition based on neural networks are largely data-driven; however, current publicly released datasets of sign languages are still several orders smaller in magnitude compared to datasets of other spoken languages used to train automatic speech recognition systems.

While summarizing the challenges facing the sign-recognition field, a recent paper identified 4 dimensions on which to classify datasets: size, continuous real-world signing, the inclusion of native signers, and signer variety (Bragg et al., 2019). Since datasets of isolated signs can only support very specific use-cases, e.g. sign language dictionaries, it is therefore important to collect continuous signing datasets (natural conversational data or at least longer utterances) from a diverse set of signers to support useful real-world applications (Albanie et al., 2021).

Existing datasets of ASL usually consist of videos of people performing continuous signs (Bragg et al., 2019; Albanie et al., 2021), e.g. How2Sign (Duarte et al., 2021), NCSGLR (Databases, 2007), ASLG-PC$_{12}$ (Othman and Jemni, 2012), CopyCat (Zafrulla et al., 2010), RWTH-BOSTON-400 and RWTH-BOSTON-104 (Dreuw et al., 2008; Dreuw et al., 2007). There are some datasets of isolated signs, e.g. ASL-LEX-2.0 (Sehyr et al., 2021), WLASL (Li et al., 2020), ASL-100-RGBD (Hassan et al., 2020), MSASL (Vaezi Joze and Koller, 2019), ASL-LEX (Caselli et al., 2017), ASLLVD (Athitsos et al., 2008), Purdue RVL-SLL (Martínez et al., 2002), etc., and fingerspelling as well, e.g. ChicagoFSWild+ (Shi et al., 2019) and ChicagoFSWild (Shi et al., 2018) . Table 1 describes some of these datasets in greater detail [1].

Data collection methodologies and apparatuses as well as the motivations behind data collection effort determine what the final publicly released datasets look like. Datasets have been collected to support sign recognition efforts (training and benchmark testing sets), generate signing avatars, and design systems for learning different sign languages. For example, motion capture datasets that make use of sensors attached to signers are often curated to generate signing avatars (Lu and Huenerfauth, 2010; Heloir et al., 2005; Berret et al., 2016). Datasets also vary on the demographic profiles of the signers and geographic regions in which they are collected. The demographic profiles can include paid professional interpreters on live TV (Forster et al., 2014; Koller et al., 2017) and research assistants hired to record (Martínez et al., 2002; Zahedi et al., 2006), ASL students, or Deaf signers, etc. Datasets can be collected in controlled laboratory settings or collected using scrapping online video libraries and sites, e.g. YouTube (Joze and Koller, 2018).

Another key aspect of the publicly released sign language datasets is their annotations. Annotations can be in the form of the closest English label or gloss, which

[1] Table 2 in (Albanie et al., 2021) enlists summary statistics of other sign language datasets.

Dataset	Year	Type	Multi	Pose	Depth	Samples	Signers	F/nF	Publication
ASL-LEX 2.0	2021	Isolated				2723	1	F	(Sehyr et al., 2021)
WLASL	2020	Isolated				21083	119	F	(Li et al., 2020)
ASL-100-RGBD	2020	Isolated			Yes	4150	22	F	(Hassan et al., 2020)
How2Sign	2020	Continuous	Yes	Yes	Yes	35000	11	F	(Duarte et al., 2021)
MS-ASL	2019	Isolated				25000	200	F	(Vaezi Joze and Koller, 2019)
ChicagoFSWild+	2019	Fingerspelling				55232	260	F	(Shi et al., 2019)
ChicagoFSWild	2018	Fingerspelling				7304	200	F	(Shi et al., 2018)
ASL-LEX	2016	Isolated				1000	1	F	(Caselli et al., 2017)
NCSGLR	2012	Continuous	Yes			1866	4	F	(Databases, 2007)
CopyCat	2010	Continuous				420	5	nF	(Zafrulla et al., 2010)
ASLLVD	2008	Isolated	Yes	Yes		3300	6	F	(Athitsos et al., 2008)
RWTH-BOSTON-400	2008	Continuous	Yes			483	4	F	(Dreuw et al., 2008)
RWTH-BOSTON-104	2007	Continuous	Yes			104	3	F	(Dreuw et al., 2007)
Purdue RVL-SLL	2002	Isolated				104	14	F	(Martínez et al., 2002)
ASL-Homework-RGBD	**2022**	**Continuous**			**Yes**	**935**	**45**	**Both**	

Table 1: Examples of published ASL datasets, with the year of release and the type of signing it contains (Isolated, Continuous, or Fingerspelling). The table indicates whether multiple camera views (e.g., front and side) were included (Multi), whether 3D human skeleton information is included (Pose), whether RGBD depth information is included (Depth), the number of videos (Samples), the number of people in the dataset (Signers), whether the signers were fluent, non-fluent, or both (F/nF), and a citation (Publication). The last row describes the ASL-Homework-RGBD dataset shared with this paper. The non-fluent ("nF") participants in the COPYCAT dataset included Deaf children with developing ASL skills.

are linguistic notations representing each sign component, or just translated text. Annotations can also demarcate signs in different manners, e.g. start and end of each handshape, sign, or a phrase/sentence. Specialized analysis software resources may also be employed, e.g ELAN (Archive, 2018), SignStream (Neidle et al., 2018; Augustine and Opoku, 2020), VIA (Dutta and Zisserman, 2019), iLex (Hanke, 2002), or Anvil (Kipp, 2017). In collection of some of the datasets, researchers also engaged Deaf annotators for a manual-sign annotation-verification step at the end (Albanie et al., 2021).

With this paper, we are releasing an annotated dataset of continuous ASL signing from 45 signers. A unique contribution of our new dataset is that it includes recordings of both fluent and non-fluent ASL signers, who are engaged in the same set of homework-style expressive signing tasks. In addition, the annotation of our dataset not only includes gloss labels and annotation of syntactic non-manual expressions, but it also includes labels as to whether specific errors have occurred in the signing, e.g., when a non-fluent signer may have omitted a linguistically required non-manual expression. Given these characteristics, our dataset may be useful for research on detection of production errors in ASL signing, e.g., in the context of educational systems, and this data may also be of interest to educational or linguistics researchers, who wish to compare ASL production among signers of various levels of fluency.

We describe the context and motivation of our work in section 2. We then describe the dataset in detail including the apparatus used, data collection methods, participant recruitment, and post-processing of the data. Finally, in section 4, we conclude with the insights we learned and some of the limitations of the dataset.

2. Context of Data Collection and Release

This is a novel dataset that has been collected as a part of a collaborative project between Rochester Institute of Technology, The City College of New York, and Hunter College (Vahdani et al., 2021; Huenerfauth et al., 2017; Zhang et al., 2016). A previous dataset of isolated ASL signs for the educational tool was released at LREC 2020 (Hassan et al., 2020).

This paper describes a video-recording corpus of students (and fluent signers) performing ASL phrases and sentences, as a part of homework assignments. This new dataset was collected to support the design of technologies to fundamentally advance partial-recognition of some aspects of ASL. For example, identifying linguistic and performance attributes of ASL without necessarily determining the entire sequence of signs, or automatically determining if a performance is fluent or contains errors made by ASL students. This research effort was aimed at enabling future computer-vision technologies to support educational tools to assist ASL learners in achieving fluency, with an automatic system providing feedback on their signing. The ASL-Homework-RGBD dataset is available to authorized users of the Databrary platform[2]. RGBD in the dataset title refers to red-green-blue color video and depth information, provided by a color and depth camera, such as the Kinect.

3. ASL-Homework-RGBD Dataset

3.1. Participants and Recruitment

We recruited 45 ASL signers to be recorded in this IRB-approved data collection effort, using electronic and paper advertisements across the Rochester Institute of Technology and National Technical Institute for the

[2] https://nyu.databrary.org/volume/1249

Deaf campus. Our participants consisted of 24 fluent signers and 21 non-fluent students.

Our fluent participants included 17 men and 7 women aged 20 to 51 (mean=25.08, median=23 years, SD=6.65). 5 of the participants self-described as Hard-of-hearing while the rest 19 self-described as Deaf/deaf. To recruit fluent ASL signers, we used the following screening questions: Did you use ASL at home growing up, or did you attend a school as a very young child where you used ASL?

Our non-fluent participants included 6 men and 15 women aged 18 to 49 (mean=23.19, median=21 years, SD=7.65). 4 of the participants self-described as Hard-of-hearing while the rest 17 self-described as hearing. To recruit non-fluent ASL signers (students who were learning the language), we used the following screening questions: Are you currently taking an introductory or intermediate course in American Sign Language, or have you completed an introductory or intermediate ASL course in the past five years?

3.2. Data Collection Procedure and Apparatus

Each participant was assigned a codename starting with "P" if they were a not-fluent signer, e.g. P01, or "F" if they were a fluent signer, e.g. F13. A paper copy of a consent form was shared with the participants which they signed. They then filled out a short demographic questionnaire.

Participants were told: *You will work on a "homework" style assignment, from an American Sign Language class, where you will need to make a video of yourself signing.* We shared a paper copy of the homework-assignment prompt that they would be attempting during the session. (Details of these prompts appear below.) Some participants, especially fluent signers, had time to complete multiple homework assignments during a single one-hour recording session visit, and other participants returned to the laboratory on multiple days for additional sessions, to complete additional assignments. The camera was 1.5m from the signer, and there was a researcher in the room with the participant. For hearing students learning ASL, this was a hearing researcher, and for Deaf fluent ASL signers, this was a Deaf ASL-signer researcher. Participants were given $40 (U.S. dollars) compensation for participating in each one-hour recording session.

When considering the prompt and preparing what they would like to sign in ASL, a hard copy of an ASL-English dictionary and some other ASL reference books were made available to participants. They were encouraged to write a script first and practice so that they could produce their signing for each video without looking at their paper. The researcher was told to make sure that there was at least 30 minutes available to do the recording, and thus, if a participant was taking over 20 minutes to prepare for their signing, the researcher needed to encourage them to finish up their preparation soon.

The researcher then made sure that the Kinect v2 camera system was working properly, that it was recording at approximately 30 frames per second (FPS), and that the system was detecting a "skeleton" pose of the participant. Each video recording was assigned a codename in the format ParticipantID-UtteranceNumber, e.g., for non-fluent participant 1 and utterance 1 the name assigned was P01U01. (In this dataset, each individual video that was produced is referred to as an utterance.)

Participants were discouraged from signing any introductory information at the beginning of their video, e.g., "Phrase Number 1." The researcher switched off recording as soon as the participant finished. Participants were strongly encouraged to use a standard starting and ending position (hands on their lap). If participants attempted a phrase multiple times, only the last video was kept.

3.3. Description of Prompts

As stimuli prompts for signers, a series of homework assignments were created, to align with concepts traditionally taught in a second-semester ASL course at the university level. Some of these prompts asked the signer to produce a sequence of 1-2 sentence videos, and other prompts asked the signer to produce a longer multi-sentence video. In total, there were 6 homework prompts, with each focusing on a set of grammatical concepts, as described below. The homework prompts are also shared with the dataset.

3.3.1. Homework 1: WH Questions and YN Questions

This assignment consisted of 10 short prompts, each of which required the signer to produce a single question. Participants were asked to use non-manual signals (e.g., facial expressions and head movements) correctly as they produced these WH and Yes-No questions. The English text descriptions (of what to ask about) encouraged the signer to produce questions that, at times, contained some fingerspelling, numbers, or pointing to locations in the signing space to refer to people.

3.3.2. Homework 2: Your Autobiography

Participants were asked to produce a multi-sentence ASL passage about themselves. Some key information that they were asked to include were their name, whether they are deaf or hearing, what languages they know, their high school and college education, some activities that they were part of in high school and college that they liked or disliked (using a contrastive structure), etc.

3.3.3. Homework 3: Describing Pets

This prompt consisted of two open questions, each of which encouraged the signer to produce a short multi-sentence passage. In the first question, they were asked to compare and contrast two pets that they have or wished they had. In the second question, they were required to invent and ask 4 questions related to pets (directing the question to the camera).

3.3.4. Homework 4: Your Home

This assignment asked signers to produce one multi-sentence video to discuss where they live, the type of home they live in, their neighborhood, where they work or go to school, their commute to work or school, and who they live with.

3.3.5. Homework 5: Pronouns and Possessives

This assignment consisted of 12 short prompts, each of which consisted of two English sentences. Participants were asked to produce a short video for each, to convey the meaning in ASL. The sentences were specifically designed to include many personal pronouns (e.g., you, me, him) and possessive adjectives (e.g, your, my, his).

3.3.6. Homework 6: Conditional Sentences and Rhetorical Questions

This assignment consisted of 12 short prompts in written English that students had to translate into ASL, to produce a short video for each prompt. The sentences were designed so that the ASL signing would likely require the signer to produce conditional phrases or rhetorical questions.

3.4. Description of Annotation Process

After each recording session, the video files were converted to the MOV format for analysis within the ELAN analysis tool (Archive, 2018) and for distribution in our dataset. Our team of annotators included both ASL interpreters (who had completed a semester-long university course in ASL linguistics) and DHH individuals with native-level fluency in ASL (who received training on the specific linguistic properties being labeled). Our annotation and analysis process consisted of a four-pass process: First, one of the ASL interpreters on the project analyzed each video. Second, it was cross-checked by another ASL interpreter on the team for accuracy. Third, it was checked by a DHH researcher on our team with native-level ASL fluency, and finally, it was checked by a faculty member with expertise in ASL linguistics.

There were 6 different groups of annotation tiers, and annotators were encouraged to go from the simplest one and gradually move to more complex tiers. We describe each group of annotation tiers in this section in a similar manner:

The first tier, *Signing Happening*, was used to just identify the times when any signing is happening. The next tier was *Timing of Glosses*. The annotators indicated exactly when each sign began and ended (when the hand begins to fall or move into the position of another sign). Annotators did not count the anticipatory movements—while the hands get into the appropriate position to begin to articulate the sign in question—as part of that sign. Similarly, the end of signs was identified as occurring prior to movement of the hands out of the position for that sign in preparation for the articulation of the following sign.

The next tier was *Labels for Glosses*. The annotator selected a gloss label based on an English word that represented the sign. The annotators worked for consistency in using a single correspondence English gloss for each ASL sign throughout our videos, but no controlled gloss-label vocabulary list was used for this initial gloss labeling. However, for a specific set of 100 key glosses that were of special interest to our research project, e.g., words relating to specific grammatical structures, annotators used a controlled vocabulary of 100 gloss labels to consistently label those signs. A larger collection of video of isolated sign productions of this same set of 100 word was previously shared in a prior dataset (Hassan et al., 2020).

There was also a *Fingerspelling* tier, on which annotators could identify any spans of fingerspelling in videos. There were also associated tiers to identify fingerspelling errors, e.g., use of ungrammatical handshapes, non-standard location of the hand in space, unnecessary and/or non-standard movement of the hand, and non-fluent speed of fingerspelling. The next tier group was for indicating *Clauses*; annotators marked where each clause began and ended.

There was also a set of tiers for *Non-Manual Signals*. The annotators were asked to indicate specific non-manual signals (facial expressions or head movements) on the timeline. The annotator was not required to align the start-time and stop-time of each facial expression with gloss boundaries. The various types of facial expressions included: NEG (to indicate signer's head shaking left-to-right as in a negative manner), WHQ (to indicate a WH-question facial expression), YNQ (to indicate a yes/no question), RHQ (to indicate a rhetorical question), COND (to indicate a conditional, or TOPIC (to indicate a topicalized phrase).

The final group of tiers was for *Non-Manual Errors*. Annotators were asked to identify any non-manual-signal errors such as missing or incorrect facial expressions or head movements. For instance, if the signer used a negative sign like NOT or NONE but failed to produce a NEG non-manual signal. The annotators used separate tiers for errors relating to the absence of Yes-No Question, WH-Question, Rhetorical Questions, Conditional, and Negative facial expressions.

Tier descriptions are provided in much greater detail in the "Instruction for Using ELAN Annotation Software," which was the annotation guide and instructions document provided to annotators in this study. This document is shared with the dataset.

3.5. Dataset Contents

The dataset includes a CSV file containing demographic data for the participants, PDF files for each of the 6 homework-assignment prompts, the annotation guide and instructions document for annotators (mentioned above), original MP4 video files, Kinect v2 ".bin" recording files, and ELAN annotation files. The ASL-Homework-RGBD dataset is available to authorized users of the Databrary platform (Huenerfauth, 2022).

4. Discussion, Limitations, and Future Work

The dataset was collected to serve as training and testing data for the development of computer-vision technologies for the creation of educational-feedback tools for ASL students, i.e., systems that could analyze a video of an ASL learner and provide them feedback on their signing (Vahdani et al., 2021). Beyond this initial project, we anticipate that computer-vision researchers working on designing algorithms to detect signing errors in videos of ASL can use this data to train or test their models (Rastgoo et al., 2021). The corpus can also be used as a benchmark dataset to evaluate the performance and robustness of algorithms to detect continuous sign recognition or some specific aspects of signing, e.g. non-manual markers.

A theme of this year's workshop is how data can be made more useful for individuals beyond the field of sign-language technologies. We anticipate that our dataset may be of interest to ASL education researchers who are investigating how the signing of ASL students compares with those of fluent signers. For instance, researchers could compare fluent and non-fluent signers across various grammatical aspects of signing, e.g., correct use of non-manual signals. Since our dataset includes annotation of when errors occur in signing, it may also be of interest to individuals training to be ASL instructors or ASL interpreting students who wish to practice their receptive skills on non-fluent signers.

There are several limitations of this dataset:

1. Each participant was not able to do all the homework assignments, leading to a variable number of homeworks and annotated videos from each participant.

2. The data collection occurred within New York State and the participants mostly consisted of young adults. Therefore, the signs included in this dataset might not represent the wide variety of demographic and regional variation in ASL signing.

3. We did not assess the level of proficiency of the signers. We broadly classified the signers into *fluent* and *non-fluent* groups. However, the actual signing fluency may be on a spectrum.

4. Since stimuli were shown in English, there is a risk that an ASL signer with lower English literacy may not have accurately understood the homework assignment text. To mitigate this, the sessions with fluent signers were conducted by a Deaf ASL signer researcher, who offered to clarify any details of the assignment. However, future work could consider assignment prompts based on images or other modalities.

5. We did not measure the level of fluency of our participants through an analysis of the videos produced or other objective measures. In future work, researchers could examine videos to assign fluency levels to participants.

6. The homework assignments, data collection, and annotation has been driven by the specific needs of our research project. Researchers investigating other questions may need to provide alternative or additional annotation in support of their work.

5. Acknowledgements

This material is based upon work supported by the National Science Foundation under award numbers 2125362, 1763569, and 1462280, and Department of Health and Human Services under award number 90DPCP0002-0100.

6. Bibliographical References

Albanie, S., Varol, G., Momeni, L., Bull, H., Afouras, T., Chowdhury, H., Fox, N., Woll, B., Cooper, R., McParland, A., et al. (2021). BBC-Oxford British Sign Language Dataset. *arXiv preprint arXiv:2111.03635.*

Archive, T. L. (2018). ELAN - the max planck institute for psycholinguistics.

Athitsos, V., Neidle, C., Sclaroff, S., Nash, J., Stefan, A., Yuan, Q., and Thangali, A. (2008). The American Sign Language Lexicon Video Dataset. In *2008 IEEE Computer Society Conference on Computer Vision and Pattern Recognition Workshops*, pages 1–8. IEEE.

Augustine, C. and Opoku, A. (2020). Signstream version 3, Jul.

Berret, B., Braffort, A., et al. (2016). Collecting and Analysing a Motion-capture Corpus of French Sign Language. In *Workshop on the Representation and Processing of Sign Languages.*

Bragg, D., Koller, O., Bellard, M., Berke, L., Boudreault, P., Braffort, A., Caselli, N., Huenerfauth, M., Kacorri, H., Verhoef, T., Vogler, C., and Ringel Morris, M. (2019). Sign Language Recognition, Generation, and Translation: An interdisciplinary perspective. In *The 21st International ACM SIGACCESS Conference on Computers and Accessibility*, ASSETS '19, page 16–31, New York, NY, USA. Association for Computing Machinery.

Caselli, N. K., Sehyr, Z. S., Cohen-Goldberg, A. M., and Emmorey, K. (2017). Asl-lex: A lexical database of american sign language. *Behavior research methods*, 49(2):784–801.

Databases, N. S. (2007). American Sign Language Linguistic Research Project (Distributed on CD-ROM.

Dreuw, P., Rybach, D., Deselaers, T., Zahedi, M., and Ney, H. (2007). Speech Recognition Techniques for a Sign Language Recognition System. In *Interspeech*, pages 2513–2516, Antwerp, Belgium, August. ISCA best student paper award Interspeech 2007.

Dreuw, P., Neidle, C., Athitsos, V., Sclaroff, S., and Ney, H. (2008). Benchmark Databases for Video-based Automatic Sign Language Recognition. In *Proceedings of the Sixth International Conference on Language Resources and Evaluation (LREC'08)*, Marrakech, Morocco, May. European Language Resources Association (ELRA).

Duarte, A., Palaskar, S., Ventura, L., Ghadiyaram, D., DeHaan, K., Metze, F., Torres, J., and Giro-i Nieto, X. (2021). How2sign: a large-scale multimodal dataset for continuous american sign language. In *Proceedings of the IEEE/CVF conference on computer vision and pattern recognition*, pages 2735–2744.

Dutta, A. and Zisserman, A. (2019). The VIA Annotation Software for Images, Audio and Video. In *Proceedings of the 27th ACM international conference on multimedia*, pages 2276–2279.

Forster, J., Schmidt, C., Koller, O., Bellgardt, M., and Ney, H. (2014). Extensions of the sign language recognition and translation corpus RWTH-PHOENIX-weather. In *Proceedings of the Ninth International Conference on Language Resources and Evaluation (LREC'14)*, pages 1911–1916, Reykjavik, Iceland, May. European Language Resources Association (ELRA).

Hanke, T. (2002). ilex-a tool for sign language lexicography and corpus analysis. In *LREC*. Citeseer.

Hassan, S., Berke, L., Vahdani, E., Jing, L., Tian, Y., and Huenerfauth, M. (2020). An isolated-signing RGBD dataset of 100 American Sign Language signs produced by fluent ASL signers. In *Proceedings of the LREC2020 9th Workshop on the Representation and Processing of Sign Languages: Sign Language Resources in the Service of the Language Community, Technological Challenges and Application Perspectives*, pages 89–94, Marseille, France, May. European Language Resources Association (ELRA).

Heloir, A., Gibet, S., Multon, F., and Courty, N. (2005). Captured Motion Data Processing for Real Time Synthesis of Sign Language. In *International Gesture Workshop*, pages 168–171. Springer.

Huenerfauth, M., Gale, E., Penly, B., Pillutla, S., Willard, M., and Hariharan, D. (2017). Evaluation of Language Feedback Methods for Student Videos of American Sign Language. *ACM Trans. Access. Comput.*, 10(1), apr.

Joze, H. R. V. and Koller, O. (2018). Ms-asl: A large-scale data set and benchmark for understanding american sign language. *arXiv preprint arXiv:1812.01053*.

Kipp, M. (2017). The video annotation research tool.

Koller, O., Zargaran, S., and Ney, H. (2017). Re-sign: Realigned end-to-end sequence modelling with deep recurrent cnn-hmms. In *Proceedings of the IEEE Conference on Computer Vision and Pattern Recognition*, pages 4297–4305.

Li, D., Rodriguez, C., Yu, X., and Li, H. (2020). Word-level Deep Sign Language Recognition From Video: A new large-scale dataset and methods comparison. In *Proceedings of the IEEE/CVF winter conference on applications of computer vision*, pages 1459–1469.

Lu, P. and Huenerfauth, M. (2010). Collecting a Motion-capture Corpus of American Sign Language for Data-driven Generation Research. In *Proceedings of the NAACL HLT 2010 workshop on speech and language processing for assistive technologies*, pages 89–97.

Martínez, A. M., Wilbur, R. B., Shay, R., and Kak, A. C. (2002). Purdue RVL-SLLL Asl Database for Automatic Recognition of American Sign Language. In *Proceedings. Fourth IEEE International Conference on Multimodal Interfaces*, pages 167–172. IEEE.

Neidle, C., Opoku, A., Dimitriadis, G., and Metaxas, D. (2018). New shared & interconnected asl resources: Signstream® 3 software; dai 2 for web access to linguistically annotated video corpora; and a sign bank. In *8th Workshop on the Representation and Processing of Sign Languages: Involving the Language Community, Miyazaki, Language Resources and Evaluation Conference 2018*.

Othman, A. and Jemni, M. (2012). English-asl Gloss Parallel Corpus 2012: ASLG-PC12. In *5th Workshop on the Representation and Processing of Sign Languages: Interactions between Corpus and Lexicon LREC*.

Rastgoo, R., Kiani, K., and Escalera, S. (2021). Sign Language Recognition: A deep survey. *Expert Systems with Applications*, 164:113794.

Sehyr, Z. S., Caselli, N., Cohen-Goldberg, A. M., and Emmorey, K. (2021). The ASL-LEX 2.0 Project: A Database of Lexical and Phonological Properties for 2,723 Signs in American Sign Language. *The Journal of Deaf Studies and Deaf Education*, 26(2):263–277, 02.

Shi, B., Del Rio, A. M., Keane, J., Michaux, J., Brentari, D., Shakhnarovich, G., and Livescu, K. (2018). American Sign Language Fingerspelling Recognition in the Wild. In *2018 IEEE Spoken Lang. Tech. Workshop (SLT)*, pages 145–152. IEEE.

Shi, B., Rio, A. M. D., Keane, J., Brentari, D., Shakhnarovich, G., and Livescu, K. (2019). Fingerspelling Recognition in the Wild with Iterative Visual Attention. In *Proceedings of the IEEE/CVF International Conference on Computer Vision*, pages 5400–5409.

Vaezi Joze, H. and Koller, O. (2019). Ms-asl: A Large-scale Data Set and Benchmark for Understanding American Sign Language. In *The British Machine Vision Conference (BMVC)*, September.

Vahdani, E., Jing, L., Tian, Y., and Huenerfauth, M. (2021). Recognizing American Sign Language Nonmanual Signal Grammar Errors in Continuous Videos. In *2020 25th International Conference on Pattern Recognition (ICPR)*, pages 1–8. IEEE.

Zafrulla, Z., Brashear, H., Hamilton, H., and Starner, T. (2010). A Novel Approach to American Sign Language (ASL) Phrase Verification Using Reversed Signing. In *2010 IEEE Computer Society Conference on Computer Vision and Pattern Recognition-Workshops*, pages 48–55. IEEE.

Zahedi, M., Dreuw, P., Rybach, D., Deselaers, T., and Ney, H. (2006). Continuous Sign Language Recognition-approaches from Speech Recognition and Available Data Resources. In *Second workshop on the rep. and proc. of sign lang.: lexicographic matters and didactic scenarios*, pages 21–24.

Zhang, C., Tian, Y., and Huenerfauth, M. (2016). Multimodality American Sign Language Recognition. In *2016 IEEE International Conference on Image Processing (ICIP)*, pages 2881–2885.

7. Language Resource References

Huenerfauth, M. (2022). An RGBD Dataset of American Sign Language Homework-Assignment Videos by Students and by Fluent ASL Signers.

Proceedings of the 10th Workshop on the Representation and Processing of Sign Languages (sign-lang@LREC 2022), pages 73–79
Language Resources and Evaluation Conference (LREC 2022), Marseille, 20-25 June 2022

MY DGS – ANNIS: ANNIS and the Public DGS Corpus

Amy Isard, Reiner Konrad
Institute of German Sign Language and Communication of the Deaf
University of Hamburg, Germany
{amy.isard, reiner.konrad}@uni-hamburg.de

Abstract

In 2018 the DGS-Korpus project published the first full release of the Public DGS Corpus. The data have already been published in two different ways to fulfil the needs of different user groups, and we have now published the third portal *MY DGS – ANNIS* using the ANNIS browser-based corpus software. ANNIS is a corpus query tool for visualization and querying of multi-layer corpus data. It has its own query language, AQL, and is accessed from a web browser without requiring a login. It allows more complex queries and visualizations than those provided by the existing research portal. We introduce ANNIS and its query language AQL, describe the structure of *MY DGS – ANNIS*, and give some example queries. The use cases with queries over multiple annotation tiers and metadata illustrate the research potential of this powerful tool and show how students and researchers can explore the Public DGS Corpus.

Keywords: German Sign Language (DGS), corpus query and visualization tools, ANNIS

1. Introduction

The DGS Corpus is a part of the DGS-Korpus project, which is a long-term project to create both a corpus and dictionary of German Sign Language (Prillwitz et al., 2008). The elicitation setting for the DGS Corpus involves two participants interacting in different ways with each other and a moderator leading the session.[1] In order to fulfil the needs of a variety of different users (Jahn et al., 2018), the data are published in different formats:

MY DGS (meine-dgs.de) – a community portal for the Deaf community and others interested in DGS, which offers video recordings of selected dialogues with optional German subtitles, and

MY DGS – annotated (ling.meine-dgs.de) – a research portal in English and German for the international scientific community, which offers an annotated corpus of DGS for linguistic research.

These resources were released and continue to be improved and extended during the life time of the DGS-Korpus project. With release 2 in September 2019 the Public DGS Corpus contained a subset of 50 hours of the DGS Corpus, release 3[2] (Hanke et al., 2020) followed in July 2020, and release 4 is in preparation.

The *MY DGS – annotated* web interface provides a list of transcripts, an index of sign types, and an index of keywords that allow the Public DGS Corpus to be accessed by topic. Each transcript consists of its video recording with time-aligned annotations and translations. All of these pages are searchable through built-in browser-based text search, but it is not possible to perform more advanced searches. The main purpose of *MY DGS – annotated* is to offer an interesting subset of the DGS Corpus data that can be used for various research options. Online transcript views and KWIC concordances of the tokens in the types list[3] entries make it possible for a researcher to browse the data before deciding to download videos and annotation files.

Although we will continue to improve the usage options of *MY DGS – annotated*, for example by introducing a text search function for translations, we were aware that this cannot replace a corpus search tool that allows for combined searches also including metadata. Therefore, we have created a third freely available option:

MY DGS – ANNIS (annis.meine-dgs.de) – a second additional research portal which allows complex queries of the annotated Public DGS Corpus[4], searching either in English or German annotations or both.

[1] About 560 hours of near-natural signing were collected from 330 participants 2010-2012; 376 hours of videos were translated into German, about 113 hours time-aligned; 92.5 hours of aligned elicitation tasks were lemmatized resulting in nearly 615,000 tokens. The total number of tokens of the DGS corpus is more than 668,000, the Public DGS Corpus has more than 374,800 tokens. For references to all relevant publications please refer to the data statement of the Public DGS Corpus (Schulder et al., 2021).

[2] `https://doi.org/10.25592/dgs.corpus-3.0`

[3] `https://www.sign-lang.uni-hamburg.de/meinedgs/ling/types_en.html`

[4] Jokes are not available in *MY DGS – ANNIS* because they have no annotations and therefore cannot be searched. They are available in *MY DGS – annotated* where all content of the Public DGS Corpus can be accessed in its entirety.

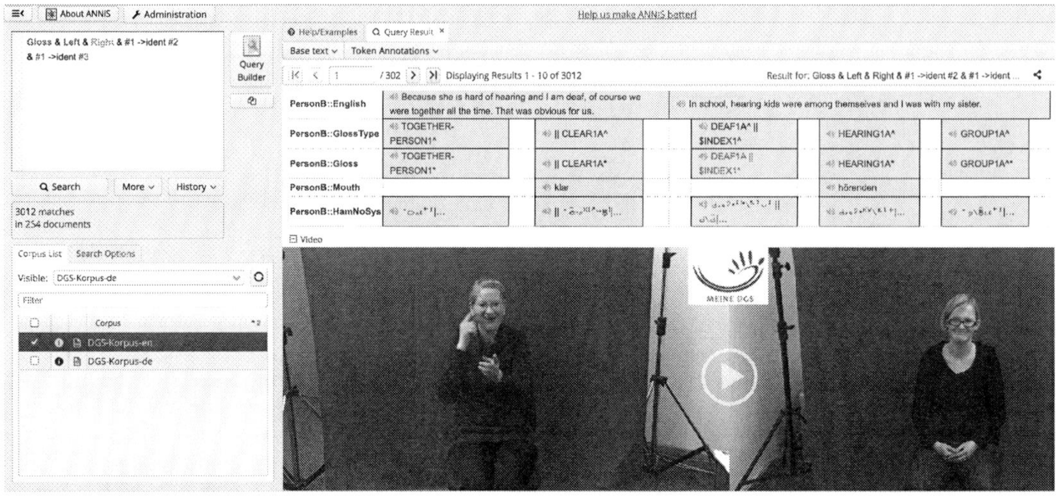

Figure 1: ANNIS display showing query results for glosses involving articulation of different signs with each hand (Query 10).

ANNIS (Krause and Zeldes, 2016) is a web browser-based search and visualization architecture for complex multi-layer linguistic corpora with diverse types of annotation. It allows the display of a corpus with multiple annotation tiers and optional linked audio or video files, as shown in Figure 1. In *MY DGS – ANNIS* the videos with the frontal perspective of the participants are displayed side by side as in the "Video AB" file in *MY DGS – annotated.*[5] Queries can be carried out using the ANNIS Query Language (AQL), which we introduce in Section 3, and the query results shown in Figure 1 are discussed in Section 4.1.

What makes *MY DGS – ANNIS* attractive is the fact that DGS data can now be searched online in a user interface that is already known to researchers working with corpora and that allows queries

- over more than one transcript,
- over more than one annotation tier,
- combining annotations with metadata (13 regions, 4 age groups, participant's code and gender),
- for form features (using HamNoSys notation of types' forms),
- with customized range of left and right neighbours (tokens), and
- with specified distance between annotations in the same tier.

ANNIS is not meant to be another content-related access point. Users will need to be somewhat familiar with the Public DGS Corpus content, its metadata, and the annotation conventions used.

In the following sections we give some background information on ANNIS (Section 2) and AQL (Section 3), followed by a description of how we transformed the data (Section 4). We then explain in more detail the advantages of exploring the Public DGS Corpus with ANNIS, and make suggestions by presenting some research use cases (Section 5).

2. ANNIS

ANNIS (Krause and Zeldes, 2016) is a browser-based tool developed at Humboldt-Universität zu Berlin, Georgetown University and Potsdam University, which allows complex queries to be carried out on corpora with multiple annotation tiers. The data may be structured as required by any particular corpus, and there are no constraints or theory-based requirements. Query results can be visualized in a number of different styles, and linked audio and/or video files can also be displayed. ANNIS is a Java software programme which can be run on a server so that free access is available to all via a web browser (ANNIS Server), or as a standalone version on an individual machine without outside access (ANNIS Desktop)[6].

Many corpora are already available online through ANNIS, from a very wide variety of domains, with many different annotations; large collections are available for example from korpling.german.hu-berlin.de/annis3 and corpling.uis.georgetown.edu/annis. The majority of these corpora are text-based, but there are also some containing video, including the Berlin Map Task corpus BeMaTac (Sauer and Lüdeling, 2016).

[5] In *MY DGS – annotated* there is an additional "Video Total" perspective showing participants from their side with the moderator between them.

[6] https://corpus-tools.org/annis/download.html

3. ANNIS Query Language

The ANNIS Query Language (AQL) is based on the concept of searching for annotation attributes and relations between them. There are a number of search operators which can be combined to form complex queries. The query operators allow searches involving:

- text, including regular expressions using the Rust library regex format
- annotations
- the hierarchical structure of the tiers
- pointing relations between nodes
- distances between nodes in the same tier
- corpus metadata

Below, we will introduce the query operators most relevant for the examples given in this paper; a full guide to AQL is available online[7]. All of the explanatory examples given in Sections 2 and 4 refer to the English version of the corpus, and each use case example in Section 5 specifies whether it refers to the English or German version of the corpus.

3.1. Annotation Text Queries

Any annotations which contain text can be searched either as exact strings using quotation marks or as regular expressions using forward slashes (/). Both may also be negated using the operator "!". For example, in Query 1 we search for all glosses which exactly match the string "TRAIN2A", in Query 2 for all glosses beginning with the string "TRAIN" and in Query 3 for all English translations which do not contain the string "train" anywhere in them.

(1) Gloss="TRAIN2A"

(2) Gloss=/TRAIN.*/

(3) English!=/.*train.*/

The operators and (&) and or (|) can be used to combine any number of search elements within queries.

3.2. Queries with the Distance Operator

The AQL dot (.) operator can be used to search for preceding or following tokens within the same tier. In corpora such as ours where there are multiple tiers, the tier on which tokens are consecutive can be specified. In Query 4 we first specify two search elements, one a gloss starting with TRAIN and the other a gloss containing arbitrary text. We then specify that the first element (referenced as #1) should directly precede the second element (referenced as #2) in the Gloss tier. It is possible to use a shortcut for this query by placing the distance operator between the two search elements, as shown in Query 5. If desired, we can also specify a distance, and search for example for two glosses starting with TRAIN which occur between one and 5 tokens apart, shown in Query 6.

(4) Gloss=/TRAIN.*/ & Gloss=/.*/ & #1.Gloss #2

(5) Gloss=/TRAIN.*/ .Gloss Gloss

(6) Gloss=/TRAIN.*/ .Gloss,1,5 Gloss=/TRAIN.*/

3.3. Query Links between Tiers

It is also possible within ANNIS for there to be links between tokens from different tiers, and AQL queries can use these links. The links are specified using the AQL operator "->" followed by the name of the link. In *MY DGS – ANNIS* we have created an "ident" link which links tokens belonging to the same participant. Query 7 combines Queries 2 and 3 and searches for a gloss starting with TRAIN which has an "ident" link to an English translation which does not contain the word "train". Query 8 uses a shortcut to express the same query. We explain in Section 4.2 how we use links in *MY DGS – ANNIS* and why they are important.

(7) Gloss=/TRAIN.*/ & English!=/.*train.*/
& #1 ->ident #2

(8) Gloss=/TRAIN.*/ ->ident English!=/.*train.*/

3.4. Metadata Queries

Metadata can be included in queries using the AQL "@*" operator. Query 9 will return results for glosses starting with TRAIN only from participants recorded in Schleswig-Holstein (SH).

(9) Gloss=/TRAIN.*/ @* RegionCode="SH"

Further explanations and examples of these queries with *MY DGS – ANNIS* are provided in the following sections.

4. Transforming the Public DGS Corpus Data for ANNIS

In order to convert the DGS Corpus data into the ANNIS format, we used Pepper, which is a software platform that allows linguistic data to be converted from one format to another (Zipser and Romary, 2010).[8] Pepper uses the interchange format Salt[9] as an abstract theory-independent interchange format, so we wrote a Pepper module to transform the DGS Corpus data into the Salt format, which can then be output as ANNIS data.

4.1. Annotation Tiers

The DGS Corpus uses a type hierarchy and double glossing (Konrad et al., 2020), where types and subtypes are linked to each other by a parent-child relation. Individual gloss tokens in the annotations may refer either to a type or a subtype.

[7] https://korpling.github.io/ANNIS/4.6/user-guide/aql

[8] https://corpus-tools.org/pepper

[9] https://corpus-tools.org/salt

We created a separate ANNIS corpus for English and for German, each of which contains the following annotation tiers for each participant[10]:

Gloss – subtypes or types used to lemmatize tokens (in English or German)

GlossType – parent types (in English or German)

HamNoSys – type citation forms in HamNoSys (phonetic notation system of signs (Hanke, 2004))

Mouth – mouthings (referring to German words and therefore only in German in both ANNIS DGS corpora) or mouth gestures (coded simply as "[MG]")

Translation – for each utterance (in English or German)

Right and Left – tokens which note whether a sign was carried out with the right or left hand. These tiers are not displayed in query results but are used to perform queries referring to a single hand, as described below.

Signs in DGS may be one- or two-handed, and there are also complex sign constructions where each hand articulates a different sign. Rather than providing one gloss tier for each hand, we have a single tier for all the glosses for one participant, so when complex signs occur, we combine the two glosses into a single token, with the two glosses separated by "||". This allows us to perform AQL queries involving distance between tokens, where we include all of the tokens belonging to a participant, regardless of which hand they used. We also have a tier containing tokens which note whether a sign was carried out with the right or left hand. In this way, we can search for example for all tokens signed with the left hand, while still allowing all sign tokens from one participant to be present in the same tier.
Query 10 uses the links between the Gloss tiers and the "Right" and "Left" tiers to find all occasions in which a participant has articulated a different sign with each hand.

(10) Gloss & Left & Right & #1 ->ident #2
& #1 ->ident #3

The query results are shown in Figure 1. In this case we have selected the English version of the corpus, and are viewing the video of the first of the 3012 results returned for Query 10. We can see the annotation tiers for the current signer (PersonB): English, GlossType, Gloss, Mouth and HamNoSys. The tiers for PersonA are not visible because they are not currently signing. The token which corresponds to the search just carried out is highlighted in red (in this case a (double) token DEAF1A || $INDEX1* in the Gloss tier) and some context is shown on either side. We can also play video by clicking on a token from any tier to play just a short segment, or by using the play button to play for as long as desired.
Once a query has been performed, it is also possible within ANNIS to see a frequency analysis of the results, as described in Section 5.1 and shown in Figure 3.

4.2. Links between Annotation Tiers

Because almost every transcript of the DGS Corpus involves two participants, we cannot rely on the timeline when running AQL queries which involve more than one tier. When both participants sign simultaneously, annotations for one participant will overlap in time with annotations for their interlocutor. We therefore created "ident" links within the ANNIS corpus between tokens pertaining to a single participant in different tiers which temporally overlap, so that queries involving more than one tier will only return results where the tiers relate to the same participant (see Section 3.3).
The need for "ident" links between tiers is illustrated by the following two queries which specify an English translation containing the word "not" and a gloss which denotes a headshake[11]. Query 11 uses temporal alignment to search for translations which include tokens of the gloss (AQL operator "_i_"), whereas Query 12 uses the links between participant tiers (our implemented link operator "->ident").

(11) Gloss=/\$GEST-NM-SHAKE-HEAD.*/
& English =/.* not .*/ & #2 _i_ #1

(12) Gloss=/\$GEST-NM-SHAKE-HEAD.*/
& English =/.* not .*/ & #1 ->ident #2

Query 11 returns 104 results including some where the translation temporally coincides with the the gloss, but the translation belongs to one participant and the gloss to the other. An example is shown in Figure 2, where the translation "No that's not right. You're right" (highlighted in purple) belongs to PersonA while the gloss $GEST-NM-SHAKE-HEAD1^ (highlighted in red) belongs to PersonB. Query 12 returns 84 results, where the translation temporally includes the target gloss token, and additionally the token and the translation belong to the same participant. If we had not included the participant links, the query results for this case would therefore have included almost 20% of false results.

4.3. Metadata

Each corpus also contains searchable metadata pertaining to the transcript (recording region and date, transcript task) and the participants (age group, gender). As described in Section 3.4, AQL queries can also include any of the corpus metadata.

[10]In addition, there is a translation tier for the moderators' utterances when they say something relevant to the general flow of conversation. There are however no Gloss, GlossType or Mouth annotations for the moderators.

[11]A nonmanual gesture identifying utterances without relevant manual activity but only headshaking to express negation.

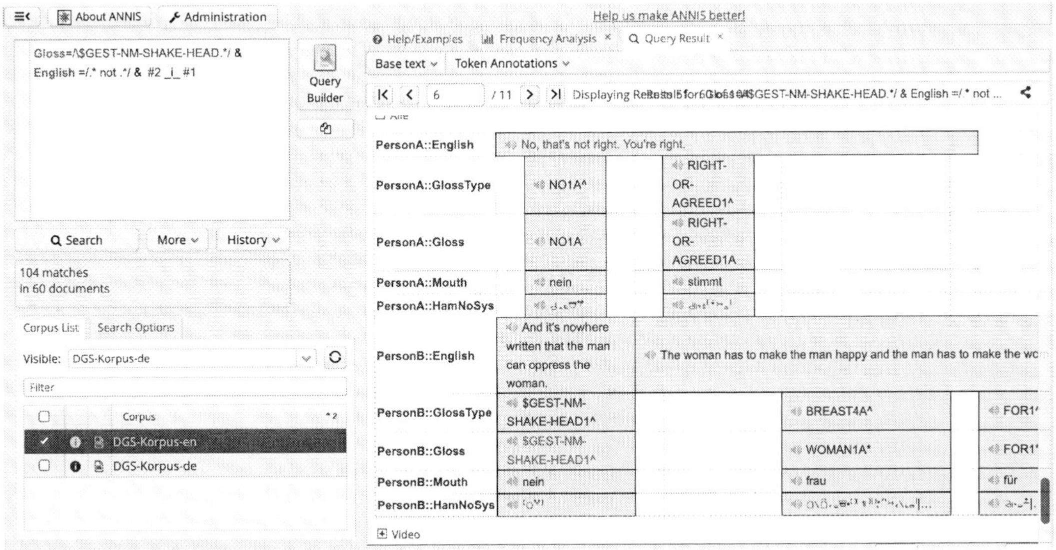

Figure 2: ANNIS display showing result of AQL query which uses temporal overlap and finds a translation from PersonA overlapping with a Gloss from PersonB (Query 11).

5. Research Use Cases with ANNIS

As described in Sections 3 and 4, ANNIS allows queries to be made over and within the different annotation tiers and metadata. The following sections contain some examples of research queries.

5.1. Lexical Negation in DGS

One could be interested in how negation is expressed in DGS with a focus on manual (lexical) signs. To identify these signs (or rather the glosses which represent them) one could search the German version of the corpus for German negation words like "nicht", "nein", or "kein" in the German translations and filter out relevant glosses within these sequences. For example, the AQL statement in Query 13 searches for "kein", "keine", "keines", "keiner", "keinem", and "keinen" in German translations and all glosses from the same participant which occur during the time covered by the translation:

(13) Deutsch =/.* kein(e[srmn]?)? .*/
& Gloss & #2 ->ident #1

Within ANNIS, the glosses included in these utterances can be displayed using the "Frequency Analysis" tool, which displays a gloss list sorted by frequency of tokens. This frequency analysis can be saved as a CSV file and further processed in a spreadsheet. Singling out unique gloss names shows that in the Public DGS Corpus, several gloss names appear that are highly relevant for expressing negation, such as KEIN (NONE), NEIN (NO), NICHT (NOT), NICHTS (NOTHING), NIEMALS (NEVER), NIEMAND (NOBODY), NIRGENDWO (NOWHERE), but also combinations with -NICHT (NOT-), KEIN-, KEINE- (NO-) and some others like the previously mentioned gesture $GEST-NM-KOPFSCHÜTTELN ($GEST-NM-SHAKE-HEAD). These glosses can be used for further queries like the one shown in Query 14:

(14) Gloss=/.*KEIN.*/ ->ident Mundbild

The query returns 1128 matches for tokens of both participants lemmatized by glosses that contain KEIN, highlighting the matched gloss and coarticulated mouthing in the ANNIS query results. The frequency analysis in ANNIS reports 227 different gloss-mouthing combinations. Fifty percent of the tokens are accompanied by a mouth gesture rather than a mouthing. In 41% the annotated mouthing starts with "kein", and in some cases the mouthing is extended (e.g. "keine Ahnung" (no idea)) or simultaneously expresses a further meaning component ("Erfahrung"; cf. Ebbinghaus (1998, 596) giving similar examples of this kind of "syntagmatic dimension" which the coarticulation of manual signs and mouthed words can take).

Knowing that in some sign languages negation is expressed by a morphemic pattern showing a characteristic alpha-movement, in the terminology of Zeshan (2006, 49-54) "irregular negatives", one could try to find these forms by searching for mouthings that contain at least two words of which the second is "nicht", for example "kann nicht", which are coarticulated with a manual sign that is deviant from the citation form. Tokens with form deviation, which in the case of alpha negation is a different movement pattern, are singled out in the Public DGS Corpus by an asterisk (*) at the end of the gloss e.g. KANN1*. The AQL statement in Query 15 returns 925 matches resulting in a frequency list of 347 sign-mouthing combinations like KANN1*/kann nicht (124 tokens) or

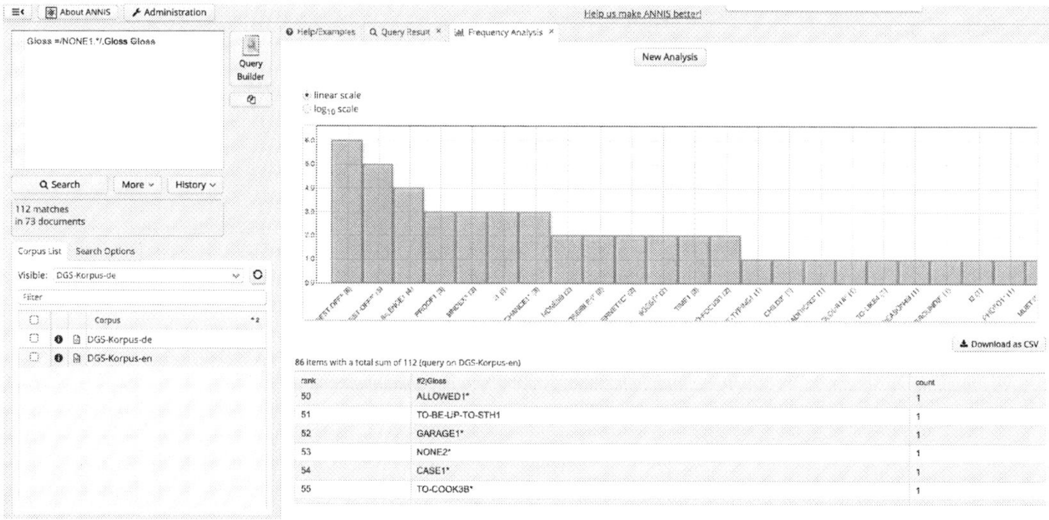

Figure 3: ANNIS display of frequency analysis for AQL query searching for Gloss tokens which follow a Gloss token NONE1 (Query 16)

BRAUCHEN1*/braucht|e|en nicht (41 tokens).[12]

(15) Mundbild=/.*[a-z] nicht.*/ & Gloss=/.**/ & #2 ->ident #1

With *MY DGS – ANNIS* we can also test a hypothesis made by Papaspyrou et al. (2008, 179). The authors state that NONE1[13] can only refer to nouns. Since the Public DGS Corpus is not part-of-speech tagged, a straightforward query searching for NONE1 tokens followed by a noun can not be run. However, we can search the English version of the corpus for the right-hand neighbours of NONE1 and have a closer look at the results. The AQL statement in Query 16 returns 112 matches.

(16) Gloss =/NONE1.*/.Gloss Gloss

Figure 3 shows the frequency anaalysis of the matches. Going through the frequency list of the right neighbour glosses, one finds glosses like ALLOWED1, CAN2A, TO-LIKE4, MUST1, GOOD1, RIGHT-OR-CORRECT1B, NONE2, and TO-COOK3B. Each of these combinations of NONE1 followed by one of these tokens are included in the same translation tag belonging to the same utterance. With a refined search like the one shown in Query 17 one can analyse the tokens in question.

(17) Gloss=/NONE1.*/.Gloss Gloss=/(ALLOWED|CAN|TO-LIKE).*/

Since the examples thus found contain a number of words whose part of speech is not noun, this suggests that the hypothesis should be modified.

5.2. Metaphorical Use of Signs

As the type forms in the Public DGS Corpus are notated in HamNoSys, one can search for form features and access all the tokens that are matched directly to that type or to one of its subtypes. To analyse the use of the brain = cognition metaphor the AQL statement in Query 18 on the English version of the corpus returns all tokens whose type has a location at the forehead region (as specified by the HamNoSys character ⌒):

(18) GlossType & HamNoSys=/.*⌒.*/ & Gloss & #3 ->ident #1 & #3 ->ident #2

The frequency list generated from this query contains over 1000 entries. Normalizing the list in a spreadsheet and sorting by type gloss reveals more than 3,500 tokens of four lexical or phonological type variants all glossed by TO-KNOW-OR-KNOWLEDGE, 148 tokens of the type TO-COMPREHEND1[14], and 10 tokens of types glossed EXPERT. But even if the type name seems to indicate a non-metaphorical use like BRAIN, one has to look for the subtypes' gloss names as they indicate conventionalized uses of the sign like MENTALLY2[15], a subtype of BRAIN1A with repeated movement.

Interested in how metaphorical uses of signs vary between age groups, one can search for a type name like EXPERT including the metadata AgeGroup and run a frequency analysis. Of course, this could also be done for region or even for signs of a single participant as they are coded by an anonymized shortname.

[12] For a more comprehensive description of how negation is annotated in the DGS Corpus see Loos and Konrad (2022).

[13] https://www.sign-lang.uni-hamburg.de/meinedgs/types/type16242_en.html

[14] https://www.sign-lang.uni-hamburg.de/meinedgs/types/type15301_en.html

[15] https://www.sign-lang.uni-hamburg.de/meinedgs/types/type13914_en.html#type26535

6. Conclusion

We presented *MY DGS – ANNIS*, a new portal which complements the existing portals available for the Public DGS Corpus by providing a freely accessible web interface which allows researchers to directly search the corpus online without the need to register, download data, or install new programs. We provide access for corpus-based research that allows complex searches to be made across the different annotation tiers and metadata information available in the Public DGS Corpus. Since the ANNIS interface is already familiar to corpus researchers, we hope that *MY DGS – ANNIS* will stimulate corpus-based research in DGS, and encourage crosslinguistic studies.

Some knowledge of the ANNIS Query Language and the DGS Corpus annotations is necessary to interact with *MY DGS – ANNIS*. There is detailed online documentation for the ANNIS software interface and query language[16], and in addition to the simple queries automatically generated for our corpora by the ANNIS software, we will provide a number of more complex example queries in the Help/Examples section of the interface. These will illustrate the use of AQL operators with the various annotation tiers, and researchers can then use these examples as a basis to search for the information in which they are interested.

7. Acknowledgements

This publication has been produced in the context of the joint research funding of the German Federal Government and Federal States in the Academies' Programme, with funding from the Federal Ministry of Education and Research and the Free and Hanseatic City of Hamburg. The Academies' Programme is coordinated by the Union of the Academies of Sciences and Humanities.

8. Bibliographical References

Ebbinghaus, H. (1998). Warum deutsche Wörter wesentliche Bestandteile der Deutschen Gebärdensprache sind. Teil I: *Das Zeichen* 45, 443-451; Teil II: *Das Zeichen* 46, 594-611.

Hanke, T., Schulder, M., Konrad, R., and Jahn, E. (2020). Extending the Public DGS Corpus in size and depth. In Efthimiou, E., et al., editors, *Proceedings of the LREC2020 9th Workshop on the Representation and Processing of Sign Languages*, pages 75–82, Marseille, France. European Language Resources Association (ELRA).

Hanke, T. (2004). HamNoSys – representing sign language data in language resources and language processing contexts. In Streiter, O. et al., editors, *Proceedings of the LREC2004 Workshop on the Representation and Processing of Sign Languages*, pages 1–6, Lisbon, Portugal. European Language Resources Association (ELRA).

Jahn, E., Konrad, R., Langer, G., Wagner, S., and Hanke, T. (2018). Publishing DGS Corpus data: Different formats for different needs. In Bono, M., et al., editors, *Proceedings of the LREC2018 8th Workshop on the Representation and Processing of Sign Languages*, pages 83–90, Miyazaki, Japan. European Language Resources Association (ELRA).

Konrad, R., Hanke, T., Langer, G., König, S., König, L., Nishio, R., and Regen, A. (2020). Öffentliches DGS-Korpus: Annotationskonventionen / Public DGS Corpus: Annotation conventions. Project Note AP03-2018-01, DGS-Korpus project, IDGS, Hamburg University, Hamburg, Germany. DOI: 10.25592/uhhfdm.822.

Krause, T. and Zeldes, A. (2016). ANNIS3: A new architecture for generic corpus query and visualization. *Digital Scholarship in the Humanities*, 31(1):118–139. DOI: 10.1093/llc/fqu057.

Loos, C. and Konrad, R. (2022). Detailed annotation and qualifiers. Project Note AP03-2021-01, DGS-Korpus project, IDGS, Hamburg University, Hamburg, Germany. DOI: 10.25592/uhhfdm.10224.

Papaspyrou, C., von Meyenn, A., Matthaei, M., and Herrmann, B. (2008). *Grammatik der deutschen Gebärdensprache aus der Sicht gehörloser Fachleute*. Seedorf: Signum.

Prillwitz, S., Hanke, T., König, S., Konrad, R., Langer, G., and Schwarz, A. (2008). DGS Corpus project – development of a corpus based electronic dictionary German Sign Language / German. In Crasborn, O., et al., editors, *Proceedings of the LREC2008 3rd Workshop on the Representation and Processing of Sign Languages*, pages 159–164, Marrakech, Morocco. European Language Resources Association (ELRA).

Sauer, S. and Lüdeling, A. (2016). Flexible multi-layer spoken dialogue corpora. *International Journal of Corpus Linguistics*, 21(3):419–438. DOI: 10.1075/ijcl.21.3.06sau.

Schulder, M., Blanck, D., Hanke, T., Hofmann, I., Hong, S.-E., Jeziorski, O., König, L., König, S., Konrad, R., Langer, G., Nishio, R., and Rathmann, C. (2021). Data statement for the Public DGS Corpus. Project Note AP06-2020-01, DGS-Korpus project, IDGS, Hamburg University, Hamburg, Germany. DOI: 10.25592/uhhfdm.1745.

Zeshan, U. (2006). Negative and interrogative constructions in sign languages: A case study in sign language typology. In Zeshan, U., editor, *Interrogative and Negative Constructions in Sign Languages*, pages 26–68. Ishara Press. DOI: 10.26530/OAPEN_453832.

Zipser, F. and Romary, L. (2010). A model oriented approach to the mapping of annotation formats using standards. In *Workshop on Language Resource and Language Technology Standards, LREC 2010*, La Valetta, Malta.

[16] https://korpling.github.io/ANNIS/4.6/user-guide/interface/index.html

Proceedings of the 10th Workshop on the Representation and Processing of Sign Languages (sign-lang@LREC 2022), pages 80–87
Language Resources and Evaluation Conference (LREC 2022), Marseille, 20-25 June 2022

Outreach and Science Communication in the DGS-Korpus Project: Accessibility of Data and the Benefit of Interactive Exchange between Communities

Elena Jahn, Calvin Khan, Annika Herrmann
Institute of German Sign Language and Communication of the Deaf
University of Hamburg, Germany
{elena.jahn,annika.herrmann,calvin.khan}@uni-hamburg.de

Abstract

In this paper, we tackle the issues of science communication and dissemination within a sign language corpus project with a focus on spreading accessible information and involving the D/deaf community on various levels. We will discuss successful examples, challenges, and limitations to public relations in such a project and particularly elaborate on use cases. The focus group is presented as a best-practice example of a what we think is a necessary perspective: taking external knowledge seriously and let community experts interact with and provide feedback on a par with academic personnel. Showing both social media and on-site events, we present some exemplary approaches from our team involved in public relations.

Keywords: public relations, science communication, sign language community, DGS-Korpus project

1. Introduction

'Just as there is science to be communicated, there is a science of communication.' (Fischhoff and Scheufele, 2013) Scientists who seek to inform the interested public about their work need to navigate through the highly exciting, yet also challenging field of science communication. In the case of the DGS-Korpus project, the dissemination of results as well as the publication and promotion of the products (the *Public DGS Corpus* and the *DW-DGS*, a digital and corpus-based dictionary of DGS[1]) to different communities is an important project goal.[2] In order to present these products and how they can be accessed or utilised, science communication and public relations are key elements.

Although science communication is by no means a young field of research, it is among the areas of research that have received the most public attention in recent years and is changing rapidly in response to new academic and technical circumstances. These developments include not only the public's changing perception of scientific research, but also more recent technical innovations and changes in dissemination platforms, such as social media channels. To an increasing extent, these platforms are being discovered by the various sciences, as they merge entertainment and information transfer. Furthermore, science communication is more and more recognised as a requirement in recent project conception and is demanded by funding parties as well as by the public at large.

Nevertheless, science communication is still under scrutiny, as it entails a history of misunderstandings and mistrust. While scientists in the past often made the argument that the public lacked the necessary background knowledge and scientific literacy to understand certain scientific work, the public repeatedly accused scientists of being detached from everyday concerns and not very trustworthy.[3] While as a result, scientists may be hesitant to open up to the public, believing their work might not be properly understood and therefore criticised, in our view, it has proved fruitful to overcome this apprehension. One reason for this is the growing awareness that both parties, science and the public, may benefit from the exchange.[4]

To provide an insight into the dissemination activities and communicative goals and challenges of our project, the remainder of this paper is structured as follows. In §2, we discuss outreach and communication strategies in a sign language corpus project with a focus on target groups (in §2.1), in particular the German D/deaf community and DGS language community, and address the benefits of use case oriented approaches (§2.2). In §3, we discuss the guiding principles that influence our work and are prominent in, but of course not limited to, our specific field of sign language research. The following guiding principles are relevant for the provision of materials and corpus data: accessibility (§3.1), diversity (§3.2) and interaction (§3.3).

[1]*DW-DGS*: 'Digitales Wörterbuch der Deutschen Gebärdensprache — Das korpusbasierte Wörterbuch DGS – Deutsch'

[2]See §2.2 for a short introduction of the *Public DGS Corpus* and the *DW-DGS*.

[3]See, for example, Weingart and Guenther (2016) on the issue of trust with respect to the field of science communication and also Bultitude (2011) for more recent events that have resulted in a decline in trust towards science. In their paper, Bubela et al. (2009) provide an overview of the development of science communication from the deficit model to the interactive model and deal with the challenges that science communication faces.

[4]See, for example, Bultitude (2011) for more reasons why science communication is beneficial.

2. Outreach and Science Communication

'Science requires the public's support. Whether it is forthcoming depends on how much the public trusts and values science.' (Fischhoff and Scheufele, 2013) While this quote refers to science in general, it is just as applicable to smaller fields of science or individual projects, as it is the case for the DGS-Korpus project. As the DGS-Korpus project aims to provide a freely accessible online corpus and dictionary for specific target groups, especially a target group that will be referred to herein as the DGS language community, the involvement of these groups is most important.[5] The DGS language community has been directly involved in the creation of the *DGS corpus* during data collection and data handling by being the source of the data as participants, by being involved in the data elicitation as interviewers, and by annotating and evaluating the data as language experts and scientists. For this reason, both products emerging from the *DGS corpus*, the *Public DGS Corpus* and the *DW-DGS*, are designed primarily with the DGS language community in mind and by actively involving experts from among them. The design of these online resources benefits from feedback of users who actively work with the resources provided by the project. Such feedback makes for a very fruitful type of extended peer review, as it highlights issues that have previously gone unnoticed, steers research in new directions, or reinforce paths already taken.

Since the DGS-Korpus project aims for a mutual exchange in which content is shared with the DGS language community and other target groups and these audiences contribute to the work of the project by means of feedback, the remaining question is: how can such an exchange be constantly optimised? As stated by Fischhoff and Scheufele (2013): '[I]f scientists want to be effective in their communication, they must understand and address the perspectives of interest groups.' One of the most important prerequisites for all outreach activities in the DGS-Korpus project is to be aware of the target group(s) that are to be addressed by certain outreach activities.

2.1. Target Groups and Communities

'Instead of relying on personal experience or anecdotal observations, it is necessary to do careful audience research to determine which frames work for the target audiences.' (Bubela et al., 2009) While this statement can be fully agreed with in theory, the practical implementation poses challenges to many academic projects due to the lack of resources to conduct such a careful audience research. However, the thorough consideration of the audience with their language preferences or needs, their preferred media channels and the content they are interested in, can save a lot of time and effort, as outreach activities can be efficiently tailored to specific target groups.

The potential audience is composed of several subgroups with diverse needs and interests. For the sake of simplicity, we adopt a broad tripartite distinction and refer to the groups as the **DGS language community, scientific communities**, and the **interested public** in this paper.

The **DGS language community** refers to those who use the language DGS, and is itself composed of many subgroups, and may comprise individuals with or without a linguistic background (DGS teachers, for example, are usually linguistically trained). Likely the largest subgroup of the DGS language community is the D/deaf community, with those who use DGS as their everyday language. Furthermore, the language community includes people who might not use DGS as their everyday language, but on a regular basis with a high level of fluency, for instance interpreters and others who work together with D/deaf people. Also included in this group are people who are not yet fully fluent in DGS, for example students, prospective interpreters, parents of D/deaf children, and signing competent researchers. An important subgroup of DGS learners are students, who might use the DGS corpus and the emerging dictionary in various ways: as additional practice material in the context of their studies, as a resource for student research papers, and - for students on site - as hired transcribers in the DGS-Korpus project.

The above-mentioned examples of subgroups within the DGS language community are not intended to be seen as an exhaustive list, as the diversity of the DGS language community is immense, which is why groups are not always clearly assignable; for example, among the group of researchers there are both D/deaf scientist and DGS learners. 'People who are deaf reflect the full range of diversity found in the general population, with added layers of complexity related to levels and type of hearing loss, parental hearing status, access and ability to benefit from auditory-enhancing technologies, language usage based on signs and/or voice, and use of visually accessible sign languages.' (Harris et al., 2009) The above statement can certainly be extended to the DGS language community as a whole.

As a scientific long-term project, the DGS-Korpus project's **scientific target groups** include D/deaf and hearing researchers from the same discipline as well as from other disciplines, such as computational linguistics, cultural or heritage studies and others.

Also, we aim to address the very diverse group that is the **interested public**, persons without or with only little background knowledge on sign languages or D/deaf culture and little to no competence in DGS. For this target group, we usually highlight the importance of corpus data with regard to the cultural heritage that this resource offers, which is interesting for society in general.

[5] See §2.1 on target groups and communities for more information on the diversity of the groups that the DGS-Korpus project seeks to address, and also briefly on how the DGS language community is composed.

2.2. Use Cases

In addition to being conscious of the different target groups and their varying needs, such as language preferences, the bidirectional approach of the DGS-Korpus project also takes into account the requirements of specific use cases. For the project, it has proven most beneficial to identify specific user profiles and needs and address them through targeted outreach activities. For our outreach activities, we consider the following questions: For what purpose do users want to use the *Public DGS Corpus* or the *DW-DGS*? How would the user interact with the product, where would they look for specific information? Which applications might users not yet be aware of, and which options should be introduced to them? Some use case examples are given below. For this, the products of our project are briefly introduced first.

Both the *Public DGS Corpus* and the *DW-DGS* are based on the *DGS corpus*, a reference corpus of DGS. The ***Public DGS Corpus*** is a freely accessible subset (50 hours) of the reference corpus, that is completely translated and was first released in 2018. The content focuses on formats that are of interest to the D/deaf community, while also covering all task formats used during the elicitation, and showing all participants (given their consent). Releases covering new features and content are published on a regular basis (Hanke et al., 2020c).[6] Annotations and translations were subjected to careful quality assurance steps (Konrad et al., 2020b) and personal information of participants and third parties was anonymised (Bleicken et al., 2016). The different publication formats for the *Public DGS Corpus*, *My DGS*[7], *My DGS – annotated*[8] and *My DGS – ANNIS*[9] were designed with the needs of different target groups in mind (Jahn et al., 2018). *My DGS* (Hanke et al., 2020b) is a community portal, in which the videos are presented (in the browser) with optional German subtitles. The website was designed to be a low-threshold interface for easy access and is aimed at the D/deaf and DGS language community primarily, but also at the public. *My DGS – annotated* (Konrad et al., 2020a) is a research portal aimed at the international scientific community, in which the videos can be watched (online) with translations, annotations and comments. It also provides several download options and metadata. A third portal, *My DGS – ANNIS* (Isard and Konrad, 2022) provides an ANNIS (Krause and Zeldes, 2016) interface for advanced corpus queries and statistics.

The ***DW-DGS***[10] is a digital dictionary, based on the *DGS corpus*, which provides a variety of information on individual sign entries, such as regional distribution and links to example sentences from the *Public DGS Corpus*. Pre-release entries are already freely accessible. The dictionary is aimed at the DGS language community foremost, but also the scientific community.

For the DGS language community, as well as researchers and also the interested public, there are a variety of possible use cases and applications for the *Public DGS Corpus* and the *DW-DGS*, for example:

The *Public DGS Corpus* can be used as a language learning resource and to train visual perception. It can also be used as a cultural and historical archive, as the videos published for open access have been specifically selected to cover topics that are of interest to the D/deaf community and those interested in their culture. Of course, the *Public DGS Corpus* can also be used for research questions in a variety of scientific disciplines: linguistic questions as well as cultural or historical questions can be investigated. Other users might be interested in the way the *Public DGS Corpus* and the *DW-DGS* are linked and how they provide additional or complementary features for users.[11]

As these use cases are not always directly attributable to one specific target group, the individual outreach actions are mostly oriented towards usage possibilities. Certainly, the target groups and their needs are taken into account, too, so that a mixture of considerations regarding the target groups and different use cases emerges to guide the outreach actions.

2.3. The Focus Group

In order to conduct a goal-oriented target group analysis of the DGS language community, and to identify different use cases of the project's products, we worked with a focus group, consisting of D/deaf experts from various regions across Germany, and D/deaf colleagues from the project. The support of D/deaf experts was crucial, as a target group cannot be determined from the projects' perspective alone, and insights from and about the DGS language community can best be provided by D/deaf experts. Since most of the members of the focus group have been involved with the project from its beginning, they are familiar with the project, its goals and values and have therefore evolved into very important consultants similar to an advisory board. They provide advice on various language-related issues, and were engaged in narrowing down subgroups within the DGS language community. As parts of their respective local D/deaf communities, the focus group communicates news and relevant information to and from the community and thus acts both as a spokesperson for the project as well as a source of feedback from the community. In this way, the focus group's role as bridges between the project and the D/deaf community is twofold: on the one hand, the focus group represents a target group, on the other hand they are an important internal element of the project's public relations work.

[6] See here for a release history of the *Public DGS Corpus*.

[7] http://meine-dgs.de

[8] http://ling.meine-dgs.de

[9] http://annis.meine-dgs.de

[10] http://www.dw-dgs.de

[11] See Müller et al. (2020) for more information on the linking of the *Public DGS Corpus* and the *DW-DGS*.

In regular meetings with the focus group, new features for the the *Public DGS Corpus*, the design and user interface of the *DW-DGS* and public relations, in particular the DGS language community as a target group, were discussed. In some cases, they themselves have taken the initiative: Some members of the group joined presentations about the DGS-Korpus projects' work as an integral part of the project team. An idea for a social media campaign including stepwise information packages in DGS video format was initiated and carried out by members of the focus group.

3. Guiding Principles

In their paper, Harris et al. (2009) postulate a list of terms of reference, 'principles and procedures that need to be considered when researchers decide to study Sign Language communities'. These terms of reference are understood as a 'code of research' that is intended to set ethical standards in interacting with the signing community. Outreach activities are of great importance when it comes to adhering to these principles and can contribute to complying with them. The basis for implementing these principles is that '[s]ign language communities' terms of reference (SLCTR) must be inclusive of the community's perspectives'. A fundamental point is that ' [i]nvestigators should take into account the worldviews of the Sign Language community' and that 'culturally competent researchers endeavor to build rapport despite differences, gain the trust of community members, and reflect on and recognise their own biases' (Harris et al., 2009, p.112). This is where outreach activities come into play.

Another general tenet that the DGS-Korpus project is committed to is the adherence to FAIR[12] (Wilkinson et al., 2016) and CARE[13] principles (Carroll et al., 2020). The FAIR principles *(Findable, Accessible, Interoperable, Reusable)* are concerned with the management of data sets for scientific (re-)use. They state that data should be both human- and machine-readable, well documented, accompanied by metadata, and easily accessible, e.g. through (persistent) identifiers, allowing data to be retrieved, accessed and exploited for further research purposes. The DGS-Korpus project strives to comply with these guiding principles, for example, by documenting work processes in detail including the publication of project notes and by providing detailed metadata and DOIs[14] as persistent identifiers. The CARE principles *(Collective benefit, Authority to control, Responsibility, and Ethics)* are a complement to FAIR that addresses the ethical implications of working with data from minority communities. The CARE principles are taken very seriously by the DGS-Korpus project. All stages of the project have involved D/deaf project members and advisors, participants were empowered through informed consent and legal control of their recordings, portals were designed to encourage use by the D/deaf and DGS language communities and the corpus was actively designed to focus on the values and world-views of those communities, while usage conditions were designed to prevent harm. For a more detailed description of how the DGS-Korpus project has implemented FAIR and CARE principles, see Schulder and Hanke (2022).

In addition to these principles and the fundamental objectives of the DGS-Korpus project to adhere to ethical principles and provide open access to as much of the data as possible, certain guiding principles are of particular importance for outreach activities. The three most important of the guidelines that govern all outreach activities on these various channels are **accessibility**, **diversity** (of campaigns and content) and **interaction** (as opposed to uni-directional information).

3.1. Accessibility

While underlying principles and guidelines are essential, they 'do not clearly address the need for the researchers to establish trust with the participants in the community and to ensure that the participants view the research as collaborative and culturally valued' (Harris et al., 2009). Outreach activities can be considered the practical implementation of the guiding principles, which are intended to build this trust. However, trust can only be generated if comprehension is enabled, and for this purpose the DGS-Korpus project strives to design all outreach activities in an accessible way.

To ensure accessibility, most of the information on the web-presence, social media posts, and announcements of events and lectures are composed in either DGS and written German or International Sign and written English. The social media platforms Facebook and Instagram as well as the German version of the website are primarily used to address the DGS language community and the public, so content on these platforms consist of a DGS video and an equivalent text in written German. Social media posts are deliberately produced in a rather informal manner, using a more general non-scientific language register. DGS guarantees access for the signing D/deaf community, but not all members of the D/deaf community in Germany are fluent in DGS, and DGS learners come with different proficiency levels, while the public usually does not have a background in signing and might also rely on German texts rather than DGS videos.

As the Twitter channel and the English version of the website are aimed at an international (research) community, contributions here are published in English and International Sign.

3.2. Diversity

Another guiding principle, which stems not only from the diversity of the target groups but also from the general aim to provide information in a variety of ways to maintain interest, is to create a multitude of diverse

[12] https://www.go-fair.org

[13] https://www.gida-global.org/care

[14] Digital Object Identifier, https://www.doi.org/

outreach campaigns, as a single campaign can never address the needs and interests of all target groups. Similarly, we find that reiterating the same campaign design for one specific target group quickly leads to a decrease of interest. Different user groups are interested in different information and seek this information in different ways and through different channels and platforms. Along with the aim to create a diverse range of activities, also comes a commitment to create activities in a manner that is as continuous as possible. The most regular contact with target groups can be held via our social media channels.

However, while social media provides a fertile platform for science communication, actual interaction is only possible to a limited extent via such platforms. Thus, our outreach activities aim at finding a balance between creating content for various (social media) channels on the one hand and, on the other hand organise exhibitions, events and lectures.[15] Some examples of activities are given below:

For those interested in the history and culture of the D/deaf community in Germany, a series of thematic specials was designed. Videos that highlight occasions or selected topics are posted on social media according to the occasion and are also published on a dedicated sub-page of *MY DGS*, where they can be accessed collectively.[16] In these specials, a teaser video shows transcripts from the *Public DGS Corpus* that correspond to the selected topic, for example the anniversaries of 9/11 or the fall of the Berlin Wall. Each video post is complemented by a link collection, leading to conversations on the topic in the *Public DGS Corpus*. The special videos are a recurring, yet diverse element on the social media platforms covered by the DGS-Korpus project and are complemented by other activities as seasonal greetings, announcements of news, and more.

Another recurring social media campaign is an annual advent calendar, with different thematic priorities, that is primarily designed to address the DGS language community and to draw attention to various features or content of the *Public DGS Corpus* or the *DW-DGS*. In terms of content, the calendars cover seasonal content associated with content from the *Public DGS Corpus* or the *DW-DGS* and thereby draws attention to features and contents of the products in an entertaining way.

As for activities outside of social media platforms, for instance, an interactive media station was placed in a permanent exhibition in a museum.[17] The exhibition displays both science and art with a focus on current research projects and emphasises interactive formats with visitors. The media station was designed to address several audiences: People with or without a background in sign languages in general, people interested in DGS specifically, international visitors, passers-by or those interested in sign languages in general or DGS specifically. To address such diverse audiences, three different question-answer games were designed for the media station. The first quiz on sign languages in general is aimed at people with little or no knowledge of sign languages or DGS and contains yes/no-questions concerned with interesting facts regarding sign languages. The second quiz builds upon the first quiz, focusing on DGS and aiming at people with or without a background in signed languages or DGS. The third quiz is aimed at persons with a fair amount of background knowledge in DGS. Here, visitors are presented with three different variants of a sign and are asked to identify for which sign in a certain region in Germany the most occurrences can be found in the *DGS corpus*.

3.3. Interaction

Outreach activities take place on various channels, including a web presence, social media channels (Facebook, Instagram and Twitter), and more interactive formats such as a variety of different events and lectures (both online or on site) or permanent exhibitions. Furthermore, occasional press contributions are part of the outreach activities. When designing outreach activities on these platforms, efforts are made to strike a balance between information and interaction. The aim of most of our dissemination efforts is to provide an indication of where to find certain information, to illustrate usage possibilities of the *Public DGS Corpus* and the *DW-DGS* and to provide general information both on the project, its products and research results. However, (science) communication is not a one-way street and the DGS-Korpus project seeks to inform, as well as to interact.

With regard to open science, the European Commission states: 'When researchers share knowledge and data as early as possible in the research process with all relevant actors it helps diffuse the latest knowledge. And when partners from across academia [...] and citizen groups are invited to participate in the research and innovation process, creativity and trust in science increases.'[18] Social media channels are a valuable means to diffuse knowledge, actual interaction and participation is only possible to a limited extent on such platforms. To ensure regular and timely responses to emails as well as messages on the different social media channels, a team of deaf and hearing people is responsible for monitoring them. However, the availability (and limits) of resources to interact is an important factor when it comes to regular interaction via so-

[15]This balance was shifted in favour of the social media channels and web presence in times of the pandemic, resulting in increased media traffic. as a flexible adaptation to the current situation. However, the future focus will be on on-site events for productive exchanges.

[16]https://www.sign-lang.uni-hamburg.de/meinedgs/extras/specials.html

[17]The Humboldt-Forum is a long-term exhibition in Berlin that was opened digitally in 2020 and on-site in 2021.

[18]https://ec.europa.eu/info/research-and-innovation/strategy/strategy-2020-2024/our-digital-future/open-science_en

cial media, as moderation on all platforms is necessary, which also entails regular monitoring. This can only be accomplished to a certain extent, therefore we attempt not to invite interaction unless we are confident that the responses can be handled. To enable direct interaction, on-site events have proven to be the better choice. Some examples of interactive events for the respective target groups are given below:

For the interested public, exhibition stands were organised several times at different events. Here, the focus of the presentation lay on the display of the project's work, for instance (film) technology used in the project was shown and supplemented with posters explaining the procedure of corpus creation, the analysis of corpus data, and the current state of work in the project. All these formats were planned in such a way that visitors could move around the stand independently and approach the colleagues from the project with questions.

For the scientific community, the releases of the *Public DGS Corpus* in particular were announced at specific events, such as a public announcement ceremony of Release 3 (Konrad et al., 2020a) as a satellite event of the thirteenth edition of the TISLR *(Theoretical Issues in Sign Language Research)* conference. Here, we mainly presented (technical) innovations and offered many opportunities to trial and test, while colleagues as well as student assistants were present to explain the new functions and to answer questions. Furthermore, poster presentations at conferences offer invaluable opportunities for direct interaction and feedback.

Events specifically targeted at the D/deaf and DGS community included exhibition stands and presentations (for example at the *Deaf Messe* (deaf fair) or the *Kulturtage der Gehörlosen* (culture days of the deaf)). These presentations mainly concentrated on the usage possibilities the products offer for the community, as well as research results and the current project status. Another example was an online event, in which the project's divisions each gave 5-minute input presentations on their current state of work during the pandemic. Student assistants and interpreters were also involved as presenters, as their work is of enormous value to the success of our project outcomes. Most of the time was reserved for feedback and questions following the input presentations. This event was conducted online and proved to be a suitable format to achieve a well-balanced mix of information and interaction.

Furthermore, the tool SIGNHUNTER was programmed to allow the community to actively participate in the collection of additional individual signs. SIGNHUNTER is meant to create a way of interacting that allows the D/deaf and DGS language community to participate in the decision of which individual signs are collected by the DGS-Korpus project by suggesting topics of interest, that are then displayed in SIGNHUNTER as word lists. From these word lists, participants can then select the concepts they are familiar with and record one or more signs and thereby add them to the database. Possible topics and concept lists for SIGNHUNTER have been suggested by the focus group, such as signs for cities and locations. (SIGNHUNTER is described in more detail in (Hanke et al., 2020a).) In the Rome Declaration on Responsible Research and Innovation, the European Commission states: 'Excellence today is about more than ground-breaking discoveries – it includes openness, responsibility and the co-production of knowledge').[19] Although the tool was not yet been widely used due to the pandemic, first tests show that by means of SIGNHUNTER, co-production of content can be actively implemented.

Last, but not least, one of the most important sources of interaction is the exchange with the focus group. To name one example of an issue where direct interaction with the focus group was of great importance and value: there is an ongoing debate about the use of the term 'mother tongue' (*Muttersprache*), that was discussed in great detail with the focus group. Suggestions comprised alternatives such as 'main language' (*Hauptsprache*) or 'base language' (*Basissprache*), but most interestingly in relation to debates in the field of spoken languages, the term 'first language' (*Erstsprache*) was not approved of by any of the members of the focus group.

4. Discussion

The discussion will be devoted to recurring issues, that we cannot resolve conclusively, but will surely continue to be relevant for future debates on how to implement public relations and dissemination into project management. The first issue concerns the effort and the benefit of outreach activities and the constant trade-off between the two. This question is related to available resources and how to manage existing resources to be as efficient as possible. The second point concerns the indirect pressure to be up-to-date at all times, which requires an enormous effort, especially when it comes to social media, as discussions and opinions on the internet are extremely dynamic. We share some reflections and experiences related to this questions below.

4.1. Available Resources

In scientific projects, the main focus is on scientific work. While outreach activities are an increasingly important part of scientific work, they are not the main focus, which is why the resources available for outreach are limited. Rarely are people in science projects solely responsible for outreach, and rarely have they had the background training to do so. As a result, a balance has to be found: on the one hand, the importance of outreach cannot be emphasised clearly enough. On the other hand, outreach activities must be in reasonable relation to the effort of the entire project and also be

[19] https://www.sis-rri-conference.eu/wp content/uploads/2014/12/RomeDeclaration_Final.pdf

feasible as such. Below, we discuss some examples of how the advantages and disadvantages of particular outreach activities have been weighed for campaigns previously conducted by the DGS-Korpus project.

When it comes to social media campaigns in particular, balancing effort and benefit is not that straightforward, as each medium entails its own requirements and contributions cannot easily be transferred from one medium to the other. This especially applies to information in a signed language, i.e. when the main format is video. Due to their different objectives, the different social media platforms are naturally also used by different target groups. For the outreach activities, however, this means that designing a post to be published on all platforms is expedient. Then again, social media posts can be created with much less effort than on-site events, for example. They are therefore well suited for establishing regular contact with our target groups.

On-site activities usually take place only once, and the amount of work is quite high in relation to the number of participants that can be addressed at a one-time event. In contrast, however, the benefits of an event on-site are usually very significant, as direct interaction with visitors can take place. A similar situation applies to contributions to a permanent exhibition (as described above): This exhibition has required more effort than one-time events, but can remain in place for a longer period of time, and will thereby reach a much larger audience. In addition, permanent exhibitions do not require project staff to be on-site during the exhibition period. However, this also means that interaction is only possible to a limited extent, for example in the form of a programmed station or the possibility of contacting project staff after the visit. In this case, the workaround approach for the DGS-Korpus project was to complement a permanent exhibition with a one-time event where a colleague from the project would give a presentation and then be available afterwards for direct interaction and questions in a *meet the scientist* format.

Another example where the decision was made in favour of the effort is the publication of project-internal project notes. The project notes offer a low-threshold access to the methods applied in the DGS-Korpus project. The advantages of publishing these papers are an increased insight into how the data in the *DGS corpus* are composed, as they provide access to project-internal processes and workflows. The target group consists of scientists from the same or others disciplines, especially those who are planning a similar project, and in principle also the interested public.

With any outreach activity, it remains a recurring consideration of whether and when an activity is profitable to undertake, especially given that the main focus of a scientific project is research. For outreach activities of the DGS-Korpus project, we work out the efforts and benefits with a focus on dissemination to the D/deaf community, and then do our best to find ways to overcome obstacles, but also not to launch campaigns that we cannot possibly do justice.

4.2. Current Trends

The DGS-Korpus project strives to be informed about current discussions, trends and developments to a certain degree in order to be able to react accordingly. Both for long-term changes, such as the increased sensitivity to gender-fair language in recent years, but also for short-term emerging issues, it might be necessary to take a stand. The challenge is that some of these developments, particularly in social media, are subject to rapid change and being up-to-date to all current changes and trends would require a constant monitoring of science-related news on the internet, while resources (as noted above) for outreach activities are limited. In addition to constant monitoring, some reactions to certain developments must follow promptly, which is not always feasible in a project whose main focus is (as it should be) on research.

Therefore, in addition to efforts and benefits of campaigns, we also try to foresee whether a reaction is appropriate and then discuss how to implement the necessary changes in accordance with the self-representation of the project.

As noted above, an example of an ongoing, but still current debate is gender-fair language, first with regard to written language, but it also refers to DGS in upcoming debates. On this issue, the DGS-Korpus project decided to follow the University guidelines for gender-fair written language, as they are in line with the values and self-image of the project. Another highly important response to contemporary developments was to provide all publications of the project with DOIs to facilitate permanent access and citation (see FAIR principles above).

5. Conclusion

In this paper, we have discussed outreach activities of the DGS-Korpus project and presented guiding principles for decision-making with regard to public relation campaigns and science communication in our field. Not only funding institutions set dissemination activities as a requirement for projects, but also society in general as well as, in our case, the D/deaf and DGS language community rightfully demand for knowledge transfer. This is why we, as a deaf and hearing team, dedicate significant effort into overcoming limitations and challenges, and aim to produce both scientific and interactive output in an accessible way.

6. Acknowledgements

This publication has been produced in the context of the joint research funding of the German Federal Government and Federal States in the Academies' Programme, with funding from the Federal Ministry of Education and Research and the Free and Hanseatic

City of Hamburg. The Academies' Programme is coordinated by the Union of the German Academies of Sciences and Humanities.

7. Bibliographical References

Bleicken, J., Hanke, T., Salden, U., and Wagner, S. (2016). Using a language technology infrastructure for German in order to anonymize German Sign Language corpus data. In Calzolari, N., et al., editors, *Proceedings of the 10th International Conference on Language Resources and Evaluation (LREC 2016)*, pages 3303–3306, Portorož, Slovenia. ELRA.

Bubela, T., Nisbet, M. C., Borchelt, R., Brunger, F., Critchley, C., Einsiedel, E., Geller, G., Gupta, A., Hampel, J., Hyde-Lay, R., et al. (2009). Science communication reconsidered. *Nature Biotechnology*, 27(6):514–518. DOI: 10.1038/nbt0609-514.

Bultitude, K. (2011). The why and how of science communication. In Rosulek, P., editor, *Science Communication*. European Commission, Pilsen.

Carroll, S. R., Garba, I., Figueroa-Rodríguez, O. L., Holbrook, J., Lovett, R., Materechera, S., Parsons, M., Raseroka, K., Rodriguez-Lonebear, D., Rowe, R., et al. (2020). The CARE principles for Indigenous data governance. *Data Science Journal*, 19(43):1–12. DOI: http://doi.org/10.5334/dsj-2020-043.

Fischhoff, B. and Scheufele, D. A. (2013). The science of science communication. *Proceedings of the National Academy of Sciences*, 110(Supplement 3):14031–14032. DOI: 10.1073/pnas.1312080110.

Hanke, T., Jahn, E., Wähl, S., Böse, O., and König, L. (2020a). SignHunter – a sign elicitation tool suitable for deaf events. In Efthimiou, E., et al., editors, *Proceedings of the LREC2020 9th Workshop on the Representation and Processing of Sign Languages*, pages 83–88, Marseille, France. ELRA.

Hanke, T., König, S., Konrad, R., Langer, G., Barbeito Rey-Geißler, P., Blanck, D., Goldschmidt, S., Hofmann, I., Hong, S.-E., Jeziorski, O., Kleyboldt, T., König, L., Matthes, S., Nishio, R., Rathmann, C., Salden, U., Wagner, S., and Worseck, S. (2020b). *MEINE DGS. Öffentliches Korpus der Deutschen Gebärdensprache, 3. Release*. Universität Hamburg, DOI: 10.25592/dgs.meinedgs-3.0.

Hanke, T., Schulder, M., Konrad, R., and Jahn, E. (2020c). Extending the Public DGS Corpus in size and depth. In Efthimiou, E., et al., editors, *Proceedings of the LREC2020 9th Workshop on the Representation and Processing of Sign Languages*, pages 75–82, Marseille, France. ELRA.

Harris, R., Holmes, H. M., and Mertens, D. M. (2009). Research ethics in sign language communities. *Sign Language Studies*, 9(2):104–131.

Isard, A. and Konrad, R. (2022). MY DGS – ANNIS: ANNIS and the Public DGS Corpus. In *Proceedings of the LREC2022 10th Workshop on the Representation and Processing of Sign Languages*, Marseille, France. European Language Resources Association (ELRA).

Jahn, E., Konrad, R., Langer, G., Wagner, S., and Hanke, T. (2018). Publishing DGS Corpus data: Different formats for different needs. In Bono, M., et al., editors, *Proceedings of the LREC2018 8th Workshop on the Representation and Processing of Sign Languages*, pages 83–90, Miyazaki, Japan. ELRA.

Konrad, R., Hanke, T., Langer, G., Blanck, D., Bleicken, J., Hofmann, I., Jeziorski, O., König, L., König, S., Nishio, R., Regen, A., Salden, U., Wagner, S., Worseck, S., Böse, O., Jahn, E., and Schulder, M. (2020a). *MY DGS – annotated. Public Corpus of German Sign Language, 3rd release*. Universität Hamburg, DOI: 10.25592/dgs.corpus-3.0.

Konrad, R., Hanke, T., Langer, G., König, S., König, L., Nishio, R., and Regen, A. (2020b). Public DGS Corpus: Annotation conventions. Project Note AP03-2018-01, Hamburg University, Hamburg, Germany. DOI: 10.25592/uhhfdm.822.

Krause, T. and Zeldes, A. (2016). ANNIS3: A new architecture for generic corpus query and visualization. *Digital Scholarship in the Humanities*, 31(1):118–139. DOI: 10.1093/llc/fqu057.

Müller, A., Hanke, T., Konrad, R., Langer, G., and Wähl, S. (2020). From dictionary to corpus and back again – linking heterogeneous language resources for DGS. In Efthimiou, E., et al., editors, *Proceedings of the LREC2020 9th Workshop on the Representation and Processing of Sign Languages*, pages 157–164, Marseille, France. ELRA.

Schulder, M. and Hanke, T. (2022). How to be FAIR when you CARE: The DGS Corpus as a case study of open science resources for minority languages. In *Proceedings of the 13th International Conference on Language Resources and Evaluation*, Marseille, France. European Language Resources Association (ELRA).

Weingart, P. and Guenther, L. (2016). Science communication and the issue of trust. *Journal of Science communication*, 15(5):C01. DOI: https://doi.org/10.22323/2.15050301.

Wilkinson, M. D., Dumontier, M., Aalbersberg, I. J., Appleton, G., Axton, M., Baak, A., Blomberg, N., Boiten, J.-W., da Silva Santos, L. B., Bourne, P. E., et al. (2016). The FAIR guiding principles for scientific data management and stewardship. *Scientific Data*, 3:160018. DOI: 10/bdd4.

Proceedings of the 10th Workshop on the Representation and Processing of Sign Languages (sign-lang@LREC 2022), pages 88–93
Language Resources and Evaluation Conference (LREC 2022), Marseille, 20-25 June 2022

MC-TRISLAN: A Large 3D Motion Capture Sign Language Data-set

Pavel Jedlička, Zdeněk Krňoul, Miloš Železný, and Luděk Müller
NTIS - New Technologies for the Information Society,
Faculty of Applied Sciences, University of West Bohemia
Univerzitní 8, 306 14 Pilsen, Czech Republic.
{jedlicka, zdkrnoul, zelezny, muller}@ntis.zcu.cz

Abstract

The new 3D motion capture data corpus expands the portfolio of existing language resources by a corpus of 18 hours of Czech sign language. This helps to alleviate the current problem, which is a critical lack of high quality data necessary for research and subsequent deployment of machine learning techniques in this area. We currently provide the largest collection of annotated sign language recordings acquired by state-of-the-art 3D human body recording technology for the successful future deployment in communication technologies, especially machine translation and sign language synthesis.

Keywords: Motion Capture, Sign Language, Human Body Pose

1. Introduction

Sign languages (SLs) are natural means of communication for deaf people. Hundreds of sign languages are used around the world today. Czech sign language (CSE) is one of sign languages in Europe and, in general, each country has one or more native sign languages (Timmermans, 2005).

Although significant progress has been made in recent years in the field of spoken language machine learning techniques, the field of SL processing struggles with a critical lack of high quality data needed for the successful application of these techniques. For comparison, WaveNet-based speech synthesis method has been trained on data set contained 10,000 utterances (about 14 hours of speech) of one professional male speaker (Vít et al., 2018). SL resources are scarce – they consist of small SL corpora usually designed for a specific domain such as linguistics or computer science. There are some motion capture data-sets for American Sign Language (ASL) and French Sign Language (Lu and Huenerfauth, 2010; Naert et al., 2017). The total recorded time of motion is up to 60 minutes in those data-sets. The situation is even worse for "small" languages like CSE.

There are techniques for the 3D reconstruction of human body pose/motion from RGB and depth images and this is a common approach for capturing human body movement (MMPose Contributors, 2020; Cao et al., 2017). Current SL data-sets are mostly video-based (Joze and Koller, 2019; Zelinka and Kanis, 2020). Although video is a natural way of capturing sign languages, these readily available data sources are ambiguous in the sense that they do not contain spatial (3D) information. For comparison SIGNUM, one of the largest video-based SL data-sets, contains approximately 55 hours of SL recordings (Koller et al., 2015), other example of large data-set is DGS-Corpus with more than 47 hours of SL recordings, see (Wolfe et al., 2022). On the contrary, one of the largest 3D motion capture data-sets contain only 60 minutes of SL recordings (Naert et al., 2017; Naert et al., 2020).

Motion capture technologies guarantee high precision recording of the signer's movements in 3D space at the cost of a more complex preparation phase compared to standard video recording. Optical marker-based motion capture has become the industry standard for capturing movement of the human body. One of the first publicly available scientific motion capture SL data-set was recorded in 2016, see (Benchiheub et al., 2016).

In (Jedlička et al., 2020), we collected the first 3D motion capture data-set for CSE, which covers the weather forecast domain. This data-set is rather limited in size and contains recordings of one signer only. 18 mocap simultaneously recording cameras were used to capture SL, which was our first step in the research towards a new concept of sign language capture in 3D. The total length of recordings was 42 minutes.

A large number of cameras eliminates the frequency of marker occlusions and thus the loss of measurements. However, this method turned out to be very time consuming and not suitable for large data and records from multiple markers. The negative aspect is its high complexity both in the recording and the post-processing phase. In principle, this approach does not allow us to get more data for a given price. Additionally, the occlusion issue is not resolved in this case. Occlusion has been shown to be a significant problem for hand markers in general, where hand poses in sign language are often in contact with each other or with the face.

In this work, We deliver a new recording protocol and a large 3D motion data-set collected using high precision optical marker-based motion capture system in order to extend the existing portfolio of language resources with Czech sign language (CSE) data. The contribution of our work can be summarized as follows:

- Proof of concept for large-scale motion capture recording by splitting hand-configuration and body recording;

- 3D motion capture protocol to cover wider domains, grammatical context and more signers. We assume proper data post-processing, annotation, and tools for data extraction from the collected data;

- The largest SL motion capture data-set of sign language consisting of recordings of continuous CSE phrases and a vocabulary of six native SL speakers from carefully selected domains, in total more than 18 hours. The data-set is available at *https://live.european-language-grid.eu/catalogue/corpus/18324*

2. Related Work

Recently, spoken language research is directed to machine learning algorithms, deep neural learning in particular. In the field of sign languages, common tasks are translation, speech recognition and synthesis (Zelinka and Kanis, 2020; Stoll et al., 2020; Gruber et al., 2021). The goal of sign language synthesis is to generate natural, natural, and intelligible video-utterances of SL based on methods capable of mimicking human SL's performance.

There are techniques developed for the pose estimation from the image or video, e.g. OpenPose (Cao et al., 2017) or MMpose (MMPose Contributors, 2020). There methods are marker-less with no restriction on the freedom of movement of the hands but the 3D precision is in principle lower than the actual 3D pose measuring provided by MoCap systems.

Some data-sets using different motion capture techniques were created in recent years (Lu and Huenerfauth, 2010; Naert et al., 2020; Jedlička et al., 2020). (Lu and Huenerfauth, 2010) recorded American SL using magnetic-based motion capture for hand and finger tracking. The evolution of motion capture data-sets collected in French SL is described in (Gibet, 2018). They recorded several MoCap data-sets in the last 15 years. All of them contain manual and non-manual components of SL.

The project HuGEx (2005) used the Vicon MoCap system in combination with Cybergloves for recording finger movements and for the body and the facial movements. The total recording time was 50 minutes. The Sign3D project ((Lefebvre-Albaret et al., 2013)) recorded the position of the body and hand with the same system in combination with the eye gaze recorded with a head-mounted oculomotor (MocapLab MLab 50-W). However, it contains 10 minutes of recorded data only. More recently in (Naert et al., 2020), the authors collected the LSF-ANIMAL corpus that composed of captured isolated signs and full sentences that can be used both to study LSF features and to generate new signs and utterances.

In contrast, we assume that we can reconstruct the hand pose and other SL components with only one technique and with minimal restrictions on signers' body movement. We rather follow SignCom ((Gibet et al., 2011)) and we use the Vicon MoCap system to record 3D pose with limited markers per hand and face. We provide a protocol suitable for acquiring large volumes of SL data using the motion capture system.

There is a continual need for a large amount of data to utilize machine learning techniques. Although the quality and size of data-sets are increasing, there is still a lack of such data. The usual size of those data-sets is between 10 and 60 minutes of recording time.

3. Objective

The aim of this research is to create a new large data-set of sign language suitable for sign language synthesis based on machine learning techniques. 3D data are essential for synthesizing new, natural, and realistic utterances of a data driven avatar (Naert et al., 2020). The problem of synthesis lies in modifying and connecting captured movements. One of the main problems is how to capture a shape and motion of human body in 3D space with sufficient precision.

By fulfilling this goal we gain the opportunity to work on large scale data. In particular, data-set contains occurrences of signs and grammar structures in natural context. This is beneficial for analysis of movement, linguistics and other phenomena in SLs. We will use the data as a ground truth for design, observations, and evaluation for new algorithms for SL synthesis.

Movement of human body during sign language utterances is very specific and complex. The movements of hands, and body, as well as facial expressions are made simultaneously in SL utterances. We assume that continuous speech is most natural manifestation of sign language. So we are solving a problem where complex movements demands specific and elaborate setup and on the other hand large volume of data is needed. Our approach to data-set acquisition attempts to meet both demands.

4. Data-set MC-TRISLAN

We have done experiments with different setups and protocols in order to find one suitable for recording large scale of motion capture data of sign language. As a result we have made the MC-TRISLAN data-set.

4.1. Methods and Experiment

The recording is divided into two separate parts, according to our protocol: One is the recording of a body movement with a simplified hand and face model, and the other one being highly detailed hand pose and movement. This division allows us to use different motion capture system settings for both recordings, each using simpler settings and therefore a reduced number of cameras. It also allows faster motion capture system preparation and fine tuning for a new SL speaker.

4.1.1. Recording Setup

We used our VICON motion capture system based on infrared high-speed cameras T-20. This system uses passive retro-reflexive markers placed on special suit or directly on body. The choice of marker sizes and their exact locations on the body of the SL speaker is crucial for precise measurement of the movement during recording. The resulting movement is modeled as a trajectories of a skeleton, which is composed of bones representing measured rigid body parts. The recording was made using 8 cameras set to frame-rate of 100 fps. This frame-rate is a compromise between need for capture SL dynamics with enough precision and increasing noise levels. Recording setup was extended with standard RGB camera for reference video at 25 fps, see Figure 3.

The cameras placement and speaker preparation depends on the type of recording. For whole body movement, we used standard VICON 3-finger body setup. The markers are located on the poles of the axis of rotation of the joints of the skeleton. Each body part is defined by at least 4 markers except the fingertips, see Fig. 1. Total number of markers tracked in full body recording is 59. Tracked fingertips are the thumb, index and pinky. The fingertips are not well defined and, in general, lost tracking can not be corrected or traced from another marker. We used 7 markers for the recording of non-manual component. This setup is used for the whole body recording of continuous speech and dictionary items, particularly for capturing all three parts at once: hand configuration (HC), position and non-manual component (Sandler and Lillo-Martin, 2006).

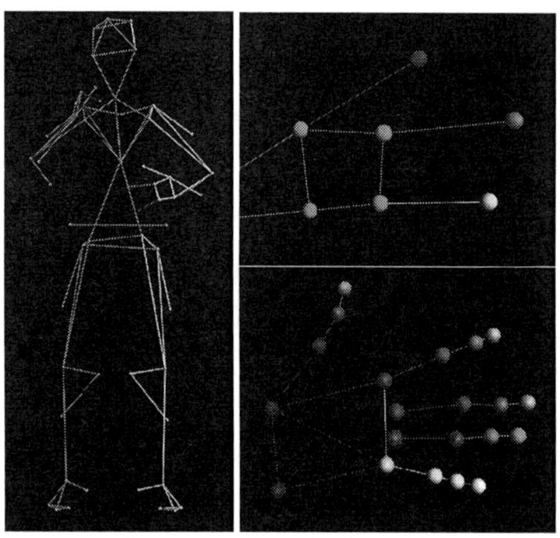

Figure 1: The marker-setups for body on left and hand pose on right. The body pose marker-setup integrates simple hand pose by 7 markers (right up). High detailed hand poses are reconstructed from hand marker-setup data (right down).

We used 21 marker setup developed specifically for hand configuration (HC) recording. There is a set of HC used in a vocabulary extended with some common HCs, see Fig. 2. HCs are recorded separately with limited arm movement. One HC is recorded at one time and the movement of the recording hand is from a relaxed position to the given HC and then back to a relaxed pose. Data are recorded for dominant hand only, we use those data also for non-dominant hand. The exact position of markers on the hand is very important for the 3D reconstruction of the hand skeleton. From the point of view of capturing all degrees of freedom, the location of the markers is not unified (Hoyet et al., 2012).

Our hand marker setup is based on our previous research (Jedlička et al., 2020). We are newly proposing a small marker for each finger joint, which is placed on the top of the hand to prevent the hand from moving as much as possible during signing. Additionally, we put one marker for each fingertip and two markers on the wrist. We used a total of 21 hemispherical markers with 4 mm diameter. The markers were attached to a skin with a double-sided adhesive tape. Note, that 7 of these markers are at the same positions as markers in the whole body setup, and therefore, can be used as reference for data composition. Motion capture cameras are placed closer to the speaker, 2 from above and 2 from below the speaker's hand, the other 4 surround the hand from the sides.

4.1.2. Data-set Design and Data Acquisition

To select suitable domains and to estimate the amount of SL recordings to cover them, we cooperated with CSE linguists, translators and native speakers. The data-set design was done so that it contains sufficient informational data, and including multiple instances of the same signs in different grammar contexts. All recordings were made twice. The possibility to choose between instances of the same movement segment is beneficial for the fine setup of synthesis (Gibet, 2018). We limited the linguistic domain to two specific fields to reduce the number of unique signs. Weather forecasts and animal descriptions from the zoological garden domain were selected by CSE linguists (Dictio Contributors, 2022), see Table 1. Linguists have provided us a list of all HCs that occur in these domains, see Figure 2. The data-set is collected from 6 native CSE speakers, who differ in body size, age, and gender.

The data-set was collected during 37 recording sessions, the recording team of each session consisted of our recording staff, an SL speaker and one or more SL quality control expert(s). The sessions were divided into two separate tasks. The first task was to record a complete set of hand configurations (HCs) that are used in the selected topics. The signer is obligated to perform each HC separately. The movement starts from the relaxed HC, then changes to the given HC and back to the relaxed HC.

The second task was to record whole body movement

Topic	Weather forecast	ZOO tour
Structure	36 individual forecasts (one forecast ~30 sec continuous speech)	20 different animals - Structured description
Vocabulary Type	diversity - cover forecast topic (3 forecasts per month)	Large sample of letters (Latin names - finger-spelling) (extensible)
Vocabulary Size	Limited (> 300 signs), Large sample of numbers	Limited (> 800 signs)
Data Characteristic	Multiple instances of the same sign in different context (frequent signs more than 20 repetitions)	Repetition of similar sign groups (biotope, food, lifespan, ...)

Table 1: Topics, vocabulary and data characteristic of MC-TRISLAN data-set.

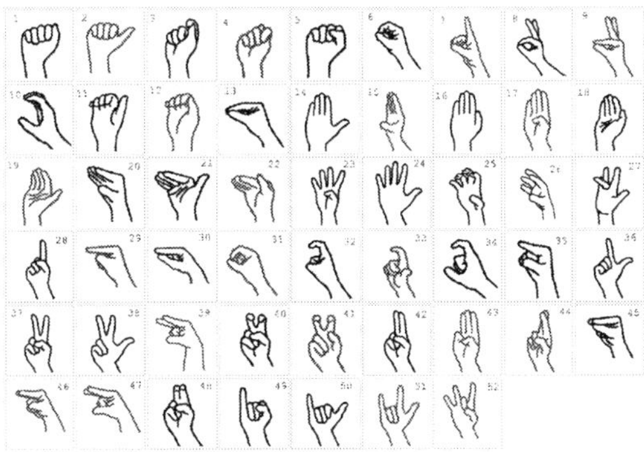

Figure 2: The list of all hand configurations.

using the 3-finger setup. This task consisted of isolated signs for vocabulary and continuous SL utterances. For each topic, the first signer was carefully selected so that his entries would serve as a template for the other signers' entries. These signers were informed of the required recorded content in advance by watching a reference video. Thus the content was the same for all signers. Instructions for each task were displayed on a large screen in front of the signer. Signers could choose whether they wanted a text template, a video or their combination. But signers had always been instructed to make the most natural and realistic sign language production possible. The signer was obliged to perform the given utterance in such a way that he started from the T-position, shifted to the rest position, performed the given utterance and finally returned through the rest position to the T-position.

4.1.3. Data Annotation

An essential step is the annotation of captured SL utterances. We used a reference video, that is time-synchronised manually and the ELAN tool, see Figure 3. The annotation of a sign is done by SL experts giving the information of the sign's meaning (gloss), and the right and the left HC. If the sign consists of more than one defined HC, the HC are annotated as a set of HC. Both the activities are very laborious and time-consuming. To successfully complete this task, we are involving several trained annotators who worked in parallel.

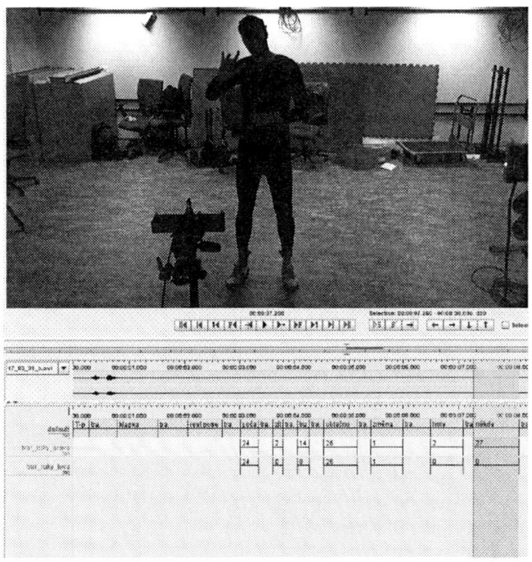

Figure 3: Example of annotation work in ELAN, we use reference video annotated by SL experts.

4.1.4. Data Post-processing

Post-processing consists of data-cleaning, whole-body motion reconstruction, and data-solving. Data-cleaning removes noise and fills gaps in the raw 3D data caused by frequent mutual occlusions of markers during signing, and other noise caused by the environment. Motion reconstruction recalculates the position of the marks on the motion of the skeletal model using a data solver.

The data of both setups was post-processed. For HC setup, we reconstructed small gaps by the interpolation standard technique as long as the trajectory was simple enough. Note, that the recording speed is 100 fps, which is fast enough to contain minimal changes in trajectory between frames. We used semi-automatic 3D reconstruction of marker trajectories and labeling, and manual cleaning of swaps and gaps. For the body parts defined by at least four markers, filling in the trajectories of the marker is well automatised because at least three points are enough to define the missing position. The body marker setup uses only one marker per fingertip and some larger gaps caused by more complex self-occlusions of body parts can obscure three or more markers in one rigid segment. Post-processing in those cases is more complicated and gaps must be filled in manually.

The full SL body movement is achieved as a composition of the body movement and corresponding data of the HCs setup. For this purpose, the annotation of HCs provides us with temporal segmentation of the recordings, see Figure 3. Thus the 3-fingertip motion in the segment provides information about dynamic changes during the performance of the HC in a particular data frame.

The middle part of the segment is always completed from reference data according to the HC(s) assigned by the annotation for each hand. We captured full fingers motion only for the transition of the given HC from and to the neutral HC. Thus, for the reconstruction of the other frames of the segment, the nearest hand pose with the smallest reconstruction error (1) were used. We consider only those frames that contain the trajectory of fingertips and where the error is below a given threshold τ. The remaining frames will have gaps in the final trajectories of high detailed hand pose.

We solved the above problem as point-set alignment via Procrustes analysis that arises especially in tasks like 3D point cloud data registration. The rigid transformation of two sets of points on top of each other minimises the total distance in 3D between the corresponding markers (Arun et al., 1987). Since the data is noisy, it minimises the least-squares error:

$$err_f = \sum_{i=1}^{N} ||R_f M_f^i + t_f - M_{rf}^i||, \tag{1}$$

where M_f and M_{rf} are current and reference frame(s) respectively as a set of N 3D points with known correspondences, R_f is the rotation matrix and t_f the translation vector for given frame f. We assume $3 \leq N \leq 7$ points of the 3-fingers setup, see Figure 1. We aligned only the rotation and translation because the 3D the transformation preserves the shape and size (same HC and SL speaker). For the non-dominant hand, we mirrored the reference frame(s) recorded for dominant hand only.

The last step of the post-processing is motion data-solving. It is a process of reconstruction of the 3D motion of the skeleton from the 3D marker trajectories. For this purpose, we use the VICON software. The skeleton is well defined to directly control the SL avatar animation or handle animation retargeting.

4.2. Discussion

The key factor for optical motion capture is the correct identification of each trajectory in 3D, so-called labeling. We chose the marker setup, that reduces the amount of occlusions and marker swaps. A lower marker count placed on the hands and a reduced number of facial markers reduce significantly the labeling complexity. This is crucial for processing large volume of data. In order to complement the data, detailed HC recording is done. This detailed HC recording uses a high number of markers that provide precise information at the cost of demanding manual post-processing. HC recording is done only once for each SL speaker and does not increase up with the number of recorded signs.

5. Conclusion

SLs are not sufficiently supported through technologies and have only fragmented, weak, or no support at all. We propose a new protocol that solves the problem of complex data-set creation and provides a procedure for obtaining sufficient diversity of SL speakers, grammar and character contexts. In contrast to the all-in-one recording setup, the body movement is recorded separately from the highly detailed recording of hand poses. This separation reduces the complexity of camera setup and data during post-processing, making SL recording more flexible and making adjustments for new SL speakers or large data easier. Data processing procedures are an integral part of the experiment. The protocol therefore provides complete instructions for the necessary post-processing and annotation.

As result, a professionally created SL data-set via state-of-the-art 3D motion capture technology is introduced. The data-set provides data for the wider research community. We have recorded 18 hours of sign language and recorded six different speakers for two different domains. This makes this data-set more versatile and useful in many different areas of research, such as other linguistic and SL analysis.

We assume our results will be beneficial for other applications such as next generation SL synthesis that uses a 3D animated avatar for natural human movement reproduction or SL analysis or gesture recognition and classification in general.

6. Acknowledgements

We want to thank staff of Institute of Special Education Studies, Palacký University Olomouc, mainly J. Langer, P. Kučera and J. Grohmannová for their cooperation in signers selection, data elicitation and linguistics support. The work described in this article has received funding from the EU project European Language Grid as one of its pilot projects and the Ministry of Education, Youth and Sports of the Czech Republic, Project No. LM2018101 LINDAT/CLARIAH-CZ. The ELG project has received funding from the European Union's Horizon 2020 research and innovation programme under grant agreement no. 825627.

7. Bibliographical references

Arun, K. S., Huang, T. S., and Blostein, S. D. (1987). Least-squares fitting of two 3-d point sets. *IEEE Transactions on Pattern Analysis and Machine Intelligence*, PAMI-9(5):698–700.

Benchiheub, M., Berret, B., and Braffort, A. (2016). Collecting and Analysing a Motion-Capture Corpus of French Sign Language. In *Workshop on the Representation and Processing of Sign Languages*, pages 7–12, Portoroz, Slovenia, January.

Cao, Z., Simon, T., Wei, S., and Sheikh, Y. (2017). Realtime multi-person 2d pose estimation using part affinity fields. In *2017 IEEE Conference on Computer Vision and Pattern Recognition (CVPR)*, pages 1302–1310.

Dictio Contributors. (2022). Online monolingual dictionary. `https://www.dictio.info/about?lang=en`.

Gibet, S., Courty, N., Duarte, K., and Le Naour, T. (2011). The SignCom System for Data-Driven Animation of Interactive Virtual Signers : Methodology and Evaluation. *ACM Transactions on Interactive Intelligent Systems* , 1(1):6.

Gibet, S. (2018). Building French Sign Language Motion Capture Corpora for Signing Avatars. In *Workshop on the Representation and Processing of Sign Languages: Involving the Language Community, LREC 2018*, pages 53–58, Miyazaki, Japan, May.

Gruber, I., Krňoul, Z., Hrúz, M., Kanis, J., and Boháček, M. (2021). Mutual support of data modalities in the task of sign language recognition. In *Proceedings of the IEEE/CVF Conference on Computer Vision and Pattern Recognition (CVPR) Workshops*, pages 3424–3433, June.

Hoyet, L., Ryall, K., McDonnell, R., and O'Sullivan, C. (2012). Sleight of hand: Perception of finger motion from reduced marker sets. In *Proceedings of the ACM SIGGRAPH Symposium on Interactive 3D Graphics and Games*, I3D '12, page 79–86, New York, NY, USA. Association for Computing Machinery.

Jedlička, P., Krňoul, Z., Kanis, J., and Železný, M. (2020). Sign language motion capture dataset for data-driven synthesis. In E. Efthimiou, et al., editors, *Proceedings of the LREC2020 9th Workshop on the Representation and Processing of Sign Languages*, pages 101–106, Marseille, France, May. European Language Resources Association (ELRA).

Joze, H. R. V. and Koller, O. (2019). Ms-asl: A large-scale data set and benchmark for understanding american sign language. In *30th British Machine Vision Conference 2019, BMVC 2019, Cardiff, UK, September 9-12, 2019*, page 100. BMVA Press.

Koller, O., Forster, J., and Ney, H. (2015). Continuous sign language recognition: Towards large vocabulary statistical recognition systems handling multiple signers. *Computer Vision and Image Understanding*, 141:108–125.

Lefebvre-Albaret, F., Gibet, S., Turki, A., Hamon, L., and Brun, R. (2013). Overview of the Sign3D Project High-fidelity 3D recording, indexing and editing of French Sign Language content. In *Third International Symposium on Sign Language Translation and Avatar Technology (SLTAT) 2013*, Chicago, United States, October.

Lu, P. and Huenerfauth, M. (2010). Collecting a motion-capture corpus of american sign language for data-driven generation research. In *Proceedings of the NAACL HLT 2010 Workshop on Speech and Language Processing for Assistive Technologies*, pages 89–97. Association for Computational Linguistics.

MMPose Contributors. (2020). OpenMMLab Pose Estimation Toolbox and Benchmark. `https://github.com/open-mmlab/mmpose`.

Naert, L., Larboulette, C., and Gibet, S. (2017). Coarticulation analysis for sign language synthesis. In Margherita Antona et al., editors, *Universal Access in Human–Computer Interaction. Designing Novel Interactions*, pages 55–75, Cham. Springer International Publishing.

Naert, L., Larboulette, C., and Gibet, S. (2020). LSF-ANIMAL: A Motion Capture Corpus in French Sign Language Designed for the Animation of Signing Avatars. In *LREC 2020*, Marseille, France, May.

Sandler, W. and Lillo-Martin, D. (2006). *Sign Language and Linguistic Universals*. Cambridge University Press (CUP), The Edinburgh Building, Cambridge CB2 2RU, UK, 02.

Stoll, S., Camgöz, N. C., Hadfield, S., and Bowden, R. (2020). Text2sign: Towards sign language production using neural machine translation and generative adversarial networks. *Int. J. Comput. Vis.*, 128(4):891–908.

Timmermans, N. (2005). *The Status of Sign Language in Europe (Integration of People with Disabilities*. Council of Europe Publications.

Vít, J., Hanzlíček, Z., and Matoušek, J. (2018). On the analysis of training data for wavenet-based speech synthesis. In *2018 IEEE International Conference on Acoustics, Speech and Signal Processing (ICASSP)*, pages 5684–5688.

Wolfe, R., McDonald, J. C., Hanke, T., Ebling, S., Van Landuyt, D., Picron, F., Krausneker, V., Efthimiou, E., Fotinea, E., and Braffort, A. (2022). Sign language avatars: A question of representation. *Information*, 13, April.

Zelinka, J. and Kanis, J. (2020). Neural sign language synthesis: Words are our glosses. In *Proceedings of the IEEE/CVF Winter Conference on Applications of Computer Vision (WACV)*, March.

Proceedings of the 10th Workshop on the Representation and Processing of Sign Languages (sign-lang@LREC 2022), pages 94–101
Language Resources and Evaluation Conference (LREC 2022), Marseille, 20-25 June 2022

A Machine Learning-based Segmentation Approach for Measuring Similarity Between Sign Languages

Tonni Das Jui, Gissella Bejarano, Pablo Rivas
Baylor University
1311 S 5th St, Waco, TX 76706
{tonni_jui1, gissella_bejaranonic, pablo_rivas}@baylor.edu

Abstract

Due to the lack of more variate, native and continuous datasets, sign languages are low-resources languages that can benefit from multilingualism in machine translation. In order to analyze the benefits of approaches like multilingualism, finding the similarity between sign languages can guide better matches and contributions between languages. However, calculating the similarity between sign languages again implies a laborious work to measure how close or distant signs are and their respective contexts. For that reason, we propose to support the lexical similarity measurement between sign languages through a video-segmentation-based machine learning model that will quantify this match among signs of different sign languages. Using a machine learning approach, the similarity measurement process can run more smoothly than a more manual approach. We use a pre-trained temporal segmentation model for British Sign Language (or BSL). We test it on three datasets, an American Sign Language (ASL) dataset, an Indian Sign Language (ISL), and an Australian Sign Language (or Auslan) dataset. We hypothesize that the percentage of segmented and recognized signs by this machine learning model can represent the percentage of overlap or similarity between British and the other three sign languages. In our ongoing work, we evaluate three metrics considering Swadesh's and Woodward's list and their synonyms. We found that our intermediate-strict metric coincides with a more classical analysis of the similarity between British and American Sign Language, as well as with the classical low measurement between Indian and British sign languages. On the other hand, our similarity measurement between British and Australian Sign language holds for part of the Australian Sign Language and not the whole data sample.

Keywords: Sign language, Similarity, Machine learning, Segmentation model

1. Introduction

Measuring the similarity of sign languages can enhance research on genealogical, social, and other relations between different signed languages and regions. Besides, it can help understand Deaf culture, origins, and evolution. As reported in (Börstell et al., 2020), one of the largest sign language databases, Glottolog 4.1[1] (Hammarström et al., 2019) contains 194 sign languages datasets whose relations are not known or analyzed enough. Measuring similarity between specific sign languages can help reuse resources in a multilingualism approach, such as in machine translation (Bapna et al., 2019). We can bridge communication gaps between signers and speakers with properly annotated sign language datasets, scaled analysis, and machine learning technology.

Sign language similarity usually focuses on measuring lexical similarity across the signs, extracting features manually and under the subjectivity of the different experts. This approach can be very time-consuming due to the exhausting visual analysis that needs to be performed by a person. In that sense, more systematic approaches can support or complement this analysis by using machine learning methods. More specifically, sign languages similarity measurement is a process that can benefit from more computational approaches such as computer vision and natural language processing. Moreover, computer-vision approaches are preferred when working with sign language processing because they are less intrusive and less laborious. For example, most recent research is obtaining good results in sign language segmentation to find temporal boundaries of signs and recognition to identify a segment of a video with a corresponding sign (Renz et al., 2021a; Renz et al., 2021b; Bull et al., 2021; Varol et al., 2021; Camgoz et al., 2020).

Our work proposes to use a segmentation model to measure the sign languages similarity. For that goal, we use a pre-trained segmentation model in one sign language, such as BSL (Cormier and Fenlon, 2014; Fenlon et al., 2011), and measure how well it can segment and recognize signs in a second sign language. We evaluate different strict-level metrics, such as raw or exact match and match, considering synonyms. We use the vocabulary provided in Swadesh's list (Swadesh, 1971), and Woodward's list (Woodward, 2000) to compare to previous and future work. Our results show relative values to the previously-reported classical similarity-measure method comparing BSL to ASL and ISL. On the other hand, even when our similarity measure between BSL and AUSLAN categorizes them as the languages of the same family, the exact value is not close to the reported classical measurement when looking at the entire sample. When analyzed by the Australian region, our calculations are closer to the classical measure in the Melbourne sample. We have organized our paper as follows. In section 2, we review the background of simi-

[1]https://github.com/glottolog/glottolog

larity measures between languages and current similarity measurements between sign languages. In section 3, we describe our datasets. We provide more details of our proposed use of a video-based machine learning model to measure similarity in section 4.1 and the calculation and analysis of the metrics in section 4.2. Later in section 5, we present results and similarity analysis.

2. Background for Sign Language Similarity

As mentioned in (Mathur and Napoli, 2011), many factors have an effect on similarities and dissimilarities across different sign languages. For this reason sign language similarity analysis often provides new information that helps linguists to study sign languages. For example, in spite of USA and UK sharing English as their spoken language, ASL is closer to French Sign Language (usually abbreviated as LSF) than to BSL (Cagle, 2010; Brooks, 2018; Mathur and Napoli, 2011). The factors that influence sign languages, can be geographic or historic ones (Cheek et al., 2002). Recent methods measure sign language similarity from a lexicostatistics perspective (Yu et al., 2018; Börstell et al., 2020). These four features are usually considered to measure similarity of signs: hand shape, location, movement, and palm orientation. Besides these features, it is worth to notice other cases of similarity. For example, signs may or may not encode the same meanings in different sign languages. For example, as reported by (Börstell et al., 2020), the NGT (Sign Language of the Netherlands) sign WAAR-A ('where') is identical to the ASL sign WHAT, while the sign WAT-A ('what') is identical to the ASL sign WHERE. This form overlap may produce cross-linguistic mismatch.

Language similarity is usually measured by the Swadesh method, which started being a list of 225 words (Swadesh, 1952) and ended up being a list of 100 universally used meanings (Swadesh, 1971). Initially, a similar process was followed to measure the similarity between a pair of sign languages. However, (Woodward, 2000) considered Swadesh's method an overestimation of the similarity measure. As mentioned by (Yu et al., 2018), Woodward highlights that the use of pointing for signs, such as pronouns and body parts, can be misleading. Woodward list was developed from swadesh list in (Woodward, 1978) but then modified to a list of 100 words (Woodward, 2000). Other work compares the similarity overlap obtained from a lexical database of 50 signs and the Swadesh list (Minton-Ryan et al., 2019). For instance, (McKee and Kennedy, 2000) reported similarity measures in three categories: identical (match in the four features), related but different (differ only in one feature), and completely different considering swadesh list. They reported 25% and 77% of identical similarity of between BSL-ASL and BSL-Auslan, respectively, and 31% and 87% including related-but-different. Similarity measures between 12% and 36% are considered families of a stock; between 36% and 81% make two sign languages of the same family, while the overlap of larger than 81% makes them dialects of the same sign language. These ranges were proposed in (Crowley and Bowern, 2010). Other previous work uses computational and more systematic approaches to measure similarity and intelligibility between and within sign languages. The work in (Hildebrandt and Corina, 2002) measures the similarity of different signs within the same sign language by asking native and hearing subjects. (Brentari et al., 2020) analyzes properties such as marking agency and number in four sign languages for their cross-linguistic similarities. (Sáfár et al., 2015) evaluates the mutual intelligibility through genre among three sign languages and the benefit of mouthing to measure the effect of the overlap between the spoken languages.

Some automatized methods include a comparison between finger-spelling only (Kishore et al., 2017) and automatic distance measures such as Dynamic Time Warping (DTW) on videos over the four previously mentioned features (Wang et al., 2014). Machine learning models for recognition, segmentation, and translation can contribute to analyzing larger corpora and with more detail. Moreover, we estimate that they would become a powerful tool to support similarity analysis of languages. More standardized and multi-sign language datasets are needed to approach these tasks.

3. Datasets and Preprocessing

In this section we describe our datasets and preprocessing methods. For ASL and Auslan, we found existing dataset. However, for ISL, we downloaded Youtube videos and match them with their transcripts. We use the python library moviepy to segment the videos according to their annotations per sentence. For testing the similarity with BSL (Schembri et al., 2013; Fenlon et al., 2011), we analyzed ASL, Auslan and ISL datasets. As we do not perform any preprocessing step for BSL, we provide details about it in section 4

3.1. ASL

We used How2Sign [2] (Duarte et al., 2021), a large-scale multi-modal and multi-view continuous American Sign Language dataset. It originally had significantly large training, testing, and validation datasets each consisting of video files and ground-truth annotation files. We work with its test set where the video files have multiple sentences in 24 fps.

In the annotation file of large-scale ASL, sentence-wise time boundary was available for each video. We represent the duration distribution of sentences in Figure 1. We sample 100 sentences that last between 1 second and 6 seconds. Along with their respective annotation or English translation, this became our final ASL dataset. We converted the video files into 25fps as 25fps was the required rate of Renz's model. There

[2] https://how2sign.github.io/

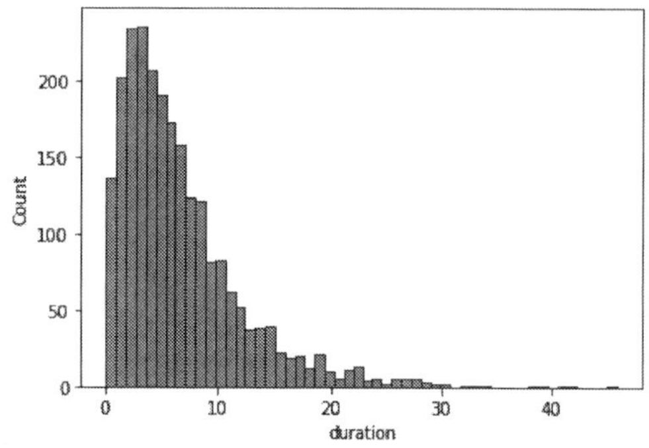

Figure 1: Duration of each sentences in seconds in x axis and Number of sentences in y axis. The majority of the sentences had no more than 10 seconds and there were no more than 100 sentences having length larger than 20 seconds.

are a total of 548 tokens (including repetition of some signs or tokens in different sentences) in the sample we took from ASL testing dataset for our experiment.

3.2. Auslan

We collected videos and their annotations in EAF files from Auslan corpus[3] mentioned in (Johnston and Schembri, 2006). The annotation files provided several tiers such as FreeTransl, LitTransl, Comments-Linzi, CLUwithinCLU etc. However, some of them were for isolated signs and some of them were for sentences. FreeTransl and LitTransl were for sentences and we took the datasets that had translations of LitTransl tier. We refined our collection criteria to be within the area of Melbourne (1 large video file containing 21 sentences), Sydney (1 large video file containing 31 sentences) and Northern Australia (3 large video files containing 66 sentences) from their collection of endangered Australian Sign Language. Similarly to ASL, we extracted a total of 118 sentences in new video files of 25 fps along with their corresponding English sentence translation in a ground-truth annotation file. There were total of 1186 tokens, including repetitions. For example, in these two sentences: "He ran. Then she ran", 5 signs) tokens are counted.

3.3. ISL

We extracted 50 video files in 30 fps from a Indian Sign Language (ISL) tutorial along with their corresponding ground-truth annotation file (was available in English translation) from (CADREE, 2020). The tutorial was in English whereas the sign representation is in ISL. There were total of 112 tokens, including repetition of some tokens in different sentences. We converted the video files to 25 fps. The process that we followed to measure the classical similarity score of ISL with BSL is addressed in Section 5.

[3]http://hdl.handle.net/2196/00-0000-0000-0000-D7CF-8

4. ML-based Segmentation Model for Similarity

We estimate the similarity by counting the number of recognized signs of one sign language that the segmentation model found even when pre-trained in another sign language. In other words, we interpret the test accuracy as the overlap between these two sign languages. This section explains the sign-segmentation model and our proposed evaluation metrics for sign language similarity analysis.

4.1. Segmentation Model

The temporal segmentation process of signs is a costly process that needs expert annotators to distinguish the boundaries or start and end of each sign in a semantic unit. Motivated by this, (Renz et al., 2021a) presents a 3D multi-stage temporal convolutional network trained as binary classification to determine if each frame is in a boundary or in a sign segment. To get the sign boundaries, they use a very well known action recognition model, I3D, to get spatio-temporal features. These spatio-temporal features are processed with a multi-stage temporal convolutional network. A classification layer on top of this feature vector generates the sign class probabilities.

Renz *et al.* propose a segmentation model trained on two datasets, BSLCorpus and PHOENIX14 (DGS) German Sign Language and tested in those 2 and BSL-1K. We take this model pretrained with BSLCorpus (Fenlon et al., 2011) learned weights. BSLCorpus is a BSL linguistic corpus that provides various types of manual annotations, and a portion of it carries individual signs with their sign categories and temporal boundaries. The BSLCorpus dataset consists of videos of 4.8 hours. The sign classification procedure followed numerous rules, including allocating lexical variations of the same word to the same class and selecting classes with less than 10 occurrences. Merging the categories for constructing a generalized training dataset focuses on priority for dominant hand. This work provides code and a pretrained model[4] in BSL that we use to test in ASL, Auslan and ISL.

They explain their results with two metrics mF1B and mF1S, which are calculated based on the correct identification of boundary positions and extent of the sign segments, respectively. They defined *boundary* as a series of the frames labeled with value of 1. Consequently frames of a sign segment are labeled with value of 0. To measure correct segment identification they work with two thresholds. One establishes the maximum distance between the middle of the ground-truth boundary and the middle of the predicted boundary. On the other hand, they count as a correct identified sign segment the value of IoU (intersection over union) of the ground-truth and predicted sign segments. Although they reach values of 68.68 and 47.71 in mF1B

[4]https://github.com/RenzKa/sign-segmentation

and mF1S, these metrics mainly focus on lengths and positions and not in the recognition of the class or sign. Moreover, they mention that semantic class labels were not fundamental to achieve good segmentation performance. From our understanding, they also used a pre-trained model on sign language recognition. Up to date this paper is written, we were not able to access details on the accuracy of the sign language recognition model. However, we hypothesise they rely on some of the most advanced sign language recognition models looking at their collaborators an their previous work.

4.2. Evaluation Metrics

To measure the similarity of two sign languages, dataset-A and dataset-B, we train or use a pre-trained model on dataset-A. The input for this model is a video of a sequence of signs and the prediction is the written or annotated signs, in a sequence as well. Then, we test this model in dataset-B and compare the prediction of sequence signs to the ground-thruth annotation. In our case, the segmentation model is trained on BSL and we will test the model for ASL, Auslan and ISL to measure the similarity between them and BSL. We represent the similarity between ground-truth annotation (part of our dataset) and the predicted-annotation (model's output) using the 3-metric measurement system with different level of strictness: EXACT_MATCH, MATCH_SYNG, MATCH_SYNGP.

```
00 : 00 : 00,312 −− > 00 : 00 : 00,815
let

00 : 00 : 01,135 −− > 00 : 00 : 01,492
forget

00 : 00 : 01,535 − − > 00 : 00 : 01,998
emotion
```

Figure 2: **The ground truth-annotation files:** These files have signs of a sentence with their corresponding boundaries.

In Figure 2 and 3, we show some examples of how the ground-truth and the prediction annotation files look like. In Figure 2, the single file (of a sentence) contains a total of three signs (after filtering stop words such as " 's", "an", "the") and the line before the sign contains the time boundaries of that single sign. The first and last boundaries of the file represent a single sentence's time boundary. We represent the corresponding prediction-annotation file for that ground-truth annotation file in Figure 3. The "WEBVTT" writing on top of the file represents that these files are in .vtt extensions. We get these files by testing the input video files (containing one sentence each) on the pre-trained sign segmentation model in BSL.

```
WEBVTT

00 : 00 : 00.440 − − > 00 : 00 : 00.920
EMPTY,DISCUSS,DIRTY,TIDY,LET,WANT

00 : 00 : 01.120 − − > 00 : 00 : 01.440
SLIP,LOW,NOT,GROW-UP,SURPRISE,SAY

00 : 00 : 01.525 − − > 00 : 00 : 01.980
LOW,SAY,ENOUGH,CLOTHES,PANIC,ANGRY
```

Figure 3: **The predicted-annotation files:** These files have multiple predicted signs of a sentence with their corresponding boundaries.

We work with continuous sign language and not isolated sign language. We look for any match throughout the sentence boundary instead of the sign boundary. According to EXACT_MATCH, there is one sign ("let") common in both files. For the sign "let" from Figure 2, "EMPTY,DISCUSS,DIRTY,TIDY,LET,WANT" are the predicted signs in Figure 3.

4.2.1. Exact Match

The ground truth annotation files have signs of a single sentence in them. We get the corresponding predicted signs in individual predicted-annotation files. Regardless of lexical ordering differences, the sentence boundaries of each prediction-annotation file should contain the matched sign if there were any matched sign between the ground-truth annotation file and prediction annotation file. For EXACT_MATCH, we first calculate the total signs throughout all the ground truth-annotation files that had any match in its corresponding prediction-annotation file. We then divide this number by the number of signs from the ground truth-annotation file. We finally represent the percentage of the ratio. Equation 1 below represents the formula to calculate metric1.

$$\text{EXACT\_MATCH} = \frac{n}{N} * 100, \quad (1)$$

where n is the number of groundtruth signs that matched with a sign from it's corresponding predicted-annotation sentence, and, N is the total number of groundtruth annotation signs.

4.2.2. Ground Truth Synonyms

MATCH_SYNG is similar to EXACT_MATCH, except we first get a set of synonyms for each word sign of ground truth-annotation files. Then, We look for the sign or any sign synonyms of that sign in the corresponding prediction-annotation files. For example, if there is a word "small" in the ground-truth annotation file, and we get a set of synonyms for that word as "{little, slight, tiny, minor}" and the prediction-annotation file contains "tiny", we calculate it as one match. Finally, we calculate the number of matches, and we divide this number by the total number of signs in the ground truth-annotation files and present its percentage. Equation 2 below represents the formula to calculate MATCH_SYNG. It is the procedure for MATCH_SYNG.

$$\text{MATCH\_SYNG} = \frac{n}{N} * 100, \quad (2)$$

where n is the number of groundtruth signs or any synonym of that sign that matched with a sign from it's corresponding predicted-annotation sentence, and, N is the total number of groundtruth annotation signs.

4.2.3. Ground Truth and Prediction Synonyms

For MATCH_SYNGP, along with considering the synonyms of ground-truth words, we also consider the synonyms of predicted words for matching. It is similar to MATCH_SYNG except that we also collect a set of synonyms for each word signs of prediction-annotation files and the synonyms of ground-truth annotation files' words. So, we look for the sign or any synonyms of a sign from ground-truth annotation files in the corresponding prediction-annotation files' words or any synonyms of that word. Finally, we calculate the number of matched signs considering the synonyms of both files. We divide this number by the number of original signs in the ground truth-annotation files and present its percentage. Equation 3 below represents the formula to calculate MATCH_SYNGP. It is the procedure for MATCH_SYNGP.

$$\text{MATCH\_SYNGP} = \frac{n}{N} * 100, \quad (3)$$

where, n is the number of groundtruth signs or any synonyms of a sign from ground-truth annotation files in the corresponding prediction-annotation files' words or any synonyms of that word that matched with a sign from it's corresponding predicted-annotation sentence, and, N is the total number of groundtruth annotation signs.

5. Experiments and Result Analysis

In this section we present the overlap of our datasets and the Woodward' and Swadesh's lists to have a better perspective and interpretation of our results. Although the two lists are traditionally identical (as woodward list was mainly developed from swadesh list), we included results for both the lists. The reason is that we compare our results to classical measurements that use swadesh list such as (McKee and Kennedy, 2000) for BSL-ASL and BSL-Auslan, and our manual calculation for ISL. However, more recent works use woodward list and there is more probability to compare our analysis with others future work. We present the values obtained for our 3-metric system and analyze which one gets closer results to classical similarity measurements. Finally we analyze Australian results by each region.

5.1. Signs from Swadesh list and Woodward list in our dataset

We have described in Section 1 that 100 signs of Swadesh list and 100 signs of Woodward list have the possibility of lexical similarity of any two sign language all over the world. The occurrences of signs from Swadesh list and Woodward list are around $1/10$ times of the total signs in our datasets (represented in Table 1).

SL	Sign entries	w_s	% Overlap	s_s	% Overlap
ASL	548	21	3%	43	7.85%
Auslan	1186	78	6.58%	156	13.15%
ISL	112	11	9.8%	10	8.93%

Table 1: Occurrences of words of sign language dataset in Woodward and Swadesh lists. Here, w_s = Occurrences of words from Woodward list # of times (including repetition in different sentences) and s_s = Occurrences of words from Swadesh list # of times (including repetition in different sentences.

In this table, total sign entries for ASL is 548. As we are working with continuous signs instead of isolated signs, it includes repetition of signs. Also, Renz's model tries to predict each sign in a sentence. So, we calculated total of how many signs we are putting as input to the Renz's model that it is trying to predict (excluding stop words such as 'a', 'the'), instead of total of how many unique words are there in the dataset. For example, from "The person is picking a pen from the other person's hand", total signs are 'person', 'is', 'pick', 'pen', 'from', 'other', 'person', 'hand' and the number is 8 (including the repetition of the word 'person', because the model is trying to that word twice). Sign entries column represent this count for all the datasets. Also, the overlap percent 3% means that from 548 signs altogether, 3% times a Woodward word appeared. The overlap column of Table 1 represents this count for all of our datasets.

5.2. Evaluation of metrics

We process three datasets, ASL, Auslan, ISL datasets for testing them on a pre-trained segmentation model in BSL. For each of these datasets, we have video files with their corresponding ground truth-annotation files and obtain the prediction-annotation files after testing. We provide a repository[5] for reproducible experiments. We analyze the similarities between ground truth-annotation files and predicted-annotations files with respect to EXACT_MATCH, MATCH_SYNG, MATCH_SYNGP. As the EXACT_MATCH does not consider any synonym sign matching, rather matches directly, we address it as stricter metric. On the other hand, MATCH_SYNGP considers synonyms of both ground-truth signs and predicted-signs which increases its possibility of getting a match per pair. Nevertheless,

[5]https://github.com/tonnidas/sign_similarity

	Woordward Similarity (in %)			Swadesh Similarity (in %)			Classic Similarity (in %)
Sign Language	EXACT_ MATCH	MATCH_ SYNG	MATCH_ SYNGP	EXACT_ MATCH	MATCH_ SYNG	MATCH_ SYNGP	
ASL	28.57	**33.33**	47.62	13.95	**23.26**	39.53	25
Auslan	23.72	**50**	57.69	34.62	**46.15**	48.72	77
ISL	0	**9.09**	9.09	0	**0**	0	7

Table 2: All numbers represent the percent for that column in that particular row. The first row after the header is for ASL dataset which matches with classical similarity measurement. There are focused two rows. First one is "Woodward similarity" that represents how many Woodward words occurrences found a match among all the Woodward words occurrences in datasets and the second one is "Swadesh similarity" which represents how many Swadesh occurrences found a match among all the Swadesh occurrences in datasets.

MATCH_SYNG is a semi-strict metric as we consider the synonyms of only ground-truth signs. Our results show that this metrics MATCH_SYNG is the more reasonable and correlated sign language similarity measurement compared to the classical method of similarity score. We compare our results with the scores of identical categorized from (McKee and Kennedy, 2000).

From Table 1, we can see that among the signs in ASL dataset, 3% of the time Woodward appeared and 7.85% of the time Swadesh words appeared. It indicates that great part of the dataset is out of Swadesh and Woodward's lists, and this also holds for both Auslan and ISL. In our Auslan dataset, the times of occurrences of Woodwards and Swadesh words were 78 and 156 respectively and in our ISL dataset, the times of occurrences of Woodwards and Swadesh words were only 11 and 10 respectively. In Table 2, we presented our results for the two datasets with respect to two lists of words: *Woodward similarity*' and *Swadesh similarity*'.

Our results show that, in general, metrics considering '*Swadesh Similarity*' are closer to the '*Classical Similarity*'. For BSL and ASL, we see in Table 2, our similarity metric, MATCH_SYNG, is 23.26% that supports the classical similarity score is 25%, which is close. It is a common assumption that ASL and BSL are similar as both American and British speak English. Nevertheless, ASL and BSL are independent sign languages, fully unique and distinct, and cannot be understood by each other's users.

We could not find a reported similarity score for ISL and BSL considering Swadesh list and Woodward list. Thus, we calculated the classical measurement value for ISL manually considering only the appeared Woodward words and Swadesh words following (McKee and Kennedy, 2000)'s method for the category of identical. This process considers four features: location, handshape, orientation and movement for each single isolated sign. If any all of the four features match with another sign of same meaning, that is considered identical. As our ISL dataset has low number of swadesh and woodward words (10 and 11), the similarity percentage according to the category of identical signs may not represent the similarity score for all 100 swadesh or woodward listed words. Thus, we considered calculating similarity score for all the features(location, handshape, orientation and movement) individually and put a score of 1 for all these features for a individual sign. If a feature is matched in both sign representations from different sign languages that has the same meaning, a score of 1 is calculated. If all four of the features are matched for a sign representation that a score of 4 is achieved. We calculate the percentage of scores by dividing the scores that is achieved with the scores that we would achieve if all of them were identical according to (McKee and Kennedy, 2000) and then we calculate the percentage.

We considered only the isolated words (manually picked) that appeared combined in both standardized Swadesh and Woodward words lists and count 10 and 11, respectively. Our calculations indicate that BSL-ISL has a 7% of classical similarity. We see in Table 2 that the similarity score between BSL and ISL, is around 9% for our MATCH_SYNG metric, which is close to the classical measurement.

Comparing BSL and Auslan, according to MATCH_SYNG, Woodward and Swadesh similarity is 50% and 46.15%, respectively. we can see that Auslan results for '*Woodward Similarity*' do not fully support its classical similarity measurement with value 77%. In spite of this result, some specific dialects of Auslan correlates better with the classical measurement as we will describe in Subsection 5.2.1.

5.2.1. Analysis of dialects in Auslan

The total proposed values of similarity measurement between BSL and Auslan in Swadesh's and Woodward's lists are distant from the classical measurement of 77%. In this section we provide a desegregated analysis on Auslan Sign Language variations and how our proposed metric calculated individually by dialect might reflect a closer relation with the classical measurement. According to (Wikipedia contributors, 2022), the reason behind this is that Sydney and Melbourne dialects of Auslan is more inclined to BSL where Northern Auslan dialect is more prone to be different than BSL. In our dataset, we collected 5 video files for a total of 3 groups dialects; 3 files from Northern (total of 654 signs), 1 file from Sydney (total of 230 signs) and another 1 file from Melbourne (total of 302 signs).

	MATCH_SYNG		(in %)
Sign Language	Swadesh Similarity	Woordward Similarity	Classic Similarity
Auslan (Northern1)	39.29	25	77
Auslan (Northern2)	45	28.57	
Auslan (Northern3)	27.59	23.53	
Total Of this 3 files	36.36	25	
Auslan (Melbourne)	55.17	75	77
Auslan (Sydney)	68	61.11	
Total Of this 2 files	63.29	68.42	

Table 3: Dis-aggregated analysis of Australian dialects

Table 3 represents the similarity rate according to MATCH_SYNG aggregated into two groups, the first one is of northern dialect and the second one is of Sydney and Melbourne (combined). We combined these two in one group as we also mentioned earlier that these two dialects may have roots in older dialectal differences from the United Kingdom. From this table, we can see that the northern group has a similarity of only 36.36% for Swadesh words and only 25% for Woodward words which is far away from the classical measurement of 77%. On the other hand, the combined Sydney and Melbourne group has a similarity of around 64% for Swadesh words and around 70% for Woodward words which is very close the classical measurement of 77%. This different results on regions and dialects of the Auslan dataset explains our results in Table 2. The sign language from northern dialects are not much similar to BSL while the Melbourne and Sydney dialects are similar which is why we can see that the overall combined Auslan results are not close to classical measurement in Table 2.

6. Conclusions and Future Work

This work proposes the similarity measurement of three pairs of sign languages: BSL vs. ASL, BSL vs. Auslan, and BSL vs. ISL. This measurement consists of interpreting the accuracy of a model trained in one sign language and tested in another as the overlap or similarity measurement. Our work emphasises on cross-linguistic matching where forms of the signs and also the assigned English gloss for the signs match. The ground truth-annotations are provided by the signers (according to ASL, Auslan, ISL dataset repositories). The segmentation model identify the temporal boundaries of each signs and then predicts the sign. As the model is pre-trained in BSL, it can only predict a sign from the testing set (ASL, Auslan, ISL) successfully when similar sign is present in BSL. So, our similarity percentage reflects what percent of signs in ASL or Auslan or ISL would a BSL signer recognize based on their lexical forms.

We introduce three accuracy metrics of different strict levels using exact matches and considering synonyms for only the ground truth and for both ground truth and predictions. We found that the intermediate-strictness metric using woodward and swadesh lists are the closer measurements to the classical one for ASL and Auslan; and woodward list for ISL.

This approach could help provide a more systematic way to measure the similarity between two sign languages. Our approach can measure the similarity of any pair of sign languages once we compare our findings with previous manually reported similarities. However, we compare our similarity metrics to previous classical measurements reported. We cannot guarantee that the same calculations were followed in all the sign languages on those classical calculations. On the other hand, we do not report more information about the BSL dataset and its overlap with Woodward's and Swadesh's lists.

Naturally, another suitable model to measure similarity can be a sign language recognition, which directly focuses on the sign. In reality, isolated signs may be influenced by other signs when used inside a sentence, and continuous signs make up the English word related to the sign.

7. Bibliographical References

Bapna, A., Cherry, C. A., Lepikhin, D. D., Foster, G., Krikun, M., Johnson, M., Chen, M., Ari, N., Firat, O., Macherey, W., Wu, Y., Cao, Y., and Chen, Z. (2019). Massively multilingual neural machine translation in the wild: Findings and challenges, July.

Börstell, C., Crasborn, O., and Whynot, L. (2020). Measuring lexical similarity across sign languages in Global signbank. In *Proceedings of the LREC2020 9th Workshop on the Representation and Processing of Sign Languages: Sign Language Resources in the Service of the Language Community, Technological Challenges and Application Perspectives*, pages 21–26, Marseille, France, May. European Language Resources Association (ELRA).

Brentari, D., Horton, L., and Goldin-Meadow, S. (2020). Crosslinguistic similarity and variation in the simultaneous morphology of sign languages. *The Linguistic Review*, 37(4):571–608.

Brooks, R. (2018). A Guide to the Different Types of Sign Language Around the World. `https://tinyurl.com/wex97vu6`, May. Accessed: 2022-05-20.

Bull, H., Afouras, T., Varol, G., Albanie, S., Momeni, L., and Zisserman, A. (2021). Aligning subtitles in sign language videos. In *Proceedings of the*

IEEE/CVF International Conference on Computer Vision (ICCV), pages 11552–11561, October.

CADREE. (2020). Simple Sentences in Indian Sign Language part 1| Simple Sentences of Everyday Usage in ISL. `https://tinyurl.com/429hzc85`, October.

Cagle, K. M. (2010). *Exploring the Ancestral Roots of American Sign Language: Lexical Borrowing from Cistercian Sign Language and French Sign Language*. ProQuest LLC.

Camgoz, N. C., Koller, O., Hadfield, S., and Bowden, R. (2020). Sign language transformers: Joint end-to-end sign language recognition and translation. In *Proceedings of the IEEE/CVF Conference on Computer Vision and Pattern Recognition (CVPR)*, June.

Cheek, C., Cheek, A., Knapp, H., and Rathmann, C. (2002). *Modality and structure in signed and spoken languages*. Cambridge University Press.

Cormier, K. and Fenlon, J. B. (2014). Bsl corpus annotation guidelines.

Crowley, T. and Bowern, C. (2010). *An Introduction to Historical Linguistics*. Oxford University Press.

Duarte, A., Palaskar, S., Ventura, L., Ghadiyaram, D., DeHaan, K., Metze, F., Torres, J., and Giro-i Nieto, X. (2021). How2sign: a large-scale multimodal dataset for continuous american sign language. In *Proceedings of the IEEE/CVF conference on computer vision and pattern recognition*, pages 2735–2744.

Fenlon, J., Stamp, R., Cooke, M., Rentelis, R., Hepner, A., Denmark, C., Parker, J., Wilkins, J., and Nelson, M. (2011). Bsl corpus project.

Hammarström, H., Forkel, R., and Haspelmath, M. (2019). glottolog/glottolog: Glottolog database 4.1, November. Type: dataset.

Hildebrandt, U. and Corina, D. (2002). Phonological similarity in american sign language. *Language and Cognitive Processes*, 17(6):593–612.

Johnston, T. and Schembri, A. (2006). Issues in the creation of a digital archive of a signed language. In *Sustainable data from digital fieldwork: Proceedings of the conference held at the University of Sydney*, pages 7–16.

Kishore, P., Kumar, D. A., Prasad, M., Sastry, A., and Kumar, E. K. (2017). similarity assessment of 30 world sign languages and exploring scope for a sign–to–sign translator. *International journal of control theory and applications*, 10:315–335.

Mathur, G. and Napoli, D. J. (2011). *Deaf around the world: The impact of language*. Oxford University Press.

McKee, D. and Kennedy, G. (2000). Lexical comparison of signs from american, australian, british and new zealand sign languages. *The signs of language revisited: An anthology to honor Ursula Bellugi and Edward Klima*, pages 49–76.

Minton-Ryan, C. A., Sorola, M., Brown, J., and Perez, P. R. (2019). A lexicostatistical study: Phonological similarity between american and malawi sign languages.

Renz, K., Stache, N. C., Albanie, S., and Varol, G. (2021a). Sign language segmentation with temporal convolutional networks. In *ICASSP 2021-2021 IEEE International Conference on Acoustics, Speech and Signal Processing (ICASSP)*, pages 2135–2139. IEEE.

Renz, K., Stache, N. C., Fox, N., Varol, G., and Albanie, S. (2021b). Sign segmentation with changepoint-modulated pseudo-labelling. *CoRR*, abs/2104.13817.

Schembri, A., Fenlon, J., Rentelis, R., Reynolds, S., and Cormier, K. (2013). Building the British Sign Language Corpus. *undefined*.

Swadesh, M. (1952). Lexico-statistic dating of prehistoric ethnic contacts: With special reference to north american indians and eskimos. *Proceedings of the American Philosophical Society*, 96(4):452–463.

Swadesh, M. (1971). *The origin and diversification of language*. Edited *post mortem* by Joel Sherzer. Chicago: Aldine.

Sáfár, A., Meurant, L., Haesenne, T., Nauta, E., Weerdt, D. D., and Ormel, E. (2015). Mutual intelligibility among the sign languages of belgium and the netherlands. *Linguistics*, 53(2):353–374.

Varol, G., Momeni, L., Albanie, S., Afouras, T., and Zisserman, A. (2021). Read and attend: Temporal localisation in sign language videos. In *Proceedings of the IEEE/CVF Conference on Computer Vision and Pattern Recognition*, pages 16857–16866.

Wang, L.-C., Wang, R., Kong, D.-H., and Yin, B.-C. (2014). Similarity assessment model for chinese sign language videos. *IEEE Transactions on Multimedia*, 16(3):751–761.

Wikipedia contributors. (2022). Auslan — Wikipedia, the free encyclopedia. `https://en.wikipedia.org/w/index.php?title=Auslan&oldid=1081044982`. [Online; accessed 25-April-2022].

Woodward, J. (1978). Historical bases of american sign language. *Understanding language through sign language research*, pages 333–348.

Woodward, J. (2000). Sign Languages and Sign Language Families in Thailand and Viet Nam. In Karen Emmorey et al., editors, *The Signs of Language Revisited*, pages 30–52. Psychology Press.

Yu, S., Geraci, C., and Abner, N. (2018). Sign languages and the online world online dictionaries & lexicostatistics. In *Proceedings of the Eleventh International Conference on Language Resources and Evaluation (LREC 2018)*.

Proceedings of the 10th Workshop on the Representation and Processing of Sign Languages (sign-lang@LREC 2022), pages 102–109
Language Resources and Evaluation Conference (LREC 2022), Marseille, 20-25 June 2022

The Sign Language Dataset Compendium: Creating an Overview of Digital Linguistic Resources

Maria Kopf, Marc Schulder, Thomas Hanke
Institute of German Sign Language and Communication of the Deaf
University of Hamburg, Germany
{maria.kopf, marc.schulder, thomas.hanke}@uni-hamburg.de

Abstract

One of the challenges that sign language researchers face is the identification of suitable language datasets, particularly for cross-lingual studies. There is no single source of information on what sign language corpora and lexical resources exist or how they compare. Instead, they have to be found through extensive literature review or word-of-mouth. The amount of information available on individual datasets can also vary widely and may be distributed across different publications, data repositories and (potentially defunct) project websites.

This article introduces the *Sign Language Dataset Compendium*, an extensive overview of linguistic resources for sign languages. It covers existing corpora and lexical resources, as well as commonly used data collection tasks. Special attention is paid to covering resources for many different languages from around the globe. All information is provided in a standardised format to make entries comparable, but kept flexible enough to allow for differences in content. The compendium is intended as a growing resource that will be updated regularly.

Keywords: Survey, Sign Languages, Corpora, Lexical Resources, Metadata

1. Introduction

Recent decades have seen a marked increase in the creation of digital resources for signed languages. This has opened up new possibilities for data driven research, such as computational and corpus linguistics, including work involving multiple languages or resources. Identifying and comparing suitable resources can still be a challenging task, however, requiring extensive literature review, web search and the use of personal contacts. The amount of information available on individual datasets can vary widely and may be distributed across different publications, data repositories and (potentially defunct) project websites. Documentation may also exist only in the local language(s) of the dataset creators, introducing additional barriers to international research. Once the information is gathered, different datasets may still be difficult to compare, as even basic meta-information like the size of a dataset may be reported in a variety of ways. These hurdles harm linguistic diversity as they discourage studies across multiple resources and favour the use of only the most well-known datasets.

To support researchers in their work, this paper introduces the **Sign Language Dataset Compendium**, an extensive overview of available digital datasets of signed languages. It covers both **corpora** and **lexical resources**, providing structured information and metadata, literature references, and pointers to where the data or more information can be obtained. It also provides an index of commonly used **corpus data collection tasks** to assist researchers in finding corpora with comparable contents. Additional topics, such as a documentation of existing annotation conventions, may be added in the future.

The entry for each corpus, lexical resource and collection task consists of the following elements:

1. a free-form description;
2. a structured info table;
3. corpus-specific task information (if applicable);
4. a list of references.

The core of each entry is the info table, which structures information using thematic categories commonly applicable to the given type of resource, such as size, linguistic information, participant demographic, data formats, licence conditions and more. The category fields follow a regular pattern, but there is enough flexibility to allow for differences in content.

The aim of the compendium is to help researchers find data that represent each language as it is used naturally by signers with L1 language proficiency. Corpora should contain (semi-)spontaneous language production rather than prepared utterances or translations of spoken language content. As such it does not cover interpreted television broadcasts or language acquisition datasets.

The compendium is available both as a website[1] and as a static document[2]. At the time of writing it describes 40 corpora, 63 lexical resources and 27 data collection tasks, covering 72 different sign languages. The compendium is intended as a growing resource that will be updated regularly.

[1] `https://www.sign-lang.uni-hamburg.de/lr/compendium/`
[2] `https://doi.org/10.25592/uhhfdm.10210`

2. Background

When looking for linguistic resources, three kinds of centralised information sources can be of relevance: curated lists, metadata repositories and data repositories. Each of these fulfil separate, if overlapping, important functions in the language data ecosystem. They will be described in the following subsections.

2.1. Curated Lists

Curated lists are resource descriptions compiled by a single author or editorial group. Commonly they strive to provide a comprehensive overview of resources that lie within their chosen scope. They describe the resources and often specify where they can be found, but do not store or host the data themselves. The compendium introduced in this article is such a curated list. There exist a number of curated lists on sign language resources. As they were created for a number of different purposes, the type of information they provide differs considerably, as does the selection of resources and languages considered. While some are being maintained, others are snapshots of a specific point in time. Originally created for the appendix of his dissertation, Konrad (2012) provides a detailed tabular overview of 34 sign language resources, identifying various linguistic properties of each resource. In her journal article, Schmaling (2012) provides a detailed overview of dictionaries for African sign languages. She focuses on print-media dictionaries, but also describes two resources providing video materials. Hartzell (2022) created an informal compilation of language resources for minority languages in Egypt, including eight resources for Egyptian Sign Language. As part of their overview website on automatic sign language processing, Moryossef and Goldberg (2021) include a table of sign language resources they consider suitable for such tasks. At the time of writing the table covers 36 resources and provides brief information regarding their size, licence, primary reference and data location. The website of the African Sign Language Resource Center[3] provides information on sign languages used in African countries. While the website is still under active development, it already contains profiles for 54 countries, offering general information on their deaf populations and used sign languages. In several cases, the profiles identify existing language resources, although not necessarily where to find them.

2.2. Metadata Repositories

Like curated lists, metadata repositories collect information about datasets without hosting the datasets themselves. Unlike curated lists, the required metadata is usually provided by the dataset creators, either through submission forms or harvested from metadata files that the creators host at dedicated locations. These metadata files must match supported formats such as Dublin Core, OLAC or CMDI. Depending on the metadata format, the design of the repository and the amount of information provided by creators, entries may provide only generic dataset information, general language dataset information or even information specific to sign language datasets. In the following we describe notable repositories that were designed specifically for language data and include entries for sign language resources.

The virtual library of the Open Language Archives Community[4] (OLAC) harvests metadata from a number of participating language archives (Simons and Bird, 2003) using the OLAC metadata standard for language data (Bird and Simons, 2001).

Similarly, the CLARIN Virtual Language Observatory[5] (VLO) collects information on language resources, tools and services (Van Uytvanck et al., 2012; Goosen and Eckart, 2014). Metadata is harvested from various CLARIN centers and a small number of other providers. It supports multiple metadata standards and can represent datasets as hierarchical structures, allowing the interlinking of dataset collections, subcollections and individual components.

The LRE Map[6] (Calzolari et al., 2010) by the European Language Resources Association (ELRA) follows a different approach. Information is collected as part of the article submission process of participating conferences and workshops. Authors publishing articles about new or updated datasets are requested to fill out a metadata form for each. The forms are kept short to encourage many authors to fill them out, so they cover fewer aspects than VLO and OLAC.

2.3. Data Repositories

Data repositories host and archive datasets and provide them together with their metadata. Often submission of data is restricted to participating organisations. Depending on the focus of the repository, the metadata standards it uses and the information provided by data creators, resource descriptions may be more or less detailed. Unlike curated lists and metadata repositories, data repositories focus on representing the data they themselves host, rather than giving a general overview of available data.

Among the data repositories tailored specifically for language resources are The Language Archive[7] (TLA), the Endangered Languages Archive[8] (ELAR), META-SHARE[9] and the commercial ELRA Catalogue[10]. TLA and ELAR are noteworthy for explicitly taking sign languages into account in their categorisation and metadata structures. Each of these repositories lists several sign language datasets.

[3] https://africansignlanguagesresourcecenter.com

[4] http://www.language-archives.org

[5] https://vlo.clarin.eu

[6] https://lremap.elra.info

[7] https://archive.mpi.nl/tla

[8] https://www.elararchive.org

[9] http://www.meta-share.org

[10] https://catalog.elra.info

3. Creating the Compendium

The Sign Language Dataset Compendium originally evolved out of two other information collection efforts led by the authors of this article. The first was the creation of the *sign-lang@LREC Anthology*[11] (Hanke et al., 2021), the proceedings archive of the *Workshop Series on the Representation and Processing of Sign Languages*. To enrich the archive with additional metadata, a literature review of its 363 publications was performed to determine which datasets and tools each article introduced or used, which languages it addressed and which project it was part of. For each of these categories, an index was created and each entry enriched with basic information, such as its licence, links to the resource or project, or language identifiers.

The second effort was the *Overview of Datasets for the Sign Languages of Europe* (Kopf et al., 2021), a public project deliverable for the EU project EASIER[12]. This expanded review of literature, dataset and project websites and personal correspondence with data creators resulted in a structured report on 67 datasets (26 corpora and 41 lexical resources) and 26 data collection tasks, covering 24 languages. Since the EASIER project aims to develop machine translation technologies for signed and spoken languages of the European Union, the report focused on resources for European sign languages that were suitable for such tasks.

While both efforts fulfilled their set goals, the limitations of their scope meant that neither could function as a general global overview of sign language datasets. To fill this gap we decided to create the compendium, which would cover resources from across the entire globe. Naturally, this increase in scale also introduced new questions regarding curation criteria (see Section 3.1), in what format the compendium should be released (see Section 3.2) and how to best summarise information (see Section 3.3).

3.1. Curation

When choosing which resources to include in the compendium, a balance must be struck between quantity and quality. On the one hand it is our goal to provide a comprehensive overview of resources for as many languages as possible, on the other hand we wish to focus on resources that can be of use to the core audience of the compendium, corpus linguists and computational linguists. Curation criteria help define which resources should be included, but also which resources should be prioritised as we work on expanding the compendium.

The starting point of the compendium are the resource descriptions of Kopf et al. (2021). However, the curation criteria for that report were designed for the European resource landscape and needs of machine translation research. For the purposes of the compendium they had to be revised.

[11] www.sign-lang.uni-hamburg.de/lrec/

[12] www.project-easier.eu/

In selecting suitable curation criteria, we had to take into account that there exist strong imbalances between languages in the size and number of available resources. To address this we chose a two-tiered approach of minimum and strict requirements. All resources must meet the minimum requirements, but if some resources for a given language also meet the strict requirements, other resources for that language are not (yet) listed.[13] The conditions are applied to corpora and lexical resources separately, so a language can be subject to strict conditions for one and minimum restrictions for the other. This regulates the number of included resources for comparatively well-resourced languages without disqualifying less-resourced languages entirely.

The curation criteria for the compendium are as follows:

General criteria for resources

1. *Must include video data*: Motion is an essential part of sign languages; still images and drawings alone are not sufficient.

2. *No sign-supported systems*: The compendium covers only sign languages, systems to support spoken language with signs are not included.

3. *No language acquisition data*: Language acquisition research is a specialised area of linguistics with different data requirements than post-acquisition research. Consequently, descriptions of acquisition datasets require a different focus, which would require an extension of the compendium structures. For the time being, such an extension is outside the scope of the compendium.

4. *No historical sign languages*: Similar to language acquisition data, data about historical languages is outside the scope of the compendium in its current phase.

5. *Data must be attainable*: There needs to be a clearly defined way of accessing the resource. This may for example be a download location or a point of contact. A resource is not included if access by third parties is generally ruled out or if it is not available for other reasons, such as a lack of points of contact or storage and file formats that can not be accessed by current computer systems.

Corpora

6. *Must be (semi-)spontaneous signing*: The corpus should predominantly represent natural use of language, rather than prepared, interpreted or translated utterances.

7. *L1 signers*: The participants should be L1 users of the language.

[13] This limitation may be revisited in the future, after sufficient coverage across languages has been achieved.

8. *Annotation*: The minimal requirements for a sign language corpus to be machine readable are a free translation and ID-glosses (Johnston, 2010). Therefore corpora must at least have a partial translation and/or gloss annotation.

9. *Size*: Monolingual corpora must include at least 5 hours (minimum) or 10 hours (strict) of sign language recordings. Multilingual corpora are exempt.

Lexical Resources

10. *Must include index*: Individual lexemes must be directly accessible through an index, e. g. of glosses, translational equivalents or phonetic description. This excludes datasets that collect many lexemes in a single recording without identifying the starting timestamps of the discrete entries.

11. *Size*: Lexical resources must cover at least 100 (minimum) or 1000 (strict) different signs. Multilingual corpora are exempt.

Data Collection Tasks

12. *Used by multiple resources*: Collection tasks are included if they were used in the creation of more than one of the corpora described by the compendium.

Developing the described criteria was an organic process that went hand in hand with the inspection of potential resources. They may be adjusted further as the compendium grows over time.

3.2. Publication Formats

The compendium will be published in two formats: As a static report and as a website.

The report is provided as a PDF document, structured similarly to Kopf et al. (2021). As such it can be used offline or printed out and individual versions are easily cited and archived. Each version is registered with its own unique persistent identifier.

The website provides dynamic access to information by making it browsable through various indices and filters. For example, in the language index, each language provides a list of all resources that contain it. To make it easier to find the correct language in the index, a text filter allows users to search for it by its various names, acronyms and identifiers (see Section 4.6). More filters will be added in future releases, as the compendium is developed further.

3.3. A Descriptive Approach to Standardisation

A central goal of the compendium is to present information in a standardised structured format that makes it easy to inspect and compare entries. Dataset factors such as size, licence or data format and linguistic information like participant demographic or annotated phenomena should always be described the same way. In practice, this proved to be a complex challenge, both due to the complexity of language resources and the varied availability of documentation. Corpus size, for example, might be specified in terms of recorded hours, number of transcribed tokens/types, file size or number of files. Even within these categories, differences could be observed in what values were reported, e. g. whether *recorded hours* counted individual camera angles as separate recordings or the same time span. For linguistic information, this variability was even more pronounced, due to the varying goals of different resources and the large variety of annotation practices in the sign language research community (cf. Kopf et al. (2022))

To address this challenge, a descriptive approach was chosen. It was started in Kopf et al. (2021) and continued for the compendium. Information for a variety of resources was gathered first and based on what information could consistently be determined for most resources, categories were defined. Within each category, descriptions were kept free-form to allow suitable documentation of each resource, although as patterns emerged, a consistent format and terminology was employed where appropriate.

The advantage of this approach is that it ensures that individual entries are not restricted by pre-defined vocabularies and categories. Its downside is that, at this stage, it does not integrate with machine-readable metadata standards and closed vocabularies as they are recommended for modern open science practices such as the FAIR principles (Wilkinson et al., 2016). However, to enable its multiple output formats (see Section 3.2) the internal formatting of compendium entries already uses a set of semantic XML tags. This tag inventory will be further extended in future to allow the extraction of machine-readable information without harming the flexibility of human-readable contents.

4. Compendium Content

The compendium is intended as a resource overview for digital sign language resources. It collects two types of datasets: corpora and lexical resources. In addition to this it compiles information on data collection tasks commonly used in the creation of different corpora. It also provides basic entries for each language.

The information provided in the compendium is compiled from public resource documentation, research articles, inspection of public data and personal correspondence with resource creators.

Each compendium entry consists of a free-form text description, a structured info table and a list of references. The categories of the info table are described in the following subsections. There are categories specific to corpora (Section 4.1), to lexical resources (Section 4.2), general dataset categories applicable to both (Section 4.3) and categories for data collection tasks (Section 4.4). In addition, corpora and tasks contain tables providing information specific to individual

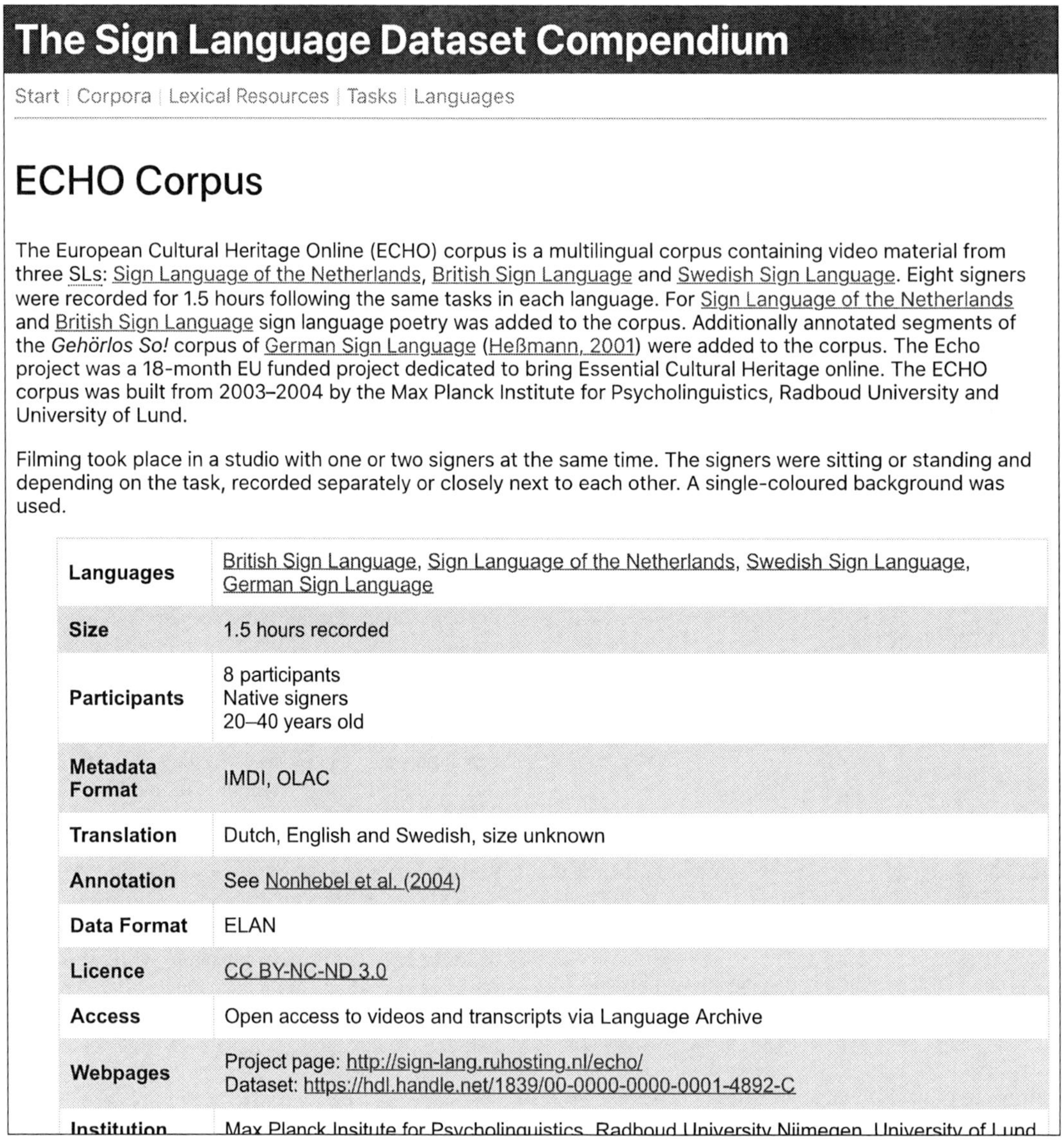

The Sign Language Dataset Compendium

Start | Corpora | Lexical Resources | Tasks | Languages

ECHO Corpus

The European Cultural Heritage Online (ECHO) corpus is a multilingual corpus containing video material from three SLs: Sign Language of the Netherlands, British Sign Language and Swedish Sign Language. Eight signers were recorded for 1.5 hours following the same tasks in each language. For Sign Language of the Netherlands and British Sign Language sign language poetry was added to the corpus. Additionally annotated segments of the *Gehörlos So!* corpus of German Sign Language (Heßmann, 2001) were added to the corpus. The Echo project was a 18-month EU funded project dedicated to bring Essential Cultural Heritage online. The ECHO corpus was built from 2003–2004 by the Max Planck Institute for Psycholinguistics, Radboud University and University of Lund.

Filming took place in a studio with one or two signers at the same time. The signers were sitting or standing and depending on the task, recorded separately or closely next to each other. A single-coloured background was used.

Languages	British Sign Language, Sign Language of the Netherlands, Swedish Sign Language, German Sign Language
Size	1.5 hours recorded
Participants	8 participants Native signers 20–40 years old
Metadata Format	IMDI, OLAC
Translation	Dutch, English and Swedish, size unknown
Annotation	See Nonhebel et al. (2004)
Data Format	ELAN
Licence	CC BY-NC-ND 3.0
Access	Open access to videos and transcripts via Language Archive
Webpages	Project page: http://sign-lang.ruhosting.nl/echo/ Dataset: https://hdl.handle.net/1839/00-0000-0000-0001-4892-C
Institution	Max Planck Insitute for Psycholinguistics, Radboud University Nijmegen, University of Lund

Figure 1: Example of a corpus entry in the compendium. Shown are the header, menu, free-form description and part of the info table. Not shown are the tables of used tasks and the list of references.

corpus-task pairs (Section 4.5). Language entries are described in Section 4.6.

All entries are interconnected, providing links between related resources, between languages and resources and between tasks and corpora. An example corpus entry can be seen in Figure 1. An example elicitation task entry including corpus-task pairs is shown in Figure 2.

4.1. Categories for Corpora

The following info table categories are provided for each corpus:

Languages: The languages used in the primary data of the corpus. Does not include languages used in annotation or translation.

Size: Size of the corpus. Depending on the information available, this may be specified as token count, type count, recording hours, number of video clips and/or file size.

Participants: Demographic information about the corpus participants. Apart from the number of participants this may include which regions they are from, age groups, gender distribution, and more. It is limited to demographic information that has been publicly documented.

Metadata Format: The file formats in which machine-readable metadata is provided by the corpus.

Translation: Which languages the primary data is translated into and how much of it has been translated.

Annotation: How much data has been annotated and which annotation conventions were used. If possible, a reference to the conventions is provided, otherwise information is paraphrased.

Data Format: The file formats in which the annotation/translation data of the corpus is provided.

4.2. Categories for Lexical Resources

The collection of lexical resources includes both lexical databases as well as electronic dictionaries. Lexical databases are language resources containing lexemes and additional information such as citation forms and translations. Dictionaries extend this information further, e. g. by documenting sign usage or sense disambiguation. As the boundaries between lexical database and dictionary are fluid, the compendium does not explicitly differentiate between the two.
Each lexical resource info table covers the following categories:

Languages: The languages used in the lexical resource. As most lexical resources can be used as bilingual dictionaries to some degree, this covers both signed and spoken languages.

Size: Number of lexical items. Items are identified as signs or types depending on the resource.

Linguistic Information: Which linguistic information is provided for lexical items, such as ID-glosses, translational equivalents, citation form video, meanings, phonetic transcription or categorisations, frequency and other statistics, list of corpus occurrences and more.

4.3. Categories for Corpora and Lexical Resources

The following info table categories apply to datasets in general, covering both corpora and lexical resources:

Licence: The licence conditions for using the dataset. These may be commonly used licences such as those by Creative Commons or custom licences defined for the dataset. A link to the licence is provided where possible.

Access: Describes how public and restricted data can be accessed. If the dataset has both public and restricted parts, this category identifies which parts of it are public.

Webpages: A list of relevant websites, such as those for the project, the research dataset, or portals for access by the general public.

Institutions: List of the universities or other organisations by which the dataset was created.

References: Important bibliographic references for the resource. If an external list of publications for the resource exist, a link to it is included here.

4.4. Categories for Data Collection Tasks

During corpus data collection, participants are guided by a series of tasks, such as retelling a story or open discussion of a given topic. The compendium lists data collection tasks used in multiple corpora. This information is intended to help with finding corpora that have comparable contents.
The info tables for data collection tasks cover the following categories:

Stimulus: Brief description of the stimulus provided to participants.

Target: The linguistic phenomena that the task is intended to elicit.

Degree of Interaction: An estimate whether the task usually results in a low, medium or high amount of interaction between participants. A reason for the degree may be given as a comment.

Duration: An estimate of how long the task usually lasts, based on instances observed in corpus data or published documentation.

Source: References to the material used in the task (e. g. books, films) or to scientific publications providing a definition of the task.

4.5. Categories for Corpus-Task Pairs

In addition to general descriptions of corpora and the data collection tasks that are used in their creation, the compendium also includes additional tables that provide information on the use of a task in a specific table. These tables contain the following categories:

 # recordings – open access: The number of recordings that are available in the publicly accessible part of the corpus.

 # recordings – closed access: The number of recordings that are only available in the non-public part of the corpus.

Data available: Links to the corpus recordings of this task, where available. Where possible these links will connect only to the given task; otherwise disambiguating notes are provided to help find the task on the referenced page.

4.6. Languages

The compendium provides an index of the languages covered by its resources. As sign languages often go by a number of different names and acronyms, each language is given an entry that lists various common names and identifiers for it:

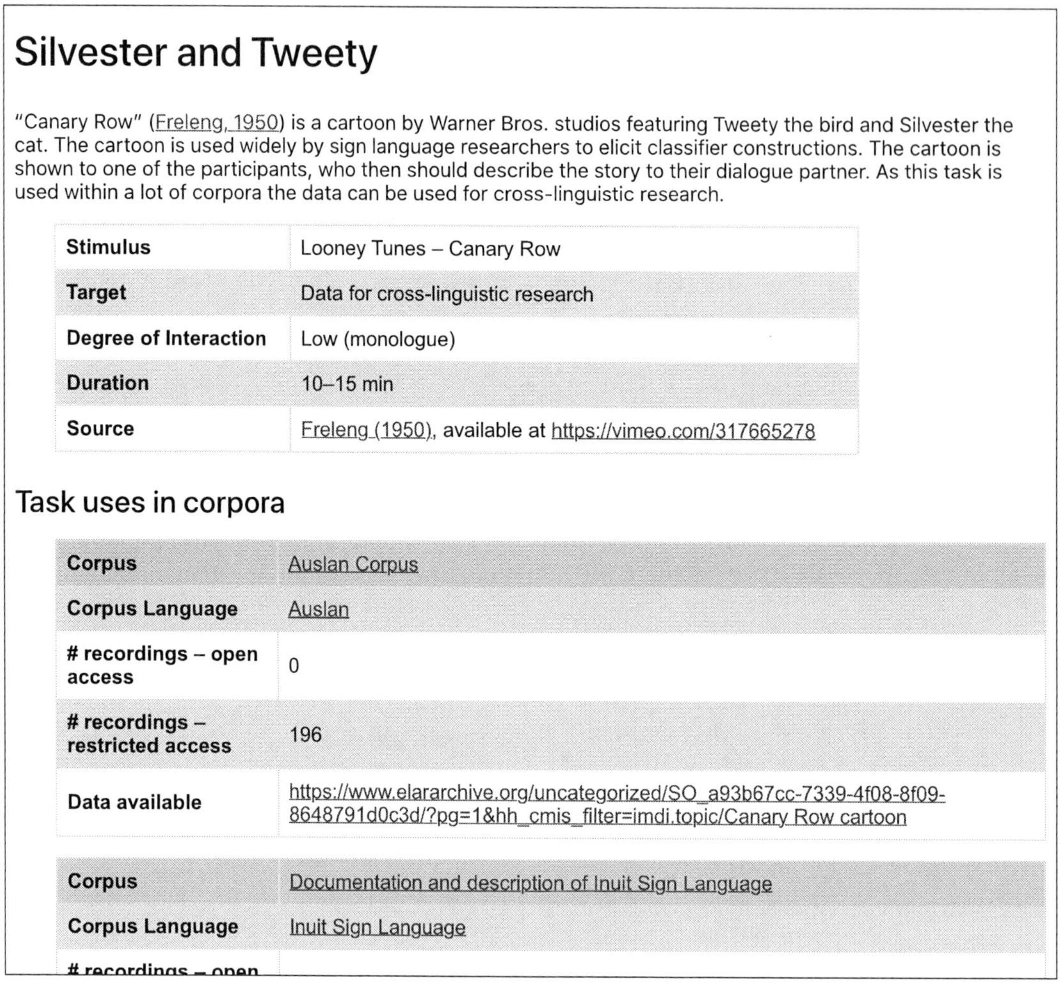

Silvester and Tweety

"Canary Row" (Freleng, 1950) is a cartoon by Warner Bros. studios featuring Tweety the bird and Silvester the cat. The cartoon is used widely by sign language researchers to elicit classifier constructions. The cartoon is shown to one of the participants, who then should describe the story to their dialogue partner. As this task is used within a lot of corpora the data can be used for cross-linguistic research.

Stimulus	Looney Tunes – Canary Row
Target	Data for cross-linguistic research
Degree of Interaction	Low (monologue)
Duration	10–15 min
Source	Freleng (1950), available at https://vimeo.com/317665278

Task uses in corpora

Corpus	Auslan Corpus
Corpus Language	Auslan
# recordings – open access	0
# recordings – restricted access	196
Data available	https://www.elararchive.org/uncategorized/SO_a93b67cc-7339-4f08-8f09-8648791d0c3d/?pg=1&hh_cmis_filter=imdi.topic/Canary Row cartoon

Corpus	Documentation and description of Inuit Sign Language
Corpus Language	Inuit Sign Language
# recordings – open	

Figure 2: Example of a data collection task entry in the compendium. Shown are the free-form description, info table and the first task use tables. Not shown are header, menu and list of references.

ISO 639-3: The unique identifier of the language in the ISO 639-3 code table.

Glottolog: The unique glottocode identifier of the language in the Glottolog database (Forkel and Hammarström, 2021).

Acronyms: Language acronyms commonly used by the language community or in research publications.

English names: English names for the language.

Local names: Names for the language used in its native region. So far this is limited to languages with a written form, which unfortunately prevents the representation of sign language names in their own language. For names written in other scripts than the latin alphabet, a transliteration is also provided.

Acronyms, English and local names are each sorted roughly by which variants are preferred within the language community and by how commonly they are used locally and in research. The most preferred English name and (where applicable) most preferred acronym of each language are shown in the language index. However, each language can still be found by all its other names, acronyms and identifiers by typing them in the provided search filter.

5. Conclusion

The *Sign Language Dataset Compendium* provides an extensive overview of corpora and lexical resources for many different signed languages from across the world. In addition it identifies a number of data collection tasks that have been used across different corpora. Information for each resource is presented in a standardised structure that is nevertheless flexible.

The compendium supports researchers in identifying language resources suitable to their needs, particularly in the case of cross-lingual research and research combining and comparing multiple resources. The compendium also highlights the imbalance in data availability across different languages while at the same time supporting the visibility of languages that are less often considered for data-driven sign language research.

The compendium is a growing resource that will be updated regularly. At the current time it contains 102 resources and 27 tasks, but more will be added over time. Various aspects of the compendium will be reevaluated as it grows, including the curation criteria and table categories described in this article. Possible improvements to the table categories that are under consideration are the addition of a recording setup category to describe factors like camera angles and the restructuring of the *linguistic information* category into more fine-grained categories.

The web format of the compendium will also receive additional feature updates. Plans for these include additional filter and sorting functions, e. g. for finding public datasets, and integrating machine-readable metadata standards.

Should you spot any inaccuracies, be able to contribute missing information or know of additional resources that should be included in the compendium, please contact us at sldc@dgs-korpus.de.

6. Acknowledgements

We would like to thank the following people for their valuable input, advice, and their information on indivdual resources: Ronice Müller de Quadros, Csilla Bartha, Eleni Efthimiou, Hope E. Morgan, Johanna Mesch, Katalin Liszi, and Thomas Troelsgård.

This work is supported in part by the EASIER (Intelligent Automatic Sign Language Translation) Project. EASIER has received funding from the European Union's Horizon 2020 research and innovation programme, grant agreement n° 101016982.

This work has in part been produced in the context of the joint research funding of the German Federal Government and Federal States in the Academies' Programme, with funding from the Federal Ministry of Education and Research and the Free and Hanseatic City of Hamburg. The Academies' Programme is coordinated by the Union of the Academies of Sciences and Humanities

7. Bibliographical References

Bird, S. and Simons, G. (2001). The OLAC metadata set and controlled vocabularies. In *Proceedings of the ACL 2001 Workshop on Sharing Tools and Resources*, pages 7–18, Toulouse, France.

Calzolari, N., Soria, C., Del Gratta, R., Goggi, S., Quochi, V., Russo, I., Choukri, K., Mariani, J., and Piperidis, S. (2010). The LREC map of language resources and technologies. In *Proceedings of the Seventh International Conference on Language Resources and Evaluation (LREC'10)*, pages 949–956, Valletta, Malta. European Language Resources Association (ELRA).

Forkel, R. and Hammarström, H. (2021). Glottocodes: Identifiers linking families, languages and dialects to comprehensive reference information. *Semantic Web*, Preprint. DOI: 10.3233/SW-212843.

Goosen, T. and Eckart, T. (2014). Virtual Language Observatory 3.0: What's new? In *Selected papers from the CLARIN 2014 Conference*, Soesterberg, Netherlands.

Hanke, T., Schulder, M., and Kopf, M. (2021). The sign-lang@LREC Anthology. Web Archive.

Hartzell, E. (2022). Egyptian minority language resources. DOI: 10.5281/zenodo.6385150.

Johnston, T. (2010). From archive to corpus: Transcription and annotation in the creation of signed language corpora. *International Journal of Corpus Linguistics*, 15(1):106–131. DOI: 10.1075/ijcl.15.1.05joh.

Konrad, R. (2012). Sign language corpora survey. DOI: 10.25592/uhhfdm.9893.

Kopf, M., Schulder, M., and Hanke, T. (2021). Overview of datasets for the sign languages of Europe. Project Deliverable EASIER D6.1, EASIER Consortium. DOI: 10.25592/uhhfdm.9560.

Kopf, M., Schulder, M., Hanke, T., and Bigeard, S. (2022). Specification for the harmonization of sign language annotations. Project Deliverable EASIER D6.2, EASIER Consortium. DOI: 10.25592/uhhfdm.9842.

Moryossef, A. and Goldberg, Y. (2021). Sign language processing. Website.

Schmaling, C. H. (2012). Dictionaries of African sign languages: An overview. *Sign Language Studies*, 12(2):236–278. DOI: 10.1353/sls.2011.0025.

Simons, G. and Bird, S. (2003). The Open Language Archives Community: An infrastructure for distributed archiving of language resources. *Literary and Linguistic Computing*, 18(2):117–128. DOI: 10.1093/llc/18.2.117.

Van Uytvanck, D., Stehouwer, H., and Lampen, L. (2012). Semantic metadata mapping in practice: the Virtual Language Observatory. In *Proceedings of the Eighth International Conference on Language Resources and Evaluation*, pages 1029–1034, Istanbul, Turkey. European Language Resources Association (ELRA).

Wilkinson, M. D., Dumontier, M., Aalbersberg, I. J., Appleton, G., Axton, M., Baak, A., Blomberg, N., Boiten, J.-W., et al. (2016). The FAIR guiding principles for scientific data management and stewardship. *Scientific Data*, 3:160018. DOI: 10.1038/sdata.2016.18.

Proceedings of the 10th Workshop on the Representation and Processing of Sign Languages (sign-lang@LREC 2022), pages 110–117
Language Resources and Evaluation Conference (LREC 2022), Marseille, 20-25 June 2022

Making Sign Language Corpora Comparable: A Study of Palm-Up and Throw-Away in Polish Sign Language, German Sign Language, and Russian Sign Language

Anna Kuder
Sign Language Interpreting Section, Department of Special Education and Rehabilitation,
Faculty of Human Sciences, University of Cologne
Section for Sign Linguistics, Faculty of Polish Studies, University of Warsaw
Krakowskie Przedmieście 26/28, 00-927 Warsaw, Poland
anna.kuder@uw.edu.pl

Abstract

This paper is primarily devoted to describing the preparation phase of a large-scale comparative study based on naturalistic linguistic data drawn from multiple sign language corpora. To provide an example, I am using my current project on manual gestural elements in Polish Sign Language, German Sign Language, and Russian Sign Language. The paper starts with a description of the reasons behind undertaking this project. Then, I describe the scope of my study, which is focused on two manual elements present in all three mentioned sign languages: palm-up and throw-away; and the three corpora which are my data sources. This is followed by a presentation of the steps taken in the initial stages of the project in order to make the data comparable. Those steps are: choosing the adequate data samples from all three corpora, gathering all data within the chosen software, and creating an annotation schema that builds on the annotations already present in all three corpora.
Even though the project is still underway, and the annotation process is ongoing, preliminary discussions about the nature of the analysed manual activities are presented based on the initial annotations for the sake of evaluating the created annotation schema. I conclude the paper with some remarks about the performance of the employed methodology.

Keywords: gesture, sign, sign language corpus, corpus linguistics, annotation, Polish Sign Language (PJM), German Sign Language (DGS), Russian Sign Language (RSL), comparative studies

1. Introduction

For many years the standard of sign language (SL) research was based only on small samples of language material and/or the researcher's (and/or his/her informant's) own linguistic intuitions. This approach based on elicited data and linguistic judgements was used both in research regarding single SLs (e.g., Zeshan, 2006), and in comparative studies of multiple SLs (e.g., Pfau and Quer, 2004). In more recent years, since the creation of the Australian Sign Language (Auslan) Corpus (Johnston, 2009) and similar projects that have followed, studies based on corpus material are becoming more common for the analysis of individual SLs. For comparative studies of multiple SLs however, the approach utilizing elicited data and linguistic judgements is still more common.
But with the growing number of available resources, more and more cross-linguistic studies are being performed with the use of data coming from two of more separate corpora. Some examples include: the comparison of negation markers in Polish Sign Language (PJM) and Auslan (Kuder et al., 2018), the comparison of information structure in Russian Sign Language (RSL) and Sign Language of the Netherlands (NGT) (Kimmelman, 2019); the comparison of body-anchored verbs and argument omission in DGS and RSL (Oomen and Kimmelman, 2019); the comparison of discourse markers in French Belgian Sign Language (LSFB) and Catalan Sign Language (LSC) (Gabarró-López, 2020).
In line with this more recent trend, I set out to perform a cross-linguistic corpus-based study of two manual elements present in three European SLs: Polish Sign Language, German Sign Language, and Russian Sign Language. As the corpora from which I draw my data were primarily created using different standards for annotation, and in different software (PJM and DGS corpora – in iLex, and RSL corpus – in ELAN), this paper details the choices faced and decisions made in the preparation phase of the large-scale cross-linguistic corpus-based study.

2. Theoretical Background & Motivation

The topic of gesture and gesticulation has been tackled more often by spoken language (SpL) than SL linguists. Gestures, defined in SpLs as "visible actions of the hand, body, and face that are intentionally used to communicate" (Kendon, 1986, 2004, following: Özyürek, 2012, p. 627), are usually seen as integrated into the communication system, being another part of language, alongside speech (Özyürek, 2012).
This view of gestures is supported by the fact that, in SpLs, gestures are most often produced in a different modality than speech (e.g., Goldin-Meadow, 2003; Kendon, 2004; McNeill, 2005). They are easily distinguishable from fully syntactic elements just by being "shown" and not "said" (note the common notion of gestures as being "non-verbal"). Elements that are being "shown" while a spoken word/clause is being uttered are called co-speech gestures. However, this is not the case for gestures accompanying SLs, in which there is no modality difference between lexical and gestural elements. The fact that both signs and gestures in SLs are "shown" has led researchers to trying to establish a more prominent relationship between them than has ever been argued for SpLs. Namely, it has been claimed that some of the elements that in SpL linguistics are referred to as gestures, when present in SLs take on a grammatical function in a process known as grammaticalization, and instead are referred to as grammatical markers. This has been stated with respect to both non-manual elements, e.g., headshaking, and manual elements, e.g., palm-up (van Loon et al., 2014).
This approach to dealing with gestural elements in SLs stems from fact that SL researchers "naturally adopted the

theoretical and analytic tools that were established in spoken language linguistics" (Lepic, 2019, p. 3). Using these tools on SL data has led them to establish strict claims about lexicalization and grammaticalization of certain elements in some SLs (i.e., multiword expressions and morphologically complex signs (Lepic, 2019)).

However, some recent large-scale corpus-based studies provide evidence that contradicts these previous claims. It has been shown that elements serving as co-speech gestures in SpLs, when studied on the basis of SL corpus data, turn out to function in SLs in a similar way they do in SpLs (e.g., Johnston, 2018; Kuder, 2021 for headshaking), suggesting that they should not have been described as grammaticalized as previously stated. If claims must be made about the nature of these elements in SLs, then adopting a usage-based framework "alleviates the burden for sign language linguists to determine whether or not linguistic constructions have become <<lexicalized>>" (Lepic, 2019, p. 1) or, in this case, grammaticalized. Instead, by focusing only on the degree of analysability (Lepic, 2019) of an element, we can compare to what extent each element has been conventionalized (e.g., Schmid, 2020).

My current project follows the corpus-based approach and applies it to manual gestural elements present in SLs, to help gain a new perspective on the analysability of gestural elements in SLs and add to the discussion about the nature and role of gestural elements in SL discourse. The project is motivated by the need to conduct comparative studies of gestures across different sign languages which has been directly expressed by other authors (here with respect to palm-up): "there have already been several insightful corpus-based treatments of the palm-up in sign, but especially valuable would be further studies that compare use of the form in different sign languages using the same analytic criteria and theoretical framework. Such an approach would be critical in distinguishing cross-linguistic patterns from language-specific particulars" (Cooperrider et al., 2018, p. 12).

3. Scope of the Study and Data Sources

My current study focuses on two manual activities present both in SLs and SpLs:

- the **palm-up** – a multifunctional manual activity taking the form of rotating one's forearms so that the palms of the hand face upward (e.g., Cooperrider et al., 2018 among others; see fig. 1);
- the action of an open hand going downward having a common meaning of "never mind" or "not important" (Bressem and Müller, 2014; see fig. 2), which I will call the **throw-away**.

Throw-away has so far only been studied for co-speech gesture (Bressem and Müller, 2014, 2017, Francis et al., 2022).

Palm-up, on the other hand, is a manual form that has received a lot of scientific attention. It has been thoroughly studied in a number of sign languages: New Zealand Sign Language (McKee and Wallingford, 2011), Sign Language of the Netherlands (van Loon et al., 2014), Danish Sign Language (Engberg-Pedersen, 2002) and American Sign Language (Conlin et al., 2003). Small-scale studies of palm-up are also present for German Sign Language (Volk, 2016) and Russian Sign Language (Bauer, 2019). Preliminary comparative corpus-based studies of palm-up were also undertaken for French Belgian and Catalan Sign Languages (Gabarró-López, 2020). There are also analyses exploring the origin and relations of the element in signed and spoken communication (Cooperrider et al., 2018).

Figure 1: A palm-up (photo from the PJM corpus).

Figure 2: A throw-away (photo from the PJM corpus).

No large-scale and entirely corpus-based study has been conducted across multiple sign languages to compare the use of these two elements, which my study will provide. My current project is based on naturalistic corpus data extracted from the PJM, DGS and RSL corpora, all of which have open-access repositories. A substantial part of the PJM corpus is made publicly accessible as the "Open Repository of the Polish Sign Language Corpus" (Wójcicka et al., 2020; Kuder et al., this volume; https://www.korpuspjm.uw.edu.pl/en). The DGS corpus project is accessible as the "Public DGS Corpus" (with three different levels of access, Konrad et al., 2020; https://www.sign-lang.uni-hamburg.de/meinedgs/ling/start_en.html) and the RSL corpus as the "Online Russian Sign Language Corpus" (Burkova, 2015; http://rsl.nstu.ru).

4. Making Datasets Comparable

As all three corpora were created separately and published in different ways, the process of making my language material comparable involved 3 main questions:

(I) Which software(s) should be used for annotation?

(II) How to choose comparable data samples?

(III) How best to create an annotation schema that builds on the annotations already present in all three corpora?

4.1 Software

All three corpus projects were created and are published in different ways. Both PJM and DGS corpora were primarily created with the use of iLex (Hanke and Storz, 2008), while RSL corpus was made using ELAN (Crasborn and Sloetjes, 2008). Using two different tools throughout the project would make comparison difficult, if not impossible. However, all files in the repositories of PJM and DGS corpora are available to download both in iLex and ELAN formats. Therefore, I decided to work with only the ELAN files throughout my whole project. Importing the RSL annotation files into iLex would have been possible but was deemed unnecessary for a project conducted by an individual. If the study was conducted by a project team that needed to work on the annotation files at the same time, then using iLex would have been recommended instead.

4.2 Data Samples

To obtain comparable results, the data samples had to be chosen carefully, as each of the corpora features a different number of recorded informants and different lengths of recorded texts. A sample of 16 informants from each corpus was picked to be annotated. Each sample is balanced out with respect to gender (8 males & 8 females), and age (4 informants – 2 males & 2 females – from each of the age groups: 18-30; 31-45; 46-60; 60+).

As the geographical division of the data in the Polish Sign Language Corpus mirrors the distribution of Poland into 16 voivodeships[1], my sample includes one informant from each part of the country. The DGS corpus is also balanced geographically, following the division of the country into 13 regions[2] which correspond to the location of current and former Deaf schools. I thus decided to include one informant from each of the regular regions and two from the three biggest ones: Berlin, Leipzig and Nürnberg. The data from the Russian Sign Language corpus was collected in two places: Moscow and Novosibirsk[3]. Therefore, I decided to include 8 informants from each of the regions in the RSL sample.

The corpora differ also when it comes to the publication format of the publicly available files: approx. half of the files from the PJM Open Repository present signers talking in pairs and half of them present single signers. In the DGS files signers are almost always presented in pairs. Most of the RSL files only show one informant at a time. Due to the different formats of the three corpora, only the material coming from a single signer will be used in the study. For the dialogical tasks which show people signing in pairs, only data coming from one informant will be annotated per task.

The next decision was to choose suitable text produced by the informants so that the final samples would be as similar as possible with respect to text types and length. This was the most challenging part of the preparation phase, as here more than elsewhere I was limited to the material present in the open access corpora repositories. My final choices are presented in table 1 below.

	dialogue	narrative/ monologue	retelling
PJM	14 texts	24 texts	37 texts
DGS	5 texts	38 texts	3 texts
RSL	1 text	42 texts	27 texts

Table 1: The distribution of text types in the data samples from three corpora.

4.3 Existing Annotations

The biggest obstacle faced in the data preparation is the fact that the annotation schemas used in the original files from all three repositories are not identical, albeit similar.

As none of the present schemas was detailed enough to provide a good template to the study of gestural elements, a new schema had to be created. It had to be developed in such a way that would make use of the existing annotations and at the same time grasp all features of the articulatory elements important from the point of view of my study. This new schema needed to be developed in such a way that it could be applied in the files coming from all three corpora.

Only the tiers appearing consistently in all three datasets could have been consistently used in the study. These were limited to: tiers for glosses for dominant and non-dominant hand, and free translation. A comparison of all tiers existing in the files prior to starting the study is presented in table 2 below.

	PJM	DGS	RSL
Glosses for dominant and non-dominant hand (signer A[4]; written in the native language)	✓	✓	✓
Glosses for dominant and non-dominant hand (signer B; written in the native language)		✓	
Glosses for dominant and non-dominant hand (signer A; written in English)		✓	
Glosses for dominant and non-dominant hand (signer B; written in English)		✓	
Free translation into the native language	✓	✓	✓
Free translation into the English		✓	
HamNoSys notation	✓		
Mouthing/mouth gesture (signer A)		✓	✓
Mouthing/mouth gesture (signer B)		✓	
Non-manual features present on head, body & face			✓

Table 2: Overview of the annotation schemas used in the open repositories of all the three corpora prior to starting the current study.

[1] https://www.korpuspjm.uw.edu.pl/en

[2] https://www.sign-lang.uni-hamburg.de/meinedgs/ling/start_en.html

[3] http://rsl.nstu.ru/site/data

[4] As the files from the DGS corpus show two informants at the same time the relevant tiers are doubled to present the annotations for both signers separately.

The tiers for glosses and translations were used in the study in their present form. No alterations were made to the glossing and translating conventions. Even though they were not identical in all three datasets, they are similar enough from the point of view of the study which is not targeted to research purely lexical elements. Some tiers present in single datasets were important from the point of view of the current study (e.g., tiers for coding mouthing and non-manual elements). In such cases, existing data could already be used as is, but needed to be annotated from scratch for the remaining datasets.

4.4 The New Annotation Schema

The new schema was build based on the reports present in the literature concerning the elements important during studying the manual gestural elements in SLs (e.g., Cooperrider et al., 2018) and my own experience in building and using SL corpora (e.g., Kuder et al., 2018). The annotation process consists of four steps: (1) identifying all occurrences of palm-up and throw-away and defining their manual form; (2) defining the non-manual features associated with a given occurrence; (3) defining the function of the occurrence; (4) delineating the clauses that the occurrences are contained in.

As all three corpora feature pre-existing glosses for the two targeted manual elements (even though they are glossed differently in each of the corpora), the base of step (1) was already pre-prepared in all three datasets. After identifying each occurrence, I coded for[5]:

a) manual type (is it a palm-up or throw-away and is it one- or two-handed),
b) manual subtype (following Kendon, 2004 and Cooperrider et al., 2018 four subtypes of palm-up were distinguished: lateral, presentational, addressed and pointing).

In the (2) step I marked:

c) placing in the signing space,
d) handshape assimilation (if present),
e) nonmanual elements on the body,
f) nonmanual elements on the head,
g) nonmanual elements on the face,
h) gaze of the signer (if distinguishable by bare eye),
i) mouthing/mouth gesture.

If it was needed any additional information was added on the tier called:

j) "comment".

Step (3) consisted of tagging for:

k) function of the palm-up,
l) function of the throw-away,
m) lexical meaning of palm-up (if present),
n) lexical meaning of throw-away (if present).

Even though the files are equipped in pre-existing glosses for both palm-up and throw-away and in written translations, during the annotation process the whole video files are inspected sign by sign. This is needed to properly grasp the context of signing, which is crucial for establishing the function of the given manual element. Ambiguous cases are discussed with signers of each language.

The functional analysis was conducted based on pre-existing corpus annotations, my knowledge of the languages, observed context of signing, and consultations with users of the three target languages. The initial set of function tags was based on literature and then later augmented while studying the data, as not all of the functions I observed were previously reported on in the literature. I ended up with approx. 50 detailed function tags, which were later grouped into four broader categories (see section 5.3 for details).

Coding each occurrence with respect to the 14 listed tiers constitutes the first round of annotation for any given file. Annotations from these tiers are being used for cross-linguistic frequency counts and analyses of correlation of form and functions of the manual elements in question (see sections 5.2 & 5.3 for preliminary results).

Step (4) of annotation (the sentential annotation) serves the purpose of distinguishing "basic articulatory chunks of propositional meaning" (Johnston, 2019). It follows the protocol for clause like units (CLUs) tagging proposed by Johnston (2019) and adapted during the creation of the Polish Sign Language Corpus. This part of annotation consists of defining the boundaries of CLUs and then distinguishing their predicates, main arguments, and peripheral elements. The predicates and arguments are tagged for the macro roles and semantic roles they exhibit in the clauses. They are also marked with tags for parts of speech and in this process, I take into consideration all issues connected with distinguishing parts of speech (PoS) in sign languages (Schwager and Zeshan, 2008) and employ a usage-based notion of PoS (Linde-Usiekniewicz and Rutkowski, 2016) which focuses on the usage of a given sign in a given context. The types of the CLUs and dependencies between the clauses are then marked for, before adding the English translation.

Therefore, this subsection of my annotation schema contains eight tiers (see also fig. 3):

o) CLU (used for marking the scope of the clause),
p) arguments in the CLU (used for marking the predicate, its arguments, and peripherals),
q) macro roles in the CLU,
r) semantic roles in the CLU,
s) part of speech,
t) sentence type
u) type of CLU,
v) CLU within CLU (used for marking dependencies between the clauses),
w) English translation (on the basis of the written translations already present in the corpora).

Data collected in this round of annotation will be used in the future stages of the project for establishing what is the position of the manual elements in question within the sign languages clauses and whether there is a correlation between the position in the clause and a specific function or meaning of palm-up and throw-away.

5. Current State of the Project

5.1 Annotated Data Sample

As the project is still ongoing, so far the material coming from 9 informants from each of the corpora was annotated with the first round of annotation. The overview of the annotated sample is presented in the tables below.

[5] Each letter corresponds to a single tier in the annotation schema – see fig. 3.

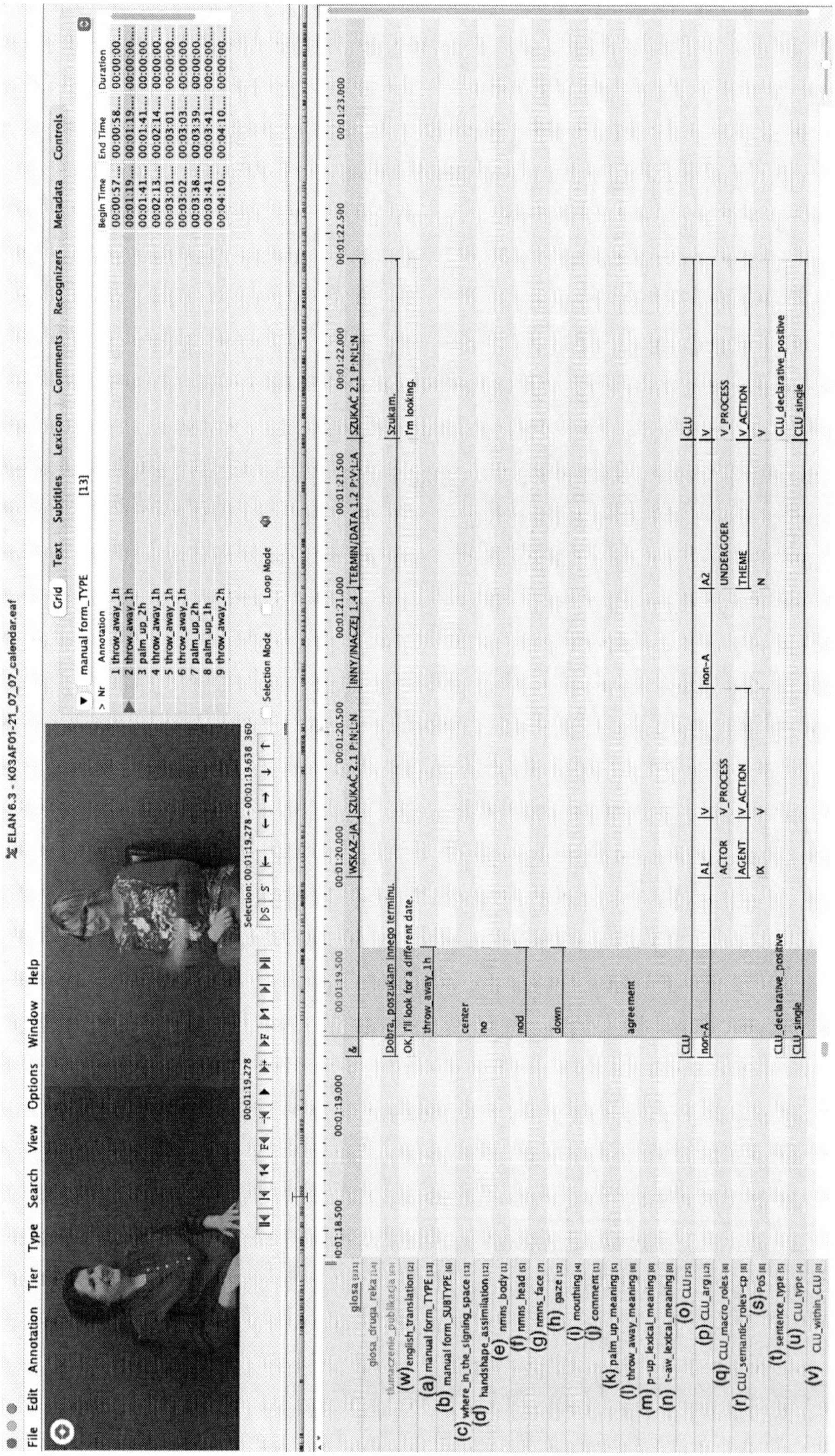

Figure 3: Annotation schema (photo from the PJM corpus).

	no. of texts	text types	length	no. of produced signs
PJM	43	retelling: 26 narratives: 9 dialogues: 8	05:37:32	20,851
DGS	27	narrative: 16 dialogues: 11	02:47:03	11,048
RSL	35	retelling: 16 narratives: 18 dialogue: 1	01:00:59	6,313

Table 3: The overview of the annotated dataset.

	gender/ age	18-30	31-45	46-60	60+
PJM	F	1	1	-	2
	M	2	1	1	1
DGS	F	1	1	-	2
	M	1	2	1	1
RSL	F	1	1	2	-
	M	2	1	1	1

Table 4: Age and gender of informants.

5.2 Preliminary Findings: Quantitative Analysis

As previously mentioned, the frequency analysis was based mostly on the pre-existing glosses present in all three corpora. However, aside from just targeting the existing glosses, I also examined the videos sign by sign, so as not to miss any instances of the manual forms (which may have been tagged with different labels than the anticipated ones). This also was needed for the functional analyses I will describe below. Fully understanding what is being signed was crucial for properly determining the functions of the manual elements, as they are heavily context based.
The frequency of the occurrence of palm-up and throw away in all three data samples is summarized in the table 5 below.

	no. of palm-ups (and as a % of all manual signs annotated)	no. of throw-aways (and as a % of all manual signs annotated)
PJM	729 (3.49%)	310 (1.49%)
DGS	734 (6.64%)	133 (1.20%)
RSL	269 (4.26%)	86 (1.36%)

Table 5: The frequency of both manual elements in the datasets.

The findings are consistent with the literature reports about the frequency of palm-up in other SLs of the world. For example, in the study of lexical frequency in British Sign Language (BSL), Fenlon and colleagues (2014) found that the percentage of palm-up occurrence stays at 5.5% making palm-up the second most frequent type of manual activity in the BSL data. They compared it to the Australian Sign Language (Auslan) data, in which the occurrence rate stays at 3.6% (Fenlon et al., 2014). In New Zealand Sign Language (NZSL), palm-up comprises 5% of all manual signs in the corpus and is the second most frequent sign type in the studied sample (McKee and Wallingford, 2011). In the next phases of the project, I will investigate the slightly higher occurrence rate of palm-up in DGS than in the other two languages.
When it comes to throw-away I have less possibilities for cross-linguistic comparison, but the percentages seem to be similar across studied languages.
What is more, these figures are consistent when checked against the whole of the PJM corpus, which currently comprises of approx. 706,233 glosses, of which palm-up is the second most common manual activity with approx. 30,558 occurrences (4.33%). Following this is throw-away with 7,134 occurrences, which put its frequency percentage at 1.01%.
The fact that the used method yields results comparable with the literature report about similar elements in other SLs shows that the chosen apparatus is working as planned.

5.3 Preliminary Findings: Qualitative Analysis

If the data prepared with the use of the newly formed annotation schema is adequate, then it will allow for a cross-modal comparison with what has been reported about palm-up and throw-away in co-speech gesture.
This can be done on the basis of the step (3) in the annotation process – the analysis of the elements' functions. As mentioned previously, all the detailed functions of the studied manual elements were grouped into four categories based on the type of function. The first three categories (van Loon et al., 2014; Bauer, 2019), which are also used to describe the functions of palm-up in co-speech gesture (cf. Ferré, 2012) are:

- Expressing modal meanings:
    - positive (e.g., agreement; revelation; surprise);
    - negative (e.g., lack of knowledge, lack of understanding, lack of interest, lack of ability; negation, surprise; annoyance; disappointment);
    - neutral (e.g., hesitation; hypotheticality; reinforcement of the stance);
- Discourse regulation: e.g., turn/topic opening or ending; response to the interlocutor's question/stance; connecting sentences;
- Conveying coherence: e.g., meta-comment; rhetorical question; self-correction.

My data suggests that all the functions performed by throw-away in all three SLs also fit into this categorisation.
The last category, labelled as "conveying lexical meaning", features all occurrences of both manual activities that were coded with lexical glosses by the original annotators. This tag was inserted in the "function" tier and the lexical meaning was specified on another annotation level (see the tiers labelled "lexical meaning of palm-up" and "lexical meaning of throw-away" in the fig. 3). The consistency of co-occurrence of palm-up and throw-away with particular lexical glosses raises an important question about the conventionalization level of the elements in question and the reports of palm-up functioning as a grammatical marker (van Loon et al., 2014). Some of the meanings consistently co-occurring with palm-up and throw-aways in the three SLs also possess different, fully lexicalized, manual forms in their lexicons (e.g., NOT-HAVE; NOT-BE; NOT-KNOW in PJM which I found to be associated with palm-up or BAD; TO-LET; DROP in DGS which I found to be

associated with throw-away). But the signers occasionally chose to substitute them with palm-up or throw-away and were understood by both the interlocutor and later by the annotators who chose to gloss the occurrence with a lexical gloss rather than a gestural marker. Future efforts within the study will be targeted towards explaining this issue within the usage-based framework (Lepic, 2019) and towards explaining the similarity of the functions of palm-up and throw-away observed in both signed and spoken modality.

6. Conclusion

The aim of this paper was primarily to show the preparation phase of a comparative corpus-based project when dealing with multiple SL corpora. The chosen methodology and annotation schema appear to be working well enough to provide adequate data to already allow preliminary conclusions about the nature of the analysed manual activities to be drawn.

The three issues connected to the topic of data comparability raised in the section 4 can be assessed as follows.

(I) Performing the annotations in ELAN was a good decision due to the very powerful search engine that is built into the software. Searching throughout annotated files is a key element of calculating the results. Searching in ELAN is more straightforward for a researcher without a programming background than searching within iLex, which requires the knowledge of SQL queries. The central database functionality of iLex was not needed for this project but would make iLex the preferred tool in any multi-annotator setting.

(II) The chosen data sample seems to be representative of the language usage as the obtained quantitative results are consistent with existing literature reports about palm-up in other SLs.

(III) The developed annotation schema, when applied to the chosen data sample, is providing adequate information about the frequency, form, and function of the two studied manual elements in all three SLs and allows for both cross-language and cross-modal comparison with the previous literature reports about the same topic in both signed and spoken languages. If anything, the schema might be too detailed. When it comes to coding for eye-gaze for example, it is unclear at this point if the corpus material is providing adequate data. It is hard to delineate the features that affect the signer's eye-gaze in the conversational data. Probably eye-gaze studies should be mainly based on the data obtained with the use of an eye tracker.

As mentioned previously, the current project is still ongoing. In order to gain a better understanding of the actual usage of the manual elements in question and to better understand the level of their conventionalisation, the next stages of my project will be devoted to conducting:

- analysis of co-occurrence of both gestures' types and subtypes with specific nonmanual markers;
- analysis of the correlation between the gestures' types and subtypes and their function;
- sociolinguistic analyses of the usage of the gestures across genders and age groups;
- CLU (sentential) coding and analysis;
- more detailed comparison of the gestures' usage between SLs and co-speech gesture.

The annotation schema has been prepared in a way that should make it possible to tackle all of these topics. However, assessing the choices and decisions made along the way will have to be done again, upon completion of the project (in the next 12 months). With the results of this further analysis, I hope to be able to add more direct claims to the discussion about the conventionalisation of palm-up and throw-away in the three studied SLs, as previously discussed in the theoretical background. If the assessment will yield positive results, in the future this project might serve as a basis for creating a blueprint for other comparative corpus-based studies.

7. Acknowledgements

My current research is financially supported by the Polish National Agency for Academic Exchange within the Bekker Programme (edition 2020): PPN/BEK/2020/1/00254.

Proofread and edited by Oliver B. Woof.

8. Bibliographical References

Bauer, A. (2019). Nonmanual components with palm-up in Russian SL. Paper presented at the *93rd LSA Annual Meeting*, New York, NY, USA.

Bressem, J. and Müller, C. (2014). The family of Away gestures: Negation, refusal, and negative assessment. In C. Müller et al. (Eds.), *Body – Language – Communication*, Berlin: De Gruyter Mouton, pp. 1592–1604.

Bressem, J. and Müller, C. (2017). The "Negative-Assessment-Construction" – A multimodal pattern based on a recurrent gesture? *Linguistic Vanguard*, 3:1–9.

Conlin, F., Hagstrom, P. and Neidle, C. (2003). A particle of indefiniteness in American Sign Language. *Linguistic Discovery*, 2(1):1–21.

Cooperrider, K., Abner, N. and Goldin-Meadow, S. (2018). The Palm-Up Puzzle: Meanings and Origins of a Widespread Form in Gesture and Sign. Frontiers in Communication, 3(23), https://doi.org/10.3389/fcomm.2018.00023.

Crasborn, O. and Sloetjes, H. (2008). Enhanced ELAN functionality for sign language corpora. In Proceedings of the 3rd Workshop on the Representation and Processing of Sign Languages: Construction and Exploitation of Sign Language Corpora. 6th International Conference on Language Resources and Evaluation (LREC 2008), pages 39–43, France, Paris, May. European Language Resource Association (ELRA).

Engberg-Pedersen, E. (2002). Gestures in signing: The presentation gesture in Danish Sign Language. In R. Schulmeister & H. Reinitzer (Eds.), *Progress in Sign Language Research: In Honor of Siegmund Prillwitz*. Hamburg: Signum, 143–162.

Fenlon, J., Schembri, A., Rentelis, R., Vinson, D. and Cormier, K. (2014). Using conversational data to determine lexical frequency in British Sign Language: The influence of text type. *Lingua*, 143:187–202.

Ferré, G. (2012). Functions of three open-palm hand gestures. *Multimodal Communication*, 1(1):5–20.

Francis, N., Grosz, P.G., Patel-Grosz, P. (2022). Analyzing the throwing away gesture as a discourse management device. Paper presented at the *DGfS-Workshop: Visual Communication. New Theoretical and Empirical Developments*, Tübingen, Germany.

Gabarró-López, S. (2020). Are discourse markers related to age and educational background? A comparative account between two sign languages. *Journal of Pragmatics*, 156:68–82.

Goldin-Meadow, S. (2003). Hearing Gesture: How Our Hands Help Us Think. Cambridge, MA: Harvard University Press.

Hanke, T and Storz, J. (2008). iLex – A database tool for integrating sign language corpus linguistics and sign language lexicography. In *Proceedings of the 3rd Workshop on the Representation and Processing of Signed Languages: Construction and exploitation of sign language corpora. International Conference on Language Resources and Evaluation* (*LREC 2008*), pages 64–67, France, Paris, May. European Language Resource Association (ELRA).

Johnston, T. (2009). Creating a corpus of Auslan within an Australian national corpus. In M. Haugh, K. Burridge, J. Mulder and P. Peters (Eds.), *Selected Proceedings of the 2008 HCSNet Workshop on Designing the Australian National Corpus: Mustering Languages*. Somerville: Cascadilla Proceedings Project, pp. 87–95.

Johnston, T. (2018). A corpus-based study of the role of headshaking in negation in Auslan (Australian Sign Language): Implications for signed language typology. *Linguistic Typology*, 22(2): 185–231.

Johnston, T. (2019). Auslan Corpus Annotation Guidelines. August 2019 Version, manuscript, Macquarie University, Sydney, Australia.

Kendon, A. (1986). Some reasons to studying gesture. *Semiotica*, 62(1-2):3–28.

Kendon, A. (2004). Gesture. Visible action as utterance. Cambridge: Cambridge University Press.

Kimmelman, V. (2019). Information structure in Sign Languages. Evidence from Russian Sign Language and Sign Language of the Netherlands. Berlin, Boston: De Gruyter Mouton.

Kuder, A., Filipczak, J., Mostowski, P., Rutkowski, P. and Johnston, T. (2018). What Corpus-based Research on Negation in Auslan and PJM Tells Us about Building and Using Sign Language Corpora. In *Proceedings of the 8th Workshop on the Representation and Processing of Sign Languages: Involving the Language Community. Language Resources and Evaluation Conference* (*LREC 2018*), pages 101–106, Miyazaki, Japan, May. European Language Resource Association (ELRA).

Kuder, A. (2021). Negation markers in Polish Sign Language (PJM), Sign Language and Linguistics, 24(1):118–131.

Kuder, A., Wójcicka, J., Mostowski, P., Rutkowski, P. (this volume). Open Repository of the Polish Sign Language Corpus: Publication Project of the Polish Sign Language Corpus. *In Proceedings of the 10th Workshop on the Representation and Processing of Sign Languages: Multilingual Sign Language Resources. Language Resources and Evaluation Conference* (*LREC 2022*), Marseille, France, June. European Language Resource Association (ELRA).

Lepic, R. (2019). A usage-based alternative to "lexicalization" in sign language linguistics. *Glossa: a journal of general linguistics*, 4(1):23:1–30. https://doi.org/10.5334/gjgl.840.

Linde-Usiekniewicz, J. and Rutkowski, P. (2016). The division into parts of speech in the Corpus-based Dictionary of Polish Sign Language. In T. Margalitadze & G. Meladze (Eds.), *Proceedings of the XVII EURALEX International Congress: Lexicography and Linguistic Diversity*. Tbilisi: Ivane Javakhishvili Tbilisi University Press, pp. 375–388.

McKee, R. and Wallingford, S. (2011). "So, well, whatever": Discourse functions of palm-up in New Zealand SL. *Sign Language & Linguistics*, 14:213–247.

McNeill, D. (2005). Gesture and Thought. Chicago: University of Chicago Press.

Müller, C. (2004). Forms and uses of the Palm Up Open Hand: A case of a gesture family? In C. Müller, & R. Posner (Eds.), *The Semantics and Pragmatics of Everyday Gestures*. Berlin: Weidler, pp. 233–256.

Oomen, M. and Kimmelman, V. (2019). Body-anchored verbs and argument omission in two sign languages. *Glossa: a journal of general linguistics*, 4(1): 42.

Özyürek, A. (2012). Gesture. In R. Pfau, M. Steinbach, & B. Woll (Eds.), *Sign Language. An International Handbook*. Berlin/Boston: De Gruyter Mouton, pp. 626–646.

Pfau, R. and Quer, J. (2004). On the syntax of negation and modals in LSC and DGS, paper presented at the *26. Jahrestagung der Deutschen Gesellschaft für Sprachwissenschaft*, Mainz, Germany.

Schmid, H.-J. (2020). The Dynamics of the Linguistic System: Usage, Conventionalization, and Entrenchment. Oxford Scholarship Online.

Schwager, W. and Zeshan, U. (2008). Word classes in sign languages. Criteria and classifications. *Studies in Language* 32(3): 509–545.

Van Loon, E., Pfau, R. and Steinbach, M. (2014). The grammaticalization of gestures in sign languages. In C. Müller et al. (Eds.), *Body – Language – Communication*. Berlin: De Gruyter Mouton, pp. 720–730.

Volk, E. (2016). Discourse functions of palm-up in German SL (DGS). Paper presented at the *FEAST conference*, Venice, Italy.

Zeshan, U. (Ed.) (2006). Interrogative and Negative Constructions in Sign Languages. Nijmegen: Ishara Press.

9. Language Resource References

Burkova, S. (2015). Russian Sign Language Corpus. Novosibirsk. http://rsl.nstu.ru/site/signlang.

Konrad, R., Hanke, T., Langer, G., Blanck, D., Bleicken, J., Hofmann, I., Jeziorski, O., König, L., König, S., Nishio, R., Regen, A., Salden, U., Wagner, S., Worseck, S., Böse, O., Jahn, E. and Schulder, M. (2020). MY DGS – annotated. Public Corpus of German Sign Language, 3rd release [Dataset]. Universität Hamburg. https://doi.org/10.25592/dgs.corpus-3.0.

Wójcicka, J., Kuder, A., Mostowski, P. and Rutkowski, P. (2020). Open Repository of the Polish Sign Language Corpus. Warsaw: Faculty of Polish Studies, University of Warsaw. https://www.korpuspjm.uw.edu.pl/en

Proceedings of the 10th Workshop on the Representation and Processing of Sign Languages (sign-lang@LREC 2022), pages 118–123
Language Resources and Evaluation Conference (LREC 2022), Marseille, 20-25 June 2022

Open Repository of the Polish Sign Language Corpus: Publication Project of the Polish Sign Language Corpus

Anna Kuder, Joanna Wójcicka, Piotr Mostowski, Paweł Rutkowski
Section for Sign Linguistics, Unit for General Linguistics and Sign Linguistics,
Faculty of Polish Studies, University of Warsaw
Krakowskie Przedmieście 26/28, 00-927 Warsaw, Poland
{anna.kuder, j.filipczak, piotr.mostowski, p.rutkowski}@uw.edu.pl

Abstract

Between 2010 and 2020, the research team of the Section for Sign Linguistics collected, annotated, and translated a large corpus of Polish Sign Language (*polski język migowy*, PJM). After this task was finished, a substantial part of the gathered materials was published online as the Open Repository of the Polish Sign Language Corpus. The current paper gives an overview of the process of converting the material from the Corpus into the Repository. If presents and explains the decisions made along the way and describes the process of data preparation and publication.

There are two levels of access to the Repository, which are meant to fulfil the needs of a wide range of public users, from members of the Deaf community, through hearing students of PJM, sign language teachers and interpreters, to users with academic background. We describe how corpus material available in open access was prepared to be searchable by text type and elicitation tasks, by sociolinguistic metadata, and by translation into written Polish. We go on to explain how access for research purposes differs from open access. We present possible ways in which data gathered in the Repository may be used by members of the signing community in Poland and abroad.

Keywords: sign language corpus, sign language data annotation, repository, corpus data publication, open access, Polish Sign Language (PJM)

1. Introduction

The Polish Sign Language Corpus project was launched in 2010 at the University of Warsaw by the Section for Sign Linguistics (SSL) of the Faculty of Polish Studies. The endeavour was undertaken for two main reasons: firstly, to document Polish Sign Language (*polski język migowy*, PJM) – the endangered language which is the main vessel of the Deaf culture in Poland. Secondly, to serve as a solid empirical foundation for detailed grammatical and lexical studies of the language (which at that time had only been analysed on the basis of small data samples or researchers' and users' intuitions). The PJM Corpus project was designed to match other modern big-scale sign language corpora that were being developed around that time in different parts of the world, e.g., in Germany[1] (Prillwitz et al., 2008), Australia[2] (Johnston, 2009), Great Britain[3] (Schembri et al., 2013) and the Netherlands[4] (Crasborn and Zwitserlood, 2008).

2. Polish Sign Language Corpus

In the 10 years of the project's development (2010-2020), we obtained elicited recordings from 150 Deaf PJM signers from all over the country. The group of informants was balanced with respect to their age, place of origin and gender. Taken together, all the frontal-view recordings of individual signers are approx. 565 hours in length, as each recording session involved two participants and lasted approx. 3-5 hours. The elicitation scenario contained approx. 24 tasks that the informants were asked to complete in a face-to-face conversation context. The elicitation materials used in the PJM Corpus project were designed in close collaboration with the German Sign Language corpus team operating at the University of Hamburg (Nishio et al., 2010).

After each recording session, the collected data was backed up, stored on the University of Warsaw servers and annotated in the iLex software (Hanke and Storz, 2008). The methodological choices made during the PJM Corpus creation are described in detail in: Rutkowski et al., 2013; Rutkowski and Łozińska, 2014; Rutkowski et al., 2017.

The annotation team consisted of approx. 20 trained Deaf signers and hearing linguists. The annotation protocol used in the PJM Corpus (overview in: Filipczak, 2014 and in section 3.2.2.2 of this text) was based on annotation schemas used in other sign language corpus projects, including the ECHO project (Nonhebel et al., 2003), Australian Sign Language Corpus (Johnston, 2010, 2019), German Sign Language Corpus (Prillwitz et al., 2008) and others. During the annotation process the team distinguished 687,971 sign tokens (which were grouped into 15,384 sign types) and inserted 1,340,536 additional tags. The latter were used to represent the following levels of linguistic analysis:

- segmentation into clause-like units (developed based on the CLU tagging methodology proposed by Johnston (2019)),
- parts of speech,
- negation (overview in: Kuder, 2021),
- transcription into HamNoSys notation (Prillwitz et al, 1989).

On the basis of these primary annotations, 67,698 PJM sentences were translated into written Polish.

While the PJM Corpus was still being annotated it served as the empirical basis for different research and educational projects. The most important ones have included: the creation of *The Corpus-based Dictionary of Polish Sign Language*[5] (Łacheta et al., 2016); detailed linguistic analyses of PJM verbs (Łozińska, 2014) and of negation (Kuder, 2021); the creation of *Sign with us 1* and *Sign with*

[1] http://www.sign-lang.uni-hamburg.de/dgs-korpus
[2] http://www.auslan.org.au/about/corpus
[3] http://www.bslcorpusproject.org
[4] http://www.ru.nl/corpusngt
[5] https://www.slownikpjm.uw.edu.pl/en

us 2[6] – two parts of an extensive multi-media PJM course for children corresponding to A1-B2 CEFR proficiency levels. A number of smaller research endeavours have included studies on different linguistic, socio-linguistic, and psycho-linguistic features of PJM and Deaf Culture that have been presented through the years at various conferences and workshops in Poland and internationally, and published in numerous papers and articles.[7]

3. Open Repository of the Polish Sign Language Corpus

The PJM Corpus project team decided to make a significant portion of the collected data publicly available, following good practices set by other corpus projects of this type (e.g., Schembri, 2008 for British Sign Language; Bono et al., 2014 for Japanese Sign Language; Jahn et al., 2018 for German Sign Language). Therefore, when the project was completed, the project team moved onto designing the most sustainable way of on-line data publication. The platform used for that purpose was entitled the *Open Repository of the Polish Sign Language Corpus* (see section 3.1 below, henceforth the Repository).

Firstly, we decided to publish only a limited number of tasks performed by each of our informants. This was related to the need to protect sensitive information shared during the recording sessions (see Crasborn, 2008 and section 3.2 for details).

Our second decision concerned publishing different types of signed texts, so as to represent different genres. Therefore, the Repository features mono- and dialogical texts (see section 3.2 for details), including retellings and narratives that were produced in response to materials eliciting the use of different language structures and expressions (e.g., depicting signs, constructed actions, expressions involving the use of sign space, negation, different types of discourse structures).

Our third decision concerned the sociolinguistic data. The portion of the PJM Corpus data published in the Repository corresponds to the entire Corpus, balanced with respect to the informants' age, place of origin and gender (as the Repository is meant to reflect regional variation and differences in signing between younger and older signers).

Lastly, we distinguished four potential Repository user groups:

- casual visitors (deaf and hearing members of the signing community and all persons interested in sign language who wish to use PJM materials created for non-professional purposes, e.g., to see the diversity of signing styles, regional variation, etc.; this group includes persons concerned with preserving PJM as an endangered language documenting Deaf Culture);
- sign language teachers and students (who are, on the one hand, interested in obtaining materials that can be used in teaching sign language – e.g., for lesson practice or homework – and, on the other hand, in studying sign language and expanding their language competences by observing signing styles of deaf people from various environments and backgrounds; Crasborn, 2008);
- sign language interpreters (who can benefit from obtaining signed videos in which the same topic is covered by informants with different signing styles, which can serve as an excellent source of training materials; Leeson, 2008);
- sign language researchers (who are especially interested in obtaining materials for conducting detailed analyses of the PJM linguistic structure and other aspects of signed communication, including for comparative studies).

Our choices informing data publication were made to match the needs of those groups (see section 3.2.1 and 3.2.2 for an overview).

3.1 Name and Visual Representation

Among one of the first choices we made before publication, was the choice concerning the name and the visual representation of the published materials. As not all of the PJM Corpus materials are publicly available, we decided its shared part should go under a different name – not to cause any confusion as to its character. A decision was thus made to call the corpus website the *Open Repository of the Polish Sign Language Corpus* and make it publicly accessible at: www.korpuspjm.uw.edu.pl/en (Wójcicka et al., 2020). The website can be accessed by scanning the QR code below. We decided to publish the Repository on the University of Warsaw servers, to ensure good quality of hosting and to minimize the financial cost of maintaining the site.

Figure 1: QR code linking to the Repository website.

Then, we developed the visual identification of the Repository, consistent with the visual identification assumptions of other projects carried out by the SSL. A separate logotype (Fig. 2) is meant to indicate that the Repository should not be confused with the PJM Corpus.

OPEN REPOSITORY OF THE POLISH SIGN LANGUAGE CORPUS

Figure 2: The Open Repository of the Polish Sign Language Corpus logotype.

The Repository webpage contains all the video files that were qualified for publication. Additionally, the page includes information on PJM, the PJM Corpus project, the SSL team and a thorough instruction on how to use the resource. All Polish written texts are translated into PJM, written English, and International Sign.

[6] https://www.gov.pl/web/edukacja-i-nauka/kurs-polskiego-jezyka-migowego-pjm

[7] https://www.plm.uw.edu.pl/publikacje/

3.2 Data Publication

After each recording session, the collected video recordings were first segmented into 24 separate clips, in line with the elicitation task schema. This segmentation into individual tasks was not limited to specific task-related productions, but rather included instructions from the moderator, follow-up questions, clarifications and nonrelevant signing and, therefore, the pre-segmented recordings contained sensitive information that should not be published. For that reason, the recorded material to be included in the Repository was carefully examined and extracted from the extensive recording sets to minimize the possibility of publicly sharing any personal data unrelated to the elicitation tasks. Additionally, in some cases our informants did not fully grasp the instruction to the given task and their signing did not fully correspond with the elicitation materials. All of these clips were excluded from publication.

What is more, we also came across a number of videos in which our informants shared some information that could potentially be demeaning for them personally and for people mentioned by them, and also uncomfortable for the users of the Repository. We share the concerns of other sign language researchers who point out the issue of the anonymization of publicly available corpus data (Isard, 2020). Since we did not want to modify our data by means of concealment methods (as it would result in having to blur out too many clips), we decided, for ethical reasons, not to publish those parts of the PJM Corpus videos that contained sensitive or uncomfortable and disturbing data (Crasborn, 2008).

Having prepared the video material, we focused on designing the way in which the data will be presented on the website. In this regard we followed the choices made by the teams publishing the British (Schembri, 2008) and Japanese (Bono et al., 2014) Sign Languge Corpora. We drew upon the idea of publishing the collected data in different ways in order to better serve the needs of different potential Repository users (see section 3). After careful considerations, we decided to create two ways of accessing the Repository:

- fully open access for all interested parties;
- access requiring previous registration, for researchers, interpreters, and teachers.

3.2.1 Open Access

To make the PJM Repository openly accessible from different angles and to fulfill the needs of various users and various research purposes, different browsing options have been provided. As shown in Figure 3, the open access mode offers three ways to search the set of video clips constituting the Repository:

- by the birthplace, age, and gender of the signer (sociolinguistic data),
- by the type and topic of discussion,
- by words present in written Polish translations.

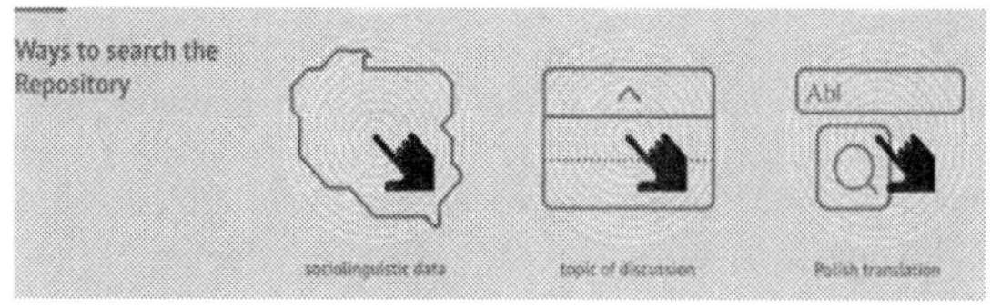

Figure 3: Three different ways to search the Repository.

After clicking the chosen icon corresponding to the particular search method, the user is presented with further options to specify the search. When browsing by sociolinguistic data, the user is presented with a map of Poland (Fig. 4), from which they can choose the part of the country they are interested in. In the next step the user is taken to the page with clips which allows a more fine-grained selection, the user can choose the interesting age range (possibilities: 18-30; 31-45; 46-60; 60+) and gender(s) of signers (as shown in Fig. 5 below).

Figure 4: Browsing through sociolinguistic data.

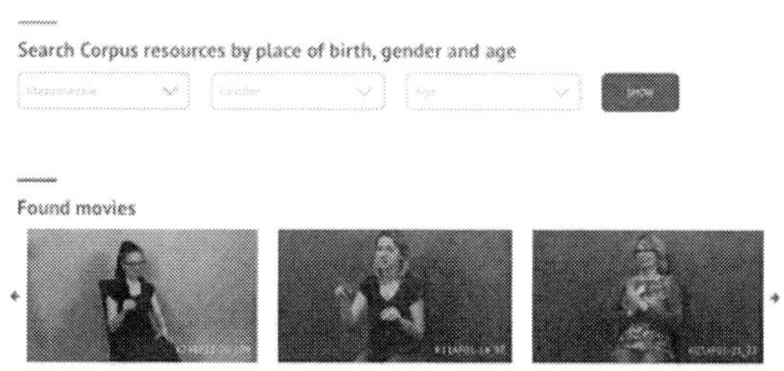

Figure 5: Selection page after browsing by sociolinguistic data.

When browsing by discussion topic, the user is presented with a list of drop-down menus to specify their selection. They can choose different text types, stimulus types, elicitation material types and, finally, specific elicitation tasks.

These search procedures reflect the extent of variation of the PJM Corpus elicitation materials. Some of the materials were designed to elicit monologue responses, other clips result from tasks that elicited conversational interaction.

In the Repository, all monologue tasks are divided into groups depending on the type of stimulus used for elicitation – either a movie clip or a drawing. Movie clips used in the elicitation showed either films/animations (therefore, eliciting narrative retelling) or a signing person (therefore, eliciting retelling of a signed story).

In the last browsing step, the user can choose the name of a specific task. To get to know which elicitation materials have been used for which task, the user should consult the detailed description in the 'how to use' section on the Repository website.
When it comes to dialogues included in the Repository, the informants either:

- discuss the interpretation of the pictures they are shown, or
- are asked to set the date for the meeting based on the calendar pages they are shown, or
- describe short comic strips to one another.

In the PJM Repository, clips with conversations show both signers performing the task simultaneously (to reflect the interactional nature of the recorded discourse). In the case of monologues, we decided to publish videos of the single informant (as shown in Fig. 6).

Figure 6: Individual video page (https://www.korpuspjm.uw.edu.pl/en/videos/178_).

When searching by Polish translations, the user is asked to type a Polish word into the search box. The search is performed in the form of a full-text search — the form of a word in the text is matched without the possibility of searching by lemmas or grammatical categories. The search results provide a list of videos that contain the given form, without specifying the precise timecode in which the written word occurs. More fine-grained search on the translation tier is possible after obtaining the "access for research purposes" – see section 3.2.2 – and using .eaf files.
After specifying their selection, the user is taken to a page listing all video clips in the Repository that meet the chosen criteria. Clicking on a particular video clip takes the user to the video individual page (Fig. 6), giving the possibility to watch the recording with Polish subtitles (based on the free translation extracted from the PJM Corpus) and providing detailed information about the clip, including the following:

- gender and age of the signer,
- the number of the recording session during which this particular clip was recorded,
- number of the task from the PJM Corpus that the clip corresponds to,
- ID of the clip,
- date of the last update,
- title of the task,
- text type
- the type of the stimulus used to elicit material.

3.2.2 Access for Research Purposes

The videos and data available in the open access mode are meant to serve the needs of general users, such as casual visitors. However, that form of access has its shortcomings from the point of view of professional users. For this reason, another type of Repository access is offered for those who wish to register. It is aimed at users with research interests who will be able to justify their need to have broader access to the Repository (for example, teachers, interpreters, or linguists). The access is granted individually by the Repository editorial team upon the receipt of an on-line request.
After obtaining the editorial team's approval and creating a personal account, the user can still use the Repository in the standard way available in the open access. Additionally, they can download the .eaf file for each of the video clips contained in the Repository, to be opened in the ELAN software (Crasborn and Sloetjes, 2008).

3.2.2.1 Annotation Files

Each .eaf file corresponds to a video with a single informant (regardless of the type of activity: monologue or dialogue). The .eaf files accessible from the Repository contain four tiers of annotation extracted directly from the PJM Corpus:

- gloss for dominant hand,
- gloss for non-dominant hand,
- HamNoSys transcription,
- free translation into written Polish.

Tiers with annotation follow the conventions applied in the PJM Corpus (see section 3.2.2.2. and Filipczak, 2014).
The dominant/non-dominant hand tier distinction is not meant to reflect the structure of particular signs, as two-handed signs are annotated on the dominant hand tier. The non-dominant hand tier is used for independent articulations (such as buoys, simultaneous signing using two hands, changing hand dominance, anticipations, perseverations, etc.). The layer with free translation was prepared for public access purposes to convey the general meaning of PJM utterances in Polish.
The .eaf files are extracted from the PJM Corpus with a custom software created to facilitate and accelerate export of iLex files according to the needs of the Repository publication team. The custom-built exporter allows to adjust annotation files with specific filters (e.g., time stamps, particular informants, chosen tasks or tiers) and additional configuration for extracting selected indexed parts of annotations or fixing Unicode encoding issues.

3.2.2.2 Annotation Conventions in the PJM Corpus and Repository

The Repository annotation conventions follow the annotation schema used in the creation of the PJM Corpus, where the videos are glossed using conventions that differentiate between lexicalized ('frozen') signs and non-lexicalized signs.
The latter group contains non-frozen signs and gestures divided in groups such as productive signs (including partly-lexicalized classifiers, glossed with the prefix *$:KL:*), phatic gestures (glossed with symbols *&* and *@*), palm-ups (glossed as *%*) and other gestures (glossed with the prefix *G:*). Fingerspelling glosses (annotated as: *A.B.C.D.*) are not treated as lexicalized.

Lexicalized forms have a hierarchical structure differentiating between types and subtypes. Types are used as labels for main glosses (Johnston, 2008) and a Polish equivalent is chosen to represent the sign's approximate meaning. Types (labeled 'Signs' in the iLex software) are written in capital letters and are always presented in the form of an uninflected Polish word. Lexical variants are distinguished by numbers: e.g., *BUS1*, *BUS2*. In the PJM Corpus, type labels are accompanied by conventionalized notations of hand configuration for the right and left hand for the most frequent form (mainly used for facilitating annotation process in identifying lexical variants): e.g., *BUS1 P:O;L:O*, *BUS2 P:CC;L:CC*, where *P:* stands for the right hand (*prawa* in Polish), *L:* stands for the left hand (*lewa* in Polish), and the letters following the colon specify a given handshape.

For searching purposes some lexical signs are grouped by using specific prefixes: e.g., *NUM:* for numerals, *IDENTYF:* for sign names.

Division into subtypes serves the purpose of differentiating between articulatory variants of the main type, including variants with modified handshapes (e.g., *CAT 1.1 P:O;L:O*, *CAT 1.2 P:Z;L:Z*), weak-hand drop (*CAT 1.3 P:O;L:Ø*, where *Ø* indicates that the hand is not in use), orientation, localization, or modification of movement. This way of formulating type glosses provides additional options when it comes to analyzing phonological and phonetical variation in signs. In the Repository files, data are represented by the main gloss accompanied with numbers for lexical variants and basic hand articulation notation.

This way of representing signed data in annotation is not identical but consistent enough with annotation methods used in other large-scale corpus projects worldwide, so it allows for comparative studies of sign language phenomena between different sign languages.

4. Conclusion

Publishing materials extracted from an existing sign language corpus is a complex, multi-dimensional process. Decisions must be made regarding the choice of materials suitable for publication, their anonymization, form of presentation and features offered to the website users.

In this paper, we have presented a detailed description of the Open Repository of the Polish Sign Language Corpus. We have focused mainly on the user perspective, but we have also explained the decisions made in the publication process. We have presented various methods of browsing and searching the published data (including the ability to download annotations in the form of .eaf files). Publication in two modes (open access without registration and registered access) is meant to serve the needs of different users.

The Repository can be used by linguists, researchers in the field of deaf studies, sign language teachers, translators/interpreters, L2 learners, and everyone interested in sign language. The Repository also serves as one of the largest available datasets documenting and archiving the language and culture of the Deaf community in Poland.

The Repository is a closed publication, but its form remains open. It is possible for it to be expanded with additional materials created in subsequent research projects.

5. Acknowledgements

The first phase of the PJM Corpus project was supported financially by Poland's National Science Center (*Narodowe Centrum Nauki*) under the project *Iconicity in the grammar and lexicon of Polish Sign Language (PJM)* (grant number: 2011/01/M/HS2/03661) and by the Foundation for Polish Science (*Fundacja na rzecz Nauki Polskiej*) under the project *Grammatical categorization through space and movement in Polish Sign Language* (grant number: 1/2009). The second phase was financed by the Polish Ministry of Science and Higher Education (*Ministerstwo Nauki i Szkolnictwa Wyższego*) under the National Program for the Development of Humanities (*Narodowy Program Rozwoju Humanistyki* – project title: *Multi-layered linguistic annotation of the corpus of Polish Sign Language (PJM)*; grant number: 0111/NPRH3/H12/82/2014).

6. Bibliographical References

Bono, M., Kikuchi, K., Cibulka, P. and Osugi, Y. (2014). A Colloquial Corpus of Japanese Sign Language: Linguistic Resources for Observing Sign Language Conversations. In *Proceedings of the 6th Workshop on the Representation and Processing of Sign Languages: Beyond the Manual Channel. International Conference on Language Resources and Evaluation* (*LREC 2014*), pages 23–31, Reykjavik, Iceland, May. European Language Resource Association (ELRA).

Crasborn, O. (2008). Open Access to Sign Language Corpora. In *Proceedings of the 3rd Workshop on the Representation and Processing of Sign Languages: Construction and Exploitation of Sign Language Corpora. 6th International Conference on Language Resources and Evaluation* (*LREC 2008*), pages 33–38, Marrakech, Morocco, May. European Language Resource Association (ELRA).

Crasborn, O. and Sloetjes, H. (2008). Enhanced ELAN functionality for sign language corpora. In *Proceedings of the 3rd Workshop on the Representation and Processing of Sign Languages: Construction and Exploitation of Sign Language Corpora. 6th International Conference on Language Resources and Evaluation* (*LREC 2008*), pages 39–43, Marrakech, Morocco, May. European Language Resource Association (ELRA).

Crasborn, O. and Zwitserlood, I. (2008). The Corpus NGT: an online corpus for professionals and laymen. In *Proceedings of the 3rd Workshop on the Representation and Processing of Sign Languages: Construction and Exploitation of Sign Language Corpora. 6th International Conference on Language Resources and Evaluation* (*LREC 2008*), pages 44–49, Marrakech, Morocco, May. European Language Resource Association (ELRA).

Filipczak, J. (2014). Anotacja korpusu PJM [The PJM Corpus Annotation Process]. In P. Rutkowski & S. Łozińska (eds.), *Lingwistyka przestrzeni i ruchu. Komunikacja migowa a metody korpusowe* [*Linguistics of space and movement. Sign language communication and corpus methods*]. Warsaw: Faculty of Polish Studies, University of Warsaw, pp. 91–105.

Hanke, T and Storz, J. (2008). iLex – A database tool for integrating sign language corpus linguistics and sign language lexicography. In *Proceedings of the 3rd Workshop on the Representation and Processing of Signed Languages: Construction and exploitation of sign language corpora. International Conference on Language Resources and Evaluation* (*LREC 2008*), pages 64–67, Marrakech, Morocco, May. European Language Resource Association (ELRA).

Isard, A. (2020). Approaches to the Anonymisation of Sign Language Corpora. In *Proceedings of the 9th Workshop on the Representation and Processing of Signed Languages: Sign Language Resources in the Service of the Language Community, Technological Challenges and Application Perspectives. International Conference on Language Resources and Evaluation* (*LREC 2020*), pages 95–100, Marseille, France, May. European Language Resource Association (ELRA).

Jahn, E., Konrad, R., Langer, G., Wagner, S. and Hanke, T. (2018). Publishing DGS Corpus Data: Different Formats for Different Needs. In *Proceedings of the 8th Workshop on the Representation and Processing of Sign Languages: Involving the Language Community. Language Resources and Evaluation Conference* (*LREC 2018*), pages 83–90, Miyazaki, Japan, May. European Language Resource Association (ELRA).

Johnston, T. (2008). Corpus linguistics and signed languages: no lemmata, no corpus. In *Proceedings of the 3rd Workshop on the Representation and Processing of Sign Languages: Construction and Exploitation of Sign Language Corpora. Language Resources and Evaluation Conference* (*LREC 2008*), pages 82–87, Marrakech, Morocco, May. European Language Resource Association (ELRA).

Johnston, T. (2009). Creating a corpus of Auslan within an Australian national corpus. In M. Haugh, K. Burridge, J. Mulder and P. Peters (eds.), *Selected Proceedings of the 2008 HCSNet Workshop on Designing the Australian National Corpus: Mustering Languages*. Somerville: Cascadilla Proceedings Project, pp. 87–95.

Johnston, T. (2010). From archive to corpus: transcription and annotation in the creation of signed language corpora. *International journal of Corpus Linguistics*, 15(1):106–131. https://doi.org/10.1075/ijcl.15.1.05joh

Johnston, T. (2019). Auslan Corpus Annotation Guidelines. August 2019 Version, manuscript, Macquarie University, Sydney, Australia, on-line at: https://www.academia.edu/40088269/Auslan_Corpus_Annotation_Guidelines_August_2019_version

Kuder, A. (2021). Negation markers in Polish Sign Language (PJM), *Sign Language and Linguistics*, 24(1):118–131. https://doi.org/10.1075/sll.00055.kud

Leeson, L. (2008). Quantum leap. Leveraging the signs of Ireland digital corpus in Irish Sign Language/English interpreter training. *The Sign Language Translator and Interpreter,* 2:231–258.

Łozińska, S. (2014), Czasownik w polskim języku migowym. Studium semantyczno-gramatyczne [Verb in PJM. Semantic and grammatic analyses]. Unpublished PhD thesis. Warsaw: Faculty of Polish Studies, University of Warsaw.

Nishio, R., Hong, S.-E., König, S., Konrad, R., Langer, G., Hanke T., and Rathmann, C. (2010). Elicitation methods in the DGS (German Sign Language) Corpus Project. In *Proceedings of the 4th Workshop on the Representation and Processing of Sign Languages: Corpora and Sign Language Technologies. Language Resources and Evaluation Conference* (*LREC 2010*), pages 178–185, Valletta, Malta, May. European Language Resource Association (ELRA).

Nonhebel, A., Crasborn, O. and van der Kooij, E. (2003). Sign language transcription conventions for the ECHO project. University of Nijmegen, Tech. Rep. 6, on-line at: https://repository.ubn.ru.nl/bitstream/handle/2066/57889/57889.pdf

Prillwitz, S., Leven, R., Zienert, H., Hanke, T. and Henning, J. (1989). HamNoSys: Version 2.0. Hamburg Notation System for sign languages. An introductory guide, Hamburg: Signum.

Prillwitz, S., Hanke, T., König, S., Konrad, R., Langer, G. and Schwarz, A. (2008). DGS Corpus Project – Development of a Corpus Based Electronic Dictionary German Sign Language / German. In *Proceedings of the 3rd Workshop on the Representation and Processing of Sign Languages: Construction and Exploitation of Sign Language Corpora. 6th International Conference on Language Resources and Evaluation* (*LREC 2008*), pages 159–164, Marrakech, Morocco, May. European Language Resource Association (ELRA).

Rutkowski, P., Łozińska, S., Filipczak, J., Łacheta, J. and Mostowski, P. (2013). Jak powstaje korpus polskiego języka migowego (PJM)? [How is the PJM Corpus created?]. *Polonica,* 33:297–308.

Rutkowski, P. and Łozińska, S., eds. (2014). Lingwistyka przestrzeni i ruchu. Komunikacja migowa a metody korpusowe [Linguistics of space and movement. Sign language communication and corpus methods]. Warsaw: Faculty of Polish Studies, University of Warsaw.

Rutkowski, P., Kuder, A., Filipczak, J., Mostowski, P., Łacheta, J. and Łozińska, S. (2017). The design and compilation of the Polish Sign Language (PJM) Corpus, In P. Rutkowski (ed.), *Different faces of sign language research*. Warsaw: University of Warsaw, Faculty of Polish Studies, pp. 125–151.

Schembri, A. (2008). British Sign Language Corpus Project: Open Access Archives and the Observer's Paradox. In *Proceedings of the 3rd Workshop on the Representation and Processing of Signed Languages: Construction and exploitation of sign language corpora. International Conference on Language Resources and Evaluation* (*LREC 2008*), pages 165–169, Marrakech, Morocco, May. European Language Resource Association (ELRA).

Schembri, A., Fenlon, J., Rentelis, R., Reynolds, S. and Cormier, K. (2013). Building the British Sign Language Corpus. *Language Documentation & Conservation,* 7:136–154

7. Language Resources References

Łacheta, J., Czajkowska-Kisil, M., Linde-Usiekniewicz, J. and Rutkowski, P. eds., (2016). The Corpus-based Dictionary of Polish Sign Language, Warsaw: Faculty of Polish Studies, University of Warsaw. http://www.slownikpjm.uw.edu.pl.

Wójcicka, J., Kuder, A., Mostowski, P. and Rutkowski, P. (2020). Open Repository of the Polish Sign Language Corpus. Warsaw: Faculty of Polish Studies, University of Warsaw. https://www.korpuspjm.uw.edu.pl/en

Proceedings of the 10th Workshop on the Representation and Processing of Sign Languages (sign-lang@LREC 2022), pages 124–131
Language Resources and Evaluation Conference (LREC 2022), Marseille, 20-25 June 2022

Functional Data Analysis of Non-manual Marking of Questions in Kazakh-Russian Sign Language

Anna Kuznetsova[1], Alfarabi Imashev[2], Medet Mukushev[2], Anara Sandygulova[2], Vadim Kimmelman[3]
[1]Charles University, [2]Nazarbayev University, [3]University of Bergen
kuzannagood@gmail.com, vadim.kimmelman@uib.no
{alfarabi.imashev, mmukushev, anara.sandygulova}@nu.edu.kz

Abstract

This paper is a continuation of Kuznetsova et al. (2021), which described non-manual markers of polar and wh-questions in comparison with statements in an NLP dataset of Kazakh-Russian Sign Language (KRSL) using Computer Vision. One of the limitations of the previous work was the distortion of the 3D face landmarks when the head was rotated. The proposed solution was to train a simple linear regression model to predict the distortion and then subtract it from the original output. We improve this technique with a multilayer perceptron. Another limitation that we intend to address in this paper is the discrete analysis of the continuous movement of non-manuals. In Kuznetsova et al. (2021) we averaged the value of the non-manual over its scope for statistical analysis. To preserve information on the shape of the movement, in this study we use a statistical tool that is often used in speech research, Functional Data Analysis, specifically Functional PCA.

Keywords: non-manuals, Functional Data Analysis, Computer Vision

1. Introduction

In sign languages, besides hand signs, multiple non-manual markers are employed, such as body and head movements, movements of facial features and direction of the eye gaze (Pfau and Quer, 2010). These features can be linguistically significant, for instance, it is frequent for different types of questions to be marked only with non-manuals, leaving the manual signs and their order the same as in statements (Cecchetto, 2012).

In Kuznetsova et al. (2021) we provided the first description of some non-manual markers in Kazakh-Russian Sign Language (KRSL) based on a dataset that was collected for an NLP task. The material for that study was taken from Kimmelman et al. (2020) and comprised of video recordings of statements and questions produced by nine native signers of KRSL.

Research on sign language is usually not automated, meaning that linguists need to manually annotate material and make their observations subjectively. We tried to test whether this can be overcome with state-of-the-art Computer Vision tools in Kuznetsova et al. (2021). Using OpenFace (Baltrušaitis et al., 2018; Baltrušaitis et al., 2013; Zadeh et al., 2017) we were able to extract face landmarks in 3-dimensional space and use them to measure eyebrow movement and head rotation angle. However, we faced the model bias, which distorted the positions of the facial landmarks with the change of the head rotation angle (see Section 2.2). Our solution was to train a simple linear regression model to predict this bias and then subtract it from the initial results of the OpenFace. We achieved relatively stable data and statistically analyzed it using a mixed-effects multivariate linear regression model. However, our analysis was not on continuous data of the movements but on discrete points that represented the mean value of the feature over the duration of the movement. The results suggest that in our KRSL dataset polar questions are marked by eyebrow raise on the whole sentence, and consecutive forward head tilts on the subject and verb (see example 1). On the other hand, wh-questions are marked by backward head tilts on the wh-sign, and by eyebrow raise on the wh-sign that can spread over the whole sentence (see examples 2, 3).

Based on these prior results, the goals of this study are the following. Firstly, we will try to improve on our bias detection model. Secondly, we will use Functional Data Analysis to analyze continuous movement of the eyebrows and head. We hope that this work will be helpful to linguists who also want to study non-manual movements in other languages because we believe that our approach can be extended to other datasets. We share the code with a step-by-step instruction on `https://github.com/kuzanna2016/non-manuals-2021`.

2. Data Extraction and Correction

For the current study, we used the same video clips and annotations as in Kuznetsova et al. (2021). The data contains recordings of 10 simple sentences with a subject and an intransitive verb, each in three forms – statement, polar question and wh-question (for example, the signed versions of "The dog is eating.", "Is the dog eating?" and "Where is the dog eating?"). At the beginning of the wh-questions, there is also a wh-sign. The sentences were produced by nine native KRSL signers, 5 deaf signers and 4 are hearing children of deaf adults (CODAs) currently working as KRSL interpreters. In total we have 270 videoclips.

1.

br_raise

head_forward head_forward

DOG EAT

'Is the dog eating?'

2.

br_raise

chin_up

WHERE CHILD DANCE

'Where the child is dancing?'

3.

br_raise

chin_up

WHEN MOM TIRED

'When was mom tired?'

2.1. Face Landmark Extraction

We firstly needed to extract face landmarks from the videoclips. We use the same method as in Kuznetsova et al. (2021) – OpenFace (Baltrušaitis et al., 2018; Baltrušaitis et al., 2013; Zadeh et al., 2017). OpenFace outputs face landmarks location in 3d space in millimetres, the location of the head with respect to the camera in millimetres, the head rotation in radians around three axes, which can be interpreted as pitch (Rx), yaw (Ry), and roll (Rz) and a confidence score from 0 to 1 for the whole frame. Only 103 frames from 12 videos had a low confidence score (< 0.8); we did not use those frames and filled in the neighbouring frames' values.

The next step in the analysis is to calculate the eyebrow distances. In Kuznetsova et al. (2021) the distance between the eyebrow points and the eye line was used. The main reason for that was that this distance is the most intuitively interpretable as the eyebrow movement is mostly vertical. We also tried other distances – distance to the upper nose point (27),[1] distance to a horizontal plane, but they did not work as well, so we will not discuss them. For distance calculations we used the following eyebrow points: outer left eyebrow – 18, inner left eyebrow – 20, inner right eyebrow – 23, outer right eyebrow – 25.

[1]The numbers correspond to the numbers used in OpenPose's output files.

2.2. Correction Model

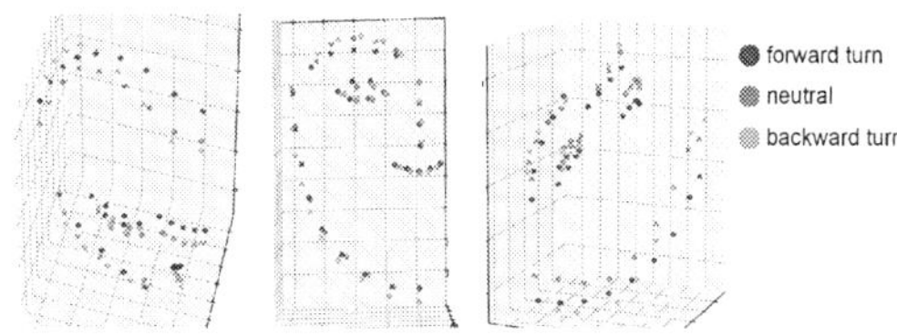

Figure 1: The behaviour of keypoints with different head turns on the test video.

As already stated in Kuznetsova et al. (2021), we found out that the OpenFace model has a rotation bias in 3d face landmarks detection. This means that the location of the points distorts with the head rotation: for instance, the eyebrows become more rounded in the backward tilt and more flat in the forward tilt (we examined this behaviour in the test video, where we recorded the head movement from the low to high pitch without the eyebrow movement, see Figure 1). We tried to eliminate this distortion using different geometrical techniques, but in the end we decided to switch to machine learning tools. The model should learn the bias distortion from the frames without eyebrow movement, then this bias can be predicted for all the frames and later subtracted from the initial distance. In Kuznetsova et al. (2021) we used a simple linear regression model to predict this bias. The training data was from the statements, specifically the manually selected videos where no eyebrow movement is present (63 sentences in total, 4414 frames). Our choice of the model was based on the observation that the distortion seems to be linear and consistent across signers – Pearson correlation coefficient between vertical head angle and the eyebrow distance to the eye line in sentences with no eyebrow raise is -0.39 for the inner distance and -0.4 for the outer distance.

This time we tried to improve the bias prediction by using a more advanced model, specifically multilayer perceptron. We believe it is sufficient for our task: it is not a deep model, can handle a moderate number of samples without overfitting and it can also capture some nonlinear dependencies. We performed hyperparameter search using cross-validation on 4 folds (test size – 25%, 1104 frames, train size – 75%, 3310 frames). The input features were the rotation angles of the head in three dimensions (pose_Rx, pose_Ry, pose_Ry in OpenFace), the cosine of the head rotation angles, the location of the head (pose_Tx, pose_Ty, pose_Tz in OpenFace), the one-hot encoded sentence and signer features. As previously mentioned in Kuznetsova et al. (2021) the big increase in quality is mostly attributed to the addition of the signer features, as the model learns individual parameters of the face of the signer. This set of features thus makes the model only applicable to our dataset and we encourage the researchers to retrain their models if they want to use our method.

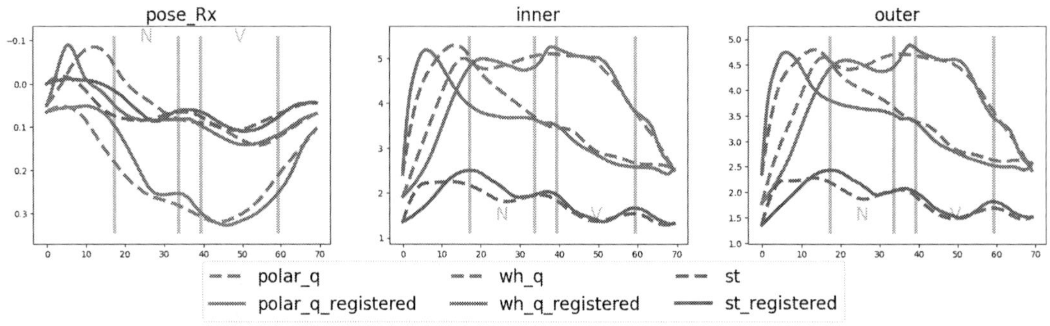

Figure 2: The mean curves of the sentence types before and after landmark registration. The red lines represent the boundaries of the hand signs.

For the experiment we used the *sklearn* library for Python (Pedregosa et al., 2018). The baseline model is the linear regression model from Kuznetsova et al. (2021) with L2 regularization (sklearn.linear_model.Ridge) and the examined model is Multi-layer Perceptron regression (sklearn.neural_network.MLPRegressor). The inner and outer eyebrow distances were predicted simultaneously.

The best result was achieved by the MLPRegressor with hidden layer size 40 – combined MSE score for inner and outer distances was 0.38, which improved on the baseline score of 1.45 for inner eyebrows and 1.36 for outer eyebrows. The best score of the model without the sentence and speaker features was 3.2 (the model had hidden layer sizes 45 and 40), which is also an improvement from the baseline score of 4 but is still significantly worse than the model with individual features.

As before, we used the trained model to predict the "default" eyebrow distance for all frames and then subtracted it from the originally computed distance.

3. Functional Data Analysis

Eyebrow movement and head rotation angle are dynamic features, therefore we want to analyse them as continuous data rather than discrete, as we did in Kuznetsova et al. (2021). In Gubian et al. (2009) Functional Data Analysis (FDA) was introduced as a tool to analyze dynamic transitions in speech signals. FDA provides the means to analyze continuous functional data like classic statistical methods analyze scalars (Ramsay and Silverman, 2002). Our main focus will be on functional principal component analysis (fPCA) – a tool that converts functional data into a scalar representation with minimum information loss. Our analysis is described by the following algorithm. Firstly, time measurements need to be transformed into function form. This can be done by using basis functions like B-splines and standard least-squares interpolation with a regularization term. Functions are normalized so that all observations have the same duration – to compare them across time. It is also possible to align functions on the landmarks – so that events in all observations coincide in time. In our case, the landmarks are the start and end frames of the hand signs. After the data preparation, fPCA, which finds a representation of the data with a smaller dimension size saving the variation. Principal components can afterwards be interpreted and analyzed with classical statistical methods, like mixed-effect multivariate linear regression. fPCA eliminates the problem of manually picking the scalar features from the dataset – in Kuznetsova et al. (2021) it was the mean across the manual signs and with fPCA we will be able to take into consideration the whole contour. In our analysis we use the *scikit-fda* library for Python (Carreño et al., 2022).

3.1. Data Preprocessing

The first step to FDA is to turn raw data points into continuous functional data. This is done by the combination of the set of functions. In our case, the most applicable set of functions is B-splines (de Boor, 1978) as the data is not periodic and can vary in shape greatly. Our data is quite noisy, therefore we do not want the function to approximate our data ideally, we want a smooth representation. This can be done by adjusting the numbers of the functions in the combination – the number of "hills" by the regularization term and by the order of the B-spline. When fitting the curves to the data we can compute the fitting error and try to minimize it when choosing the hyperparameters, however, visual inspection is still a valuable step. Based on both methods, we set the number of basis functions at 14 and the order of functions at 3, because it smoothes the data enough, saving the important features.

We want to align our functions on the start and end of the hand signs because we need to determine which constituent is marked by the non-manual and because we have different numbers of signs: there is an additional wh-word sign at the beginning of the wh-questions. We extracted the boundaries of the signs

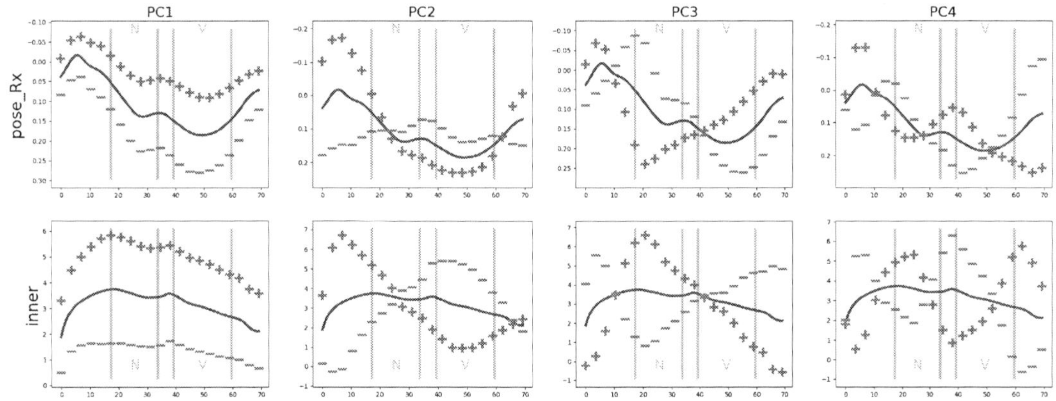

Figure 3: The perturbation graphs for the top 4 principal components. The solid curve is the mean of the dataset. Lines with the '+' sign are the curves where the principal component was added to the mean and lines with the '-' sign are the curves where the principal component was subtracted from the mean. The weight of the principal component is equal to the standard deviation of the dataset weights for that principal component.

from the manual annotation and we aligned them to the mean of those boundaries across all sentences (17.27 – the start of the noun, 33.71 – the end of the noun, 39.33 – the start of the verb, 59.46 – the end of the verb).

The importance of landmark registration is described in the document entitled Time normalisation and landmark registration in the additional material from Gubian et al. (2015)[2]. In the analysis of formant curves the authors claim that although overall non-registered results go in the same direction with the registered results, the effectiveness of the obtained principal components (see Section 3.2 on fPCA) decreased. The principal components from non-registered data described less variance and tried to incorporate the boundaries information which can be explicitly done with landmark registration.

The effect of the landmark registration can be seen in Figure 2 where the mean of each sentence type is plotted before and after registration. The peaks of the wh-questions have been moved to the left, which reflects the position of the wh-sign at the beginning of the sentence, while polar questions and statements have been slightly moved to the right as the mean positions of the hand signs are influenced by the wh-questions and are skewed to the right. Moreover, the peaks in all sentence types became more pronounced as they became more aligned. Moreover, it is clear from the figure that inner and outer eyebrow movement do not differ much, so we will not discuss outer eyebrow movement separately.

3.2. Functional PCA

With registered and smoothed data we can perform fPCA. One of the applications of PCA is dimensionality reduction. PCA provides principal components (usually vectors) and their weights for each data point so that the sum of the dataset mean and the weighted sum of the principal components will reconstruct the data point. For data point x_i the formula

$$mean + s_i^1 * PC_1 + s_i^2 * PC_2 .. + s_i^n * PC_n,$$

where s_i^n – is the score of the nth principal component for that data point and PC_n is the nth principal component, will produce the best approximation of x_i. Principal components are ranked from the most informative to least, so the first principal component will capture the biggest variance in the dataset. This feature is the reason why PCA is used in dimensionality reduction: using only some of the first principle components the data can be expressed with some percent of the saved variance. Functional PCA has the same output but principal components are in function form (Jolliffe and Jackson, 1993). Functional principal components are modifying functions that work like the regular principal components. To reconstruct a function from the dataset we need to add functional principal components multiplied by their weights to the mean curve. We performed fPCA independently on our three features. The first four principal components explain 93-96% of the variance (Table 1).

	PC1	PC2	PC3	PC4	Total
head rotation	69%	14%	6%	4%	93%
inner brows	83%	7%	4%	2%	96%

Table 1: The explained variance ratios of the principal components.

Functional principal components are modifiers of the mean curve; therefore the best way to look at them and interpret them are perturbation graphs (Figure 3). The

[2]https://github.com/uasolo/FDA-DH/blob/master/paper/TimeRegistration.pdf

perturbations are defined as variations over the mean: we add (lines with '+' sign) and subtract (lines with the '-' sign) each principal component from the mean curve (the solid line) with the weight equal to the standard deviation of the dataset weights for that principal component. We can interpret these lines as the borderline cases of the principal component modification.

In Figure 3 we can see that PC1 mainly alters the amplitude of the movement and to some extent the bulge of the curve both in eyebrow and head rotation cases. Next we will explore the eyebrow movement components. PC2 seems to distinguish between curves that have the eyebrow raise before the noun and the curves which have the eyebrow raise on the verb. PC3 acts as a separator between curves with one main raise on the noun and gradual decline to the end of the sentence and curves with slight raise before the noun and a plunge on the noun. The last component is more complicated with more than one peak, it will be harder to interpret it correctly. Still, PC4 either has a raise on the noun and a slightly lower raise at the end of the verb or two raises: one before the noun and one before the verb. As for the head movement, PC2 distinguishes between an almost flat movement with a small bump between noun and verb and a raise before the noun with a deep plunge on noun and verb. PC3 has either a raise before the noun and a plunge until the end of the sentence or a raise on the noun and a decline towards the verb with a small hump between the noun and the verb. Finally, PC4 has very subtle differences and the least amplitude of the changes: it separates the high rise before the noun from the small rise on the noun and a big hump between the noun and the verb and a more smooth hump there.

3.3. Statistical Analysis

In the previous section we obtained valuable discrete features for all sentences – scores of the principal components, which we can analyse with the standard statistical tools. We will repeat the analysis made in Kuznetsova et al. (2021) with some alterations. The analysis is made in R. The model that we are using is a mixed-effects multivariate linear regression (Baayen et al., 2008; Bates et al., 2015). The fixed predictor variables for the model are sentence type (categorical, three levels: statement, polar question, wh-question), group (categorical, deaf vs. hearing), and all the interactions between the two predictors. The random variables are participant (with a random slope for sentence type or part of sentence), and sentence (with a random slope for the group). We also use the *lme4* package (Chung et al., 2015) with the help of the *blme* package (Chung et al., 2013) to achieve convergence with a small number of levels for the random effects. The significance of the group feature was calculated with the *ANOVA* function from the car package (Fox and Weisberg, 2019). We have three levels in our sentence type feature, therefore we would need to test three hypotheses and account for the multiple comparison problem. In Kuznetsova et al. (2021) we overcame this problem with the orthogonal contrast: we compared statements with wh-questions and the mean of the statements and wh-questions with the polar questions. The features were the distances and the concept of the mean of the distances is intuitive, however, when the features are principal components, the mean of the principal components is more complicated. That is why we decided to make a more complicated analysis with a pairwise comparison. We use the *multcomp* package (Hothorn et al., 2008) to do this. We used Tukey Contrasts and the p-values were adjusted with the single-step method (Bretz et al., 2016). We made separate models for the inner eyebrow distance, for the outer eyebrow distance and for the vertical head rotation angle, and for each principal component, producing a total of 15 models. The result of the models is discussed in Section 4.

4. Results

4.1. Eyebrow Movement

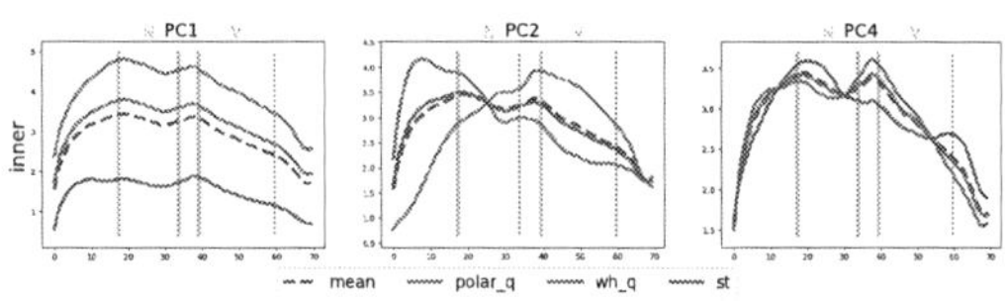

Figure 4: Mean curves of the eyebrow movement for each sentence type reconstructed with the significant principal components separately.

From visual inspection of the mean curves (Figure 2) we come to the same conclusion as in Kuznetsova et al. (2021): polar questions are marked by the eyebrow raise on the noun and verb with some nods in-between, while wh-questions are marked by the eyebrow raise on the wh-sign at the beginning of the sentence and gentle eyebrows lowering to the end of the sentence. Statements have some eyebrow movement but the amplitude is much lower and it may be the effect of the inconsistency of marking across signers. We will report only on the significant features; the full results of the statistical analysis can be found with the code.

The first principal component has a significant impact in distinguishing between polar questions and statements: in inner and outer eyebrows the p-value is < 0.001; and wh-questions and statements: in inner eyebrows the p-value is 0.0498. The mean PC1 score for the polar questions is 9.74 for the inner eyebrows and 6.94 for the outer eyebrows, while for the statements it is -11.65 for inner and -9.27 for outer and for the wh-questions it is 2.54 and 2.78 respectively. According to the shape of the perturbation graph (Figure 4), polar questions have a big amplitude raise and statements have a low eyebrow raise with a flatter curve, while wh-questions are close to the mean.

The second principal component is also significant, but for the distinction between the polar and wh-questions. For both the inner and outer eyebrows the p-value is < 0.001. The mean PC2 score for the polar questions is -6.06 and -4.79, and for the wh-questions it is 4.83 and 3.78 for inner and outer eyebrows respectively. Polar questions thus have a more gentle raise to the verb and wh-questions have a sharp raise before the noun, on the wh-sign (Figure 4).

The fourth principal component also has a significant impact, but the least one. It distinguishes between the wh-questions and statements. For the inner eyebrows the p-value is 0.0501 and for the outer it is 0.0273. The mean PC4 score for the wh-questions is 1.23 for the inner eyebrows and -1.37 for the outer, and for the statements it is -1.53 and 1.28. In the Figure 4 it is a very subtle difference, statements deviate slightly from the mean curve in three positions, on the sign boundaries, while wh-questions have a more pronounced deviation in the beginning, on the wh-sign, and a raise before the verb.

Thus, we confirm the previous observations that polar questions are marked by eyebrow raise on the noun and verb, while wh-questions are marked by eyebrow raise at the beginning of the sentence on the wh-sign.

4.2. Head Movement

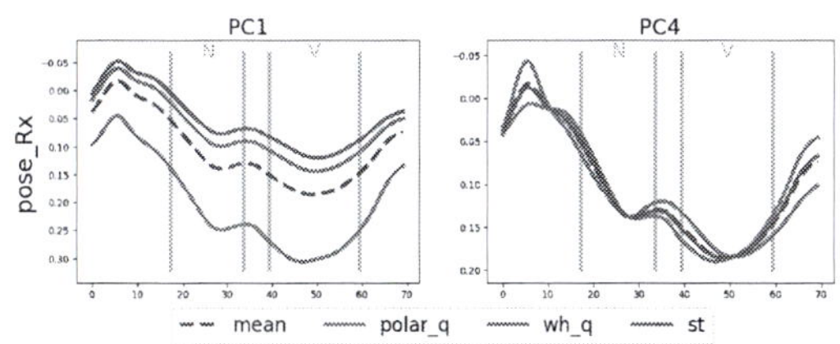

Figure 5: Mean curves of the vertical head rotation for each sentence type reconstructed with the significant principal components separately.

From visual inspection of the data, wh-questions seem to be marked with the backward tilt on the wh-sign, polar questions have a forward tilt on the noun and verb, and statements have small movements that resembles quick nods on the noun and the verb.

The statistical analysis shows that the first principle component significantly impacts the separation between wh-questions and polar questions (p-value $<$ 0.00291) and statements and polar questions (p-value 0.0016). The mean score of the first component for wh-questions is 0.3, for polar questions – -0.82, for statements 0.47, which means that polar questions have a deep forward tilt on the sentence peaking at the noun and verb, while wh-questions and statements have a more flattened movement (Figure 5, the first column).

The next significant principal component is the fourth principal component. Statement and wh-questions differ significantly (p-value is 0.00229) and so do wh-questions and polar questions (p-value is 0.02667). The mean scores of the fourth principal component are -0.1 for polar questions, 0.12 for wh-questions and -0.02 for statements. According to the perturbation graph (Figure 5, the second column), this means that wh-questions have a pronounced backward tilt at the beginning of the sentence on the wh-sign, and a nod between the noun and the verb, while statements and polar questions do not have a backward tilt in the beginning. We come to the same conclusion that the polar questions are marked with a continuous forward tilt on the noun and verb and the wh-questions are marked with a backward tilt on the wh-sign.

4.3. Deaf/hearing Differences

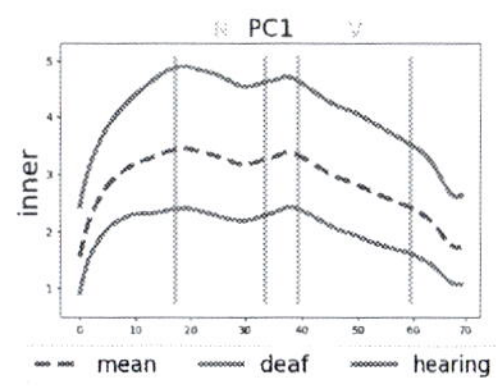

Figure 6: Mean curves of the eyebrow movement for the sentences with deaf and hearing signers reconstructed with the significant principal components separately.

In Kuznetsova et al. (2021) we did not find any statistically significant differences between the deaf and hearing signers. This time we can report that there are differences in some principal components.

The eyebrow movement has shown some significant differences in the first principal component for both the inner eyebrows and the outer eyebrows (p-values are 0.02764 and 0.03632 respectively). The first component mean scores for the inner eyebrows are -7.49 for the deaf signers and 10.31 for the hearing signers, for the outer eyebrows – -8.85 and 12.18. Figure 6 shows that in the first component the hearing signers tend to have higher eyebrow raise than the deaf signers.

5. Discussion

5.1. FDA and Sign Languages

The main source of the Functional Data Analysis techniques for this study was the website hosted by Michele Gubian. In his works, Gubian explores how FDA can be applied to speech research; however, he points out that FDA can be applied to other types of uni- or multi-dimensional continuous signals. We took inspiration from this and were able to translate his approach to sign language prosody. We believe that FDA has significantly improved our analysis. Firstly, we were able to analyse sentences with different durations and different number of signs with landmark registration. Secondly, with fPCA we were able to take into account the whole sentence contour, rather than some handpicked features. The principal components that we obtained were interpretable and it was easy to explore the visualisations. We hope that our work will increase interest in applying computer vision tools and FDA to sign language data. Section 5.2 has some practical advice to those who would like to try this approach.

5.2. Applying to Naturalistic Data

This study was made with the materials that were collected for NLP tasks in a constrained way and with a small number of signers. Moreover, almost half of the signers were hearing children of deaf adults, which means that the sample was not homogeneous, which is reflected in the differences between deaf and hearing signers. This makes our dataset far from naturalistic and we cannot guarantee that this approach will work on naturalistic data.

However, we believe that it is still possible and we encourage researchers to test it. We suggest finding materials in corpus where sign boundaries and non-manuals are already annotated. Various non-manual markers can be obtained with OpenFace, including head rotation in three axes, head movement, eye aperture, eye gaze, mouthing and eyebrow movements. We advise to obtain the frames with no non-manual markers from the same materials and same signers to use in the correction model, if the non-manuals in question can be modified by the head rotation. When using the correction model the id of the material and the id of the signer should be used as categorical features (like we used the sentence id and the signer id). The following analysis can be done with FDA or another framework, depending on the aims of the study. Lastly, we recommend inspecting frames with low confidence scores from OpenFace as they can damage the results of the correction model and the subsequent analysis. Frames with low confidence scores should not be included in the correction model training set, but they can be used in other steps if their values are filled in by the neighboring values or the mean of the neighboring values.

5.3. Data Manipulation

We understand that our approach of correcting the OpenFace results can introduce unwanted noise to the data and it would be more reliable to modify the predictor. The approach of putting a correction model on top of the predictor is indirect and subjective, as the features that we use only reflect our empirical observations, while the predictor has important internal states that can directly solve the problem. Although OpenFace is a state of the art tool the problem of general 3D reconstruction from a single camera is challenging, especially when the camera is not constrained, and the reconstructed 3D shape is not always going to be accurate and will be affected by rotation up to a point. We did not try other models that can perform 3D reconstruction of the face landmarks and did not modify the original model. We also did not retrain it on our data because we do not have the resources to annotate it for this task. If there are other solutions, we would encourage to try them out in subsequent research.

5.4. Availability of the Code

We produced a script which captures all elements of the data preparation, including the bias detection model, Functional Data Analysis and statistical analysis for further research on non-manual markers in sign languages. The script is freely available on GitHub with a step-by-step instruction: `https://github.com/kuzanna2016/non-manuals-2021`.

6. Conclusions

In this study, we (1) re-tested and improved techniques for eyebrow distance extraction using computer vision tools and (2) introduced FDA as a tool to analyse dynamic shapes of non-manuals. We supported the conclusions about the non-manual marking of the questions in the KRSL dataset from Kuznetsova et al. (2021) with the new analysis. In the KRSL dataset the wh-questions are marked with a backward head tilt and an eyebrow raise on the wh-word while polar questions are marked with a forward head tilt and an eyebrow raise on the noun and verb. We also found a difference between the deaf and hearing signers: the hearing signers tend to have more expressive non-manuals, meaning that the manuals have a bigger amplitude and the features are more pronounced.

Furthermore, this study demonstrates that computer vision techniques can be applied for sign language linguistic research, specifically research on non-manuals. Although these tools are very useful, they also have limitations. For example, the OpenFace model distorts face landmarks when the head is rotated. We have found one solution to this problem. We train an additional model on top of the predicted results to predict the errors and then we subtract the errors from the OpenFace output.

Moreover, we used a new statistical tool for linguistic analysis: Functional Data Analysis. It was already proven to be a great tool for spoken language phonetics and this study provides evidence that it can also be used for sign language prosody. FDA provides a way to work with continuous data, to shift curves and to extract features from these curves using functional principal component analysis. The translation of continuous data into scalar points helps analyse this data with standard statistical procedures.

We hope that our research will be useful in solving the problem of quantitative analysis of sign language linguistic features.

7. Bibliographical References

Baayen, H., Davidson, D., and Bates, D. (2008). Mixed-effects modeling with crossed random effects for subjects and items. *Journal of Memory and Language*, 59:390–412, 11.

Baltrušaitis, T., Robinson, P., and Morency, L.-P. (2013). Constrained local neural fields for robust facial landmark detection in the wild. In *2013 IEEE International Conference on Computer Vision Workshops*, pages 354–361.

Baltrušaitis, T., Zadeh, A., Lim, Y. C., and Morency, L.-P. (2018). Openface 2.0: Facial behavior analysis toolkit. In *2018 13th IEEE International Conference on Automatic Face Gesture Recognition (FG 2018)*, pages 59–66.

Bates, D., Mächler, M., Bolker, B., and Walker, S. (2015). Fitting linear mixed-effects models using lme4. *Journal of Statistical Software*, 67(1):1–48.

Bretz, F., Hothorn, T., and Westfall, P. (2016). *Multiple Comparisons Using R*. Chapman and Hall/CRC.

Carreño, C. R., Suárez, A., Torrecilla, J. L., Berrocal, M. C., Manchón, P. M., Manso, P. P., Bernabé, A. H., Fernández, D. G., Yujian Hong, and Rodríguez-Ponga Eyriès, P. M. (2022). Gaa-uam/scikit-fda: Version 0.5. `https://doi.org/10.5281/zenodo.4406983`.

Cecchetto, C. (2012). Sentence types. In Roland Pfau, et al., editors, *Sign language: An international handbook*, pages 292–315. De Gruyter Mouton.

Chung, Y., Rabe-Hesketh, S., Dorie, V., Gelman, A., and Liu, J. (2013). A nondegenerate penalized likelihood estimator for variance parameters in multilevel models. *Psychometrika*, 78:685–709, 10.

Chung, Y., Gelman, A., Rabe-Hesketh, S., Liu, J., and Dorie, V. (2015). Weakly informative prior for point estimation of covariance matrices in hierarchical models. *Journal of Educational and Behavioral Statistics*, 40:136–157, 04.

de Boor, C. (1978). *A Practical Guide to Splines*. Springer New York.

Fox, J. and Weisberg, S. (2019). *An R Companion to Applied Regression*. Sage, Thousand Oaks CA, third edition.

Gubian, M., Torreira, F., Strik, H., and Boves, L. (2009). Functional data analysis as a tool for analyzing speech dynamics - a case study on the french word c'était. In *Interspeech 2009*. ISCA, September.

Gubian, M., Torreira, F., and Boves, L. (2015). Using functional data analysis for investigating multidimensional dynamic phonetic contrasts. *Journal of Phonetics*, 49:16–40, March.

Hothorn, T., Bretz, F., and Westfall, P. (2008). Simultaneous inference in general parametric models. *Biometrical Journal*, 50(3):346–363, June.

Jolliffe, I. T. and Jackson, J. E. (1993). A user's guide to principal components. *The Statistician*, 42:76–77.

Kimmelman, V., Imashev, A., Mukushev, M., and Sandygulova, A. (2020). Eyebrow position in grammatical and emotional expressions in kazakh-russian sign language: A quantitative study. *PLOS ONE*, 15(6):e0233731, June.

Kuznetsova, A., Imashev, A., Mukushev, M., Sandygulova, A., and Kimmelman, V. (2021). Using computer vision to analyze non-manual marking of questions in KRSL. In *Proceedings of the 1st International Workshop on Automatic Translation for Signed and Spoken Languages (AT4SSL)*, pages 49–59, Virtual, August. Association for Machine Translation in the Americas.

Pedregosa, F., Varoquaux, G., Gramfort, A., Michel, V., Thirion, B., Grisel, O., Blondel, M., Müller, A., Nothman, J., Louppe, G., Prettenhofer, P., Weiss, R., Dubourg, V., Vanderplas, J., Passos, A., Cournapeau, D., Brucher, M., Perrot, M., and Duchesnay, E. (2018). Scikit-learn: Machine learning in python.

Pfau, R. and Quer, J. (2010). Nonmanuals: their prosodic and grammatical roles. In Diane Brentari, editor, *Sign Languages*, pages 381–402. Cambridge University Press.

Ramsay, J. and Silverman, B. (2002). *Applied Functional Data Analysis: Methods and Case Studies*. Springer New York.

Zadeh, A., Baltrušaitis, T., and Morency, L.-P. (2017). Convolutional experts constrained local model for facial landmark detection. *ArXiv e-prints*, arXiv:1611.08657.

Proceedings of the 10th Workshop on the Representation and Processing of Sign Languages (sign-lang@LREC 2022), pages 132–138
Language Resources and Evaluation Conference (LREC 2022), Marseille, 20-25 June 2022

Two New AZee Production Rules Refining Multiplicity in French Sign Language

Emmanuella Martinod, Claire Danet, Michael Filhol
Université Paris-Saclay, CNRS, Laboratoire Interdisciplinaire des Sciences du Numérique (LISN), 91400, Orsay, France
{emmanuella.martinod, claire.danet, michael.filhol}@lisn.upsaclay.fr

Abstract

This paper is a contribution to sign language (SL) modeling. We focus on the hitherto imprecise notion of "Multiplicity", assumed to express plurality in French Sign Language (LSF), using AZee approach. AZee is a linguistic and formal approach to modeling LSF. It takes into account the linguistic properties and specificities of LSF while respecting constraints linked to a modeling process. We present the methodology to extract AZee production rules. Based on the analysis of strong form–meaning associations in SL data (elicited image descriptions and short news), we identified two production rules structuring the expression of multiplicity in LSF. We explain how these newly extracted production rules are different from existing ones. Our goal is to refine the AZee approach to allow the coverage of a growing part of LSF. This work could lead to an improvement in SL synthesis and SL automatic translation.
Keywords: AZee, Sign language, Formal representation, Multiplicity, Plural

1. Introduction

The framework of this study is sign language (SL) formal description with the AZee model (Filhol et al., 2014). One of the outcomes of SL formal description is the potential use for SL generation with an avatar.

Current approaches are often elaborated based on spoken languages, which are linear systems (see (Hadjadj et al., 2018) for a review of existing systems). This may pose some fundamental problems since SLs are multi-linear visual-gestural languages. In contrast, AZee aims at integrating all the forms and phenomena observable in SL. It is a corpus-based approach that defines systematic links between observed forms and interpreted meanings.

This article deals with a specific problem related to one of these form–meaning associations: the case previously marked as "Multiplicity", which covered a vague notions of plurality. We propose a systematic study of this phenomenon in French Sign Language (LSF).

After briefly presenting the basics of the AZee approach, its production rules system, and a methodology to identify them (section 2), we will introduce the notion of `multiplicity` and explain why it needs refinement (section 3). Then, we will present the LSF data we analyzed (section 4) and detail the application of the methodology (section 5). We expose the obtained results, i.e. two new production rules (section 6). We will discuss this contribution (section 7) and finish with some propositions for future studies (section 8).

2. The AZee Approach

AZee is a formal approach for representing SL utterances and discourse. This is done by constructing recursive expressions that combine *production rules* applied to arguments.

Production rules are systematic links between observable forms (a set of articulators and the way they are synchronized or arranged in time) and semantic functions (an interpretation of such observable forms, i.e. their meaning). The forms can be parameterised with arguments, which can be mandatory or optional (Hadjadj et al., 2018). For example, rule `vêtement` associates the meaning "clothing" with the form given in figure 1, and has no arguments. Rule `all-of`, with list argument *items*, creates the meaning of a set containing all the *items*, focusing on the set as a whole (McDonald and Filhol, 2021).[1] The associated form is the concatenation of each item in *items*, recursively produced in an accelerated manner.

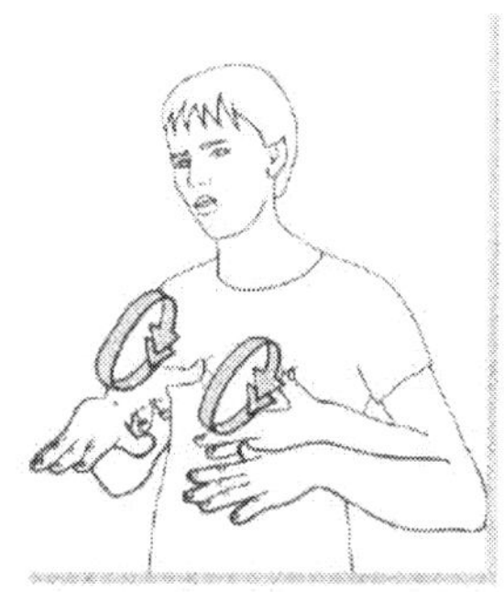

Figure 1: Form of production rule `vêtement` (IVT, 1997)

The set of all identified production rules is called the production set. It is then possible to combine them and build tree-structured expressions that represent complex utterances in SL, called *discourse expressions*. The AZeefication process consists in elaborating an AZee expression to represent a given SL utterance. This has recently been done on the corpus of real-life short news items *40 brèves v2* (Challant and Filhol, 2022), totalling 120 AZee discourse expressions covering 1 hour of signed discourse.

AZee provides a corpus-based methodology to identify production rules through the analysis of SL data. It consists in alternating search criteria of form and meaning until regular form–meaning associations are determined. In general,

[1] For information, the language of the name of the production rules (French and English here) is arbitrary, as any gloss can potentially be.

form observations are done on videos with the naked eye, which is the case in the work reported here, although additional software measurements would be possible for more accurate data, in particular for better analysis of dynamics. Meaning interpretation, though, is assumed to be performed by a human in the process. We explain the steps of the process below (Hadjadj et al., 2018), as we will be applying it later in section 5:

1. start with a form or meaning criterion X to explore;
2. locate and list all occurrences of X in a selected SL corpus, and let N_{occ} be the number of occurrences;
3. for each occurrence of X listed, add description elements:
    - elements of interpretation if X is a form criterion;
    - elements of form if X is a semantic criterion;
4. identify groups of at least two occurrences with similar description elements, and let:
    - N_{gp} be the number of identified groups;
    - N_{out} be the number of occurrences not included in any group;
5. if all of the following conditions are satisfied:
    - X is a meaning criterion;
    - $N_{gp} = 1$;
    - N_{out} is less than a threshold, e.g. 15% of N_{occ};

    then the form elements defining the unique group $X.1$ can be considered invariant, and we define a new production rule associating X with the invariant form, and this iteration stops;
6. if this iteration has not stopped, for each group $X.k, k \in 1..N_{gp}$:
    - if X is a meaning that can already be expressed using known production rules justifying the form $X.k$ or, conversely, $X.k$ is a meaning that can already be expressed using known production rules justifying the form X, then no new rule is to be found, nor any new search to be fired;
    - otherwise, recursively apply this methodology with a new iteration starting with the criterion defining group $X.k$.

3. The `Multiplicity` Issue

The AZeefication of the *40 brèves v2* corpus (LIMSI and LISN, 2022a) mentioned above resulted in some phenomena that AZee could not represent. In the AZee expressions, the authors have filled the parts covering those instances with an "ellipsis", using a dummy rule application and marking it with `%E`. Many of these ellipses were tentatively marked as `multiplicity` when concerning the expression of plurality.

For instance, Figure 2 shows two examples of motion repetition labeled `multiplicity`. Arrows show the trajectory of movement repetitions, and crosses stand for each of

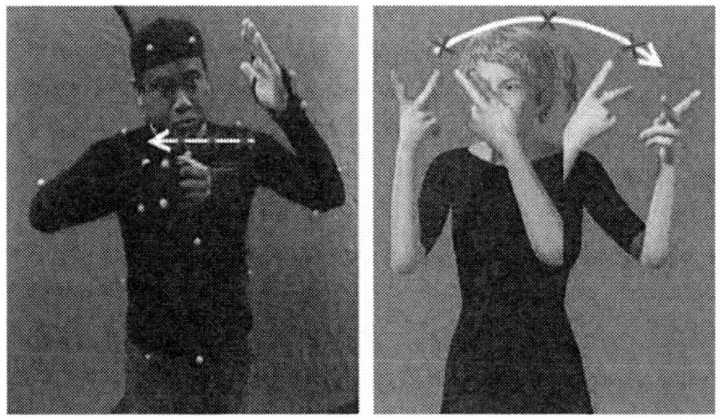

Figure 2: Two examples of motion repetition with different forms and meaning. Left side: from *Mocap1*: i0611, 00:09:32 ; Right side: from *Rosetta-LSF*: RST_X0047.demonstrateur1.mp4 00:03:60

these repetitions. On the left side, the signer represents a series of three aligned poles. His left hand stands for a roof while his right hand shows the set of successive aligned poles. On the right side, the virtual signer repeats three times the sign for "*town*" in LSF, with the meaning "towns everywhere".

Previous work in SL linguistics also mentions movement repetition as a strategy for expressing plurality in some SLs (Pfau and Steinbach, 2006; Kuhn, 2015). Although differences between SLs have been observed (Perniss et al., 2007; Steinbach, 2012; van Boven, 2021), it appears to be a possible strategy in LSF as well (Sallandre et al., 2021). However, these studies often use as examples a few isolated signs but there is no systematic analysis based on a corpus of SL data.

The problem with the `multiplicity` instances is that while the meanings might be captured with a common notion of quantity (count, duration, repetition...), no stable invariant form can be associated with it. Looking at figure 2, we can observe that in the left case, the trajectory is straight whereas in the right case, the trajectory is in contrast a circular one. In terms of meaning, finer distinctions seem also to be possible: the example on the left means for the geometric alignment to be interpreted, as opposed to that on the right. It would be wrong to interpret the towns as aligned on a circle.

Our objective was to clarify what rules should account for these repetitions and better define the "multiplicity" phenomenon with true form–meaning pairs extracted from SL data. To do this, we chose to apply the methodology for the extraction of production rules, starting from the most salient element that seems common to all cases in question, i.e. the repeated movement criterion (R), which we define as follows:

R Succession of deliberate motion strokes similar in path, by a same or symmetric body part, with no other significant motion in between. By *similar*, we mean to allow for geometric translation, symmetry and scaling.

We will apply the methodology to two different LSF video sets, which we present below.

Figure 3: Screenshot of a video from *Mocap1* corpus

4. Data

Available LSF corpora are scarce. The corpora we selected, *Mocap1* (LIMSI and CIAMS, 2020) and *Rosetta-LSF* (LIMSI and LISN, 2022b) are downloadable from Ortolang. They offer the advantage of containing two different discourse genres.

4.1. *Mocap1*

Mocap1 is a corpus of LSF recorded with a motion capture system and an HD camera. It was designed with the goal of carrying out multidisciplinary studies in Movement Sciences, Linguistics, and Computer Science.
This corpus is composed of 5 different tasks. The task on which we focused is a description task of 25 images, performed by eight deaf signers facing the camera, as shown in Figure 3. 94 videos out of 187 video files corresponding to this task were analyzed.
The nature of these data is challenging for the formal representation of LSF since they are descriptions of spatialized elements, where the signers use less lexical signs but instead rely on the iconic representation potentialities of their language.

4.2. *Rosetta-LSF*

Rosetta-LSF is an LSF corpus captured by a motion capture system (Vicon) with retroreflective markers recording at 100 Hz and a head-mounted oculometer (MocapLab MLab 50-W) recording at 50 Hz and rendered as a 3D avatar animation (Figure 4). This 3D rendering in good quality allows us to see the necessary details (movement, facial expression, gaze, etc.) to do the analysis. It was designed in the framework of a French public/private project that studied accessibility solutions for audiovisual content (Bertin-Lemée et al., 2022).
In contrast with *Mocap1*, the news titles translation task was chosen among the four of the ROSETTA project. This constitutes a list of nearly 194 news titles from a French public information channel. News content exhibits clean language, deals with any topic, which makes it a more conventional nature of the data.

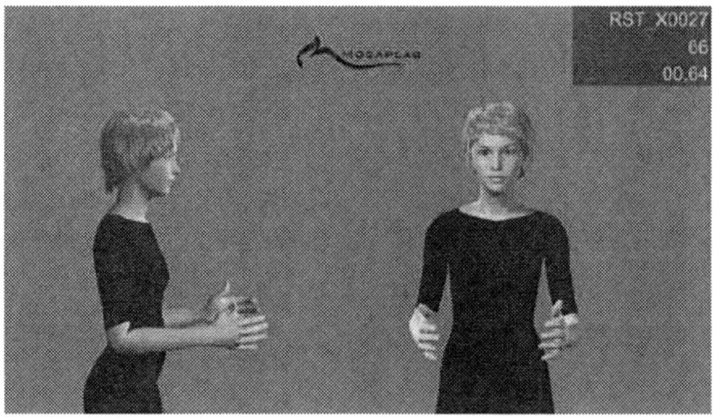

Figure 4: Screenshot of a video from *Rosetta-LSF*

5. Applying the Methodology

This section follows the methodology presented in section 2, starting with the form criterion R.

Iteration R

The first step is to identify and list all occurrences of criterion R (form criterion defined above, of a repeated movement) in the selected corpus. We found 756 occurrences (640 in *Mocap1* and 116 in *Rosetta-LSF*). For each occurrence of R, we then indicate elements of interpretation since R was a form criterion. For instance: a set of countable and counted elements.
After the description of the occurrences, 25 groups of at least two entries could be constituted on the basis of similar features, covering a significant portion of the list but leaving out 52 entries. We summarise this below:

- $N_{occ} = 756$
- $N_{gp} = 25$
- $N_{out} = 52$

Of the 25 groups formed, we give the first ten in size below, with the common semantic feature defining them and examples.

R.1 Set of countable but uncounted elements (448 entries)
Examples: "many flowers on the ground", "rows of trees", "companies"

R.2 Set of countable and counted elements (157 entries)
Example: "four chairs set around a table", "three people"

R.3 Set of uncounted countable and numerous elements (57 entries)
Example: "laying of tiles", "carpet mesh"

R.4 Permanence of a capacity/function for an object (25 entries)
Example: "curtain opening", "mechanical arm motion"

R.5 Wood (9 entries)

R.6 Clothing (8 entries)

R.7 Salt (6 entries)

R.8 Construction (5 entries)

R.9 Wine (5 entries)

R.10 House (3 entries)

...

Following the methodology requires that we now take each of these groups separately and either recognise a meaning–form association already accounted for by other rules of the known production set, or explore further by going through the steps again, starting with the criteria defining the group. All groups numbered R.5 and up happen to be trivial cases of known signs (dictionary entries) for which we already have a production rule justifying the observed form. For example R.6, whose form is that of figure 1, is easily explained with an application of rule `vêtement`. These groups need therefore not be explored any further.
In contrast, the other groups R.1 to R.4 must be explored recursively because no trivial way can be found to justify form R with a combination of known rules that would match the meaning defining the group. We do this below for R.1 and R.2, the last two R.3 and R.4 being marked as future research and not covered in this paper. For every cascading iteration, we report on the values for N_{occ}, N_{gp} and N_{out}, followed by a definition of each formed group in the iteration.

Iteration R.1

This iteration starts with a search for all occurrences meaning "set of countable, but uncounted, elements." The result of this search follows:

- $N_{occ} = 427$
- $N_{gp} = 2$
- $N_{out} = 21$

Most of the occurrences include either or both of the following conditions on a repeated motion:

(a) attenuation of precision or amplitude over the repetitions

(r) relocation of the successive repetitions

The two groups formed in this iteration are given below.

R.1.1 Repetition of a movement with (a) and (r)
Example: "shelves", the repeated movement being that for each flat shelf under the previous (see Fig. 5)

R.1.2 Repetition of a movement without (a) or without (r)
Example: "traffic jam", repetition of the shape of a car with forward relocation

This is not a stopping case, and none of those groups can be entirely accounted for with known rules. Two new iterations, one for each group, are necessary. They are presented below.

Iteration R.1.1

Search for form: repeated movement with attenuation and relocation.

- $N_{occ} = 406$
- $N_{gp} = 2$
- $N_{out} = 96$

We found two groups defined by meaning in this iteration.

R.1.1.1 Set of countable but uncounted elements without any order
Examples: "towns" (Fig. 2) (right), "roofs"

R.1.1.2 Set of countable but organized uncounted elements
Example: "poles", "shelves"

This is still not a stopping case. Two new iterations are necessary, one for each of those groups.

Iteration R.1.1.1

Search for meaning: set of uncounted, unordered countables.

- $N_{occ} = 49$
- $N_{gp} = 1$
- $N_{out} = 1$

A unique group formed:

R.1.1.1.1 Repetition of a movement along a circular path, with attenuation
Example: "towns" in Fig. 2 (right)

Because a unique group formed in an iteration started with a meaning criterion, and only one out of 49 occurrences falls out of the group (below 15% threshold), this is a stopping case. As explained in step 5 of the methodology, a new production rule, named `mult-around`, can now be defined. It associates meaning R.1.1.1 with form R.1.1.1.1, depending on a signed *item* and an optional location *loc* (default is neutral space in front of signer). A stand-alone specification is given in the result section recap.

Iteration R.1.1.2

Search for meaning: set of organized uncounted countables.

- $N_{occ} = 223$
- $N_{gp} = 1$
- $N_{out} = 4$

A unique group formed:

R.1.1.2.1 Repetition of a movement along a straight path, with attenuation
Example: "shelves" (Fig. 5)

Again this is a stopping case of the methodology. A new production rule is defined: `mult-in-a-row`, depending on a signed *item* and a *path* along which the items are placed. See the result section for a full specification.

This terminates iteration R.1.1.

Iteration R.1.2

Search for form: repeated movement without attenuation or without relocation.

- $N_{occ} = 37$
- $N_{gp} = 1$
- $N_{out} = 11$

A unique group formed:

R.1.2.1 Set of items, with exact count known
Example: "four chairs positioned at [...]"

The meaning defining R.1.2.1 can be constructed using the known `all-of` rule applied to the item list, which creates an expression meaning the set of items, focusing on the set as a whole. Such expression generates a form compatible with R.1.2.1, which means that R.1.2.1 needs no further exploration.

This being the only group in the iteration, no further exploration is needed for R.1.2. This indeed terminates R.1 all together.

Iteration R.2

Search for meaning: set of countable and counted elements.

- $N_{occ} = 156$
- $N_{gp} = 3$
- $N_{out} = 1$

Three groups formed:

R.2.1 repeated and relocated movement without attenuation
Example: "four plates"

R.2.2 repetition of a movement where each hand realizes an item
Example: "both sides of a river"

R.2.3 repetition of a movement with a hold and a blink between each repetition
Example: "two lamps"

We notice that all groups are defined by forms that we can already generate with combinations of existing rules such as `all-of`, `simultaneous`, `each-of` or `place-object` (McDonald and Filhol, 2021), which match the meaning of the current criterion R.2.
No groups are left to explore under iteration R.2. And as we said above, R.3 and R.4 are left for future research, which makes this the end of exploration R.

6. Results

Figure 6 provides a summary of the study. It allowed the identification of two new regular form–meaning associations. This constitutes two new production rules, as detailed below (section 61). We will test these new production rules by applying them to other data (section 62).

Figure 5: Example of R.1.1: movement repeated with attenuation and relocation, from *Mocap1*: i0812, 00:34:17

6.1. Two New Production Rules

`mult-around` discovered in iteration R.1.1.1

- arguments: signed *item*, point location *loc* (default is in front of signer)
- meaning: multiple instances of *item* scattered or spread out on a surface around *loc*, with the exact count unknown
- form: *item* repeated along an arc trajectory sweeping around *loc*, with attenuation of the movement

`mult-in-a-row` discovered in iteration R.1.1.2

- arguments: signed *item*, *path*
- meaning: multiple instances of *item* aligned along *path*, with the exact count unknown
- form: *item* repeated along *path*, with attenuation of the movement

6.2. Evaluation of the New Production Rules

To evaluate our newly extracted production rules, we applied them to another LSF corpus, the *40 brèves v2*. Indeed, (Challant and Filhol, 2022) initially found 207 occurrences of cases labeled `multiplicity` in this data. We have reviewed them to identify the occurrences now covered by our two production rules. In total, 63.5% of these cases are now covered by our new production rules. More precisely, 36.5% are `mult-around` occurrences, and 27% are `mult-in-a-row` occurrences: their form and meaning correspond to these rules.
Figure 7 shows examples of each of the two production rules in this data (`mult-around`, and `mult-in-a-row`). As in Figure 2, arrows stand for the trajectory of movement repetitions. On the left, the signer repeats the item for "dead," and, on the center, the signer repeats the item for "inhabitant,".
Another outcome of this study is that it allows increasing the portion of LSF phenomena AZee can cover. In total, including the two new production rules, 96.1% of the

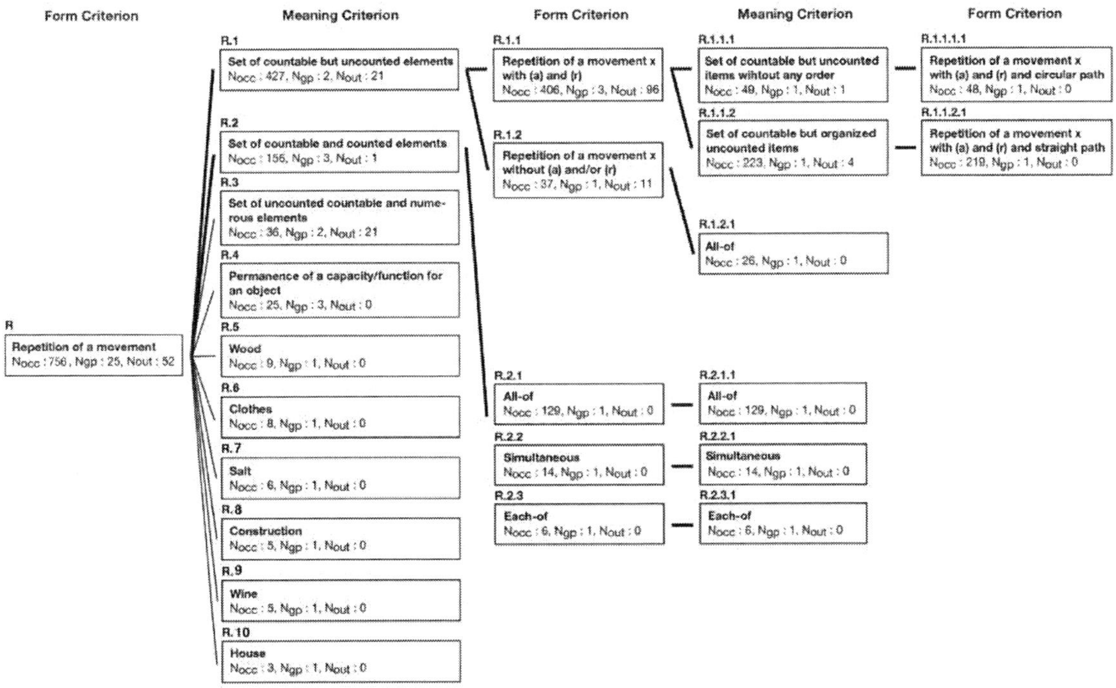

Figure 6: Overview of AZee production rules extraction process from R

LSF discourse from the *40 brèves v2* can be formally represented with AZee.

7. Discussion

In addition to enriching the existing production set, this study to us also exhibits the precision of the existing rules, which we explain in this section.

In our work, 70.27% of R.1.2 occurrences are occurrences of an existing rule we already mentioned, `all-of`.

This observation means that `all-of` is both formally and semantically close to the two rules that were finally highlighted. As a reminder, Rule `all-of`, its arguments, and its meaning are given hereinafter (McDonald and Filhol, 2021):

- All-of (*items*): Set of *items*, with focus on the set as a whole

In other words, this rule presents the association between the form of a list of items produced in an accelerated manner, and a meaning corresponding to "Set of items, with focus on the set as a whole".

From the meaning point of view, the two new production rules (i.e., `mult-around` and `mult-in-a-row`), on one side, and `all-of` on the other, are disjoint subsets of the previously labeled `multiplicity`. Our application of methodology highlighted that this assumption was not supported by the data. `all-of` creates the meaning of a set containing *items*, focusing on the set as a whole. But in the case of `mult-around` and `mult-in-a-row`, it is the same item that is repeated, and this item is necessarily countable and not counted, and either without any order or aligned.

From the form point of view, some cues are decisive in differentiating `all-of` from our two new production rules: the attenuation of the amplitude (or precision) of the repeated movement and the presence of a relocation of movement repetitions.

This observation overall underlines the semantic finesse of the different production rules, in line with semantic nuances observed in LSF.[2]

8. Conclusion and Prospects

The present study provided a better understanding of regular form–meaning associations regarding movement repetition in LSF. This contributes to enriching and refining the AZee LSF production set by adding two new production rules. This contributes to increase the ever growing proportion of the language that AZee can describe. Other studies could be conducted on the basis of this one.

Firstly, groups left unexplored (R.3 and R.4) might lead to other new production rules.

Secondly, among the initial 207 occurrences in *40 brèves v2*, we noticed that 36.7% are similar to what we observed in N_{out} from R.1.1 in our data. These occurrences displayed a specific type of relocation resulting from an alternation of movement of both hands. Moreover, this form seems to often refer to the same element. Indeed,

[2]In this regard, we notice that `mult-in-a-row` captures the possibility in LSF to project time into the signing space. Indeed, items repeated along *path* can represent items aligned in space, or repeated in time.

Figure 7: Examples of new production rules in *40 brèves v2*

in our data, 53.6% of these cases of specific relocation concerned the item *"people"* in LSF. In *40 brèves v2*, it represents 36.25%. Thus, these occurrences seem to share a similar form criterion. This subset could also be submitted to another iteration to reveal a possible specific form–meaning association.
Thirdly, we intend to test our two new production rules using a small-scale experimental study. Image stimuli containing only various multiplicities of entities (disordered or aligned) will be presented to a deaf signer equipped with a motion capture system. Their task will be to describe this plurality of entities. This will allow us to verify that the form cues included in the two rules (attenuation of movement and specific trajectories) are systematically verified in production.
Finally, AZeefication of more data in LSF could also be a good evaluation of these two new rules and the AZee system in general.

9. Acknowledgement

This work has been funded by the Bpifrance investment "Structuring Projects for Competitiveness" (PSPC), as part of the Serveur Gestuel project (IVès and 4Dviews Companies, LISN — University Paris-Saclay, and Gipsa-Lab — Grenoble Alpes University).

10. Bibliographical References

Bertin-Lemée, E., Braffort, A., Challant, C., Danet, C., Dauriac, B., Filhol, M., Martinod, E., and Ségouat. (2022). Rosetta-LSF: an Aligned Corpus of French Sign Language and French for Text-to-Sign Translation. In *LREC 2022, 13th Conference on Language Resources and Evaluation, Representation and Processing of Sign Languages*, Marseille, France.

Challant, C. and Filhol, M. (2022). A First Corpus of AZee Discourse Expressions. In *LREC 2022, 13th Conference on Language Resources and Evaluation, Representation and Processing of Sign Languages*, Marseille, France.

Filhol, M., Hadjadj, M., and Choisier, A. (2014). Non-Manual Features: The Right to Indifference. In *International Conference on Language Resources and Evaluation, 6th Workshop on the Representation and Processing of Sign Languages: Beyond the Manual Channel*, page 49–54, Reykjavik, Iceland.

Hadjadj, M., Filhol, M., and Braffort, A. (2018). Modeling French Sign Language: a proposal for a semantically compositional system. In *Proceedings of the Language Resources and Evaluation Conference*, page 4253–4258, Miyazaki, Japan.

IVT. (1997). *La Langue Des Signes, Dictionnaire Bilingue LSF-Français*, volume 2. International Visual Theatre, Paris.

Kuhn, J. (2015). *Cross-categorial singular and plural reference in sign language*. Ph.D. thesis, New York University.

McDonald, J. and Filhol, M. (2021). Natural synthesis of productive forms from structured descriptions of sign language. *Machine Translation*, 35(3):363–386.

Perniss, P. M., Pfau, R., and Steinbach, M. (2007). *Visible Variation: Comparative Studies on Sign Language Structure*. Walter de Gruyter.

Pfau, R. and Steinbach, M. (2006). Pluralization in sign and in speech: A cross-modal typological study. *Linguistic Typology*, 10(2):135–182.

Sallandre, M.-A., Zribi-Hertz, A., and Perini, M. (2021). La Langue des Signes Française (LSF). *Projet Langues et Grammaire en Ile-de-France*.

Steinbach, M. (2012). Plurality. In Markus Steinbach Roland Pfau et al., editors, *Sign language: An international handbook*, 37 6, page 112–136. De Gruyter Mouton, Berlin.

van Boven, C. (2021). Phonological restrictions on nominal pluralization in sign language of the netherlands: evidence from corpus and elicited data. *Folia Linguistica*, 55(2):313–359.

11. Language Resource References

LIMSI and CIAMS. (2020). *MOCAP1*. ISLRN 502-958-837-267-9.

LIMSI and LISN. (2022a). *40 brèves*. v2, ISLRN 988-557-796-786-3.

LIMSI and LISN. (2022b). *rosetta-lsf*. ISLRN 535-376-670-927-5.

Proceedings of the 10th Workshop on the Representation and Processing of Sign Languages (sign-lang@LREC 2022), pages 139–143
Language Resources and Evaluation Conference (LREC 2022), Marseille, 20-25 June 2022

Language Planning in Action: Depiction as a Driver of New Terminology in Irish Sign Language

Rachel Moiselle and Lorraine Leeson
Trinity College Dublin, Centre for Deaf Studies
moisellr@tcd.ie, leesonl@tcd.ie

Abstract

In this paper, we examine the linguistic phenomenon known as 'depiction', which relates to the ability to visually represent semantic components (Dudis, 2004). While some elements of this have been described for Irish Sign Language, with particular attention to the 'productive lexicon' (Leeson and Grehan, 2004; Leeson and Saeed, 2012; Matthews, 1996; O'Baoill and Matthews, 2000), here, we take the analysis further, drawing on what we have learned from cognitive linguistics over the past decade. Drawing on several recently developed domain-specific glossaries (e.g., Science Technology Engineering Math[1] (STEM), Covid-19[2], political domain, Sexual, Domestic and Gender Based Violence (SDGBV)-related vocabulary) we present ongoing analysis indicating that a deliberate focus on iconicity, in particular, elements of depiction, appears to be a primary driver. We also outline some potential implications from Deaf-led glossary development work in the context of Machine Translation goals, for example, for work in progress on the Horizon 2020 funded SignON project.[3]

Keywords: Irish Sign Language, Depiction, Glossary Development, Sign Language Machine Translation

1. Introduction and Background

Sign languages are not universal. They are naturally developing human languages (Fenlon and Wilkinson, 2015), which are typologically diverse; each sign language has its own lexicon and grammar.

1.1 Irish Sign Language

Irish Sign Language (ISL) is the indigenous sign language of Ireland. It is used by some 6,500 deaf people on the island of Ireland: 5,000 in the Republic and 1,500 in the North (Leeson and Saeed, 2012).

ISL is the third official language of Ireland, following adoption of the Irish Sign Language Act (2017). As Mohr and Leeson (in press) note, while formal recognition of ISL is a recent phenomenon, we can trace reference to signing in Ireland to at least the eighteenth century. Thus, ISL is not a 'new' language. (and see Leonard and Conama (2020) for additional discussion of same).

ISL has had many influences, arising from contact with British Sign Language (BSL), French Sign Language (LSF), ASL, French and English. Additionally, we can say that other influencing factors include gesture, educational policy (which has impacted on the language in many ways; see, for example, McDonnell and Saunders 1993), and new technologies.

1.2 Depiction

Sign languages are expressed in the visual-gestural modality, drawing upon a range of articulators to express and perceive a linguistic message (Vermeerbergen, Leeson and Crasborn 2007). Iconicity is a phenomenon that has received a great deal of attention in the sign language literature historically (e.g., Klima and Bellugi 1979, Brennan, Hughes and Lawson 1984, Brennan 1990, etc.).

Many terms in sign languages exhibit iconic mappings. Indeed, the iconic correspondences of many signs are clear even to non- signers. However only one set of these signs are said to have the ability to visually represent semantic components - depicting signs (Liddell 2003). In employing depiction, signers 'provide information about what an entity or event is like, what it looks like, or even what it acts like' (Thumann 2013, p. 316).

Depiction is not a phenomenon unique to sign languages. Speakers can also leverage depiction in taking on the role of other people, quoting their speech or imitating their actions. It can also have a significant semantic and possibly even grammatical role in a sentence (Lu and Goldin-Meadow 2018).

Dudis (2007) discusses the distinction between signs that depict and those that do not. The ASL sign for 'bird' (which is identical in ISL) is presented by Dudis as exemplifying an iconic but non-depicting sign: 'the manual articulator corresponds to the beak, its location to the location on the bird's head, and so forth. Yet, the sign does not function to describe what the bird looks like, nor does it function to describe the actions of a bird' (Dudis 2007, p. 1).

In contrast, Dudis illustrates how a signer describing a new light fixture in a kitchen known to the addressee, is an example of a depicting sign. Through the creation of a conceptual blend including a previously established mental space, Dudis explains that the signer depicts many features of this light fixture including its 'general bowl-like shape', 'the direction towards which certain sides of the fixtures or facing', 'the location...upwards and slightly away from the signer' (Dudis 2007, p. 11–12).

This example is indicative of how Dudis describes depiction in ASL as observed through the selective projection of Real-Space elements (Real Space meaning mental conceptualisations of a signer's current surrounding physical environment, which include the 'setting, vantage point, temporal progression, the subject, and the body' in

[1] https://www.dcu.ie/islstem
[2] https://www.irishdeafsociety.ie/irish-sign-language-for-covid19-related-vocabulary
[3] https://signon-project.eu

combination with 'cognitive abilities including the ability to partition the body into several meaningful zones, to compress the setting and the time of the scenes being depicted, and to create simultaneous blends (Dudis 2007, p.19).

Dudis writes that from a cognitive linguistic perspective, 'when ASL verbs and constructions are shown to have components that depict semantic features, depiction becomes a focus of grammatical analysis' concluding his work by stating that it 'demonstrates the significant potential through further analysis for elucidating the role depiction has in ASL grammar' (Dudis 2007, p. 29). This statement provides significant justification and incentive for research on this linguistic phenomenon, particularly in relation to language development/evolution.

Against this backdrop, we note that in recent years we have seen a significant focus on the development of new terminology in sign languages in a variety of domains including (for ISL) terms around sexual, domestic and gender based violence (SDGBV); STEM; Covid-19; and political concepts.

1.3 Depiction: A Gesture Studies Approach

Identifying a gestural substrate for signs is not the same as saying that sign languages are 'just' gesture. Indeed, as Wilcox (2004) writes:

'Positing a gesture-language interface does not deny that signed languages are unique in important ways. Suggesting that signed languages are kin to gestures, or that developmental paths may lead from gesture to language, doesn't mean that signed languages are merely gestures. It simply means that the remarkable family resemblance between signs and gestures, and the tight integration of speech and gesture, point to a common ancestor' (Wilcox 2004, p. 67).

Drawing on the canon of gesture studies - and analysing this through a cognitive linguistic lens - provides us with contemporary and cutting-edge analytical tools through which to define and describe depiction strategies. This work also facilitates us in understanding the linguistic ideologies that help drive contemporary community decision making around new vocabulary, an issue that draws significant community interest and engagement (e.g., see Kusters, Green, Moriarty and Snoddon (2020)). In the Irish context, for example, a webinar organised by the Centre for Deaf Studies in September 2021 to discuss new vocabulary in ISL drew an audience of over 100 deaf people.

Our work in this space will also provide robust descriptions that can feed into the computational work required to prepare the machine translation element of the SignON communication.

1.4 SignON

SignON aims to reduce the communication gap between deaf, hard of hearing, and hearing individuals through a user-centred and community-driven approach, involving stakeholder-led user profiles from its inception.

To achieve this goal, the consortium is developing the SignON free and easy-to-use application and open-source framework to improve daily face-to-face communication and facilitate the fair, unbiased, and inclusive spread of information and digital content.

Funded by the European Commission's Horizon 2020 programme, the SignON consortium is developing SLMT approaches across a range of signed and spoken/written languages: ISL, Dutch Sign Language (NGT), Flemish Sign Language (VGT), Spanish Sign Language (LSE), as well as English, Dutch and Spanish oral languages. SignON is a project in progress that runs from 2021-2023 and comprises 17 partners from across Europe.

Through collaboration with European Deaf and hard-of-hearing communities, SignON researchers are (re)defining use cases and co-designing and co-delivering the SignON service and application. This communication service will be more than an advanced translation system: SignON aims to deliver signed conversations via a life- like avatar built with the latest graphic technologies.

At the heart of the SignON consortium's approach is a commitment to co-construction. From conception to implementation, Deaf community views are built into our approach. The SignON consortium includes deaf advocacy organisations and deaf academics.

The overall objective of the project is the fair, unbiased, and inclusive spread of information and digital content in European society.

2. In Progress Linguistic Analysis of New Terminology ISL

As stated above, we are in the process of conducting a first pass linguistic analysis of new terminology in Irish Sign language from a variety of domain-specific glossaries: STEM, Covid-19, political domain, and SDGBV related vocabulary. Specifically, we are analysing these glossaries to identify the role of depiction within these vocabularies, and to define the depiction strategies for the purposes of the SignON project.

As part of our general analysis, our work will involve empirical data collection; we have recently received research ethics approval to conduct three focus groups with the following cohorts:

1. Deaf interpreting students at the Centre for Deaf Studies who were involved in generating the ISL sexual, domestic, and gender-based violence glossary as part of the Erasmus+ Justisigns 2 project and the ISL political signs glossary developed in partnership with the Houses of the Oireachtas (Irish legislature) across 2021.
2. Individuals involved in other glossary development processes (e.g., the DCU STEM glossary project; the Covid-19 glossary project; confirming the SDGBV glossary for the Erasmus+ Justisigns 2 project; those engaged in pushing for vocabulary use shifts (e.g., Black Lives Matter)).
3. Deaf community members who are interested in the topic of language change and new vocabulary.

These focus groups will be held between April-November 2022. The purpose of conducting focus groups with those who were actively engaged in the vocabulary development process is to gain insight into conscious linguistic motivation around the prevalence of features we observed, of which depiction is a primary example. A focus group with Deaf community members who were not involved in these vocabulary development processes will help us document broader views around features that are preferred/disliked and will likely help us explore how gendered, generational, and perhaps other views may intersect with linguistic accessibility judgements.

Our key aims for the focus groups are as follows:

- To identify the guiding principles and linguistic motivators in the development of these new terms;
- To provide sociological context to the linguistic features identified in our feature analysis of the terms;
- To identify key concerns and views within the Deaf community of new (and continuously developing) terminology in a variety of different domains: SDGBV, STEM, Covid-19, and political domain.
- To stimulate a conversation with consideration of macro-level equality, diversity, and inclusion related matters in recent changes to the ISL lexicon (e.g., signs regarding race and ethnic groupings which tend to be contested).

Our key research questions, therefore, are as follows:

1. What were the linguistic motivations in the development process of new vocabulary in the domains considered for Irish Sign Language?
2. Were any sociological factors considered in the development of these new signs?
3. What are the views in the Deaf community in relation to how new terminology is/should be developed?
4. What bodies/groups in the community should be consulted?
5. Are there any key concerns regarding the development of new signs? If so, what are these? How could they be ameliorated?
6. How could feedback processes for proposed vocabulary items best be negotiated?
7. How/where/should/could new signs be shared with the community?

Horizon 2020 beneficiaries such as SignON are encouraged to make their research data findable, accessible, interoperable, and reusable (FAIR) and to follow the principle of data being 'as open as possible as closed as necessary'. In line with this ethos, we intend-and have research ethics approval- to film these focus groups, which will be conducted through ISL, and archive them online so they function as an open dataset (with the express permission of all participants).

ISL is an under-resourced minority language, particularly in terms of digital content. Our focus groups will be capturing conversations about ISL terminology in ISL. Most linguistic research into ISL is published in English: thus, archiving these focus groups will serve as a mechanism towards the process of repatriating the language to the community of origin in this area of research.

2.1 Data

Our analysis of the vocabulary is a work in progress. We have begun a preliminary analysis of vocabulary in the domain of DSGBV drawn from the Justisigns 2 project.[4] This glossary presents 80 SL terms in this domain, drawn from the Istanbul Convention: Action against violence against women and domestic violence. The Justisigns 2 project team is taking a co-construction approach to the glossary development process – draft items were shared with the wider community and currently, key stakeholder representatives are finalising terms that will be published in summer 2022.

Our analysis of new terminology in ISL, and this SDBV vocabulary specifically, is also at an interim stage.

Our goal is to identify key drivers underpinning new vocabulary development, specifically to explore whether (and if so, to what degree) depiction is one such driver. We will cross check this analysis with the focus groups.

2.2 Initial Analysis – Framework

Our linguistic analysis follows two distinct phases:

Phase 1: Feature Analysis

1. ***Initialisation:*** where the first letter of the English word is represented by a fingerspelled item from the ISL alphabet (McDonnell 1997).
2. ***Depiction:*** relates to the ability to visually represent semantic components (Dudis 2007).
3. ***Arbitrary:*** whereby no element of the form of the sign resembles aspects of its meaning (Meir and Tkachman 2018).
4. ***Mouthing:*** where the corresponding word of the surrounding spoken language is voicelessly mouthed (Boyes Braem and Sutton-Spence 2001).
5. ***Metaphor:*** 'the use of an item from one semantic domain in a different semantic domain in order to characterise the latter in terms of the former (Meir and Cohen 2018, p.1).
6. ***Metonymy:*** 'a cognitive and linguistic process through which we use one thing to refer to another' (Littlemore 2015, p.1).
7. ***Body Partitioning:*** where the signer subdivides their body to represent a number of different actors at the same time (Dudis 2004).
8. ***Simultaneity***: where distinct lexical elements that are bound together in some form of syntactic relationship are produced independently and simultaneously in autonomous channels (Miller 1994).
9. ***Compounding:*** 'a compound is a combination of two free morphemes that form a new sign/word with a different (but related) meaning' (Sutton-Spence and Woll 1999, p.102).

Phase 2: Depiction Analysis

The framework that is being used in this research follows an integrated approach. We combine a taxonomy of gesture studies definitions of depiction which has been developed by English (forthcoming) following the work of, e.g. Müller (1998), Mason Carro, Groudbeek and Kramer

[4] https://justisigns2.com

(2016, 2017), and Hwang et al. (2017). Key elements include:

1. ***Handling:*** a transitive action involving imitating operating a tool or device.
2. ***Enactment:*** an intransitive action which entails imitating an action with no object use.
3. ***Portrayal:*** hands embody the item they portray.
4. ***Molding:*** hands sculpt a 3D shape. Two sub-groups are distinguished: static and dynamic. Molding static gestures enclose a shape with no movement involved while molding dynamic gestures depict an object's shape with hands in motion.
5. ***Drawing:*** the hand traces a shape or a trajectory.
6. ***Personification:*** Personification entails participants becoming the entity they wish to represent by "mapping the body of a non-human entity onto the human body, using the human head to represent parallel locations on a non-human head, the human body to represent a non-human body, and human appendages to represent nonhuman appendages" (Hwang et al., 2017 p. 576).
7. ***Placing:*** These gestures place an imaginary item in gesture space or inform about a spatial relation between two or more imaginary items.
8. ***Other:*** All other gestures are classified as "other".

We have added sign language specific considerations including how embodiment plays out in the semantic presentation of linguistic concepts and the significance of point of view (e.g., as in two possible signs for 'rape' illustrated in examples[5] 1 and 2 below, and see Leeson and Seed (2020)).

Example 1: RAPE (1) (ISL) - Agentive perspective[6]

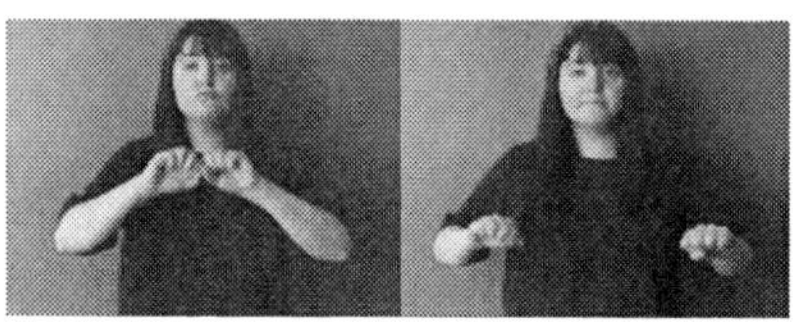

(a) RAPE 1 (onset) (b) RAPE 1 (offset)

Example 2: RAPE (2) (ISL) - Patient perspective

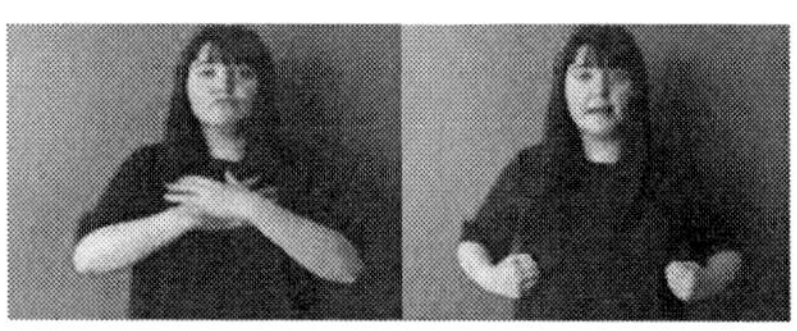

(a) RAPE 2 (onset) (b) RAPE 2 (offset)

Adopting a gesture studies approach to the analysis of depiction in a sign language is novel. Work in this arena to date has tended to define depiction categories with reference primarily to sign language specific linguistic forms, for example depicting verbs (classifiers), surrogate space (role shifts, constructed dialogue), token space, buoys (Cormier et al. 2012, Liddell 2003, Thumann 2013).

Our intent in adopting this integrated method to defining depiction strategies is twofold. Firstly, bringing a broader lens by including additional gesture dimensions will facilitate robust descriptions and categorisations of depiction. Secondly, this analysis will also provide a thorough examination of the relationship between the gestural substrate of ISL and depiction. We are also hopeful that we can build on the work of others, like Smith and Hofmann (2020) in identifying patterns of co-occurrence of features.

2.3 Initial Thoughts

This work represents an opportunity to delve into a period of deliberate language planning in progress. Our first pass analysis of this data points to a high incidence of depiction. We have identified depiction in 63% of established lexical items considered and in 91% of newly proposed lexical items. Thus far in our analysis, depiction has co-occurred with embodiment 100% of the time. We have observed instances of (proposed) semantic bleaching, specifically the lessening in iconic immediacy in visceral signs. For example, the third possible sign that was suggested for the term 'rape' does not make use of the body as the previous two proposed terms did, but rather makes use of a classifier. Interestingly, this sign was rejected by the stakeholder group signing off on the final lexicon to be adopted, with Examples 1 and 2 maintained.

Example 3: Rape (3) (ISL) - Classifier

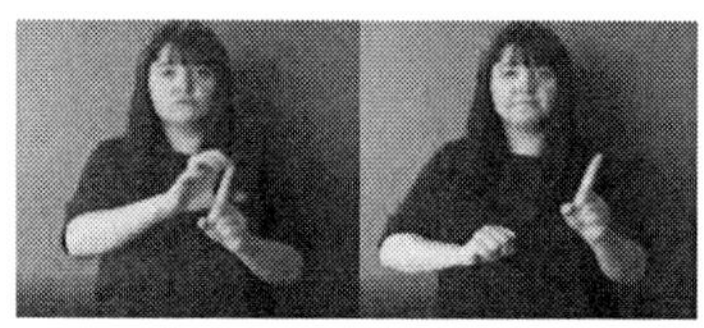

(a) RAPE (onset) (b) RAPE (offset)

2.4 Next Steps

Our primary focus over the coming months is to continue our data analysis and conduct our empirical data collection: engaging with those involved in the generation of new lexical items for special purpose glossaries and the Irish Deaf community at large through our planned focus groups. These are presented for the purpose of discussion and debate in addition to the purpose of gaining insights into the drivers of lexical creation in ISL (and prime discussion for other SLs).

While the knowledge we intend to gain from this work is important in its own right in relation to the role of linguistic motivation in language evolution, it is also is intended to serve a more immediate practical purpose: providing robust linguistic descriptions of depiction that will feed into the computational work required to prepare the machine element of the SignON partners until the end of the lifecycle of the project in 2023 and possibly beyond.

[5] https://www.youtube.com/channel/UCVaVfZvPa16NWvjaupUmHeA for a full list of glossary terms

[6] Agentive and patient perspectives refer to distinct thematic roles denoting the initiator of some action and the entity affected by some action respectively (Saeed 2015).

3. Acknowledgements

This work is supported by the SignON Project. SignON has received funding from the European Union's Horizon 2020 research and innovation programme, grant agreement number 101017255.

4. Bibliographical References

Boyes Braem, P., and Sutton-Spence, R. (eds.) (2001). *The Hands Are the Head of the Mouth. The Mouth as Articulator in Sign Languages*. Hamburg: Signum Press.

Brennan, M. (1990). *Word Formation in British Sign Language*. Stockholm: University of Stockholm.

Brennan, M., Hughes, G., and Lawson, L. K. (1984). *Words in Hand: a structural analysis of the signs of British Sign Language*. Edinburgh: Edinburgh BSL Research Project.

Cormier, K., Quinto-Pozos, D., Sehyr, Z., and Schembri, A. (2012). Lexicalisation and de-lexicalisation processes in sign languages: Comparing depicting constructions and viewpoint gestures. *Language & Communication* 32 (4), 329-348.

Dudis, P. (2004). Body partitioning and real-space blends. *Cognitive Linguistics* 15 (2), 223-238.

Dudis, P. (2007). Types of depiction in ASL. Manuscript, Gallaudet University.

English, E. (forthcoming) *Can you mold, handle or portray it? Iconicity and metaphor in depiction strategies in co-speech gesture.* PhD Dissertation. Dublin: CLCS, Trinity College Dublin.

Fenlon, J., and Wilkinson, E. (2015). Sign languages in the world. In A. Schembri and C. Lucas (Eds.), *Sociolinguistics and Deaf communities*. Cambridge: Cambridge University Press, 5–28.

Government of Ireland (2017). Irish Sign Language Act. URL: https://beta.oireachtas.ie/en/bills/bill/2016/78/.

Hwang, S.O., Tomita, N., Morgan, H., Ergin, R., İlkbaşaran, D., Seegers, S., Lepic, R., Padden, C. (2017). Of the body and the hands: patterned iconicity for semantic categories. *Language and Cognition*, 9(4), 573–602.

Klima, E.S., and Bellugi, U. (1979). *The Signs of Language*. Cambridge, Mass. Harvard University Press.

Kusters, A., Green, M., Moriarty, E., and Snoddon, K. (Eds.) (2020). *Sign Language Ideologies in Practice*. Berlin: De Gruyter Mouton.

Leeson, L., and Grehan, C. (2004). To the lexicon and beyond: The effect of gender on variation in Irish Sign Language. In M. Van Herreweghe and M. Vermeerbergen (Eds.), *To the lexicon and beyond: Sociolinguistics in European deaf communities*. Washington DC: Gallaudet University Press, 39–73.

Leeson, L., and Saeed, J.I. (2012). *Irish Sign Language*. Edinburgh: Edinburgh University Press.

Leeson, L., and Saeed, J.I. (2020). Embodiment in ISL Passives. *Teanga* (11), 48–66.

Leonard, C., and Conama, J.B. (2020) In Search of ISL's Pre-History. The Complex Origins of Irish Sign Language(s)? *Teanga* (11), 1-17.

Liddell, S.K. (2003). *Grammar, Gesture, and Meaning in American Sign Language*. Cambridge: Cambridge University Press.

Littlemore, J. (2015). *Metonymy*. Cambridge University Press.

Lu, J. C., and Goldin-Meadow, S. (2018). Creating images with the stroke of a hand: Depiction of size and shape in sign language. *Frontiers in psychology*, 9.

Masson-Carro, I., Goudbeek, M., and Krahmer, E. (2016). Can you handle this? The impact of object affordances on how co-speech gestures are produced. *Language, cognition and neuroscience*, 31(3), 430–440. DOI: 10.1080/23273798.2015.1108448.

Masson-Carro, I., Goudbeek, M., and Krahmer, E. (2017). How what we see and what we know influence iconic gesture production. *Journal of nonverbal behavior*, 41(4), 367–394.

Matthews, P.A. (1996). *The Irish Deaf Community – Volume 1*. ITE, Dublin.

McDonnell, P., and Saunders, H. (1993). Sit on Your Hands: Strategies to Prevent Signing. In R. Fischer and H. Lane (Eds.), *Looking Back: A Reader on the History of Deaf Communities and their Sign Languages*. Hamburg: Signum Verlag. pp. 255–260.

Meir, I., and Cohen, A. (2018). Metaphor in sign languages. *Frontiers in psychology*, 9, 1025.

Meir, I., and Tkachman, O. (2018). Iconicity. In Oxford Research Encyclopedia of Linguistics.

Miller, C. (1994). Simultaneous Constructions in Quebec Sign Language. In M. Brennan and G.H. Turner (eds.), *Word Order Issues in Sign Language*. Working Papers. International Sign Linguistics Association, pp. 89–112.

Mohr, S. and Leeson, L. (in press). Ireland's Third Language: Irish Sign Language. In Ray Hickey (ed.) Oxford Handbook of Irish English. Oxford: Oxford University Press.

Müller, C. (1998). Iconicity and gesture. In S. Santi, I. Guaïtella, C. Cavé, and G. Konopczynski (Eds.), *Oralité et gestualité* Paris: L'Harmattan, pp. 321–328.

Müller, C. (2014b). Gestural modes of representation as techniques of depiction. In C. Müller, A. Cienki, E. Fricke, S. H. Ladewig, D. McNeill, & J. Bressem (Eds.), *Body – language – communication. An international handbook on multimodality in human interaction* (pp. 1687-1702). Berlin: De Gruyter Mouton

O'Baoill, D., and Matthews, P.A. (2000). *The Irish Deaf Community, Volume 2: The Structure of Irish Sign Language*. Dublin: ITE.

Ortega, G., and Özyürek, A. (2020). Systematic mappings between semantic categories and types of iconic representations in the manual modality: A normed database of silent gesture. *Behavior research methods*, 52, 51–67.

Saeed, J. I. (2015). *Semantics*. John Wiley and Sons.

Smith, R. and Hofmann, M. (2020). A Lexical Frequency Analysis of Irish Sign Language. *Teanga* (11), 18–47.

Sutton-Spence, R., and Woll, B. (1999). *The linguistics of British Sign Language: an introduction*. Cambridge University Press.

Thumann, M. (2013). Identifying Recurring Depiction in ASL Presentations. *Sign Language Studies*, 13, 316–349.

Vermeerbergen, M., Leeson, L., and Crasborn, O. (eds.) (2007). *Simultaneity in Signed Languages*. Amsterdam: John Benjamins.

Wilcox, S. (2004). Gesture and language: Cross-linguistic and historical data from signed languages. *Gesture*, 4(1), 43–73.

Proceedings of the 10th Workshop on the Representation and Processing of Sign Languages (sign-lang@LREC 2022), pages 144–147
Language Resources and Evaluation Conference (LREC 2022), Marseille, 20-25 June 2022

Facilitating the Spread of New Sign Language Technologies across Europe

Hope E. Morgan[1], Onno Crasborn[1] Maria Kopf[2] Marc Schulder[2] Thomas Hanke[2]
[1] Centre for Language Studies, Radboud University;
[2] Institute of German Sign Language and Communication of the Deaf, University of Hamburg

[1]{hope.morgan, onno.crasborn}@ru.nl
[2]{maria.kopf,marc.schulder,thomas.hanke}@uni-hamburg.de

Abstract

For developing sign language technologies like automatic translation, huge amounts of training data are required. Even the larger corpora available for some sign languages are tiny compared to the amounts of data used for corresponding spoken language technologies. The overarching goal of the European project EASIER is to develop a framework for bidirectional automatic translation between sign and spoken languages and between sign languages. One part of this multi-dimensional project is that it will pool available language resources from European sign languages into a larger dataset to address the data scarcity problem. This approach promises to open the floor for lower-resourced sign languages in Europe. This article focusses on efforts in the EASIER project to allow for new languages to make use of such technologies in the future. What are the characteristics of sign language resources needed to train recognition, translation, and synthesis algorithms, and how can other countries including those without any sign resources follow along with these developments? The efforts undertaken in EASIER include creating workflow documents and organizing training sessions in online workshops. They reflect the current state of the art, and will likely need to be updated in the coming decade.

Keywords: sign language resources, sign language corpora, sign language lexicons, training

1. Introduction

Various inputs are needed to develop functional workflows for language technologies. These technologies are varied, including visual recognition of signed utterances, cross-lingual transfer and naturalistic avatars. Annotated corpora associated to rich lexical databases have an important role to play. In the case of sign languages, these corpora have to be annotated manually, as there is no way of doing so automatically yet. Unlike video data with interpreters or videos from signers of various skill levels on social media (Bragg et al. 2019, De Meulder 2021, Leeson 2021), high quality linguistic corpora more often include the natural language use of fluent deaf signers and conversational rather than monologic discourse. Even more importantly, they contain detailed time-aligned linguistic data rather than merely translations. Yet, there are many well-known challenges with using these corpora, including the fact that they are rather small compared to what language engineers for spoken languages work with, and that their content is very diverse, leading to low type-token ratios. This leads to challenges for many language technologies that rely on significant quantities of training data. The problem we focus on here is that for many European countries there are still very few annotated corpora at all.

Two current projects, EASIER[1] and SignON[2] (each running from 2021-2023), both endeavor to advance the automatic translation of sign languages. These two projects have some overlapping and some complementary goals. One of the notable aspects of the EASIER project is a concerted effort to focus on language documentation datasets; specifically, how to integrate them into the translation workflow and how to make sure that datasets from under-resourced languages are not overlooked presently and in the future. In this paper, we describe the steps that EASIER has taken and will take to do this.

Even within EASIER's core sign languages, Sign Language of the Netherlands (NGT), German Sign Language (DGS), British Sign Language (BSL), French Sign Language (LSF), Greek Sign Language (GSL), Italian Sign Language (LIS), and Swiss German Sign Language (DSGS), there is substantial variation with respect to the size and nature of language resources available. These languages were pragmatically selected because of expertise in the languages or use of the datasets among the project partners. Other European sign languages for which sizeable corpora and lexicons are available include Swedish Sign Language (SSL), Finnish Sign Language (FinSL), and Polish Sign Language (PJM).

Plans to address the inclusion of large datasets, as well as partial or new datasets from various languages are addressed below. EASIER will direct special attention on how to support linguists and deaf communities in countries with partial datasets or new projects to create sign resources that are commensurate with emerging European standards. The following sections sketch how we aim to achieve this.

2. Overview of Datasets for Sign Languages in Europe

At the onset of the EASIER project, it was recognized that preparing datasets in other languages would be important, not only for potential benefit to the current project (as data inputs), but well into the future. This desire to include more sign languages also dovetails with the ethical consideration to not leave out smaller or less-resourced languages in Europe from participating in technological advances.

However, at the beginning of the project, there was no comprehensive or current survey of these datasets. Therefore, the first step was to gather information about all the known sign language resources in the EU that would meet the needs of the EASIER pipeline. This was accomplished in the report *Overview of the Datasets for the Sign Languages of Europe* (Kopf, Schulder, and Hanke 2021) which identifies and describes 26 corpora and 41 lexical resources covering 24 sign languages.

[1] https://www.project-easier.eu

[2] https://signon-project.eu

By clarifying the existing resources of these languages, it will be possible to build a bridge for them to participate in at least some parts of a machine translation pipeline, giving these languages a head start when it comes to further developing or integrating resources to ultimately enable full two-way translation.

One of the findings in the Kopf et al. (2021) report was that high-quality training data for language technologies does not yet exist for the majority of European SLs. Fragmented and small datasets can be found for approximately half of the European SLs; for the rest no suitable resources could be identified.

3. Harmonizing Existing Datasets

Having identified quality datasets, the next challenge is to make sure their contents are machine-readable. Over the decades, as new language corpus projects were implemented, they borrowed some methods and annotation conventions from previous documentation projects starting with Johnston's seminal work on Auslan (Johnston 2010), but each team also developed their own conventions and notations along the way. The EASIER project recognized that each of these idiosyncratic systems would need to be translated into a common interchange format in order to be usable for language technology pipelines.

In order to understand exactly how the datasets differed, the report *Specification for the Harmonization of Sign Language Annotations* (Kopf et al. 2022) analyzed each available set of annotation conventions and the associated annotations of the available corpora for over 20 aspects, including segmentation, compounds, repetition, name signs, directional verbs, etc. This report also summarizes the notation of non-manuals and compares handshape coding across corpora.

With a much clearer picture of how the corpus resources of European sign languages both align and differ in their notation, the report then proposes a basic single unified interchange format that would be able to encode the information relevant to the EASIER translation pipeline. Because this format must be easily and unambiguously parsable by software, we propose using a JSON container structure to encode signs and other linguistic units (buoys, fingerspelling, etc.).

This interchange format will continue to develop as converters for individual corpora are written. The initial effort and most work by project partners within EASIER will be given to converting corpus data from the six core project sign languages. However, the EASIER project would also like to be able to incorporate data from other sign languages. This would allow the inclusion of more languages in the translation system as well as providing additional training data. Even outside of the EASIER system, use of the interchange format could support and speed up the integration of datasets into technology pipelines and the use of multiple datasets in quantitative linguistic studies.

With the detailed picture of relevant sign language resources in Europe and the basic interchange format established, the next issue is how to facilitate the entry of this data into the EASIER pipeline for resource managers. These managers include language documentation teams, institutions with national corpora, and possibly individual researchers. There are three broad audiences among them: (1) those that already have relatively large-scale resources that are richly coded, (2) those with partial language resources (e.g., a good online dictionary, but no corpus), and (3) those who have just recently or will soon start language documentation projects. For each of these audiences, it should be determined what they need to know to be able to integrate their data with the EASIER pipeline.

There are only a few examples of the first type of audience that are not already in the EASIER or SignON project. Among them are the datasets for SSL, FinSL, and PJM mentioned above. Given that expertise was developed in these countries to create large-scale annotated corpora, significant capacity-building has already taken place. This makes it likely that resource managers for these languages will be able to use our published documentation to develop their own converters for the interchange format with minimal input from the EASIER project partners. However, the other two audiences may need further support. The EASIER project therefore designed a specific work package to reach out to these groups, described next.

4. Extending to Other Sign Languages

In this section, we describe the steps to extend the fruits of the EASIER project to reach more sign languages. This is a long-term endeavor that will not be realized within the short timeframe of this project, but we hope will prepare sign language resources to be ready for the next steps in machine translation in the future.

4.1 Defining the "Minimal Contents" for a New Language Dataset

For the two audiences who do not already have relatively rich corpora and/or lexical resources – that is, those with partial language resources and those who have just recently or will soon start language documentation projects – it is important to provide guidance on what it would entail to create, modify, or update resources to be ready for inclusion into the machine translation pipeline based on what we currently know. One important question to address is how large datasets should be in order to lead to translations that match the quality of those for the seven project languages.

This question remains difficult to answer in terms of exact quantities, but an indication of the size can promote resource development throughout Europe, in the sense that grant applications and lobbying efforts would have something they can refer to, and new documentation projects can work with tangible benchmarks in the near term, even if these continue to evolve in the future.

Therefore, a report is planned to provide an overview of what would be minimally necessary based on current standards and best practices: what are the ranges for size in terms of hours of annotated and non-annotated interaction, and associated lexical resources? This report will thus provide recommendations for both the creation and coding of *corpora* (i.e., linguistic, technical, and ethical criteria) and *lexical resources* (e.g., software, quantity, ID-glossing, phonological coding, etc.). The report is currently in production and will be published on the EASIER website in 2022.

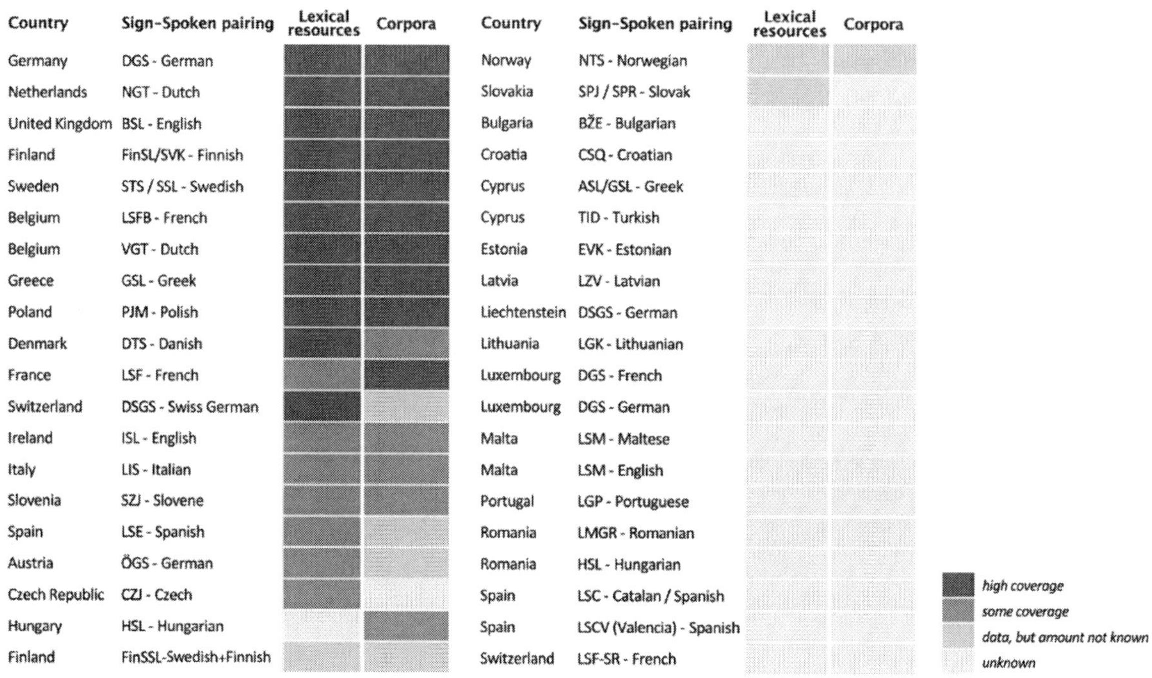

Figure 1: Chart of European sign language resources shown in sign-spoken language pairs; data is based on the selection criteria and findings in Kopf et al. (2021).

4.2 Locating New Language Documentation Projects

The immediate scope of EASIER is all sign languages in the EU (plus the UK, which at the time of submitting the project proposal was still an EU member). Ultimately, these technologies will become available as open source tools for any sign language. Those countries who stand to benefit most are the few who already have existing datasets while countries with fewer resources and who have not invested in sign language documentation projects are at a disadvantage.

In order to determine which countries and sign languages may need specific support, the survey report by Kopf et al (2021) described in §2 was used to create a list of all sign languages in Europe, categorizing the availability of lexical resources and corpora that meet the criteria set up for their possible integration into the EASIER pipeline in terms of quantity and – roughly – quality. This is illustrated in Figure 1, showing four levels of resources: high coverage resources (dark blue), resources with some coverage (light blue), resources that exist but the extent is not known (dark yellow), and no resources found (light yellow).

What we can observe in this overview is that most languages with high or medium coverage are already participating in machine translation projects, in either SignON or EASIER, while most with partial resources and whose extent is not known are not involved in these projects. These 'partial resource' languages will be able to take advantage of the relevant portions of the definition of minimal contents for datasets in §4.1 and the workflow documents in §4.3.

In addition, there are a striking number of European sign languages with no language resources at all. Therefore, one current task in EASIER is to discover whether any new language documentation projects are underway or planned in the future for those languages colored yellow in the chart. This involves a two-pronged approach, reaching out to (i) researchers in those countries to find out about possible projects within academic institutions and (ii) contacting representative members of the European Union of the Deaf to connect with potential projects led by deaf community and other social institutions outside of academia. This also involves an online media effort to request help from the public on identifying projects. To the extent that this uncovers sign language resources not currently in the Kopf et al. (2021) report, we will make updates in a new version. Any new or in-progress documentation projects can take advantage of our report on minimal contents for language datasets, the workflow documents, and training sessions for new documentation, discussed next.

4.3 Workflow Documents for New and Existing Datasets

The LREC workshop series *Representation and Processing of Sign Languages* along with a series of other European workshops (e.g., Crasborn 2010, Cormier et al. 2016) has resulted in a substantial body of knowledge regarding sign language resource creation. Written output of those events has been collected in the 'sign-lang@LREC Anthology'.[3] The many hundreds of papers there constitute a valuable source of information for universities and deaf associations starting the creation of new sign language resources. However, this collection is bewilderingly diverse, and it can be difficult for language resource managers to extract key information. For that reason, another aim in EASIER is to compile the most essential information on how to

[3] https://www.sign-lang.uni-hamburg.de/lrec/

create valuable SL resources into a set of workflow documents that can serve as a starting guide. These documents will cover linguistic questions (e. g. granularity of annotation) as well as technological questions (e.g., studio setup).

4.4 Training Sessions for New Documentation

The workflow documents mentioned above will be accompanied by online training sessions, where linguistic and technical aspects, tools and open issues can be discussed and researchers can provide support to each other.

One of the workshops will specifically focus on how to deal with the translation of neologisms. As the pipeline developed in EASIER will include a post-editing environment for humans it will be possible to provide high-quality translations that even take into account the use of new terms in either the spoken or the signed language. Sign language interpreters come across neologisms and challenging vocabulary on a day-to-day basis, and the aim is to bring them together, discuss existing solutions across European SL productions and see how they can enrich the machine translation output.

4.5 Infrastructure to Automatically Analyze Other Datasets

Lastly, a hurdle for the creation of automatic analyses may be a lack of technological infrastructures within smaller projects. Therefore, EASIER will support data creators with video processing services in the form of an infrastructure running on high-performance clusters. In this way, less-resourced research projects can use state-of-the-art 2D pose estimation techniques which then again can be used to feed sign language translation pipelines and other sign language technologies, e.g., classifiers for the verification of manual annotation.

5. Conclusion

Language technologies for signed languages are in an emerging state, where initial application areas are explored and served with the latest of technical advances in computer vision, machine translation, and animation. These developments are foreseen to increase in speed over the coming decade. It is our responsibility as developers to look beyond the 'test languages' that we currently can work with, and that have benefited from major investments in language resources over the last ten to twenty years. The present efforts within the EASIER project to increase the scope to all of Europe's sign languages that we described in this paper will hopefully contribute to best practices in this field when it comes to extending the use of technologies to less-resourced languages. Although the focus of EASIER lies within Europe, modern practices in sharing both software and research data will hopefully further broaden its impact throughout the world.

6. Acknowledgements

This work is supported in part by the EASIER (Intelligent Automatic Sign Language Translation) Project. EASIER has received funding from the European Union's Horizon 2020 research and innovation programme, grant agreement n° 101016982.

This work has in part been produced in the context of the joint research funding of the German Federal Government and Federal States in the Academies' Programme, with funding from the Federal Ministry of Education and Research and the Free and Hanseatic City of Hamburg. The Academies' Programme is coordinated by the Union of the Academies of Sciences and Humanities

7. Bibliographical References

Bragg, D., Koller, O., Bellard, M., Berke, L., Boudreault, P., Braffort, A., Caselli, N., Huenerfauth, M., Kacorri, H., Verhoef, T., Vogler, C. and Ringel Morris, M. (2019). Sign language recognition, generation, and translation: An interdisciplinary perspective. In *The 21st international ACM SIGACCESS conference on computers and accessibility*, pp. 16–31. DOI: 10.1145/3308561.3353774

Cormier, K., Crasborn, O. and Bank, R. (2016). Digging into Signs: Emerging Annotation Standards for Sign Language Corpora. In *Proceedings of the 7th Workshop on the Representation and Processing of Sign Languages: Corpus Mining*. Paris: European Language Resources Association (ELRA), pp. 35–40. https://www.sign-lang.uni-hamburg.de/lrec/pub/16015.html

Crasborn, O. (2010). The Sign Linguistics Corpora Network: Towards standards for signed language resources. In N. Calzolari, K. Choukri, B. Maegaard, J. Mariani, J. Odijk, S. Piperidis, M. Rosner, and D. Tapias (Eds.). Valletta, Malta: European Language Resources Association (ELRA), pp. 457–460. https://aclanthology.org/L10-1009

De Coster, M., Shterionov, D., Van Herreweghe, M. and Dambre, J. (2022). Machine Translation from Signed to Spoken Languages: State of the Art and Challenges. arXiv preprint. DOI: 10.48550/arXiv.2202.03086

De Meulder, M. (2021). Is "good enough" good enough? Ethical and responsible development of sign language technologies. In *Proceedings of the 1st International Workshop on Automatic Translation for Signed and Spoken Languages (AT4SSL)*, pp. 12–22. https://aclanthology.org/2021.mtsummit-at4ssl.2

Jantunen, T., Rousi, R., Rainò, P., Turunen, M., Moeen Valipoor, M. and García, N. (2021). Is There Any Hope for Developing Automated Translation Technology for Sign Languages? In *Multilingual Facilitation*, pp. 61–73. DOI: 10.31885/9789515150257

Johnston, T. (2010). From archive to corpus: Transcription and annotation in the creation of signed language corpora. In *International Journal of Corpus Linguistics*, 15(1), pp. 106–131. DOI: 10.1075/ijcl.15.1.05joh

Kopf, M., Schulder, M. and Hanke, T. (2021). D6.1 Overview of Datasets for the Sign Languages of Europe. Technical report, Universität Hamburg. DOI: 10.25592/uhhfdm.9560

Kopf, M., Schulder, M., Hanke, T. and Bigeard, S. (2022). D6.2 Specification for the Harmonization of Sign Language Annotations. Technical report, Universität Hamburg. DOI: 10.25592/uhhfdm.9841

Leeson, L. (2021). Deliverable 1.1: Case Studies and Evidence Analysis. Report, Trinity College Dublin. https://signon-project.eu/publications/public-deliverables/

Proceedings of the 10th Workshop on the Representation and Processing of Sign Languages (sign-lang@LREC 2022), pages 148–153
Language Resources and Evaluation Conference (LREC 2022), Marseille, 20-25 June 2022

ISL-LEX v.1: An Online Lexical Resource of Israeli Sign Language

Hope E. Morgan[1], Wendy Sandler[2], Rose Stamp[3], Rama Novogrodsky[2]
[1]Radboud University, [2]University of Haifa, [3]Bar Ilan University
hope.morgan@ru.nl, wsandler@research.haifa.ac.il, rose.stamp@biu.ac.il, rnovogr1@univ.haifa.ac.il

Abstract

This paper describes a new online lexical resource and interactive tool for Israeli Sign Language, *ISL-LEX v.1*. The dataset contains 961 non-compound ISL signs with the following information: subjective frequency ratings from native signers, iconicity ratings from native and non-native signers (presented separately), and phonological properties in six domains. The selection of signs was also designed to reflect a broad distinction between those signs acquired early in childhood and those acquired later. ISL-LEX is an online interface built using the SIGN-LEX visualization (Caselli et al. 2022), and is intended for use by researchers, educators, and students. It is therefore offered in two text-based versions, English and Hebrew, with video instructions in ISL.

Keywords: Israeli Sign Language, ISL, lexical database, lexicon, lexical network, phonological coding, ISL-LEX, SIGN-LEX

1. Introduction

While linguistics research on Israeli Sign Language (ISL) has been active and productive for many years (Meir and Sandler 2004; Nespor and Sandler 1999; Meir 2001; Meir and Sandler 2007; Lepic et al. 2016; Dachovsky et al. 2018; Sandler 2018; Fuks 2021, etc.), efforts to produce ISL language resources and make them publicly available have only recently gotten underway. This is in part due to a shift in focus by the global academic community toward greater open access and publicly available datasets. In alignment with this goal, we report here on a new lexical resource of Israeli Sign Language, *ISL-LEX v.1*.

Lexical databases have many important uses. They are crucial for testing hypotheses and controlling variables in psycholinguistic studies regarding language processing and acquisition, and for pedagogical applications, such as curriculum development and assessment. They also can be used to support dictionary making, contain information to facilitate different types of linguistic analysis, and track ID-glosses in corpus annotation.

ISL-LEX is an online interface and search tool associated with a lexical database of ISL. This interface portrays 961 lexical signs of Israeli Sign Language in a visual network of phonological relations; that is, signs are grouped and colored by the degree of similarity to other signs (**Figure 1**). ISL-LEX also contains a video of each sign, detailed phonological information, and ratings for sign frequency and iconicity. The content data was created for projects at University of Haifa in Israel, while the online interface is part of the SIGN-LEX interactive web-based platform (Caselli et al. 2022). This platform has a unique visualization, search features, and scatterplot views to aid language research, language learning, and teaching.

This is one of the few quantitative datasets of ISL in general, and the first to be made available to the public. It is accessible in English and Hebrew through parallel versions of the interactive online platform, as well as in standalone datasets for download (see §3). This paper provides a description of ISL-LEX v.1, including the digital resources associated with it, a description of the interface, its versions in English and Hebrew, details about the contents, the raw data in OSF (Open Science Framework), and future plans.

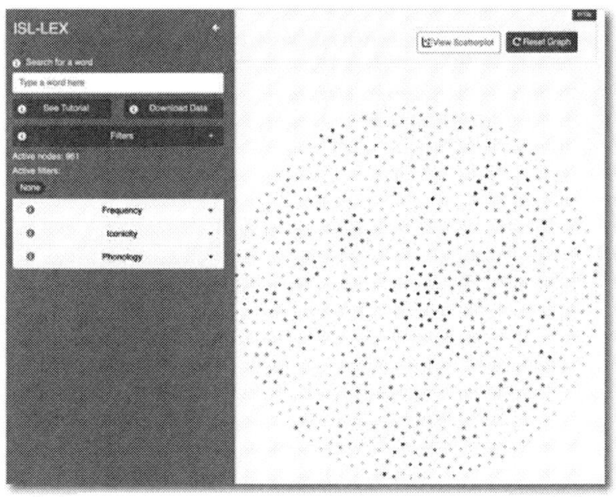

Figure 1: The ISL-LEX interface

2. Digital Resources Associated with ISL-LEX

There are four independent but associated sources of data related to ISL-LEX: (i) the 'landing page' website, (ii) the interface itself, (iii) the raw downloadable data, and (iv) associated articles about the content.

The first is the **landing page website** at https://sites.google.com/view/isl-lex. This site provides attribution, instructions, permissions, and contact information for the project. It is also the "front door" entry point to ISL-LEX. The second and main resource, **ISL-LEX** itself, is a web-based interface using the SIGN-LEX platform, located at this URL (but customarily accessed via the landing page): https://asl-lex.github.io/isl-lex/index.html. The third source of data is the **raw data** in comma-separated values (CSV) format in two files, one for English and one for Hebrew. This data is available on OSF: https://osf.io/jmwyx/. The fourth type of resource are **publications** that describe the data in greater depth; that is, the methods used to collect the data and detail about the coding in Novogrodsky and Meir (2020) and in Morgan et al. (in prep).

3. A Multilingual Resource

In keeping with the theme of the LREC 2022 workshop, ISL-LEX is notable for being available in two written languages, English and Hebrew, as well as in ISL in informational videos. The online interface can toggle between English and Hebrew by clicking the button in the upper-right hand corner of the main interface (Fig. 2). Also, the raw data is available in both languages.

Figure 2: Toggle between English and Hebrew

This satisfies a goal for ISL-LEX to be a resource for both international researchers and for various audiences within Israel, including linguists, teachers and students of ISL, parents of deaf children, and others (uses for linguists and teachers focusing on acquisition questions are addressed further in Novogrodsky and Meir, 2020). It is important to point out that the translations used to label signs in both English and Hebrew in ISL-LEX should be treated with some caution. While deaf signers were involved in assigning them, translations between any two languages can be fraught and may fail to convey the exact semantic scope and patterns of use specific to each language. For example, in ISL two different signs are translated to "love" in Hebrew and English. One sign denotes love for inanimate objects and the other sign denotes love for animate beings. The glossing conventions address this to some extent by using numbers for signs with one gloss translation in the written language but different meanings in ISL; e.g. LOVE1, LOVE2 (see Novogrodsky and Meir 2020 for more details). A new corpus project for ISL, the *ISL Corpus Project* (ISLCP; Stamp 2022), will help to clarify the usage of ISL signs and assign ID-glosses to the lexicon for corpus annotation. See §7 for future plans with this resource.

4. Description of the ISL-LEX Interface

ISL-LEX is one of the SIGN-LEX web-based interfaces (Caselli et al. 2022; see also Acknowledgements). This interface has three main components: (1) a **visualization** of all the signs; (2) a **filter** component that has various ways to search and sort signs based on the phonology, frequency, iconicity as well as specific glosses; and (3) a **scatterplot** tool that presents the scalable data (frequency, iconicity, neighborhood density) in individual XY plots. These components are dynamically-linked with each other in order to isolate particular types of data for various research and pedagogical applications.

The visualization presents all signs in the dataset as a network of relations based on phonological relatedness. Fifteen phonological feature types were selected to build the visualization. Edges (lines) between nodes (individual signs) are shown when the cursor is placed over a node; the connecting lines represent signs that match on fourteen out of fifteen features (for a description of features in ISL-LEX, see §5.6 and Morgan et al., in prep). The colors of nodes also reflect related clusters of signs that share phonological properties. A complex network modularity algorithm was used to aid the final form of the visualization, transforming the data into clusters.

5. Contents of ISL-LEX

5.1 Description of the Signs

The ISL-LEX dataset consists of 961 Israeli Sign Language signs. The signs come from two datasets: (i) 467 signs from the ISL Child Development Inventory (CDI) project (Novogrodsky and Meir 2020) and (ii) 494 signs that were selected randomly from a master list of 4,233 signs. These signs were collected for an online dictionary of ISL (https://www.isl.org.il) produced by the former Institute for the Advancement of Deaf Persons in Israel (IADPI; this organization re-formed as Ma'agale Shema, מעגלי שמע). The collection of the IADPI dictionary list was a collaborative effort by deaf Israeli signers, led by Sara Lanesman, the late linguist Irit Meir, and the director of the IADPI, Yael Kakon.

5.2 Videos of Signs

The videos of signs in the ISL-LEX interface are stored in Vimeo and connected with links to the interface. These videos are the same ones used for the phonological coding and for obtaining the frequency and iconicity ratings. Most of the videos, 798 out of 961, originate from the IADPI video dictionary of ISL just mentioned, while the other 163 videos were filmed at the University of Haifa for the last author's research project on ISL-Hebrew bimodal bilingualism in Israeli children (the 'BIBI' project, funded by the Israeli Science Foundation Grant No. 1068/16).

5.3 Subjective Frequency Ratings

All 961 signs have subjective frequency ratings that are an average of ratings provided by 19 deaf native signers (that is, deaf signers who acquired ISL as a first language), following a methodology similar to previous studies in sign languages (Mayberry et al. 2013; Caselli et al. 2017; Sevcikova Sehyr et al. 2021). Specifically, ISL signs were rated on a Likert scale from 1–7. Each video of a sign was presented along with a digital form for responses, using Google Forms. These instructions, translated here in English, were given in written Hebrew prior to the task: "The purpose of this questionnaire is to rate signs according to their frequency of use. How frequently is the sign used on daily basis? Our scale ranges from 1 to 7, where 7 represents the highest frequency, and 1 represents the lowest frequency."

Frequency ratings for the 467 CDI signs (see also Novogrodsky and Meir 2020) were collected first, followed approximately a year later by ratings for the second dataset of 494 signs (those selected from the IADPI dictionary). At least 15 out of 19 raters for each dataset are the same people, but the exact number is not recoverable due to an anonymization step. In both groups, it was found that some signers gave the same response for nearly every sign (1 person in the CDI group, 2 people in the IADPI group). These were excluded in the final ratings; i.e. they are not included in the final 19 raters nor are they in the ISL-LEX data.

In ISL-LEX, custom searches can be made by using a slider that selects signs with specific degrees of frequency. Signs in the dataset generally received high ratings. Altogether, the CDI signs have an average rating of 5.97, while signs selected from the IADPI's list have an average frequency rating of 5.42. Note that frequency of signs is based on subjective frequency judgements. The relations between the current frequency measures and frequency measure that is derived from corpus data awaits future studies.

5.4 Iconicity Ratings

A subset of the data, 467 signs, was rated for iconicity as part of the ISL-CDI project and on-going research by the last author. Signs were rated by two groups, sign-naïve participants (labelled as 'NonNative' in ISL-LEX) and native signers.

The sign-naïve ratings are reported in Novogrodsky and Meir (2020). Participants were 41 sign-naïve adults (27 females, 14 males) who speak Hebrew as their native language with a mean age of 32 (SD = 12, Min–Max: 21–67). Each ISL-CDI sign was presented as a video along with a Hebrew translation. Each participant rated it on a computer using a scale of 1–7, with 1 as absolutely non-iconic and 7 as very iconic. The instructions were given in written Hebrew prior to the task. The translation in English is: "Sign languages tend to be iconic. That is, sometimes the shape of the sign resembles the shape of the object or entity in reality, or the movement of the sign is reminiscent of the action that the sign represents. Sometimes the sign is arbitrary and not-iconic. This means no connection between the sign and the concept it represents. Our scale ranges from 1 to 7, where 7 represents the highest degree of iconicity, and 1 represents the lowest iconicity size."

The native signer participants were 11 ISL signers (7 females, 4 males) with a mean age of 32 (SD = 10, Min–Max: 20–53). They were from different areas of Israel (north, center, and south), and belonging to a mid-high socioeconomic group (Novogrodsky and Meir 2020). The task was the same as with the sign-naïve participants.

In ISL-LEX, custom searches can be made for 'Native' and 'NonNative' ratings separately to create a selection of signs on the basis of degree of iconicity. Note that while these ratings differ, they show high correlations ($r = .71$, $p < .001$) (Novogrodsky and Meir 2020).

5.5 Acquisition Data

The signs in ISL-LEX are also meant to broadly reflect different stages of language acquisition because one reason they were gathered and coded was to address research questions about phonological complexity and acquisition (Morgan et al. 2019).

Approximately half of the signs in ISL-LEX v.1 (467 signs, 48.6%) are found in the ISL-CDI, an assessment tool for evaluating child acquisition of ISL, which is modeled on the MacArthur–Bates Communicative Developmental Inventory (Fenson et al. 1994). This assessment tool is described further in Novogrodsky and Meir (2020). It consists of 563 total signs. Novogrodsky and Meir demonstrate that this inventory of ISL signs was able to reveal developmental stages of expanding vocabulary capacity in 34 native ISL child signers, from 8 months to 7yrs old. That is, acquisition of the inventory increased dramatically for children between 18–29 months, and reached ceiling for children at 50 months old and older (i.e. around 4yrs old). Therefore, this collection of signs broadly reflects early-acquired signs in ISL. For example, it includes signs for '*mother*', '*father*', '*sleep*', '*water*', '*more*', etc.

What about the 96 signs in the ISL-CDI that are not in ISL-LEX? These are primarily compound signs, including 70 compounds and 15 signs whose compound status was uncertain; e.g. UGLY (מכוער), GAS-STATION (תחנת דלק), BEACH (חוף ים). Compounds were removed because the phonological coding system is based on components of single words.[1,2] Also excluded were two highly polysemous signs whose lexical distinctiveness from other signs in the dataset was in doubt and one sign with inadvertently complex morphology ('to film oneself').

The other 494 signs in ISL-LEX (51.4%) were chosen to complement this set of early-acquired ISL signs by reflecting a cross-section of the ISL lexicon, including many that would presumably be acquired later, after early childhood. This set of signs was selected from the master list of 4,233 signs in the dictionary of ISL. This was done by generating a list of 500 random numbers from 1–4,233 and matching those numbers to the index number for each sign. Excluded from this list (and replaced with a new batch of random signs in a second round) were: compounds, duplicates to the signs in the set of ISL-CDI signs, signs in the list whose videos could not be located in the online dictionary, and signs that were too similar in both form and meaning to signs already in the dataset.

In ISL-LEX, signs with a master index 2–555 are from the CDI signs and those with an index 556–1054 are from the ISL dictionary's master list. The interface does not currently allow custom searches on the basis of these two groups, but the data in OSF also contains these index numbers.

5.6 Phonological Coding

The phonological coding system is described in further detail in Morgan et al. (in prep), and summarized here. It has six overall phonological domains, each with a several formational types that occur in the database as fields. The six domains are (1) **articulator** with four fields, (2) **handshape** with nine fields, (3) **orientation** with two fields, (4) **location** with six fields, (5) **core articulatory movement** with nine fields, and (6) **manner of movement** with nine fields. These are listed in Table 1.

The phonological coding structure was created by the first author, based in part on a previous analysis of contrastive features in Kenyan Sign Language (KSL) (Morgan 2022). That analysis was contextualized within current theoretical models of sign language phonology for each parameter and feature (Sandler 1989, 2012; Brentari 1998; Kooij 2002). It also drew on comparisons of features found in other sign languages, such as ASL, Sign Language of the Netherlands, Hausa Sign Language, and others. Therefore, this coding schema is grounded in both theoretical and descriptive phenomena in sign language phonology.

The coding was done in a FileMaker Pro database created by the first author and performed by two coders: the first author, who is a hearing signer not conversant in ISL (but fluent in other sign languages) and a deaf native ISL signer, Debbie Menashe. The two coders met repeatedly for training sessions that were first mediated by an interpreter,

---

1 Other lexical databases of sign languages with phonological coding, such as the Global SignBanks (Crasborn et al. 2020, Cassidy et al. 2018) also treat compounds in a similar way by coding the phonology of each sign in a compound separately.

2 We did not include the singleton signs from compounds in the dataset because only the concepts as compounds were tested in the ISL-CDI. It is not known how children used these signs or whether they would recognize them as one sign or separate signs.

but later largely held through direct communication. As the coding progressed, these sessions became two-way discussions about the phenomena represented by the coding and Menashe's intuitions about categories of form—both at the level of fields themselves and values within the fields. Gradually, values like specific handshapes, locations, and movement types that did not fit the existing values were changed to fit ISL, and were added as new values in the database.

domain/parameter	field
articulator	number of hands
	symmetry of the moving hands
	symmetry of handshapes
	hands cross or connected
handshape	handshape dominant (h1)
	ending handshape (h1)
	handshape non-dominant (h2)
	initialized
	selected fingers
	flexion
	spread/stacked
	thumb position
	thumb contact (aperture)
orientation	palm orientation
	finger direction*
location	major area
	location 1
	location 2
	laterality
	contact (yes, no)
	contact type
articulatory movement	path movement (yes, no)
	axis of path movement 1
	axis of path movement 2*
	setting change 1
	setting change 2*
	handshape change (yes, no)
	handshape change type
	orientation (yes, no)
	orientation movement
manner of movement	path shape 1
	path shape 2
	syllables
	repeated exact
	alternating
	bidirectional/unidirectional
	displaced iteration
	switch dominance
	switch orientation
	trill

Table 1: Forty phonological fields in ISL-LEX (*in dataset, but not included as filter option in the interface)

However, it is important to point out that the coding was not then followed by a systematic phonological analysis to determine which units are phonemic in ISL (as it was in Morgan 2022 for KSL). Therefore, this coding should be viewed as "quasi-phonemic." That is, while it is likely many of the values in ISL-LEX are phonological units in ISL, probably not all of them are. The coding of the ISL dataset reflects a conservative approach to determining phonological structure because characteristics that could not be confidently assigned to a category are coded in the raw datasets as "unsure". This helps to highlight and demarcate important areas for future phonological research in ISL. It also demonstrates a principle expressed in Morgan (2022) that it is beneficial to use lexical databases as active tools for research and not only repositories of finished analyses. From this perspective, it is helpful to maintain (i) fields with information that is expressly phonetic as well as phonemic, and (ii) fields that may contain redundant information. For example, in ISL-LEX there is a field to indicate the presence or absence of path movement as well as several additional fields for details about the path (i.e. shape, axis, setting change).

6. Description of the Raw Data in OSF

In the ISL-LEX interface and on the landing page website a 'download data' button directs users to a repository on the Open Science Framework website where CSV files for English and Hebrew data can be downloaded (DOI: 10.17605/osf.io/jmwyx).

The CSV files have 961 records (i.e. 'rows' representing signs) and 52 fields (i.e. 'columns'). In addition to the 40 phonological fields shown in Table 1, there are fields for master index, glosses in English and Hebrew, compound status (all are single), the name of the video file, the unique Vimeo link to the video, one field for frequency ratings, two for iconicity ratings (Native and NonNative), and three fields for handshape image filenames.

In the event of minor changes to the ISL-LEX v.1 data, such as the correction of errors, new CSV files will be added to this repository, while older versions will also be maintained in OSF for archiving purposes.

7. Conclusion and Future Directions

In summary, ISL-LEX is a new resource of ISL signs that brings the results of linguistic research out of the university and into the public sphere. It is presented in a dynamic, searchable, online interface that has applications for research, teaching, and language learning (for research see Caselli and Pyers, 2017). Creating this resource was a highly collaborative endeavor, with input and cooperation from many individuals and institutions in Israel and United States.

While it is a relatively small dataset, it contains a lot of new information per sign, and is set to expand in a second version with input from a new natural language corpus in Israel (Stamp et al. 2022a, b). In fact, the data in ISL-LEX v.1 is serving as the initial input to a SignBank for ISL that is dynamically-linked to the corpus for purposes of managing ID-glosses and guiding annotation. In time, the ISL Corpus and SignBank will yield an expanded dataset of ISL signs derived from usage that can become the basis for ISL-LEX v.2.

8. Acknowledgements

The original work on the SIGN-LEX platform (initially for ASL-LEX v.1, v.2) was supported by the grants from National Institutes of Health DC010997 to Karen Emmorey and San Diego State University, a Tufts University Faculty

Research Award to Ariel Cohen-Goldberg, and a Tufts University Graduate Research Award to Naomi Caselli. Additional awards include: (i) NSF Award BCS-1918556 to Zed Sevcikova Sehyr and Karen Emmorey; (ii) NSF Awards BCS-1625954 to Karen Emmorey; (iii) NSF Awards BCS-1625793 and BCS-1918252 to Naomi Caselli; and (iv) NSF Awards BCS-1625761 and BCS-1918261 to Ariel Cohen-Goldberg.

Funding for the content of ISL-LEX was supported by an Israeli Science Foundation grant to Rama Novogrodsky (ISF grant No. 1068/16; the *Bimodal Bilingualism* project) and a European Research Council (ERC) grant to Wendy Sandler, under the European Union's Seventh Framework Programme, grant agreement No. 340140 (*Grammar of the Body* project). Additional support for the website and dissemination was supported by an ISF grant to Rose Stamp (ISF grant No. 2757/20; *ISL Corpus project*) and an internal grant from the Data Sciences Institute (DSI).

9. Bibliographical References

Brentari, D. (1998). *A prosodic model of sign language phonology*. Cambridge, MA: MIT Press.

Caselli, N., Sevcikova Sehyr, Z., Cohen-Goldberg, A. M., and Emmorey, K. (2017). ASL-LEX: A lexical database of American Sign Language. *Behavior Research Methods 49*(2), 784–801. DOI:10.3758/s13428-016-0742-0

Caselli, N., Sevcikova Sehyr, Z., Cohen-Goldberg, A. M., Emmorey, K., Pandit, S., Cao, X., Fantes, M., Simeon, J. (2022). *SIGN-LEX: Interactive visualizations for sign language lexicons*. SIGN-LEX. http://www.sign-lex.org/

Cassidy, S., Crasborn, O., Nieminen, H., Stoop, W., Hulsbosch, M., Even, S., Komen, E., and Johnston, T. (2018). Signbank: Software to support web based dictionaries of sign language. In *Proceedings of the Eleventh International Conference on Language Resources and Evaluation (LREC 2018)*. https://www.aclweb.org/anthology/L18-1374

Caselli, N. K., and Pyers, J. E. (2017). The road to language learning is not entirely iconic: Iconicity, neighborhood density, and frequency facilitate acquisition of sign language. *Psychological science*, *28*(7), 979-987. DOI: 10.1177/0956797617700498

Dachkovsky, S., Stamp, R. and Sandler, W. (2018). Constructing Complexity in a Young Sign Language. *Frontiers in Psychology 9* (2202). DOI: 10.3389/fpsyg.2018.02202

Fenson, L., Dale, P. S., Reznick, J. S., Bates, E., Thal, D. J., Pethick, S. J., Tomasello, M., Mervis, C. B., and Stiles, J. (1994). Variability in early communicative development. *Monographs of the society for research in child development*, i–185. https://www.jstor.org/stable/1166093

Fuks, O. (2021). The distribution of handshapes in the established lexicon of Israeli Sign Language (ISL). *Semiotica 2021* (242), 101–122. DOI: 10.1515/sem-2019-0049

Kooij, E.v.d. (2002). *Phonological categories in Sign Language of the Netherlands: The role of phonetic implementation and iconicity*. LOT (Netherlands Graduate School of Linguistics).

Lepic, R., Börstel, C., Belsitzman, G., and Sandler, W. (2016). Taking meaning in hand: Iconic motivations in two-handed signs. *Sign Language and Linguistics 19*(1), 37–81. DOI: 10.1075/sll.19.1.02lep

Mayberry, R. I., Hall, M. L., and Zvaigzne, M. (2014). Subjective frequency ratings for 432 ASL signs. *Behavior Research Methods 46* (2), 526–539. DOI: 10.3758/s13428-013-0370-x

Meir, I. (2001). Motion and Transfer: The analysis of two verb classes in Israeli Sign Language. In V. Dively (Ed.) *Signed Languages: Discoveries from international research*. Washington D.C.: Gallaudet University Press, 74–87.

Meir, I. and Sandler, W. (2004). *Śafah ba-merḥav: eshnav la-śafat ha-simanim ha-Yiśre'elit (Language in Space: a window onto Israeli Sign Language*). Haifa, Israel: University of Haifa Press. (in Hebrew).

Meir, I., and Sandler, W. (2007). *A language in space: The story of Israeli Sign Language*. Psychology Press.

Morgan, H. E. (2022). *A Phonological Grammar of Kenyan Sign Language*. Boston/Berlin: De Gruyter Mouton.

Morgan, H. E., Sandler, W., and Novogrodsky, R. (in prep). *Phonological coding in a lexical database of Israeli Sign Language, ISL-LEX v.1*.

Morgan, H. E., Novogrodsky, R., and Sandler, W. (2019). Phonological complexity and frequency in the lexicon: A quantitative cross-linguistic study. Paper presented at Theoretical Issues in Sign Language Research 13. Hamburg, Germany, Sept 2019.

Nespor, M. and Sandler, W. (1999). Prosodic Phonology in Israeli Sign Language. *Language and Speech* 42 (2&3), 143–176. DOI: 10.1177/00238309990420020201

Novogrodsky, R. and Meir, N. (2020). Age, Frequency and Iconicity in early sign language acquisition: Evidence from the Israeli Sign Language MacArthur-Bates Communicative Developmental Inventory. *Applied Psycholinguistics*, 1–29. 10.1017/S0142716420000247

Sandler, W. (1989). *Phonological representation of the sign: Linearity and nonlinearity in American Sign Language*. Dordrecht, Holland: Foris Publication.

Sandler, W. (2012). The phonological organization of sign languages. *Language and Linguistics Compass 6* (3), 162–182. DOI: 10.1002/lnc3.326

Sandler, W. (2018). The body as evidence for the nature of language. *Frontiers in Psychology.* DOI: 10.3389/fpsyg. 2018.01782

Sevcikova Sehyr, Z., Caselli, N., Cohen-Goldberg, A. M., and Emmorey, K. (2021). The ASL-LEX 2.0 Project: A database of lexical and phonological properties for 2,723 signs in American Sign Language. *Journal of Deaf Studies and Deaf Education*. DOI: 10.1093/deafed/enaa038

Stamp, R., Ohanin, O. and Lanesman, S. (2022a). The corpus of Israeli Sign Language. Paper presented at LREC 2022. Marseille, France, June 2022.

10. Language Resource References

Caselli, N., Sevcikova Sehyr, Z., Cohen-Goldberg, A. M., and Emmorey, K. (2021). ASL-LEX. https://asl-lex.org/index.html

Crasborn, O. et al. (2020). *Global Signbank*. Radboud University, Nijmegen. https://signbank.science.ru.nl

Institute for the Advancement of Deaf Persons in Israel (IADPI). *ISL Dictionary*. Currently hosted by Ma'agale Shema: https://isl.danfishgold.com/#he-3SI (original site is offline: https://www.isl.org.il).

ISL-LEX. (2022). https://sites.google.com/view/isl-lex; https://asl-lex.github.io/isl-lex/index.html

Morgan, H. E., Novogrodsky, R., and Sandler, W. (2022). ISL-LEX 1.0: A database of phonological and lexical properties for 961 signs in Israeli Sign Language. DOI: 10.17605/OSF.IO/JMWYX

Stamp, R., Ohanin, O. and Lanesman, S. (2022b). *The Corpus of Israeli Sign Language.* Bar-Ilan University, http://islcorpus.co.il (landing site launched in 2022).

Proceedings of the 10th Workshop on the Representation and Processing of Sign Languages (sign-lang@LREC 2022), pages 154–158
Language Resources and Evaluation Conference (LREC 2022), Marseille, 20-25 June 2022

Towards Large Vocabulary Kazakh-Russian Sign Language Dataset: KRSL-OnlineSchool

Medet Mukushev[1], Aigerim Kydyrbekova[1], Vadim Kimmelman[2], Anara Sandygulova[1]
[1]Department of Robotics and Mechatronics, School of Engineering and Digital Sciences
Nazarbayev University, Nur-Sultan, Kazakhstan
[2]Department of Linguistic, Literary, and Aesthetic Studies
University of Bergen, Bergen, Norway
{mmukushev, aigerim.kydyrbekova, anara.sandygulova}@nu.edu.kz
vadim.kimmelman@uib.no

Abstract

This paper presents a new dataset for Kazakh-Russian Sign Language (KRSL) created for the purposes of Sign Language Processing. In 2020, Kazakhstan's schools were quickly switched to online mode due to COVID-19 pandemic. Every working day, the El-arna TV channel was broadcasting video lessons for grades from 1 to 11 with sign language translation. This opportunity allowed us to record a corpus with a large vocabulary and spontaneous SL interpretation. To this end, this corpus contains video recordings of Kazakhstan's online school translated to Kazakh-Russian sign language by 7 interpreters. At the moment we collected and cleaned 890 hours of video material. A custom annotation tool was created to make the process of data annotation simple and easy-to-use by Deaf community. To date, around 325 hours of videos have been annotated with glosses and 4,009 lessons out of 4,547 were transcribed with automatic speech-to-text software. KRSL-OnlineSchool dataset will be made publicly available at https://krslproject.github.io/online-school/

Keywords: sign language dataset, kazakh-russian sign language, sign language processing

1. Introduction

Sign Language Processing (SLP) combines three related research and development directions, such as automated Sign Language recognition, generation, and translation, with the goal of developing technological solutions that will help break down communication barriers for the Deaf community and sign language users (Bragg et al., 2019). To date, more than half of published vision-based research for SLP utilizes isolated sign language data with a limited vocabulary size (Koller, 2020). However, the real-world value of SLP solutions demands continuous signing recognition, which is significantly harder than individual sign recognition due to co-articulation (the end of one sign affecting the beginning of the next), depiction (visually representing or enacting content), and generalization (Bragg et al., 2019). There are considerable limitations in publicly available sign language datasets that restrict the strength and applicability of recognition systems trained on them. Limitations of datasets include the size of the vocabulary, which is mostly related to expensive annotation methodologies, or datasets that only include isolated signs, which are insufficient for most real-world use cases involving continuous signing (Bragg et al., 2019). As a result, in order to progress SLP, realistic, generalizable, and extensive datasets are required.

This paper proposes a new large-scale KRSL dataset created for the needs of SLP. The objective of KRSL-OnlineSchool is to address shortcomings of commonly used datasets such as lack of continuous signing and small vocabulary size. KRSL-OnlineSchool's main advantage is in its large vocabulary size, extensive gloss annotation, and high number of recorded videos.

In 2020, classes in Kazakhstan's schools were quickly switched to online mode due to COVID-19 pandemic. Every working day, the El-arna TV channel was broadcasting video lessons for grades from 1 to 11 with sign language translation. This opportunity was used to create a large corpus consisting of video recordings of online school's translations to sign language performed by 7 interpreters. We collected more than 1,000 hours of raw video recordings which were later pre-processed and divided into categories by subject and grade. At the end we obtained 890 hours of cleaned videos with sign language. Additionally, web-based annotation tool was created to make the process of data annotation simple and easy-to-use by deaf annotators. To date, around 325 hours of videos were annotated with glosses and 4,009 lessons out of 4,547 were transcribed with automatic speech-to-text software. Thus, this paper makes the following contributions:

- we release the first large-scale Kazakh-Russian Sign Language dataset consisting of 4547 video lessons (890 hours), translated by 7 signers, and divided into categories by subject and grade;
- we release transcripts for 4009 lessons collected with automatic speech-to-text software (a total of 1 million sentences);
- we release more than 39,000 gloss annotations of 30-seconds video segments (a total of 325 hours).

Datasets	Language	Signers	Vocabulary	Samples	Duration (h)
RWTH-BOSTON-400 (Dreuw et al., 2008)	ASL	4	483	843 sentences	-
SIGNUM (Agris and Kraiss, 2010)	DGS	25	450	780 sentences	55,3
RWTH-PHOENIX 2014T (Camgoz et al., 2018)	DGS	9	2887	8,257 sentences	10,96
Video-Based CSL (Huang et al., 2018)	CSL	50	178	25,000 videos	100
BSL-1K (Albanie et al., 2020)	BSL	40	1064	1M sentences	1,060
How2Sign (Duarte et al., 2021)	ASL	11	15,686	35,000 sentences	80
KRSL-OnlineSchool	**KRSL**	**7**	**20,000**	**1M sentences**	**890**

Table 1: Datasets used for Continuous Sign Language Recognition. This list excludes datasets of isolated signs. For KRSL-OnlineSchool vocabulary we counted unique words with at least 20 samples in transcripts

The remainder of this paper discusses related work, followed by descriptions of our methodology for the data collection. We then introduce the data itself and provide some statistics. The paper concludes with guidelines for future work utilizing collected dataset.

2. Related Work

Sign language datasets are critical for progressing the goals of Sign Language Recognition. RGB datasets captured with conventional cameras, for example, have practical use in real-world scenarios. These collections include videos of either isolated or continuous signing. Table 1 presents an overview of the most commonly used sign language datasets that are appropriate for the problem of Continous Sign Language Recognition with an inclusion of KRSL-OnlineSchool.

RWTH-Phoenix-Weather-2014T (Camgoz et al., 2018) is a German Sign Language (DGS) dataset used as a benchmark for most recent works in SLP. It features nine signers who performed sign language translations of the weather forecast on TV broadcasts. RWTH-Boston-400 (Dreuw et al., 2008) is one of the first CSLR benchmark datasets for American Sign Language (ASL). But it has only four signers present in the videos. In contrast, Video-Based CSL (Chinese Sign Language) (Huang et al., 2018) provides a large number of participants (n=50) involved in collecting the dataset. At the same time, they are all recorded in the same recording settings, and most participants seem to be unfamiliar with sign language as they sign in slow and artificial ways without involving any facial expressions. SIGNUM (**?**) is a signer-independent CSLR dataset of DGS with all participants being fluent in DGS and are either deaf or hard-of-hearing. However, all videos were shot with a single RGB camera in a supervised condition with the same lighting and uniform blue background.

These concerns of existing datasets limit the accuracy and robustness of the models developed for SLR and their contribution to the challenges of real-world signing. More recent datasets aim to address most challenges of the previous datasets: BSL-1K (Albanie et al., 2020) provides the largest number of annotated sign data, while How2Sign (Duarte et al., 2021) provides the largest vocabulary size. Similar to older datasets, they were either recorded in a controlled lab environment or extracted from the TV broadcast. From this perspective, KRSL-OnlineSchool is the sign language dataset that includes large vocabulary size and extensive gloss annotation needed for training recognition models.

3. Dataset Collection

The KRSL-OnlineSchool dataset consists of phrases and sentences in KRSL recorded as a synchronous interpretation of online lessons on various subjects for various grades (1-11 grades of primary, secondary and high school). KRSL is the sign language used in the Republic of Kazakhstan. KRSL is closely related to Russian Sign Language (RSL). While no official research comparing KRSL with RSL exists, they show a substantial lexical overlap and are entirely mutually intelligible (Kimmelman et al., 2020). Figure 1 shows the overview of our data collection methodology.

3.1. Video Collection Process

Every working day during the academic year, from September 2020 to May 2021, the El-arna national TV channel was broadcasting video lessons for grades from 1 to 11 with sign language translation. Lessons were live broadcast both on TV and channel's website from 9 AM till 5 PM, with an average duration of 10-12 minutes per lesson. We set up a computer with screen recording software and were recording online classes for 9 months. Table 2 shows a total number of collected lessons divided into subjects category.

The next step included a need to crop signers' region from the extracted videos and splitting videos into lessons by subjects and grades. We utilized OpenCV library for video processing and wrote custom scripts to perform this task. At the end we collected 890 hours of clean videos divided into 4,547 video lessons. Extracted videos have a resolution of 230x264 pixels. English lessons had to be discarded as they had no sign language translation.

3.2. Annotation Process

We have collected two types of annotations for our dataset, full text transcriptions of lessons and gloss annotation of short clips. Table 3 shows a total number of collected lessons presented by grade level and their number of transcripts.

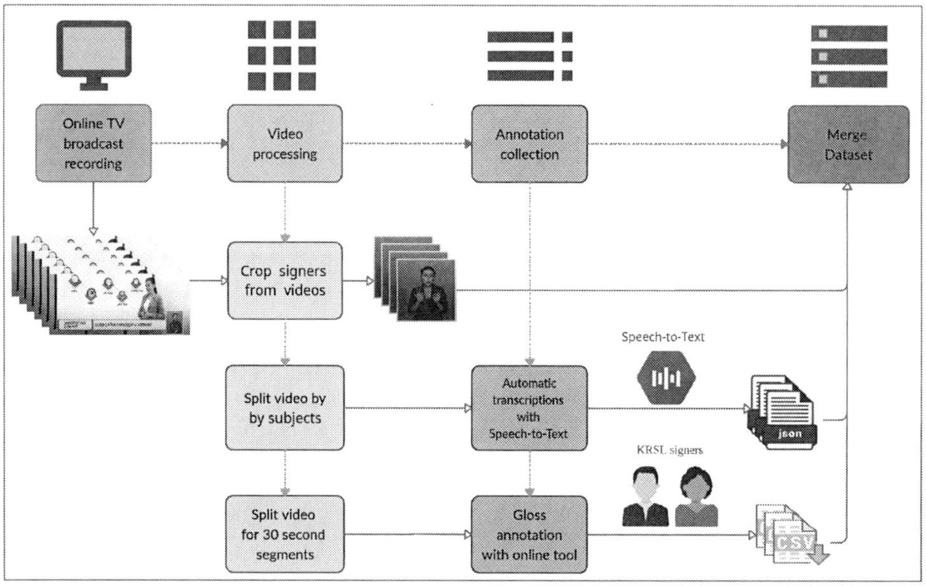

Figure 1: Dataset collection methodology

	Subject name	Videos
1	Literacy education	76
2	Math	602
3	Second language	794
4	Natural science	129
5	World science	91
6	Digital literacy	43
7	History	357
8	Kazakh language	538
9	World history	216
10	Algebra	298
11	Informatics	178
12	Geography	248
13	Chemistry	193
14	Literature	100
15	Geometry	185
16	Physics	263
17	Biology	236
Total		**4547**

Table 2: List of subjects in dataset

Grade	Videos	Transcripts
1	249	205
2	318	257
3	334	288
4	325	282
5	366	349
6	344	292
7	484	441
8	513	457
9	584	522
10	518	468
11	506	448
Total	**4547**	**4009**

Table 3: Number of lessons by grade

At first we utilized Kaldi ASR library (Povey et al., 2011) to collect full text transcriptions of lessons. However, this approach was not very convenient, as it required to extract audio streams from videos and splitting them into small segments. Later these segments were passed to automatic speech recognition algorithm, which then provided transcriptions for each segment. We then decided to utilize YouTube's captioning software which automatically recognized and synced captions for each video. We wrote custom script using the YouTube API to download transcriptions for all lessons.

For gloss annotation, we divided videos into small 30-seconds clips in order to make the gloss annotation process simpler for deaf annotators. To date, a total of 325 hours of videos or 39,000 segments were uploaded and annotated using a custom web-based annotation tool.

We realized that it was necessary to send videos to annotators, to receive their annotations as well as keep track of their progress and time spent for monetary compensation (8 USD per hour). It was decided to implement a web-based annotation tool (https:surdobot.kz). Annotators were provided with login and password to enter the system. The tool has a simple user interface, which shows a random clip and a text area to enter recognized glosses. Functionality of the tool also includes options to play, stop video clip, change playback speed, and submit annotation. Annotators also have options to view all clips they have processed and edit them if needed. Videos were divided and uploaded into online annotation tool as soon as they were processed. Thus, we have first annotated videos recorded in September, October and November of 2020. For annotation process we hired 8 annotators, 5 of whom are deaf and 3 are professional KRSL translators.

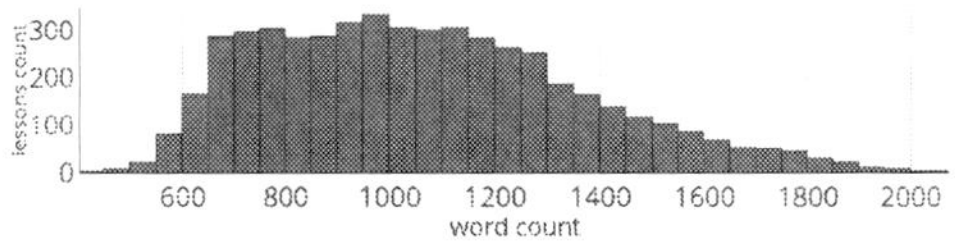

Figure 2: Full text transcripts length for each lesson

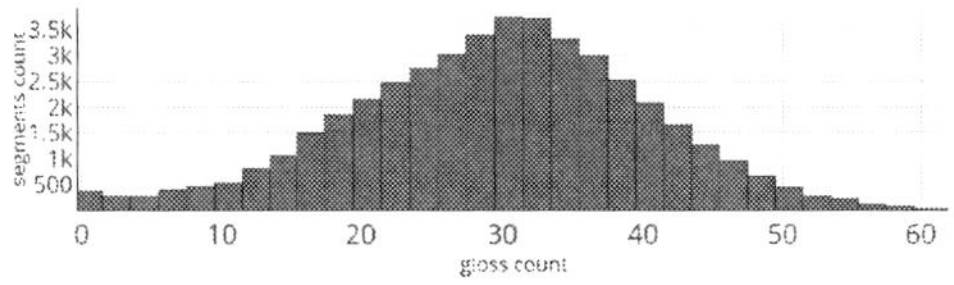

Figure 3: Gloss annotation length for each 30 second clip

4. Results

We collected 890 hours of video lessons divided into 4547 lessons. Around 325 hours of videos were annotated with glosses and 4,009 lessons out of 4,547 were transcribed with automatic speech-to-text software. For KRSL-OnlineSchool vocabulary we counted unique words with at least 20 samples in transcripts which give us a size of vocabulary of more than 20,000 words.

Figure 2 shows a word count in full text transcriptions of the lessons. An average word count of one lesson is around 1,000 words. Transcripts shorter than 800 words were mostly lessons for primary school classes, as they had shorter duration.

Figure 3 shows a gloss count in 30-seconds clips. An average gloss count of one clip is around 30 glosses. There are more than 1,000 unique glosses with at least 150 repetition for each. We are currently continuing the gloss annotation process with an aim to fully annotate all 890 hours of videos.

We have extracted 25 most frequently used words and glosses from both annotations. Figures 4 (words) and 5 (glosses) demonstrate these results. As we can see, there are some samples that appear in both charts. For example, most frequent token in both cases is "this". Also, "minus", "equal", "today", "correct", "exercise", "number", "words", "answer", "need", "watch" tokens are common for two charts. This shows us that both

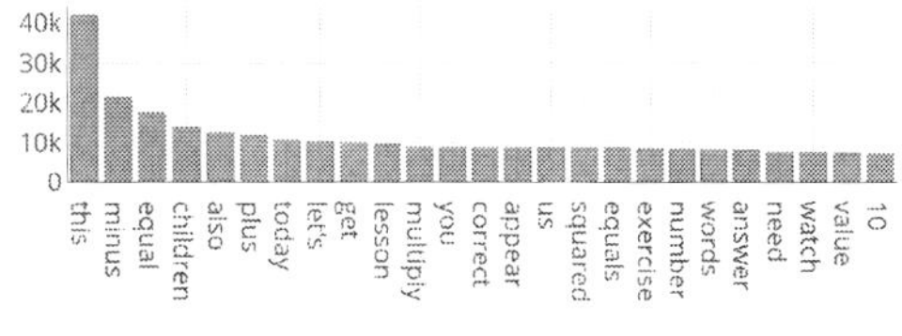

Figure 4: Top words in full text transcripts

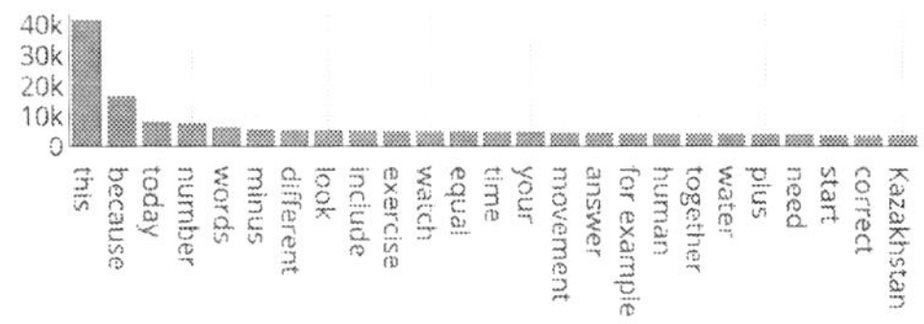

Figure 5: Top glosses in gloss annotations

automatic transcriptions and manual gloss labeling can be used for dataset annotation. We believe that number of correlating tokens will increase when the rest of the dataset is annotated with glosses.

Additionally, we have extracted 20 most frequently used 2-grams from both annotations. Figures 6 (words) and 7 (glosses) shows these results. There were fewer matching examples compared to top words-glosses charts. Some matching examples include "lesson today", "correct answer", "next assignment", "equals minus" were common for both charts.

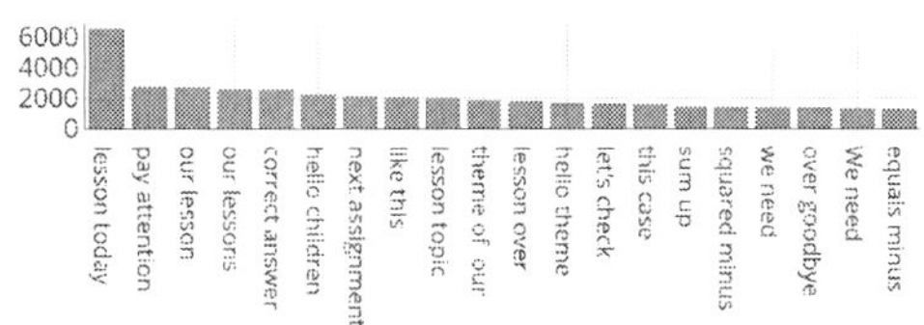

Figure 6: Top 2-grams for text transcriptions

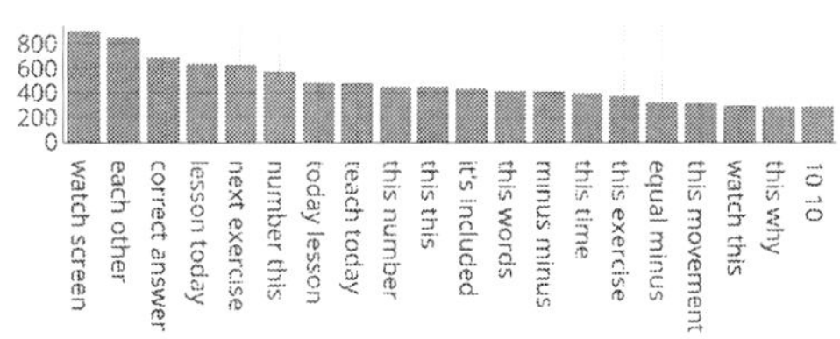

Figure 7: Top 2-grams for gloss annotations

5. Conclusion

We have presented a new dataset for Kazakh-Russian Sign Language created for the purposes of Sign Language Processing. It is a large-scale dataset that includes a large vocabulary size and extensive gloss annotation needed for training recognition models. It is one of the largest collected sign language dataset with more than 890 hours of videos, 325 of which are manually annotated with glosses and 1 million sentence transcripts. This dataset can be utilized for experiments on weakly supervised Sign Language translation models by training a large teacher model with the help of gloss annotated data, which can later be evaluated on transcribed data.

6. Acknowledgements

This work was supported by the Nazarbayev University Faculty Development Competitive Research Grant Program 2019-2021 "Kazakh Sign Language Automatic Recognition System (K-SLARS)" under award number 110119FD4545.

7. Bibliographical References

Agris, U. v. and Kraiss, K.-F. (2010). SIGNUM Database: Video Corpus for Signer-Independent Continuous Sign Language Recognition. In Philippe Dreuw, et al., editors, *Proceedings of the LREC2010 4th Workshop on the Representation and Processing of Sign Languages: Corpora and Sign Language Technologies*, pages 243–246, Valletta, Malta, May. European Language Resources Association.

Albanie, S., Varol, G., Momeni, L., Afouras, T., Chung, J. S., Fox, N., and Zisserman, A. (2020). BSL-1K: Scaling up co-articulated sign language recognition using mouthing cues. In *European Conference on Computer Vision*, pages 35–53. Springer.

Bragg, D., Koller, O., Bellard, M., Berke, L., Boudreault, P., Braffort, A., Caselli, N., Huenerfauth, M., Kacorri, H., Verhoef, T., et al. (2019). Sign Language Recognition, Generation, and Translation: An Interdisciplinary Perspective. In *The 21st International ACM SIGACCESS Conference on Computers and Accessibility*, pages 16–31. ACM.

Camgoz, C. N., Hadfield, S., Koller, O., Ney, H., and Bowden, R. (2018). Neural sign language translation. In *Proceedings of the IEEE Conference on Computer Vision and Pattern Recognition*, pages 7784–7793.

Dreuw, P., Neidle, C., Athitsos, V., Sclaroff, S., and Ney, H. (2008). Benchmark Databases for Video-Based Automatic Sign Language Recognition. In *Proceedings of the Sixth International Conference on Language Resources and Evaluation (LREC'08)*, pages 1–6, Marrakech, Morocco, May. European Language Resources Association.

Duarte, A., Palaskar, S., Ventura, L., Ghadiyaram, D., DeHaan, K., Metze, F., Torres, J., and Giro-i Nieto, X. (2021). How2Sign: A Large-scale Multimodal Dataset for Continuous American Sign Language. In *Proceedings of the IEEE/CVF conference on computer vision and pattern recognition*, pages 2735–2744.

Huang, J., Zhou, W., Zhang, Q., Li, H., and Li, W. (2018). Video-based sign language recognition without temporal segmentation. *arXiv preprint arXiv:1801.10111*.

Kimmelman, V., Imashev, A., Mukushev, M., and Sandygulova, A. (2020). Eyebrow position in grammatical and emotional expressions in Kazakh-Russian Sign Language: A quantitative study. *PLOS ONE*, 15(6):1–16, 06.

Koller, O. (2020). Quantitative Survey of the State of the Art in Sign Language Recognition. *arXiv preprint arXiv:2008.09918*.

Povey, D., Ghoshal, A., Boulianne, G., Burget, L., Glembek, O., Goel, N., Hannemann, M., Motlicek, P., Qian, Y., Schwarz, P., Silovsky, J., Stemmer, G., and Vesely, K. (2011). The Kaldi Speech Recognition Toolkit. In *IEEE 2011 Workshop on Automatic Speech Recognition and Understanding*. IEEE Signal Processing Society, December.

Proceedings of the 10th Workshop on the Representation and Processing of Sign Languages (sign-lang@LREC 2022), pages 159–164
Language Resources and Evaluation Conference (LREC 2022), Marseille, 20-25 June 2022

Towards Semi-automatic Sign Language Annotation Tool: SLAN-tool

Medet Mukushev[1], Arman Sabyrov[1], Madina Sultanova[1], Vadim Kimmelman[2], Anara Sandygulova[1]
[1]Department of Robotics and Mechatronics, School of Engineering and Digital Sciences
Nazarbayev University, Nur-Sultan, Kazakhstan
[2]Department of Linguistic, Literary, and Aesthetic Studies
University of Bergen, Bergen, Norway
{mmukushev, arman.sabyrov, madina.sultanova, anara.sandygulova}@nu.edu.kz
vadim.kimmelman@uib.no

Abstract

This paper presents a semi-automatic annotation tool for sign languages namely SLAN-tool. The SLAN-tool provides a web-based service for the annotation of sign language videos. Researchers can use the SLAN-tool web service to annotate new and existing sign language datasets with different types of annotations, such as gloss, handshape configurations, and signing regions. This is allowed using a custom tier adding functionality. A unique feature of the tool is its automatic annotation functionality which uses several neural network models in order to recognize signing segments from videos and classify handshapes according to HamNoSys handshape inventory. Furthermore, SLAN-tool users can export annotations and import them into ELAN. The SLAN-tool is publicly available at https://slan-tool.com.

Keywords: Sign language, sign language annotation, multimedia annotation tools

1. Introduction

Most of the existing sign language datasets use sentence-level translations and glossing for annotation of sign language (SL) data. Glossing is a simplified notation system used to transcribe sign language with written words in a spoken language. Additionally, some corpora can also be enhanced with annotations of handshape configurations, mouthing cues and other non-manual markers, or keypoint locations of the body. However, such extra annotations are not common for all datasets. As sign languages make use of the rich visual modality by employing hand gestures, facial expressions, body and head orientation and movement, this information is lost if only textual annotations are provided.

In contrast to automatic speech recognition, no computational tools exist to conduct semi-automatic sign language annotation. As a result, annotating sign language corpora is a time-consuming manual operation. Furthermore, there are no widely accepted annotation standards. Bragg et al. (2019) highlight the lack of a standardized annotation system and annotation granularity. As a result, experts are unable to merge sign language datasets. It is vital to provide uniform annotations as input for Natural Language Processing (NLP) and Machine Translation (MT) systems in order to train accurate and dependable models (Bragg et al., 2019). Because there is no technology to automatically tag or annotate sign language data in the quality required for linguistic annotation, corpus developers have been compelled to manually annotate the data. (Kopf et al., 2021).

There is a need for a web-based program, that provides the required flexibility to automate accurate, customizable analysis and data annotation. To address this, we developed a semi-automatic tool tailored for annotation of sign language videos. We propose the Sign Language ANnotation-tool (SLAN-tool) that semi-automatically divides videos into segments with active signing, identifies handshape configurations, and enables users to edit and export annotations. Our main contributions are as follows:

- SLAN-tool provides a web-based service for manual and semi-automatic SL annotation. The tool is freely available at https://slan-tool.com.
- We developed a neural network model to find segments of active signing in longer videos. This can help to work with shorter versions of the video and decrease annotation time.
- SLAN-tool provides extended handshape configuration classification model with more than 80 handshape classes. For the ease of use, they are divided into categories according to HamNoSys (Schmaling and Hanke, 2001) notation system.

2. Related work

There are various video annotation software packages available that are often used for sign language annotation.

ELAN (Wittenburg et al., 2006) is a tool for annotating audio and video recordings. A user can add an extensive list of textual comments to audio and/or video recordings using ELAN. An annotation can be a phrase, a word, a gloss, a comment, a translation, or a description of anything seen in the media. Annotations could be produced on several layers, known as tiers, that could be integrated hierarchically. An annotation might be time-aligned to the media or link to

other annotations that already exist. Annotation output is Unicode text, and annotation documents are saved in XML format (EAF). ELAN is free and open source (GPLv3), and it may be installed on Windows, macOS, and Linux. Crasborn and Sloetjes (2008) enhanced it specifically for sign language corpora annotation.
Neidle et al. (2001) proposed SignStream, which is aimed to make linguistic annotation and analysis of video data easier. It may be used to annotate handshapes and show non-manual characteristics. SignStream is only available for MacOS versions and is released under the MIT license.
iLex (Hanke and Storz, 2008) is a corpus and sign language lexicography analysis software that integrates characteristics from empirical sign language lexicography and sign language dialogue transcription. It assists the user in constructing an integrated vocabulary while working on the transcription of a corpus and provides a number of additional features. MacOS binaries for iLex are available for installation.
There are several works focusing on automatic annotation of Sign Languages. Chaaban et al. (2021) presented an automatic annotation system for face and body annotations such mouthing, head direction, and sign position. Furthermore, their system was able to automatically splits signs based on hand movements. De Coster et al. (2019) developed a gloss suggestion system based on OpenPose (Cao et al., 2019) keypoint extraction library. It provides annotation suggestion for a selected video clip by showing top 5 predictions.

3. Methodology

First, we discuss the user requirements collecting approach that was utilized to acquire system needs. Following that, we will go into the system design and user interfaces that were created based on the requirements that were obtained. Finally, we cover neural network models that are employed for automated annotation of signature segments and categorization of handshapes.

3.1. User requirements

We began by studying and comparing current sign language annotation tools. There are various options, the most common of which is ELAN. ELAN includes a lot of features. Simultaneously, it has a severe learning curve for first-time users.
Following preliminary study, the goal of this project was clear: to present researchers with a specialized tool for semi-automatic annotation of sign language recordings. The major aims were to provide a web-based interface for the annotation tool and semi-automatic annotation generating modules. We conducted interviews with potential users of the system, including sign language researchers and data annotators, to get high-level abstract needs. The following user needs were gathered:

- to upload and play the selected video on the main page;
- to send uploaded videos to the annotation generation module for processing;
- to view generated annotations in relevant tiers on main page;
- to adjust and update generated annotations (change predicted class, adjust segmentation boundaries, etc.);
- to add custom tiers for annotation if needed;
- to export and import generated annotations (JSON, CSV, ELAN format);
- to share results of the annotation with other people.

3.2. User Interface (UI) and functionality

The annotation tool's UI consists of the main page and supplementary pop-up windows with menu choices. The main page is divided into four sections: control functions, video player, annotation tiers, and supplementary visualization.

1. The control functions area needs to have the following buttons: Upload video, Process video, Export/import annotation file, Save project, Share project, Annotate.
2. The video player area needs to display the uploaded video and a timeline underneath it.
3. The additional visualization area needs to display information that is not suitable for tiers.
4. The annotations tiers area needs to display a predefined list of tiers such as translation, gloss, right handshape, left handshape. Additional tiers can be added by users when needed.

3.3. System design

System design requirements are more thorough definitions of the functions, services, and operational limitations of a software system. The system requirements specify precisely what should be implemented. To make it more convenient for users, we decided to create a web-based solution. It assists in the avoidance of issues associated with the installation of certain software libraries and the availability of computing resources. The annotation tool was decided to be accessible via preferred web browsers and to feature an easy-to-use UI. The cloud servers undertake automatic annotation of the videos. Figure 1 shows an overview of the Sign Language Annotation tool's architecture. Figure 2 shows the proposed User Interface for SLAN tool.

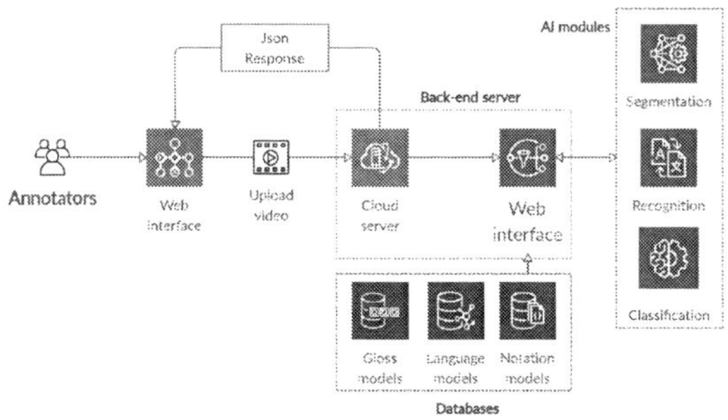

Figure 1: Overview of the Sign Language Annotation tool's Web service.

Figure 2: Proposed User interface for annotation tool.

3.4. Neural network models

3.4.1. Signing segmentation model

The fundamental concept is to assist annotators in automatically locating and working with active areas of the video. This can help to improve the efficiency and speed of annotation for long sign language videos. It was decided to identify video segments when signing happens i.e. a signing segment. This task may be compared to an action recognition task. To this end, the segmentation task involves recognizing frame boundaries in videos to separate them into meaningful units. These units can be a series of glosses or subtitle-units matched to sign language videos. To train detection algorithms, both techniques require annotated sets of videos.

3.4.2. Handshapes classification model

Handshape images gathered from the large handshape dataset (Koller et al., 2016) are divided by HamNoSys annotation, yielding 84 classes and 101 098 samples in total. On a test set, the training strategy on all classes performed poorly in terms of generalization. As a result, we devised a method that first determines the category of the handshape image. A category is a set of handshape configuration classes that are comparable to one another. After identifying the category, another model is utilized to determine the class handshape inside the category. We tried numerous tactics in order to find the optimal one that outperformed on the test set.

4. Implementation

The SLAN-tool was built with a variety of Open Source libraries and software technologies. The SLAN-source tool's code will be published under the BSD-2 clause license.

4.1. Annotation tool

User interface is implemented with HTML5, CSS3, JS, JQuery and Bootstrap library. Back-end processing is implemented with Python programming language, Django framework, Flask machine learning framework, and PostgreSQL database. AWS S3 is used as a cloud server. Networking is performed with Gunicorn and Nginx.

4.2. Classification Models

Sign segmentation and Handshape classification models have been pre-trained using the TensorFlow (Abadi et al., 2016) and PyTorch (Paszke et al., 2019) machine learning frameworks to recognise and classify sign language videos automatically.

4.2.1. Sign Language Segmentation

In order to train our model we divide sign language videos into three categories: signing-start, signing-end, no-signing segments. For training the model we have extracted videos for each category from three different datasets, KRSL (Imashev et al., 2020), WLASL (Li et al., 2020) and Dicta-Sign–LSF–v2 (Belissen et al., 2020), which were manually labeled.

We used R(2+1)D (Tran et al., 2018) action recognition model, which is highly accurate and at the same time significantly faster than other approaches. Its accuracy comes in large parts from an extra pre-training step which uses 65 million automatically annotated video clips. Its speed comes from simply using video frames as input. Many other state-of-the-art methods require optical flow fields to be pre-computed which is computationally expensive.

4.2.2. Handshape Configuration Classification

We implemented several strategies to discover the best one that has better performance over a test set.

First, every 4 neighbour classes were merged as shown in Figure 3.A, and the training process included 36 categories. The model is fine-tuned by changing hyper-parameters and as a result, it is under-fitting. It showed poor performance on the training set, so both training and validation accuracy was not higher than 30%.

Second, we consolidated classes by HamNoSys rows, thus each category in this strategy has 11–22 classes. Figure 3.B presents an illustration of that strategy. This approach also did not show promising results. Both training and validation accuracy did not exceed 40%.

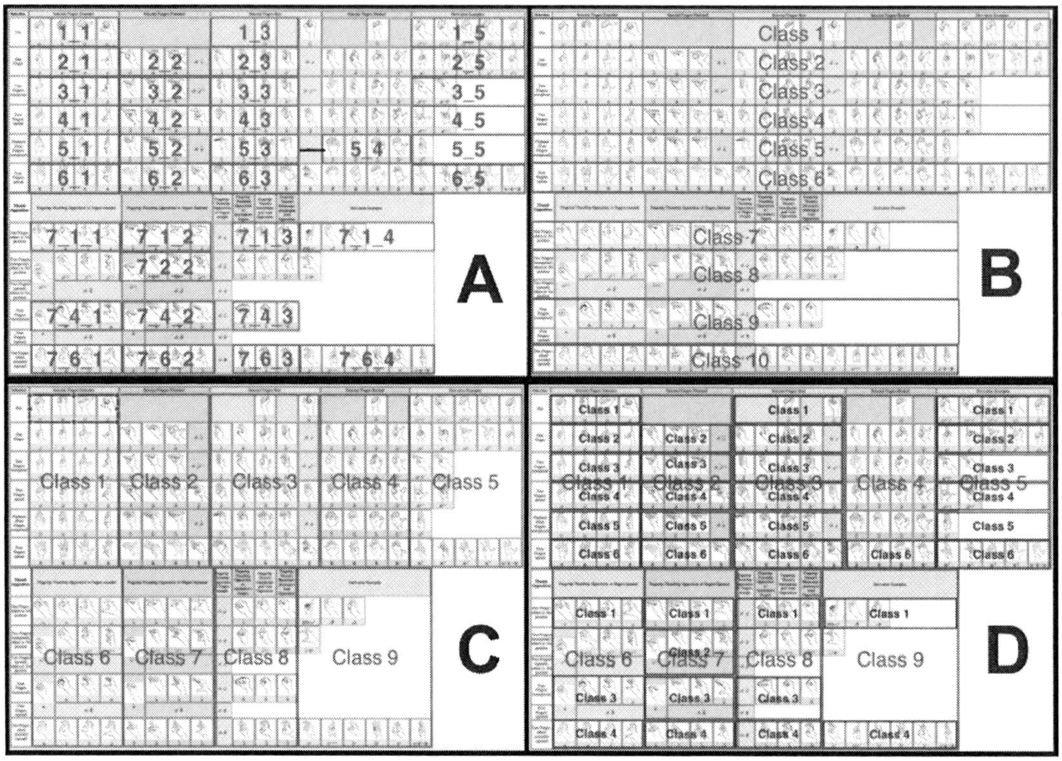

Figure 3: Different strategies for handshape categories based on HamNoSys Handshape Chart (Hanke, 2010)

	Sub-category classes (1 - 6)	Total images	Train images	Validation images
1	6	59056	47243	11813
2	5	5758	3998	998
3	6	9433	7543	1890
4	1	154	N/A	N/A
5	6	3951	3159	792
6	3	8416	6732	1684
7	4	4916	3931	985
8	3	6825	5460	1365
9	2	2487	1989	498

Table 1: Sub-category classes of Categories

Results present high bias and low variance which are indicators of the under-fitting again. Since it could happen due to model simplicity, EfficientNet-B5 (Tan and Le, 2019) model architecture was replaced by EfficientNet-B7 (Tan and Le, 2019). Additional training for more time or epochs in this step also shows poor validation accuracy.

Finally, we come to the best way, of consolidating classes into categories presented in Figure 3.C. By this strategy, we start with training a model on 9 large categories. To improve the model accuracy optimizers, their learning rates, decay, and other hyper-parameters were carefully selected. Accordingly, only after the identification of the handshape category, we start training by sub-categories which are described in the first strategy. As it can be seen from Figure 3.D we have 1-6 sub-category classes inside each category (Table 1). Afterwards, the result of this step is a total of 8 models which give different sub-categories where each has 4 classes. Furthermore, each sub-category trained only on at most 4 classes. This approach demonstrates the best generalization from the beginning, while all previous ones have failed.

4.3. Demonstration

The main page consists of 4 areas: control functions, video player, annotation tiers, and an additional visualization. The annotations tiers area display a predefined list of tiers such as text and handshapes. There are buttons to add and remove custom tiers. On the right panel handshapes menu is shown when users work with a handshape annotation tier. Figure 4 shows current interface of the SLAN tool.

5. Usability testing

In order to conduct usability testing, we invited 3 sign language data annotators. The participants are experienced in using a web-based annotation tool SurdoBot (https://surdobot.kz) for gloss annotation of sign language videos. It is a custom built tool that was used to annotate short clips of KRSL dataset.

We performed 1 hour individual Zoom sessions in which the participants were asked to annotate short sign

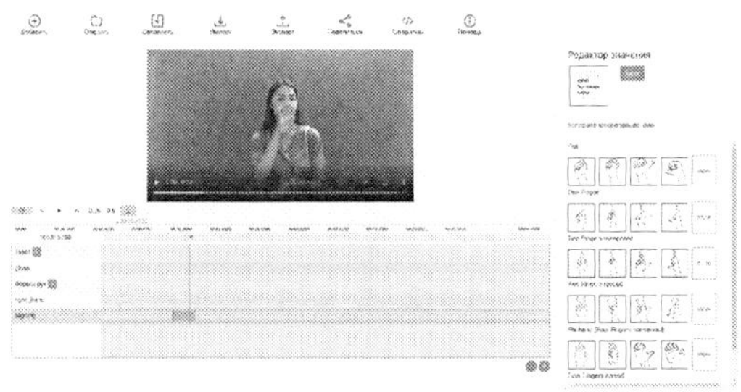

Figure 4: Current UI of the SLAN tool.

language video clips. We performed two test scenarios. First, we compared SLAN-tool to the service they used before for sign language data annotation. Next, after they got familiar with the SLAN-tool, we asked them to compare manual annotation to automatic annotation. Below are details of both scenarios.
The procedure of the usability test was specifying a task and asking the users to speak aloud their thinking process. The following tasks were specified:

- Could you please annotate the video by writing its translation in a written form?
- Could you please annotate regions of individual signs?
- Could you please annotate several handshape configurations?
- Since SLAN tool provides an automatic handshape annotation functionality, could you please launch it?
- What do you think about the layout and user interface in general?

Overall, the participants had some difficulties with adding tiers and gloss annotation for the first time. These issues were mainly because they had been using a simpler tool which had only one functionality. We have changed the instructions section by adding the "Help" button to the main menu. After that, when the participants had difficulties with any functions of the tool, they were able to quickly find instructions.
Another suggestion from most participants was to change the input method. We added options to directly enter annotations next to the selected segment. It helped to increase annotation speed and made the process more convenient.
Regarding the automatic annotation functionality, all the participants agreed that it makes annotations process easier and faster. After automatic annotation, the participants just needed to edit and adjust the selected segments only.

6. Discussion

The SLAN-main tool's goal is to provide a convenient functionality that does not require any further software installation. All users have to do is go to the website and upload their videos. The web service is freely accessible and does not involve the use of additional computing resources on the client's site. Currently, the service is hosted on an AWS dedicated server. The SLAN-tool can be used in conjunction with the ELAN-tool. It supports export and import in the same format as the ELAN software. For example, the SLAN-tool may be used to automatically annotate a sign language video and then export the results to ELAN for further annotations.
There are several use cases of the SLAN-tool:

- Automatic annotation: SLAN-tool can be used to automatically divide signing videos into shorter segments. Then for each segment the tool can identify handshape configurations and annotate them. Later these annotations can be exported to other tools such as ELAN for additional processing.
- Gloss notation: if the user needs to quickly annotate a sign language video it can be done in SLAN-tool by adding custom glossing tiers. When combined with the segmentation model, the annotation process takes shorter time as the user only needs to focus on active segments.

Currently, the main limitation is the computational resources available for the SLAN-tool. We are using a self-hosted server with 2 GPUs for video processing. For this reason, users have limitation on the duration of annotated videos. In future, we plan to migrate to a cloud-based server where researcher will be able to automatically annotate longer videos.

7. Conclusion

Our proposed tool automatically annotates some features in sign language videos and enables researcher to extend annotations for their datasets. With the help of SLAN-tool, researchers will have faster and cost effective annotation process.
SLAN-tool, as for now, has 2 models for automatic annotation: segment detection and handshape configuration classification. Other functionalities, such as hand orientation, location and movement are planned to be released.
Additionally, the tool will support automatic spotting of the most common signs (their detection and classification). Also, we will release all source codes, so that researchers can use tool on their computers if needed.

8. Acknowledgements

This work was supported by the Nazarbayev University Faculty Development Competitive Research Grant Program 2019-2021 "Kazakh Sign Language Automatic Recognition System (K-SLARS)". Award number is 110119FD4545.

9. Bibliographical References

Abadi, M., Barham, P., Chen, J., Chen, Z., Davis, A., Dean, J., Devin, M., Ghemawat, S., Irving, G., Isard, M., Kudlur, M., Levenberg, J., Monga, R., Moore, S., Murray, D. G., Steiner, B., Tucker, P., Vasudevan, V., Warden, P., Wicke, M., Yu, Y., and Zheng, X. (2016). TensorFlow: A System for Large-Scale Machine Learning. In *Proceedings of the 12th USENIX Conference on Operating Systems Design and Implementation*, OSDI'16, page 265–283, USA. USENIX Association.

Belissen, V., Braffort, A., and Gouiffès, M. (2020). Dicta-Sign-LSF-v2: Remake of a continuous French Sign Language dialogue corpus and a first baseline for automatic sign language processing. In *Proceedings of the 12th Language Resources and Evaluation Conference*, pages 6040–6048, Marseille, France, May. European Language Resources Association.

Bragg, D., Koller, O., Bellard, M., Berke, L., Boudreault, P., Braffort, A., Caselli, N., Huenerfauth, M., Kacorri, H., Verhoef, T., et al. (2019). Sign language recognition, generation, and translation: An interdisciplinary perspective. In *The 21st International ACM SIGACCESS Conference on Computers and Accessibility*, pages 16–31.

Cao, Z., Hidalgo Martinez, G., Simon, T., Wei, S., and Sheikh, Y. A. (2019). OpenPose: Realtime Multi-Person 2D Pose Estimation using Part Affinity Fields. *IEEE Transactions on Pattern Analysis and Machine Intelligence*.

Chaaban, H., Gouiffès, M., and Braffort, A. (2021). Automatic Annotation and Segmentation of Sign Language Videos: Base-level Features and Lexical Signs Classification. In *VISIGRAPP*.

Crasborn, O. and Sloetjes, H. (2008). Enhanced ELAN functionality for sign language corpora. In *Proceedings of the 3rd Workshop on the Representation and Processing of Sign Languages at LREC*, pages 39–43, Marrakech, Morocco. European Language Resources Association.

De Coster, M., Van Herreweghe, M., and Dambre, J. (2019). Towards automatic sign language corpus annotation using deep learning. In *Proceedings of the 6th Workshop on Sign Language Translation and Avatar Technology*.

Hanke, T. and Storz, J. (2008). iLex–A Database Tool for Integrating Sign Language Corpus Linguistics and Sign Language Lexicography. In *Proceedings of the 3rd Workshop on the Representation and Processing of Sign Languages at LREC*, pages 64–67, Marrakech, Morocco. European Language Resources Association.

Hanke, T. (2010). HamNoSys 4 Handshapes Chart. Drawings by H. Zienert, O. Jeziorski, A.Hanß.

Imashev, A., Mukushev, M., Kimmelman, V., and Sandygulova, A. (2020). A dataset for linguistic understanding, visual evaluation, and recognition of sign languages: The K-RSL. In *Proceedings of the 24th Conference on Computational Natural Language Learning*, pages 631–640.

Koller, O., Ney, H., and Bowden, R. (2016). Deep Hand: How to Train a CNN on 1 Million Hand Images When Your Data is Continuous and Weakly Labelled. In *Proceedings of the IEEE Conference on Computer Vision and Pattern Recognition*, pages 3793–3802.

Kopf, M., Schulder, M., and Hanke, T. (2021). Overview of Datasets for the Sign Languages of Europe, July.

Li, D., Rodriguez, C., Yu, X., and Li, H. (2020). Word-Level Deep Sign Language Recognition from Video: A New Large-Scale Dataset and Methods Comparison. In *Proceedings of the IEEE/CVF Winter Conference on Applications of Computer Vision*, pages 1459–1469.

Neidle, C., Sclaroff, S., and Athitsos, V. (2001). SignStream: A tool for linguistic and computer vision research on visual-gestural language data. *Behavior Research Methods, Instruments, & Computers*, 33(3):311–320.

Paszke, A., Gross, S., Massa, F., Lerer, A., Bradbury, J., Chanan, G., Killeen, T., Lin, Z., Gimelshein, N., Antiga, L., Desmaison, A., Köpf, A., Yang, E., DeVito, Z., Raison, M., Tejani, A., Chilamkurthy, S., Steiner, B., Fang, L., Bai, J., and Chintala, S., (2019). *PyTorch: An Imperative Style, High-Performance Deep Learning Library*. Curran Associates Inc., Red Hook, NY, USA.

Schmaling, C. and Hanke, T. (2001). HamNoSys 4.0. *Interface definitions. ViSiCAST Deliverable D5-1.*

Tan, M. and Le, Q. (2019). EfficientNet: Rethinking Model Scaling for Convolutional Neural Networks. In *Proceedings of the 36th International Conference on Machine Learning*, pages 6105–6114. PMLR.

Tran, D., Wang, H., Torresani, L., Ray, J., LeCun, Y., and Paluri, M. (2018). A Closer Look at Spatiotemporal Convolutions for Action Recognition. In *2018 IEEE/CVF Conference on Computer Vision and Pattern Recognition*, pages 6450–6459.

Wittenburg, P., Brugman, H., Russel, A., Klassmann, A., and Sloetjes, H. (2006). ELAN: a Professional Framework for Multimodality Research. In *Proceedings of the Fifth International Conference on Language Resources and Evaluation*, Genoa, Italy. European Language Resources Association.

Proceedings of the 10th Workshop on the Representation and Processing of Sign Languages (sign-lang@LREC 2022), pages 165–172
Language Resources and Evaluation Conference (LREC 2022), Marseille, 20-25 June 2022

Resources for Computer-Based Sign Recognition from Video, and the Criticality of Consistency of Gloss Labeling across Multiple Large ASL Video Corpora

Carol Neidle[1], Augustine Opoku[1], Carey Ballard[1], Konstantinos M. Dafnis[2], Evgenia Chroni[2], Dimitris Metaxas[2]
[1]Boston University, [2]Rutgers University
[1]Boston University Linguistics, 621 Commonwealth Ave., Boston, MA 02215
[2]110 Frelinghuysen Road, Piscataway, NJ 08854

carol@bu.edu, augustine.opoku@gmail.com, cmball@bu.edu, kd703@cs.rutgers.edu, etc44@cs.rutgers.edu, dnm@cs.rutgers.edu

Abstract

The WLASL purports to be "the largest video dataset for Word-Level American Sign Language (ASL) recognition." It brings together various publicly shared video collections that could be quite valuable for sign recognition research, and it has been used extensively for such research. However, a critical problem with the accompanying annotations has heretofore not been recognized by the authors, nor by those who have exploited these data: There is no 1-1 correspondence between sign productions and gloss labels. Here we describe a large, linguistically annotated, video corpus of citation-form ASL signs shared by the ASLLRP—with 23,452 sign tokens and an online Sign Bank—in which such correspondences are enforced. We furthermore provide annotations for 19,672 of the WLASL video examples consistent with ASLLRP glossing conventions. For those wishing to use WLASL videos, this provides a set of annotations making it possible: (1) to use those data reliably for computational research; and/or (2) to combine the WLASL and ASLLRP datasets, creating a combined resource that is larger and richer than either of those datasets individually, with consistent gloss labeling for all signs. We also offer a summary of our own sign recognition research to date that exploits these data resources.

Keywords: ASL, isolated sign recognition, gloss labels, ASLLRP, WLASL, ASLLVD

1. Goals of this Paper

There are several interrelated goals of this paper:

1) To disseminate information about resources shared by the American Sign Language Linguistic Research Project (**ASLLRP**), which can be used for linguistic and computational research. These resources have recently been expanded, with new download functionalities.

2) To bring to the attention of the many sign recognition researchers who have been using (or who may wish to use) the valuable video data from the **WLASL** (Li et al., 2020) serious issues resulting from inconsistent text-based gloss labeling of signs in that dataset, which adversely affects the use of these data for computer learning.

3) To share an alternative set of gloss labels for a large subset of the WLASL data, which follow annotation conventions consistent with those used for ASLLRP data. This provides internally consistent gloss labeling for the WLASL, offering added value to this large set of videos. This also makes it possible to combine WLASL data with any of the ASLLRP datasets, giving rise to a dataset larger and richer than either.

Given space limitations, this paper does not aim to present a comparative survey of datasets available for ASL research, nor an overview of the large literature dealing with *desiderata* for sign language annotation.

2. Introduction

Deficiencies in the quality and accuracy of annotated sign language corpora are a key limitation for progress on sign recognition research (Bragg et al., 2019). Research based on gloss labels for signs faces a serious challenge, given that: (1) there is no 1-1 correspondence between English words and ASL signs; and (2) there are also no established glossing conventions shared by the ASL/research community. As an integral part of the research conducted by the American Sign Language Linguistic Research Project (ASLLRP), we have, from the outset of our research, established conventions to ensure a 1-to-1 correspondence between gloss label and ASL sign production, which is essential for use in computational research. See Neidle, Thangali & Sclaroff (2012) for discussion of challenges in establishing glossing conventions, and Neidle & Opoku (2022) for further details about our annotations.

There is widespread recognition of the requirement for unique text-based gloss labels to represent signs. This is enforced in all serious corpus research. We have implemented these principles since the mid-1990s; see, e.g., Neidle (2002). Many others have also written about these and other important issues involved in sign language annotation (e.g., Johnston, 2010; Orfanidou, Woll, and Morgan, 2015; Cormier, Crasborn, and Bank, 2016).

Major problems arise, however, when researchers use datasets where 1-1 gloss label to sign correspondences have not been enforced; or when multiple datasets using inconsistent glossing are combined. This is the situation for the WLASL (Li et al., 2020), which brings together multiple, publicly shared, ASL video corpora from different sources—thus offering a potentially valuable resource for research. However, internal consistency of labeling is not even enforced within the individual collections that are combined.

3. The WLASL Dataset

Li et al. (2020) claim that the WLASL is "by far the largest public ASL dataset to facilitate word-level sign recognition research." They report that it contains "2,000 common different words in ASL" (although for reasons discussed below, the count of distinct gloss labels does not necessarily correlate with the number of distinct signs).

The WLASL brings together data shared publicly on the Web from different sources; various types of metadata, including a gloss label for each video, are also provided. As they explain: "We select videos whose titles clearly describe the gloss of the sign." However, basing sign identification on filenames is problematic, since there is no standard convention for associating an English-based gloss label with an ASL sign, and no 1-1 relationship between English words and ASL signs; there is also considerable variability in how gloss labels are used. As a result, there are cases where multiple WLASL examples of a single ASL sign are glossed with different English words, as in the sign glossed sometimes as *woman* and sometimes as *lady*, shown in **Figure 1**. Conversely, there are many cases where the same English gloss is used for totally different ASL signs, as shown in **Figure 2** for the gloss label *close*: the sign on the left is a verb, the opposite of 'open,' whereas the sign on the right is an adjective, meaning 'near'. Another example is shown in **Figure 3**, for *mean*. The sign on the left is a verb in ASL meaning 'to signify,' whereas the sign on the right is an adjective meaning 'unkind'. They classify these as 'dialectal variants,' but that is not correct; and the designation of dialectal variants throughout the WLASL dataset is highly problematic.

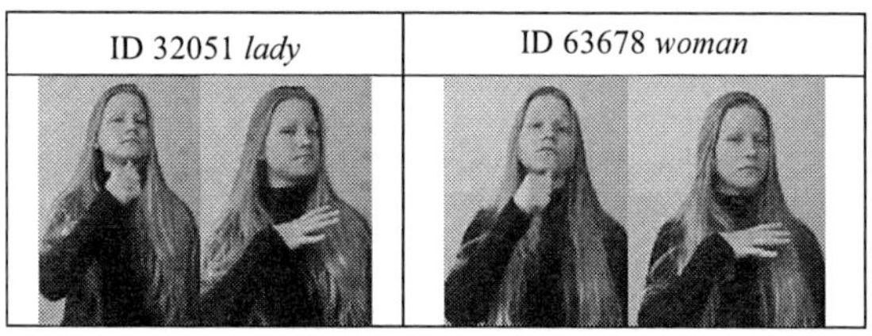

Figure 1. WLASL: same ASL sign, different English glosses

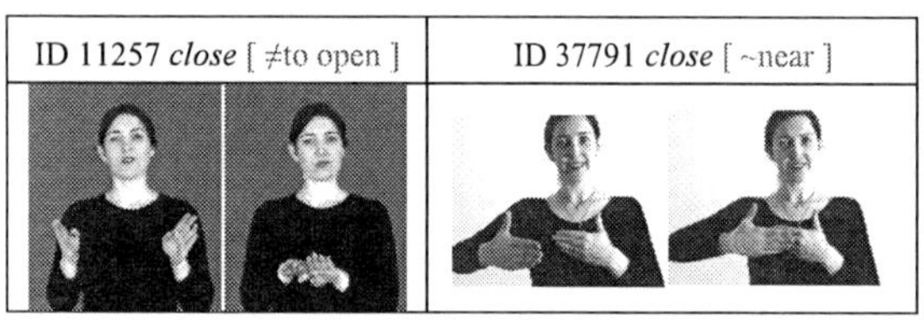

Figure 2. WLASL: same English gloss, different ASL signs

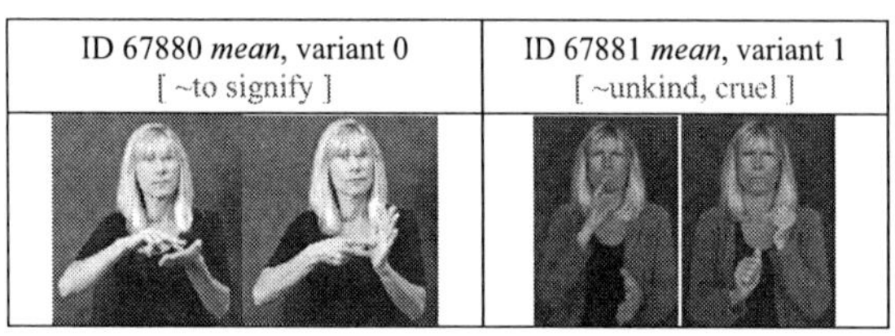

Figure 3. Supposed Dialectal Variants in WLASL

The issues exemplified above are pervasive in the WLASL data, posing critical obstacles to using this dataset reliably for computational research, despite the fact that it has been widely used (e.g., Hassan, Elgabry, and Hemayed, 2021; Maruyama et al., 2021; Boháček and Hrúz, 2022; Ebrahimi and Ebrahimpour-komleh, 2022); for a partial list of research based on these data, see https://paperswithcode.com/dataset/wlasl.

This surely explains, at least in part, the low recognition rates that have been reported (e.g., less than 63% for top-10 accuracy on 2,000 words/glosses (Li et al., 2020)).

We have illustrated these problems with the WLASL data in some detail precisely because this dataset has been widely used in recent sign recognition research, and also because, as discussed below, the consistent gloss labels we are providing for use with the WLASL data can greatly increase the value of these data.

4. Other Datasets for Sign Recognition

Another dataset used extensively in recent vision-based ASL sign recognition research is our **ASLLVD**; see below. For example, de Amorim & Zanchetti (2021) introduced 2 datasets "derived from one of the most relevant sign language datasets–the American Sign Language Lexicon Video Dataset (ASLLVD)." Several other papers tested new sign recognition methods on datasets including the ASLLVD (Theodorakis et al. (2014): computational phonetic modeling; Elakkiya & Selvamani (2019): "three subunit sign modeling"; Lim et al. (2019): use of CNNs to train hand models; Bilge et al. (2022): new machine learning method; Kumar et al. (2028): sign recognition using computer vision and neural networks; Rastgoo et al. (2022): a combination of neural network methods; among others).

Other datasets used in recent computational research include the recently introduced large-scale **How2Sign dataset of American Sign Language** (Duarte et al., 2021; Duarte et al., 2022); and the **MS-ASL Large-Scale Data Set and Benchmark for Understanding ASL** (Joze, Vaezi, and Koller, 2018). This last article also reviews older benchmark datasets, including the **Purdue RVL-SLLL ASL database** (Kak, 2002) and the **RWTH-BOSTON** datasets (Dreuw et al., 2008). It is worth noting that the RWTH-BOSTON data were collected at Boston University through the ASLLRP; those videos are included in our current, much larger, data collection, described next.

5. ASLLRP Resources

We describe here ASL data made available through the[1] ASLLRP, including isolated signs (**23,452** sign videos, corresponding to distinct signs, from **33** different signers) and continuous signing corpora (**2,651** utterances, containing a total of **20,560** signs available as video clips segmented from those utterances and in their utterance context, from **19** different signers). It incorporates data collected at Boston University and at the Rochester Institute for Technology (under the supervision of Matt Huenerfauth), as well as videos shared by DawnSignPress. Including the citation-form signs and continuous signing corpora, we have a total of **44,012** sign tokens corresponding to **3,542** distinct signs (not including fingerspelled signs, classifiers, and gestures).

[1] This incorporates our **ASLLVD, American Sign Language Lexicon Video Dataset** (Athitsos et al., 2008; Neidle, Thangali, and Sclaroff, 2012), with >3,300 citation-form signs, produced by 1-6 native ASL signers, for a total of almost 9,800 tokens.

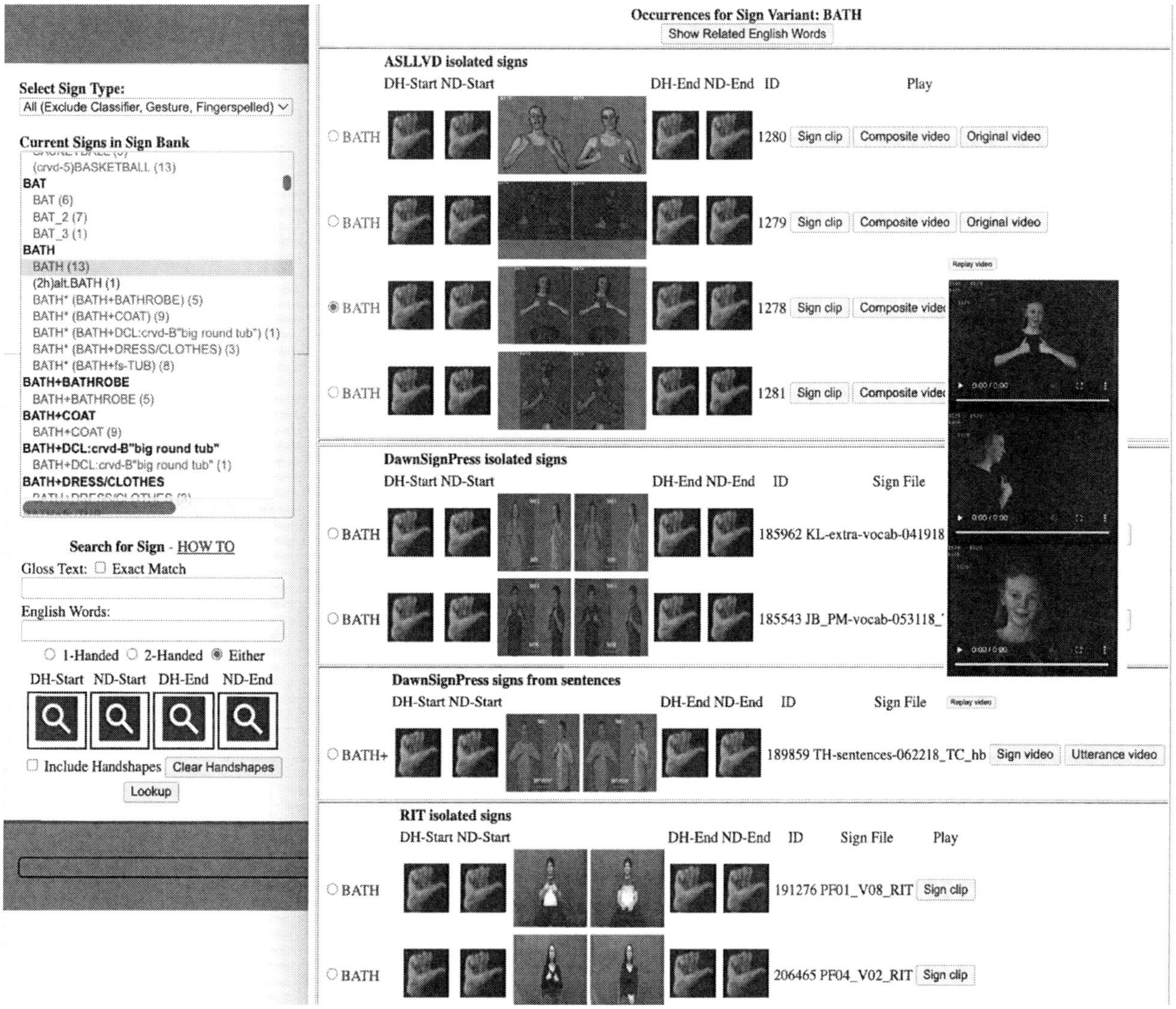

Figure 4. Screen shot showing Sign Bank Interface for Searching and Viewing ASL Sign Variants

The data can be searched, browsed, and downloaded. We have enforced, to the best of our ability, consistency in labeling throughout our corpora. Sign-level annotations include gloss labels, annotations of sign type (lexical, loan, fingerspelled, classifier, number, and name signs, as well as gestures and compounds), and phonological properties (e.g., information about hand configurations on the 2 hands). Utterances include sentence-level information about such things as non-manual behaviors and grammatical markings, translations, etc..

5.1 ASLLRP Continuous Signing Corpus

Our continuous signing data can be accessed here: https://dai.cs.rutgers.edu/dai/s/dai. The data can be browsed or searched based on various sign-level and utterance-level properties.

Download options are available for:

- **American Sign Language Linguistic Research Project (ASLLRP) SignStream® 3 Corpus**
  - **47** files with a total of **2,124** utterances; **17,528** sign tokens; and **5** signers

See https://dai.cs.rutgers.edu/dai/s/runningstats for further statistics.

Linguistic annotations for the signs and utterances that can be downloaded are available in XML format. These utterances can also be viewed and further analyzed and annotated within SignStream®, an application we have developed for analysis of visual language data, shared on the Web (http://www.bu.edu/asllrp/SignStream/3/ ; a major new update has just been released).

5.2 ASLLRP Sign Bank

An online ASLLRP Sign Bank (Neidle et al., 2018; Neidle, Opoku, and Metaxas, 2022) is also available: https://dai.cs.rutgers.edu/dai/s/signbank. It is possible to search based on various criteria, and to view, for specific signs, both examples from our citation-form sign datasets and segmented signs from our continuous signing corpora (viewable either individually or in their sentential context). **Figure 4** illustrates the interface. It is currently possible to download the citation-form sign datasets and videos from our website for use in sign recognition research, with the ability to download segmented Sign Bank examples from our continuous signing corpora to be provided from the same site in the near future. Datasets currently available for download, with accompanying annotations:

- **Boston University American Sign Language Lexicon Video Dataset (ASLLVD)**
  - **9,748** sign tokens; **6** signers
- **Rochester Institute of Technology (RIT) Dataset**
  - **11,801** sign tokens; **12** signers
- **DawnSignPress (DSP) Dataset**
  - **1,903** sign tokens; **15** signers

Further statistics are available here:
https://dai.cs.rutgers.edu/dai/s/runningstats

Linguistic annotations for the videos are available in Excel and csv formats. ASLLRP Sign Bank annotations are explained in http://www.bu.edu/asllrp/rpt20/asllrp20.pdf, Neidle & Opoku (2022), with further description of our general annotation conventions in Neidle (2002, 2007).

6. Alignment of Annotations for WLASL

We selected 19,672 sign videos from the WLASL dataset. (Some examples were excluded for one of several reasons, including poor quality of the signing or the video, the presence in the video of a string of signs rather than a single sign, the unavailability of the videos in question, cases where the hands were not within the visible region, etc.) A spreadsheet, at https://dai.cs.rutgers.edu/dai/s/aboutwlasl, provides, for signs already in our Sign Bank, annotations consistent with the rest of the ASLLRP dataset. See **Figure 5**. In cases where the specific signs do not already exist in the ASLLRP dataset, new glosses that follow our existing conventions and that do not conflict with any existing gloss labels were assigned; we will continue to use the same labels for additional examples that may be added to our Sign Bank in the future.

Figure 6 illustrates how WLASL gloss labeling compares with ASLLVD gloss labels for the sign with ASLLVD class label 'COP'. As is evident, the three different WLASL gloss labels in column 1 (corresponding to possible designations for such a person in English: *cop, police, policeman*) are used indifferently in the WLASL dataset for all occurrences, with no distinction made at all in the gloss labels for the handshape variation that potentially occurs with this sign. In some cases, multiple gloss labels are associated with identical WLASL video examples that bear distinct video IDs. See also "Why Alternative Gloss Labels Will Increase the Value of the WLASL Dataset" (Neidle and Ballard, 2022).

These alternative gloss labels are shared on the Web. So, it would be straightforward to use these labels in conjunction with the WLASL videos and other associated metadata. It is therefore also straightforward to combine the ASLLRP data with the WLASL data for research on sign recognition, to expand the number of examples and distinct signers per sign and to extend the vocabulary beyond what is contained only in one or the other of these datasets.

7. Sign Recognition Research using the Modified-Gloss WLASL Data

Recent research by our group has made use of the revised WLASL annotations in conjunction with the WLASL data, combined with the ASLLVD.

7.1 Bidirectional Skeleton-Based Isolated Sign Recognition using Graph Convolution Networks (GCNs)

Dafnis et al. (2022b) report on a new skeleton-based learning method for isolated sign recognition involving explicit detection of the start and end frames of signs trained on the ASLLVD dataset. Using linguistically relevant parameters based on skeleton input, this method employs a bidirectional learning approach within a Graph Convolutional Network (GCN) framework. For 18,141 videos of 1,449 lexical signs from the WLASL dataset (with a minimum of 6 examples per sign)—with revised gloss labeling as described earlier in this paper—we achieved a success rate of 77.43% recognition accuracy for top-1 and 94.54% for top-5, outperforming other state-of-the-art approaches. A comparison with the TRN method of Zhou et al. (2018) and the SL-GCN (SAM-SLR-v2) method of Jiang et al. (2021) *on this same WLASL dataset with revised gloss labeling* is shown in **Figure 7**.

gloss	video_id	CLASS	MAIN ENTRY	[entry/variant]
cop	13244	COP	COP	COP
cop	13246	COP	COP	COP
cop	13247	COP	COP	COP
cop	13249	COP	COP	COP
cop	13252	COP	COP	COP
cop	13253	COP	COP	COP
police	43519	COP	COP	COP
police	43525	COP	COP	COP
police	43527	COP	COP	COP
police	43528	COP	COP	COP
police	43531	COP	COP	COP
police	43534	COP	COP	COP
police	43535	COP	COP	COP
policeman	43536	COP	COP	COP
policeman	43538	COP	COP	COP
policeman	43539	COP	COP	COP
cop	13245	COP	COP	COP_2
cop	13248	COP	COP	COP_2
cop	13250	COP	COP	COP_2
police	43522	COP	COP	COP_2
police	43523	COP	COP	COP_2
police	43526	COP	COP	COP_2
police	43529	COP	COP	COP_2
police	43532	COP	COP	COP_2
police	43533	COP	COP	COP_2
police	66306	COP	COP	COP_2
policeman	43537	COP	COP	COP_2
policeman	43540	COP	COP	COP_2
policeman	43542	COP	COP	COP_2
policeman	67087	COP	COP	COP_2
police	43524	COP	COP	COP_3

Figure 5. Excerpt from spreadsheet establishing correlations between WLASL signs (glossed as in Column 1) and ASLLRP-based gloss labels (with class labels used as the basis for our sign recognition research)

7.2 Combining Data from the WLASL and ASLLVD Datasets

In more recent work, Dafnis et al. (2022a) have been combining the WLASL data used in Dafnis et al. (2022b) with lexical signs from the ASLLVD dataset, again selecting those signs for which we had a minimum of 6 examples per sign—this time from those *combined* datasets; we ended up with **1,480** total signs (and **22,853** total video examples). There is an additional challenge involved in combining these datasets, because signers in the WLASL are standing, whereas the ASLLVD signers are seated; see **Figure 8**. It should be noted that this makes the combined dataset especially valuable, since in the real world, signers may be either sitting or standing.

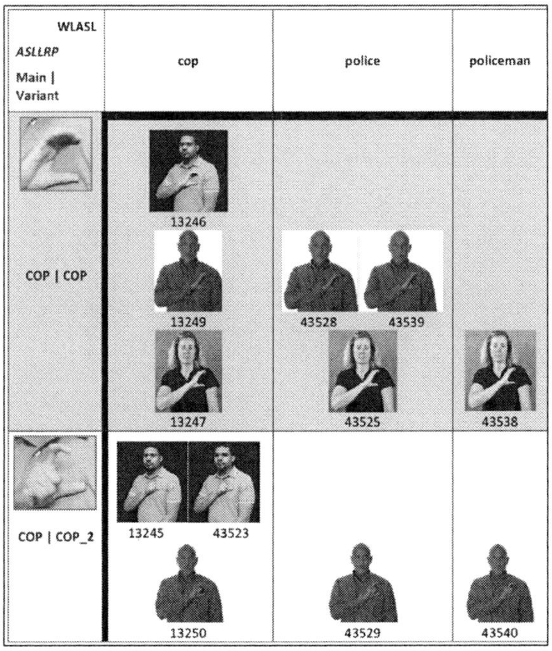

Figure 6. Comparison of WLASL and ASLLRP labeling of signs and sign variants. The WLASL labels ***cop***, ***police***, and ***policeman*** are used indifferently for these examples; the ASLLRP class label COP is used for all of them, with variant labels COP *vs.* COP_2 distinguishing the handshapes.

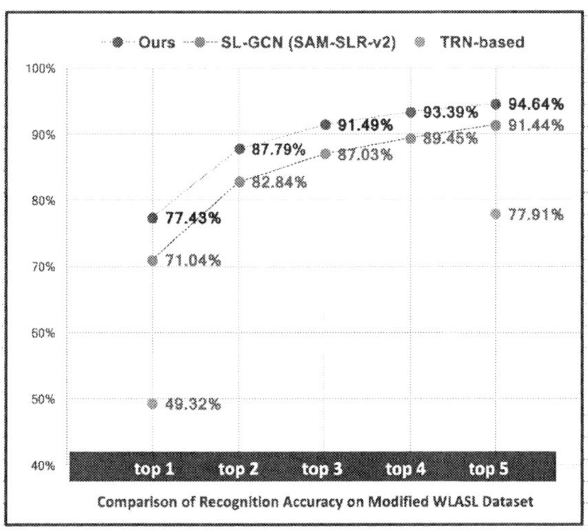

Figure 7. Comparison of Recognition Accuracy for 18,141 videos of 1,449 Lexical Signs in the WLASL Dataset with Modified Gloss Labeling

Figure 8. Pooling examples from ASLLVD and WLASL

Sign Types	Min. # samples per sign	Total # distinct signs (class labels)	Total # samples	Top-1	Top-5
Lexical	**6**	1,480	22,853	**78.54%**	**94.72%**
Lexical	**12**	983	18,362	**84.23%**	**96.69%**
All *	**6**	1,502	23,016	**78.70%**	**94.79%**
All *	**12**	990	18,482	**84.70%**	**96.56%**

* **Includes lexical signs, loan signs, and compounds**

Figure 9. Sign Recognition Accuracy for Different Sets of Signs (all with WLASL & ASLLVD combined)

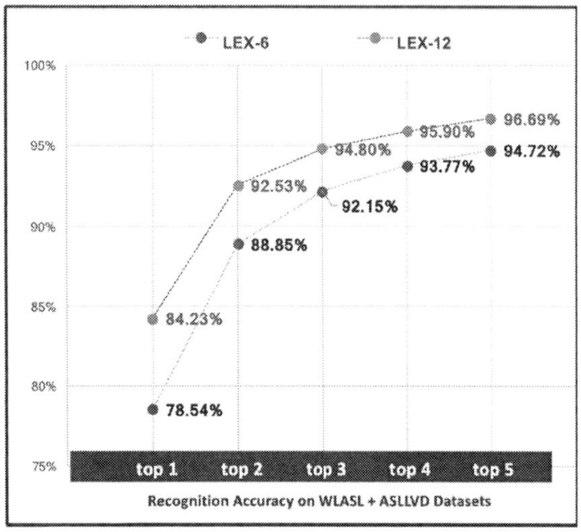

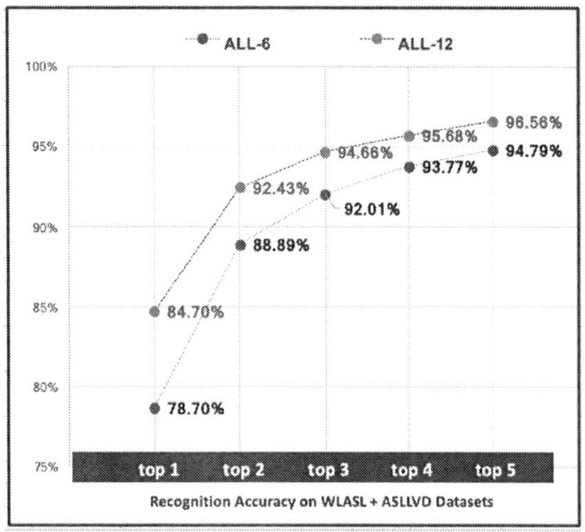

Figure 10. Sign Recognition Accuracy for Different Datasets (WLASL & ASLLVD combined): **for lexical *vs.* all signs (incl. compounds & loan signs) with minimum of 6 or 12 samples**

This research is based on a spatial-temporal GCN architecture for modeling skeleton keypoints, with use of both the forward and backward data streams for joints and bones for isolated sign recognition, following Dafnis et al. (2022b).

In preliminary results—with further improvements anticipated as our research proceeds—we achieved a success rate of **78.54%** for top-1, and **94.72%** for top-5; see the top graph in **Figure 10**.

We also explored how increasing the minimum number of examples per sign from **6** to **12**—thereby also decreasing the total number of signs from **18,362** total examples to **983**, the number of distinct signs for which we have at least that many examples, resulting in a more balanced dataset overall—improved recognition accuracy.

Furthermore, we expanded the set of signs considered from the combined datasets to include loan signs and compounds, in addition to lexical signs,[2] thereby increasing the number, of total examples for which we have at least 6or 12 examples per sign to **23,016**, representing **1,502** distinct signs, or **18,482** representing **990** signs, respectively. The sign recognition accuracy achieved by fusion of the forward and backward video streams is shown in **Figure 9** and **Figure 10**. This research is reported in Dafnis et al. (2022a), but for present purposes, we offer these examples of the usefulness of the consistent gloss labeling across the ASLLVD and WLASL datasets in enabling sign recognition research on the larger and richer combined dataset.

8. Benchmark Datasets

Details about the datasets used for our published research on sign recognition, including identification of videos used for training, validation, and testing, are available on our website: http://www.bu.edu/asllrp/signrec.html.

9. Conclusions

Thus, our belief is that the spreadsheet we provide with internally consistent gloss labeling for the WLASL greatly increases the value of that dataset for use in research. The fact that these gloss labels are also consistent with those used for the ASLLRP Sign Bank (i.e., the ASLLVD and other available ASLLRP data) makes it possible to use these datasets in combination, resulting in a resource that is substantially larger and richer than those datasets individually. The preliminary research on sign recognition reported in Section 7 gives an indication of the promise offered by this approach.

Furthermore, the high accuracy with which a sign can now be recognized from video within the top-5 makes this technology potentially useable in applications, such as search by video example (from the signer's webcam or a video clip identified by the user) in an all-ASL dictionary, where a user could be presented with 5 choices and asked to confirm the selection. Our research group is, in fact, currently working to develop such functionality.

10. Acknowledgments

For invaluable assistance with this project, we thank Indyaloreal Oliver, Gregory Dimitriadis, and Douglas Motto. We are grateful to Matt Huenerfauth for carrying out the ASLLRP Sign Bank data collection at RIT, with the help of Abraham Glasser, Ben Leyer, Saad Hassan, and Sarah Morgenthal; and to DawnSignPress for sharing video data for the ASLLRP Sign Bank. See http://www.bu.edu/asllrp/people.html for a list of the

[2] Lexical signs still represented a very large proportion of this expanded 'All' dataset; the total number of signs did not increase by a large amount. As shown here, this expansion made only a negligible difference in the recognition accuracy. However, it should be noted that the current methodology did not take advantage of the linguistic constraints on the internal structure of lexical signs, something we plan to explore further in the future, as this has proven to increase recognition accuracy in our prior research (Neidle et al., 2013; Dilsizian et al., 2014).

many, many, many people who have made important contributions to the research that gave rise to the materials described here. We also gratefully acknowledge Stan Sclaroff, Vassilis Athitsos, Ashwin Thangali, Joan Nash, Ben Bahan, Rachel Benedict, Naomi Caselli, Elizabeth Cassidy, Lana Cook, Braden Painter, Tyler Richard, Tory Sampson, and Dana Schlang for collaboration on the development of the ASLLVD dataset. The work reported here has been supported in part by grants from NSF: no. 2040638, 1763486, 1763523, and 1763569. Any opinions, findings, or conclusions expressed in this material are those of the authors and do not necessarily reflect the views of the National Science Foundation.

11. Bibliographical References

Athitsos, V., Neidle, C., Sclaroff, S., Nash, J., Stefan, A., Yuan, Q., and Thangali, A. (2008). The American Sign Language Lexicon Video Dataset. *Proceedings of the IEEE Workshop on Computer Vision and Pattern Recognition for Human Communicative Behavior Analysis*. http://vlm1.uta.edu/~athitsos/publications/athitsos_cvpr4hb2008.pdf.

Bilge, Y.C., Cinbis, R.G., and Ikizler-Cinbis, N. (2022). Towards Zero-shot Sign Language Recognition. *IEEE Transactions on Pattern Analysis and Machine Intelligence, July 2009*. doi: 10.1109/TPAMI.2022.3143074.

Boháček, M. and Hrúz, M. (2022). Sign Pose-based Transformer for Word-level Sign Language Recognition. *Proceedings of the IEEE/CVF Winter Conference on Applications of Computer Vision Workshops (WACVW)*. pp. 182-191. https://ieeexplore.ieee.org/document/9707552.

Bragg, D., Koller, O., Bellard, M., Berke, L., Boudreault, P., Braffort, A., Caselli, N., Huenerfauth, M., Kacorri, H., Verhoef, T., Vogler, C., and Ringel Morris, M. (2019). Sign Language Recognition, Generation, and Translation: An Interdisciplinary Perspective. *Proceedings of the 21st International ACM SIGACCESS Conference on Computers and Accessibility (ASSETS '19). Association for Computing Machinery*, New York, NY. doi: 10.1145/3308561.3353774.

Cormier, K., Crasborn, O., and Bank, R. (2016). Digging into Signs: Emerging Annotation Standards for Sign Language Corpora. *Proceedings of the Workshop on Representation and Processing of Sign Languages: Corpus Mining.* 10th International Conference on Language Resources and Evaluation (LREC). European Language Resources Association (ELRA). Portorož, Slovenia, May 2016.

Dafnis, K.M., Chroni, E., Neidle, C., and Metaxas, D. (2022a). Isolated Sign Recognition using ASL Datasets with Consistent Text-based Gloss Labeling and Curriculum Learning. *Proceedings of the 7th International Workshop on Sign Language Translation and Avatar Technology: The Junction of the Visual and the Textual (SLTAT 2022).* 13th International Conference on Language Resources and Evaluation (LREC). European Language Resources Association (ELRA). Marseille, France, June 2022.

Dafnis, K.M., Chroni, E., Neidle, C., and Metaxas, D.N. (2022b). Bidirectional Skeleton-Based Isolated Sign Recognition using Graph Convolution Networks. *Proceedings of the 13th International Conference on Language Resources and Evaluation (LREC).* European Language Resources Association (ELRA). Marseille, France, June 2022.

de Amorim, C.C. and Zanchetti, C. (2021). ASL-Skeleton3D and ASL-Phono: Two Novel Datasets for the American Sign Language. *arXiv:2201.02065*. doi: 10.48550/arXiv.2201.02065.

Dilsizian, M., Yanovich, P., Wang, S., Neidle, C., and Metaxas, D. (2014). A New Framework for Sign Recognition based on 3D Handshape Identification and Linguistic Modeling. *Proceedings of the 9th International Conference on Language Resources and Evaluation (LREC).* European Language Resources Association (ELRA). Reykjavik, Iceland, May 2014. http://www.lrec-conf.org/proceedings/lrec2014/pdf/1138_Paper.pdf.

Dreuw, P., Neidle, C., Athitsos, V., Sclaroff, S., and Ney, H. (2008). Benchmark Databases for Video-Based Automatic Sign Language Recognition. *Proceedings of the 6th International Conference on Language Resources and Evaluation (LREC).* European Language Resources Association (ELRA). Marrakech, Morocco, May 2008. http://www.lrec-conf.org/proceedings/lrec2008/pdf/287_paper.pdf.

Duarte, A., Palaskar, S., Ventura, L., Ghadiyaram, D., DeHaan, K., Metze, F., Torres, J., and Giró-i-Nieto, X. (2021). How2sign: a large-scale multi- modal dataset for continuous American Sign Language. *Proceedings of the Conference on Computer Vision and Pattern Recognition (CVPR),* 2021. Dataset website: https://how2sign.github.io.

Duarte, A., Albanie, S., Giró-i-Nieto, X., and Varol, G. (2022). Sign Language Video Retrieval with Free-Form Textual Queries. *Arxiv 2201.02495v1.* doi: 10.48550/arXiv.2201.02495.

Ebrahimi, M. and Ebrahimpour-komleh, H. (2022). Rough Set with Deep Neural Network for Sign Language Recognition. *TechRxiv. Preprint.* doi: 10.36227/techrxiv.19255742.v1.

Elakkiya, R. and Selvamani, K. (2019). Subunit sign modeling framework for continuous sign language recognition. *Computers and Electrical Engineering, 74*, pp. 379–390. doi: 10.1016/j.compeleceng.2019.02.012.

Hassan, A., Elgabry, A., and Hemayed, E. (2021). Enhanced Dynamic Sign Language Recognition using SlowFast Networks. *Proceedings of the 17th International Computer Engineering Conference (ICENCO).* pp. 124-128. doi: 10.1109/ICENCO49852.2021.9698904.

Jiang, S., Sun, B., Wang, L., Bai, Y., Li, K., and Fu, Y. (2021). Skeleton aware multi-modal sign language recognition. *Proceedings of the IEEE/CVF Conference on Computer Vision and Pattern Recognition (CVPR)* Workshops, 2021, pp. 3413-3423.

Johnston, T. (2010). From archive to corpus: Transcription and annotation in the creation of signed language corpora. *International Journal of Corpus Linguistics, 15*(1), pp. 106-131. doi: 10.1075/ijcl.15.1.05joh.

Joze, H., Vaezi, R., and Koller, O. (2018). MS-ASL: A large-scale data set and benchmark for understanding American Sign Language. *arXiv preprint arXiv:1812.01053.* doi: 10.48550/arXiv.1812.01053.

Kak, A.C. (2002). Purdue RVL-SLLL ASL Database for Automatic Recognition of American Sign Language. *Proceedings of the IEEE Int. Conf. on Multimodal Interfaces (ICMI).* https://dl.acm.org/doi/abs/10.1109/ICMI.2002.1166987.

Kumar, S.S., Wangyal, T., Saboo, V., and Srinath, R. (2018). Time Series Neural Networks for Real Time Sign Language Translation. *Proceedings of the 17th IEEE International Conference on Machine Learning and Applications (ICMLA), 2018,* pp. 243-248. doi: 10.1109/ICMLA.2018.00043.

Li, D., Rodriguez, C., Yu, X., and Li, H. (2020). Word-level deep sign language recognition from video: A new large-scale dataset and methods comparison. *Proceedings of the IEEE/CVF winter conference on applications of computer vision*, 2020. pp. 1459-1469.

Lim, K.M., Tan, A.W.C., Lee, C.P., and Tan, S.C. (2019). Isolated sign language recognition using Convolutional Neural Network hand modelling and Hand Energy Image. *Multimedia Tools and Applications (2019), 78*, pp. 1-28. doi: 10.1007/s11042-019-7263-7.

Maruyama, M., Ghose, S., Inoue, K., Prathim Roy, P., Iwamura, M., and Yoshioka, M. (2021). Word-level Sign Language Recognition with Multi-stream Neural Networks Focusing on Local Regions. *Arxiv abs/2106.15989.* doi: 10.48550/arXiv.2106.15989.

Neidle, C. (2002). SignStream™ Annotation: Conventions used for the American Sign Language Linguistic Research Project. American Sign Language Linguistic Research Project Report No. 11: Boston University, Boston, MA. http://www.bu.edu/asllrp/asllrpr11.pdf.

Neidle, C. (2007). SignStream™ Annotation: Addendum to Conventions used for the American Sign Language Linguistic Research Project. American Sign Language Linguistic Research Project Report No. 13: Boston University, Boston, MA. http://www.bu.edu/asllrp/asllrpr13.pdf.

Neidle, C., Thangali, A., and Sclaroff, S. (2012). Challenges in Development of the American Sign Language Lexicon Video Dataset (ASLLVD) Corpus. *Proceedings of the 5th Workshop on the Representation and Processing of Sign Languages: Interactions between Corpus and Lexicon,* 9th International Conference on Language Resources and Evaluation (LREC). European Language Resources Association (ELRA). Istanbul, Turkey, May 2012. https://open.bu.edu/handle/2144/31899.

Neidle, C., Thangali, A., Nash, J.P., and Sclaroff, S. (2011). Exploiting phonological constraints for handshape inference in ASL video. *Proceedings of the 2013 IEEE Conference on Computer Vision and Pattern Recognition (CVPR), June 2011*, pp. 521-528. https://www.semanticscholar.org/paper/Exploiting-phonological-constraints-for-handshape-Thangali-Nash/5e404d87b84cb5db11fb6a0c01291ff59528dceb.

Neidle, C., Opoku, A., Dimitriadis, G., and Metaxas, D. (2018). NEW Shared & Interconnected ASL Resources: SignStream® 3 Software; DAI 2 for Web Access to Linguistically Annotated Video Corpora; and a Sign Bank. *Proceedings of the 8th Workshop on the Representation and Processing of Sign Languages: Involving the Language Community.* 11th International Conference on Language Resources and Evaluation (LREC). European Language Resources Association (ELRA). Miyagawa, Japan, May 2018. https://open.bu.edu/handle/2144/30047.

Neidle, C. and Ballard, C. (2022). Why Alternative Gloss Labels Will Increase the Value of the WLASL Dataset Boston, MA: Boston University, ASLLRP Project Report No. 21. http://www.bu.edu/asllrp/rpt21/asllrp21.pdf.

Neidle, C. and Opoku, A. (2022). Documentation for Download of ASLLRP Sign Bank Citation-Form Sign Datasets. Boston, MA: Boston University, ASLLRP Project Report No. 20. http://www.bu.edu/asllrp/rpt20/asllrp20.pdf.

Neidle, C., Opoku, A., and Metaxas, D. (2022). ASL Video Corpora & Sign Bank: Resources Available through the American Sign Language Linguistic Research Project (ASLLRP). *arXiv:2201.07899.* doi: 10.48550/arXiv.2201.07899.

Orfanidou, E., Woll, B., and Morgan, G., eds. (2015). *Research Methods in Sign Language Studies: A Practical Guide,* West Sussex, UK: John Wiley & Sons.

Rastgoo, R., Kiania, K., and Escalerab, S. (2022). Word separation in continuous sign language using isolated signs and post-processing. *Arxiv 2204.00923v3.* doi: 10.48550/arXiv.2204.00923.

Theodorakis, S., Pitsikalis, V., and Maragos, P. (2014). Dynamic–static Unsupervised Sequentiality, Statistical Subunits and Lexicon for Sign Language Recognition. *Image and Vision Computing, 32*(8), pp. 533-49. doi: 10.1016/j.imavis.2014.04.012.

Zhou, B., Andonian, A., Oliva, A., Torralba, A. (2018). Temporal Relational Reasoning in Videos. In: Ferrari, V., Hebert, M., Sminchisescu, C., Weiss, Y. (eds) *Computer Vision – ECCV 2018. ECCV 2018. Lecture Notes in Computer Science, vol 11205.* Springer, Cham. doi: 10.1007/978-3-030-01246-5_49.

Proceedings of the 10th Workshop on the Representation and Processing of Sign Languages (sign-lang@LREC 2022), pages 173–180
Language Resources and Evaluation Conference (LREC 2022), Marseille, 20-25 June 2022

Signed Language Transcription and the Creation of a Cross-linguistic Comparative Database

Justin M. Power[1], David Quinto-Pozos[1], Danny Law[1]
[1]The University of Texas at Austin
305 E. 23rd Street STOP B5100, Austin, TX 78712, USA
justinmpower@utexas.edu, davidqp@austin.utexas.edu, dannylaw@austin.utexas.edu

Abstract

As the availability of signed language data has rapidly increased, sign scholars have been confronted with the challenge of creating a common framework for the cross-linguistic comparison of the phonological forms of signs. While transcription techniques have played a fundamental role in the creation of cross-linguistic comparative databases for spoken languages, transcription has featured much less prominently in sign research and lexicography. Here we report the experiences of the Sign Change project in using the signed language transcription system HamNoSys to create a comparative database of basic vocabulary for thirteen signed languages. We report the results of a small-scale study, in which we measured (i) the average time required for two trained transcribers to complete a transcription and (ii) the similarity of their independently produced transcriptions. We find that, across the two transcribers, the transcription of one sign required, on average, one minute and a half. We also find that the similarity of transcriptions differed across phonological parameters. We consider the implications of our findings about transcription time and transcription similarity for other projects that plan to incorporate transcription techniques.

Keywords: multi-sign-language resources, transcription, cross-linguistic comparison, HamNoSys

1. Introduction

Over the past two decades, signed language data in various forms have become increasingly available and widely accessible. Numerous online dictionaries are available for individual signed languages; many of these dictionaries have been created by researchers and have been used in scholarly research (e.g., Stumpf et al., 2020; Caselli et al., 2016; Hochgesang et al., 2020). These resources typically include thousands of entries with videos of sign articulations and with other representations of the forms of signs—such as images, transcriptions, and theoretically-informed coding schemes. Several corpus projects have also been started during the past two decades for, inter alia, Australian Sign Language (Johnston & Schembri, 2007), *Deutsche Gebärdensprache* (Prillwitz et al., 2008), British Sign Language (Schembri et al., 2013), and *Russkiy Zhestovyi Yazyk* (Russian Sign Language, Kimmelman et al., 2022). New approaches using recently-developed software, such as OpenPose (Cao et al., 2021), promise to increase the amount and the type of data—as well as the precision of the data—that are available to researchers in the future (e.g., Kimmelman et al., 2020).

Although there has been a marked increase in the amount of signed language data available, cross-linguistic comparative resources are still few in number. Websites such as spreadthesign.com have made it possible to visually compare signs across dozens of languages—though it is unclear whether the data presented in such resources are representative of each respective signing community because the methodologies used to collect data are not always well described. Recent large-scale comparisons of lexical signs (Yu et al., 2018) and of manual alphabets (Power et al., 2020) have used such websites as sources of cross-linguistic data. The network of SignBank dictionaries, which uses a common approach and format (Crasborn et al., 2020; Hochgesang, 2022), offers the possibility of large-scale cross-linguistic comparison in the future (Börstell et al., 2020). In addition to the coding system developed for the Global Signbank, scholars have begun to collaborate on the development of a common phonological coding scheme for resources in American Sign Language (Becker et al., 2020). And, the Dicta-Sign project has created a framework for comparing basic vocabulary and connected signing across four signed languages[1] (Hanke et al., 2010). Despite these welcome advances in the creation of comparable phonological representations, currently, there are extremely few open cross-linguistic comparative databases that include easily comparable representations of the forms of signs.

The challenge of creating a comparative framework for cross-linguistic data confronts scholars of both signed and spoken languages (Forkel et al., 2018). However, scholars of spoken languages have inherited practical orthographies as well as a transcription system, the International Phonetic Alphabet (IPA), which has been used for more than a century to represent hundreds of spoken languages in precise phonetic detail (Albright, 1958); and, the IPA is itself based on alphabetic symbols with millennia-old histories. With the benefit of this inheritance, transcription techniques have played a fundamental role in the creation of cross-linguistic comparative databases for spoken languages and in the possibility of extending those comparisons to new languages (e.g., Greenhill et al., 2008). In contrast, all currently used systems for writing signed languages have short histories, and the transcription of signed language data using one of these systems is not widely practiced (Hochgesang, 2014). In sum, transcription has featured much less prominently in the creation of cross-linguistic resources for signed languages.

Here we report the experiences of the Sign Change project[2] in using transcription techniques to create a cross-linguistic comparative database of basic vocabulary across 13 signed languages. Begun in September 2020, this three-year project aims to make its comparative database open to scholars at the end of the project in mid-2023. To create the comparative database, we have used the transcription system HamNoSys to represent the forms of signs in a uniform system (Hanke, 2004). By using transcription techniques, our aim has been to make the database

[1] British, German, French, and Greek Sign Languages.

[2] See the project website: liberalarts.utexas.edu/lrc/sign-change.

expandable with transcribed data from other signed languages and with data produced within other projects.

In this paper, we report information that concerns two aspects of signed language transcription—namely, transcription time and transcription similarity. That is, first, following a training period in which research assistants learned to transcribe signs in HamNoSys, how much time, on average, is required for those research assistants to complete transcriptions of signs? And, second, once completed, how similar are the transcriptions that were produced by multiple trained transcribers? In exploring these aspects of the transcription process, we aim to inform future projects that use transcription techniques to create cross-linguistic signed language resources.

We report the results of a small-scale study in which we compare two trained transcribers after one year of experience transcribing signs. Thus, although the study is small in scale, it provides a window into the transcription process through the lens of relatively well-trained transcribers. We explore the factors which affected the dimensions of transcription time and similarity, such as the phonological complexity of a sign and the number of symbols systematically required in a HamNoSys transcription. We note a relationship between the number of symbols required in a transcription and the amount of time needed for that transcription. We find that particular phonological parameters of the sign, such as handshapes, were transcribed with a greater degree of similarity than other parameters, such as movement. Finally, we discuss the practical implications of the study for a project that incorporates transcription techniques. We also discuss the theoretical issues raised by the study and propose future research that would compare the transcription process across signed and spoken languages.

2. Methods

2.1 Transcribers

The two transcribers in this study (hereafter transcriber-1 and transcriber-2) were undergraduate research assistants who worked on a part-time basis (up to 10 hours per week). At the time of the study, transcriber-1 had completed three years of a four-year degree program in linguistics, and transcriber-2 was in the final semester of a four-year program in audiology. In their courses of study, both transcribers had been trained to use the International Phonetic Alphabet, and both were second-language adult learners of American Sign Language (ASL) who had taken multiple courses in that language at the undergraduate level. The ASL coursework for each transcriber totaled approximately 225 face-time hours of instruction over an 18-month period; transcriber-1 had also assisted a deaf instructor with first-semester courses for an additional 270 hours of exposure to classroom ASL. Prior to their training in HamNoSys transcription, neither transcriber had been trained in any signed language transcription system, and neither had any knowledge of HamNoSys.

Both transcribers completed an initial training period of approximately one month. The training period, which was conducted by the first author, included weekly hour-long sessions that focused on the transcription of one sign parameter per week (i.e., handshape, orientation, location, movement). For lesson material, we used the *HamNoSys 4 Handshape Chart* (Hanke et el., 2010) and the *HamNoSys 4.0 User Guide* (Smith, 2013). Using video data, the transcribers then practiced transcription techniques during the week following each session. After their initial training period, both transcribers received ongoing training on an as-needed basis, as well as feedback on their transcriptions.

The training program instructed the transcribers to produce relatively narrow transcriptions. A comparison of a relatively broad versus a relatively narrow HamNoSys transcription is given in (1); the transcriptions are aligned to group parameters in a visually distinctive way. The transcription in (1a), which is taken from Hanke (2018), represents a relatively broad transcription. The location of the hand at the beginning of the sign is close to the right side of the forehead; this relationship is indicated in (1a) by the three symbols 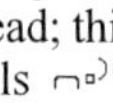, which respectively represent the forehead, the right side, and closeness. In the relatively narrow transcription in (1b), there are seven additional symbols—the open and close parenthesis symbols group the five number symbols (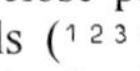), which represent the fingers that are close to the forehead as well as the finger part symbol (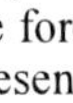), which represents the tips of the fingers.

(1) a.  'Hamburg' *DGS*
b. 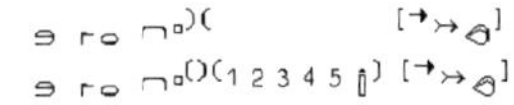

At the time of the study, transcriber-1 had completed 13 months in the project, and transcriber-2 had completed 12 months. By that time, the transcribers had each gained experience transcribing more than 1,000 basic vocabulary signs from multiple sign languages, including ASL, British Sign Language, *Lengua de Señas Mexicana*, *langue des signes française*, *Nederlandse Gebarentaal*, *Langue des signes de Belgique francophone*, and others; and they had experience editing many hundreds of transcriptions that had been completed by other transcribers.

2.2 Signs

For the study, we selected 100 basic vocabulary signs from *Vlaamse Gebarentaal* (VGT, or Flemish Sign Language), a language that, prior to the study, neither transcriber had had experience transcribing. We used the VGT Signbank (Vlaams GebarentaalCentrum, 2018) as a source for basic vocabulary signs in *Vlaamse Gebarentaal*. Table 1 shows the concepts that were included in the study. Sixty-three (63) of the signs in the table were articulated with one hand, and 37 were articulated with two hands. Only one sign had two parts[3]: the sign meaning 'dull' (i.e., blunt) is composed of parts meaning 'not' and 'sharp'.

Because entries in the VGT Signbank do not include information about part of speech, in order to organize the 100 concepts by part of speech (as in Table 1) we had to rely on the part of speech of the Flemish translation of each sign. That is, we had to assume that the sign meaning 'mother' in *Vlaamse Gebarentaal* shares the same part of speech as the word *moeder* in Flemish—namely, noun. Given problems classifying signs into word classes in some sign languages (Schwager & Zeshan, 2008), this assumption represents a potential limitation of our study.

[3] In our database, each sign part is transcribed in a separate row, such that each row has only one value per parameter.

Part of speech	Concepts
Noun (n=45)	animal, ant, back, belly, bird, child, cloud, day, dog, ear, earth, egg, eye, father, feather, fingernail, fire, fish, flower, fly, fog, foot, fruit, hair, hand, heart, knee, man, meat (2), moon, mother, name (2), night, nose, person, stone, tongue, tooth, tree, water, wife, woman, year
Verb (n=19)	bite, blow, breathe, burn, come, count, cry, cut, die, do, drink, eat, fall, fight, float, flow, fly, know, play
Adjective (n=26)	all, bad (2), big (2), black (2), cold (2), dirty, dry, dull, fat, few, five, four, good, green, heavy, new, old, three (2), two, white, yellow
Adverb (n=7)	far, how, not, what, where, who, yesterday
Pronoun (n=3)	he, I, you

Table 1: Concepts used in the study, organized by part of speech. (2) = two variants of the relevant concept.

In addition to their organization in part of speech categories, the concepts in Table 1 can be grouped into semantic and semiotic categories. For example, five of the signs in our data represent colors: black (2 variants), green, white, and yellow; five signs refer to numerals: five, four, three (2 variants), and two; and thirteen concepts in the noun category refer to a part of the body: back, belly, ear, eye, fingernail, foot, hair, hand, heart, knee, nose, tongue, and tooth. Sixteen of the signs in the table are thought, according to Parkhurst & Parkhurst (2003), to be non-iconic vocabulary items: bad (2 variants), black (2 variants), father, good, green, how, mother, name, new, old, play, what, where, white, who, and year.

2.3 Transcription

In advance of the study, we prepared two identical copies of an online spreadsheet in which the transcribers were instructed to complete their transcriptions. For each sign, the spreadsheet included columns for the concept in English, a translation of the concept in Flemish (taken from the VGT Signbank), and the link to the VGT Signbank entry page for each sign. In addition, the spreadsheet had separate columns for each sign parameter and for symmetry, for the number of hands used to articulate a sign, and for whether the signer appeared to be right- or left-dominant. Finally, the spreadsheet also had a column in which the transcribers were instructed to record the amount of time (in minutes and seconds) that it took them to complete each sign transcription.

The transcribers only had access to their own copy of the spreadsheet; they were asked not to consult with one another while completing their transcriptions. They used a web-based HamNoSys input tool (http://www.sign-lang.uni-hamburg.de/hamnosys/input/) to compose their transcriptions, which they subsequently copied into their spreadsheet. They were allowed to complete their transcriptions at their own pace during a two-week period: transcriber-1 completed the 100 transcriptions over the course of six days, while transcriber-2 took five days to complete the transcriptions.

2.4 Comparison Methodology

We used Levenshtein distance to pairwise compare the difference between transcriptions. We normalized the resulting distance scores by dividing each score by the length, ignoring spaces, of the longer string in the relevant pairwise comparison. We then subtracted the normalized scores from 1 in order to have a measure of the similarity of each pair of strings. Consider, for example, the transcriptions in (2), which are taken from the study data.

(2) a. 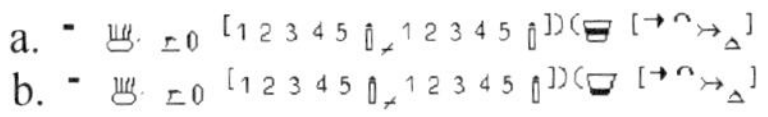 'big' *VGT*

There is only one difference between the transcriptions in (2a-b)—namely, the location symbols [HamNoSys] and [HamNoSys], which represent different heights in the neutral space in front of the signer; thus, the Levenshtein distance for this comparison is 1. Each transcription consists of 28 symbols (handshape=2 symbols, orientation=2, location=17, movement=6, symmetry=1). The normalized Levenshtein distance between the two strings is thus 1/28≈0.036; and the similarity score is 1-0.036≈0.964.

Consider now the transcriptions in (3). There are 5 differences between the transcriptions in (3a-b): one difference in the orientation parameter ([HamNoSys] vs. [HamNoSys]), one difference and one additional symbol in the location parameter ([HamNoSys] vs. [HamNoSys]), and again one difference and one additional symbol in the movement parameter ([HamNoSys] vs. [HamNoSys]). The length of the longer string (3b) in this comparison is 21. Thus, the normalized Levenshtein distance between the two strings is 5/21≈0.238; and the similarity score is 1-0.238≈0.762.

(3) a. 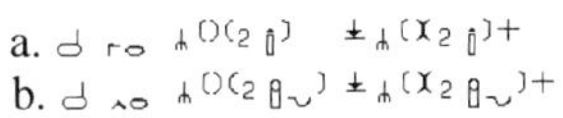 'nose' *VGT*

We used Python (Van Rossum & Drake, 2009) and the pandas library (McKinney, 2010) to perform the comparisons. For statistical analyses, we used NumPy (Harris et al., 2020), SciPy (Virtanen et al., 2020), and researchpy (Bryant, 2021). Figures were produced using Matplotlib (Hunter, 2007).

3. Results

In this section, we report the results of our two main analyses—namely, of the time required per transcription and of the similarity of the transcriptions produced by the two transcribers. As part of the timing results, we highlight selected factors that evidently affected the rate at which the transcribers completed their transcriptions.

3.1 Transcription Time

Taken together, the two transcribers averaged 95.2 seconds (SD=38.1) per transcription—roughly, one minute and a half. But, they completed their transcriptions at different rates. On average, transcriber-1 (M=82.2 seconds, SD=26.7) completed each transcription at a significantly faster rate, according to a Welch's t-test, than did transcriber-2 (M=108.3 seconds, SD=43.1), $t(166.6) = -5.1$, $p < .001$. At present, we have not attempted to count the number of errors in the transcribers' transcriptions or to assess the relationship between errors and speed.

3.1.1 Effect of the Number of HamNoSys Symbols on Transcription Time

Intuitively, the more symbols that are required by HamNoSys for a transcription, the longer it will take on average to complete that transcription. In our data, there is, as expected, a significant positive correlation between the number of symbols used in a transcription and the time it took to complete the transcription, $r(200) = .72, p < .001$.

In consequence of this general feature of the transcription process, one-handed signs were transcribed more quickly than two-handed signs: on average, one-handed signs were transcribed in 84.8 seconds (*SD*=31.4), while two-handed signs were transcribed in 113.1 seconds (*SD*=41.8). There is a significant correlation between the number of hands used to articulate a sign (1 or 2) and the amount of time needed per transcription, $r(200) = .36, p < .001$. This correlation is expected because there is a systematic difference in the number of symbols required by HamNoSys to transcribe one- versus two-handed signs. HamNoSys minimally requires one extra symbol—namely, a symmetry symbol—to transcribe two-handed versus one-handed signs. And, for any parameter in a two-handed sign that is asymmetrical, at least four extra symbols are required: three meta-symbols to show which is the dominant and which is the non-dominant hand, and at least one symbol to represent the non-dominant parameter.

3.1.2 Effect of Grammatical, Semantic, or Semiotic Features and Transcription Time

There is an evident relationship in our data between the grammatical, semantic, or semiotic features of certain concepts and the average number of symbols that were used to transcribe signs representing those concepts. In consequence, there is a difference in the average amount of time required to complete a transcription based on features of the concept. Table 2 reports the average number of symbols used in a transcription and the average time per transcription, broken down by part of speech and by selected semantic and semiotic categories for the 100 concepts included in the study. The non-iconic signs in Table 2 are those concepts in our data that, according to Parkhurst & Parkhurst (2003), may represent non-iconic concepts in four European signed languages and in regional varieties of *Lengua de Signos Española*; see Section 2.2.

Part of speech	Mean symbols per transcription	Mean time (seconds)
Pronoun (n=6)	12.0 (6.0)	63.2 (16.9)
Adverb (n=14)	14.4 (4.8)	72.4 (13.0)
Verb (n=38)	17.7 (7.1)	89.7 (31.6)
Adjective (n=52)	18.2 (8.6)	96.1 (43.4)
Noun (n=90)	23.6 (10.7)	102.8 (38.1)
Semantic category		
Numeral (n=10)	7.8 (2.5)	59.9 (16.0)
Body part (n=26)	20.3 (7.8)	91.2 (31.3)
Color (n=10)	18.5 (9.5)	100.2 (41.8)
Semiotic category		
Non-iconic (n=18)	20.2 (9.1)	97.6 (34.2)

Table 2: Average transcription time (in seconds) and length of the transcription in selected grammatical, semantic, and semiotic categories; standard deviations are provided in parentheses in the two rightmost columns.

If we take the number of HamNoSys symbols used to transcribe a sign as a rough estimate of the phonological complexity of that sign—that is, if we assume that increased phonological complexity will require, on average, more symbols to transcribe—then the results in Table 2 suggest that phonological complexity is unevenly distributed across certain parts of speech and across certain semantic categories in *Vlaamse Gebarentaal*. For example, pronouns and numeral signs in that language were transcribed using relatively few symbols, whereas nouns, body part signs, and non-iconic signs were transcribed using comparatively more symbols.

In sum, there are at least two factors that affected the time per transcription in this study—namely, the transcriber and whether a sign was one- or two-handed. In addition, our results suggest that the grammatical, semantic, or semiotic features of a concept may affect the phonological complexity of a sign—as measured by the number of symbols required to transcribe the sign—and, thus, the average amount of time required for a transcription.

3.2 Transcription Similarity

Using the comparison methodology outlined in Section 2.4, we measured the similarity of each pair of transcriptions that were produced for the same concept. The average similarity of a pair of full transcriptions was 0.69 (*SD*=0.18) for all 100 pairs. The distribution of similarity scores for all 100 transcription pairs is shown in the histogram in Figure 1.

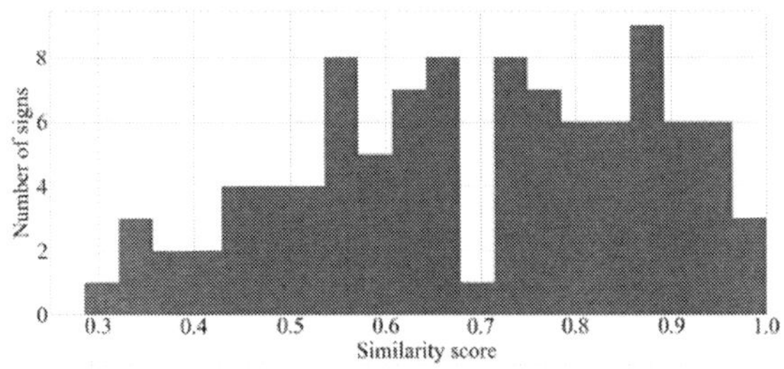

Figure 1. Distribution of similarity scores of full transcriptions for all 100 pairs of signs.

Just two pairs of transcriptions were exactly the same, but fifteen pairs scored 0.9 or higher according to our similarity metric and 84 pairs were at least 0.5 similar.

Similarity was not evenly distributed across all parts of the full transcriptions; that is, some parameters were more similarly transcribed than others. Our approach to organizing transcriptions in a spreadsheet (see Sec. 2.3) allowed us to individually compare the sign parameters (handshape, orientation, location, and movement) and other global aspects of the signs, such as symmetry, the number of hands used to articulate the sign, and hand dominance.

We first report our results pertaining to the last two of these global aspects of the sign. With respect to their coding of the number of hands used to articulate a sign, the two transcribers differed in only one comparison. This difference was apparently a mistake: one transcriber coded the sign as being produced with one hand, but then also used a symmetry symbol in the transcription, which is a type of symbol that is only used to transcribe two-handed signs. Thus, this transcriber likely thought the sign was articulated with two hands, but mistakenly coded the sign as being produced with one hand. The transcribers differed in four comparisons with respect to hand dominance. In two of these four differences, the signs are articulated using two hands; the signs are also symmetrical. Hence it would be challenging (and perhaps impossible) to determine hand dominance solely based on the articulations of these two signs. When viewing other signs in the data set produced by the same signer, it becomes clearer that the signer is likely left-dominant. In the two other comparisons in which the transcribers came to differing conclusions about hand dominance, the signs are articulated with the left hand.

Figure 2 shows the distribution of similarity scores across transcriptions of handshape, orientation, location, movement, and symmetry. Note first that there is a relationship between the number of symbols used to transcribe each parameter and the distribution of scores. For example, an orientation transcription for a one-handed sign requires exactly two symbols: one symbol to represent the orientation of the back of the palm and one symbol to represent the relative orientation of the palm. Hence, using our comparison methodology, the similarity scores can only be 0 (both symbols different), .5 (one symbol different and one identical), and 1.0 (both symbols identical); and the distribution of similarity scores in Figure 2 largely reflects these possible scores.

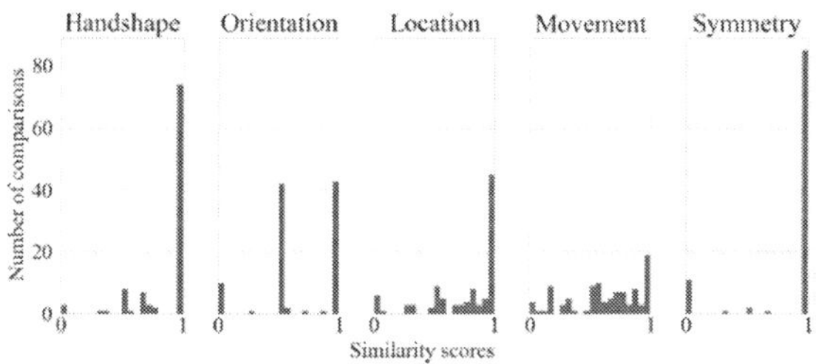

Figure 2: Comparison of the distributions of similarity scores for the transcriptions of four parameters and of symmetry.

In addition to the general relationship in HamNoSys between certain parameters and the number of symbols used to transcribe them, there was also an imbalance in our data in the number of symbols used to transcribe each parameter. For example, whereas handshape transcriptions comprised on average 2.8 symbols (*SD*=1.7), movement transcriptions comprised 8.8 symbols (*SD*=5.7) on average. Intuitively, if more symbols are needed to transcribe a given parameter, then there is a greater number of opportunities for differences across transcriptions and, perhaps, a greater number of differences. However, we found no significant correlation in our data between the average length of a pair of transcriptions and the average similarity score for that pair, $r(100) = -.01$, $p = .90$. In addition, there was no significant correlation between these factors when separately considering each parameter. Among the four main parameters, the strongest correlation was found for movement, but even this correlation is weak and is not significant: $r(100) = .16$, $p = .11$.

On average, transcriptions of handshapes (*M*=.88, *SD*=.24) and of symmetry values (*M*=.87, *SD*=.32) scored highest for similarity, followed by locations (*M*=.76, *SD*=.30), orientations (*M*=.67, *SD*=.33), and movements (*M*=.63, *SD*=.29). Consider the difference in similarity scores between transcriptions of handshapes and of movements. Although, as we have seen, more symbols were used on average in our data to transcribe movements than to transcribe handshapes, there was only a weak correlation between the number of symbols used to transcribe a parameter and the similarity score for that parameter. Hence the difference in the average similarity scores of handshape transcriptions versus scores of movement transcriptions (0.88-0.63=0.25) at best can be only partly explained by the difference in the average number of symbols used to transcribe the two parameters. Thus, these results may suggest that it is comparatively easier, in a sense, to accurately transcribe handshapes than it is to accurately transcribe movements.

4. Discussion

In this section, we consider how the results in Section 3 might inform future projects that incorporate transcription methods. We also discuss questions raised by our results that pertain to the phonological features of signs and the transcription process.

Before highlighting the practical lessons that can be gleaned from our study, it is important to note one preliminary point. First, our study was designed to compare two transcribers and their transcriptions prior to any subsequent editing of those transcriptions. For each sign, the current study resulted in two transcriptions that were not edited by any other individual. Thus, the results of the study differ in two ways from the results that we aim for in our project. Although just one transcriber in our project completes an initial transcription of a sign, that transcription is edited by at least two other members of the transcription team in successive stages. Our aim is to arrive at one best transcription of a sign, rather than multiple, unedited transcriptions of that sign.

4.1 Transcription Time in the Creation of a Comparative Database

Our analyses in Section 3 focused on the amount of time it took for the transcribers to complete transcriptions and on the similarity of their transcriptions. With respect to the time required for transcriptions, our results may reflect a relatively conservative estimate (approx. 1.5 minutes per transcription; see König & Langer, 2009, who report that one minute of *DGS* text requires 135 to 200 transcription minutes, depending on the details included in the transcription). Why is our estimate relatively conservative? As briefly discussed in Section 2.1, our project aims to produce narrow transcriptions in HamNoSys that, for example, in a sign involving contact, provide details about the exact part of the hand (or parts of the hands in two-handed signs) that make contact with the body or with the nondominant hand. Our approach to transcription will tend to require a greater number of symbols per transcription than will an approach that systematically aims at broad transcriptions. And, as we have shown in Section 3.1, there is a relationship in our data between the number of symbols used to transcribe a sign and the time it takes to complete a transcription.

This general finding about the relationship between transcription time and the number of symbols required by HamNoSys has several consequences for any project that incorporates transcription methods. For instance, the balance of one- versus two-handed signs in a dataset will affect the amount of time required to transcribe that dataset using HamNoSys and, perhaps, using other sign transcription systems. In our data, one-handed signs were transcribed on average in under 1.5 minutes, while it took nearly 2 minutes on average to transcribe two-handed signs (84.8 seconds versus 113.1 seconds, see Sec. 3.1). That average difference of 28.3 seconds can result in large differences in the time necessary to complete transcriptions in a project with a large dataset. Compare, for example, one dataset of 2,000 signs with a balance of one- versus two-handed signs that matches our dataset (63% vs. 37%) and a second dataset of 2,000 signs with an equal balance (50% vs. 50%). Based on our results, we estimate that the first dataset would require 29.7 hours for the one-handed signs (1260 signs * 84.8 seconds) and 23.2 hours for the two-handed signs (740 signs * 113.1 seconds). For the second dataset, we estimate 23.6 hours for the one-handed signs (1000 * 84.8 seconds) and 31.4 hours for the two-handed signs (1000 * 113.1 seconds). The difference in time required for the two datasets is thus estimated at 2.1 hours for the initial draft transcriptions (55 hours – 52.9 hours).

Our results also suggest that the type of vocabulary that comprises a dataset can affect the amount of time it will take to transcribe that dataset. In Section 3.1, we showed that signs representing numerals and pronouns—signs that have been thought to be articulatorily simple—required the least amount of time to transcribe on average (approx. 1 minute for both categories); whereas signs representing nouns and colors both required more than 100 seconds on average to transcribe.

Finally, personal characteristics of the transcribers themselves will inevitably affect the time required to transcribe a dataset. In our study, the transcribers were asked not to focus too carefully on their speed—though by asking them to record the time required for each transcription, the study contained an implicit emphasis on speed. Because the study did not include a target transcription, but rather compared the similarity of each pair of transcriptions, we cannot measure the relationship between transcription time and accuracy.

Given our timing results, how long would it take to produce first draft transcriptions for datasets of various sizes that are similar to our dataset (i.e., datasets with similar balances of one- versus two-handed signs and with similar types of vocabulary)?

Number of signs	Time (hours)
1000	26.5
2000	52.9
5000	132.3
10000	264.6

Table 3: Estimated transcription time required for datasets of various sizes.

In our discussion of transcription time, we have not considered the time required for the editing process; nor have we discussed the potential use of avatar technology or of software such as OpenPose (Cao et al., 2019) in both the transcription and editing processes. Although the editing process was not the focus of the current study, based on the experience of our project, that process is at least as time-consuming as the first-draft transcription process.

4.2 Transcription Similarity

Our study compared the similarity of a pair of transcriptions; it did not attempt to directly measure the accuracy of transcriptions in comparison with target transcriptions. For purposes of this discussion, however, we will take the similarity score as a proxy for accuracy; that is, we will assume that higher similarity scores reflect more accurate transcriptions because, while possible, it is nevertheless unlikely that two transcribers would independently make similar mistakes in the transcription of a sign. Hence any agreement in their transcriptions likely reflects transcription accuracy.

As we have seen, there were differences in similarity scores across parameters: for example, handshape transcriptions showed higher similarity scores than did movement transcriptions (0.88 versus 0.63). Why were some parameters transcribed more accurately than others? In Section 3.2, we argued that the difference in the number of symbols used to respectively transcribe these parameters (on average, 2.8 versus 8.8) at best only partly explains the difference in accuracy. Recall that, overall, there was no significant relationship between the average number of symbols in a pair of transcriptions and their similarity score.

There may be multiple factors that influence the relative reliability of transcribing handshape versus transcribing other parameters, including factors concerning the perception of parameter values and factors related to characteristics of the transcription system. Regarding the former, handshapes might be perceived more categorically than orientations, locations, and movements. Efforts to determine if categorical perception exists in signed language have found that handshape shows traditional patterns of categorical perception for native signers of ASL, but the same is not true for location (Emmorey et al., 2003). Although the transcribers in this study were not native signers, they each had had a substantial amount of exposure to ASL before being trained in transcription. That exposure could have influenced their ability to transcribe handshapes in categorical ways.

Alternatively, the transcribers might have perceived other parameters, such as location and movement, in a more gradient fashion. For example, two typical locations in sign articulations are the right side of the forehead and the cheek; but, locations in-between these two typical locations can also serve as valid locations for a sign in discourse (Russell et al., 2011). The variability of location values during signing—as a result of phonetic and sociolinguistic factors, among others—might have been differently perceived by the two transcribers. A similar argument could be made for movement values in signs.

The options available within a transcription system might also have an influence on which symbols are used to transcribe parameter values. In the example of forehead-to-cheek variants that was given above, HamNoSys includes several options for coding different locations (e.g., beside the eyebrows, eyes, and cheek) that could correspond to signer productions. However, there might be other locations, orientations, and movements that do not correspond to signer productions—and vice versa. These mismatches between productions and symbols could result in less reliability across transcribers.

Yet another possible factor in the reliability of handshape transcription could be linked to the focus on handshapes during the learning of a signed language. Sign language curricula typically stress the importance of handshape values; often, handshapes charts feature prominently in such curricula. Signed language games that rely on handshape contrasts (e.g., so-called ABC handshape games in ASL) could serve to make a learner hypersensitive to the handshape parameter, which could lead to increased inter-transcriber reliability of handshape transcriptions.

Finally, handshape symbols in HamNoSys iconically represent the forms of handshapes in a way that is independent of any other articulatory aspect of the sign. That is, the symbol ⅆ represents a handshape with an extended index finger—whether the handshape is produced in space, in contact with the body, at various heights, or with various orientations. In contrast, orientations are arguably more challenging to transcribe because the second symbol in an orientation transcription (e.g., ˄⌓) represents the orientation of the palm with respect to the direction of the back of the hand. Thus, orientation symbols are arguably less iconic than handshape symbols, and they may be more challenging to transcribe.[4] In sum, transcription reliability could be influenced by factors that are linked to the properties of sign parameters and to the perception of those parameters. They could also be influenced by factors that are associated with characteristics of signed language learning. And, they may be affected by differences in the iconicity of HamNoSys symbols.

5. Conclusions and Future Research

The results of this study raise intriguing questions about the general process of transcription across signed and spoken languages. Is more time required to transcribe signs or words? Based on the third author's experience transcribing lexical data from many of the spoken languages of Mesoamerica, the transcription of spoken words in IPA requires much less time than the time it took in our study to produce transcriptions in HamNoSys. However, the type of narrow phonetic transcriptions produced by the signed language transcribers in our study are arguably much more fine-grained than the type of phonemic transcriptions that are typically produced for a word list with the basic vocabulary of a spoken language.

A second intriguing comparison with spoken language transcription concerns transcription similarity. In Section 4, we suggested that, because certain parameters such as handshape may be more categorically perceived than other parameters (Emmorey et al., 2003), it may be easier, in a sense, to assign categorical symbols to certain parts of sign articulations. It has been shown that stop consonants in English, for example, are more categorically perceived than vowels (Fry et al., 1962). Could there also be an imbalance in transcriber reliability across differing classes of speech sounds?

6. Acknowledgements

This research has been supported by NSF grant BCS-1941560 "Regularity and Genetic Relatedness in Sign Languages". As always, any opinions, findings, and conclusions or recommendations expressed here are those of the authors and do not necessarily reflect the views of the National Science Foundation.

7. References

Albright, R.W. (1958). The International Phonetic Alphabet: Its Backgrounds and Development. Reprinted in *International Journal of American Linguistics*, 24(1).

Becker, A., Catt, D., and Hochgesang, J.A. (2020). Back and Forth between Theory and Application: Shared Phonological Coding Between ASL Signbank and ASL-LEX. In *Proceedings of the 9th Workshop on the Representation and Processing of Sign Languages*, 1–6. Marseille, France. European Language Resources Association (ELRA).

Börstell, C., Crasborn, O., and Whynot, L. (2020). Measuring Lexical Similarity across Sign Languages in Global Signbank. In *Proceedings of the 9th Workshop on the Representation and Processing of Sign Languages*, 21–26. Marseille, France. European Language Resources Association (ELRA).

Bryant, C. (2021). researchpy Documentation, release 0.3.2. researchpy.readthedocs.io/_/downloads/en/latest/pdf/

Cao, Z., Hidalgo, G., Simon, T., Wai, S.-E., and Sheikh, Y. (2021). OpenPose: Realtime Multi-Person 2D Pose Estimation Using Part Affinity Fields. *IEEE Computer Society*, 43(1):172–186.

Caselli, N.K., Sehyr, Z.S., Cohen-Goldberg, A.M., and Emmorey, K. (2016). ASL-LEX: A lexical database of American Sign Language. *Behavior Research Methods*, 49:784–801.

Crasborn, O., Zwitserlood, I., van der Kooij, E. and Ormel, E. (2020). *Global Signbank Manual, version 2*. Radboud University, Centre for Language Studies.

Forkel, R., List, J.-M., Greenhill, S.J., Rzymski, C., Bank, S., Cysouw, M., Hammarström, H., Haspelmath, M., Kaiping, G.A., and Gray, R.D. (2018). Cross-Linguistic Data Formats, advancing data sharing and re-use in comparative linguistics. *Scientific Data*, 5:180205.

Fry, D.B., Abramson, A.S., Elmas, P.D., and Liberman, A.M. (1962). The identification and discrimination of synthetic vowels. *Language and Speech*, 5(4):171–189.

Greenhill, S.J., Blust, R., and Gray, R.D. (2008). The Austronesian Basic Vocabulary Database: From Bioinformatics to Lexomics. *Evol. Bioinformatics*, 4:271–283.

Hanke, T. (2004). HamNoSys – Representing Sign Language Data in Language Resources and Language Processing Contexts. In *Proceedings of the Workshop on the Processing of Sign Languages (LREC 2004)*, 1–6. Lisbon, Portugal. European Language Resources Association (ELRA).

Hanke, T. (2010). HamNoSys 4 Handshapes Chart. https://www.sign-lang.uni-hamburg.de/dgs-korpus/files/inhalt_pdf/HamNoSys_Handshapes.pdf

Hanke, T., König, L., Wagner, S., and Matthes, S. (2010). DGS Corpus & Dicta-Sign: The Hamburg studio setup. In P. Dreuw, et al., (Eds.), *Proceedings of the Fourth*

[4] Our thanks to one of the reviewers for suggesting that the iconicity of handshape symbols may affect the relative accuracy with which handshapes are transcribed.

Workshop on the Representation and Processing of Sign Languages: Corpora and Sign Language Technologies (LREC 2010), 106–109. Valletta, Malta. European Language Resources Association (ELRA)

Hanke, T. (2018). HamNoSys – Hamburg Notation System for Sign Languages. Hamburg, Germany: Universität Hamburg. https://www.sign-lang.uni-hamburg.de/dgs-korpus/files/inhalt_pdf/HamNoSys_2018.pdf

Harris, C.R., et al. (2020). Array programming with NumPy. *Nature*, 585:357–362.

Hochgesang, J.A. (2014). Using Design Principles to Consider Representation of the Hand in Some Notation Systems. *Sign Language Studies*, 14(4):488–542.

Hochgesang, J.A. (2022). SLAASh ID Glossing Principles, ASL Signbank and Annotation Conventions, Version 3.2. https://doi.org/10.6084/m9.figshare.12003732.v4.

Hochgesang, J.A., Crasborn, O., Lillo-Martin, D. (2018). Building the ASL Signbank: Lemmatization Principles for ASL. In N. Calzolari, et al., (Eds.), *Proceedings of the Eleventh International Conference on Language Resources and Evaluation (LREC 2018)*, 69–74. Miyazaki, Japan. European Language Resources Association (ELRA).

Hunter, J.D. (2007). Matplotlib: A 2D graphics environment. *Computing in Science & Engineering*, 9(3):90–95.

Johnston, T. and Schembri, A. (2007). Testing language description through language documentation, archiving and corpus creation: The case of indicating verbs in the Auslan Archive Corpus. In P. K. Austin, et al., (Eds.), *Proceedings of Conference on Language Documentation and Linguistic Theory*, 145–154. London: SOAS.

Kimmelman, V., Imashev, A., Mukushev, M., Sandygulova, A. (2020). Eyebrow position in grammatical and emotional expressions in Kazakh-Russian Sign Language: A quantitative study. *PLoS ONE*, 15(6):e0233731.

Kimmelman, V., Komarova, A., Luchkova, L., Vinogradova, V., and Alekseeva, O. (2022). Exploring Networks of Lexical Variation in Russian Sign Language. *Frontiers in Psychology*, 12:740734.

König, S. and Langer, G.. (2009). Signs fiction? Ein Wörterbuch DGS – Deutsch wird entwickelt. *Das Zeichen*, 81:82–89.

McKinney, W. (2010). Data structures for statistical computing in Python. In S. van der Walt and J. Millman (Eds.), *Proceedings of the 9th Python in Science Conference*, 56–61. Austin, TX: SciPy 2010.

Parkhurst, S. and Parkhurst, D. (2003). Lexical Comparison of Signed Languages and the Effects of Iconicity. *Work Papers of the Summer Institute of Linguistics, North Dakota Session*, 47:1–17.

Power, J.M., Grimm, G.W., and List, J.-M. (2020). Evolutionary dynamics in the dispersal of sign languages. *Royal Society Open Science*, 7:191100.

Prillwitz, S., Hanke, T., König, S., Konrad, R., Langer, G., and Schwarz, A. (2008). DGS Corpus Project – Development of a Corpus Based Electronic Dictionary German Sign Language / German. In O. Crasborn, et al. (Eds.), *Proceedings of the Sixth International Conference on Language Resources and Evaluation (LREC 2008)*, 159–164. Marrakesh, Morocco. European Language Resources Association (ELRA).

Russell, K., Wilkinson, E. and Janzen, T. (2011). ASL sign lowering as undershoot: A corpus study. *Laboratory Phonology*, 2(2):403–422.

Schembri, A., Fenlon, J., Rentelis, R., Reynolds, S., and Cormier, K. (2013). Building the British Sign Language Corpus. *Language Documentation & Conservation*, 7:136–154.

Schwager, W. and Zeshan, U. (2008). Word classes in sign languages: Criteria and classifications. *Studies in Language* 32(3):509–545.

Smith, R., (Ed.). (2013). HamNoSys 4.0 User Guide. Institute of Technology Blanchardstown, Ireland. https://robertsmithresearch.files.wordpress.com/2012/10/hamnosys-user-guide-rs-draft-v3-0.pdf.

Stumpf, M.R., Pizzio, A.L., Lucinda, J.O., Quadros, R.M. de, and Crasborn, O. (2020). SignBank da Libras. *Fórum Linguístico*, 17(4):5475–5487.

Van Rossum, G. and Drake, F.L. (2009). *Python 3 reference manual*. Scotts Valley, CA: CreateSpace.

Virtanen, P., et al. (2020). SciPy 1.0: Fundamental Algorithms for Scientific Computing in Python. *Nature Methods*, 17(3):261–272.

Yu, S., Geraci, C., and Abner, N. (2018). Sign Languages and the Online World Online Dictionaries & Lexicostatistics. In N. Calzolari, et al., (Eds.), *Proceedings of the Eleventh International Conference on Language Resources and Evaluation (LREC 2018)*, 4235–4240. Miyazaki, Japan. European Language Resources Association (ELRA).

8. Language Resource References

Crasborn, O., et al., (Eds.). (2020). *Global Signbank*. Radboud University, Nijmegen. signbank.science.ru.nl.

Hochgesang, J.A., Crasborn, O., and Lillo-Martin, D. (2020). ASL Signbank. New Haven, CT: Haskins Lab, Yale University. https://aslsignbank.haskins.yale.edu/.

Vlaams GebarentaalCentrum. (2018). VGT Signbank. Gent, Belgium. https://vlaamsegebarentaal.be/signbank.

Proceedings of the 10th Workshop on the Representation and Processing of Sign Languages (sign-lang@LREC 2022), pages 181–186
Language Resources and Evaluation Conference (LREC 2022), Marseille, 20-25 June 2022

Integrating Auslan Resources into the Language Data Commons of Australia

River Tae Smith, Louisa Willoughby, Trevor Johnston
Monash University
Melbourne, Australia
{river.smith, louisa.willoughby, trevor.johnston}@monash.edu

Abstract

This paper describes a project to secure Auslan (Australian Sign Language) resources within a national language data network called the Language Data Commons of Australia (LDaCA). The resources are Auslan Signbank, a web-based multi-media dictionary, and the Auslan Corpus, a collection of video recordings of the language being used in various contexts with time-aligned ELAN annotation files. We aim to make these resources accessible to the language community, encourage community participation in the curation of the data, and facilitate and extend their uses in language teaching and linguistic research. The software platforms of both resources will be made compatible with other LDaCA resources; and the two will also be aggregated and linked so that (i) users of the dictionary can view attested corpus examples for an entry; and (ii) users of the corpus can instantly view the dictionary entry for an already glossed sign to check phonological, lexical and grammatical information about it, and/or to ensure that the correct annotation gloss (aka 'ID-gloss') for a sign token has been chosen. This will enhance additions to annotations in the Auslan Corpus, entries in Auslan Signbank and the integrity of research based on both.

Keywords: Auslan, signed language dictionaries, signed language corpora, data repositories, language documentation, linking corpora and lexicons

1. Introduction

This paper describes a project to secure Auslan resources within a national digital network called the Language Data Commons of Australia (LDaCA). Auslan is the signed language of the deaf community in Australia. The aim is to make these resources readily accessible to the language community, encourage community participation in the on-going curation of them, and facilitate and extend their uses in Auslan language teaching and linguistic research.

We begin by describing the purpose and principles behind the LDaCA initiative. This is followed by an overview of the two Auslan resources: Auslan Signbank[1] and the Auslan Corpus[2]. We then continue with more specific information about securing, aggregating and linking these two resources, and the desired outcomes of the project.

We then describe how we intend to achieve these goals in terms of data management (including community participation) and software development. We summarise previous work to develop software for related signed language data storage and research. These are compared with software development which is already underway or is planned as part of the restructure of the Auslan language resources so that they are seamlessly integrated into the LDaCA network.

[1] https://auslan.org.au/
[2] https://www.elararchive.org/dk0001/

2. The Language Data Commons of Australia (LDaCA)[3]

Australia has amassed significant collections of language data concerning Australian Indigenous languages, the signed language of the **deaf** community, languages of the Pacific region, and of Australian English. Many of these collections remain under-utilised or at risk and are difficult to access for researchers and communities. These collections need to be hosted on durable infrastructure that ensures that those collections are given perennity and security. LDaCA will address this by working with key groups to capitalise on existing infrastructure to secure vulnerable and dispersed language collections of written, spoken, multimodal and **signed** text. Moreover, LDaCA will link these collections with improved analysis environments for new research outcomes.
LDaCA aims to establish a sustainable long-term repository for ingesting and curating language data collections of national significance: to democratise access to Australia's rich linguistic heritage through enabling those collections to become more FAIR while following the CARE principles[4]; and to demonstrate how to balance research needs with preserving community rights. It also aims to develop the computational capa-

[3] The Language Data Commons of Australia (LDaCA) is a sub-part of the Humanities and Social Sciences Research Data Commons (HASS RDC) which is itself part of the large Australian Research Data Commons (ARDC) initiative

[4] Further information about the CARE Principles for Indigenous Data Governance can be found on the GIDA website (https://www.gida-global.org/care)

bilities, technical infrastructure and support services to analyse language collections at scale.
The overall LDaCA project will build connections to other research data collections in the humanities and social sciences in Australia by developing APIs and text analytics tools that can be applied to any of these collections; by facilitating text analysis of aggregated administrative data collections; and by developing a community-driven approach for governance of Indigenous language collections as well as the signed language of the Australian deaf community (Auslan).

3. The Auslan Resources

The two major Auslan language resources that exist are Auslan Signbank (Johnston, 2004) and the Auslan Corpus (Johnston, 2008). They are perfect examples of the type of language resources which are the focus of the LDaCA initiative.

3.1. Auslan Signbank

Auslan Signbank is an online dictionary of Auslan. Entries consist of a form-based sequence of Auslan headsigns as videos with accompanying definitions in Auslan and English. It is thus a true dictionary of a sign language not simply an English word list with each word equated with a sign.
A lexical database of Auslan was begun in 1984 by one of the authors of this paper (Johnston, 2001) and it slowly migrated over various programs and platforms. In 2004, the first online iteration of the dictionary was released, Auslan Signbank.
Currently there are c. 7,500 sign entries in Auslan Signbank of which c. 5,000 are viewable by all visitors to the site. The remaining c. 2,500 are in development and can only be viewed by registered users with special access. Auslan Signbank is thus not a static repository of lexical information. The web-based format was designed to enable on-going change to the content by the editor/lexicographer without any need for discrete editions. For example, sign entries can be deleted, corrected, or created (including showing or hiding entries in the public portal). This includes phonological, semantic, and grammatical information about each sign. These changes are informed by on-going linguistic research, input from Auslan teachers or interpreters, and deaf community feedback.
Since its creation Auslan Signbank has had no official long-term institutional home and hosting site. Thus, its future was insecure until an appropriate repository could be established.

3.2. Auslan Corpus

The Auslan Corpus is a collection of digital video recordings of deaf users of Auslan using the language in various contexts. Many of the recordings have time-aligned annotation files; thus, the Auslan Corpus is not just a collection of video recordings.
The Auslan Corpus was one of the first digital video archives of a signed language that was collected with the express purpose of creating a machine-readable linguistic corpus in the modern sense. It was collected as part of a three-year Endangered Languages Documentation Program project (2004-2006) which resulted in the deposit of the Auslan Corpus in the Endangered Languages Archive (ELAR) in 2008. One hundred participants from Australia's five largest cities were filmed. This yielded approximately 150 hours of edited clips. At the time of deposit $<$50 clips had been annotated for glosses and literal and free translations.
Over the fourteen years since its initial deposit, hundreds of thousands of annotations have been added to the corpus during a number of research projects and are not part of the original or current ELAR resource (Examples include Ferrara & Johnston 2014; Gray, 2013; Hodge & Ferrara 2014; Hodge & Johnston 2014; Johnston 2012, 2013, 2018, 2019; Johnston et al. 2015, 2016.). Today about 200 clips have been annotated in detail, with roughly 200 more annotated sporadically. In the current working corpus, there are approximately 105,000 sign token gloss annotations, but 385,000 linguistic annotations in total. These annotations include part-of-speech tagging, morphemic tagging, clause tagging and grammatical role tagging.

4. Auslan/LDaCA project

The Auslan/LDaCA project will significantly increase research opportunities in Auslan language and linguistics using these two aggregated and linked resources. The project has been briefly summarised above. It has three phases which focus on (i) **securing language data collections**, (ii) **aggregating and linking collections**, and (iii) **enhancing their research potential and facilitating new research, especially text data analysis environments**. The LDaCA project has several streams and hubs based on the language resources and expertise associated with each of its partner organisations and associated language repositories[5]. At the Monash University hub of LDaCA, the focus is on Auslan and other signed languages of Australia and its region, and on co-speech gesture and multimodal language research.

4.1. Phase 1: Securing Language Data Collections

The first phase is particularly relevant to Auslan. Until this project, Auslan Signbank did not have any long-term institutional home or hosting site and its future was not secure. Its ownership and hosting had migrated with the chief investigator (Trevor Johnston) over many

[5]The project partners are: The University of Queensland, Australian National University, Monash University, The University of Melbourne, The University of Sydney, AARNet, First Languages Australia (FLA), Australian Institute for Aboriginal and Torres Strait Islander Studies (AIATSIS), PARADISEC,ARC Centre of Excellence for the Dynamics of Language (CoEDL), Digital Observatory (Queensland University of Technology), CLARIN.

separately funded research projects across multiple institutions. Without a long-term institutional home for Signbank, it is difficult not only to simply secure the data but also to support editing, and improvements and additions to enhance its usability and accessibility for learners and teachers of Auslan, Auslan/English interpreters, deaf community members, and language researchers; as well as to prepare its underlying data structure for linking with the Auslan Corpus. Tweaking of the software and the design of the dictionary webpages will be made to include and then distinguish each type of sign form that are possible, such as (i) conventional lexical signs of Auslan, (ii) gestures used by both deaf Auslan-users and hearing Australian English speakers; (iii) conventional signs of the sign languages of Indigenous Australia; and (iv) conventional signs found in any deaf community sign language anywhere around the world.

With respect to Phase 1 the Auslan Corpus as it currently exists (with enriched annotation files that have been created since 2008) also had no institutional home. The reason is that these newer annotation files are not part of the ELAR deposit from 2008. Partly because there has been no easy way to manage version control as various research projects add or change annotations to existing files, these enhanced or project-specific annotations files have instead been saved and backed up privately by Trevor Johnston and other Auslan researchers.

The first phase of the Auslan/LDaCA project started in early 2022 when the long term hosting of both resources at Monash University was secured. Work has begun on re-configuring the resources to conform to the LDaCA data protocols.

4.2. Phase 2: Aggregating and Linking Language Collections

The second phase is again of particular relevance with regard to the Auslan resources. Since its creation the Auslan Corpus has been completely separate from Auslan Signbank, and vice versa. The two need to be linked both for the benefit of the language community itself, and to maximise the utility of the data contained within each.

With respect to the language community, deaf and hearing teachers of Auslan, deaf students and their teachers in schools, and hearing learners of Auslan (school children, adults, and parents of deaf children), and trainee Auslan interpreters, have all on multiple occasions asked to access the Auslan Corpus to simply get more exposure to the language or to have more examples of particular constructions to use in teaching. Auslan Signbank also needs to be linked to the Auslan Corpus to unlock the full potential of the latter as a resource for the teaching and learning of Auslan. Linking will make it possible for teachers and learners to jump from an entry in Auslan Signbank to attested examples from the Auslan Corpus. This is particularly useful for students to appreciate the ways the actual production of a sign in context can vary from its citation form due to (i) phonological processes found in continuous signing (which are not unlike those found in continuous speech), and (ii) morphological processes that change the shape of signs in systematic ways to express various meanings.

We envisage that Auslan textbooks and classroom resources will link to Signbank and the Auslan Corpus to provide vocabulary lists and resources for students, and that teachers and students will access the dictionary and the corpus both for explicit teaching in class and private study.

With respect to language researchers, linking will have practical advantages. A unique identifying gloss (known as the 'ID-gloss') is used for each sign form entry in Signbank. It was quickly realised when the first annotations of the corpus in ELAN were being made that the Signbank site could be used by annotators to view ID-glosses and thus ensure consistency in corpus glossing. Linking the two resources by exploiting the common data point (the ID-gloss) so that (i) users of the dictionary can view attested corpus examples for an entry; and (ii) users of the corpus can instantly view the dictionary entry for an already glossed sign to check phonological, lexical and grammatical information about it, and/or to ensure the correct ID-gloss for a sign token is chosen. This will enhance additions to the annotations in the Auslan Corpus, entries in Auslan Signbank and the integrity of research based on both.

4.3. Phase 3: Enhancing and Facilitating the Research Potential of Language Resources

The aggregation of the data in Auslan Signbank and the Auslan Corpus will improve the research potential of both datasets, as well as enable new and accelerated research into unexplored aspects of the lexicon and grammar of the language. In this phase we will develop specialist tools for text analytics and extend the text analytics workbench to enable large-scale computational analysis of written, spoken, multimodal and signed language data, and to share those workflows with other researchers. Thus, once the annotation environment for the Auslan Corpus has been streamlined, researchers should be able to take advantage of LDaCA text analytics tools to enhance their research.

These developments will also serve to enhance the accuracy of phonology description the dictionary and corpus, and facilitate the management of other multimedia resources, such as co-speech gesture data, Australian Indigenous signed language data, and, ultimately, data from potentially any signed language. It will also enhance the research potential of these resources.

4.4. Software Development

4.4.1. Previous Work

Over its lifetime, the user interface and functionality of Auslan Signbank has been consistently improved and updated. For example, in 2008 a major overhaul of the Signbank site created new data fields to accommodate import of data from Prof. Johnston's existing FileMaker lexicon. These new data fields were visible to logged-in researchers and lexicographers who could then edit them. In 2014, the ability to add video definitions in Auslan was added, meaning that headsigns could be given definitions in both English and Auslan. In other words, after ten years the web-based dictionary has started to evolve into the first true monolingual signed language dictionary—Auslan signs can now be defined and explained in Auslan itself.

Previous attempts have been made to enable online access and annotation of ELAN annotation files (EAFs). One such attempt using the Auslan Corpus was Cassidy and Johnston (2009), which described the approach of converting EAF files into an RDF-based format which could more easily be communicated over HTTP. The new LDaCA corpus storage solution described, in part, in this paper would make this kind of intermediate format unnecessary. While online collaborative corpus editing is not planned for the Auslan/LDaCA project, it is an avenue ripe for later projects in this area.

4.4.2. This Project

Nationally significant collections of sign language data of Australia and its region will be secured as preservable digital objects using Arkisto Platforms standards, a combination of the Oxford Common File Layout (OCFL) and RO-Crate, and access protocols for Australian researchers and communities will be developed. This will involve using Signbank – the online dictionary of Auslan – and the Auslan Corpus, and working with sign language and gesture researchers, to deposit annotated multimodal video data and dictionary resources. Deliverables include migration of selected sign language data collections into RO-Crate/OCFL formats, the development of access protocols and resources for Australian researchers and communities, including Auslan teachers and deaf Australians. This work package is led by Monash University.

4.4.3. Current State of Auslan Signbank

The existing Signbank, both Auslan and subsequent forks for other languages, is written in Python, using the Django web framework. Django is an easy-to-use web framework, which includes a built-in object-relation mapping library (ORM). While Django's ORM has served the needs of Auslan Signbank till now, it necessitates high coupling between the dictionary and website content. The ORM stores all data in a single PostgreSQL database, the architecture of which is partially described in Cassidy et al. (2018). Prior to March 2022, Auslan Signbank was hosted by A/Prof. Cassidy, who developed the original Signbank, at Macquarie University. In February 2022, it was moved to temporary hosting, funded by Monash/LDaCA. This temporary hosting is planned to end in August 2022, when a new version of Auslan Signbank will become available to the public. The final hosting solution has not been confirmed, but it is expected to use Monash-managed AWS cloud resources. The auslan.org.au URL will remain in use, and existing links will be redirected where possible.

4.4.4. Signbank Next

The Auslan/LDaCA project has begun a ground-up redesign of Signbank, Signbank Next, which will incorporate modern web development best-practices, including WCAG accessible design standards[6] while delivering on existing functionality described in Cassidy et al. (2018). Signbank Next will be built with Javascript and NextJS, an open-source web development framework.

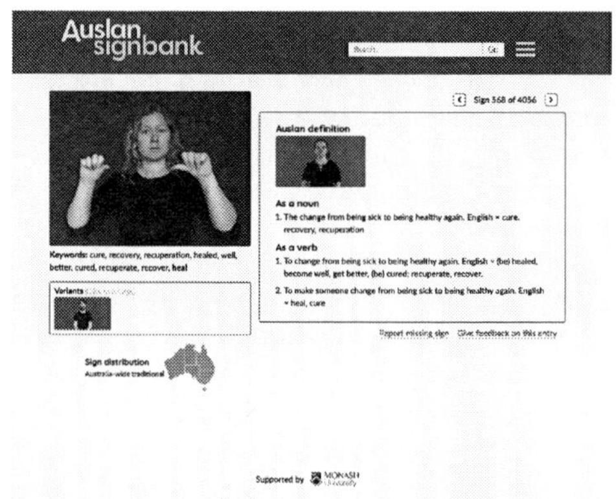

Figure 1: Signbank Next dictionary entry.

In contrast to the Django version of Signbank, and with some similarity to the FileMaker one, Signbank Next will use document storage (i.e., MongoDB). Document storage is well suited to dictionaries, as the amount of relational information is minimal in such applications. Each headsign, usually a video or picture, will be stored with all related information, eliminating the need for complex joins to construct a dictionary page. Document storage has high efficiencies of scale and will easily maintain speed as Signbank grows.

After the architectural redesign, improvements will be made to existing Signbank functionality. Headsigns have historically been sorted according to a manually curated 'sign number', which was used to order signs by their phonology. With each sign added to Signbank, it becomes increasing likely that sign numbers must be reassigned in bulk to make space for new entries. Sorting based on existing phonology fields will be implemented, and the 'sign number' field removed. This has the added benefit of opening the door to custom sorting

[6]https://www.accessibility.org.au/guides/what-is-the-wcag-standard/

orders, which would be invaluable as non-Auslan signs are added to Signbank.

More advanced searching and filtering will also be implemented. Currently, a manual tagging system is used to track problematic entries and missing or low-quality videos. This system is error prone and incorrectly tagged entries can be easily missed. Text search capabilities are similarly lacking; regular expressions are not supported, and queries only attempt to match from the start of a translation. These issues will be addressed with a combination of more comprehensive filters and the addition of an advanced query syntax.

4.4.5. Unified LDaCA Search Portal

The LDaCA corpora will share a corpus search portal, Oni. Information about the Auslan Corpus will be provided on the Auslan Signbank website, but users will directed to access it through Oni. The Oni search portal will provide a user interface for browsing and filtering its corpora and will enable text search across multiple corpora simultaneously, limited by the text available in the search index. This project will include scripts to add the corpus' English free translation tiers, where they exist, into the Oni search index.

To conform with other LDaCA resources, the Auslan Corpus will be transformed to fit the Arkisto Platform standards. These standards focus on sustainable and scalable data management. This will also allow the Auslan Corpus to leverage Arkisto-compatible tools, including data description software and web portals to accept new data from the public.

4.4.6. Dictionary Lookup Within ELAN

Global Signbank (Crasborn et al., 2018) has created two methods to aid the annotation of sign language against an instance of Signbank. Global Signbank can generate an ELAN controlled vocabulary from entries, requiring manual updates from the user as the Signbank is updated. The more recent innovation in this area is ELAN's 'lexicon service'[7], which allows ELAN to log into Signbank with a user's login details and download a local cache of compressed headsign videos. Once this cache has been created, one can search Signbank from within ELAN. This kind of interoperability is a great quality-of-life improvement for corpus annotators, who can quickly confirm glossing accuracy and improve data consistency, and researchers, who can quickly compare citation forms with real usage in their data.

Lexicon service compatibility will be added after the first release of Signbank Next, with possibility of augmenting the service with live API calls in the future, without needing to download all entries ahead-of-time.

4.4.7. Corpus Lookup From Signbank

Going the other direction, finding attested examples of Signbank entries in the corpus, will be achieved by constructing a search index over the corpus' ELAN glossing tiers. This index will map from ID glosses in the annotation onto their timestamps. To ensure proper access control checks can be made, users will be required to link their Signbank and Oni accounts. This work will benefit any current, or future, corpora that include ELAN annotation files by allowing gloss searches from within the regular Oni search portal.

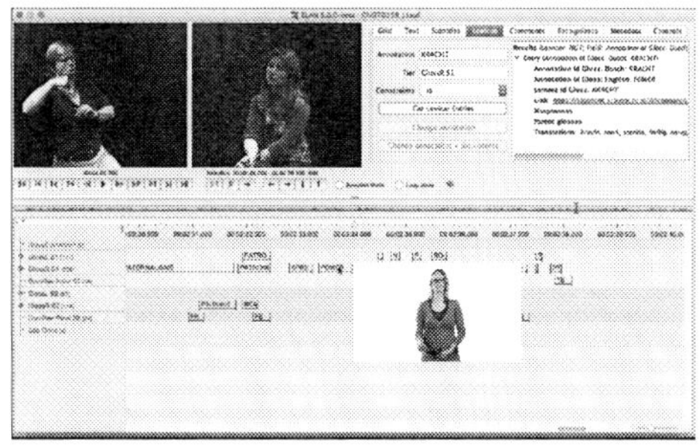

Figure 2: The ELAN lexicon service in use.

5. Conclusion

A new version of Auslan Signbank will be released, hosted by Monash University. The Auslan Corpus will also be made available to both researchers and the general public via Oni, a repository for digital multimodal language data created in partnership between five Australian universities and seven institutions concerned with language preservation and research. It will aid the development of a portal and associated backend infrastructure for multilingual corpus search and access, which will enable sign language and gesture researchers to deposit annotated multimodal video data and dictionary resources, focusing on Australia and its region. It will use Signbank—the online dictionary of Auslan—and the Auslan Corpus as testbed collections. This project involves an interdisciplinary team including data scientists, linguists, and educators. Importantly, it also includes the establishment of a formal deaf community based mechanism to advise on the curation and augmentation of these Auslan resources into the future.

The online, interlinked Signbank and Auslan Corpus will be a boon for Auslan teachers and learners at all levels across Australia. These are extremely valuable resources for language learners to see how words/signs are used in context and to understand how grammatical features of sign languages—such as facial expression or the movement path of the sign—can modify the meaning of a particular sign. It also allows both teachers and learners to better understand subtle shades of meaning between two signs that may have similar meanings in English by seeing the different environments in which they are used.

[7] Available since version 5.0.0b, documented in the ELAN manual

6. Acknowledgements

This research is being supported by LDaCA and Monash University. The original Auslan Signbank was created, and maintained for over a decade, by A/Prof. Steve Cassidy.

7. Bibliographical References

Cassidy, S. and Johnston, T. (2009). Ingesting the Auslan corpus into the DADA annotation store. In *Proceedings of the Third Linguistic Annotation Workshop on - ACL-IJCNLP '09*, pages 154–157, Suntec, Singapore. Association for Computational Linguistics.

Cassidy, S., Crasborn, O., Nieminen, H., Stoop, W., Hulsbosch, M., Even, S., Komen, E., and Johnston, T. (2018). Signbank: Software to Support Web Based Dictionaries of Sign Language.

Crasborn, O., Zwitserlood, I., Kooij, E. V. D., and Schüller, A. (2018). Global SignBank manual. Radboud University, Centre for Language Studies.

Ferrara, L. and Johnston, T. (2014). Elaborating Who's What: A Study of Constructed Action and Clause Structure in Auslan (Australian Sign Language). *Australian Journal of Linguistics*, 34(2):193–215, April.

Gray, M. (2013). Aspect marking in Australian Sign Language: a process of gestural verb modification. Macquarie University.

Hodge, G. and Ferrara, L. (2013). Showing the story: enactment as performance in Auslan narratives. University of Melbourne.

Hodge, G. and Johnston, T. (2014). Points, Depictions, Gestures and Enactment: Partly Lexical and Non-Lexical Signs as Core Elements of Single Clause-Like Units in Auslan (Australian Sign Language). *Australian Journal of Linguistics*, 34(2):262–291, April.

Johnston, T., Cresdee, D., Schembri, A., and Woll, B. (2015). FINISH variation and grammaticalization in a signed language: How far down this well-trodden pathway is Auslan (Australian Sign Language)? *Language Variation and Change*, 27(1):117–155, March.

Johnston, T., van Roekel, J., and Schembri, A. (2016). On the Conventionalization of Mouth Actions in Australian Sign Language. *Language and Speech*, 59(1):3–42, March.

Johnston, T. (2001). The lexical database of Auslan (Australian Sign Language). *Sign Language & Linguistics*, 4(1-2):145–169, December.

Johnston, T. (2012). Lexical Frequency in Sign Languages. *Journal of Deaf Studies and Deaf Education*, 17(2):163–193, April.

Johnston, T. (2013). Formational and functional characteristics of pointing signs in a corpus of Auslan (Australian sign language): are the data sufficient to posit a grammatical class of 'pronouns' in Auslan? *Corpus Linguistics and Linguistic Theory*, 9(1):109–159, May. De Gruyter Mouton.

Johnston, T. (2018). A corpus-based study of the role of headshaking in negation in Auslan (Australian Sign Language): Implications for signed language typology. *Linguistic Typology*, 22(2):185–231, August.

Johnston, T. A. (2019). Clause constituents, arguments and the question of grammatical relations in Auslan (Australian Sign Language): A corpus-based study. *Studies in Language*, 43(4):941–996, December.

8. Language Resource References

Johnston, T. (2004). *Auslan Signbank*. Royal Institute for Deaf and Blind Children & Catalyst Training Systems.

Johnston, T. (2008). *Auslan Corpus*. London: SOAS, Endangered Languages Archive.

Proceedings of the 10th Workshop on the Representation and Processing of Sign Languages (sign-lang@LREC 2022), pages 187–191
Language Resources and Evaluation Conference (LREC 2022), Marseille, 20-25 June 2022

Capturing Distalization

Rose Stamp[1], Lilyana Khatib[2] & Hagit Hel-Or[2]
[1]Bar-Ilan University, [2]University of Haifa
Bar-Ilan University, Department of English Literature & Linguistics, University of Haifa, Computer Science department
rose.stamp@biu.ac.il, lilyanakhatib0@gmail.com, hagit@cs.haifa.ac.il

Abstract

Coding and analyzing large amounts of video data is a challenge for sign language researchers, who traditionally code 2D video data manually. In recent years, the implementation of 3D motion capture technology as a means of automatically tracking movement in sign language data has been an important step forward. Several studies show that motion capture technologies can measure sign language movement parameters – such as volume, speed, variance – with high accuracy and objectivity. In this paper, using motion capture technology and machine learning, we attempt to automatically measure a more complex feature in sign language known as distalization. In general, distalized signs use the joints further from the torso (such as the wrist), however, the measure is relative and therefore distalization is not straightforward to measure. The development of a reliable and automatic measure of distalization using motion tracking technology is of special interest in many fields of sign language research.

Keywords: motion capture, distalization, proximalization, Kinect Azure, Israeli Sign Language

1. Introduction

Sign language users exploit different articulators of their body for linguistic purposes, including the face, head, torso, and the hands. In spoken language research, linguists use a range of sophisticated computer programs in the analysis of speech. However, until relatively recently, sign language researchers lacked the equivalent type of technology for measuring different aspects of visual languages. With the introduction of infra-red motion capture technology to the field of sign language linguistics, researchers can track movement in an automatic way. Motion capture has been used as a tool for analyzing a range of sign language phenomena; for example, distinguishing between verb types (Malaia et al., 2008), lexical signs and constructed action (Stamp et al., 2018a), signs first mentioned and repeated signs (Stamp et al., 2018b), etc.

In this paper, we focus on one specific feature in sign language, described as distalization. Distalization refers to the process of distancing the joint engaged in the movement further from the body (Meier et al., 2008; Poizner et al., 2000). Some signs are produced with joints closer to the body, known as proximalized signs – typically, these joints are the shoulder and the elbow, while distalized signs are produced with joints further from the body, such as the wrist and finger joints (see Figure 1). In some cases, the same sign may exist in two variations: one proximal and one distal.

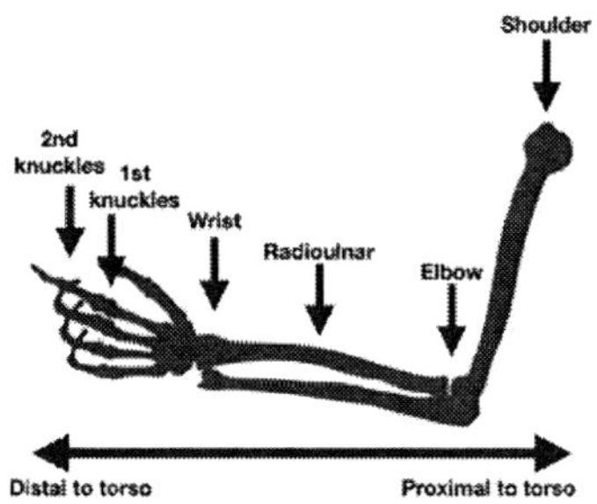

Figure 1: Distalization of joints

For example, the sign meaning 'understand' in Israeli Sign Language (Figure 2) can be produced proximally (left) and distally (right). In the distal example, the movement originates at the wrist, while in the proximal example, the movement originates from the elbow. However, distalization is relative, and therefore, while the wrist joint is distal in the sign for 'understand', it is proximal for the sign 'donkey', in comparison to the distal form produced at the finger joints. The choice of distal or proximal variants has been associated with a number of factors including fluency and sonority (Mirus et al., 2000; Napoli & Liapis, 2019), as well as the indexing of different social identities, such as gender and sexuality (Blau, 2017; Moges, 2020).

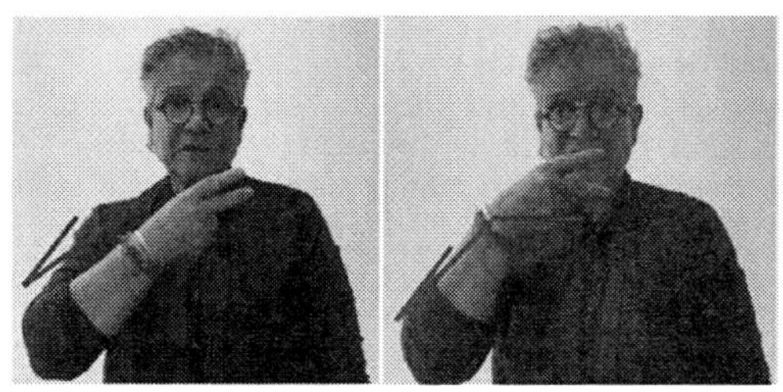

Figure 2: Proximalized sign (left) and distalized sign (right) for 'understand'

In this study, we implement 3D motion capture technology and computational modelling to automatically detect distal and proximal signs. We hope that this offers linguists a potential alternative to the manual coding of 2D video data, which has often been adopted in previous studies (e.g., Blau, 2017).

2. Distalization

Distalization is an important measure in sign language research; the measure appears in studies on sign language production and perception, first and second language acquisition and studies on language variation and change. In studies on sign language production, the movement of the most proximal joint, the shoulder, is shown to exert the greatest amount of energy and therefore use of distal joints has been associated with ease of articulation. Proximal signs are associated with non-nativity and are engaged in communication from a distance (Sandler & Lillo-Martin, 2006), suggesting that proximalization aids in the process of sign language perception. The choice between distal and proximal joints, therefore, is a balance between ease of articulation and ease of perception (Napoli & Liapis, 2019). There is an important link between ease of articulation and language acquisition and language variation and change. Studies show that learners of a sign language, both children and adults, begin by using proximal signs and then shift to distal signs as they increase their motor control (Gesell, 1929; Jensen et al., 1994; Meier et al., 2008). Therefore, distalization is an indicator of sign language fluency. For example, in a study examining signers of American Sign Language, fluent signers tended to reduce effort through distalization (Napoli et al., 2011).

Furthermore, distalization may influence the overall size of signing. Proximal signs, using the shoulder or elbow joints, are claimed to give an overall impression of larger signing. Movement around the wrist joint, in contrast, can give an impression of smaller signing. As a result, distal signs are often used to communicate something private or whispered (Brentari, 1999), while proximal signs are associated with conveying anger or excitement. Moreover, distalized forms may be used to index different social identities, including sexuality (Blau, 2017) and gender (Moges, 2020). In interviews conducted with female-bodied masculine ASL signers, Moges (2020) found that participants associated proximalization with masculinity, and participants were shown to proximalize their own signing when projecting a more masculine identity. The relationship between sign size and gender has not always been clear in the literature; some research claims that women sign bigger than men, i.e., that women tend to proximalize (De Santis, 1977), and other research suggests the opposite (Eichmann, 2004). In a recent study, implementing motion capture technology, it was shown that women's signing is characterized by a larger signing space than men's signing (Stamp et al., in prep.). The feature of distalization has also been associated with indexing gay identities in several studies (Blau, 2017; Fitzgerald, 2004; Michaels, 2008, 2015; Murray, 2002). In contradiction to this though, some researchers claim that gay-indexed styles of signing are characterized by a larger use of the signing space (Michaels, 2008, 2015), suggesting that distalization may not directly correlate with sign size.

The measurement of distalization however is not straightforward. It involves tracking the movement of several joints (e.g., finger joints, wrist, elbow, and shoulder), as well as measuring the degree of rotation around each joint. Manual coding of distalization is not optimal; data is usually based on 2D videos (often obscuring the observation of rotational movement around the joints), it is often coded subjectively, and it is considerably time-consuming and error prone. Therefore, the development of a reliable and automatic measure of distalization using motion tracking technology is of special interest in the fields of articulation and perception, acquisition, as well as language variation.

In the next section, we outline the tool utilized for tracking movement in this study, Microsoft Kinect Azure.

3. Motion capture in sign language research

Microsoft Kinect is a camera and body-tracking sensor system originally designed for video game play. Kinect (*Microsoft: 'Kinect for Xbox One'*, 2018) uses the time-of-flight (ToF) principle, in which the distance to an object is determined by the time it takes for the light emitted from the infrared light projector to reach the object and return to the camera's sensor (Foix et al., 2011; Hansard et al., 2012; Shotton et al., 2011). This enables the recognition of human bodies in the scene and an estimation of their locations in 3D space (see Figure 3). The Kinect camera also records standard RGB (red-green-blue) videos and audio. The advantages of using Kinect for motion capture in sign language research is that the device is inexpensive and non-invasive (therefore, causing minimal interference with signing).

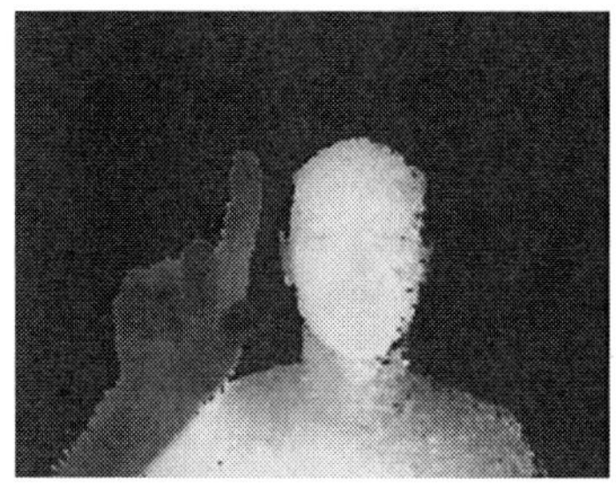

Figure 3: A depth image representing distance from the camera for every point in the human figure (bright points are more distant)

In addition, when a participant is recorded, the system uses the depth image to extract a skeleton representation of the participant computed per frame (Shotton et al., 2011). The skeleton data is composed of 32 major skeleton joints of the human body, connected by line segments (see Figure 4). For every frame, the system outputs the 3D location of each of the skeleton joints (a triplet x,y,z, in meters, given in the camera's frame of reference).

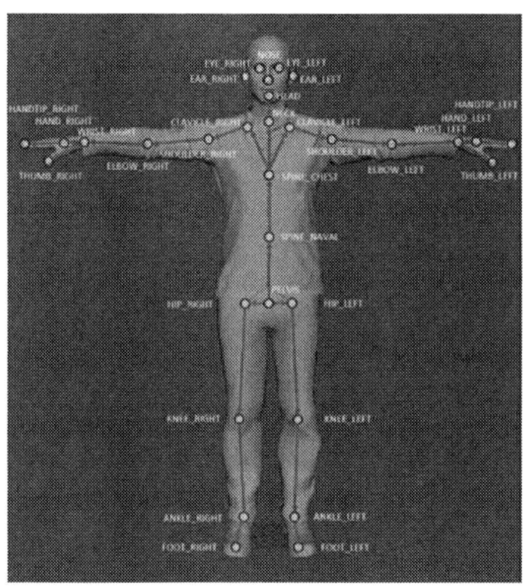

Figure 4: The joints tracked using Kinect Azure (Microsoft Kinect, 2019)

4. Methodology

Two adult female models were recruited to elicit training data (Mean age: 39 years). The models produced a set of Israeli Sign Language signs which are known to vary in terms of distalization (Stamp et al., 2021). The models were recorded using Microsoft Kinect Azure while signing two versions of the same sign (distal & proximal).

The full recording sessions were parsed into segments, comprising of single signs. Each sign was processed and analyzed using specialized code which we developed; the skeleton was extracted per frame and then spatio-temporal features were computed over all frames in the segment. Prior to computing the measurements, the skeletons were normalized to a standard size using the method in Weibel et al. (2016) to eliminate size effects.

The most noticeable features of distalization include the angles of the arms and therefore we focused on extracting movement parameters from four joints: the shoulder, elbow, wrist, and hand joints (see Figure 5). The position of each joint is given in each time frame as 3D coordinates: X, Y and Z. Thirteen features were extracted from these coordinates and used in the training:

- Speed, mean and standard deviation of:
  - Elbow angular change between frames (A)
  - Elbow twist between frames (B)
  - Wrist angular change between frames (C)
  - Hand angular change between frames (D)
- Volume:
  - Fingers

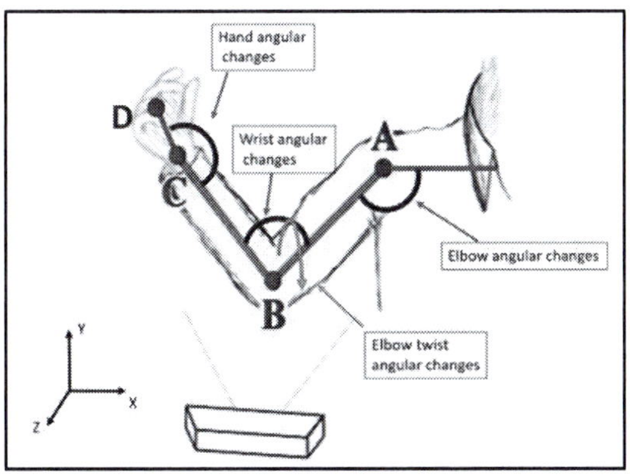

Figure 5: Visual representation of the joint movements

The twist at the elbow measures the angle of rotation of the elbow-wrist bone around the axis of rotation defined by the elbow-shoulder bone. See OSF for the calculation of angle of twist at the elbow joint in MatLab script: https://osf.io/q3h6r/. For each feature, the mean, std and average speed were calculated across all frames in the sequence. The set of features computed per video segment, formed a *feature vector* to be used in the machine learning algorithm.

5. Results

The data consisted of 350 samples, which were split into 50% distal and 50% proximal (our classification labels). A feature vector was created for each of the samples as described above. To assess the capability of predicting whether a sign is distally or proximally signed, we trained a machine learning model. We used the Random Forest model (Breiman, 2001; Ho, 1998), which is a collection of decision trees whose weights are learned from examples in the training set. We used 100 trees with unlimited depth. Gini was used as the split criterion at the nodes of the decision trees. We ran the test using a 10-folds validation design. Thus, the data was divided into 10 equal parts, and for each part, the samples were withheld from the rest of the data which were used to train the Random Forest model. The withheld samples were then tested for distalization using the trained model and the accuracy of correct prediction was determined. The process was repeated independently for each of the 10 parts resulting in 10 values of accuracy. Following this approach, we achieved a mean accuracy of 71% (std: 8.0).

In order to enhance the model performance, we reduced the dimensionality of the input feature vector by performing feature ranking (Guyon & Elisseeff, 2006) and removing the least informative features:

1. Hand angle mean
2. Elbow standard deviation
3. Elbow twist angle standard deviation
4. Volume of finger joint

Re-running the model with the remaining nine features using the same 10-fold validation design, we achieved an accuracy ranging between 80%-82%, with a mean accuracy of 81.35%. In other words, the model was able to predict if a new input segment was distal or proximal with 81% accuracy. The 19% of misses were a combination of false positives and false negatives (as displayed below, Figure 6). The data with highlighted misses can be accessed in OSF: https://osf.io/q3h6r/.

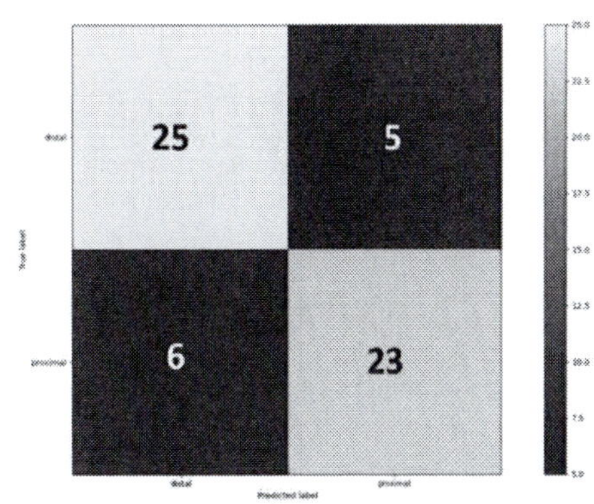

Figure 6: Distribution of the proximal and distal signs, showing 5 false positives (distal signs categorized as proximal) and 6 false negatives (proximal signs categorized as distal)

There may be several reasons why the model classified some of the samples incorrectly. In some cases, the arm joint was not captured well by the Kinect camera. In other cases, the skeleton was tracked well but the distal forms involved finger movement, which generally is not tracked well using Kinect. Finally, although a 10-folds design was used for cross-validation, the dataset is very small and therefore, more training data is required to reach a higher accuracy.

The most predictive features of distalization were standard deviation of the angular changes of the wrist and hand and the least predictive were the features depending on speed (as shown in Figure 7).

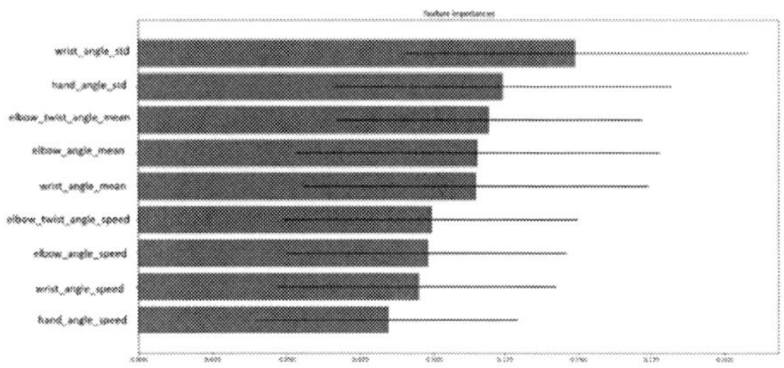

Figure 7: Features which predict distal or proximal signs, in order of their contribution to the prediction.

6. Conclusion

Distalization is a complex measure, in which the features involved are not fully understood. In this paper, we show that motion capture technologies can be implemented to measure distalization in an automatic and objective way. The model reached an accuracy of over 80% in predicting whether a sign is distal or proximal. More work needs to be done to improve the model; however, these preliminary findings suggest that motion capture can be an important tool in the automatic processing of sign language data. In addition, our initial findings point to the importance of the standard deviation of the wrist and hand movements as a predictor of such a movement. Interestingly, our model showed that volume (signing size) was not an important predictor of distal or proximal signs, despite the close relationship between distalization and signing size in the literature. Future studies should test the model on a larger dataset and implement more accurate tracking tools which enable finger joint tracking.

7. Acknowledgements

Thanks to Klil Eden and Nadav Eichler for their help in this project. Funding for this project was supported by an Israeli Science Foundation grant to Dr. Rose Stamp (2757/20; ISL Corpus project).

8. Bibliographical References

Blau, S. (2017). Indexing Gay Identities in American Sign Language. *Sign Language Studies*, *18*(1), 5–40.

Breiman, L. (2001). Random forests. *Machine Learning*, *45*(1), 5–32.

Brentari, D. (1999). *A Prosodic Model of Sign Language Phonology.* Cambridge, MA: MIT Press.

Eichmann, H. (2004). *Do women sign bigger? A research project investigating gender-specific differences in the articulatory realisation of signs in German Sign Language (DGS).* [MA thesis]. University of Bristol.

DeSantis, S. (1977). Elbow to Hand Shift in French and American Sign Languages. Paper presented at the Conference on New Ways of Analyzing Variation, Georgetown. University, Washington, DC.

Fitzgerald, A. (2004). *Gay sign variation in ISL.* [Diploma in Irish Sign Language /English Interpreting.].

Foix, S., Alenyà, G., & Torras, C. (2011). Lock-in Time-of-Flight (ToF) Cameras: A Survey. *IEEE Sensors Journal.* https://doi.org/10.1109/JSEN.2010.2101060

Gesell, A. (1929). Maturation and Infant Behavior Pattern. *Psychological Review*, *36*(4), 307–319. https://doi.org/10.1037/h0075379

Guyon, I., & Elisseeff, A. (2006). An Introduction to Feature Extraction. In I. Guyon, M. Nikravesh, S. Gunn, & L. A. Zadeh (Eds.), *Feature Extraction: Foundations and Applications* (pp. 1–25). Springer. https://doi.org/10.1007/978-3-540-35488-8_1

Hansard, M., Lee, S., Choi, O., & Horaud, R. (2012). *Time of Flight Cameras: Principles, Methods, and Applications.* Springer. https://doi.org/10.1007/978-1-4471-4658-2

Ho, T. K. (1998). The random subspace method for constructing decision forests. *IEEE Transactions on Pattern Analysis and Machine Intelligence*, *20*(8), 832–844. https://doi.org/10.1109/34.709601

Jensen, J. L., Schneider, K., Ulrich, B. D., Zernicke, R. F., & Thelen, E. (1994). Adaptive Dynamics of the Leg Movement Patterns of Human Infants: I. The Effects of Posture on Spontaneous Kicking. *Journal of Motor Behavior*, *26*(4), 303–312. https://doi.org/10.1080/00222895.1994.9941686

Malaia, E., Borneman, J., & Wilbur, R.B. (2008). Analysis of ASL motion capture data towards identification of verb type. STEP '08: Proceedings of the 2008 Conference on Semantics in Text Processing, 155-164.

Meier, R. P., Mauk, C. E., Cheek, A., & Moreland, C. J. (2008). The Form of Children's Early Signs: Iconic or Motoric Determinants? *Language Learning and Development*, *4*(1), 63–98. https://doi.org/10.1080/15475440701377618

Michaels, P. A. (2008). *The cultural and linguistic study of gay sign variation in the deaf gay community.* [PG Dip thesis,]. Durham University.

Michaels, P. A. (2015). *A study of the identity, culture and language of a sample of the deaf gay male community in Britain.* [MA thesis]. Durham University.

Microsoft Kinect (Version Azure). (2019). [[Computer software].]. https://docs.microsoft.com/en-us/azure/kinect-dk/body-joints

Mirus, G., Rathmann, C., & Meier, R. P. (2000). Proximalization and Distalization of Sign Movement in Adult Learners | Semantic Scholar. *Psychology.* https://www.semanticscholar.org/paper/Proximalization-and-Distalization-of-Sign-Movement-Mirus-Rathmann/33b71e49670ab10dd006a41b64caf4570b66209e

Moges, R. (2020). The Signs of Deaf Female Masculinity: Styles of Gendering/Queering ASL. In K. Hall & E. Barrett (Eds.), *The Oxford Handbook of Language and Sexuality.*

https://doi.org/10.1093/oxfordhb/9780190212926.013.64

Murray, E. (2002). *Gay sign variation in Irish Sign Language.* [Diploma in Irish Sign Language Teaching. Dublin]. University of Dublin, Trinity College.

Napoli, D. J., N. Sanders, and R. Wright. 2011. *Some aspects of articulatory ease in ASL.* Presented at Stony Brook University.

Napoli, D. J., & Liapis, S. (2019). Effort reduction in articulation in sign languages and dance. *Journal of Cultural Cognitive Science*, *3*(1), 31–61. https://doi.org/10.1007/s41809-019-00027-3

Poizner, H., Brentari, D., Tyrone, M. E., & Kegl, J. (2000). The structure of language as motor behavior: Clues from signers with Parkinson's disease. In K. Emmorey & H. Lane (Eds.), *The signs of language revisited: An anthology to honor Ursula Bellugi and Edward Klima* (pp. 432–452). Lawrence Erlbaum.

Sandler, W., & Lillo-Martin, D. (2006). *Sign Language and Linguistic Universals*.

Shotton, J., Fitzgibbon, A., Cook, M., Sharp, T., Finocchio, M., & Moore, R. (2011). IEEE Computer 46 Society Conference on Computer Vision and Pattern Recognition. In J. Shotton, A. Fitzgibbon, M. Cook, T. Sharp, M. Finocchio, & R. Moore (Eds.), *Proceedings CVPR: Vol. 56(1)* (pp. 1297-1304.).

Stamp, R., Hel-Or, H., Cohn, D., Raz, S. & Sandler, W. (2018a). Kinect-ing the dots: Motion capture technologies and the sign language lexicon. Paper presented at the International Congress of Linguists (ICL) conference. University of Cape Town, South Africa. July 3rd, 2018.

Stamp, R., Dachkovsky, S., Hel-Or, H., Cohn, D., Raz, S. & Sandler, W. (2018b). A Kinematic Study of Phonetic Reduction in a Young Sign Language. Paper presented at the 8th Conference of the International Society for Gesture Studies (ISGS). Cape Town, South Africa. July 5th, 2018.

Stamp, R., Ben-Israel, A., Hel-Or, H., & Raz, S. (2021). It's just a gay thing: A comparative kinematic analysis of gestures and signs in Israel. Accepted as a paper at the 27th Lavender Languages & Linguistics conference. San Francisco, 21-23rd May 2021.

Stamp, R., Khatib, L., Eden, K., Ben-Israel, A., Cohen, D., Hel-Or, H., Karpova, V., & Raz, S. (in prep.). Embodiment of gender in sign language: A comparative kinematic analysis.

Weibel, N., Hwang, S.-O., Rick, S., Sayyari, E., Lenzen, D., & Hollan, J. (2016). Hands That Speak: An Integrated Approach to Studying Complex Human Communicative Body Movements. *2016 49th Hawaii International Conference on System Sciences (HICSS)*, 610–619. https://doi.org/10.1109/HICSS.2016.82

Proceedings of the 10th Workshop on the Representation and Processing of Sign Languages (sign-lang@LREC 2022), pages 192–197
Language Resources and Evaluation Conference (LREC 2022), Marseille, 20-25 June 2022

The Corpus of Israeli Sign Language

Rose Stamp, Ora Ohanin & Sara Lanesman
Bar-Ilan University
Department of English Literature & Linguistics
rose.stamp@biu.ac.il

Abstract

The Corpus of Israeli Sign Language is a four-year project (2020-2024) which aims to create a digital open-access corpus of spontaneous and elicited data from a representative sample of the Israeli deaf community. In this paper, the methodology for building the Corpus of Israeli Sign Language is described. Israeli Sign Language (ISL) is the main sign language used across Israel by around 10,000 people. As part of the corpus, data will be collected from 120 deaf ISL signers across four sites in Israel: Tel Aviv and the Centre, Haifa and the North, Be'er Sheva and the South and Jerusalem and the surrounding area. Participants will engage in a variety of tasks, eliciting a range of signing styles from free conversation to lexical elicitation. The dataset will consist of recordings of over 360 hours of video data which will be used to conduct sociolinguistic investigations of language contact, variation, and change in the near term, and other linguistic analyses in the future.

Keywords: Israeli Sign Language, corpus, lexical database, corpus project, language contact, language change

1. Introduction

Corpora provide spontaneous, naturalistic data against which claims about the structure and use of a given language can be tested. The need for sign language corpora is of paramount importance because they remain under researched compared to spoken languages. Furthermore, it is important to widen the set of languages represented in corpus linguistics (McEnery & Ostler, 2000). While there has been a surge in sign language corpora creation since the turn of the century, with the addition of over twenty around the globe (Kopf et al., 2021), there are still many sign languages without existing corpora, especially those located in the Middle East. To add to the diversity of sign language corpora and to better understand sign language variation in Israel more specifically, the Corpus of Israeli Sign Language project was launched in 2020.

The Corpus of Israeli Sign Language is a four-year project (2020-2024) funded by the Israeli Science Foundation and hosted by Bar-Ilan University. The primary objective of the project is to conduct sociolinguistic studies on language contact, variation, and change in Israeli Sign Language (ISL), as described in Section 2. To achieve this, a machine-readable digital corpus of spontaneous and elicited data from the Israeli deaf community will be created. The project is led by Dr. Rose Stamp, together with her research team, Ora Ohanin and Sara Lanesman, who are native signers of ISL. In this paper (in Section 3), we outline the methodologies for collecting a representative sample of language data from the ISL deaf community, including the sampling method, stimuli, and task procedures. The methodology follows other sign language corpora around the world, drawing on a combination of tasks used in the British Sign Language (BSL) Corpus Project, the German Sign Language (DGS) Corpus Project and others.

Finally, in Section 4, we describe the related resources, including the project's website, the lexical database hosted by Global SignBank, and the online network-based visualization website, ISL-LEX. The Corpus of ISL will provide one of the first large-scale datasets of a young sign language and will serve as a key resource for researchers investigating ISL structure and usage.

2. Israeli Sign Language & the Deaf Community

Compared to other countries, Israel has a unique abundance of sign languages, which emerged naturally within the last hundred years (Meir & Sandler, 2008). The main sign language used in Israel is Israeli Sign Language (ISL), with an estimated 10,000 users. It is the language of the National Deaf Association, the education system, and sign language interpreting. ISL is a relatively young sign language, roughly about 90 years old, which arose with the formation of the deaf community in Israel around the 1930s, beginning with the establishment of the first school for the deaf in 1932 in Jerusalem. Many of the first generation ISL signers, who are now the older population in Israel, immigrated from Europe, North Africa and the Asia and were illiterate or semi-literate when ISL first emerged. Today, in contrast, younger deaf people, who are the third or fourth generations of ISL signers, are multilingual and are exposed to a variety of signed, spoken and written languages. The deaf ISL community has undergone rapid changes due to increased mobility, exposure to different languages within the education system, and changes in social communication and technology. These changes have led to increased contact between languages and language varieties. The creation of the Corpus of ISL is an opportunity to capture the linguistic variation and to find clues to the social demographic forces involved.

The aim of this project entitled "A corpus-based sociolinguistic study of sign languages in Israel" is not just to create a corpus of ISL, but also to address important research questions regarding language contact, variation, and change. The project presents a systematic investigation of language contact in three different situations: (1) contact between ISL regional varieties, (2) contact between ISL and Arabic, and (3) contact between ISL and a local sign language used in Kufr Qassem.

In the first contact situation, we look at how increased mobility in recent years might have had an influence on sign language varieties across Israel. It is claimed that regionally distinct varieties exist in ISL; for example, there are at least two variants for the sign 'hospital', one associated with signers from Tel Aviv, and one associated with signers from Haifa (see Figure 1).

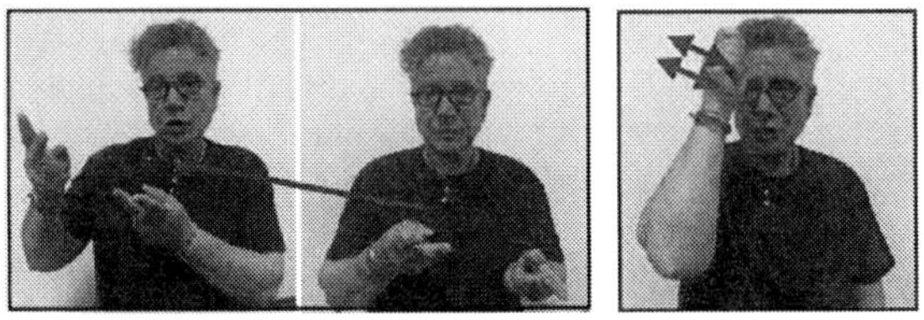

Figure 1: Two variants for the sign 'hospital': (left) in Tel Aviv and (right) in Haifa

Studies show that increases in mobility and changes in communication patterns might result in a decline in the use of such regionally distinct signs (McKee & McKee, 2011; Stamp et al., 2014). This has been shown to lead to long-term language change (Trudgill, 1986), in particular dialect levelling, in which signers reduce their use of regionally marked variants in favour of variants that are distributed over a wider geographical area (Kerswill, 2003). In this first study, we explore whether there is any evidence of language change in ISL because of increased contact between language varieties.

In the second study, we look at the unique contact situation between ISL and Arabic. For many years, deaf children from Arabic-speaking families were educated in the Jewish sector, and they were exposed to ISL and Hebrew. Nowadays, deaf children from Arabic-speaking families either attend mainstream schools alongside their hearing peers or schools in which ISL and Arabic are the main languages of instruction. While the effects of contact between ISL and Hebrew have been described previously (Meir & Sandler, 2008), few studies have focused on the contact situation between ISL and Arabic. In addition, deaf children in Arab communities are exposed to Arabic in its diglossic form. In other words, children are exposed to two distinct forms: one colloquial spoken variety and one formal written variety (Saiegh-Haddad, 2012). We investigate the contact situation between ISL and the two distinct varieties of Arabic and how each variety might affect the other.

The third study investigates the language contact situation in Kufr Qassem, an Arabic-speaking community situated in the Southern Triangle area in Central Israel, around 20 kilometers northeast of Tel-Aviv. Younger deaf people in Kufr Qassem are exposed to two sign languages: ISL, as the dominant sign language used across Israel and Kufr Qassem Sign Language (KQSL), a local sign language used only by the deaf community in Kufr Qassem (Kastner et al., 2014). KQSL emerged around 90 years ago when a high number of deaf people were born into the local community. First generation signers were relatively isolated and unaffected by other sign languages, as many did not attend school or live outside of the local community. However, the situation for third generation signers is very different. Because of increased mobility as well as changes to the instruction language used in the school for deaf children in Kufr Qassem, deaf people are now exposed to many languages, including KQSL, ISL, Arabic, Hebrew, etc. This has led to drastic language shift within this community. Recent findings suggest that younger deaf signers in Kufr Qassem are dominant in ISL, and that the continuation of KQSL is under threat from language shift (Stamp & Jaraisy, 2021). The aim of this third study is to investigate the influence of ISL on smaller sign language communities across Israel, using Kufr Qassem as our case study.

To conduct sociolinguistic investigations, such as these, on language contact, variation, and change in ISL, it is crucial to analyze language data from a representative sample of the Israeli deaf community. The corpus will serve as a large-scale dataset of ISL, which will be digitalized, annotated and made publicly available for research as well as applied purposes.

3. Methodology

At the time of writing this paper, data collection is currently underway and therefore, in the following section, we describe the methods as planned, rather than based on what we have collected to date.

3.1 Participants

To collect a representative sample of the ISL deaf community, thirty deaf ISL signers will be recruited from four key sites across Israel. The sites represent the major areas in Israel, including Tel Aviv and the Centre, Haifa and the North, Be'er Sheva and the South and Jerusalem (the capital city) and the surrounding area. These sites were selected because they contain adequate numbers of deaf signers, and because they represent sites which vary in terms of their signing varieties (e.g., the sign for 'hospital' between Tel Aviv and Haifa). Deaf fluent signers of ISL were recruited; no criteria based on family background were required (native and non-native signers are included), however, metadata regarding this was collected from each individual, as described below.

Israel is a relatively small country and therefore many individuals spend time in multiple sites during their lifetimes. As a result, participants were filmed in the site in which they lived the most within the last ten years. In each site, ten participants were recruited in three age groups: younger (18-39), middle-aged (40-59), and older (60+). During the selection of participants, gender, social class, ethnicity (e.g., Jewish, Arab) and family origin (e.g., Moroccan, German) were considered, taking a representative sample when possible. See Table 1 for participant characteristics.

Region	**Age groups**			**Gender**	
	Young (18-39)	**Middle (40-59)**	**Older (60+)**	**Male**	**Female**
Haifa & the North	10	10	10	15	15
Tel Aviv & the Centre	10	10	10	15	15
Greater Jerusalem	10	10	10	15	15
Be'er Sheva & the South	10	10	10	15	15
Total	40	40	40	60	60

Table 1: Participant characteristics

Four deaf fieldworkers were recruited, one in each site. All fieldworkers are deaf native ISL signers who live in the respective target sites and have good contacts with the local deaf community. Their role was to identify and recruit ISL signers who live in the local community. In addition, a deaf fieldworker coordinator was recruited to oversee the data collection process and to serve as the consistent interviewer in one of the tasks (described in Section 3.2).

A technique of network sampling was used, in which fieldworkers began by recruiting people they know, then asked these people to recommend other individuals who matched the project criteria (Milroy & Gordon, 2003). In this way, participants were filmed in pairs consisting of two individuals who know each other.

A Deaf Advisory Committee was set up, consisting of six deaf ISL signers from different backgrounds, who are active and prominent figures in the Israeli deaf community. The committee serves as a consultation board for various issues related to variation in ISL, stimuli selection, website design, etc. In addition, Professor Adam Schembri, who was the PI for the BSL Corpus Project and consultant on several other corpora, is the International Consultant on this project, and he is providing us with advice on methodological issues, lemmatization, and glossing at various stages in the project.

3.2 Stimuli & Procedure

The Corpus of ISL follows the methodologies outlined in other sign language corpora, and, in particular, those from the BSL Corpus Project and the DGS Corpus Project.

The data were collected in two stages: first, an online meeting between each participant and the fieldworker, and then a 3-hour sociolinguistic interview, conducted in pairs onsite. Based on Labov's classic sociolinguistic interview (1972), we included seven language tasks which elicit a range of signing styles from spontaneous to elicited, including:

Stage 1 (online, one-to-one meeting):

1. short questionnaire about name signs,
2. lexical elicitation task,

Stage 2 (onsite, filmed in pairs):

1. personal narrative,
2. free conversation,
3. retelling of the events shown in a video clip,
4. questions and answers about language variation and change,
5. retelling of the events shown in short video clips,

As part of stage one, each participant met with the fieldworker online to complete two of the seven language tasks. In most cases, this was completed using the online platform, Google Meet. An online format was preferred because the commencement of filming coincided with the COVID pandemic when filming in person was not possible. During this meeting, participants first completed a consent form and video sharing consent form to agree that their data can be made openly accessible. Then, participants completed a 43-item questionnaire about their language background, education, language preferences, etc. The items in the questionnaire were largely based on the questionnaire used in the BSL Corpus Project; however, it was adapted for the purposes of the Israeli deaf community and translated into Hebrew and Arabic. The questionnaires were completed using Google Forms. Following this, participants were asked about their name sign (name signs refer to the visual name given to members of the deaf community). Three questions were asked: (1) what is your name sign in ISL? (2) what is the reason for your name sign? (3) has your name sign stayed the same throughout your lifetime? As part of this project, we plan to conduct a diachronic analysis of name signs, similar to other studies (e.g., Börstell, 2017; McKee & McKee, 1999).

Finally, participants were asked to give their sign variants for a list of concepts. The aim of the lexical elicitation task was to elicit participant's preferred variants for the concepts known to vary considerably and to investigate how this variation patterns across different social groups. Participants were encouraged to give their preferred variant(s) and to mention other variants they know or have seen. For this reason, individual meetings were preferred to avoid the influence of one participant's answers upon another's. The concepts on the list were selected because they are known to show considerable variation in ISL and because the variation is claimed to be associated with social factors, such as a signer's age, gender, ethnicity, religion, regional background, and so on. The list was compiled with the help of the online ISL dictionary[1], which includes multiple variations for the same concept, and consultation with the Deaf Advisory Committee. In the end, the lexical elicitation task consisted of two slides acting as trials, followed by 145 slides for the actual task elicitation. Each slide showed a picture together with the sign's closest Hebrew and Arabic equivalent translations representing each of the target concepts (e.g., a coloured orange square with the Hebrew word כתום and Arabic برتقالي to elicit the sign for 'orange'). See Figure 2 below.

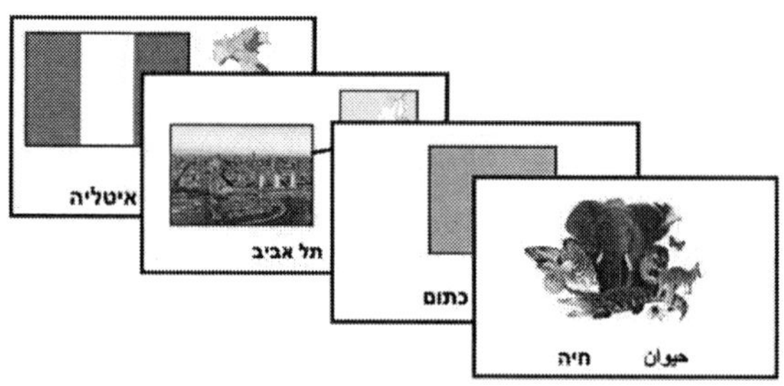

Figure 2: Example of the slides used in the Lexical Elicitation Task

In the second stage, a sociolinguistic interview was carried out. This consisted of the five remaining tasks, filmed at each site over a duration of three hours. Participants were filmed in pairs with another signer from the same age group and region. Filming took place in the local deaf club and on some occasions, in a classroom at Bar-Ilan University (for participants from the Tel Aviv site). The PI, the fieldworker

[1]The ISL dictionary was originally created by The Institute for the Advancement of Deaf Persons in Israel (IADPI) and is now hosted by Maggalei Shemae (https://isl.danfishgold.com/#he-3SI).

coordinator, and the fieldworker themselves were present at all filming sessions. For the personal narrative task, participants were informed in advance that they should think of a personal narrative lasting 5 minutes. Each participant was filmed telling their narrative to their interlocutor. After 5 minutes, participants were informed, in a non-intrusive way, that their time had run out (but that they were able to conclude their story briefly). Then, participants switched, and the other participant told their narrative. Following this, both participants engaged in free conversation (Task 2). Participants were left in front of the cameras with no intervention for thirty minutes. The aim of this task is to elicit data as naturalistic as possible (Labov, 1972).

In the third task, participants took turns watching an excerpt from a movie clip and they were asked to retell the events to their interlocutor. One participant watched an excerpt from Charlie Chaplin's The Lion's Cage (The Circus, 1928) and the other watched an excerpt from an animated cartoon called Snack Attack (2012). Both movies were selected because they contain no dialogue and, while they are different storylines, they both elicit a range of sign language features including constructed action, character reference, and use of classifiers. The Lion's Cage, specifically, has also been used for elicitation in previous ISL projects and therefore it has been shown to be a successful form of elicitation and the data elicited in the corpus can be compared to previous elicitations (e.g., Stamp et al., 2018). To avoid issues related to memory, participants were first shown the whole clip from start to finish and then they were shown the clip in parts and asked to retell the events directly after each section they watched. After all the parts were retold and participants had fully internalized the storyline, they were asked to retell the whole story from start to finish. Participants were also informed that their partners would complete a comprehension task after their retelling, which involved ordering five movie stills in chronological order of the events as they were described. Awareness of the comprehension task encouraged participants to be more detailed in their retellings.

In task four, participants were interviewed about their patterns of language use, their attitudes towards different language varieties, and about their own examples of language variation and change in ISL. The fieldworker coordinator served as the consistent interviewer in each filming site. The interview was conducted with both participants simultaneously. Questions were modified from the BSL Corpus Project interview after consultation with their team. They included questions such as: Do you think there are differences in signing between older and younger ISL signers? If you moved to a new location in Israel, would change your signing to accommodate to those in the new location? The interview lasted 20 minutes.

In the final task, participants watched three excerpts from Sylvester and Tweety's Canary Row (1950) cartoon (a total of six altogether). Each excerpt ranged in duration from 18-31 seconds. After watching each excerpt, they retold the events to their interlocutor. As part of a comprehension task, the interlocutor was given three pictures, each representing one of the excerpts, and was asked to identify the picture which most resembled what they understood from the retelling. Canary Row was selected specifically because the data is comparable with other sign language corpus projects including those in Germany, Spain, Poland and the Netherlands (Kopf et al., 2021). At the end of filming, all participants were compensated for their time.

At the time of writing (May 2022), over half of our participants (n=72) completed the online tasks and 32 were filmed face-to-face, completing all tasks.

3.3 Data Collection Technologies

For onsite filming, we used three high-definition digital video cameras to provide a close-up of each individual as well as one camera positioned to include both participants in the frame (see Figure 3 below). When necessary, portable studio lighting was used to ensure that the best images of the participants were captured.

Figure 3: Three angles of the cameras: one close up view of each participant, and a third camera positioned to capture both participants

In addition, two Microsoft Kinect Azure cameras were used to track the motion of participants whilst retelling the two elicited narratives. The Kinect Azure cameras consist of an RGB camera and an infrared camera (Brown Kramer et al., 2020). The system supplies a skeleton representation of the participant, consisting of X, Y, Z coordinates of 32 major skeleton joints connected by line segments. These are used to calculate a variety of movement measures such as signing speed, volume, variance, etc., which can be compared across participants, social groups, and even languages. Motion capture has also been ultilized in other sign language corpus projects such as the DGS corpus project.

3.4 Data Coding

The completed data collection is estimated to consist of 360 hours of recordings (120 participants x 3hrs). The corpus will be annotated by students and research assistants, using ELAN, a video annotation software (Crasborn & Sloetjes, 2008).

4. Related Resources

The corpus will be made publicly available via the corpus **website**: www.islcorpus.co.il. The website, which is currently under construction, will follow the format of other open-access corpora, in which it will be possible to search and download the data by request. A copy of all of the elicitation materials can be found on **Open Science Framework** (https://osf.io/yma98/).

The corpus data will provide the dataset for future versions of an online lexical database known as **ISL-LEX**. ISL-LEX, created by the SIGN-LEX team in the US (Caselli et al., 2022) in collaboration with ISL research teams in Israel, is an online interface and search tool associated with an existing lexical database of ISL. It provides network-based visualizations of ISL signs based on phonological characteristics, as shown in Figure 4 (https://sites.google.com/view/isl-lex). In its current version, ISL-LEX contains 961 signs grouped and colored by the degree of similarity to other signs (Morgan et al., 2022). In the next version, ISL-LEX will expand by using the dataset collected as part of the Corpus of ISL.

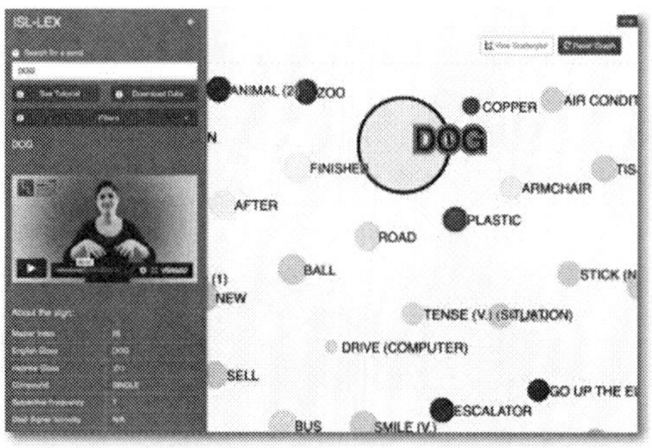

Figure 4: Example of ISL-LEX

Videos of individual signs and their ID-glosses from the corpus will be stored in an online lexical database hosted by **Global SignBank** (Crasborn et al., 2020). SignBank is a lexical database for managing ID-glosses and information about the sign form, which is dynamically-linked with ELAN for ease of coding. The database is available in three languages: English, Hebrew, and Arabic (see Figure 5 below). The goal of the multilingual format is to make the database as widely accessible as possible, and especially to different deaf communities across Israel. Data from ISL-LEX version 1.0 served as the initial input into the ISL database.

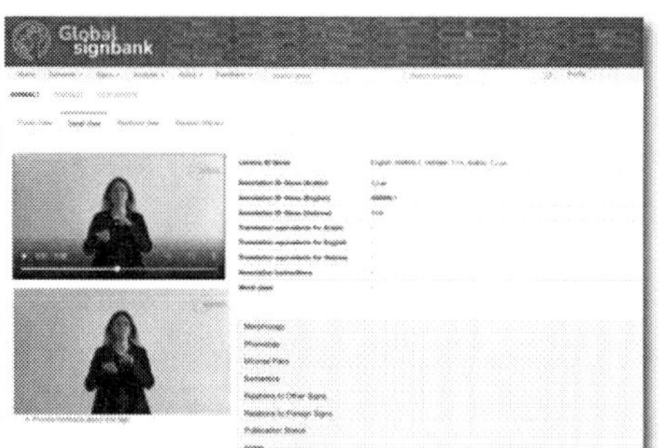

Figure 5: View of the ISL dataset as displayed in Global SignBank

5. Conclusion

In this paper, the project aims, methodologies, and the related resources were presented. The Corpus of ISL joins many other sign language corpus projects launched in the last twenty years, however, this corpus offers a unique addition by providing a corpus of a relatively young sign language. The corpus will first and foremost serve as a resource for researchers, allowing on-going and new projects on ISL contact, variation, and change. Further to this, the corpus will provide a vital open-access resource for teachers, interpreters, students, and hearing parents of deaf children.

6. Acknowledgements

We express our gratitude to the fieldworkers, the Deaf Advisory Committee, and all the deaf participants involved in the corpus filming. We also thank Professor Adam Schembri for his support as our International Consultant. Finally, a special thanks to the SIGN-LEX and Global SignBank teams for their support and collaboration.

Funding for building the Corpus of ISL was supported by an Israeli Science Foundation grant to Dr. Rose Stamp (2757/20; ISL Corpus project) and an internal Data Sciences Institute (DSI) grant, Bar-Ilan University, awarded in 2020-2021.

7. Bibliographical References

Börstell, C. 2017. Types and trends of name signs in the Swedish Sign Language community. *SKY Journal of Linguistics*, 30 (2017), 7-34.

Brown Kramer J., Sabalka L., Rush B., Jones K., Nolte T. (2020). *Automated depth video monitoring for fall reduction: A case study*. Proceedings of the IEEE/CVF Conference on Computer Vision and Pattern Recognition (CVPR) Workshops; Seattle, WI, USA. pp. 294-295

Crasborn, O., & Sloetjes, H. (2008). Enhanced ELAN functionality for sign language. *Proceedings of LREC 2008, Sixth International Conference on Language Resources and Evaluation*. pp.39-43.

Kopf, M., Schulder, M. & Hanke, T., (2021). Overview for datasets for the sign languages of Europe. EASIER report. University of Hamburg. https://doi.org/10.25592/uhhfdm.9560

Kastner, I., Meir, I., Sandler, W., & Dachkovsky, S. (2014). The emergence of embedded structure: Insights from Kafr Qasem Sign Language. *Frontiers in Psychology*, *5*, 525, pp. 1-15. https://doi.org/10.3389/fpsyg.2014.00525

Kerswill, P. (2003). Dialect levelling and geographical diffusion in British English. In: P. Trudgill, D. Britain, & J. Cheshire, (Eds.). In P. Trudgill, D. Britain, & J. Cheshire (Eds.), *Social Dialectology: In Honour of Peter Trudgill*. (pp. 223-244.). John Benjamins.

Labov, W., (1972). Sociolinguistic Patterns. Philadelphia: University of Pennsylvania.

Lucas, C., Bayley, R., & Valli, C. (2001). *Sociolinguistic Variation in American Sign Language*. Gallaudet University Press.

McEnery, T., & Ostler, N. (2000). A New Agenda for Corpus Linguistics—Working with all of the World's Languages. *Literary and Linguistic Computing,* 15(4), pp. 403-419.

McKee, R.L. & McKee, D. (1999). Name signs and identity in New Zealand sign language. In Metzger, Melanie (ed.), *Bilingualism and identity in Deaf communities*, pp. 3–40. Washington, DC: Gallaudet University Press.

McKee, R., & McKee, D. (2011). Old Signs, New Signs, Whose Signs? Sociolinguistic Variation in the NZSL Lexicon. *Sign Language Studies*, *11*(4), pp. 485–527.

Meir, I., & Sandler, W. (2008). *A Language in Space: The Story of Israeli Sign Language*. Routledge. https://www.routledge.com/A-Language-in-Space-The-Story-of-Israeli-Sign-Language/Meir-Sandler/p/book/9780805862652

Milroy, L., & Gordon, M. (2003). *Sociolinguistics: Method and Interpretation*. Wiley.

Morgan, H., Sandler, W., Stamp, R. & Novogrodsky, R. (2022). ISL-LEX v.1: An Online Lexical Resource of Israeli Sign Language. Proceedings of the LREC conference (June 25th 2022), Marseilles, France.

Saiegh-Haddad, E., (2012). Literacy Reflexes of Arabic Diglossia. *Current Issues in Bilingualism*, no. 5: pp. 43-55.

Schembri, A., Fenlon, J., Rentelis, R., Reynolds, S., & Cormier, K. (2013). Building the British Sign Language Corpus. *Language Documentation and Conservation 7,* pp. 136-154.

Stamp, R., & Jaraisy, M. (2021). Language Contact between Israeli Sign Language and Kufr Qassem Sign Language. *Sign Language Studies*, *21*(4), pp. 455–491. https://doi.org/10.1353/sls.2021.0007

Stamp, R., Schembri, A., Fenlon, J., Rentelis, R., Woll, B., & Cormier, K. (2014). Lexical Variation and Change in British Sign Language. *PLOS ONE*, *9*(4), e94053. https://doi.org/10.1371/journal.pone.0094053

Stamp, R., Hel-Or, H., Cohn, D., Raz, S. & Sandler, W. (2018). Kinect-ing the dots: Motion capture technologies and the sign language lexicon. Paper presented at the International Congress of Linguists (ICL) conference. University of Cape Town, South Africa. July 3rd, 2018.

Trudgill, P. J. (1986). *Dialects in contact*. Blackwell.

8. Language Resource References

Caselli, N., Sevcikova Sehyr, Z., Cohen-Goldberg, A. M., Emmorey, K., Pandit, S., Cao, X., Fantes, M., Simeon, J. (2022). *SIGN-LEX: Interactive visualizations for sign language lexicons*. SIGN-LEX. https://www.sign-lex.org

Crasborn, O., Zwitserlood, I., van der Kooij, E., & Ormel, E. (2020). *Global Signbank*. Radboud University, Nijmegen. https://signbank.science.ru.nl.

Institute for the Advancement of Deaf Persons in Israel (IADPI). *ISL Dictionary*. https://isl.danfishgold.com/#he-3SI

Stamp, R., Ohanin, O. & Lanesman, S. (2022). *The Corpus of Israeli Sign Language.* Bar-Ilan University, http://islcorpus.co.il (landing site launched in 2022).

Proceedings of the 10th Workshop on the Representation and Processing of Sign Languages (sign-lang@LREC 2022), pages 198–201
Language Resources and Evaluation Conference (LREC 2022), Marseille, 20-25 June 2022

Segmentation of Signs for Research Purposes: Comparing Humans and Machines

Bencie Woll, Neil Fox, Kearsy Cormier
Deafness, Cognition and Language Research Centre; University College London; UK
49 Gordon Square, London WC1H 0PD, UK
{b.woll, neil.fox, k.cormier}@ucl.ac.uk

Abstract

Sign languages such as British Sign Language (BSL) are visual languages which lack standard writing systems. Annotation of sign language data, especially for the purposes of machine readability, is therefore extremely slow. Tools to help automate and thus speed up the annotation process are very much needed. Here we test the development of one such tool (VIA-SLA), which uses temporal convolutional networks (Renz et al., 2021a, b) for the purpose of segmenting continuous signing in any sign language, and is designed to integrate smoothly with ELAN, the widely used annotation software for analysis of videos of sign language. We compare automatic segmentation by machine with segmentation done by a human, both in terms of time needed and accuracy of segmentation, using samples taken from the BSL Corpus (Schembri et al., 2014). A small sample of four short video files is tested (mean duration 25 seconds). We find that mean accuracy in terms of number and location of segmentations is relatively high, at around 78%. This preliminary test suggests that VIA-SLA promises to be very useful for sign linguists.

Keywords: sign language, segmentation, temporal convolutional networks, annotation

1. Introduction

The production of sign language annotations - the input needed for linguistic analysis and for training of machine learning models - is a necessary step in analysis. In sign language annotations, linguists extract and code visual linguistic, paralinguistic and non-linguistic features from video. For most purposes, annotation of sign language videos requires the isolation of each individual sign. Temporal segmentation and motion descriptions of continuous signing are generally carried out by linguists using annotation tools such as ANVIL (Kipp, 2001), ELAN (Wittenburg et al., 2002), or iLex (Hanke, 2002). From these, linguistic models can be built, corpora supplied to those working on machine recognition, and searchability made possible for other users (Chaaban et al., 2021). However, annotation (especially temporal segmentation) is time consuming, monotonous and error prone (Quer & Steinbach. 2019); errors can be mitigated but this is even more time consuming.

The segmentation of continuous signing presents many challenges. In addition to the significant time required for this work, the results are often extremely variable because annotators use different criteria to estimate the beginnings and ends of signs. As well as noting the lack of agreement on standardised annotation systems, Bragg et al. (2019) point out that annotators must also be extensively trained to reach sufficient proficiency in the desired annotation system; training is expensive, constraining the set of people who can provide annotations beyond the already restricted set of fluent signers; and the absence of commonly used written forms for sign languages prevents access to methods that use parallel text corpora to learn corresponding grammar and vocabulary, and more generally prevents the leveraging of ubiquitous text resources. Thus, automating the task of annotation – or even subparts of this task - would lead to substantial savings of time, and increase the robustness of the analyses. Such an approach, for example, might include doing a first pass using computer vision algorithms to segment videos of continuous signing into individual signs. This would increase the amount of data available, have a substantial impact on the design of research by linguists, and have an impact on how we design our research. Additionally, even if there were no substantial speed advantage for automated segmentation, it would likely provide other important advantages, since computer annotation is much cheaper; and because of the monotony of segmentation work, sparing the investment of human resources on this task would in any case be beneficial.

In this paper we compare the amount of time needed and accuracy achieved by experienced sign language researchers when segmenting continuous signing into individual signs occurring within naturalistic interaction among users of British Sign Language (BSL), to a newly developed sign segmentation tool (VIA-SLA) (Renz, Stache, Fox, Varol & Albanie, 2021; Renz, Stache, Albanie & Varol, 2021) This tool, VIA-SLA, is a Sign Language Annotator adapted from the VGG Image Annotator (VIA) from the Visual Geometry Group at University of Oxford. VIA-SLA was developed as part of a multidisciplinary research project (ExTOL – End-to-End translation of BSL) - a strategic collaboration between BSL linguists and computer vision software engineers who specialise in machine learning (https://cvssp.org/projects/extol/). This collaboration has enabled a focus on the development of tools that are potentially of greatest interest to linguists; in turn, the development of such tools will ultimately make available more annotated data for use by those interested in automated processing of any sign language.

We have also been working with our vision science colleagues to develop a second tool which identifies individual signs following segmentation, but this is not described in the present paper.

General descriptions and estimates of the time needed for segmentation of sign language texts are outlined below, followed by the description of VIA-SLA, a new tool for sign language segmentation using temporal convolutional networks (Renz et al., 2021a, b). Then human and machine are compared in relation to time needed and accuracy of segmentation, using samples taken from the BSL Corpus (Schembri et al., 2014). Approaches to repair of errors in automated segmentation are discussed, together with recommendations for future developments.

2. Time Needed For Human Segmentation

Segmentation and basic annotation of sign language data by humans has been described as being incredibly slow (Johnston 2010; Crasborn 2015; Fenlon et al., 2015), although there are very few direct estimates or descriptions of time needed in the literature. One exception is Crasborn (2015) who notes that it takes around 200 times real time for basic ID glossing of sign language data (i.e. 3 to 4 hours for just one minute of sign language video). ID glosses are unique identifiers of particular signs. This estimate assumes that there is a lexical database which already contains the required ID glosses and their citation form and translation equivalents; if such a database does not exist or if new entries need to be created for the signs identified, then the amount of time needed is even longer. The amount of time required for segmentation in particular depends on the annotation method. Following an initial viewing of the relevant video clip, some annotators prefer to go through the video doing all of the segmentation first, and then go through the video a second time inserting ID-glosses; others segment and then immediately gloss the segmented element before proceeding to the next segment boundary. The practice followed for annotation of the BSL Corpus (Schembri et al., 2013), for example, has been to segment an entire file, creating 'blank' annotations, and then go back, identify each sign, and add an ID gloss. This staged approach is used with the BSL Corpus (Schembri et al., 2013) and Polish Sign Language (PJM) Corpus (Mostowski, et al. 2018). Mostowski, et al. (2018) note that the segmentation stage alone takes around 60 times real time for a skilled human annotator – i.e., it takes around 1 hour to segment one minute of sign language video data.

3. Methods

VIA-SLA is accessible via the Google Chrome browser, available at the following link:
https://www.robots.ox.ac.uk/~vgg/research/signsegmentation/. At the time of testing this initial version of VIA-SLA, video files for processing had to be under one minute in length and under 5MB in size. Scaling-up of the time and file size limitations are currently under discussion. The limit can be expanded; however, this would require the host server to commit GPUs to segmentation, and internet access will need to be reliant, robust and fast. Such issues as storage of videos after processing will also need to be addressed.

Figure 1 illustrates the task of temporal sign segmentation using an example of a continuous signing from the BSL Corpus.

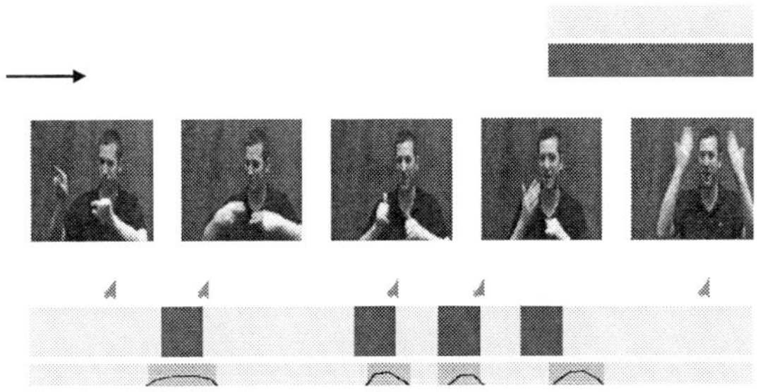

Figure 1. Example of of temporal sign segmentation. Ground truth and predictions of the model are shown. Sign segments are indicated in grey; boundaries in blue. Image from Renz, K., Stache, N. C., Albanie, S., & Varol, G. (2021) with permission.

The videos used for the present analysis were selected from BSL Corpus videos (https://bslcorpusproject.org/); examples are shown in Figure 2.

Figure 2. Examples of signers from the BSL Corpus.

The videos were cropped to ensure that they were under one minute. We then used VLC to convert the videos into MP4 files (exported as .mpg and the file extension renamed as .mp4). Since many of the corpus videos had been used as training data in the development of VIA-SLA, for the purpose of the present analysis we report only on video files taken from interview data which had no gloss annotations and thus had not been used for training.

The video files were loaded into ELAN, and the time taken by the second author, a deaf native signer of BSL, with extensive experience of annotation in ELAN, to do "blank" annotations (coding just the start and end of each sign) was recorded. The criteria for coding start and end points were those used in all BSL Corpus research. The start point for a sign was identified as the point when the hand or hands appear to start moving away from articulating the previous sign. This is signalled by a change in direction, orientation, and/or handshape. The end point for a sign was identified as the point when the hand appears to start moving towards articulating the following sign. Again, this is signalled by a change in direction, orientation, and/or handshape. A sign sequence was normally considered to be finished when the hands begin a return to a rest position or when it was clear that the signer's turn was finished. For details, see Cormier et al. (2017).

After completing this stage, the same videos were loaded into VIA-SLA, and the time taken to complete segmentation of each video was recorded. It should of course be noted that the speed of segmentation by VIA-SLA varies depending on the size of the graphics processing unit (GPU) at the server side which processes the annotation. It also depends on the quality and speed of the internet connection used to transmit and receive the data. Therefore, the figures given here are exemplars only. Once segmentation was completed, the files were exported as ELAN files (.csv files), and each .csv was loaded into the same .eaf file that had been used to manually annotate the same video. CSV files were used because of uncertainty about merging two ELAN files or exporting a tier into a second ELAN file.

4. Analyses

Using this merged .eaf file containing both human and machine annotations, we compared the two tiers, examining the numbers of segments, the start and end points of each segment, and the number of segmentations considered acceptable (See Figure 3 for an example). For any segmentation to be considered acceptable, there had to be a degree of similarity (defined as within 100 milliseconds of the sign boundary) between the predicted machine annotations compared with the Ground Truth (human annotations). Intelligibility was also checked to see whether the machine-processed segments were individually intelligible: i.e. that the predicted annotation did indeed contain something that was identifiable as a single sign (as opposed to e.g. parts of two or more signs).

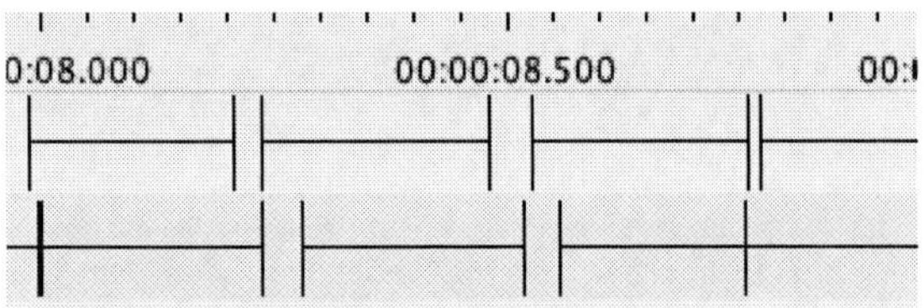

Figure 3: Merged ELAN file showing segmentation boundaries created by human (top) and by machine (bottom).

5. Results

We report here results from analysis of four videos, ranging in length from 14-40 seconds (mean 25 seconds). The time needed for human segmentation ranged from 480 seconds for the shortest clip to 1200 seconds for the longest (mean 840 seconds). The time needed for automated segmentation ranged from 21 to 73 seconds. Unsurprisingly VIA-SLA performed segmentation much faster than the human annotator. The number of segments in each video annotated by the human ranged from 24 to 89, and the number of segments predicted by VIA-SLA ranged from 29 to 86. 100 milliseconds has been used previously in identifying correct segmentation by human coders (Fenlon et al., 2007); this window has been determined to be an acceptable threshold. Even with experienced annotators, variation of a few frames occurs in annotations of 25 fps videos (Hanke et al 2012). Comparing human and machine annotations, the number of segments which were within 100 milliseconds of the boundaries identified by the human annotator, and judged as recording a single sign, ranged from 20 to 68.

Prediction accuracy was calculated as the percentage of human annotations matched by accepted machine annotations. This figure ranged from 74% to 83% for the four samples. For details see Table 1.

Video number	Duration (sec)	Time Manual Segmentation (sec)	Tool Predictions (sec)	No of Manual Segments	No of Predicted Segments	Predicted Segments Accepted	% Prediction Accuracy
1	14.5	480	21	24	29	20	83.3
2	40	1200	73	89	86	68	76.4
3	27	1020	59	42	39	31	73.8
4	19	660	26	31	35	24	77.4
Mean	25.1	840	44.8				77.7

Table 1: Comparing segmentation time and accuracy between human and machine.

6. Discussion

Although these are preliminary results and on a very small sample of data, it should be noted that use of VIA-SLA for segmentation took 5.3% of the time needed for manual segmentation, and that the mean prediction accuracy of VIA-SLA was around 78%.

There are a number of possible reasons for why prediction accuracy is only 78%. One reason relates to fingerspelling, i.e. the use of the manual alphabet. BSL has a two-handed fingerspelling system, and each letter roughly has the same phonology as two-handed lexical signs, unlike one-handed fingerspelling systems where the phonologies of one-handed lexical signs differ markedly from fingerspelled forms (Cormier et al. 2008). VIA-SLA at this stage does not discriminate between signs and fingerspelling. When we annotate fingerspelling in BSL, we use one gloss for the full or partially fingerspelled word, while VIA-SLA at present identifies each letter as one segment. One modification that is currently being worked on is to identify where a fingerspelled word appears, identify it as such and include this feature in future development of VIA-SLA. It is possible that the presence of fingerspelling had an impact on prediction accuracy, as illustrated in Video Number 1. As can be seen in Figure 4, while the upper tier, segmented and glossed manually, indicated a single segment, consisting of fingerspelling of B-S-L: "FS:BSL", VIA-SLA predicted 3 annotations, one for each letter: -B-, -S- and -L-.

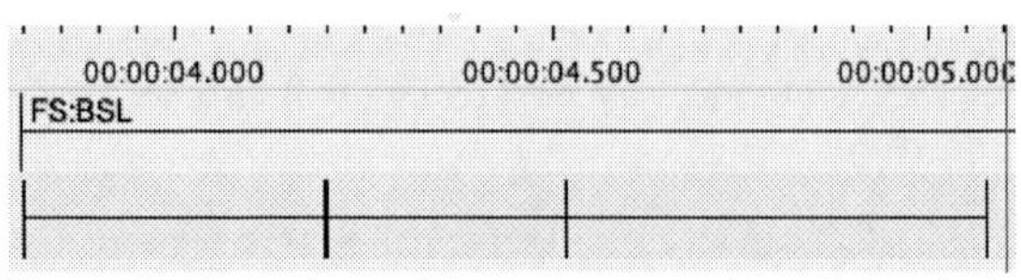

Figure 4: Comparison of human segmentation of the single fingerspelled item "BSL" (top) with segmentation into 3 items by VIA-SLA (bottom).

Other reasons for differences between manual and machine segmentation include cases where the tool has failed to identify a change of sign. This occurs where, for example, two signs that are very similar in manual features, but with different mouthings, occur one after the other.

We have not calculated the amount of time required for human editing of VIA-SLA output to correct segmentation errors. This might be done directly in the VIA-SLA output or after the segmented output has been imported into ELAN. Improved integration of VIA-SLA output into ELAN (merging files or exporting a tier into a second ELAN file) would streamline the process of integrating automated segmentation with further annotation of ELAN file.

7. Conclusion

Only preliminary analyses have been presented here, in order to check basic features, especially since VIA-SLA is still a prototype in the developmental stage. Much more testing is needed with more and longer videos and with videos in other sign languages. Other important next steps include measuring how long it takes a human to correct the machine annotations so that can be taken into account as well. Nevertheless, the VIA-SLA can already be seen to offer advantages and demonstrate positive progress for those concerned with analysis of sign language data. If performance and reliability can continue to improve, such a tool will ultimately prove very useful for sign linguists.

8. Acknowledgements

This work was supported by the UK Engineering and Physical Sciences Research Council ('ExTOL: End to End Translation of British Sign Language', EP/R03298X/1).

9. Bibliographical References

Bragg, D., Koller, O., Bellard, M., Berke, L., Boudreault, P., Braffort, A., Caselli, N., Huenerfauth, M., Kacorri, H., Verhoef, T. and Vogler, C., (2019) Sign language recognition, generation, and translation: An interdisciplinary perspective. In *The 21st international ACM SIGACCESS conference on computers and accessibility* (pp. 16-31).

Chaaban, H., Gouiffès, M., & Braffort, A. (2021, February). Automatic Annotation and Segmentation of Sign Language Videos: Base-level Features and Lexical Signs Classification. In *VISIGRAPP*.

Cormier, K., Schembri, A., & Tyrone, M. E. (2008). One hand or two? Nativisation of fingerspelling in ASL and BANZSL. *Sign Language and Linguistics, 11*(1), 3-44. doi:10.1075/sl&l.11.1.03cor

Crasborn, O. A. (2015) Transcription and notation methods. In Orfanidou, E., Woll, B., & Morgan, G. (2014). *Research methods in sign language studies: A practical guide*. John Wiley & Sons. 74-88.

Fenlon, J., Denmark T, Campbell R, Woll B (2007) *Seeing sentence boundaries. Sign Language & Linguistics* 10:2, 117-200

Fenlon, J., Schembri, A., Johnston, T., & Cormier, K. (2015). Documentary and corpus approaches to sign language research. In E. Orfanidou, B. Woll, & G. Morgan (Eds.), *The Blackwell guide to research methods in sign language studies* (p156-172). Oxford: Blackwell.

Hanke, T. (2002) iLex - A tool for sign language lexicography and corpus analysis. In M. G. Rodríguez & C. P. S. Araujo (Eds.), *Proceedings of the third International Conference on Language Resources and Evaluation, Las Palmas de Gran Canaria, Spain.* (pp. 923–926). Paris: ELRA.

Hanke, T. Matthes, S, Regen, A. & Worseck S. (2012). Where does a sign start and end? Segmentation of continuous signing. Conference Paper at the *5th Workshop of the Representation and Processing of Sign Languages: Interactions between Corpus and Lexicon (LREC 2012, Istanbul).*

Johnston, T. (2010). From archive to corpus: transcription and annotation in the creation of signed language corpora. International Journal of Corpus Linguistics, 15(1), 104-129.

Kipp, M. (2001). Anvil-a generic annotation tool for multimodal dialogue. In *Seventh European Conference on Speech Communication and Technology*.

Mostowski, P., Kuder, A., Filipczak, J., & Rutkowski, P. (2018). Workflow Management and Quality Control in the Development of the PJM Corpus: The Use of an Issue-Tracking System. In M. Bono, E. Efthimiou, S.-E. Fotinea, T. Hanke, J. Hochgesang, J. Kristoffersen, J. Mesch, & Y. Osugi (Eds.), *Proceedings of the Eleventh International Conference on Language Resources and Evaluation (LREC 2018)* (pp. 133-138). Paris: ELRA.

Quer, J., & Steinbach, M. (2019). Handling sign language data: The impact of modality. *Frontiers in psychology, 10*, 483| https://doi.org/10.3389/fpsyg.2019.00483

Renz, K., Stache, N. C., Albanie, S., & Varol, G. (2021). Sign language segmentation with temporal convolutional networks. In *ICASSP 2021-2021 IEEE International Conference on Acoustics, Speech and Signal Processing (ICASSP)* (pp. 2135-2139). IEEE. https://arxiv.org/abs/2011.12986

Renz, K., Stache, N. C., Fox, N., Varol, G., & Albanie, S. (2021). Sign Segmentation with Changepoint-Modulated Pseudo-Labelling. 2021 IEEE Conference on Computer Vision and Pattern Recognition Workshops (CVPRW'21). https://arxiv.org/abs/2104.13817

Schembri, A., Fenlon, J., Rentelis, R., Reynolds, S., & Cormier, K. (2013). Building the British Sign Language corpus. *Language Documentation & Conservation, 7*, 136-154.

Wittenburg, P., Brugman, H., Russel, A., Klassmann, A., & Sloetjes, H. (2006). ELAN: A professional framework for multimodality research. In *5th international conference on language resources and evaluation (LREC 2006)* (pp. 1556-1559).

10. Language Resource References

Cormier, K., Fenlon, J., Gulamani, S., & Smith, S. (2017). BSL Corpus Annotation Conventions, v. 3.0, https://bslcorpusproject.org/wp-content/uploads/BSLCorpus_AnnotationConventions_v3.0_-March2017.pdf. Deafness, Cognition and Language Research Centre, University College London.

Schembri, A., Fenlon, J., Rentelis, R., & Cormier, K. (2014). British Sign Language Corpus Project: A corpus of digital video data and annotations of British Sign Language 2008-2014 (Second Edition). London: University College London. http://www.bslcorpusproject.org

Proceedings of the 10th Workshop on the Representation and Processing of Sign Languages (sign-lang@LREC 2022), pages 202–211
Language Resources and Evaluation Conference (LREC 2022), Marseille, 20-25 June 2022

Sign Language Video Anonymization

Zhaoyang Xia[1], Yuxiao Chen[1], Qilong Zhangli[1]
Matt Huenerfauth[2], Carol Neidle[3], Dimitris N. Metaxas[1]
[1] Rutgers University, [2] Rochester Institute of Technology, [3] Boston University
[1] 110 Frelinghuysen Road, Piscataway, NJ 08854,
[2] 152 Lomb Memorial Drive, Rochester, NY 14623
[3] Boston University Linguistics, 621 Commonwealth Ave., Boston, MA 02215
zx149@rutgers.edu, yc984@cs.rutgers.edu, qz181@scarletmail.rutgers.edu
matt.huenerfauth@rit.edu, carol@bu.edu, dnm@cs.rutgers.edu

Abstract

Deaf signers who wish to communicate in their native language frequently share videos on the Web. However, videos cannot preserve privacy—as is often desirable for discussion of sensitive topics—since both hands and face convey critical linguistic information and therefore cannot be obscured without degrading communication. Deaf signers have expressed interest in video anonymization that would preserve linguistic content. However, attempts to develop such technology have thus far shown limited success. We are developing a new method for such anonymization, with input from ASL signers. We modify a motion-based image animation model to generate high-resolution videos with the signer identity changed, but with preservation of linguistically significant motions and facial expressions. An asymmetric encoder-decoder structured image generator is used to generate the high-resolution target frame from the low-resolution source frame based on the optical flow and confidence map. We explicitly guide the model to attain clear generation of hands and face by using bounding boxes to improve the loss computation. FID and KID scores are used for evaluation of the realism of the generated frames. This technology shows great potential for practical applications to benefit deaf signers.

Keywords: Motion Estimation, ASL, Sign Language, Anonymization, Image Animation

1. Introduction

We present here a new method for anonymizing American Sign Language (ASL) videos. Our approach is based on a state-of-art image animation model (Siarohin et al., 2021) to generate a video expressing the linguistic message of the original signer, as articulated by the hands, arms, and face, but retargeted to appear as though the signing is produced by a different person whose image is used as the source for generating the new video. In order to generate high-resolution videos with articulate hand gestures and accurate facial expressions, we enhance the model by using an asymmetric encoder-decoder structured image generator for high resolution image generation and designing a new Hand & Face Focused Loss function for better generation of hand gestures and facial expressions. Our method generates promising results for sign language video anonymization.

2. The Need for Video Anonymization

American Sign Language (ASL) is the natural language that serves as the primary means of communication within the Deaf Community in the United States and parts of Canada. In parallel with manual signing, signed languages use the nonmanual channel—facial expressions and movements of the head and upper body—to express many types of linguistic information, including syntactic marking of, e.g., negation, topics, question status, and clausal type (Baker-Shenk, 1985; Kacorri and Huenerfauth, 2016; Neidle et al., 2000; Coulter, 1979; Valli and Lucas, 2000). Thus, the face, in particular, cannot be obscured to achieve anonymity (e.g., for communicating about sensitive topics, such as medical, legal, or controversial issues) without loss of critical linguistic information.

Although there have been a number of writing systems developed for sign language (Arnold, 2009), there is no standard written form for ASL. Communicating in written English is, in principle, an option for preservation of privacy; however, this is often dispreferred by native signers, who may be less proficient and less comfortable in English than in ASL.

Many Deaf signers have expressed interest in a tool that would preserve linguistic information while allowing the signer's identity to be disguised (Lee et al., 2021). This could be used to enable, for example: anonymous peer review for academic submissions in ASL; neutrality in a range of multimodal ASL-based tools, making possible anonymized definitions in an ASL dictionary; or neutrality in interpreting situations, including messaging. It could also increase participation in video-based AI databases (Bragg et al., 2020), which are quite valuable for research.

3. Previous Approaches to Privacy Preservation

Various approaches to enabling preservation of privacy in ASL videos have been explored. See Isard (2020) for a detailed overview.

3.1. Concealment of Part or All of the Face

There have been attempts to disguise the face in various ways. They all suffer from the same unavoidable problem: that facial expressions convey essential linguistic information, which is degraded or lost by concealment. For example, in Bragg et al. (2020), a tiger-shape filter was used to disguise the signer's face, as shown in Figure 1. However, the absence of facial expression resulted, unsurprisingly, in severely diminished comprehension. Likewise, blocking out certain regions of the face, as in Figure 2, results in loss of critical linguistic information (Bleicken et al., 2016).

Figure 1: Tiger-shape filter used to protect signer privacy, taken from Figure 2 of Bragg et al. (2020)

Figure 2: Anonymized video frames from Swiss broadcast footage, from Figure 1 of Camgöz et al. (2021)

3.2. Sign Animation Controlled by Users

Heloir and Nunnari (2016) and Efthimiou et al. (2015) explored providing instructions to enable signers to manipulate virtual humans to generate anonymous messages in sign language. However, these technologies are difficult to master, and it usually takes a long time for non-experts to produce reasonable messages.

3.3. Reproduction of the Original Signing

Several approaches have also been taken to reproduce the original signer's production, to preserve anonymity.

3.3.1. Actors

Use of actors as a way to share information from signed videos when privacy must be preserved has been considered . However, as Isard (2020) points out (§3.2.1):

> For total anonymity, short examples from a corpus can be reproduced by a human actor. In this case complete anonymity is assured, but there are several disadvantages as a result. The process is very labour-intensive, requiring not only the time of the signer but also of a studio and technicians to carry out the recording. In addition, no matter how well the second signer copies the original, some information will be lost. Performativity is a vital part of sign language and it is impossible to fully separate the affective and grammatical functions of facial expressions.

3.3.2. Avatars

In principle, a signer can be replaced by a cartoon-like character replicating what the original person had signed. However, the state-of-the-art in avatar generation (see, e.g., Bragg et al. (2019)) does not make it possible to automate this process; human intervention is required. Furthermore, there are serious technical difficulties such that the use of avatars usually results in dispreferred, unrealistic results (Kipp et al., 2011).

3.3.3. Skeleton-based AI Approaches to Image Generation

As deep learning technology has developed, some researchers have used image-to-image transformation models for sign language anonymization. Recent work such as AnonSign (Saunders et al., 2021) uses a combination of VAEs and GANs to generate sign language frames with different identities. Accurate skeleton keypoints are used as constraints for image generation. A style loss is proposed to generate human appearance of different identities. The results are encouraging.

However, the generation quality and accuracy of the hand gestures and facial expressions largely depend on the skeleton keypoints. In sign language, hand movements are often rapid, causing blurring in the video frame. Occlusions of the face happen frequently. Pre-trained human pose estimation models are trained on datasets unrelated to sign language, which have different statistical properties. As a result, they may not transfer well when applied to sign language videos (a problem known as *domain gap*). All these problems make it difficult to obtain accurate keypoint information. State-of-the-art models, such as AlphaPose (Li et al., 2018; Fang et al., 2017; Xiu et al., 2018), can get a rough estimation over bounding boxes. But the accuracy and robustness of handshape estimation remain questionable. See figure 3 for failed cases of AlphaPose on the ASLLRP DSP dataset (see Section 6.1).

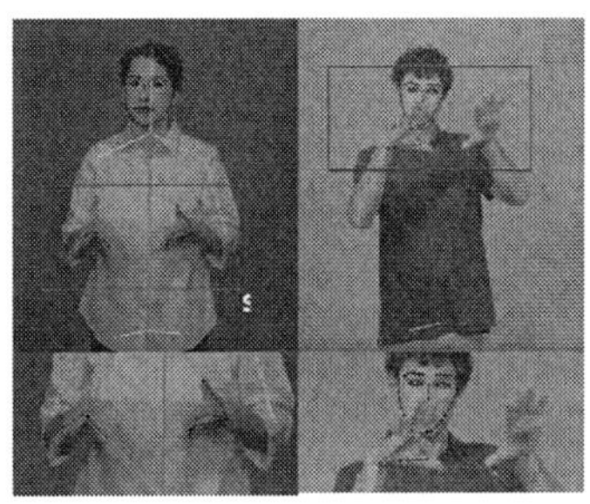

Figure 3: Failed cases of the AlphaPose human pose estimator on ASLLRP DSP dataset.

3.3.4. Facial Expression Transfer using Motion-based Animation Models

Recent work (Lee et al., 2021) applies the facial expression transfer method of Siarohin et al. (2019) for sign language anonymization. The signer's face in videos is replaced by another person's face with the facial expressions transferred. Thus, linguistic meanings are preserved while the identity of the signer in the video changes. Signers provided positive feedback with respect to this application. However, since in Lee et al. (2021) only the face has been transferred, the extent of the anonymization is limited.

3.3.5. Unsupervised Image Animation

Another way to reproduce signing is by using an unsupervised image animation model (Siarohin et al., 2021) to transfer the whole body in sign language videos. We have been the first to explore this approach to sign language anonymization. We present here enhancements to our method that we have introduced to overcome some of the problems we had encountered previously. For example, we are now able to generate high-resolution anonymized videos, with good visual representations of the hands and face, in a computationally efficient and robust way. This method has advantages over other approaches in that (1) it enables anonymization of the whole body (including clothing), without being limited to the face; and (2) it does not require (error-prone) extraction of skeletons from videos.

4. Challenges

Sign language video anonymization is extremely challenging. Accurate hand configurations and movements and detailed facial expressions are essential to preservation of linguistic meaning. Although video animation with retargeting offers many advantages over the other approaches described above, there are several difficult challenges that would need to be overcome.

4.1. Resolution & Computing Cost

The linguistically essential information is concentrated in the face, hands, and arms, although these regions make up only a small portion of the entire video frame. Rapid hand movements can result in blurring if the resolution is not optimal. Thus, high-quality videos are required as input to the model in order to preserve important information. The generated frames also need to be of high resolution for high image quality. However, for the unsupervised animation model, if we directly use the entirety of the high-resolution frames as input, the computation cost is high, and this may not be feasible if the training set contains a large number of videos. Furthermore, generating high-resolution images in one stage is not stable and degrades the image quality.

4.2. Information Density from Hands & Face

In sign language videos, hand movements and facial expressions carry important linguistic meanings. However, they occupy a relatively small part of the total frame as compared to the torso. Therefore, the information density is unbalanced in sign language videos. During training, generative neural network models calculate the difference between the generative frames and the ground truth to compute the loss function, which is important to enable the model to produce better results. Although loss function designs vary, the loss computation usually focuses on the whole image and neglects the small parts. This makes anonymization of sign language videos very challenging because the hands and face, with significantly higher information density than the torso, are neglected by the model.

4.3. 3D Hand Gesture Estimation

Hand gestures in sign language videos are complex movements with a high degree of freedom. For generation of sign language handshapes, 2D hand information is not adequate because of self-occlusion, blurriness from rapid hand movements, and the complex structure of the hands. Therefore, obtaining accurate 3D handshapes would greatly benefit anonymization of sign language videos. However, estimating 3D hand gestures from 2D images or videos is an extremely difficult problem. Pretrained models do not work well on videos in the wild because of the domain gap (explained in Section 3.3.3). The absence of 3D hand information makes hand generation in anonymized sign language videos very challenging.

5. Model Overview & Innovations to Address some of these Challenges

An overview of our methodology for sign language anonymization is presented in Section 5.1. In 5.2.1, we address the problem of computing efficiency for high-resolution image generation by using an asymmetric encoder-decoder structured image generator. In 5.2.2, we introduce a new focused L_1 loss function, which focuses on the the hands and face to improve their appearance in the generated images (given their importance in sign language and the challenges just mentioned with respect to information density). In Section 7, we will demonstrate that these innovations improve the quality of the generated videos.

5.1. Model Overview

Our approach uses 2 inputs. The first is a video sequence of a person signing an utterance (the driving video), while the second is the source image to be used for anonymization; we retarget the movements of the ASL signer in the driving video to a new video sequence based on the source image. The result is an anonymized video of the input utterance. To achieve this goal, we use a novel deep learning methodology that consists of training and inference phases.

5.2. Training Phase

As shown in Figure 4(A), during training, a pair of frames, S_H and D_H, is randomly chosen from the input utterance video sequence, which we term the high-resolution video sequence. To improve the efficiency and the quality of the generated anonymized video, we use a multiresolution approach. In the first stage, S_H and D_H are downsampled to half-size resolution images, S_L and D_L. To obtain an improved motion representation in latent space, we define an intermediate frame R. This conceptual frame is used to improve

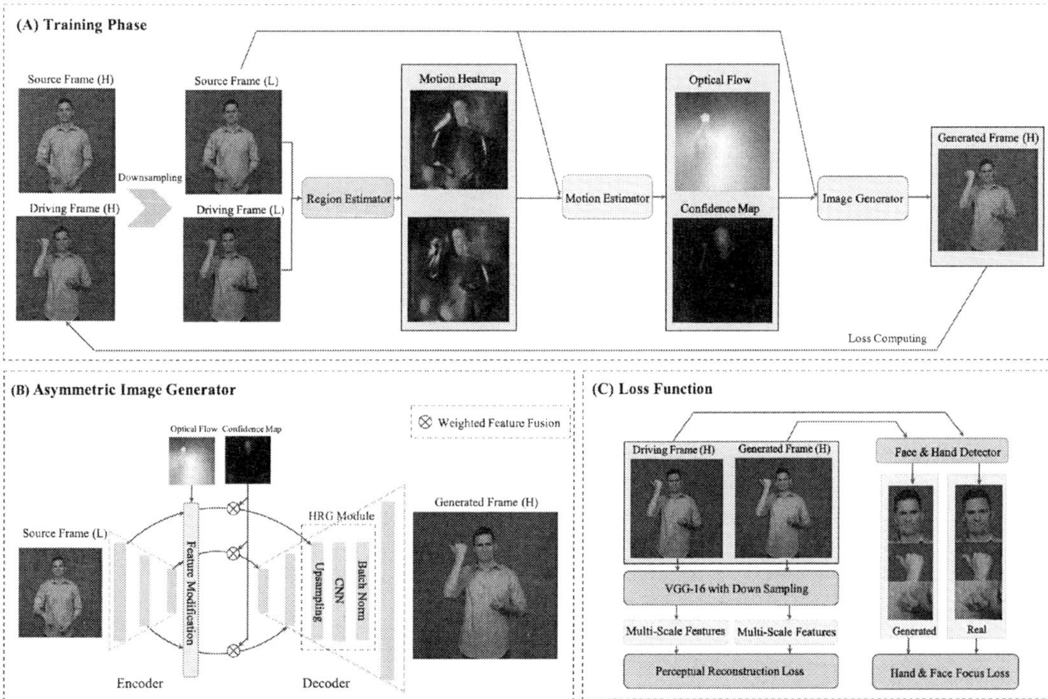

Figure 4: **Method Overview: Phase I - Training.** (A) Model is trained to generate the driving frame from the source frame. First, 2 high-resolution (H) frames are downsampled to low-resolution (L). Then the region motion estimator predicts the motion heatmap and coarse motion representation between these 2 frames. The dense motion estimator estimates the dense optical flow and confidence map from the heatmaps, coarse motion representation, and source image. The image generator outputs a high-resolution generated frame. (B) The image generator is an asymmetric encoder-decoder structured network with a High-Resolution Generation (**HRG**) module. The encoder takes the low-resolution source frame to obtain multiscale latent feature maps. The estimated optical flow is used to modify the feature maps. The confidence maps serve as the weights for latent feature fusions in the skip connections. The decoder along with the **HRG** module generates a high-resolution frame. (C) Multiscale perceptual loss based on VGG-16 and the Hand & Face Focused Loss ($\boldsymbol{L}_{\mathbf{HF}}$), designed for better generation of face and hands, are computed between the high-resolution generated frames and the driving frames.

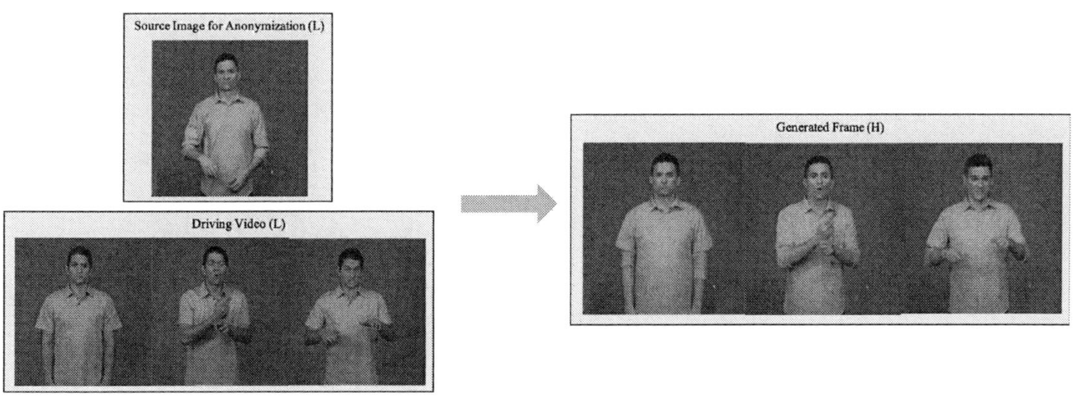

Figure 5: **Method Overview: Phase II - Inference.** In the inference phase, the source image for anonymization and the extracted frames from the driving video are input to the model. All the images are of low resolution. The model predicts the optical flow and confidence map between the source image and each frame in the driving video. The encoder-decoder takes the source image as input and outputs the high-resolution generated frames with the help of the estimated optical flow and confidence map.

the estimation of the foreground motion difference between frames S_L and D_L. The region motion estimator is used to estimate the motion heatmap M_K of k regions between the reference frame R and these 2 frames, S_L and D_L. The affine transformation matrix $A^k_{D_L \leftarrow R}$, $A^k_{S_L \leftarrow R} \in R^{2\times 3}$ of the region k between the reference frame R and D_L, S_L is computed using principal component analysis (PCA) (Wall et al., 2003) on the heatmaps M_k.

Thus, the foreground motion between the anonymization source frame S_L and the frame from the driving video D_L is modeled as an affine transformation and can be computed by equation 1.

$$A^k_{S_L \leftarrow D_L} = A^k_{S_L \leftarrow R} \begin{bmatrix} A^k_{D_L \leftarrow R} \\ 0 \quad 0 \quad 1 \end{bmatrix}^{-1} \tag{1}$$

In addition, we predict another affine transformation matrix $A^k_{S_L \leftarrow D_L}$, $k = 0$ for the background motion by taking S_L and D_L into an encoder and predict the six parameters of the affine matrix using a network-based regression operation.

The motion estimator takes the source image, the motion heatmap representation, and the foreground and background affine transformation matrices to predict the dense optical flow $O(z)$ between S_L and D_L. $O(z)$ is considered as a weighted summation of all the affine transformations, given by following formula 2, where z represents the (x, y) coordinates of a pixel, $W^k(z)$ is the weight matrix predicted by motion estimator:

$$O(z) = \sum_{k=0}^{K} W^k(z) A^k_{S_L \leftarrow D_L} \begin{bmatrix} z \\ 1 \end{bmatrix} \tag{2}$$

The network also outputs a confidence map C for each pixel, indicating the pixels that need to be inpainted during the image generation stage.

The last step in the training phase is to use the image generator to reconstruct the high-resolution driving frame D_H based on the source image S_L, the estimated dense optical flow, and the confidence map between S_L and D_H. The loss function is computed between D_H and the generated frame $\hat{D}_H$.

5.2.1. Asymmetric Image Generator with HRG

As already mentioned, in the first stage of our approach, the input frames are downsampled to half-resolution for initial estimation of the motion representation between the 2 selected video sequence frames. However, our goal is to generate a high-resolution image (of the same resolution as the driving video) for the final generated ASL video sequence. Therefore, the information from the high-resolution input video frames is crucial during the image generator phase.

To generate the desired high-resolution video images, we design our image generator as an asymmetric encoder-decoder structured network. Figure 4(B) gives details of our proposed asymmetric image generator. The source frame S_L is input to the encoder, so that the multiscale latent feature maps can be obtained. The estimated optical flow is used to modify each feature map. The multiscale deformed feature maps contribute to the input of each layer in the decoder through skip connections. Therefore, for each layer of the decoder, the input is a weighted summation of the output features from the previous layer and the multiscale deformed feature maps through the skip connections. The weight matrix for this feature fusion approach is decided by the predicted confidence maps.

The High-Resolution Generation (**HRG**) module—which contains an upsampling layer, a convolutional layer, and a batch norm layer—is added before the final output layer in the decoder. This **HRG** module increases the width and height in the latent feature space. Therefore, our decoder does not learn a trivial solution to increase the resolution, such as interpolation. The generated frame $\hat{D}_H$ is of the same resolution as D_H. The loss function is computed between these 2 high-resolution frames. This asymmetric encoder-decoder structure with the **HRG** module addresses the problem of computation cost and improves the quality of the generated images.

5.2.2. Loss Function

The model is trained to minimize 3 loss functions, including: the multiresolution perceptual loss $\boldsymbol{L_{\mathrm{MP}}}$, the equivalence loss $\boldsymbol{L_{\mathrm{Eq}}}$, and the Hand & Face Focused $\boldsymbol{L_1}$ Loss ($\boldsymbol{L_{\mathrm{HF}}}$); see equation 3. Figure 4(C) demonstrates the computation of $\boldsymbol{L_{\mathrm{MP}}}$ and $\boldsymbol{L_{\mathrm{HF}}}$. In particular, $\boldsymbol{L_{\mathrm{HF}}}$ is designed to explicitly guide the model to generate fine-grained and accurate hand movements and facial expressions:

$$L = \lambda_1 L_{\mathrm{MP}} + \lambda_2 L_{\mathrm{Eq}} + \lambda_3 L_{\mathrm{HF}} \tag{3}$$

where λ_1, λ_2 and λ_3 are the loss function weights.

Multiresolution Perceptual Loss (L_{MP}): This loss function forces the model to reconstruct images with similar high-level features extracted from a pretrained VGG-19 network (Johnson et al., 2016; Wang et al., 2018). The generated frame $\hat{D}_H$ and driving frame D_H are input to a downsampling operator F_l. The differences between the feature maps extracted by the i-th layer of the VGG-19 network are calculated and serve as the reconstruction perceptual loss.

$$L_{\mathrm{MP}}(\hat{D_H}, D_H) = \sum_l \sum_i |V_i(F_l \cdot \hat{D_H}) - V_i(F_l \cdot D_H)| \tag{4}$$

Equivariance Loss (L_{Eq}): This loss function is used to improve the model's robustness and stability for estimating the affine transformation matrix. $\tilde{X}$ is image X transformed by $\tilde{A}$, and $\tilde{A}$ is some random geometric transformation used for data augmentation.

$$L_{\mathrm{Eq}} = |A^k_{X \leftarrow R} - \tilde{A} A^k_{\tilde{X} \leftarrow R}| \tag{5}$$

Hand & Face Focused L_1 **Loss** (L_{HF}): In sign language videos, accurate and clear hand gestures and facial expressions are essential for expression of linguistic meaning. Therefore, the model needs to focus especially on the area around the hands and face, which suggests that the generation quality of these areas needs to contribute more to the loss function. To achieve that, we explicitly guide the model to focus more on the hand and face areas by computing the loss within the hand and face bounding boxes. The bounding boxes are produced using AlphaPose (Li et al., 2018; Fang et al., 2017; Xiu et al., 2018). This loss computation is implemented by constructing weighted masks of both the hands H_r, H_l and the face F based on bounding boxes, calculated in equation 6:

$$L_{\mathrm{HF}} = |(\hat{D_H} - D_H) * (H_l + H_r + F)| \quad (6)$$

The Hand & Face Focused L_1 Loss allows for capture of more details of the hands and face, thereby improving generation of hand gestures and facial expressions.

5.3. Inference Phase

Figure 5 illustrates the Inference Phase. Our model is capable of generating high-resolution videos using the low-resolution source image and driving videos. First, we extract the frames from the driving video. We estimate the bounding box of the human body and make sure the body pose in the source image is roughly aligned with those in the driving video for best results. Then, we input each pair of source image and driving frames to the model and estimate the optical flow and confidence map between them. The encoder takes the source image as input for anonymization and obtains the latent feature map. The latent feature map is then modified using the estimated optical flow and confidence map in the same manner as in the training phase. The decoder outputs the high-resolution generated frames, which preserve the identity of the source image but have the motion in the driving frames.

6. Experiments

6.1. Datasets

We trained our model on the American Sign Language Linguistic Research Project (ASLLRP) Continuous Signing Corpora (Neidle et al., 2018; Neidle and Opoku, 2021) `https://dai.cs.rutgers.edu/dai/s/dai`: (1) the BU SignStream® 3 Corpus, and (2) the DSP dataset, generously contributed by DawnSignPress (DawnSign Press, 2022). We selected 527 videos from each of the 2 ASLLRP datasets. We use 90% of the data for training and 10% for testing. Each video contains a continuous signed sentence. We trained our model on each dataset separately.

6.2. Implementation Details

We trained our model on 8 RTX6000 GPUs with a batch size of 24. The input images are cropped and resized to $(768, 768)$. For both models, we set the training epoch numbers at 100. The region number parameter k is set to 30. The learning rate is set to be $2e^{-4}$ at the beginning, and decreases at the epoch of 60 and 90.

7. Results

Figures 6 and 7 illustrate some of our results from the 2 ASLLRP corpora.

EFFECTS ON REALISM FROM ENHANCED HIGH-RESOLUTION IMAGE GENERATION (**HRG**) AND THE HAND & FACE FOCUSED L_1 LOSS FUNCTION ($\boldsymbol{L_{\mathrm{HF}}}$)

HRG	L_{HF}	FID ↓	KID ↓
✓	✓	**50.10**	**0.026**
✓		51.30	0.027
	✓	58.95	0.042
		57.47	0.038

HRG	L_{HF}	FID ↓	KID ↓
✓	✓	**91.54**	**0.060**
✓		92.33	0.062
	✓	98.56	0.063
		97.98	0.068

Table 1: KID and FID scores on the ASLLRP DSP dataset (top) and the ASLLRP SignStream® 3 Corpus (bottom). The ✓ marks the modifications used with the model. The best results are highlighted in bold.

7.1. Quantitative Evaluation

We used Fréchet Inception Distance (FID) (Parmar et al., 2022; Heusel et al., 2017) and Kernel Inception Distance (KID) (Bińkowski et al., 2018) as metrics to evaluate the quality of the generated images. These metrics measure the discrepancy between the generated and real frames.

For each of the 2 datasets, we randomly sample frames from test videos to construct the test image dataset. For each model, we select driving video and source image pairs to generate anonymized videos. Then, we randomly sample frames from these anonymized videos and construct the generated image set. Finally, we calculated the FID and KID scores between the test image set and generated image sets. The table 1 shows the effects of 2 aspects of our model on the realism of the results. Lower FID and KID scores indicate that the generated image is more similar to the real image set, and thus is considered to be more realistic. Our modifications improve the realism of the generated images. In particular, with the **HRG** module, our method is able to generate high-resolution images and achieve more realistic results. The improvements from using the Hand & Face Focused L_1 Loss are not reflected in the KID and FID scores. This is reasonable because this modification is intended to improve the quality of small parts in the image, which the KID and FID scores neglect.

FID and KID scores measure the overall generation quality of the images. They do not reflect the image details and cannot assess the preservation of linguistic meaning. In order to show that our method improves the generation of facial expressions and hand gestures, we compare the generated images in the next section.

7.2. Qualitative Evaluation

We focus on the quality of facial expressions and hand gestures in the generated frame. First, we compare hand gesture generation with and without the

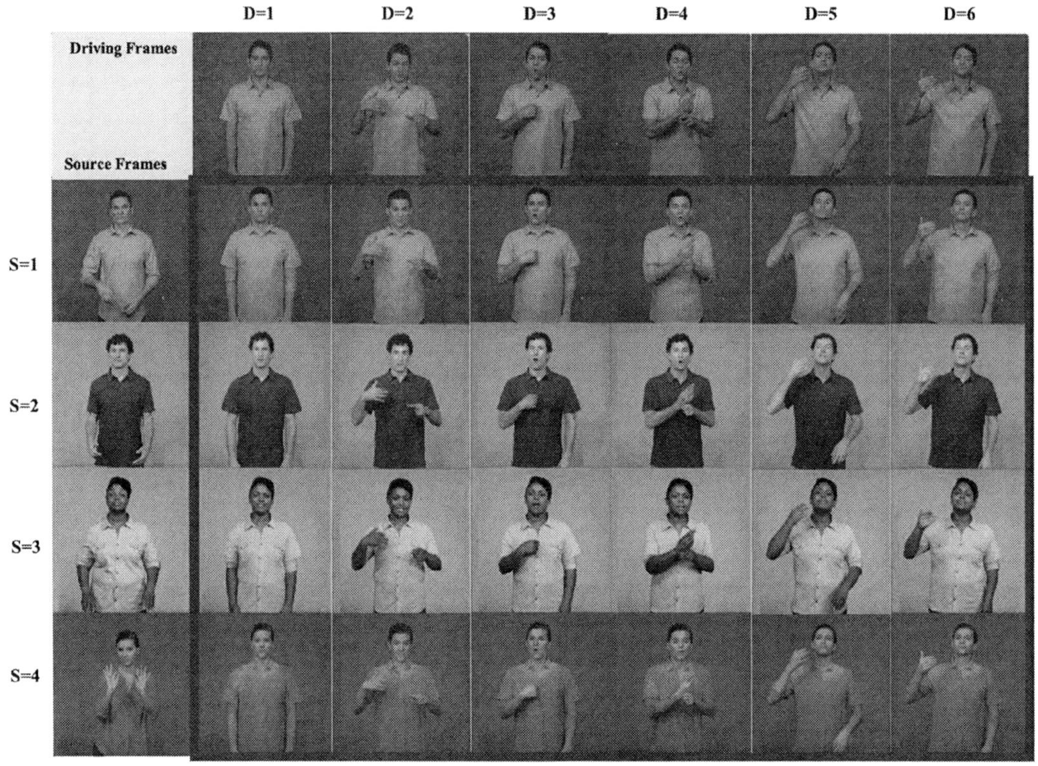

Figure 6: **Anonymization examples from the ASLLRP DSP dataset**. Our method takes the driving frames from a sign language video sequence as the motion reference and generates a new sign language video with the human appearance and body pose taken from the designated source frame. In this example, 6 driving frames $D = 1...6$ are selected from a video sequence. We use four source frames $S = 1, 2, 3, 4$ to provide the human appearance and body pose for the generated anonymized video sequence. So, Row 1 shows frames from the original signer; Column 1 shows four different source images providing the appearance to be used for the anonymized versions driven by the signing from Row 1; those generated images are shown in the rest of the frames in each row.

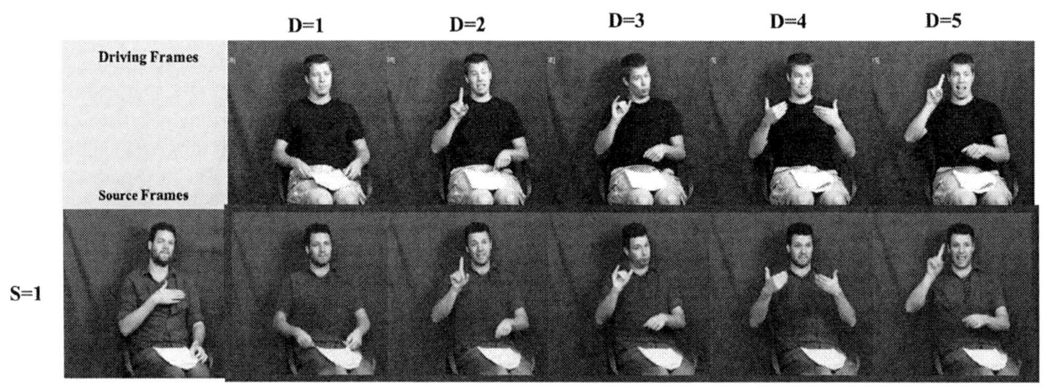

Figure 7: **Anonymization examples from the ASLLRP SignStream® 3 Corpus**. Display is similar to Figure 6

HRG modification and Hand & Face Focused L_1 Loss ($\boldsymbol{L}_{\mathbf{HF}}$) function. As seen in the sample results shown in Figure 8, the **HRG** modification improves the quality and clarity of the images. The $\boldsymbol{L}_{\mathbf{HF}}$ Loss adds more details to the hand configuration and further improves the hand appearance in the generated videos.

In Figure 9, our full model gives the clearest face generation. The **HRG** modification increases accuracy of details around the eyes and mouth in the generated videos. In particular, the improved model is able to generate wrinkles and teeth. Moreover, the generated faces have higher resolution than the low-resolution input videos. The $\boldsymbol{L}_{\mathbf{HF}}$ Loss helps with preservation of facial expressions and alleviates possible facial distortions.

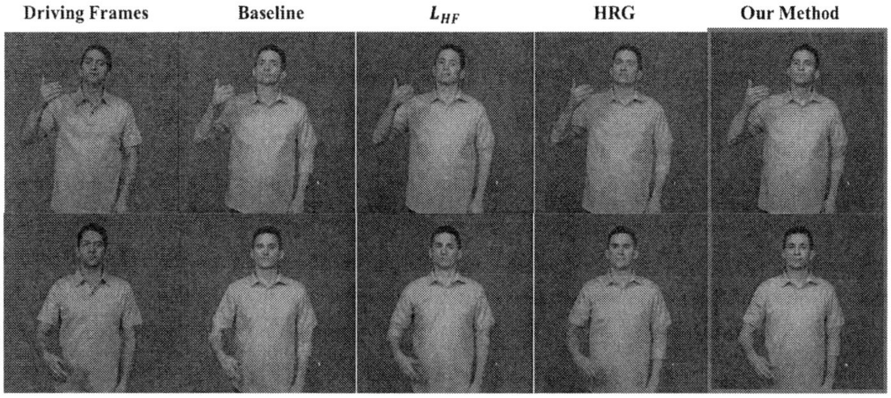

Figure 8: Comparison of Hand Gesture Generation for different models. In particular, the signer's handshape is generated best in the images shown in the red box, where the model incorporates both **HRG** and Hand & Face Focused L_1 Loss ($\boldsymbol{L}_{\mathbf{HF}}$).

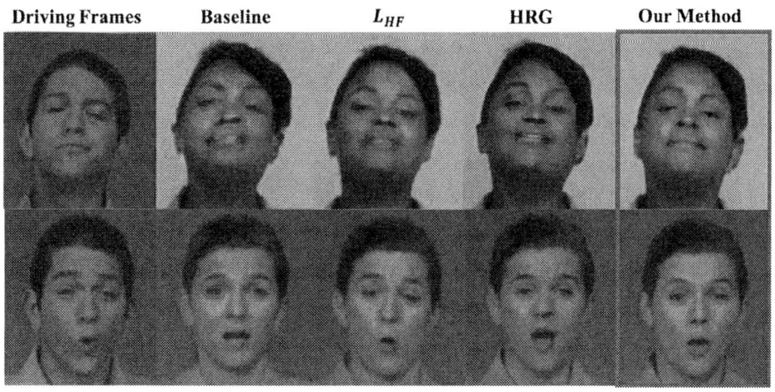

Figure 9: Comparison of Facial Expression Generation for different models. The best results are those in the red box, where the model incorporates both **HRG** and Hand & Face Focused L_1 Loss ($\boldsymbol{L}_{\mathbf{HF}}$).

8. Conclusions & Directions for Future Research

We have been developing methods for anonymizing ASL videos with input from Deaf signers. For example, Lee et al. (2021) reports on user studies with Deaf signers who evaluated our earlier experiments using facial expression transfer for purposes of video anonymization. They evaluated the extent to which the anonymized videos looked natural, succeeded in transmitting the linguistic information, and disguised the identity of the original signer. They also commented on the extent to which they would find it useful to be able to anonymize videos in this way for various purposes. Although the overall feedback was quite positive, the fact that only the face was anonymized presented a serious drawback to that technology. We have thus been developing new methods, as presented here, to enable full-body anonymization. Here we described several innovations that we developed in order to overcome challenges involved in image animation with retargeting to anonymize sign language videos. Preliminary user interviews indicate that our new method is extremely promising. With respect to the success in disguising the identity of the signer, one Deaf signer commented: "Unrecognizable – amazing work! I could not recognize the original signer, yet it kept the signing style. Impressive!" However, there are still some cases where the handshape or facial expression is not generated perfectly in certain frames, because of issues just discussed, including the fact that we are not doing any explicit 3D modeling. We will continue to refine our methods to improve these remaining glitches, after which we will conduct another set of comprehensive user studies with Deaf signers for quantitative evaluation of the degree to which the identity has been successfully disguised and of the comprehensibility and naturalness of the resulting anonymized signing.

9. Acknowledgments

We are grateful to Augustine Opoku, Carey Ballard, Indya-loreal Oliver, Lutece Dekker, Gregory Dimitriadis & Douglas Motto for important contributions. This research has been supported in part by NSF grants 2040638, 1763486, 1763523, 2125362 & 1763569. Any opinions, findings, or conclusions expressed here are those of the authors and do not necessarily reflect the views of the National Science Foundation.

10. References

Arnold, R. W. (2009). *A proposal for a written system of American Sign Language*. Gallaudet University.

Baker-Shenk, C. (1985). The facial behavior of deaf signers: Evidence of a complex language. *American Annals of the Deaf*, 130(4):297–304.

Bińkowski, M., Sutherland, D. J., Arbel, M., and Gretton, A. (2018). Demystifying MMD GANs. *arXiv preprint arXiv:1801.01401*.

Bleicken, J., Hanke, T., Salden, U., and Wagner, S. (2016). Using a language technology infrastructure for German in order to anonymize German Sign Language corpus data. In *Proceedings of the Tenth International Conference on Language Resources and Evaluation (LREC'16)*, pages 3303–3306, Portorož, Slovenia, May. European Language Resources Association (ELRA).

Bragg, D., Koller, O., Bellard, M., Berke, L., Boudreault, P., Braffort, A., Caselli, N., Huenerfauth, M., Kacorri, H., Verhoef, T., et al. (2019). Sign language recognition, generation, and translation: An interdisciplinary perspective. In *The 21st international ACM SIGACCESS conference on computers and accessibility*, pages 16–31.

Bragg, D., Koller, O., Caselli, N., and Thies, W. (2020). Exploring collection of sign language datasets: Privacy, participation, and model performance. In *The 22nd International ACM SIGACCESS Conference on Computers and Accessibility*, pages 1–14.

Camgöz, N. C., Saunders, B., Rochette, G., Giovanelli, M., Inches, G., Nachtrab-Ribback, R., and Bowden, R. (2021). Content4all open research sign language translation datasets. In *2021 16th IEEE International Conference on Automatic Face and Gesture Recognition (FG 2021)*, pages 1–5. IEEE.

Coulter, G. R. (1979). *American Sign Language typology*. Ph.D. thesis, University of California, San Diego.

DawnSign Press. (2022). DawnSign-Press (2022) About Us. *DawnSignPress Website*. `http://www.dawnsign.com/about-us`.

Efthimiou, E., Fotinea, S.-E., Goulas, T., and Kakoulidis, P. (2015). User friendly interfaces for sign retrieval and sign synthesis. In *International Conference on Universal Access in Human-Computer Interaction*, pages 351–361. Springer.

Fang, H.-S., Xie, S., Tai, Y.-W., and Lu, C. (2017). RMPE: Regional multi-person pose estimation. In *ICCV*.

Heloir, A. and Nunnari, F. (2016). Toward an intuitive sign language animation authoring system for the deaf. *Universal Access in the Information Society*, 15(4):513–523.

Heusel, M., Ramsauer, H., Unterthiner, T., Nessler, B., and Hochreiter, S. (2017). Gans trained by a two time-scale update rule converge to a local nash equilibrium. In I. Guyon, et al., editors, *Advances in Neural Information Processing Systems*, volume 30. Curran Associates, Inc.

Isard, A. (2020). Approaches to the anonymisation of sign language corpora. In *Proceedings of the LREC2020 9th Workshop on the Representation and Processing of Sign Languages: Sign Language Resources in the Service of the Language Community, Technological Challenges and Application Perspectives*, pages 95–100.

Johnson, J., Alahi, A., and Fei-Fei, L. (2016). Perceptual losses for real-time style transfer and super-resolution. In *European conference on computer vision*, pages 694–711. Springer.

Kacorri, H. and Huenerfauth, M. (2016). Continuous profile models in ASL syntactic facial expression synthesis. In *Proceedings of the 54th Annual Meeting of the Association for Computational Linguistics (Volume 1: Long Papers)*, pages 2084–2093.

Kipp, M., Nguyen, Q., Heloir, A., and Matthes, S. (2011). Assessing the deaf user perspective on sign language avatars. In *The proceedings of the 13th international ACM SIGACCESS conference on Computers and accessibility*, pages 107–114.

Lee, S., Glasser, A., Dingman, B., Xia, Z., Metaxas, D., Neidle, C., and Huenerfauth, M., (2021). *American Sign Language Video Anonymization to Support Online Participation of Deaf and Hard of Hearing Users*. Association for Computing Machinery, New York, NY, USA.

Li, J., Wang, C., Zhu, H., Mao, Y., Fang, H.-S., and Lu, C. (2018). Crowdpose: Efficient crowded scenes pose estimation and a new benchmark. *arXiv preprint arXiv:1812.00324*.

Neidle, C. and Opoku, A. (2021). Update on Linguistically Annotated ASL Video Data Available through the American Sign Language Linguistic Research Project (ASLLRP). In *ASLLRP Project Report No. 19*, Boston University, Boston, MA.

Neidle, C. J., Kegl, J., Bahan, B., MacLaughlin, D., and Lee, R. G. (2000). *The syntax of American Sign Language: Functional categories and hierarchical structure*. MIT press.

Neidle, C., Opoku, A., Dimitriadis, G., and Metaxas, D. (2018). New shared & interconnected ASL resources: SignStream® 3 software; DAI 2 for web access to linguistically annotated video corpora; and a Sign Bank. In *8th Workshop on the Representation and Processing of Sign Languages: Involving the Language Community, Miyazaki, Language Resources and Evaluation Conference 2018*.

Parmar, G., Zhang, R., and Zhu, J.-Y. (2022). On aliased resizing and surprising subtleties in gan evaluation. In *CVPR*.

Saunders, B., Camgoz, N. C., and Bowden, R. (2021). Anonysign: Novel human appearance synthesis for sign language video anonymisation. *arXiv preprint arXiv:2107.10685*.

Siarohin, A., Lathuilière, S., Tulyakov, S., Ricci, E., and Sebe, N. (2019). First order motion model for image animation. *Advances in Neural Information Processing Systems*, 32:7137–7147.

Siarohin, A., Woodford, O. J., Ren, J., Chai, M., and Tulyakov, S. (2021). Motion representations for articulated animation. In *Proceedings of the IEEE/CVF Conference on Computer Vision and Pattern Recognition*, pages 13653–13662.

Valli, C. and Lucas, C. (2000). *Linguistics of American Sign Language: An introduction*. Gallaudet University Press.

Wall, M. E., Rechtsteiner, A., and Rocha, L. M. (2003). Singular value decomposition and principal component analysis. In *A practical approach to microarray data analysis*, pages 91–109. Springer.

Wang, T.-C., Liu, M.-Y., Zhu, J.-Y., Tao, A., Kautz, J., and Catanzaro, B. (2018). High-resolution image synthesis and semantic manipulation with conditional gans. In *Proceedings of the IEEE conference on computer vision and pattern recognition*, pages 8798–8807.

Xiu, Y., Li, J., Wang, H., Fang, Y., and Lu, C. (2018). Pose Flow: Efficient online pose tracking. In *BMVC*.

Author Index

Alva-Manchego, Fernando, 1
Aonuki, Yurika, 59

Ballard, Carey, 165
Bejarano, Gissella, 1, 94
Berke, Larwan, 67
Bianchini, Claudia S., 42
Bigeard, Sam, 9
Börstell, Carl, 16
Brosens, Caro, 24

Cerna-Herrera, Francisco, 1
Chen, Yuxiao, 202
Chevrefils, Léa, 42
Chizhikova, Anastasia, 29
Choubsaz, Yassaman, 37
Chroni, Evgenia, 165
Contesse, Adrien, 42
Cormier, Kearsy, 198
Crasborn, Onno, 37, 144

Dafnis, Konstantinos M., 165
Danet, Claire, 42, 132
De Durpel, Hannes, 24
de Quadros, Ronice, 48
Dimou, Athanasia-Lida, 9
Doan, Patrick, 42

Efthimiou, Eleni, 9

Filhol, Michael, 53, 132
Fotinea, Stavroula-Evita, 9
Fox, Neil, 198

Gale, Elaine, 67
Goulas, Theodore, 9

Hall, Kathleen Currie, 59
Hanke, Thomas, 9, 102, 144
Hassan, Saad, 67
Hel-Or, Hagit, 187
Herrmann, Annika, 80
Huamani-Malca, Joe, 1
Huenerfauth, Matt, 67, 202

Imashev, Alfarabi, 124
Isard, Amy, 73

Jahn, Elena, 80
Janssens, Margot, 24
Jedlička, Pavel, 88
Johnston, Trevor, 181
Jui, Tonni Das, 94

Khan, Calvin, 80
Khatib, Lilyana, 187
Kimmelman, Vadim, 29, 124, 154, 159
Konrad, Reiner, 73
Kopf, Maria, 9, 102, 144
Krňoul, Zdeněk, 88
Krusser, Renata, 48
Kuder, Anna, 110, 118
Kuznetsova, Anna, 124
Kydyrbekova, Aigerim, 154

Lanesman, Sara, 192
Law, Danny, 173
Lee, Sooyeon, 67
Leeson, Lorraine, 139

Martinod, Emmanuella, 132
McDonald, John, 53
Metaxas, Dimitri, 165, 202
Moiselle, Rachel, 139
Morgan, Hope, 144, 148
Mostowski, Piotr, 118
Mukushev, Medet, 124, 154, 159
Muller, Ludek, 88

Neidle, Carol, 165, 202
Novogrodsky, Rama, 148

Ohanin, Ora, 192
Opoku, Augustine, 165

Power, Justin, 173
Poy, April, 59

Quinto-Pozos, David, 173

Rébulard, Morgane, 42
Rivas, Pablo, 1, 94

Rutkowski, Paweł, 118

Sabyrov, Arman, 159
Saito, Daniela, 48
Sandler, Wendy, 148
Sandygulova, Anara, 124, 154, 159
Schulder, Marc, 9, 102, 144
Seita, Matthew, 67
Siyavoshi, Sara, 37
Smith, River Tae, 181
Soleimanbeigi, Farzaneh, 37
Stamp, Rose, 148, 187, 192
Sultanova, Madina, 159

Thomas, Chloé, 42
Tian, Yingli, 67
Tolmie, Nico, 59

Vacalopoulou, Anna, 9
Vandamme, Thijs, 24
Vasilaki, Kyriaki, 9
Verstraete, Sam, 24
Vesik, Kaili, 59

Willoughby, Louisa, 181
Wójcicka, Joanna, 118
Woll, Bencie, 198

Xia, Zhaoyang, 202

Zelezny, Milos, 88
Zhangli, Qilong, 202

Association for Computational Linguistics
209 N. Eighth Street
Stroudsburg, Pennsylvania 18360

ISBN 978-1-7138-6137-9

CURRAN ASSOCIATES INC.
proceedings
.com